Mr. Remigis

CANADA'S CENTURY

SECOND EDITION

CANADA'S CENTURY

SECOND EDITION

ALLAN S. EVANS
Former Head of History
Emery Collegiate Institute
Weston, Ontario

I. L. MARTINELLO
Head of History
C. W. Jefferys Secondary School
Downsview, Ontario

McGRAW-HILL RYERSON LIMITED
Toronto Montreal New York Auckland
Bogotá Cairo Caracas Hamburg Lisbon
London Madrid Mexico Milan New Delhi
Paris San Juan São Paulo
Singapore Sydney Tokyo

CANADA'S CENTURY SECOND EDITION

ISBN 0-07-548858-2

7 8 9 10 BG 7 6 5 4 3

Printed and bound in Canada

Every reasonable effort has been made to find copyright holders of illustrations and quotations. The publishers would be pleased to have any errors or omissions brought to their attention.

CANADIAN CATALOGUING IN PUBLICATION DATA

Evans, Allan S., date-
Canada's century

2nd ed.
Includes index.
ISBN 0-07-548858-2

1. Canada - History. 2. Canada - Politics and government. I. Martinello, I. L. (Ilario Larry), date- . II. Title.

FC170.E92 1987 971 C87-094527-0
F1026.E92 1987

DISCLAIMER

This text has been prepared for use in school curriculum. It is not a legal handbook. References to the law and the Charter of Rights and Freedoms are accurate to the date of publication. Readers requiring advice for actual legal problems are urged to consult a competent lawyer.

Cover Photograph by Michael Kohn/*Saturday Night*

Buttons from the private collection of Donald Gray

Illustrations for second edition by Warren MacDonald

CONTENTS

PREFACE

DEVELOPING STUDENT SKILLS

We hope that you will find this study of modern Canadian history to be interesting and *useful*. Much of the factual content should prove helpful to you, both now and in the future. For example, you should benefit from knowing your legal rights and responsibilities and the workings of our political system and government.

But we believe that the *process* of learning these things will be just as valuable to you as the actual information itself, if not more so. We are referring here to the potential improvement of your learning skills through the study of history. These skills will be necessary for you to proceed successfully, not just in school but also in your jobs and careers.

As a comparison, consider the idea of a physical workout. There is much publicity these days about the benefits of physical fitness. Part of the benefit and enjoyment of a workout comes from the actual *doing* of the exercises. This *doing* can be compared to learning the factual content of this course. But perhaps even more important are the after-effects of a workout. Your muscles firm up, your endurance increases and your whole attitude about yourself and your activities changes. This can be said to be like developing your learning skills (not just increasing your knowledge). By *being* fit, or by learning *how* to learn, you are not merely doing an activity. You are building yourself up in preparation for even larger, more interesting challenges.

INTRODUCTION

AN APPROACH TO PROBLEM-SOLVING

One of the main goals of education is to help the student become a responsible, independent learner and problem-solver. Whether at school or at work, you will face situations in which you must identify a question or a problem and find a suitable answer. For example: *Should Canada try to become less dependent on the United States?* or *Is it worthwhile trying to expand my business into the Vancouver market?* To tackle and solve such problems, you need a variety of skills, which you can learn to develop in school, and specifically, through the study of history.

Just what are these skills? And which of them are appropriate for your needs? There are probably several ways to express and organize these skills; here is one, using as an example the application of such skills to the question of Canadian–American relations. As you read along, you might think of other applications, either to the same question or to the business decision regarding Vancouver.

Step 1

FUNCTION
Identifying the Problem To a shooter, this is like selecting the target. Only then does the aiming and firing of the rifle have any focus or purpose.

APPLICATIONS
What is the present state of Canadian–American relations? (Let us assume that you find that there is a high degree of Canadian dependence.)

Step 2

FUNCTION
Posing the Key Questions About the Issue

APPLICATIONS
In what ways is Canada dependent on the United States? Just how dependent are we in each of these areas? Why has this situation developed? What are the effects of this situation? And are they good or bad? Can we do anything about this situation? If so, what? How would we benefit? If we can't do anything, why can't we?

Step 3

FUNCTION
Collecting the Data Here you are like a detective or an investigative reporter.

APPLICATIONS
Where can I find information to help me answer these questions? Should I develop my search in any particular order? What information is there?

Step 4

FUNCTION
Evaluating the Data

APPLICATIONS
How thorough have I been in my search? What sources have I used? Are they equally good? (reliable? prejudiced?) How can I organize all this material? (What headings should I use? What order should I follow?) Which material is most important? Least important? Is some material questionable? (incomplete? distorted?) Is any important data missing?

Step 5

FUNCTION
Analyzing the Data

APPLICATIONS
What evidence shows strong Canadian dependence on the United States? What data tends to show otherwise? Can I develop charts or graphs to illustrate my main points? Can I explain why certain things have happened? Can I see and explain their effects? Is my data factual or merely someone's opinion or hope?

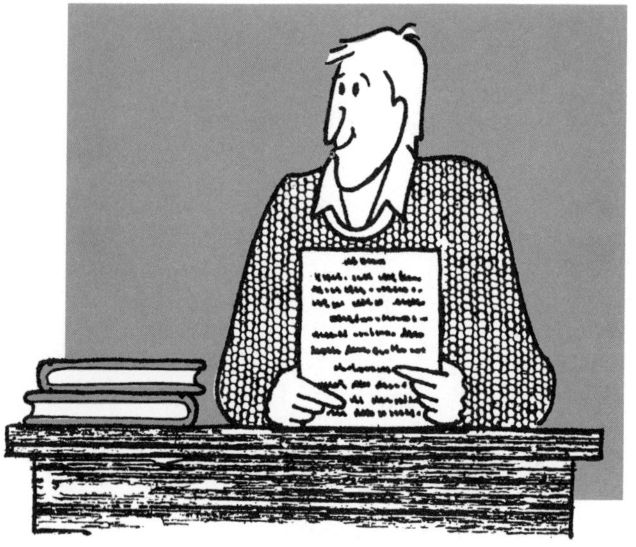

Step 6

FUNCTION
Solving the Problem

APPLICATIONS
What are the possible answers or solutions to the main questions? What are the advantages and disadvantages of each? What is likely to happen if action is taken on this issue? What risks are involved in implementing various possible solutions? Do the possible benefits justify such risks? Would a particular action be not only "good" or "bad" but also "right" or "wrong"?

Step 7

FUNCTION
Applying the Solution Let us assume that your inquiry has led to this conclusion: YES, Canada *is* too dependent on the United States and *should* act to reduce this dependence.

APPLICATIONS
Make a presentation to your class on your findings (the problem and your proposed solution). Submit a research project to your teacher on the above. Organize a school assembly on the above. Write letters to the appropriate officials expressing your ideas. (This could include members of parliament, cabinet ministers or even the premier of your province or the prime minister.) Organize a petition to publicize your concern and to urge action by the authorities. Participate in or organize a peaceful demonstration at an appropriate time and place to communicate your views.

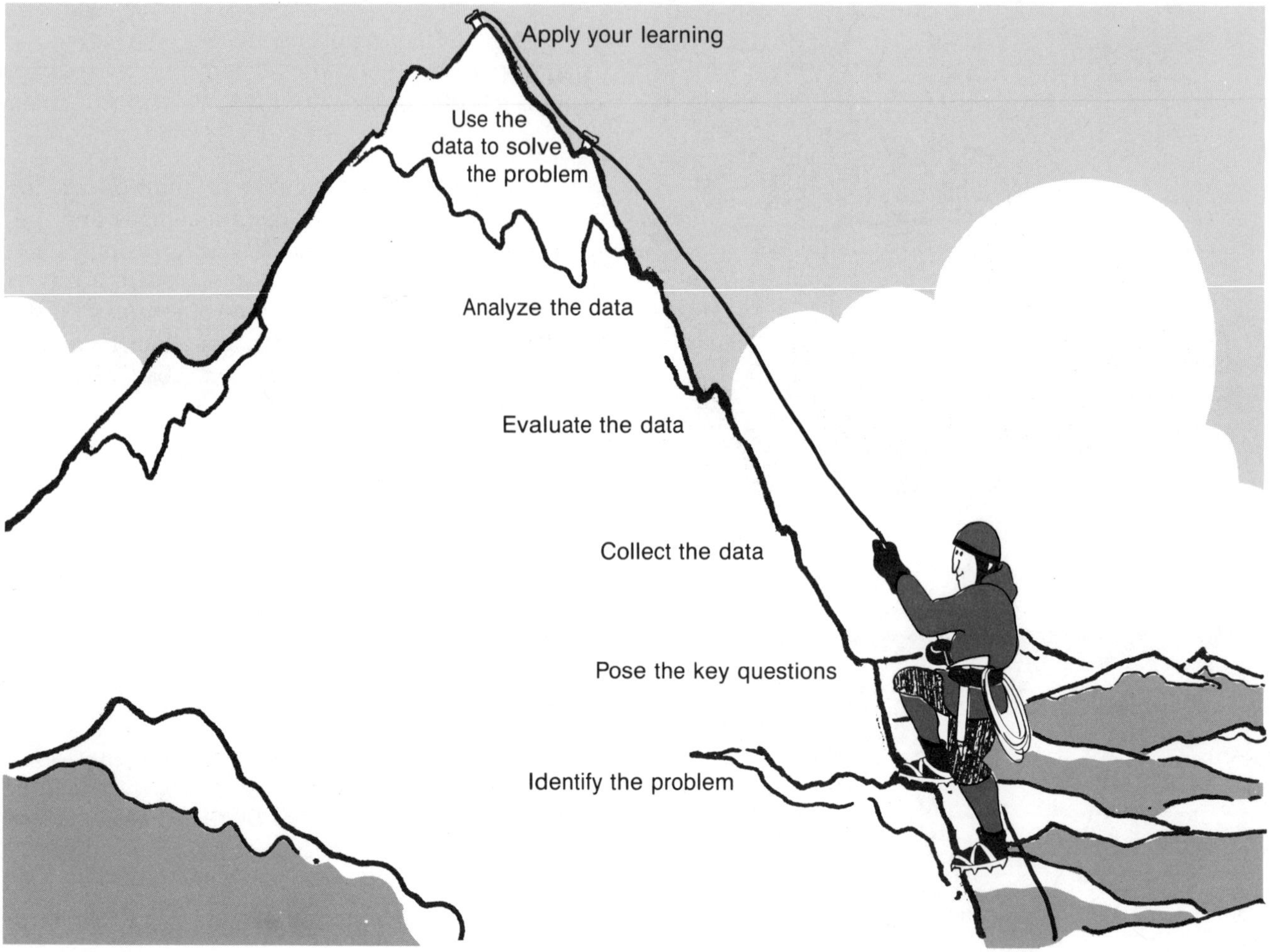

DEVELOPMENT OF LEARNING SKILLS

If you think back on the process you have just gone through, you will realize that your activities could be broken down into certain main skill areas. Learning skills are essential for all of us — in school, at work, in our social relationships, indeed, in almost all aspects of our lives. By learning these skills we are able to make sense of the vast amount of information we encounter daily.

In this textbook, we have chosen to concentrate on six main skill areas. At this stage in your education, you should be developing your "know-how" in each of these categories to the maximum of your potential. We have expressed these skills in the form of questions which you should ask yourself. When you can confidently answer "yes" to them, you will know that you are well on the way to developing your learning abilities.

Throughout the textbook we have introduced materials and/or exercises dealing with these skills. To help you find these, we have developed a system of symbols. The symbols will appear beside the items to which they are related. The chart below names the six skills on which we will be concentrating. As well, it shows the symbol and outlines the nature of each skill.

FOCUSSING on the topic or problem

- Am I clearly aware of what the topic *is*?
- What exactly must I know about it?
- Do I understand the meaning of key terms related to the topic?
- What questions should I ask about the material?
- What is the purpose of each question?
- How will I know when I have the important knowledge and ideas?
- Is there a special theme or purpose to this topic?

RESEARCHING the topic

- How can I use the textbook most effectively? (note index, table of contents, headings, etc.)
- What other sources are available to me? (magazines, newspapers, reference books, government, business, the community, etc.)
- Do I know how a library is set up? (card system, vertical files, periodicals index, etc.)
- What is the difference between a "primary" and a "secondary" source? Is one more reliable than the other? Is one more difficult to find?

ORGANIZING the material

1·2·3

- How will I plan my research of the topic?
- How can I put the data together from my various sources?
- Can my data be separated under certain headings? (economics, military, etc.)
- In what order should I present my material? (time sequence? order of importance? etc.)
- Is my material related to the key questions identified when I *focussed* on the topic?

COMMUNICATING the material

- ▶ Have I taken clear, complete notes?
- ▶ Can I talk effectively to other people about my topic? (by interviewing, discussing, debating, presenting, etc.)
- ▶ Can I express my findings clearly in writing? (essays, hand-outs, etc.)
- ▶ Could I express them audio-visually? (with charts or graphs, a video, an overhead, an audio tape, films, slides, etc.)

ANALYZING the topic or problem

- ▶ Can I now break down this topic into its component parts?
- ▶ Can I see the causes of things and also their effects?
- ▶ Can I separate the facts of the case from mere opinion or belief?
- ▶ Can I identify and state the main points of an argument?
- ▶ Can I make some conclusions, or express points of view, on the topic? Can I grade these in terms of their importance? Of their strength or validity?
- ▶ Can I support my conclusions with relevant evidence? With good logic?
- ▶ Can I estimate the accuracy or value of my conclusions?
- ▶ Can I judge the "good" or "bad," the "right" or "wrong" of an issue?

APPLYING your knowledge

- ▶ Can I state a probability or general rule as a result of my findings?
- ▶ Can I make a prediction about future developments on the topic or problem?
- ▶ Of what use are my discoveries or conclusions? (How can I connect them to the real world?)
- ▶ How might I act on my findings?

Perhaps you have noticed that there is a kind of hierarchy to this skill-building process. By this we mean that the one stage leads to the next, each becoming more important and somewhat more difficult. Your plan should be to:

1 become more aware of these skill areas,
2 honestly assess (perhaps with your teacher's help) your own present ability in each main area,
3 step into the process at whatever point is appropriate to your needs and abilities,
4 work toward the ultimate goal of being skillful in the areas of *analyzing* and *applying* your knowledge. This is what it's all about! GOOD LUCK!

unit one

THE GOVERNMENT OF CANADA

TOPIC ORGANIZER

THEME ORGANIZER

- Government around us: The role of government in our daily lives
- Levels of government: The three levels of government in Canada
- Our Constitution: The rules government plays by
- The federal government: The structure of our federal system
- The people who lead us: The role of the prime minister and the cabinet
- The legislative branch: The role of our lawmakers
- Elections: The democratic process
- Political parties: How and why groups organize
- Provincial governments: Protecting regional interests
- Municipal governments: Protecting local interests
- The system of taxation: Paying for government services

INTRODUCTION

How do you react to the prospect of studying government and politics? Many high-school students would say that this subject is dull, boring and tiresome. This attitude may be due to the way government and politics have been studied in the past. Too often the "machinery" of government is what was stressed. This included how a bill is passed, the seating arrangement in the House of Commons, the qualifications of voters and so on. Of course, knowing these things will help you to understand how we are governed. However, the true study of government and politics is much more exciting. It includes an analysis of how power is gained and how it is used. Whether we talk about gaining power in a high-school student council election or becoming a member of parliament in Ottawa, the process is similar.

The humourist Oscar Wilde defined a politician as "an animal who can sit on a fence and yet keep both ears to the ground." Stop for a moment. What does that definition mean? Do you agree with it? Why or why not? Government has also been described as an art, "the art of making people live together in peace and with reasonable happiness." Do you agree that governing is an art? Can you give reasons why this is so? When you study government, you are also studying people. For all of these reasons, the study of government and politics should be far from boring. In fact, it can be interesting and exciting.

Today, more than ever before, it is vital for Canadians to understand their country and how it is governed. We are faced with serious problems. These include maintaining our freedom and rights and our balance of trade and problems with inflation and unemployment. These are issues that we will have to face as citizens. They are also issues that only government can deal with effectively.

UNIT PREVIEW QUESTIONS

As you study this unit, keep these questions in mind; they will serve as a focus for your reading. You may want to return to them when you have finished the unit.

1. Why is government necessary? Try to imagine life without governments and laws.
2. Canada has three levels of government, each with different responsibilities. This is called a federal system. Why does Canada not have only one level of government?
3. Our political leaders can have a much greater influence on our lives than actors or rock stars. How many Canadian prime ministers can you name? Discuss the impact political leaders have on our daily lives.
4. The Charter of Rights and Freedoms gives Canadians many new rights. Can you see any problems, or disagreements, that the Charter may cause?
5. The monarch is considered to be only a figurehead, or symbol. Does the Queen have any real function in our system of government?
6. It has been argued that our political leaders must have "media appeal" to be elected. What

qualities would you look for in a good prime minister?

7 The salary and expenses of a member of parliament are often the subject of discussion. Compare the working day routine of an MP with his or her salary. Do you think MPs are overpaid or underpaid?

8 The role of the Senate in our government is a continuing issue. Should our Senate be abolished?

9 Of the three levels of government, Canadians are least familiar with local government. Compare the services of your municipal government with those of the federal government. Which are more important to you?

10 Recent estimates show that Canadians pay over fifty percent of their income to the government in the form of various taxes. Are Canadians overtaxed? If so, which services should government reduce or eliminate to cut back on taxes?

chapter 1

THE GOVERNMENT OF CANADA

TOPIC ORGANIZER | **PAGE**

THEME ORGANIZER

- The need for government: Government all around us
- Types of government: From dictatorship to democracy
- Canada's Constitution: From the BNA Act to the Constitutional Act
- Levels of government: Canada as a federal system
- Powers of government: Who makes, enforces and interprets our laws

INTRODUCTION

In the scene opposite, you are looking at a typical street in any one of a hundred towns and cities across Canada. At first glance, not much that is out of the ordinary appears to be happening. This chapter, however, is all about government and its impact on *you* and on the way you live. Examine this scene more closely. What do you see that is the result of some government action? In countless ways, large and small, governments and the laws they make affect you every day of your life.

Three centuries ago, the Englishman Thomas Hobbes used these words to describe what life would be like without government:

> During that time when men live without a common power (a government) to keep them all in awe, they are in that condition which is called war, and such a war is of every man against every man. . . . In such a condition there is no place for industry . . . no culture of the earth . . . no navigation . . . no knowledge of the face of the earth; no account of time, no arts, no letters, no societies; and which is worst of all, continual fear and danger of violent death, and the life of man solitary, poor, nasty, brutish and short.

1 What problems does Hobbes say a society will have if there is no "common power" (or government) to keep order?
2 How will the presence of a government prevent these problems?

Since that time, many writers have used this theme in their books. You may have read the book, *Lord of the Flies*, by William Golding. Perhaps you have seen the film of the book. It tells the fictional (made up) story of school boys who survive a plane wreck on a coral island. The boys struggle to survive by getting

CITY PARK
NO BIKES IN PARK
STOP
BANK
PUBLIC LIBRARY
KEEP CLEAN
KEEP CLEAN
CANADA POST
POLICE

used to one another and to their surroundings. Television and the movies have also used this theme. There are endless stories of plane-crash or shipwreck survivors on deserted islands who must organize a mini-society. What do all of these stories have in common? In all cases, one of the very first actions of the survivors is to pick leaders. In other words, they form a government. Government is one of the necessities of life. There is no human society known that does not have some way of choosing leaders or forming a government.

Before reading on, study the chart of key words and ideas that follows.

KEY WORDS AND IDEAS IN THIS CHAPTER

Term	Meaning	Sample Use
BNA Act	the British North America Act, passed in 1867	The BNA Act defines the powers of the federal and provincial governments.
constitutional monarchy	a country ruled by a monarch whose power is limited by law	Canada today is an example of a constitutional monarchy.
democracy	a country in which the government rests in the hands of the majority	Literally, democracy means "the people rule." In modern democracies, the people rule through their elected representatives.
dictatorship	a country in which the government rests in the hands of one person or group	Germany under Hitler was an example of a dictatorship.
executive power	the powers of a government to enforce the laws of the land	In Canada, the executive power rests in the hands of the prime minister and the cabinet.
federalism	a type of government in which several regions are brought together under one central government; the regions keep their regional and local governments	Canadian federalism is described in the BNA Act. Section 91 of the Act defines the federal powers. Section 92 defines provincial powers.
judicial power	the power of the government to decide the justness of a law and punish lawbreakers	In Canada, the highest judicial power is held by the Supreme Court.
legislative power	the power of a government to pass laws	In Canada, the legislative power rests in the hands of Parliament.

THE GOVERNMENT OF CANADA

Thomas Hobbes's description of society without government sounds very frightening. Does he exaggerate the importance of government? Consider the question from a very personal point of view. How does government affect YOU? Select an average day in your life. You go to school, you eat, you work, play and sleep. It does not look like government has any effect on you. Examine your routine a little more closely. If you made a detailed list of your daily activities, it might include many of the following: turning on the radio or television, eating meat and vegetables, walking on sidewalks or riding in a car or bus or on a bicycle, mailing a letter, buying clothes and going to school.

Each of these activities is controlled in some way by some level of government. Explain what role the

TORONTO'S BEST MUSIC

HOT HITS

LW	TW	TITLE	ARTIST	ALBUM	WKS. ON
1	1	Mony Mony	Billy Idol	Vital Idol	7
2	2	Only In My Dreams	Debbie Gibson	Out Of The Blue	9
3	3	Bad	Michael Jackson	Bad	9
4	4	Lost In Emotion	Lisa Lisa & Cult Jam	Spanish Fly	6
6	5	Causing A Commotion	Madonna	Soundtrack — "Who's That Girl"	6
10	6	Try	Blue Rodeo	Outskirts	5
5	7	I Heard A Rumour	Bananarama	Wow	8
16	8	(I've Had) The Time Of My Life	Bill Medley/Jennifer Warnes	Soundtrack — "Dirty Dancing"	4
9	9	Brilliant Disguise	Bruce Springsteen	Tunnel Of Love	6
11	10	Here I Go Again	Whitesnake	Whitesnake	7
12	11	It's A Sin	Pet Shop Boys	Actually	4
7	12	Paper In Fire	John Cougar Mellencamp	The Lonesome Jubilee	9
14	13	Little Lies	Fleetwood Mac	Tango In The Night	7
20	14	Casanova	Levert	The Big Throwdown	3
17	15	The One I Love	R.E.M.	Document	6
21	16	I Think We're Alone Now	Tiffany	Tiffany	3
13	17	Together (The New Wedding Song)	Joey Gregorash	Together/Various	17
18	18	Stay With Me	Tu	Tu	6
19	19	Last Of The Red Hot Fools	The Jitters	The Jitters	5
8	20	Where The Streets Have No Name	U2	The Joshua Tree	7
24	21	Heaven Is A Place On Earth	Belinda Carlisle	Heaven On Earth	2
25	22	Contact	Platinum Blonde	Contact	5
29	23	We'll Be Together	Sting	Nothing Like The Sun	2
15	24	La Bamba	Los Lobos	Soundtrack — "La Bamba"	15
28	25	U Got The Look	Prince	Sign 'O' The Times	2
—	26	Pop Goes The World	Men Without Hats	Pop Goes The World	1
23	27	Who Will You Run To	Heart	Bad Animals	9
30	28	Should've Known Better	Richard Marx	Richard Marx	2
22	29	Didn't We Almost Have It All	Whitney Houston	Whitney	11
26	30	When Smokey Sings	ABC	Alphabet City	12

HOW THE GOVERNMENT AFFECTS YOUR LIFE

1·2·3 Read carefully the above chart listing the most popular songs on a recent singles chart. You may recognize a number of the tunes. Now try to answer the following questions:

- Which of these songs are sung by Canadians?
- Which of these songs were written by Canadians?

At this point, you may be saying to yourself, "Hey, this is fun, but what does the singles chart have to do with the study of government and politics?" This exercise was intended to make one point: Much of what we do in our daily lives is even the songs on the singles chart. There is a Canadian law regarding the amount of Canadian content that radio and television stations must broadcast. At least 60 percent of all the music broadcast by a radio station must be written, produced or sung by Canadians. When you buy records, you are directly influenced by what you hear on the radio. So the record you choose may be influenced by the Canadian-content-in-broadcasting law. There are many such laws that touch our lives without our ever being aware of them. You can see the influence that our government has on our affairs, be they small matters or large.

government plays in these activities. More and more in our complex society, government regulates (makes rules about) our daily activities.

Here are some of the things that are looked after by various governments in Canada.

- ▶ transportation and communication
- ▶ health, education, welfare, social security
- ▶ business and labour
- ▶ wages and prices
- ▶ development of natural resources
- ▶ foreign trade
- ▶ agricultural production

These are all recent additions to the power of government. The government can also make you do things you may not want to do, such as:

- ▶ make you pay taxes and fines
- ▶ require you to sell your home
- ▶ forbid you to travel to certain places
- ▶ force you to leave the country
- ▶ suspend your rights
- ▶ send you to jail
- ▶ send you to war

This trend of increased government regulation is likely to continue in the future.

Most people agree on the need for government. There is widespread disagreement as to what kind of government is best. The types of governments can be reduced to two: One is "government of the many"; the other, "government of the few." Of course, "government of the few" can take many forms. The power to govern can rest in the hands of one person or group. This is called a dictatorship. Dictators are not bound by rules of law or by constitutions. They ARE the law. Recent examples of dictatorships include the governments of Adolf Hitler in Germany and Muammar Qaddafi in Libya.

Another form of one-person rule is monarchy. In this system the ruler inherits the position of power. The monarch lives within the rule of law. Centuries ago, the monarch was all-powerful, much like a modern-day dictator. King Louis XIV of France once stated, "L'etat — c'est moi!" "The state — I am the state!"

In time, the role of the monarchy decreased as the power of assemblies elected by the people grew. These elected assemblies, or parliaments, eventually limited the powers of the monarchs by law. Where a parliament and the monarch ruled together under law, the government became known as a constitutional monarchy. In most such arrangements, the role of the monarchy continued to decline. Its duties became mostly symbolic. The British Commonwealth is an example of a constitutional monarchy today.

In some countries the power to govern rests in the hands of a privileged class. This group may be thought superior because of birth or wealth or intelligence. Such a government by the "best" citizens is called an aristocracy.

FORM OF GOVERNMENT

What form of government do we have in Canada? In theory, Canada is a monarchy. The British North America Act states:

> The Executive government and Authority of and over Canada is hereby declared to continue and be vested in the Queen.

The BNA Act was passed in Britain in 1867. At that time Canada remained almost a colony of Britain. As Canada matured and gained her independence, the role of the monarchy became very small. In practice, then, Canada is a democracy, a "government of the many." All citizens have a voice in choosing their leaders. The word democracy comes from two Greek words, DEMOS (people) and KRATOS (power); in other words, the people rule.

In some countries, the combination of strong national pride and strong religious beliefs has led to the control of the government by religious leaders. An example of this is modern-day Iran, which is dominated by Moslem religious leaders called ayatollahs. This type of government is called a theocracy.

Obviously, in a country the size of Canada, it is impossible for each citizen to rule directly. The people, therefore, choose representatives. They govern in our place. These members of government meet in a parliament. In this place, new laws are discussed. For this reason, Canada's system is known as parliamentary government. Canada's Parliament consists of the following: elected representatives who sit in the House of Commons; an appointed Senate; and the governor general, who represents the Queen. Together they are responsible for making and enforcing the laws of the land.

THE LEVELS OF GOVERNMENT IN CANADA

In 1867, when the Fathers of Confederation created a new Canada, they faced the question, "What form of government shall we have?" The sheer size of the country dictated the answer. Canada was a huge country with a scattered population. The people of the Maritimes, Quebec, Ontario and the West saw themselves as groups having their own history, culture and economic interests. They felt strongly about protecting their unique traditions. Each region was willing to join in political union with the rest of Canada, but not at the expense of its own interests.

Even today these local and regional loyalties remain strong. A person from Halifax considers himself a Canadian, but also a proud Nova Scotian. A person in Burnaby shares a common bond with all Canadians, but she may also talk of the differences between British Columbians and all other Canadians. What has allowed these regional differences to continue? It is the unique form of government created in 1867 that we call Canadian federalism.

Three levels of government were created in Canada. Each has its own responsibilities. The federal government, through its Parliament in Ottawa, looks after matters that concern all the people in Canada. These include defence and international agreements. The provincial governments, through their own legislatures, look after affairs that concern only the people in their provinces. Hospitals and schools are two examples of these. Municipal or local governments take care of matters of a purely local nature, such as local roads and sewers.

This system lets Canada unite a huge territory. At the same time, it should allow people of different regions to follow their own interests, religion and way of life and to use their own language.

The Government of Canada

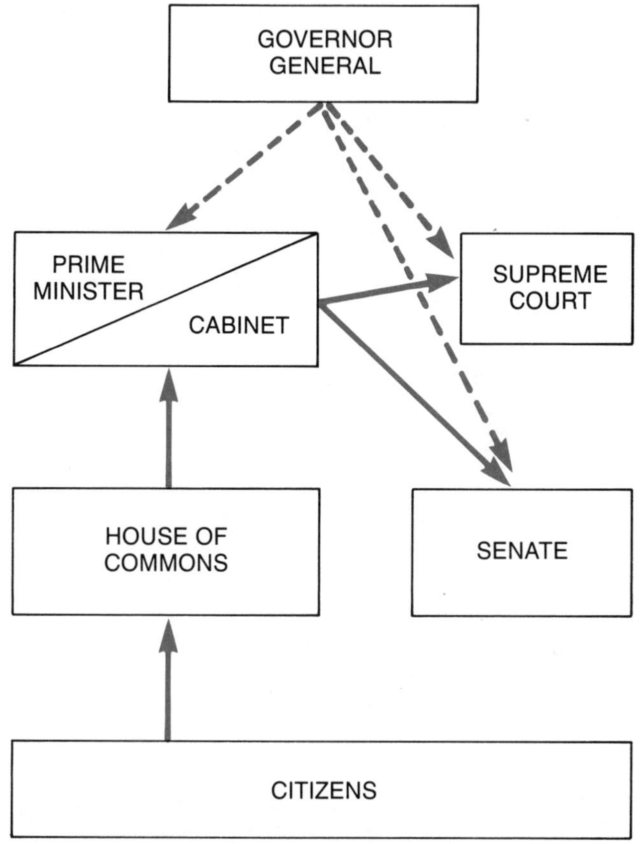

THE CONSTITUTION OF CANADA

Have you ever belonged to a school club or been a member of a sports team? If so, among the first things you learned were the rules of the club and the rules of the game. It would not be possible to have organized events without rules that everyone understood and followed. What is true for school clubs and teams is just as true for societies and countries.

The system of rules a society must live by is called a constitution. Very simply, a constitution is a set of basic laws and customs. The constitution of the National Hockey League sets down the rules that teams and players must follow. The Constitution of Canada sets down the rules our governments must follow, as well as the rights of those who are governed.

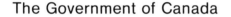

In some countries, such as the United States, the entire constitution was planned and written at a single place and time. In others, such as Great Britain, the constitution has evolved from various customs over many centuries. As a result, it may be largely unwritten. Canada, because of its British and American heritage, has a constitution that is partly written and partly unwritten.

Since 1867 the written part of Canada's Constitution has consisted of the British North America Act. We will use the short form, BNA Act, in referring to it. As we will see in the next several chapters, the BNA Act defined the powers of government and the division of these powers between the federal and provincial governments. The BNA Act, however, was an act of British Parliament. This meant that if Canadians wished to change, or amend, their Constitution, they would have to ask Britain to do so. In fact, since 1867 the act was amended more than twenty times.

Over the years the feeling grew that a constitution for Canadians should be an act of the Canadian Parliament. It should be written and changed in Canada. Finally, in 1982, the Canada Act was passed, giving Canada its own Constitution. The new Constitution added the following features to the existing BNA Act:

Prime Minister Pierre Trudeau looks on with obvious satisfaction as Queen Elizabeth II signs the constitutional proclamation in Ottawa.

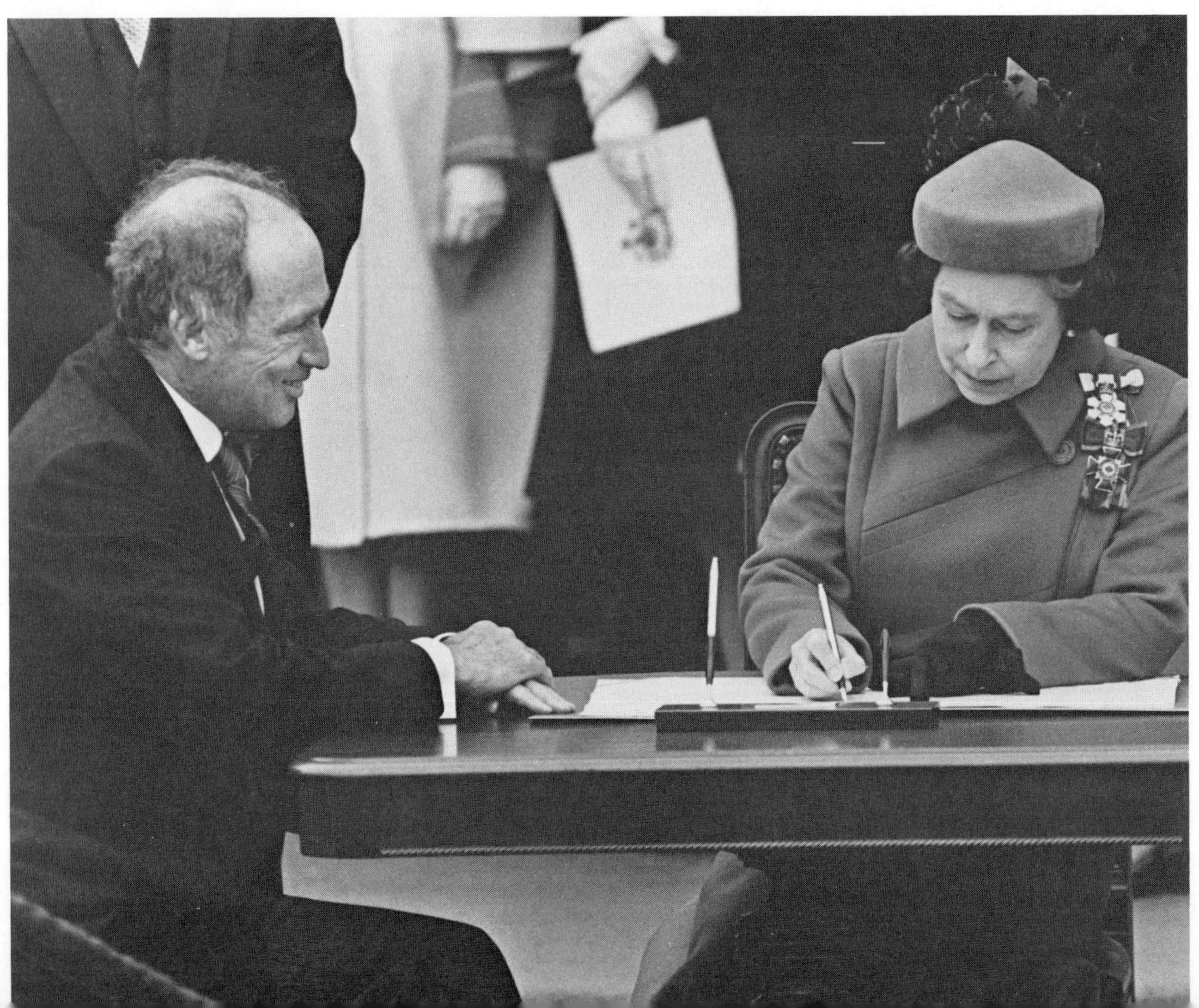

THE CONSTITUTION ACT 1982

PART I: THE CANADIAN CHARTER OF RIGHTS AND FREEDOMS

For a long time Canadians have had many rights and freedoms. For the first time in our history, these rights are now written down and protected by a Constitution.

A Democratic Rights

All Canadian citizens of legal age are guaranteed the following rights:

1 The right to vote in federal or provincial elections
2 The right to run for office in these elections
3 Neither the House of Commons nor the provincial legislatures can sit for longer than five years, except under special circumstances.
4 There must be an annual sitting of Parliament and the provincial legislatures.

B Fundamental Freedoms

Everyone is guaranteed the following freedoms:

1 Freedom of conscience and religion
2 Freedom of thought, belief and expression, including freedom of the press and other media
3 Freedom of peaceful assembly
4 Freedom of association

C Legal Rights (See page 75)

D Mobility Rights

1 All Canadian citizens have the right to enter, remain in or leave Canada.
2 Every Canadian citizen has the right to move, take up residence or seek a job in any province.

E Official Language Rights

Every citizen has the right to use English or French in dealing with the federal government. New Brunswick, Quebec and Manitoba also protect the use of English and French in their legislatures and courts.

F Minority Language Education Rights

Canadian citizens educated in English may send their children to English schools in Quebec. In the other nine provinces, any citizen whose mother tongue is French may send his or her children to French schools.

G Equality Rights

The rights and freedoms of this Charter are guaranteed to all citizens. There is no discrimination based on race, ethnic origin, religion, sex or age.

H Aboriginal Rights

The right of Canada's native peoples — Indians, Inuit and Metis—including their treaty rights, are guaranteed by this Charter.

PART II

I Equalization and Regional Disparities

Both federal and provincial governments agree to try to provide equal opportunities for all Canadians and reduce regional economic inequalities. The federal government will continue to make equalization payments for this purpose.

J Natural Resources

The provinces are given control over the exploration, development and management of natural resources. The provinces may also pass laws regarding the export of nonrenewable resources (such as oil and coal) from one province to another. They are also entitled to raise indirect taxes on these resources.

K Amendments to the Constitution

Perhaps the greatest roadblock to the creation of the new Constitution was the disagreement over how to make changes, or amendments, to it in the future. A formula was finally agreed upon. It states that any amendment must have the agreement of the Parliament of Canada, plus seven provinces whose total population represents at least 50 percent of the population of Canada.

Any province that does not approve a particular amendment may "opt out," and the changes will not apply to that province. No more than three provinces may opt out of an amendment.

For some matters, such as those affecting the monarchy and the Supreme Court, the agreement of the federal government and all provinces is required.

THE MEECH LAKE ACCORD

The Constitution Act of 1982 possessed one major flaw: It was agreed to by only nine of Canada's ten provinces. The one holdout was a key one, the Province of Quebec. René Lévesque and his Parti Québécois government refused to sign the new Constitution, insisting on greater powers for Quebec, powers which Pierre Trudeau's federal government refused to concede.

With a new federal government led by Brian Mulroney and a new Quebec provincial government under Robert Bourassa, negotiations to bring Quebec into the constitutional fold resumed. On April 30, 1987, during a conference at Meech Lake, Quebec, a tentative agreement was signed between the federal government and all ten provincial premiers. The Meech Lake Accord, as it is known, brings Quebec into the Constitution and provides for some major changes in federal–provincial powers. The major features of the Accord include the following:

- recognition of Quebec as a "distinct society" within Canada.
- increased control of immigration to Quebec and the other provinces.
- an increased voice to the provinces on the appointment of Supreme Court judges and Senators.
- the provincial option to drop out of national shared-cost programs (programs jointly financed by federal and provincial governments).

The Accord has become a controversial issue in Canadian politics. On one hand, its supporters point out that it finally brings Quebec into the Constitution. On the other hand, critics claim that it weakens the

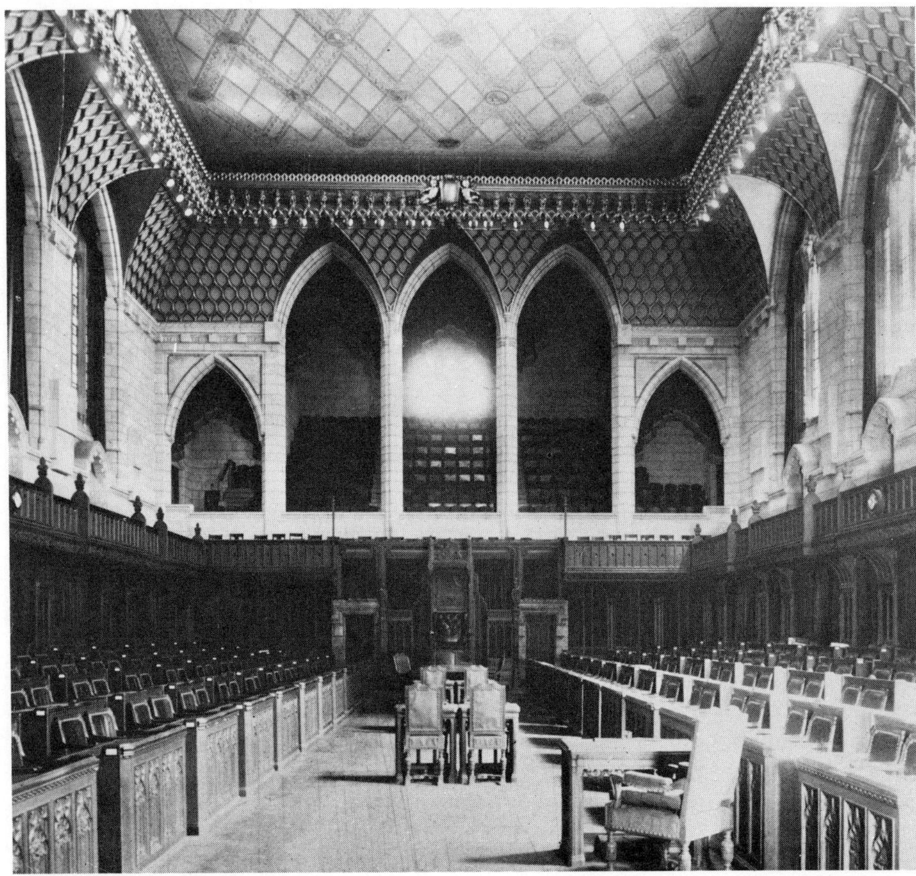

The House of Commons, Ottawa. The speaker's chair is in the centre of the photograph. The members of the government sit in the seats on the speaker's right. The Opposition sits on the left. The party leaders sit front row centre, opposite each other.

federal government by giving too much power to the provinces. Other objections have come from women's groups and native people's groups who fear that the Accord, by seeming to give special powers to the provinces, may weaken their rights under the Charter of Rights and Freedoms. To date, Canada's federal and provincial governments are in unanimous agreement on the Meech Lake Accord.

THE POWERS OF GOVERNMENT IN CANADA

All governments, from the student council at your school to federal government in Ottawa, exercise three basic powers. The first is the power to make laws and regulations. This is called legislative power. Once a law is passed, it must be carried out and enforced. That is, people must be made to follow the law. This is known as executive power. Finally, the government must have the power to punish those who break the laws. This is called the judicial power.

As we have seen, Canada is a democracy. In order to keep our system as democratic as possible, we have divided these powers among different groups. In our federal government, the legislative power is given to the House of Commons and the Senate. The executive power rests with the governor general, the prime minister and the cabinet. The judicial power is in the hands of the Supreme Court and other lower courts throughout the land. This area will be discussed in a later chapter on the law.

BUILDING YOUR LEARNING SKILLS

FOCUSSING ON THE ISSUE

1 What key ideas about the nature of government are presented in this chapter? Select four, and compare them with those your classmates have chosen.

2 Formulate five questions, the answers to which will help you remember some of the key ideas in this chapter. One example might be, "In what way is a monarchy different from a dictatorship?"

3 The following terms appeared in this chapter. Try to recall their meanings and how they were used.

aristocracy	federalism
BNA Act	judicial power
constitutional monarchy	legislative power
democracy	monarchy
dictatorship	Parliament
executive power	Supreme Court

RESEARCHING

1 Make a study of a twentieth-century dictator. Possible choices include Adolf Hitler, Benito Mussolini, Josef Stalin and Idi Amin. Provide an analysis of the dictator's background, personality and how he or she came to power. Also explain how this individual's actions qualify him or her to be called a dictator.

2 Try to find out if your favourite radio station is following the rules for Canadian content in broadcasting. Listen to one hour on the radio, and try to figure out what percentage of the programming was Canadian.

3 It has been said that the countries that have democratic governments are in the minority. With the help of your teacher and the encyclopedia, try to make a list of the countries around the world that are democracies. What percentage of the world's nations are run democratically?

ORGANIZING

1 Draw up a chart for the following activity: Make a list of the various types of governments found around the world. List at least three strong points and three weak points for each form of government.

2 As a follow-up to the above, rank these governments from best to worst, in your opinion. Compare your rankings with those of your classmates.

3 Refer to the picture of a street scene on page 5. Make a list of the various activities in which there is government involvement.

COMMUNICATING

1 Organize a daily "radio news" show for the class, in which the top international, national, regional and local news is reported. Different students in the class may take turns producing this show.
2 Imagine that you are a newspaper reporter. Write a column on the top news story of the week. Select a topic that involves the federal and/or provincial government.
3 Contact a member of one of your school clubs (student council or the chess club). Ask for a copy of the club's constitution. Report to your class on the main features of this constitution.
4 Organize a House of Commons debate on what Canada should do about international terrorism.

ANALYZING

1 It is usually argued that Hitler's Germany was a dictatorship because it was run by one man. Yet, Hitler was initially elected by the people with an overwhelming majority vote. Is a country a democracy if it votes for its government, even though all the powers of government rest in the hands of one man?
2 The Canadian content ruling was designed to promote Canadian performers on radio and television. Do you think it is fair of the government to force the public to see and hear Canadian performers, even though they may not be the very best available?
3 If the government wants to build a road or an airport, it has the power to expropriate (or buy up) any property it needs. This was the case in Pickering, Ontario, when the federal government decided to build a new airport. Dozens of homeowners were forced to sell their homes and farms and move out. Do you feel the government should have such power?
4 Organize a class conference on the issue of the Meech Lake Accord. The class should be organized into groups with each representing a different interest group affected by this agreement. Included should be groups representing women's interests, native people's interests, Quebec's point of view, and the point of view of strong federalists. Before this class conference is called, each group should do research on their area of interest. Contemporary newspapers, vertical file material and specific organizations can be the source of this research.

APPLYING YOUR KNOWLEDGE

1 Thomas Hobbes described the situation that might exist if a society had no government. Of course, every society today has a government, so his theory may be difficult to prove. Society does come close to a state of "no government," however, in several situations. It might be argued that during rioting and wars no real laws or authority exist. Try to discover what occurred in the rioting in major US cities during the 1960s. Study the behaviour of soldiers during wartime. Is Hobbes right?
2 To successfully complete the following assignment, you will have to apply the knowledge you gained in this first chapter. Imagine that you and your classmates have been shipwrecked on a deserted island. The chances of an immediate rescue are remote. You will have to organize a society. Your first task is to organize a government and make laws.

Among the things you must decide are the following:

- ▶ What form of government shall we have?
- ▶ How will leaders be selected?
- ▶ Who will be allowed to choose leaders?
- ▶ What laws will we make regarding private property, equality of the sexes, job opportunities, freedom of speech and education?
- ▶ What will happen to those who break the law? For these tasks, the class may be broken up into several committees, each responsible for making recommendations. The recommendations can then be debated and the best ones adopted.

chapter 2

THE FEDERAL GOVERNMENT

TOPIC ORGANIZER **PAGE**

THEME ORGANIZER

- The governor general: symbol of monarchy
- The prime minister: the most powerful Canadian
- The cabinet: Are the best people in charge?
- The members of Parliament: A day in the life of an MP
- The Senate: Do we still need a Senate?
- The right to vote: cornerstone of our democratic system
- Political parties: What do our main parties stand for?
- Interest groups: Can minorities pressure governments?

INTRODUCTION

When we speak of the federal government, we are referring to the Parliament in Ottawa. The BNA Act, which is part of Canada's new Constitution, stated that "There shall be one parliament for Canada, consisting of the Queen, an upper house styled the Senate, and the House of Commons."

The BNA Act also mentioned what the powers of this Parliament would be. Section 91 of the act stated:

> *Section 91 — Powers of Parliament*
> 91. It shall be lawful for the Queen, by and with the Advice and Consent of the Senate and House of Commons, **to make Laws for the Peace, Order, and good Government of Canada**, in relation to all Matters not coming within the Classes of Subjects by this Act assigned exclusively to the Legislatures of the Provinces; and for greater Certainty, but not so as to restrict the Generality of the foregoing Terms in this Section, it is hereby declared that (notwithstanding anything in this Act) the exclusive Legislative Authority of the Parliament of Canada extends to all Matters coming within the Classes of Subjects next hereinafter enumerated; that is to say,—
>
> 1. The Public Debt and Property
> *Replaced in 1949 by: 1. The amendment from time to time of the Constitution of Canada, except as regards matters coming within the classes of subjects by this Act assigned exclusively to the Legislatures of the provinces, or as regards rights or privileges by this or any other Constitutional Act granted or secured to the Legislature or the Government of a province, or to any class of persons with respect to schools or as regards the use of the English or the French language, or as regards the requirements that there shall be a session of the Parliament of Canada at least once*

each year, and that no House of Commons shall continue for more than five years from the day of the return of the writs for choosing the House; provided, however, that a House of Commons may in time of real or apprehended war, invasion or insurrection be continued by the Parliament of Canada if such continuation is not opposed by the votes of more than one-third of the members of such House.

1A. *The Public Debt and Property. (Renumbered, 1949.)*
2. The Regulation of Trade and Commerce.
2A. *Unemployment Insurance. (Added, 1940.)*
3. The raising of Money by any Mode or System of Taxation.
4. The borrowing of Money on the Public Credit.
5. Postal Service.
6. The Census and Statistics.
7. Militia, Military and Naval Service, and Defence.
8. The fixing of and providing for the Salaries and Allowances of Civil and other Officers of the Government of Canada.
9. Beacons, Buoys, Lighthouses, and Sable Island.
10. Navigation and Shipping.
11. Quarantine and the Establishment and Maintenance of Marine Hospitals.
12. Sea Coast and Inland Fisheries.
13. Ferries between a Province and any British or Foreign Country or between Two Provinces.
14. Currency and Coinage.
15. Banking, Incorporation of Banks, and the Issue of Paper Money.
16. Savings Banks.
17. Weights and Measures.
18. Bills of Exchange and Promissory Notes.
19. Interest.
20. Legal Tender.
21. Bankruptcy and Insolvency.
22. Patents of Invention and Discovery.
23. Copyrights.
24. Indians and Lands reserved for the Indians.
25. Naturalization and Aliens.
26. Marriage and Divorce.
27. The Criminal Law, except the Constitution of Courts of Criminal Jurisdiction, but including the Procedure in Criminal Matters.
28. The Establishment, Maintenance, and Management of Penitentiaries.
29. Such Classes of Subjects as are expressly excepted in the Enumeration of the Classes of Subjects by this Act assigned exclusively to the Legislatures of the Provinces.

And any Matter coming within any of the Classes of Subjects enumerated in this Section shall not be deemed to come within the Class of Matters of a local or private Nature comprised in the Enumeration of the Classes of Subjects by this Act assigned exclusively to the Legislatures of the Provinces.

The Parliament of Canada can make laws about things not listed under Section 91. Many things have happened since 1867. The writers of the Constitution could not have foreseen cars, airplanes, televisions, world wars and depressions. Laws have had to be passed dealing with these matters. Parliament has taken its right to do so from the "Peace, Order and Good Government" clause of Section 91.

Before reading on, study the chart of key words and ideas that follows.

KEY WORDS AND IDEAS IN THIS CHAPTER

Term	Meaning	Sample Use
bureaucracy	organization made up of people at different levels of power, in this case, officials in a government administration	The bureaucracy in Canada's government influences decisions made by our elected officials. This is due to their vast knowledge and experience.
cabinet solidarity	cabinet unity once the majority in the cabinet has reached a decision; every member is expected to publicly support that decision or resign	Rather than break cabinet solidarity, a minister will sometimes resign from the cabinet if he or she disagrees with a decision.
caucus	a private meeting of members of the House of Commons who belong to the same political party	Caucus is the place where MPs can express their own opinions on the issues of the day. In the House of Commons, they are expected to follow the party line.

lobbying	the attempt by certain groups to influence members of Parliament	In Ottawa, offices are set up on a full-time basis by certain groups. They are staffed by individuals whose only job is lobbying MPs.
political spectrum	the various shades of political philosophy or ideas held by different political parties in a country	In Canada the political spectrum extends from the conservative "right" to the socialist "left."
pressure groups	certain organized groups that try to persuade government to make decisions that favour their interests	The Canadian Manufacturers' Association and the Canadian Labour Congress are examples of two powerful pressure groups operating in Ottawa.

THE EXECUTIVE BRANCH

In our federal government, the power to carry out and enforce the law is given to the prime minister and the cabinet. The governor general has these powers to a lesser extent.

THE GOVERNOR GENERAL

A century ago the governor general, as the Queen's representative, played a major role in Canada's affairs. Today his or her role is mainly a symbolic, formal one. The main duty is to make sure that the government carries on. For example, if the prime minister died suddenly, the governor general would find a replacement. In this matter, he or she would accept the advice of Parliament. A similar duty may arise following an election. If no party has a clear majority, it is up to the governor general to pick a prime minister. Again, this would be done on the advice of the elected members of Parliament.

Another duty of the governor general is to sign into law all bills passed in Parliament. However, this is a mere formality (an act done because it is the custom). The governor general cannot refuse to sign a bill.

The governor general also performs official social and ceremonial duties. These include the opening and closing of Parliament and greeting foreign heads of state. In sum, the governor general is the symbol of the British tradition in our system of government.

The throne chair in the Senate. This chair is used only by the reigning monarch or the governor general. It is a symbol of the respect given the Crown in Canada.

Until 1952 the governors general of Canada were British. They were chosen from among well-known people in British public life. Since then the custom has been to select Canadians for this position. The distinguished Canadians who have held this office include:

- Vincent Massey (1952–1959)
- Georges Vanier (1959–1967)
- Roland Michener (1967–1974)
- Jules Léger (1974–1978)
- Edward Schreyer (1978–1984)
- Jeanne Sauvé (1984–)

IS THE MONARCHY (REPRESENTED BY THE GOVERNOR GENERAL) NECESSARY TO CANADA?

YES:

- The monarchy is a symbol of our ties with Great Britain.
- The monarchy is a symbol of our British parliamentary heritage.
- The monarchy links Canada with the other 35 Commonwealth countries. They too accept the queen as their head.
- Most people enjoy the pomp and pageantry connected with royalty. It adds colour to the political scene.
- The queen is above petty politics. She is able to remain neutral. This is an important quality in a symbolic head of state.
- If we abolish the monarchy, we will have to replace it with another position (perhaps a presidency).

NO:

- The monarchy is only a symbol. It has no real role in our system of government.
- The monarchy is a throwback to the old days, when the upper classes ran governments. It goes against the spirit of democracy.
- The monarchy is an issue that divides Canadians. French-Canadians are almost totally against it.
- The role of the monarchy in our government confuses people from other countries. They have a hard time understanding our stress on the *symbolic* nature of the Queen and governor general.

THE PRIME MINISTER

The most powerful position in Canada's government is that of prime minister. It might surprise you to learn that the position of prime minister is not even mentioned in the BNA Act. This is one of the clearest examples of an institution (in the British parliamentary system) that developed from custom.

The BNA Act merely says that "There shall be a Council to aid and advise the Government of Canada, to be styled the Queen's Privy Council for Canada." The leader of this privy council (now the cabinet) is called prime minister.

The duties of the office are not outlined. The role of prime minister has changed a lot since 1867. As we have seen, the role of government has greatly increased since Confederation. At the same time, the direct influence of the monarchy has decreased. The result has been a continual growth in the power of the prime minister.

Electing a Prime Minister In the United States, citizens vote directly for their president. We do not vote for a prime minister in federal elections. The person

SOME RECENT PARTY LEADERS

Examine closely the backgrounds of Liberal and Conservative party leaders in the charts on pages 19 and 20.

1 From what provinces do the majority of Liberal leaders come? How might this affect their political support in elections?

2 What seems to be the professional and educational background of most party leaders? Do you feel this suitably qualifies them for the position of prime minister?

3 Which of the leaders actually became prime minister?

4 Examine the background of each leader. Try to calculate the areas of the country that might support him in an election. Now try to check your predictions with the actual results of the federal elections in which these leaders ran.

The official residence of the prime minister in Ottawa.

LIBERAL PARTY LEADERS IN THE TWENTIETH CENTURY

Name	Age When Elected	Home Province	Selected Leader	Parliamentary Experience	Education	Profession	Religion	Ancestry
Wilfrid Laurier	45	Quebec	1887	MLA, 1871–1874; MP, 1874; cabinet minister, 1877	College-Assumption	lawyer	Catholic	French
W.L. Mackenzie King	45	Ontario	1919	MP and cabinet minister, 1908–1911 (Department of Labour)	University of Toronto, Harvard	civil servant/ industrial relations advisor	Presbyterian	Scottish
Louis St. Laurent	66	Quebec	1948	cabinet minister	Laval University	laywer	Catholic	French
Lester Pearson	60	Ontario	1958	cabinet minister, 1948–1957	University of Toronto, Oxford	civil servant	United Church	Irish
Pierre Trudeau	48	Quebec	1969	cabinet minister, 1967–1968	University of Montreal, Harvard, École des sciences politiques, London School of Economics	lawyer/ professor	Catholic	French/ English
John Turner	54	British Columbia	1984	cabinet minister, 1968–1976	University of British Columbia, Oxford	lawyer	Catholic	English

CONSERVATIVE PARTY LEADERS, 1927–1976

Name	Age When Elected	Home Province	Elected Leader	Parliamentary Experience	Education	Profession	Religion	Ancestry
R.B. Bennett	57	New Brunswick, Alberta	1927	Alberta MLA, 1909–1911; member of Parliament, 1911–1917, 1921, 1925–1927	Dalhousie University	lawyer	United Church	English
R.J. Manion	56	Ontario	1938	MP, 1917–1935; cabinet minister, 1921, 1926, 1930–1935	University of Toronto	physician	Catholic	Irish
J. Bracken	59	Manitoba	1942	premier of Manitoba, 1922–1943	Ontario Agricultural School, Guelph; University of Illinois	agricultural scientist	United Church	Scottish/ Irish/ English
G.A. Drew	54	Ontario	1948	premier of Ontario, 1943–1948	University of Toronto, Osgoode Hall Law School	lawyer	Anglican	English
J.G. Diefenbaker	61	Saskatchewan	1956	member of parliament, 1940–1956	University of Saskatchewan	lawyer	Baptist	German/ Scottish
R.L. Stanfield	53	Nova Scotia	1967	MLA, 1949–1967; premier of Nova Scotia, 1956–1967	Dalhousie University, Harvard Law School	lawyer	Anglican	English/ Welsh
J. Clark	37	Alberta	1976	member of parliament, 1972–1976	University of Alberta	politician	Catholic	Irish/ Scottish
Brian Mulroney	45	Quebec	1983	none	St. Francis Xavier, Laval	lawyer, business-person	Catholic	Irish

who becomes prime minister must first be chosen leader by his or her own party. The leader must also be elected to Parliament in his or her own riding. If the leader's party then wins the greatest number of seats in the House of Commons, he or she will become Prime Minister.

Our political system has been affected in many ways by the American experience. One example is the way Canadian political parties choose their leaders. The age of television has turned political conventions into glamourous spectacles. As a result, the person with the best "television image" and "charisma" (strong appeal) may be chosen leader. Real issues and answers can be ignored in favour of personalities. In the elections of 1958 and 1968, John Diefenbaker and Pierre Trudeau had dynamic public images. Their opponents, Lester Pearson and Robert Stanfield, could not match this appeal. This lack of "charisma" likely played a part in the election defeat of their parties.

When a party is about to elect a new leader, a convention is called. Local party branches from across the country send delegates to this convention. The delegates vote for a new leader from the list of

Past and Present Party Leaders: left: John Diefenbaker, PC, former prime minister; bottom left; Ed Broadbent, federal NDP, Stephen Lewis, provincial (Ontario) NDP; right: John Turner, Liberal leader and former prime minister.

announced candidates. Obviously, these delegates will be subject to great pressure from the candidates, who want to win their support.

THE THINKING STUDENT'S PRIME MINISTER

1 Which three of the following have the physical appearance of your ideal prime minister?
  - *a* Mavis Wilson
  - *b* Margaret Thatcher
  - *c* Chaviva Hosek
  - *d* Iona Campagnolo
  - *e* Corey Hart
  - *f* Lily Munro
  - *g* Jan Tennant
  - *h* Jesse Jackson
  - *i* John Diefenbaker
  - *j* Lester Pearson

2 Name two other people whose physical appearance comes closest to that of your ideal prime minister.

3 In age, the prime minister should be:
  - *a* under 33
  - *b* between 34 and 46
  - *c* between 47 and 60
  - *d* over 60

4 Of which party (if any) should the prime minister be leader?
  - *a* Liberals
  - *b* Conservatives
  - *c* the NDP
  - *d* the Social Credit
  - *e* the Rhinoceros party
  - *f* an entirely new party

5 The cultural heritage of the prime minister should be:
  - *a* English-Canadian
  - *b* French-Canadian
  - *c* German-Canadian
  - *d* Italian-Canadian
  - *e* Other

6 How important are each of the following for a prime minister? List in order from the most important to the least.
  - *a* university education
  - *b* religion
  - *c* bilingual ability
  - *d* non-political occupation
  - *e* significant personal wealth
  - *f* wealth earned, not inherited

7 Would you object to a prime minister who was:
  - *a* an atheist
  - *b* a muslim
  - *c* a protestant
  - *d* a Jew
  - *e* a Roman Catholic

8 Which one of the following would be the most appropriate non-political occupation of a prime minister?
  - *a* lawyer
  - *b* business executive
  - *c* professor
  - *d* labour union executive
  - *e* farmer
  - *f* minister
  - *g* doctor
  - *h* engineer
  - *i* athlete

9 What should the marital status of a prime minister be?
  - *a* married
  - *b* single
  - *c* doesn't matter

10 Of what sex should the prime minister be?

THE PRIME MINISTER IN OFFICE

The prime minister has vast power to exercise. It is his or her task to make most of the key appointments in government. The prime minister chooses cabinet ministers, Supreme Court justices, ambassadors and important civil servants. As leader of the cabinet, the prime minister makes government policy. The leader of the largest party in the House of Commons is also responsible for deciding the passage of bills into law. A prime minister must call an election at least once every five years. Within this limit, however, it is up to the prime minister to decide on the date of a federal election.

The prime minister also represents Canada in other countries. The prime minister and the cabinet must decide foreign policy and negotiate international agreements. Beyond our own borders, the image of Canada and Canadians is often created by the prime minister.

In short, the well-being of Canada both at home and abroad rests with the prime minister.

These photographs show some of the duties of the prime minister. Above, meeting with External Affairs Minister Joe Clark. Left, with Governor General Jeanne Sauvé meeting the Queen. Below, meeting reporters after a caucus decision.

THE CABINET

One person could not possibly handle the duties of government. The prime minister selects certain members of his or her party to help out with these tasks. This group, together with the prime minister, forms the cabinet. Each cabinet minister is responsible for a certain department, such as Defence, Finance or External Affairs. Each such responsibility is called a portfolio. In addition, there are several members of the cabinet who have no specific duties but are used as "troubleshooters" in other departments. These are called ministers without portfolio.

Each minister must answer to Parliament for the affairs of his or her department. He or she must introduce bills, explain the policies and answer questions for that area of responsibility.

Cabinet ministers also take part in deciding general government policy. These debates take place behind closed doors and are kept secret. Although there is often great disagreement, once a decision has been reached, each minister must publicly support it. If a member refuses to do so, he or she must resign from the cabinet. This principle is called cabinet solidarity.

George Hees explains why he resigned from the cabinet in 1963:

> Dear Mr. Prime Minister:
>
> As you know, I have been extremely concerned for some time about our defence policy and our relations with the United States.
>
> I have outlined to you, to my colleagues, and to the caucus of the Conservative party why I consider that our present defence policy does not either fulfill our international commitments or provide for the security of our country. I have also stated clearly that I consider that the present attitude of the government cannot but lead to a deterioration [worsening] of our relations with the United States.
>
> I had hoped that the views which I expressed would lead to changes in policy which would permit me to remain a member of the government. However, since that time there has been no indication of such change. I feel these matters to be of vital importance to the welfare and security of our country, and therefore I have no alternative but to tender my resignation as a member of your Cabinet.
>
> I do not propose to be a candidate in the forthcoming election.
>
> Yours sincerely,
> *signed*, George Hees

A CABINET APPOINTMENT

In recent years, more and more women have entered politics and gained prominent cabinet positions. The Honourable Judy LaMarsh joined the Pearson cabinet in 1963.

> As usual, I had to wait to see the prime minister. At lunch, nerves had overcome me, and I remember fretting because I had spilled soup down the front of my light suit and had nothing with me as a change. What a way to enter the office of the prime minister elect!
>
> Pearson asked me to sit down and we chatted for a moment or two about the election, and then he told me that he wanted me to serve in the cabinet as minister of national health and welfare. I was stunned. What raced through my mind was the size and importance of the portfolio and the amount of important work laid out for it. I wanted to be in the cabinet, but I had decided by the time I arrived there that I wasn't going to do just any old job—one which calls for no real contribution, but just to be there. I wasn't going to find myself a sop to women voters, and as each day had passed between the election and this interview I got firmer and firmer in my mind about this. (Whether if such a job had been offered to me I would have had the strength to turn it down is another question, which happily I have never had to answer.) From the night of the election, I had heard that many members had rushed to Ottawa to hang around to be "available" for a call from the prime minister and to jog his memory by their presence. . . . This must be the most difficult time for any prime minister, for the less one deserves reward for his contribution to victory, the more vocal he is in claiming it. And if he pressures enough, he often gets it. There is an old Cockney expression that covers the situation, one I often heard derisively repeated at home over the years. "It's the squeaky wheel wot gets the grease." Another is: "It's the coats and pants wot does the work, and the vest wot gets the gravy."

In selecting members for the cabinet, the prime minister must choose someone from the House of Commons or the Senate. Normally, too, the prime minister will choose members of his or her own party. During times of national emergency, such as war, members of the Opposition may be invited to join the cabinet. This happens rarely.

On the surface, it would seem that the prime minister's task in selecting the cabinet is quite simple. After all, why not simply choose the best people from his or her own party? In fact, the process is not quite so simple. Canada is a large country. Different regions have their own interests. Canada is also a multicultural country. Our population has a variety of languages, religions and ethnic backgrounds. The prime minister must take these factors into account. He or she must also include in the cabinet the strong people within his or her own party. They must be balanced by people with administrative skill. As we can see, choosing a cabinet is not an easy task.

Barbara McDougall was Minister of State for Finance from 1984 to 1986.

A RECENT FEDERAL CABINET

	Province of constituency	**Religion**	**Previous occupation**
Prime minister	Saskatchewan	Protestant	laywer
Minister of agriculture	Alberta	Protestant	farmer; teacher
Minister of citizenship and immigration	Ontario	Protestant	accountant
Minister of defence production	Quebec	Catholic	lumberman
Minister of finance and receiver general	Ontario	Protestant	lawyer
Minister of fisheries	PEI	Protestant	farmer
Minister of justice and attorney general	BC	Catholic	lawyer
Minister of labour	Ontario	Greek Orthodox	businessperson
Minister of mines and technical surveys	Quebec	Catholic	farmer
Minister of national defence	BC	Protestant	soldier
Minister of national health and welfare	Ontario	Protestant	accountant
Minister of national revenue	Nova Scotia	Protestant	lawyer
Minister of northern affairs and national resources	Saskatchewan	Protestant	teacher
Postmaster general	Quebec	Protestant	lawyer; businessperson
Minister of public works	Ontario	Protestant	lawyer
Secretary of state of Canada	Quebec	Catholic	lawyer; businessperson
Secretary of state for external affairs	BC	Protestant	lawyer
Solicitor general	Quebec	Catholic	lawyer
Minister of trade and commerce	Manitoba	Protestant	lawyer
Minister of transport	Ontario	Protestant	manufacturer
Minister of verterans affairs	New Brunswick	Protestant	lawyer
Minister without portfolio	Newfoundland	Catholic	lawyer
Associate minister of national defence	Quebec	Catholic	businessperson

In the preceding chart, what indications are there that religious, language and regional differences have been taken into account by the prime minister in the choice of a cabinet?

THE LEGISLATIVE BRANCH

THE MEMBERS OF PARLIAMENT

How many of the following questions could you answer:

- Who is your member of Parliament?
- What is the name of the riding he or she represents?
- How long has he or she represented your riding?
- What specific things has he or she accomplished for your riding?

If we were to look at the electoral map of Canada, the entire country would look like a huge jigsaw puzzle made up of 282 pieces. In fact, Canada is divided into 282 electoral districts, called ridings or constituencies. Each riding sends one representative to the House of Commons. Each representative is called a member of Parliament.

The House of Commons is the highest body in our parliamentary system. It can pass or reject bills, make cabinet ministers account for their actions and even force the government to resign. In practice, members of parliament realize that they were elected partly because of the appeal of their party or party leader. They will hesitate to vote against the wishes of their party. As a result, in most cases the vote in the House of Commons will be along party lines. To ensure this solidarity (working together as a unit), each party appoints a party whip. His or her main job is to make sure members attend the House of Commons for

Once a Baptist minister, Tommy Douglas entered politics at the height of the Depression. After serving in Ottawa for ten years he returned to Saskatchewan in 1944. He led the Co-operative Commonwealth Federation (CCF, the forerunner to the NDP) to a landslide victory. Douglas remained premier for 17 years. In 1961, the CCF merged with organized labour to form the New Democratic Party (NDP). Douglas became party leader and held that position until 1971. Douglas remained in the House of Commons until 1979. From there he travelled across the country speaking to Canadians advocating socialism. Douglas retired from politics in 1983 after nearly 50 years of public service. He passed away in 1986.

important votes and to persuade them to support the party's point of view. As you can see, when one party wins a clear majority of seats in the House of Commons, it usually gets its own way in running the affairs of state.

Your member of parliament seems to be caught in a delicate position. On the one hand, he or she was elected by the voters in your riding to represent their interests in the House of Commons. On the other hand, he or she is expected to faithfully support the party's position on important issues in the House. Does the ordinary MP have any significant role in the parliamentary system?

The Caucus The one area where your member of parliament is not expected to be a "yes person" is in a caucus meeting. The elected members of each party consult regularly, usually once every week, in a private meeting called the caucus. It is a secret session. No minutes are kept. In such meetings, individual MPs are free to state their own points of view on issues. The party leaders try to explain their programs to their followers. The MPs can debate policies and try to gather support for their local and regional interests. Obviously, many disagreements will come up. But once a decision has been reached in caucus, each party member is expected to support the decision in the House of Commons.

The Life of an MP On the surface, being a member of Parliament does not seem difficult. The sessions of Parliament are usually short (the longest on record was 174 days). MPs do not usually have to spend more than six or seven months in Ottawa. During their stay they are often asked to free luncheons and have a chance to rub shoulders with famous people from all over the world. On top of this, some MPs seem to take their jobs casually and rarely contribute to Commons debates.

On the other hand, a member of Parliament who takes his or her job seriously carries a heavy burden. A member of Parliament has a number of responsibilities calling for his or her attention. For one thing, an MP is elected to represent his or her riding. This means that, on the average, an MP looks after the needs of over 83 000 voters. The MP has other things to consider. He or she must weigh regional and national interests when making a decision. Of course, there is also the pressure to follow party policies.

The Daily Routine of a Member of Parliament The life of an MP may not be all that glamorous. Here is a typical day:

09:00 Arrives at office. Answers mail, makes telephone calls for an hour or two. Handles a great many requests: for example, from young people in the riding who want photographs or from the elderly who are worried about old-age pensions.

11:00 Attends committee meetings. Our MP may be a member of one or more parliamentary committees.

12:00 Lunch

13:00 Returns to office. Speaks to visitors or voters from the riding.

14:00 The House of Commons usually meets in the afternoon and evening. Our MP tries to attend both question periods.

16:00 Works on speech for the evening question period.

17:30 Dinner

20:00 Evening debate in the House of Commons

Salaries of MPs Have you ever wondered what a member of Parliament earns for all this work? Examine closely the following chart (these are 1985 figures):

Annual salary—$52 815
Tax-free allowance—$17 640
Travel-expense allowance—$50 000
Constituency office allowance—$9 750
Constituency travel allowance—$1 000
Staff salaries—$86 600

In addition, all MPs have free mailing privileges. Those members of Parliament with special duties get additional allowances:

Prime minister's allowance—$60 300
Cabinet minister's allowance—$40 400
Leader of the Opposition—$41 600
Speaker of the House—$41 600

These salaries are subject to an annual increase that is 1 percent lower than the inflation level.

THE SENATE

The House of Commons is the only elected body in our parliamentary system. Yet there is another seemingly powerful body called the Senate. The Senate was created in 1867. There were several reasons for this action. For one thing there was tradition. British Parliament had its House of Lords. This body could put a check on the people's representatives, the House of Commons. At that time it was felt that ordinary voters were not necessarily wise enough to choose a good government. Also, elections for members of the House of Commons came at least once every five years. It was likely that many new, inexperienced members would be elected each time. The Senate, whose members were appointed for life, could provide stability to the government.

Another factor to consider was Canada's regional interests. Representation in the House of Commons is based on population. So the provinces with the largest population, Ontario and Quebec, have a great advantage in the House. They can often get their way. The wishes of the smaller provinces can be ignored. Representation in the Senate is organized in this way:

Maritimes	24
Quebec	24
Ontario	24
West	24
Newfoundland (1949)	6
Northwest Territories (1975)	1
Yukon (1975)	1
	104

In this way, each region of Canada is equally represented. Each region can hope to have its own interests defended.

Senators are appointed by the governor general on the advice, of course, of the prime minister and the

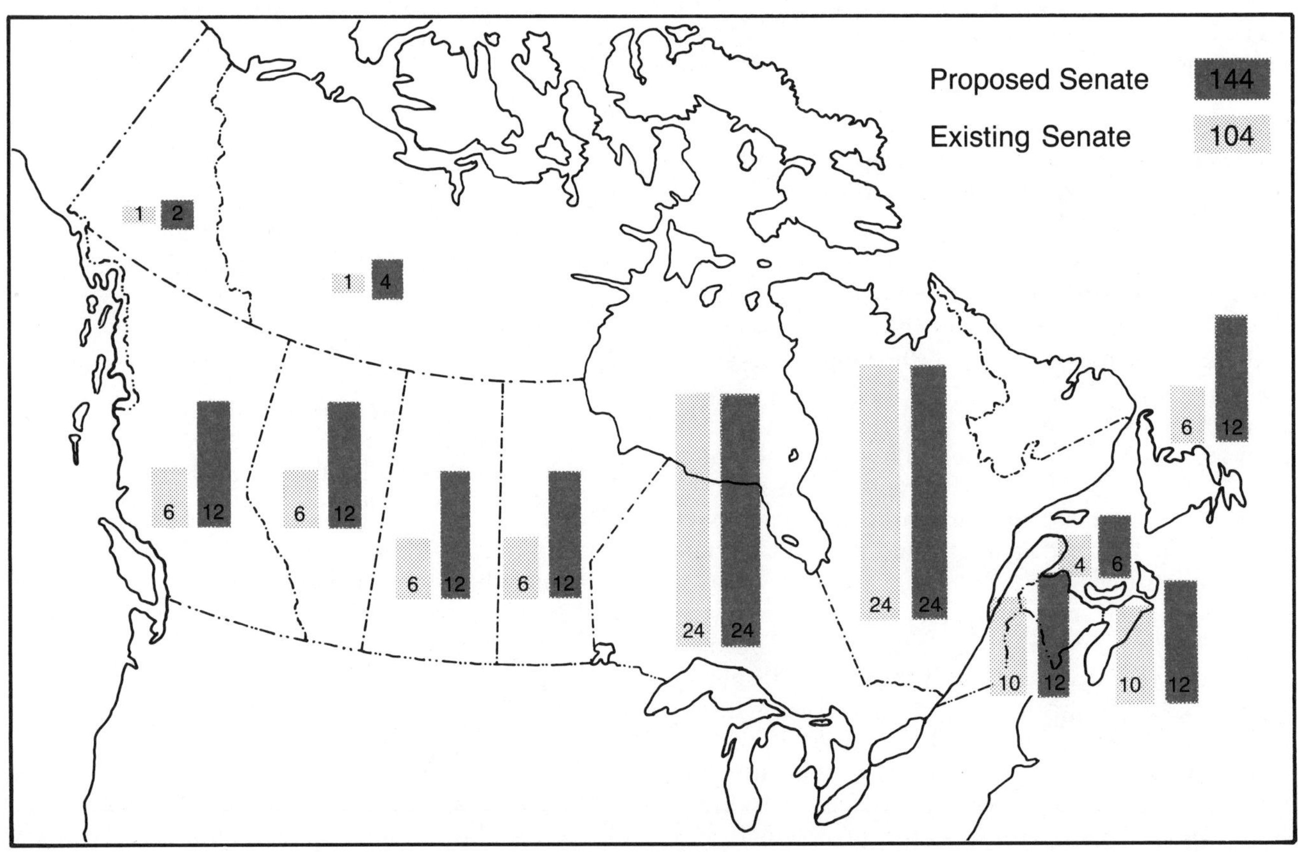

cabinet. To become a Senator, one must be at least thirty years old and own property valued at at least $4000. Today this is not a great deal of wealth. In 1867, $4000 was worth much more. This was one way of making sure that only the "better" classes would be senators.

Originally, senators were appointed for life. They could be removed only if they committed a serious crime, became bankrupt or failed to attend Senate sessions. In 1965, a bill was passed making the retirement age for all future senators seventy-five. Those already appointed would continue to sit for life. Senators are paid an annual salary of $54 000, plus an expense allowance of $8000.

DO WE REALLY NEED A SENATE?

Those who favour keeping the Senate argue that many of the original reasons for its creation still exist. We need a check on government activities, stability and protection of regional interests. Even many of the defenders, however, agree that some reform of the Senate may be useful. Some of the most common suggestions are:

1 Since the Senate represents regions, Senate appointments should be made by the provinces. This would also remove the criticism that appointment to the senate is a reward given by the party in power for past services.
2 Appointments should include people from all walks of life, not just politicians. This would help give the Senate a broader point of view.
3 Rules regarding compulsory attendance should be passed. Senators, after all, are well paid. The Senate is sometimes regarded as a "social club" where attendance and debate are minimal.
4 Make the Senate an elected body like the House of Commons. Senators' views would then carry greater authority, since they would actually represent the people.

 What do you think?

In theory, the Senate has the same duties as the House of Commons. It can pass or reject any bill passed by the House of Commons (except money bills). It may even introduce its own legislation. Senators may be asked to sit on committees to study legislation. Often, too, a member of the cabinet will be selected from the Senate.

In practice, however, the Senate is not equal to the House of Commons. The main reason is that the Senate is not an elected body. It is not responsible to the people. The Senate has become a place where party workers are rewarded for their loyalty and service. Until the election of 1984, the Liberal party had been in power in Canada for all but six years since 1935. As a result, the Senate is largely filled with Liberal supporters. These factors tend to reduce the prestige of the Senate. Its views no longer have a great influence on the government.

In view of the many different opinions regarding the usefulness of the Senate, the Special Joint Committee on Senate Reform was set up. In 1984 this committee made its report. Here are its main recommendations:

1 The Senate should be expanded from 104 seats to 144.
2 Members of the Senate should be elected to nine-year terms.
3 Once his or her term expires, a senator cannot be re-elected.

The distribution of Senate seats across Canada would be made as shown on the map on page 28.

IMPORTANT TERMS

Here are some of the important terms used in the organization of the House of Commons:

Speaker: Any debating group needs an impartial (fair to both sides) referee. This person makes sure that proper rules and procedures are followed. In the House of Commons, this is the job of the Speaker. He or she must be a member of the House. The Speaker is nominated by the prime minister and then chosen by the members of Parliament.

Floor Plan of the House of Commons

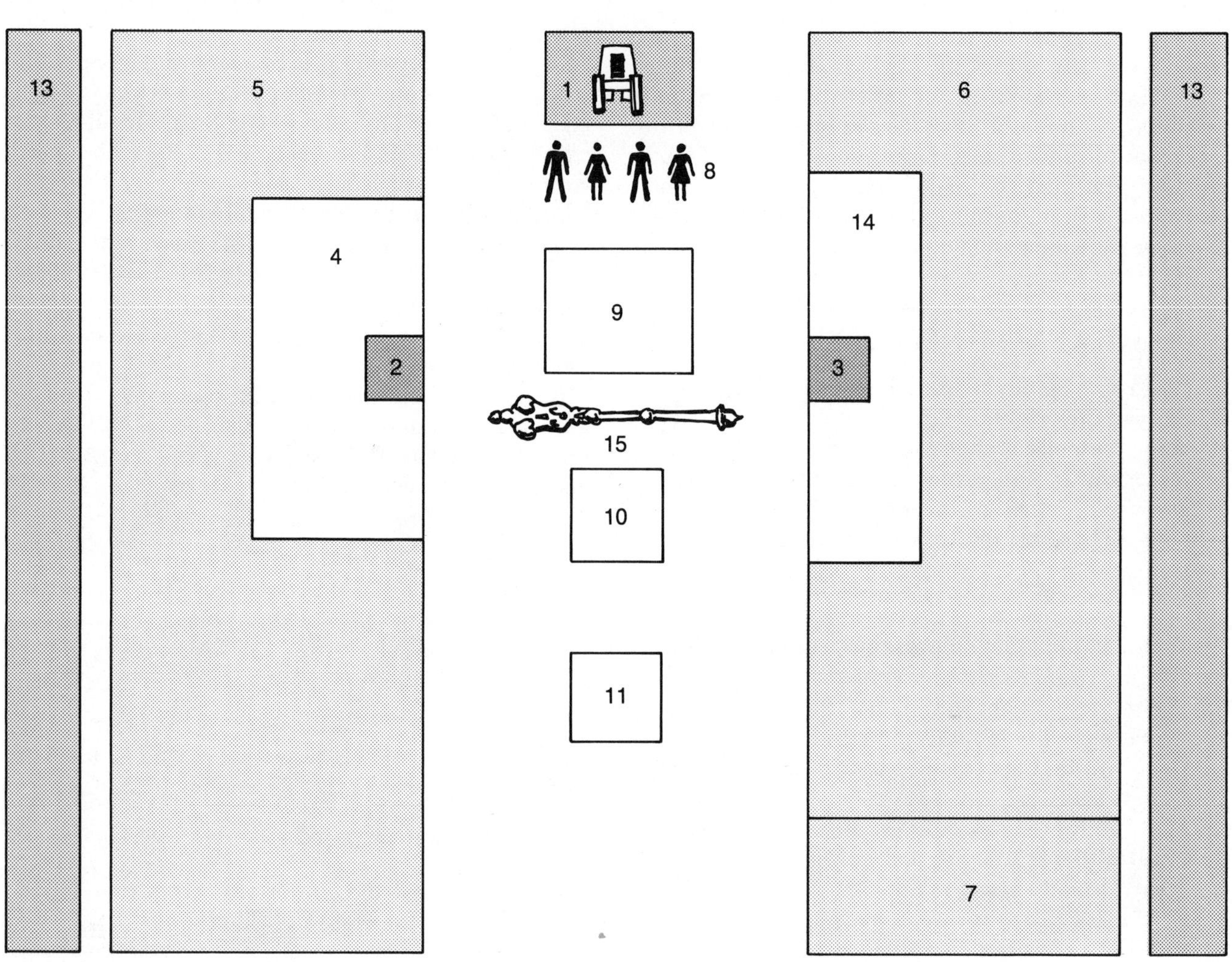

1. Speaker
2. Prime Minister
3. Leader of the Opposition
4. Cabinet
5. Back benchers — Government party
6. Back benchers — members of the Opposition party
7. Members of the other Opposition party
8. Page boys and page girls
9. Clerk's table
10. Sergeant-at-arms
11. Hansard reporter
12. Press gallery
13. Visitors' galleries
14. Shadow Cabinet (Opposition)
15. Mace

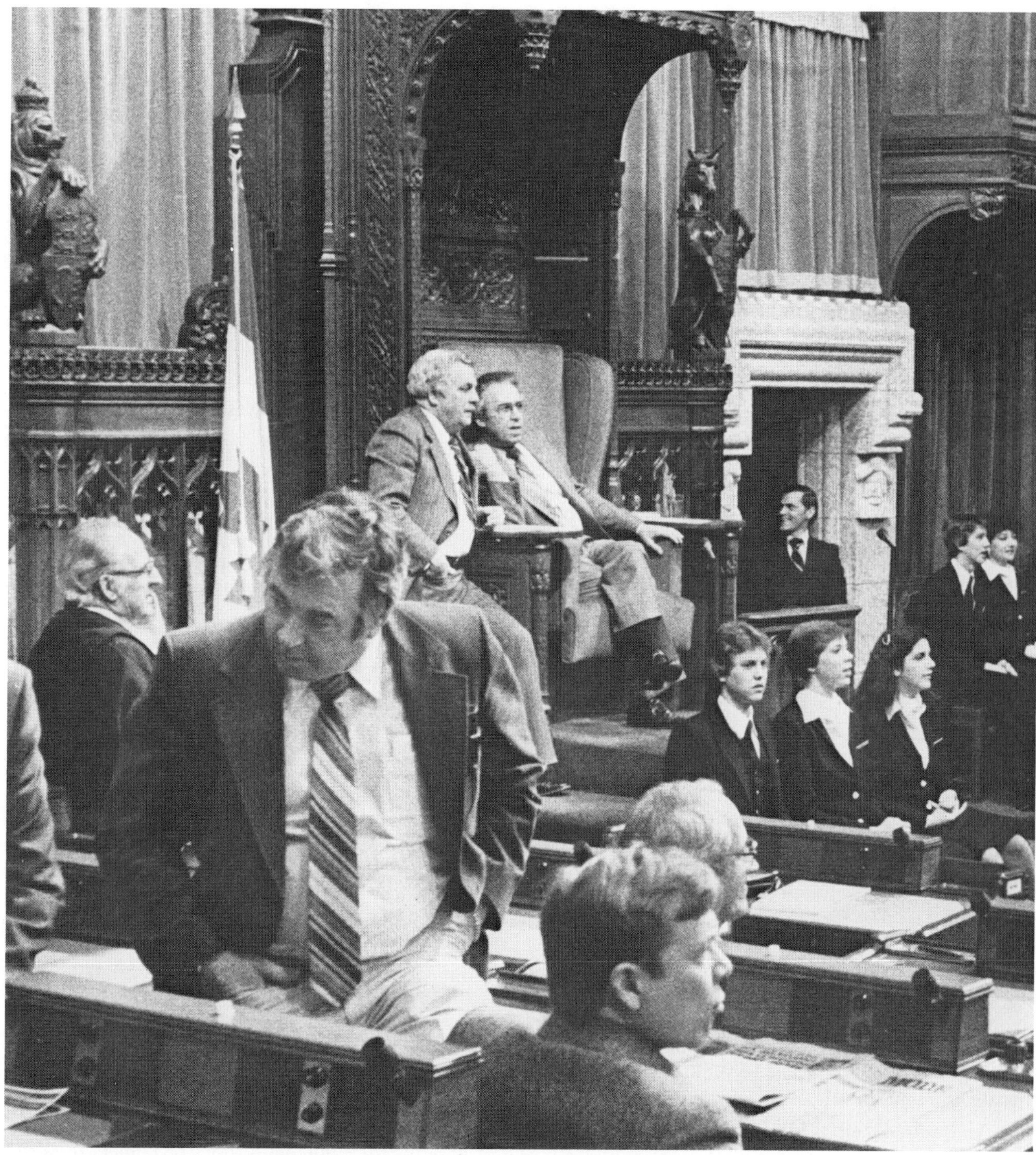

Deputy Speaker Denis Ethier, MPs and pages wait for Question Period to begin in the House of Commons.

Backbenchers: Backbenchers are members of Parliament who do not have a specific government responsibility. They do not sit on the cabinet. They are expected to support their party during debate.

Leader of the Opposition: The leader of the second-largest party in the House of Commons is called the leader of the Opposition. All non-government parties are known as "Her Majesty's Loyal Opposition." Their role is to criticize and try to improve government legislation.

Pages: If you attend a session of Parliament, you will notice a number of young people around the Speaker's throne. They are called pages. It is their duty to run errands for the members of Parliament; for example, they carry messages.

Hansard: The daily debates in the House of Commons are recorded in a publication called *Hansard*. Copies of *Hansard* are available through the Queen's Printer, Ottawa.

PASSING A BILL

The main task of Parliament is to create new laws. The responsibility for this falls mainly on the government. At the opening of a session of Parliament the governor general reads the Speech From the Throne. The speech is, in fact, written by the prime minister and cabinet. It outlines the government's plans for new laws for the upcoming session. Most bills discussed in Parliament are government bills, that is, bills introduced by a cabinet minister. If a government bill should be defeated in the House of Commons, it is traditional for the government to resign. This is because the government stakes its credibility on such bills. The principle of this is that the government should continue in power only so long as it has the support of the House of Commons. As you might imagine, great pressure is put on individual MPs to vote along party lines.

It is possible for ordinary MPs to introduce bills of their own. These are called private members' bills. These bills may deal with matters of local or national interest. However, the government usually takes no real position on these bills. Furthermore, very little time is allowed in Parliament for private members' bills. An "early death" is the fate of most such bills.

The procedure for passing any bill in Parliament is the same. A bill introduced in the House of Commons must go through three readings. If it is passed, it will go on to the Senate. Here, too, it is read three times. If it is passed by the Senate, it will go on to the governor general. He or she then signs it, and it becomes law. If the bill is rejected by the Senate, it will go back to the House of Commons and begin the process again.

THE JUDICIAL BRANCH

We have studied the role of the legislative and executive branches of Canada's federal government. The third branch of our government is the judicial branch. As we have seen, the legislative branch, headed by the House of Commons and the Senate, makes our country's laws. The executive branch, headed by the prime minister and the cabinet, ensures that these laws are carried out. For any law to be effective, however, penalties must be imposed on those who break the law. In this system, the judicial branch decides if a law has been broken and what penalty should be imposed if it has.

The judicial branch is headed by the Supreme Court of Canada. It is the highest court of appeal in our country. Its decisions are always final and can have very important consequences. The Supreme Court usually rules on matters that affect the Constitution or the rights of individual citizens. It can make decisions on a great variety of issues. It might decide, for example, whether a traffic ticket must be printed in both French and English. It could also rule on whether off-shore resources belong to an individual province or the federal government.

The Supreme Court is made up of nine individuals headed by a chief justice. It is felt that the decisions of the judicial branch should not be subject to political considerations. Because of this, judges in Canada are appointed and not elected. This is unlike the United States, where all judges, with the exception

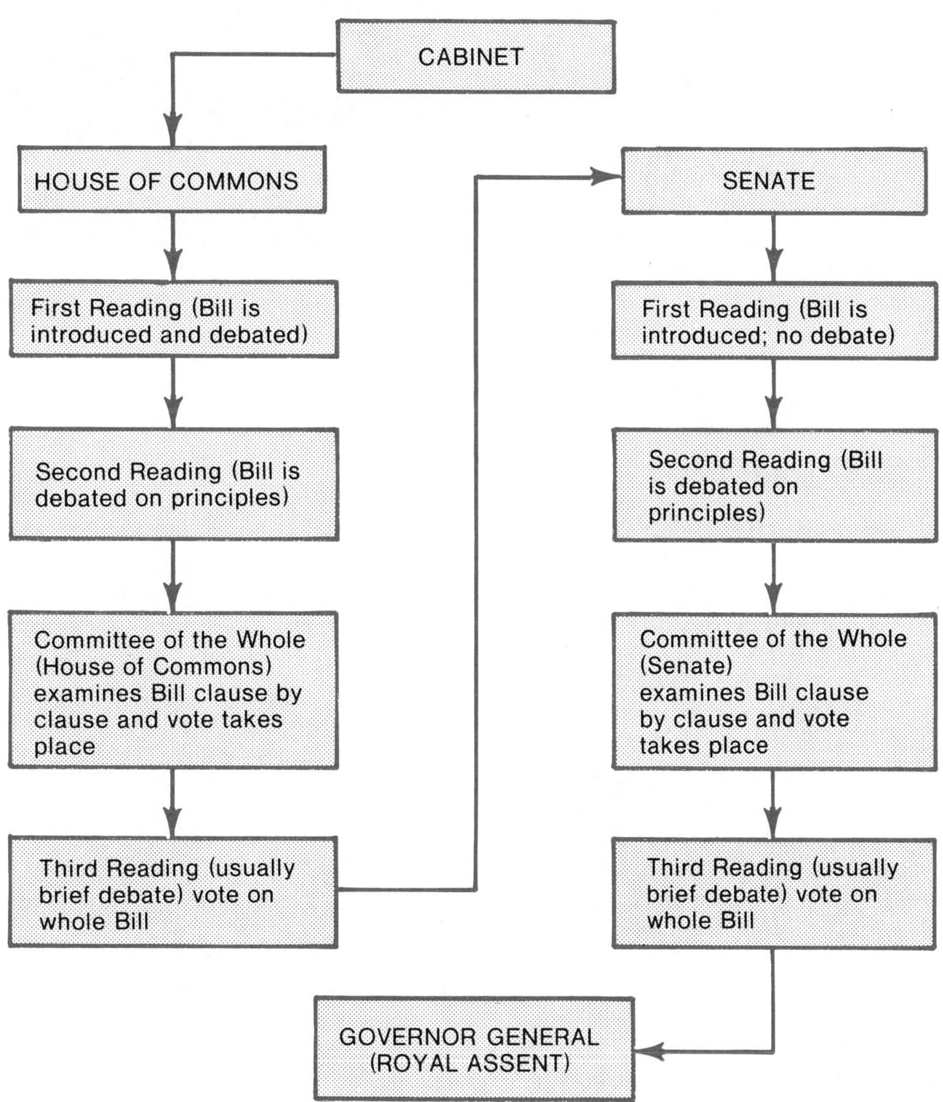

of their Supreme Court, are elected by the voters. The Canadian Supreme Court is appointed by the governor general on the advice of the prime minister and the cabinet.

When the Supreme Court makes a decision, a simple majority vote of 5–4 is all that is needed. Its decisions, however, often have long-lasting significance. Because of this, each of the nine judges gives a great deal of time and thought to each decision.

It is expected that the Supreme Court will play a very prominent role in the future of Canada. Its role will be especially important in matters affecting the Constitution and the new Charter of Rights and Freedoms.

HOLDING A NATIONAL ELECTION

Voting for our representatives in the House of Commons is the most important political decision most of us will ever make. It has been said that Canadians are truly "free" only once every four or five years. That is, on the day they vote for a new government. After that, until the next election, they are subject to the decisions of their representatives. This statement may only be a partial truth. Yet it does show how important it is to have informed citizens who choose their representatives wisely. Even so, in each federal election, over a million Canadians do not vote. Often many of these same people complain loudly about how badly their government is run.

Unlike the United States, Canada does not hold its federal elections at predetermined times. The prime minister may dissolve Parliament and call for a national election at any time within five years of the last election.

As soon as an election is called, the political parties in each of Canada's 282 ridings swing into action. The major parties will nominate a candidate for each riding. In addition, there may be a number of independent candidates (those who have no party attachments). In some ridings, as many as seven or eight candidates might seek election.

The moment the prime minister calls an election, the governor general officially sets in motion the wheels of the election machinery. The chief electoral officer, a permanent civil servant, begins to prepare the details.

THE USUAL STEPS IN A NATIONAL ELECTION

1 The election is set for a Monday. If the Monday is a holiday, then it is held on a Tuesday.
2 Returning officers are appointed to be in charge of elections in each riding in Canada.
3 The returning officers appoint enumerators in each riding. Enumerators go from door-to-door to make a list of the eligible voters in the riding.
4 The lists of eligible voters are printed and posted in public places.

Ballot box

5 The candidates are officially nominated and begin campaigning.
6 On election day, the polling stations are open from 08:00 to 19:00.
7 Each voter is given a ballot on which to secretly mark her or his choice.
8 The ballots are counted. Each party sends a representative, called a scrutineer, to make sure the ballots are counted fairly. By midnight, the winner is usually known.

WHO IS ELIGIBLE TO RUN?

The Canada Elections Act states that any person may be eligible to run for election to the House of Commons who is:

- a Canadian citizen;
- of the age of eighteen or older.

There are, however, a number of people who are not eligible for office. They include:

- anyone found guilty of corrupt practice during an election;
- members of a provincial legislature, sheriffs or Crown attorneys, while they are holding office;
- anyone holding office or employed by the government of Canada.

As you can see, a great number of Canadians are free to run for office. However, to be official, their nomination must have two things. It must have the signatures of at least ten voters in the candidate's riding. It must also be accompanied by a $200 deposit. The candidate will lose this deposit if he or she receives less than half as many votes as the winner. For example, if candidate X wins the riding with 10 000 votes, candidate Y must receive at least 5000 votes or lose his or her deposit.

WHO CAN VOTE?

Long before the actual voting day, an official voters' list is made up by the returning officer and the enumerators. The list is then posted in public places (for example, on telephone poles or tree trunks). The list includes the names and addresses of eligible voters.

The Canada Elections Act also specifies who can vote in Canadian federal elections. The franchise (or vote) is given to Canadians who

- are eighteen years of age or over;
- are Canadian citizens;
- have been living in Canada for 12 months before the election.

Some citizens are denied the right to vote. These include:

- the chief electoral officer and the assistant chief electoral officer;
- the returning officer for each riding (except in case of a tie);
- judges appointed by the federal government;
- people in mental institutions;
- people in prison;
- those found guilty of corrupt acts involving an election.

POLITICAL PARTIES

There is a common saying that when three people get together to talk politics, they will come up with four different opinions. While this is an exaggeration, it does point out one of the problems of a democracy. If there are so many different opinions among Canadians, how can any common action be taken? Imagine for a moment the situation in the House of Commons if each member insisted on having things his or her own way. There would be few, if any, bills passed. Debates in the House would be endless. We would not have effective government in Canada.

Under these conditions, you can see why political opinions and ideas must be organized under broad categories. This is the role of political parties. Each political party has a political philosophy, or point of view. Within this common set of beliefs, there is still room for shades of opinion. Because of political parties, large groups of people can organize and gain control of the government. In this way, they will be able to make laws. Naturally, these should satisfy the majority of people in the country.

THE POLITICAL SPECTRUM

Left	Centre	Right
We should change social conditions as quickly as possible.	Change should take place, but at a cautious pace.	Traditions should be kept and the present system maintained.
Key industries, transportation facilities and natural resources should be in the hands of the government.	Some form of government management of the economy is necessary.	Business and industry should be kept in the hands of individuals.
Government should take care of the needy.	There are many different approaches to caring for the needy.	Government should not interfere in the lives of individuals.
Society is not bound by tradition.	Tradition is important, but change must be accepted if it is the will of the majority.	Traditions must be respected.
The rights of individuals have the highest priority.	Law and order is important, but the rights of individuals come first.	Law and order have the highest priority.

CANADIAN GENERAL ELECTIONS 1867–1984
Party Standings in the House of Commons

Date of Election		Party Standings							
	Cons.	Libs.	Prog.	UFA	CCF NDP	SC	SCR	Other	Total Seats
Aug.-Sept. 1867	101	80							181
July-Sept. 1872	103	97							200
January 1874	73	133							206
September 1878	137	69							206
June 1882	139	71							210
February 1887	123	92							215
March 1891	123	92							215
June 1896	89	117						7	213
November 1900	78	128						8	214
November 1904	75	139							214
October 1908	85	133						3	221
September 1911	133	86						2	221
December 1917	153	82							235
December 1921	50	117	64					4	235
October 1925	116	101	24					4	245
September 1926	91	116	13	11				14	245
July 1930	137	88	2	10				8	245
October 1935	39	171			7	17		11	245
March 1940	39	178			8	10		10	245
June 1945	67	125			28	13		12	245
June 1949	41	190			13	10		8	262
August 1953	51	170			23	15		6	265
June 1957	112	105			25	19		4	265
March 1958	208	49			8				265
June 1962	116	100			19	30			265
April 1963	95	129			17	24			265
November 1965	97	131			21	5	9	2	265
June 1968	72	155			22		14	1	264
October 1972	108	109			31		15	1	264
July 1974	95	141			16		11	1	264
May 1979	136	114			27	5		1	282
February 1980	103	147			32				282
September 1984	211	40			30			1	282

1. Cons. *(Conservatives)*
2. Libs. *(Liberals)*
3. Prog. *(Progressives)*
4. UFA *(United Farmers of Alberta)*
5. CCF/NDP *(Co-operative Commonwealth Federation/New Democratic Party)*
6. SC *(Social Credit)*
7. SCR *(Social Credit* Ralliement. *After the 1968 election, this party became the federal Social Credit party. The SCR designation is maintained in the above chart to show that all Social Credit members of Parliament after 1965 have been elected from Quebec.)*
8. Other *(Independents — not allied with any political party)*

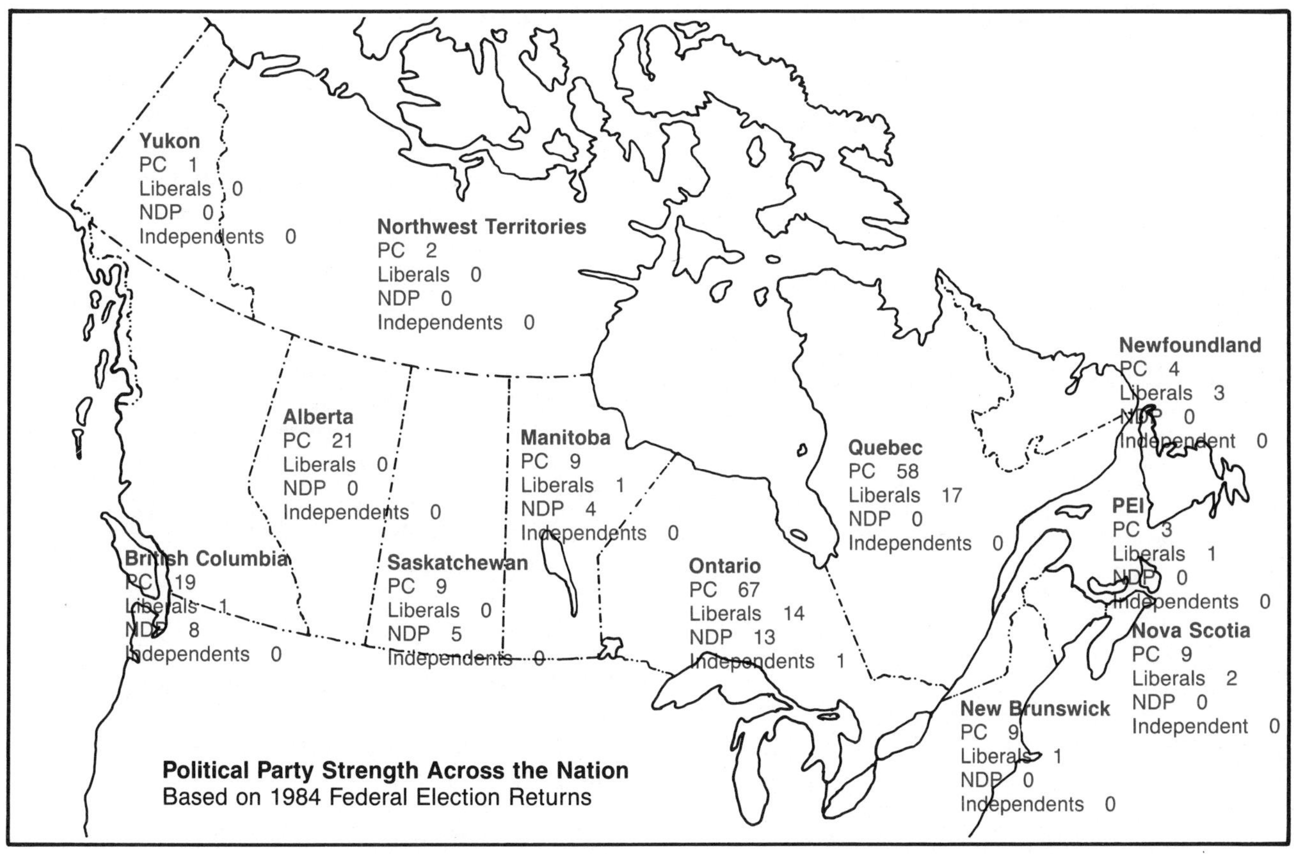

Political Party Strength Across the Nation
Based on 1984 Federal Election Returns

Political parties have several other useful roles. They help identify and describe issues that face Canadians. Political parties try to persuade the majority of people to follow their point of view. To do this, they educate the public in matters of national interest. After an election, the winning party organizes the government and drafts new laws. The losing parties must organize effective opposition. They become "watchdogs" who ensure that the party in power does not become irresponsible.

Obviously, in a democratic system, more than one political party is necessary. In fact, in any democratic country, there is no limit to the number of political parties. In some countries, as many as a dozen or more political parties run candidates for office. In the United States, just two parties, the Republican and the Democratic, have any real success. In Canada only the Conservative and Liberal parties have ever formed a national government. At various times, however, the New Democratic and the Social Credit parties have had strong voices in government decisions.

The main goal of each party is to gain power. To do this, it must appeal to the majority opinion in the country. This makes it very difficult for any party with extreme, or radical, points of view to be elected. Most parties, therefore, tend to have very moderate opinions and policies. Many people, in fact, accuse our major parties of having exactly the same philosophy of government. Actually, there is a range of political opinion, which allows voters to see the differences between the parties and so be able to make a decision. This range of opinion is sometimes called the political spectrum.

THE ROLE OF INTEREST GROUPS

One reason why a member of Parliament tries to do a good job is that he or she wants to be re-elected. This usually means that representatives will vote according to the wishes of the voters in their riding. However, the government and the individual MPs are often subject to pressures of which many Canadians are not aware. We will look at several of the powerful groups that influence government decisions. There are hundreds of such groups in Canada. They range from labour unions and farming associations to representatives of individual businesses. Any group of people that tries to persuade the government to carry out certain actions is an interest group. Their aims may also be for the good of Canada. First and foremost, however, they seek what is good for their group.

THE MASS MEDIA

Over the years, one of the strongest groups affecting government decisions has been the mass media. They include newspapers, radio and television. Politicians know that their careers are affected by the amount and the type of coverage that the media gives to them. The media may also come out strongly for or against certain bills. In this way, they can influence public opinion. One example of where this is done is the editorial pages of newspapers. In these pages, the personal views of the publishers are stated. As well, certain "letters to the editor" are printed. These can give the impression that a large part of the public is either for or against certain policies. The editorial pages of the larger Canadian newspapers can have a great influence on government decisions.

However, the media are not all-powerful. Many people do not bother to read the news and editorial parts of the newspapers, nor do they listen to the personal viewpoints expressed on radio and television. Many other readers and listeners simply come to their own conclusions on the issues. A good example of this occurred during the 1974 federal election. The three major Toronto newspapers, *The Toronto Star, The Globe and Mail*, and *Sun* all supported the Progressive Conservative party. Yet on election day, the public gave its support to the Liberal party.

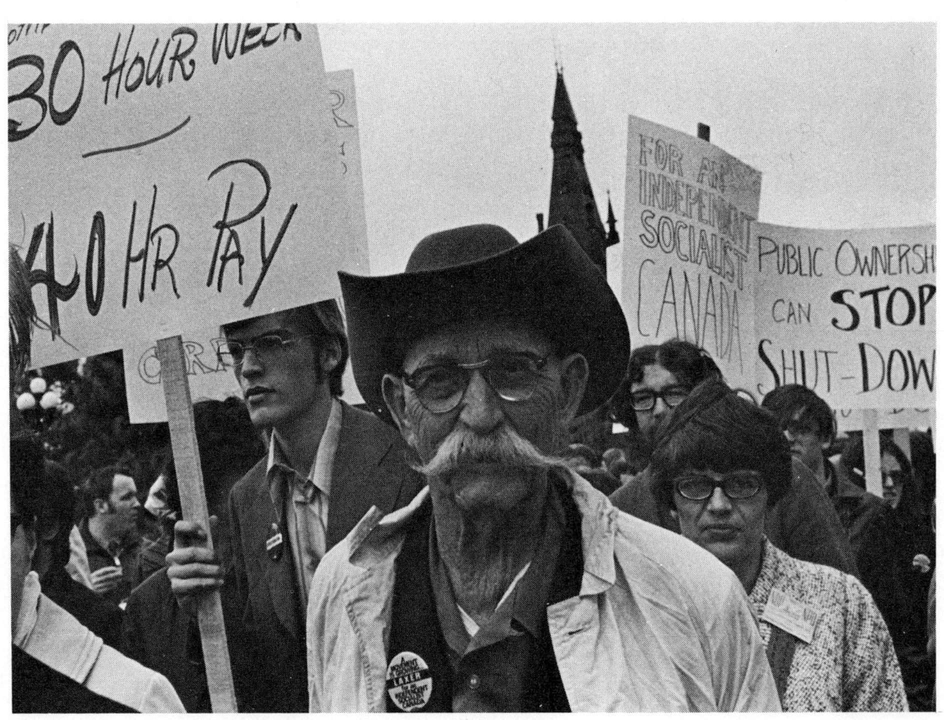

PRESSURE GROUPS

The best known interest groups are those that have special organizations to put pressure on the government. These include the Canadian Manufacturers' Association and the Canadian Labour Congress. There are also strong organizations for doctors, teachers, farmers, authors and many more. The tactic used by these groups to pressure the government is called lobbying. Lobbyists are people who try to influence the government to make a decision in their favour. Some groups hire professional lobbyists, who actually have offices in Ottawa.

THE CIVIL SERVICE

Our elected representatives create policies and pass new laws. The less exciting task of putting these policies and laws into practice is left to the group of government employees known as civil servants. The members of the civil service are sometimes called bureaucrats. They form the largest group of employees in the country. It is estimated that there are over 1000 civil servants for each member of Parliament. The total number of civil servants at all levels of government in Canada is over 500 000.

Civil servants at the highest level do more than carry out policies. They often directly influence the making of policies. This is largely due to the stability of their position. Cabinet ministers may come and go. They are, after all, elected members. They may be defeated at the next election. When a new minister takes over a portfolio, he or she will probably rely on the advice and experience of the deputy minister. This civil servant has been on the job for years. In most cases, these deputy ministers stay on the job, whether a Conservative or Liberal government takes over. This gives continuity to the ministry. Otherwise, it might well end up in chaos when there is a change of government.

At one time, when a new party won an election, it appointed civil servants. This usually meant great changes. As we have seen, the result could be chaos. In 1918 the government passed the Civil Service Act. It set up examinations for government jobs. Most government employees are now chosen on the basis of these tests. These exams are difficult, and candidates must know a great deal about their chosen field to pass them. Today most candidates must be fluent in both English and French. If a non-bilingual person is chosen for a bilingual position, that person must agree to become bilingual. Classes in French or English and exams are given by the government. Most senior civil servants probably know more about their fields than their elected superiors, the cabinet ministers. It has been said that the country might survive an emergency without an elected government but not without a civil service.

BUILDING YOUR LEARNING SKILLS

FOCUSSING ON THE ISSUE

1 What are the key ideas, or concepts, presented in this chapter? Choose at least five and compare them with those chosen by your classmates.

2 Do you recall the following facts?

a The number of elected members in the House of Commons is:
i 282 *ii* 284 *iii* 102

b What is the voting age in Canadian federal elections?

c The number of members in the Senate is decided on a regional basis. True or false?

d Canada's written constitution is known as:
i NHL Act *ii* NBA Act
iii BNA Act *iv* CFL Act

3 The following terms appeared in this chapter. Try to recall their meaning and how they were used.

aristocracy	leader of the Opposition
backbencher	legislative
bureaucrats	lobbying
caucus	minister without portfolio
civil servant	monarchy
constituency	the political spectrum
dictatorship	Parliament
enumerator	party whip
executive	private member's bill
interest group	Speech From the Throne
judicial	

RESEARCHING

1 Select one of Canada's prime ministers as the subject of a biographical study. Be sure to include information on his personal background and career, his successes and disappointments and any lasting achievements.
2 Do a research study on the construction of Canada's Parliament buildings. In your study, include the destruction by fire of the Parliament buildings in 1916 and their subsequent reconstruction.
3 Conduct a study of the salaries of elected officials in Canada. Using an organizational chart, compare the salaries of your members of Parliament, the members of your provincial assembly and the members of your local council.
4 Why has Canada not elected a female prime minister in the 120 years since confederation?

1·2·3

ORGANIZING

1 Make a list of the characteristics you think a good leader should possess. Rank these characteristics in importance. Which of these characteristics do you think our current prime minister possesses?
2 At the beginning of this chapter the powers of our federal government are listed. Select what you consider to be the five most important powers. Compare your choices with those of your classmates.
3 Using a bar graph, chart the success of Canada's three main political parties during the last five federal elections.
4 Review the last federal election by regions. Using an organizational chart, compare the success of Canada's three main political parties in Atlantic Canada, Quebec, Ontario and the West.

COMMUNICATING

1 Write a letter to your local member of Parliament. Make a list of several current social and political issues. Ask your MP to explain his or her position on these issues.
2 Debate the proposition: The governor general is a vital part of our system of government.
3 Canada's Senate is once again the subject of political debate. Working in groups of four, present an argument in class defending one of these positions:
- ▶ The Senate should be maintained as it is.
- ▶ The Senate should be reformed according to the recommendations of the 1984 report of the special joint committee.
- ▶ The Senate should be abolished.

ANALYZING

1 In a recent debate on capital punishment, the members of Parliament decided to vote according to their own consciences rather than follow the wishes of their constituents. Do you feel MPs should continue to have this freedom? Why or why not?
2 Our system of representative government has a number of problems. One of these is unequal representation. Some ridings with a sparse population cover thousands of square kilometres. In such ridings, a member of Parliament may represent only 10 000 people. In large urban centres, another member may represent as many as 150 000 people. What are the arguments in favour of and against maintaining such a system? How can this inequality of representation be overcome?
3 The prime minister faces a number of pressures when choosing a cabinet. These include regional interests, religious and ethnic concerns and party pressures. Should the prime minister ignore these factors and simply choose the best person for the job? Explain your answer.
4 The Supreme Court of Canada has the power to declare laws unconstitutional and, as such, nonexistent. Should a non-elected body such as the Supreme Court have the power to override decisions made by Canada's elected leaders?
5 Because of the influence of the media, physical appearance is becoming increasingly important as a factor in choosing our leaders. Compare the pictures of Canada's national party leaders on page 21. Which individual do you think looks most like a leader? Explain your choice.

APPLYING YOUR KNOWLEDGE

1 The mass media (radio, television, newspapers) can be very influential in determining the success or failure of a politician or a political party. Collect the editorial comments from your newspaper for a period of one week. Analyze the paper's stand on political issues. Which political party does it seem to support?

2 Passing legislation in the House of Commons can create problems, especially if there is a minority government. (A minority government is one in which no party has more than half the seats in the House of Commons.) Here is a classroom simulation that can demonstrate these problems: Divide the class into parties. Make sure that there is a minority government in power. The opposition should be divided into at least two parties. The government must now attempt to pass a bill (for example, raising the drinking age to twenty-one). What compromises and deals must be made in order for the government to succeed?

3 Here is another simulation: Your caucus is about to meet to discuss its stand on the controversial issue of abolishing the annual seal hunt. Assume that every member of the class belongs to the same political party. Divide the class in such a way that:

- Some members represent the Atlantic provinces fishing community;
- Some members represent an area in Ontario where the synthetic furs industry has created many jobs;
- Some members represent the western provinces, where the International Fund for Animal Welfare has taken out full-page ads condemning the seal hunt, and the newspaper editorials have also been against the hunt;
- About 30 percent of the members of the caucus are neutral.

Set aside a block of time to discuss the issue in caucus. What decision does your caucus make?

chapter 3

PROVINCIAL AND MUNICIPAL GOVERNMENTS

TOPIC ORGANIZER	PAGE
▶ Provincial Governments	44
▶ Municipal Governments	49

THEME ORGANIZER

- ▶ Federalism: Which level, federal or municipal, has more power?
- ▶ Regionalism: Diversity is the spice of Canadian life.
- ▶ Equalization: Should the "have" regions pay for the "have-nots"?
- ▶ Taxation: Can we ever reduce taxes?
- ▶ Local government: Municipal government touches our lives daily.

INTRODUCTION

Canada is a federal state. The Fathers of Confederation set up federal and provincial governments and divided certain powers between them. The BNA Act gave the provinces the following powers:

Section 92—Exclusive Powers of Provincial Legislatures

92. In each Province the Legislature may exclusively make Laws in relation to Matters coming within the Classes of Subjects next hereinafter enumerated; that is to say,—

1. The Amendment from Time to Time, notwithstanding anything in this Act, of the Constitution of the Province, except as regards the Office of Lieutenant-Governor.
2. Direct Taxation within the Province in order to the Raising of a Revenue for Provincial Purposes.
3. The borrowing of Money on the sole Credit of the Province.
4. The Establishment and Tenure of Provincial Offices and the Appointment and Payment of Provincial Officers.
5. The Management and Sale of the Public Lands belonging to the Province and of the Timber and Wood thereon.
6. The Establishment, Maintenance, and Management of Public and Reformatory Prisons in and for the Province.

7. The Establishment, Maintenance, and Management of Hospitals, Asylums, Charities, and Eleemosynary Institutions (almshouses) in and for the Province, other than Marine Hospitals.
8. Municipal Institutions in the Province.
9. Shop, Saloon, Tavern, Auctioneer, and other Licences in order to the raising of a Revenue for Provincial, Local, or Municipal Purposes.
10. Local Works and Undertakings other than such as are of the following Classes: —
(a) Lines of Steam or other Ships, Railways, Canals, Telegraphs, and other Works and Undertakings connecting the Province with any other or others of the Provinces, or extending beyond the Limits of the Province:
(b) Lines of Steam Ships between the Province and any British or Foreign Country:
(c) Such Works as, although wholly situate within the Province, are before or after their Execution declared by the Parliament of Canada to be for the general Advantage of Canada or for the Advantage of Two or more of the Provinces.
11. The Incorporation of Companies with Provincial Objects.
12. The Solemnization of Marriage in the Province.
13. Property and Civil Rights in the Province.
14. The Administration of Justice in the Province, including the Constitution, Maintenance, and Organization of Provincial Courts, both of Civil and of Criminal Jurisdiction, and including Procedure in Civil Matters in those Courts.
15. The Imposition of Punishment by Fine, Penalty, or Imprisonment for enforcing any Law of the Province made in relation to any Matter coming within any of the Classes of Subjects enumerated in this Section.
16. Generally all Matters of a merely local or private Nature in the Province.

As you can see, the provinces have responsibility for many areas. How are they governed? In effect, the governments of the provinces are a miniature version of the federal government (see the chart on page 44). In the provinces, the lieutenant-governor replaces the governor general. An elected legislature replaces the House of Commons. Voting procedures and party organizations are much the same. The only real difference is the lack of a Senate in the provincial governments.

Before reading on, study the chart of key words and ideas that follows.

KEY WORDS AND IDEAS IN THIS CHAPTER

Term	Meaning	Sample Use
deficit budgeting	a financial policy whereby the government plans to spend more than it takes in through taxation	Canadian governments practise deficit budgeting. They borrow money to make up for the deficit in their budgets. Paying back these loans costs hundreds of millions of dollars yearly.
national debt	the amount of money spent by the federal government over what it has received in tax revenues	Canada's national debt stands at over $30 billion.
regional disparity	refers to the fact that some provinces and regions of Canada are more prosperous than others	The federal government tries to lessen regional disparity by aiding "have-not" provinces with grants and subsidies.
shared responsibilities	although federal and provincial governments have their own specific areas of responsibility, on some occasions they divide these responsibilities	Some examples of shared responsibilities are unemployment insurance, old-age pensions and immigration policies.
tariff	a tax placed on imports coming into Canada from other countries	Tariffs are paid by the importer and collected by the federal government.

PROVINCIAL GOVERNMENTS

FEDERAL–PROVINCIAL RELATIONS

You might conclude from Sections 91 and 92 of the BNA Act that the federal and provincial governments have their own areas of responsibility. On the surface, there is no cause for dispute. Yet over the years, major areas of conflict have come up between the two levels of government. One problem area is taxation. The makers of the BNA Act, which was Canada's first Constitution, gave the most important tax sources to the federal government. They did so because it seemed that the federal government would have the greatest expenses. Since 1867, however, a number of provincial responsibilities once considered "inexpensive" and "unimportant" have changed. Health and welfare are two examples. Back in 1867, these were not considered important government responsibilities. Since the Great Depression of the 1930s, however, very costly government programs have been set up in these areas. There was no mention of these areas in the BNA Act. The Supreme Court of Canada decided that the provinces should look after them. Health and welfare came under the "Property and civil rights" clause of the BNA Act.

The demand for more schools, better roads, and other provincial services continued to grow. The provinces would soon be responsible for the largest expenses. The federal government still had the largest taxing powers. There were two answers. One dealt with money supply. The provinces agreed to give the federal government some of their own taxing powers, such as the inheritance tax. The federal government agreed to share the cost of a number of expensive programs in return. It also agreed to give grants to the needy provinces.

A second solution was to let the federal and provincial governments share some responsibilities. One example is unemployment insurance. It was a provincial responsibility. In 1940, the provinces agreed to turn control of unemployment insurance over to the federal government. Other shared responsibilities are listed below.

SOME RESPONSIBILITIES SHARED BY FEDERAL AND PROVINCIAL GOVERNMENTS

HEALTH AND WELFARE

Federal old-age pensions, unemployment insurance

Provincial hospitalization, vaccines, tuberculosis tests, sanitoria

AGRICULTURE

Federal experimental farms, loans to farms

Comparison of Federal and Provincial Governments

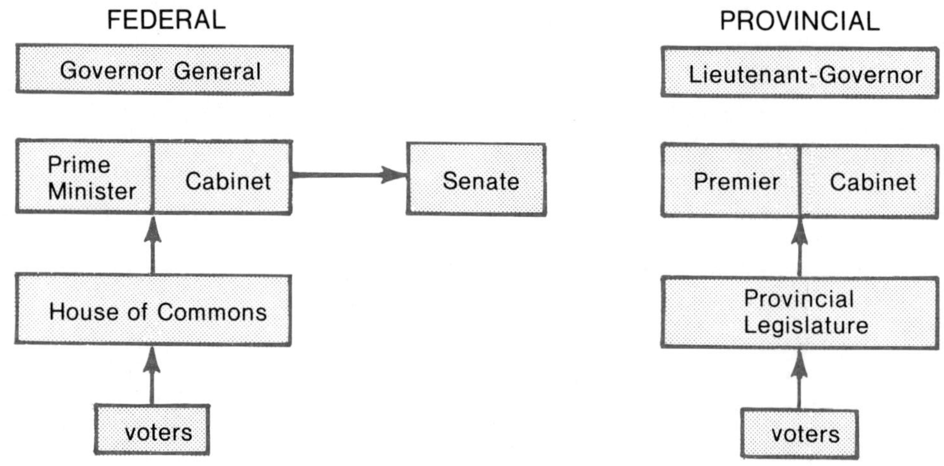

Provincial agricultural colleges, marketing boards

IMMIGRATION

Federal quotas on immigrants, checks on suitability of immigrants, financial assistance for transportation, education

Provincial acceptance of proportion of the national quota, selection and direction of immigrants to areas where needed

HIGHWAYS

Federal financial help to provinces for selected major highways

Provincial major roads between municipalities

PROVINCIAL PREMIERS VOICE REGIONAL CONCERNS

Despite the intentions of the Fathers of Confederation and the BNA Act, tensions often arise between provincial and federal governments. The differences between the regions of Canada partly account for this. The various provinces complain that the federal government is not sensitive to their needs and desires. Since 1867, the gap between the wealthy provinces and the "have-not" provinces has widened.

On February 10, 1969, a Constitutional Conference was called in Ottawa by Prime Minister Trudeau. The Premiers of the ten provinces attended. They took this opportunity to voice their regional points of view.

Premier Louis Robichaud of New Brunswick spoke for the Maritimes:

> Over the years you people from other parts of the country have heard of this problem of economic disparity in our country, which affects us more perhaps than in any other part of Canada.
>
> Over the years we argued that something dramatic should be done to alleviate [make lighter] the burden that the residents of the Atlantic area have to support.
>
> Over the years successive governments and people in this country have been listening to us with very sympathetic ears, and over the years a lot of patch work, I should say, has been done.
>
> It is most humiliating for us to appear before this august body and before the Canadian nation and appear like beggars. We are not beggars. We do not want to be beggars. We simply want our fair share of the national wealth. . . .
>
> Our taxes are double what they are in Ontario. In fact, the municipal taxes and the provincial taxes are double. That is not all. We, for instance, buy a car in the Atlantic provinces. Everybody has a car. It is no longer a luxury to have a car. It is a necessity of life. We buy a car which is manufactured in Ontario. We pay $300 to $400 more than the resident of Ontario has to pay for a car, just to buy it; and after that car is purchased, then we have to pay much higher taxes than the resident of Ontario has to pay in taxes to operate his car.
>
> Now, in so many areas we are—let us put it bluntly—somewhat discriminated against. Why? Because of transportation problems, of course, but I am wondering if something really dramatic should not be done, and now. I do not think we can wait any longer.
>
> I do not know what the solution is, but let us think for a moment of the abolition of tariffs between the United States and Canada . . . along the Atlantic border with the United States. . . . If that were feasible, do you know what it would mean? It would mean that every resident of the Atlantic provinces would save approximately $1000 for the purchase of a car —$1000 for the purchase of a car per citizen.

John Robarts, premier of Ontario, presented Ontario's case:

> I would like to make it very clear that Ontario has always supported the principle of equalization in our country. I did not realize all the beds in Newfoundland were made in Ontario, nor that all the breakfast food that is eaten there is manufactured in Ontario, but we do realize and understand full well that Ontario's prosperity is based on a whole range of factors. Some of them are just the luck of geography, some of them are the gift of God, and some just the fact that we happen to be part of that great country called Canada.
>
> We recognize this and we are at all times prepared to do our part in ensuring that we have something at least approaching minimum standards across Canada. There must be some meaning to being a Canadian, regardless of

> where you live, regardless of the economic circumstances of the particular area in which you live. This is a very fundamental and a very basic problem.

Alberta Premier Harry Strom stated the West's point of view:

> The economy of the West is based to a very large degree upon the production of certain raw resources . . . when Westerners examine the federal government's priorities in industrial development, the order which they see is the following: the manufacturing industries in eastern and central Canada, the raw resource industries of eastern and central Canada, then, the raw resources industries of western Canada and finally, the manufacturing industries of western Canada.
>
> This order of priorities is not a figment of our imagination.
>
> What western Canadians legitimately desire, if economic justice is to prevail within Confederation, is that our raw resource industries be given the same priority as the manufacturing industries of eastern and central Canada.
>
> We desire this equality of priority to be demonstrated not simply in conference communiqués but in concrete ways. . . .
>
> It is time the federal government recognized the harmful effect of the tariff system on the West, and indeed on the economic health of the nation.
>
> For us, the tariff system symbolizes the economic imbalance of Confederation.
>
> We see the logic of protecting infant industries, but some of the "infants" are now eighty years of age and we are tired of paying their pensions.
>
> If the federal government is prepared to use its influence to secure entrance to foreign markets for Canadian producers, we want it to work as hard on behalf of the raw resource industries of the West. . . .

Premier W.A.C. Bennett spoke for British Columbia:

> In the light of burgeoning provincial responsibilities, particularly in the fields of education, health, and welfare, British Columbia can see no other alternative if provincial responsibilities are to be met than for the federal government to withdraw from the direct tax fields of personal and corporate income taxes and succession duties or estate taxes.
>
> When those changes have been made, it is our view the Constitution should restrict the spending power of the federal government to those matters under its jurisdiction. . . .
>
> I want to emphasize that the stresses within the nation at the present time are primarily economic and financial in nature. If we are to achieve that high destiny to which I am sure all of us around this table believe Canada is called, then we must do more to bring about economic opportunity for all citizens in all regions of Canada.
>
> I am not minimizing the importance of such matters as language, culture and constitutional review generally. But I am saying that if we are to have and develop the kind of Canada we all unquestionably desire, then the scope of our vision must embrace the economic facts of life in Canada, which call for a frank appraisal of what national policy should be adopted to improve the situation. British Columbia believes the solution lies in direct assistance to persons — to people — of low income rather than through large unconditional payments to certain provincial governments.

1. What seem to be the main complaints and suggestions of these premiers?
2. With which position do you most agree? Why?

PAYING FOR GOVERNMENT

Have you ever heard the expression that "nothing in this world is certain but death and taxes"? Benjamin Franklin said this more than 200 years ago. Modern health standards have increased our life span. But taxes seem to go up at an ever-increasing rate. Although paying taxes often hurts, they pay for the government services we are used to receiving. No Canadian would seriously argue that we should do away with police forces, schools, hospitals, postal service and garbage collection. Yet these are but a few of the hundreds of services government provides. A century ago, many of these services did not seem important and were not even provided by government. Today Canadians are demanding more and improved government services. Can we afford them?

The current budget of our federal government is over $40 billion per year. Canada's national debt

CURRENT ESTIMATES

PROVINCIAL BUDGET DOLLAR

REVENUE | **EXPENDITURE**

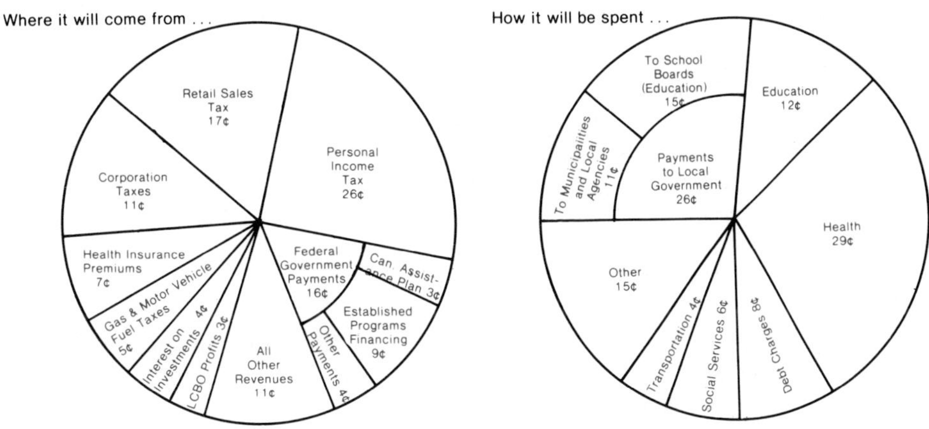

FEDERAL BUDGET DOLLAR

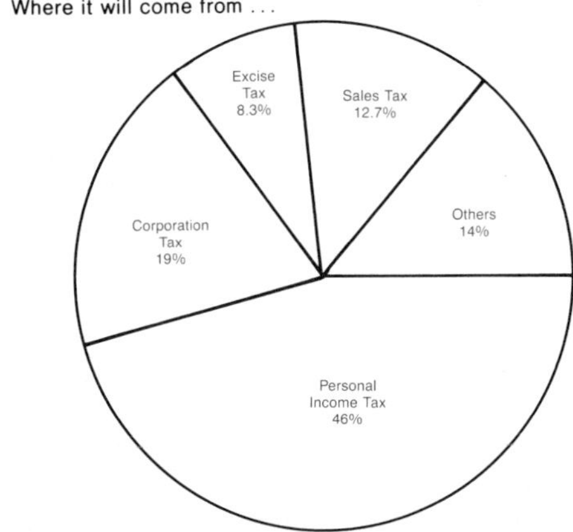

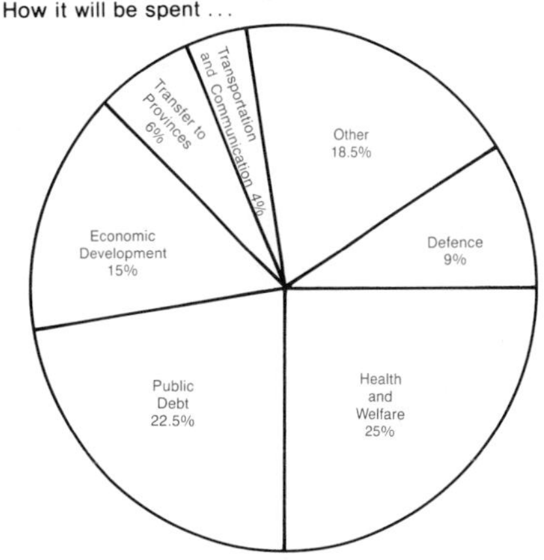

stands at over $190 billion dollars. This means that every man, woman and child in Canada would have to pay $7600 to pay off the national debt. These figures do not include all the expenses that are borne by provincial and municipal governments. Where do the various governments get the money to pay for all the services they provide?

The BNA Act gives the federal government the power to collect the following kinds of taxes:

Personal Income Tax: This tax is based on a person's annual earnings. It provides the government's largest source of revenue today.

Corporation Tax: This is a tax imposed on the income of a corporation or business.

Sales Tax: This is an indirect tax paid by the merchant on his or her total sales for the year. The buyer is usually not aware that he or she is paying for it. The amount is already included in the purchase price of an item.

Excise Tax: This is another type of indirect sales tax. Excise taxes are paid by a manufacturer to the government before he or she sells a product. An example of an excise tax is the tax on liquor.

Tariff: This is an import tax placed on goods coming in from other countries. The tax is paid by the importer.

Provincial governments also need money to pay for services they give. Their tax sources are not as great as the federal government's. The BNA Act allows provinces to raise money through the selling of various kinds of licences (e.g., automobile, pet, hunting, fishing), corporation income tax, liquor tax, sales tax (e.g., on gasoline). As well, the provinces have the power to collect two other kinds of taxes:

Direct Sales Tax: This is different from ordinary sales tax. It is paid directly by the consumer when an item is bought. Most provinces have direct sales taxes ranging from 5 percent to 11 percent. Alberta is an example of a province that has no sales tax.

Inheritance Tax: When someone dies and leaves property to his or her heirs, they must pay a tax on the value of the property.

The third level of government, the municipal, provides some of the most expensive services we use. Municipal governments operate schools, police departments, sanitation departments and public transit. Most of the money for these services comes from property taxes. Property taxes are paid on land and the value of the buildings on the land.

Even with all the taxes available to them, governments at all three levels find it hard to balance their budgets. Like many ordinary Canadians, they make a practice of spending more money than they receive. This is called deficit budgeting. The governments must then borrow money to pay their debts. They borrow from other countries or institutions. Canadian governments at all levels have borrowed a lot in recent years. A large part of our tax money goes to paying back our loans. It has been estimated that the federal government alone spends millions of dollars

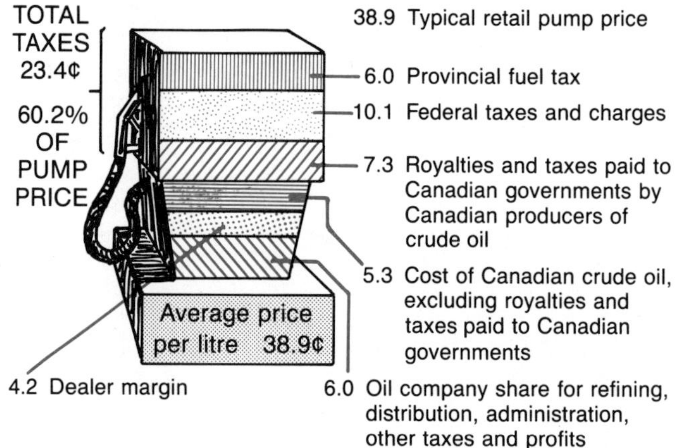

THE HIDDEN TAX BITE

We may accept taxes as being inevitable. Yet most of us are not aware of just how much of our income goes back to the government in the form of taxes. A large portion of the price of any item we buy is made up of taxes. In the diagram above, we see the impact of various taxes on the price of gasoline. How much would a litre of gas cost without federal and provincial taxes? As well, taxes will take an additional 75 percent bite of any future oil price increases.

each day just to pay back the interest on the money it has borrowed. This issue concerns many economists, especially in times of slow economic growth.

MUNICIPAL GOVERNMENTS

Canada is one of the very few countries in the world with three major levels of government. We have already studied the workings of the federal and provincial governments. The third level is the local, or municipal, government. In many ways, this may be the most important of the three. Municipal governments deal with matters that have a direct effect on us. Often, decisions of our federal or provincial governments do not touch us directly. Scarcely a day goes by, however, when each of us does not make use of the services provided by local governments. Which of the following services have you used in the past week?

- public parks
- golf courses
- zoos
- libraries
- arenas
- schools
- sidewalks
- roads
- buses or subways
- garbage disposal

These and many more are the responsibility of municipal governments. You can see the importance of these governments. Yet many voters don't act as though they know this. For federal and provincial elections, the voter turnout is usually close to 70 percent. Examine the figures for recent municipal elections:

WHAT PERCENT OF VOTERS VOTED IN MUNICIPAL ELECTIONS

City	% of Eligible Voters Who Voted
St. John's, Newfoundland	59%
Halifax, Nova Scotia	47%
Saint John, New Brunswick	40%
Montreal, Quebec	32%
Toronto, Ontario	34%
Winnipeg, Manitoba	54%
Saskatoon, Saskatchewan	35%
Edmonton, Alberta	42%
Vancouver, British Columbia	43%

Unfortunately, these figures are typical of municipal elections in cities and towns right across Canada.

ORGANIZATION OF MUNICIPAL GOVERNMENTS

Section 92, Article 8, of the Act gives the legislature of each province the right to make laws about municipal institutions. This means that municipal decisions must be approved by the government of the province. It also means that there is a wide variety of municipal governments. The type of government a community has will vary from province to province. It will also depend on the size of the community.

Toronto City Hall

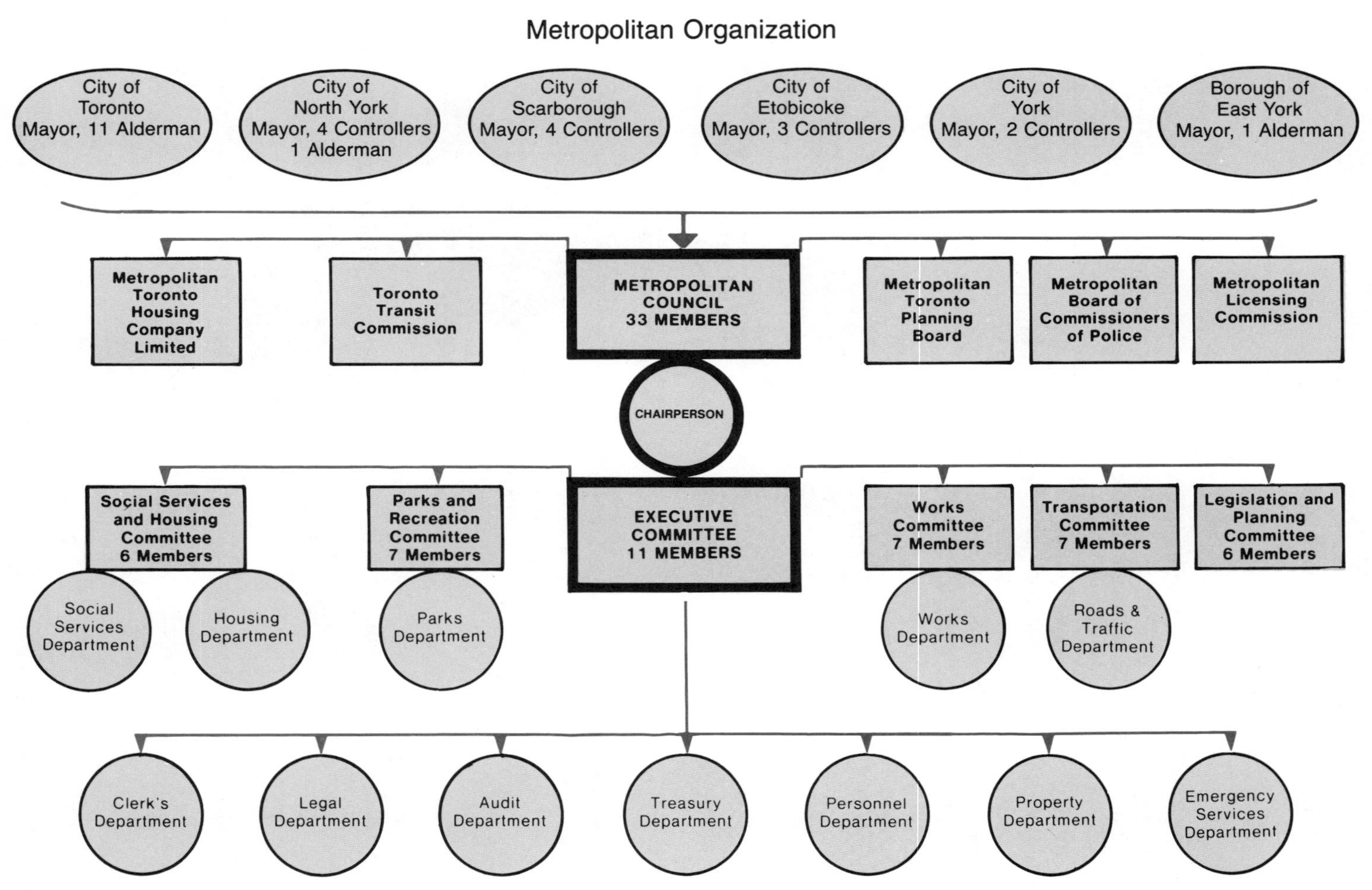
Metropolitan Organization
City of Toronto Mayor, 11 Alderman
City of North York Mayor, 4 Controllers 1 Alderman
City of Scarborough Mayor, 4 Controllers
City of Etobicoke Mayor, 3 Controllers
City of York Mayor, 2 Controllers
Borough of East York Mayor, 1 Alderman
Metropolitan Toronto Housing Company Limited
Toronto Transit Commission
METROPOLITAN COUNCIL 33 MEMBERS
Metropolitan Toronto Planning Board
Metropolitan Board of Commissioners of Police
Metropolitan Licensing Commission
CHAIRPERSON
Social Services and Housing Committee 6 Members
Parks and Recreation Committee 7 Members
EXECUTIVE COMMITTEE 11 MEMBERS
Works Committee 7 Members
Transportation Committee 7 Members
Legislation and Planning Committee 6 Members
Social Services Department
Housing Department
Parks Department
Works Department
Roads & Traffic Department
Clerk's Department
Legal Department
Audit Department
Treasury Department
Personnel Department
Property Department
Emergency Services Department

HOW YOUR LOCAL GOVERNMENT AFFECTS YOUR LIFE

1·2·3 Read the following list of events that might occur in the near future:

- A curfew of 22:00 is placed on anyone under the age of seventeen.
- The government of Canada agrees to sell nuclear reactors to Rumania.
- Your city firefighters go on strike.
- Gasoline prices will rise 10 percent this year.
- Your house is expropriated to make way for a new road.
- The government agrees to lower transportation costs of Canadian goods travelling across the country.
- There is a bus and subway strike that is likely to last for weeks.
- The city's water purification system malfunctions, and the city may be without water for days.
- The government calls a conference with leading business, labour and political figures to study the economy.
- There has been a rash of burglaries in your neighbourhood, but the police department is understaffed and can't spare extra officers to patrol the area.

List the above events in the order of their importance to *you*. After you have completed your list, try to find out which events are the responsibility of the federal, which of the provincial, and which of the municipal government. The chances are that many of the items at the very top of your list come under the responsibility of the municipal government.

LOCAL GOVERNMENT TERMINOLOGY (ONTARIO)

City:	a built-up area with a minimum population of 15 000 people
Town:	a built-up area with a minimum population of 2000
Village:	a built-up area with a minimum population of 500
Board of Control:	in cities of over 100 000 people; a board of control consists of the mayor and a small number of controllers; controllers are full-time officials responsible for looking after the city budget and departments
Mayor:	the head of the municipal council in city government
Reeve:	basically, a reeve has the same duties as a mayor; he or she is elected in townships, towns, and villages
Alderman:	an alderman is an elected member of a town council; usually he or she represents a particular area of the town or city

METRO TORONTO

In Ontario, the Department of Municipal Affairs set up a special board, the Ontario Municipal Board (OMB) to help look after local government. The OMB has great powers. One of its duties is to approve spending by each municipality.

The City of Toronto presented a special challenge for local government. Originally the area consisted of the city of Toronto and the five boroughs around it — East York, Etobicoke, York, Scarborough and North York. Each borough had, and continues to have, its own mayor and council. (In recent years, Scarborough, North York, Etobicoke and York have become cities in their own right.)

The rapid growth of the area created problems. Transportation, sewage, water supply, road building and taxation were all strained. The metropolitan system of government was created to ease the problems. The metropolitan government works in co-operation with the borough governments and looks after an area of 1500 km^2.

SHARED RESPONSIBILITY

Service	Metro Responsibility	Local Responsibility
Recreation and community services	Regional parks (ravines, waterfront, islands, zoo) Golf courses Regional libraries	Neighbourhood parks and playgrounds Recreation programs Community centres and arenas Neighbourhood libraries
Road construction and maintenance	Expressways Major arterial roads (Bridges, grade separations, snow removal and street cleaning are the responsibility of the government in whose jurisdiction the road lies.)	Minor arterial roads Neighbourhood access roads Street lighting Sidewalks
Traffic control	Traffic regulation, crosswalks and pavement markings are the responsibility of the government in whose jurisdiction the road lies. Traffic lights are a metropolitan responsibility, irrespective of the jurisdiction of the road.	
Water supply	Purification, pumping and trunk distribution system (Water is supplied wholesale by the metropolitan corporation to the area municipalities, who retail it to the consumer.)	Local distribution system
Water pollution control	Sanitary trunk sewer system and disposal plants (Storm drainage is primarily a local responsibility except on metropolitan roads and in a few cases where major storm sewers are required.)	Local connecting sewer system
Garbage collection and disposal	Disposal	Collection
Public education	School sites, attendance areas and building programs Operating and capital costs	Operation of school system
Health	Chronic and convalescent hospitals	Public health services
Licensing and inspection	Businesses	Dogs and dog pound Marriages Buildings
Planning and development control	Except for zoning, which is a local responsibility, planning and development control are shared by the metropolitan and area municipalities on the same basis as other shared responsibilities.	

YOUR ROLE IN LOCAL GOVERNMENT

Unfortunately, too large a segment of the public is unaware of the role of local government. They do not understand how it works. They seem happy to let others look after the programs and services for which they are paying. How can this be improved? The simplest way is for each citizen to become involved in the political process. Of course, we may not all be able to run for office. But we can inform ourselves about what is being done by those in office. How?

- Read the newspapers.
- Attend council meetings.
- Attend court sessions.
- Help a candidate in a local election.
- Talk to your candidate about your concerns.

You will probably find that politics is more exciting than you might have imagined.

BUILDING YOUR LEARNING SKILLS

FOCUSSING ON THE ISSUE

1 State at least four key ideas discussed in this chapter.

2 Do you recall the following facts?
- *a* The section of the BNA Act that looks after provincial matters is:
  i 99 *ii* 92 *iii* 91
- *b* The current budget of our federal government is about:
  i $10 billion *ii* $20 billion
  iii $40 billion *iv* $100 billion
- *c* A tax paid directly by the consumer when purchasing an item is called an indirect sales tax. True or false?

3 The following terms were used in this chapter. Try to recall their meanings and how they were used.

alderperson
board of control
deficit budgeting
excise tax
inheritance tax
lieutenant-governor
mayor
reeve
tariff

RESEARCHING

1 Leaders of our federal government are usually well known by most people. Elected officials at other levels of government are often less well known. Find out the following:
- *a* The name of your current provincial premier and the party he leads
- *b* The name of the leader of the Opposition in your provincial government
- *c* The name of the elected member of your provincial riding
- *d* The name of your mayor

2 Obtain a recent copy of the income tax tables. The percentage of income payable in taxes (federal and provincial) for each of these yearly earnings is:
a $10 000 *b* $24 000 *c* $60 000

3 Find out what the sum of the current federal and provincial deficit is.

1·2·3 ORGANIZING

1 Make a list of the services provided by your municipal government. Rank them in order of their usefulness or importance to you.

2 The diagram on page 48 shows the breakdown of taxes on a litre of gasoline. Make a summary of the amount earned by the federal and provincial governments and the producer. Who gets the most money?

3 The diagram on page 47 shows the sources of income and expenditures of the provincial government. List, in order, the three greatest sources of provincial expense.

4 Is your municipality considered a village, a town or a city? What is the organization of your local government? Make a chart of the various committees who look after the government of your community.

COMMUNICATING

1 Invite your representative in city council or your school trustee to come to your class and explain his or her duties as an elected official.

2 Hold a provincial conference in your class by dividing the class into representatives of the different provinces of Canada. Discuss the issues that unite and separate us today.

3 Debate the proposition: Governments should never have a deficit. They should only spend as much as they take in.

ANALYZING

1 Regional disparity is a fact of life in Canada. Do you agree with the principle that the wealthier provinces—Alberta, British Columbia, and Ontario—should share their wealth with the less fortunate provinces? What actions should the federal government take to equalize the national wealth? How would this affect you personally?

2 Education is a provincial responsibility according to the BNA Act. One of the effects of this is that there is a great variety of educational policies and standards from one end of the country to the other. If you were to move to another province, the subjects and the contents of the courses of study might be much different from what you are now taking. Should there be *one* educational system for all of Canada?

3 The voter turnout in Canada for elections at all levels of government is among the lowest in the world. In Australia there is a $12 fine for not voting. There the voter turnout is much higher. Should Canada adopt a similar system to encourage voters to participate in the electoral process?

APPLYING YOUR KNOWLEDGE

1 Canadians often complain that they are taxed too highly. What could the government do to reduce taxes? What additional sources of revenue could the government introduce in order to reduce taxes?

2 Do some research on Adam Smith and find out what his principles of just taxation were. Apply Smith's principles to Canada's tax system and decide which taxes are just and which unjust, based on Smith's principles. Do you agree or disagree with Smith?

3 For the following list of government responsibilities, decide whether each falls under federal, provincial or municipal control:

agriculture	direct taxes
mining	prisons
oil	post office
hospitals	civil law
sewers	defence
education	printing money
divorce	property taxes
marriage	

unit two

THE LAW

TOPIC ORGANIZER

THEME ORGANIZER

- Without laws, we would live in a society where might makes right.
- The Criminal Code outlines the nature of criminal offences as well as their punishment.
- Canadian criminal law is built on custom and precedent as well as the provisions of the Criminal Code.
- In our society, there are many crimes without victims or with willing victims.
- The new Charter of Rights and Freedoms strengthens and expands the legal rights of Canadians.
- The jury system is the safeguard of our legal rights.
- The new Young Offenders Act is the subject of great controversy in Canada.
- Why do people become criminals? The experts and the public disagree.
- The question of the morality of capital punishment is one of the continuing issues of Canadian life.
- Although the government of Canada has increasingly protected the consumer, the warning, "Let the buyer beware," is a rule that still applies in many situations.

INTRODUCTION

"Missing clerk wanted in million-dollar computer fraud"
"Police officer killed by unknown gunman"
"Man holds score of hostages in bank holdup attempt"
"Terrorism now considered the crime of the 80s"
"Moncton police force demands return of death sentence"
"Mounties nab suspects in drug bust"

Headlines such as these greet us almost every day in newspapers across Canada. They leave readers with the impression that crime is on the increase. Statistics seem to bear out the fact that crime is a growing problem in Canada. Over the past ten years, criminal offences have more than doubled. Violent crimes such as murder, rape and robbery are the ones that get the most public attention. Yet by far the largest number of offences committed by Canadians do not involve violence. They may involve the use of drugs or alcohol. They may be simple automobile offences. Indeed, some crimes are committed by people who do not even know they are breaking the law.

On the whole, Canadians know a good deal about the law. They know they must not steal or murder. They know they must not drive beyond the speed limit or drive without a licence. Yet there are hundreds of laws that Canadians either do not know about or do not understand. If you break such a law, you will still be punished. Our courts say that "ignorance of the law is no excuse."

It is important, then, for Canadians to know as much as they can about the law. However, even lawyers do not have knowledge of all the laws at their fingertips. As an ordinary citizen, you cannot be expected to know all the laws. You should, however, know how the law operates and what rights and duties you have under the law. This may be of vital importance to you.

In this unit we will examine criminal and civil law in Canada. You will be asked to actively participate in making decisions about laws in case studies. We will also look at your rights as Canadians, the role of the police, our court system and our method of punishing convicted criminals. One chapter will focus on crimes committed by young people.

UNIT PREVIEW QUESTIONS

As you study this unit, keep these questions in mind; they will serve as a focus for your reading. You may want to return to them when you have finished the unit.

1. What constitutes a crime?
2. Why do people become criminals?
3. What are our new rights and how are we protected under the Charter of Rights and Freedoms?

4 Does the Young Offenders Act treat youthful criminals too lightly?
5 Do the police have too much power in our country?
6 Would the return of capital punishment reduce the murder rate?
7 Does our prison system treat criminals too softly?
8 Should the government take a greater role in preventing merchandisers from taking advantage of consumers?

chapter 4

YOU AND THE LAW

TOPIC ORGANIZER **PAGE**

THEME ORGANIZER

- ▶ The legal definition of a crime
- ▶ The classes of crime: Summary conviction and indictable offences
- ▶ Crimes without victims: Are there really such things?
- ▶ The Charter of Rights and Freedoms: Giving us rights we always thought we had
- ▶ The jury system: The complicated system of jury selection
- ▶ The trial: The nature of evidence

INTRODUCTION

If every person on earth were a hermit and had no contact with other people, there would be no need for laws. Fortunately, human beings live in social groups. This helps each person in the group live a better life. But this also means that people must work and co-operate with each other. Unfortunately, it seems that some people in society behave in anti-social ways. Some individuals become irritable, some angry, some selfish, some aggressive and some even violent. These hostilities may be turned against other persons or groups in society. Laws are made to protect people from the "bad" actions of others. In effect, the idea of law is to put limits on people's greed, drives and emotions. As individuals, we all have certain freedoms and rights. Sometimes, for the protection of society, the law places limits on these rights. As a famous judge once pointed out, "Your right to swing your fist ends at the point where the other fellow's nose begins."

Imagine for a moment what your world would be like without laws. None of your possessions would be safe—your radio, television, stereo player, bicycle or even your clothes. Someone bigger, stronger or faster could take them from you. Even your person could not be safe from attack. The law of the jungle, "might makes right," would take over.

We may not always agree with the laws we live by. In fact, we may not always know what the laws are. However, we are expected to live by these laws. Ignorance is no real excuse and no guarantee against being charged. As we saw in an earlier chapter, in a democracy like Canada, our elected representatives make the laws for the good of the majority. If we feel that a certain law is unfair, we have the right to appeal it or work to change it. We do not have the right to break it.

In Canada there are two kinds of law we live by: criminal law and civil law. Criminal law protects society against illegal acts. It protects everyone's person and property against other individuals. It also provides punishment for those who break the law. Civil law deals with the rights of and agreements and contracts between individuals. The court only acts as a referee in solving disputes.

Before reading on, study the chart of key words and ideas that follows.

KEY WORDS AND IDEAS IN THIS CHAPTER

Term	Meaning	Sample Use
Charter of Rights and Freedoms	a part of our Constitution listing the rights and safeguards Canadians receive under the law	Canada's Charter of Rights and Freedoms was passed in 1982 by the government of Pierre Trudeau.
common law	a body of law developed in England in the time of King Henry II, based on decisions made by his travelling justices	English common law is the basis of the legal system of Canada.
habeas corpus	a writ of law that protects an individual against being jailed illegally or for an unreasonable period of time without trial	If an accused person is not brought before a judge within a reasonable period of time, a lawyer can have him or her released from jail with a writ of habeas corpus.
indictable offences	crimes that are considered to be serious offences	Armed robbery is one example of an indictable offence.
Civil Code	a body of law developed in France during the time of Napoleon; is in the form of a written code	The Civil Code is the basis of Quebec's provincial laws.
criminal law	the segment of the law that deals with offences against an individual or society	The Criminal Code of Canada deals with criminal law.
precedent	a decision made by a judge in a certain case, which becomes the basis for future court decisions dealing with similar cases	Precedent is used in Canada alongside the Criminal Code of Canada.
Supreme Court	the highest court in Canada; is composed of nine judges	The Supreme Court hears appeals in serious criminal and civil rights cases. It also interprets the BNA Act.
trial by jury	a trial before a group of citizens selected to hear a case against an accused person and give a verdict	People accused of serious crimes, such as murder, must have a trial by a jury.

CRIMINAL LAW

Eastview High School was holding its annual charity drive. The students of Ms. Wesley's Grade 10 history class decided to organize a car wash as their contribution. Rob Randall, a student in the class, had received his driver's licence the month before. He offered to drive his teacher's car to be washed. Ms. Wesley realized her teaching duties would prevent her from taking the car herself, so, after a moment's hesitation, she agreed to Rob's offer.

Following Ms. Wesley's instructions, Rob found her car. His eyes popped! It was a European sports car, the kind he had been dreaming about ever since he first saw it on the cover of *Auto Magazine*. From the moment he sat behind the wheel, he experienced a feeling of power and freedom. Maybe this would be as close as he would ever come to driving such a car again. Who would know if he just went for a little spin around the block first? The car handled like a dream. He pressed a little harder on the accelerator, and the car surged forward. But it hit a small pothole and veered to the right. Unable to brake in time or straighten the wheels, Rob saw himself heading for a ditch. The car hit the ditch, rolled over once and became wedged against a telephone pole. It was all over in a flash. Rob, shaken but unhurt, jumped out. As he surveyed the damage, he became frightened. What would he do now? He couldn't go back to school. He ran.

That evening Rob was arrested by the police and charged with "taking a motor vehicle without consent." Is Rob Randall a criminal?

For an action to be considered a "crime" in Canada it is generally subject to the following conditions:

1 It must be forbidden by the Criminal Code of Canada.
2 The accused must have intended to commit the offence.
3 The accused must be able to understand the nature of the action and its consequences.

Does Rob Randall's action qualify as a crime?

Most types of crime in Canada are dealt with in the Criminal Code of Canada. The Code explains the nature of an offence, sets punishments and tells how criminal proceedings must take place. Alongside the Criminal Code is the body of precedent. Precedent refers to decisions made in certain cases by courts in the past. In any new cases of a similar kind, the courts may take the precedents into account. In addition to the Criminal Code, the Narcotic Control Act bans such drugs as marijuana, opium and cocaine, while the Food and Drugs Act controls hallucinogenic drugs such as LSD. Under these two acts, the trafficking, importation and possession of a whole range of drugs are illegal and entail criminal penalties.

As we have seen, three conditions must exist for an action to be considered a crime. Often, however, it is difficult to determine if an accused person *intended* to commit a crime. It is also hard to prove that the person understood the nature of his or her actions. In fact, it is impossible for certain people to commit a crime. The Criminal Code tells us that:

CHILD UNDER TWELVE

12. No person shall be convicted of an offence in respect of an act or omission on his part while he (or she) was under the age of twelve years.

Which of the following, if any, are guilty of committing a crime? What might be their defence? What do you think the verdict would be?

A An eleven-year-old was babysitting a three-year-old child. She noticed him playing with a book of matches. She took the matches away and warned him about the dangers of playing with matches. A short while later, she again caught him with the matches in his hands. Angry now, she turned on the stove and put his hands on the hot burners. The young child suffered second-degree burns. The girl claimed she was trying to teach the child a lesson.

SOME UNUSUAL LAWS

- In Canada the law forbids payment in pennies of a debt larger than 25¢.
- In St. Stephen, New Brunswick, pretending to be drunk is against the law.
- In Prince Edward Island, it is illegal to have a parrot in your possession.
- In Alberta, you may not paint wooden ladders.
- In the Yukon, it is illegal to catch fish with an unbaited hook.
- In Kingston, Ontario, there is a law against removing worms from a public park without written permission.
- In Pictou, Nova Scotia, a man cannot kiss any woman, even his wife, on Sunday.
- In the Northwest Territories, it is against the law to keep chickens in the same shed as a milk cow.
- It is against the law to stage a cattle drive through the streets of St. John's, Newfoundland, after 08:00.
- In Montreal, it is against the law to water your garden when it is raining.
- In Saanich, B.C., it is unlawful to let a cow walk more slowly than 4 km/h on the highway.
- In Prince Albert, Saskatchewan, two people may not ride bicycles side by side.
- In Manitoba, it is an offence to sell garter snakes or elks' teeth without a permit.

B A young man who had taken LSD was accused of killing his father-in-law. He stabbed his father-in-law many times with a knife, claiming the man was the devil and was after him.

C A man had threatened to kill his wife on a number of previous occasions. One night he went out to a tavern. He returned home in a drunken state and actually killed her.

The verdicts:

A In this case, although the babysitter was aware of what she was doing, the courts decided to dismiss the charges because of her intentions and her age.

B Insanity was accepted as a defence in this case. The jury ruled that the young man's mind was so twisted from the effects of the drug that he had no criminal intent.

C The defence pleaded that since the man was drunk, he was not capable of knowing right and wrong. He was, in effect, in a state of temporary insanity. This defence was rejected. It was concluded that a person who goes out intending to kill, knowing it is wrong, and does kill, cannot escape punishment by making himself drunk before doing it.

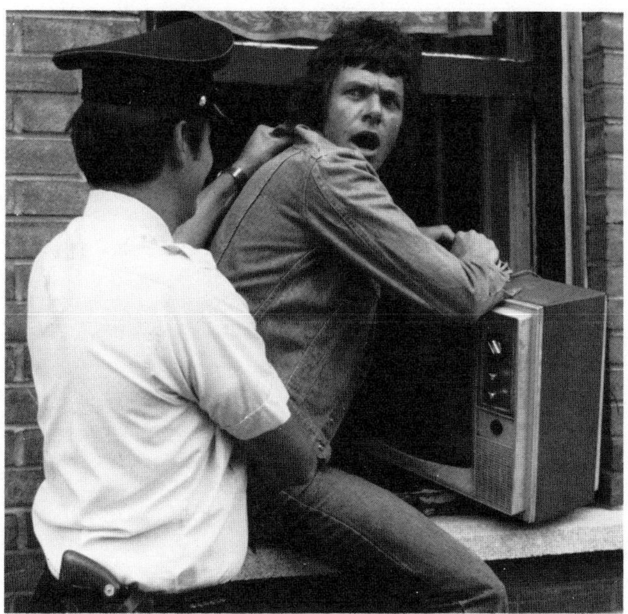

Police apprehend a thief.

ERASED CHALK MARKS — YOUTH ACQUITTED

Court follows precedent

TORONTO—The court today acquitted a youth charged with erasing a police chalk mark from the tire of a car parked on the street outside his home.

The youth's lawyer pointed to an Ontario Court of Appeal decision that had ruled that a motorist might erase the police mark from his or her own car or, with the owner's permission, from another car.

The youth admitted that he had erased chalk marks from his own car and also from his neighbour's car parked outside their homes, but his lawyer argued that this act was not against the law because of the appeal court ruling.

CLASSES OF CRIMES

The Criminal Code divides crimes into two classes:

1 Offences punished on summary conviction
2 Indictable offences

SUMMARY CONVICTIONS

Offences punishable on summary conviction are usually not very serious. Most motor vehicle offences come under this class. So do charges of common assault, juvenile delinquency and vagrancy, among others. In such cases, following a summons to appear in court, the accused is tried by a magistrate without a jury.

Some Common Offences Below are some examples of offences punishable by summary conviction.

OPERATION OF MOTOR VEHICLE, VESSEL OR AIRCRAFT WHILE IMPAIRED OR WITH MORE THAN 80 MG ALCOHOL IN BLOOD.

237. Every one commits an offence who operates a motor vehicle or vessel or operates or assists in the operation of an aircraft or has the care or control of a motor vehicle, vessel or aircraft whether it is in motion or not,

Average Annual Homicide Rates per 100 000 Population, by Province, 1980–1986

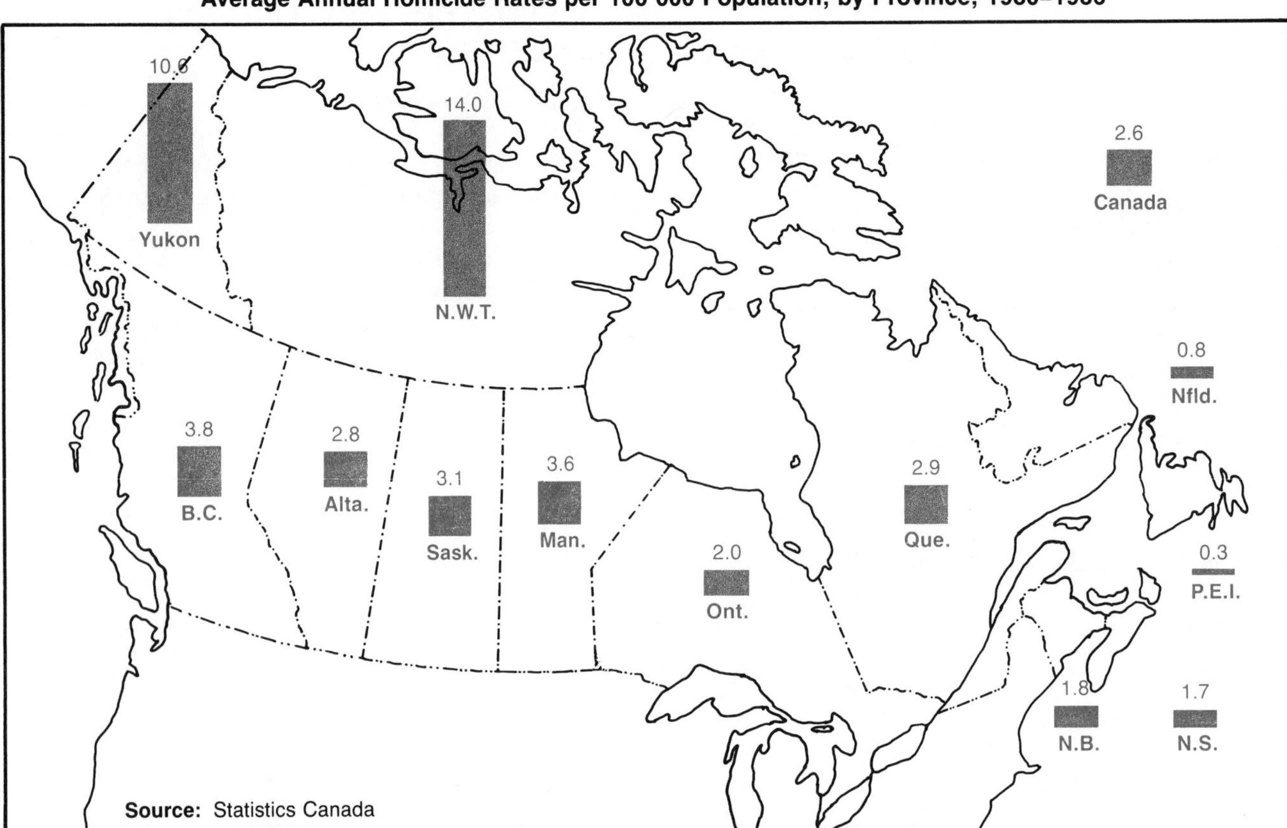

Use a bar graph to organize the information on the map showing the homicide rate in Canada. On the map showing the homicide rate in Canada rank the provinces from those with the lowest to those with the highest rate. Use the same procedure with the information on the map showing criminal code offences in Canada. Are there any trends noticeable from these statistics? Discuss the possible reasons for this.

(*a*) while his ability to operate the vehicle, vessel or aircraft is impaired by alcohol or a drug; or

(*b*) having consumed alcohol in such a quantity that the concentration thereof in his blood exceeds eighty milligrams of alcohol in one hundred millilitres of blood. 1985, c. 19, s. 36.

PUNISHMENT — Impaired driving causing bodily harm — Impaired driving causing death — Previous convictions—Conditional discharge.

239. (1) Every one who commits an offence under section 237 or 238 is guilty of an indictable offence or an offence punishable on summary conviction and is liable,

(*a*) whether the offence is prosecuted by indictment or punishable on summary conviction, to the following minimum punishment, namely,

(i) for a first offence, to a fine of not less than three hundred dollars,

(ii) for a second offence, to imprisonment for not less than fourteen days, and

(iii) for each subsequent offence, to imprisonment for not less than ninety days;

(*b*) where the offence is prosecuted by indictment, to imprisonment for a term not exceeding five years; and

(*c*) where the offence is punishable on summary conviction, to imprisonment for a term not exceeding six months.

Late one evening, a drunk driver went off the road and wound up in a field. A police officer found him "sleeping it off" behind the wheel, with the car sitting on its side. The driver was charged with impaired driving, even though the car was off its wheels. The magistrate decided that if a driver is

Rate per 100 000 Population of Criminal Code Offences, by Province, 1986

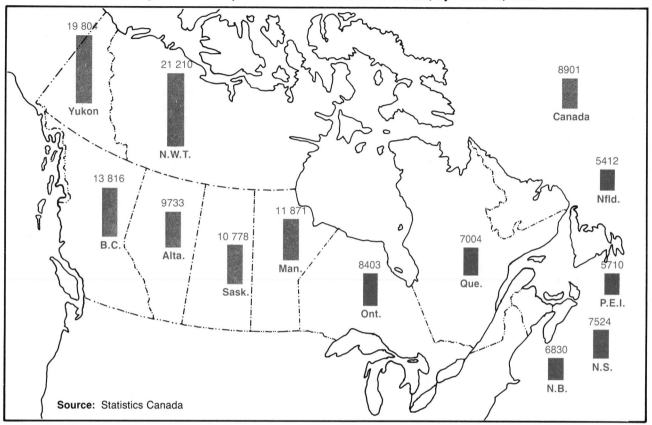

19 804
Yukon
21 210
N.W.T.
13 816
B.C.
9733
Alta.
10 778
Sask.
11 871
Man.
8403
Ont.
7004
Que.
8901
Canada
5412
Nfld.
5710
P.E.I.
7524
N.S.
6830
N.B.

Source: Statistics Canada

behind the wheel with the intention of driving, he or she may be charged. The automobile does not actually have to be in motion.

What would be the decision where a drunken person is found sleeping in the back seat of his or her car?

ASSAULT—

244. (1) A person commits an assault when

(*a*) without the consent of another person, he applies force intentionally to that other person, directly or indirectly;

(*b*) he attempts or threatens, by an act or gesture, to apply force to another person, if he has, or causes that other person to believe upon reasonable grounds that he has, present ability to effect his purpose; or

(*c*) while openly wearing or carrying a weapon or an imitation thereof, he accosts or impedes another person or begs.

A man weighing barely 40 kg started an argument with a man more than twice his size in a neighbourhood bar. The large man realized the smaller man was drunk and refused to get into a fight. He called the manager, who in turn called the police. As he was being led away, the small man turned to the larger man and threatened to "knock his block off." He was charged with assault.

The magistrate found the man not guilty. He felt that, because of his size and his opponent's size, there was little reason to believe the little man could carry out his threat. If, however, a gun or a knife had been used in the threat, he certainly would have been found guilty.

What would be the decision if the larger man had verbally threatened the smaller man?

INDICTABLE OFFENCES

Indictable offences are more serious crimes. They are placed in three different categories, depending on the court in which they are being tried.

Class A This includes the most serious types of crimes, such as murder or treason. These crimes must be tried by a jury in the Supreme Court. In Class A crimes, a preliminary hearing is held. The hearing is to determine if there is a reasonable amount of evidence to put the person on trial. If there is not sufficient evidence, the charges are dropped.

Class B These are less serious crimes, such as theft under $200. These are tried by a magistrate. The trial proceeds in the same way as a summary conviction case.

Class C This includes all other indictable offences, such as burglary, theft and kidnapping. The accused may choose to be tried by a magistrate, a judge alone or a judge and jury. If he or she selects trial by judge or trial by judge and jury, there must also be a preliminary hearing.

Before the trial Before a trial takes place, the accused is asked to plead "guilty" or "not guilty" to the charges. If the plea is "guilty," there is usually no need for a trial. However, the magistrate will still ask the Crown attorney, who prosecutes the case, to present his or her evidence. If the magistrate decides the evidence is not sufficient, he or she may change the defendant's plea to "not guilty." A trial will then be held.

If the accused pleads "not guilty," the case will go through the normal procedure. In Nova Scotia, any persons who are to be tried by judge and jury must have the charges against them examined by a grand jury. The grand jury decides if there is enough evidence to put the accused on trial. If it decides the evidence is not sufficient, the accused will be released.

Some Common Offences The following are some examples of indictable offences:

> ACCESSORY AFTER THE FACT
> 23.(1) An accessory after the fact to an offence is one who, knowing that a person has been a party to the offence, receives, comforts or assists him for the purpose of enabling him to escape.
> (2) No married person whose spouse has been a party to an offence is an accessory after the fact to that of-

Procedure in Criminal Cases

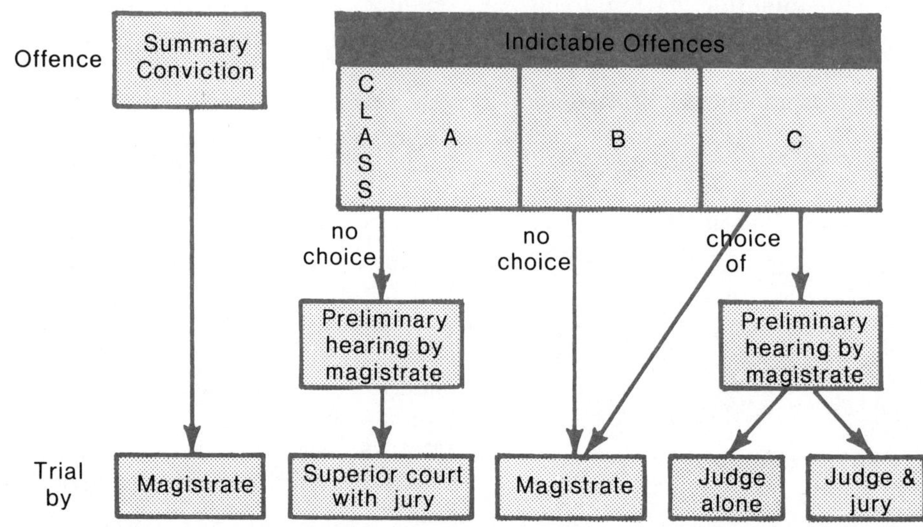

fence by receiving, comforting or assisting the spouse for the purpose of enabling the spouse to escape.

A group of friends went to a tavern. One of the men had a reputation for causing trouble when he had too much to drink. His friends knew this. Later in the evening the man started a fight with the bartender. He hit the bartender several times before his friends caught him, got him out of the tavern and drove off in their car. They were all arrested and charged. The man was charged with assault causing bodily harm. His friends were charged with being accessories after the fact. They were found guilty. On what grounds would the judge find them guilty?

ARSON—Fraudulently burning personal property.
389. (1) Every one who wilfully sets fire to
(a) a building or structure, whether completed or not,
(b) a stack of vegetable produce or of mineral or vegetable fuel,
(c) a mine,
(d) a well of combustible substance,
(e) a vessel or aircraft, whether completed or not,
(f) timber or materials placed in a shipyard for building, repairing or fitting out a ship,
(g) military or public stores or munitions of war,
(h) a crop, whether standing or cut down, or
(i) any wood, forest, or natural growth, or any lumber, timber, log, float, boom, dam or slide,
is guilty of an indictable offence and is liable to imprisonment for fourteen years.

A woman had an old wooden shed in the back yard of her property. Tearing it down would require too much time and effort. She decided to get rid of it by burning it. A neighbour called the fire department, which promptly answered the call and put out the blaze. The woman was charged with arson, found guilty and fined. The woman argued that it was her building and she could do what she wanted with it. Why did the judge reject this argument?

MURDER.
212. Culpable homicide is murder
(a) where the person who causes the death of a human being
(i) means to cause his death, or
(ii) means to cause him bodily harm that he knows is likely to cause his death, and is reckless whether death ensues or not;
(b) where a person, meaning to cause death to a human being or meaning to cause him bodily harm that he knows is likely to cause his death, and being reckless whether death ensues or not, by accident or mistake causes death to another human being, not withstanding that he does not mean to cause death or bodily harm to that human being; or
(c) where a person, for an unlawful object, does anything that he knows or ought to know is likely to cause death, and thereby causes death to a human being, notwithstanding that he desires to effect his object without causing death or bodily harm to any human being.

A man had a violent argument with his wife. She ran away from home and went to stay with her mother. The man, angry that his mother-in-law would take sides in the argument, blamed her for the quarrel and decided to take action. He took his rifle, went to his mother-in-law's home and shot at her through the open window. The bullet missed the mother-in-law but killed a neighbourhood woman who was visiting. The man pleaded that he did not intend to murder the other woman. The court, however, found him guilty of murder. On what basis did it make this decision?

CRIMES WITHOUT VICTIMS

Thus far, we have studied crimes where the victim is either society in general or individuals within society. We can easily see the need for laws that protect us from assault and injury and our property from theft or destruction. Indeed, the very definition of a crime suggests that someone or something is being harmed by the criminal.

Yet there are thousands of cases in our courts every year where there is no apparent victim. The criminals in these cases appear not to be hurting others, but only themselves. Some very common examples of this are involvement with drugs, alcohol, suicide, vagrancy and prostitution. Can you think of others? If these actions seem to harm only the offender, why are there laws against them? Let us examine a few of these crimes in more detail.

Drugs The laws against drugs fall into two categories:

1 laws against trafficking
2 laws against possession

POSSESSION OF NARCOTIC—Offence.
3. (1) Except as authorized by this Act or the regulations, no person shall have a narcotic in his possession.
(2) Every person who violates subsection (1) is guilty of an indictable offence and is liable
(a) upon summary conviction for a first offence, to a fine of one thousand dollars or to imprisonment for six months or to both fine and imprisonment, and for a subsequent offence, to a fine of two thousand dollars or to imprisonment for one year or to both fine and imprisonment; or
(b) upon conviction on indictment, to imprisonment for seven years.
TRAFFICKING—Possession for purpose of trafficking—Offence.
4. (1) No person shall traffic in a narcotic or any substance represented or held out by him to be a narcotic.
(2) No person shall have in his possession any narcotic for the purpose of trafficking.
(3) Every person who violates subsection (1) or (2) is guilty of an indictable offence and is liable to imprisonment for life.

Drugs are also classified as "hard" or "soft." "Hard" drugs are of the addictive type, such as heroin and cocaine. "Soft" drugs are non-addictive, such as marijuana and hashish. Since 1972, some of the soft drugs, such as amphetamines, have been removed from the Narcotic Control Act. They are now placed under the Food and Drug Act. Penalties under this act are less severe.

A commission headed by Gerald LeDain investigated the effects of various drugs. It recommended that the penalties for soft drugs be reduced. Some groups in society are actively pushing for the legalization of marijuana. They claim it is no more harmful than cigarette smoking. Their opponents disagree strongly. Many of them say that cigarettes, too, are harmful and should also be made illegal.

The courts have quietly reduced the penalties against marijuana users. In 1969 one person in four convicted of marijuana use was jailed. Today, few if any users are jailed. Small fines have become the rule.

Hard drugs are a greater problem. These drugs are very expensive. Addicts often spend up to $500 a day to supply their habits. Many become involved in criminal activities such as theft and prostitution to buy drugs. Drug addicts are a major reason for the existence of organized crime in Canada and the United States.

During the time of Prohibition, in the 1920s, selling alcoholic beverages was illegal. To get around the law, people made illegal whisky. Organized crime grew quickly on the profits from smuggling whisky. In time, the law was changed to make the sale of alcoholic beverages legal.

Will the same thing happen to drugs? What changes in the present law do you think should be made?

Vagrancy The Criminal Code defines a vagrant as one who "supports himself in whole or part by gaming or crime and has no lawful profession or calling by which to maintain himself." The law may also convict persons of vagrancy if they have a previous record of sex offences and are found loitering in a public place, such as a park or schoolground.

Begging in the streets, or "panhandling," may also be considered vagrancy. Therefore, it is against the law.

For a long while "wandering abroad" without a visible means of support qualified a person as a vagrant. A person could not be caught just doing nothing. Much of the reason for this law stemmed from the hard times of the Depression (see Unit 3, Chapter 9). Thousands of unemployed people roamed the streets without a dime in their pockets. Occasionally, they broke into homes or stores and stole to support themselves. The vagrancy laws gave police the right to arrest suspicious individuals before a crime could be committed.

WHO IS THE REAL VICTIM?

It can be argued that, in fact, all these crimes do have victims. An alcoholic can make life miserable for his or her family. A drug addict may sustain criminal elements in society. A prostitute may contribute to the lowering of morals in society. A panhandler helps lower society's productivity because he or she depends on others and contributes nothing.

There is another side to the issue. Some argue that in a free society, persons should be free to do as they please unless it interferes with someone else's rights. They argue that these laws make moral judgements on someone else's conduct. They believe that it is not the business of the law to judge morality. Lastly, they point out that drug and alcohol addiction are forms of sickness. Addicts should be treated in hospitals and clinics rather than in courts and prisons.

Do you think there is such a thing as a crime without a victim? If so, how should the law treat these offences?

YOUR RIGHTS BEFORE THE LAW

Most Canadians know little about their own rights. Most of what we think we know is based on American television. Until the passage of the Canadian Charter of Rights and Freedoms in 1982 many of the rights we took for granted were not protected by law.

There are thousands of laws in existence in Canada. It would be impossible for the average person to be familiar with all of them. You should, however, make an effort to be familiar with your rights before the law. It will help if you are arrested, rightly or wrongly, for breaking the law.

THE PROCESS OF LAW

Let us suppose the police suspect you of having committed a theft of over $500 from the store where you work part-time. The following is the sequence of events that might occur.

THE ARREST

A police officer comes to your door and asks you to go along with him or her.

YOU: Why should I?

OFFICER: Just come along.

At this point, the police officer has not made a lawful arrest and you do not have to go along. The officer must tell you that you are under arrest and what the charge is. If you go along willingly, you cannot claim later that an unlawful arrest was made.

If the officer asks you questions, you may want to answer. However, anything you say can be used against you in a court of law. It is wise to have a lawyer present. At the same time, you do not have to answer any questions (except your name, age and address if you want to be released). Nor do you have to show the officer your wallet, money or identification. If the arrest is unlawful, the officer cannot hold you for questioning. However, do not use force to resist arrest, even if you are innocent of the crime. If the arrest was lawfully made, you could be charged with resisting arrest.

Police officers in Canada have the right to arrest

SOME RIGHTS WE DID NOT HAVE BEFORE 1982

- The police did not have to read you your rights if they arrested you.
- The police did not have to inform you that you have the right to a lawyer.
- Any statement you made to the police, even if they had not informed you of your rights, still might be admissible in a court of law.
- Evidence, even if gathered illegally by the police, may still be used against you in court.
- Under the narcotics laws, police officers could search any property (except your home) without a specific search warrant.
- The RCMP could be issued with a Queen's writ of assistance, which entitled them to enter and search your home without a warrant.
- A police officer did not have to tell you you were under arrest—unless you asked.
- A police officer did not have to tell you the charge against you—unless you asked.

SOME NEW LEGAL RIGHTS

- You have the right to be secure against unreasonable search and seizure. (Police now have to have reasonable grounds for obtaining a search warrant.)
- You have the right to be informed of the reason for your arrest and told of your right to a lawyer.
- You have the right to be tried within a reasonable time.
- You have the right not to testify against yourself.

THE ROLE OF THE POLICE

Canada's police have one of society's most difficult jobs. On the one hand, they are supposed to protect society from criminals. On the other hand, they are often subjected to abuse from the very people they are trying to help. Besides upholding the law, the police also provide, free of charge, a number of social services not really within their jurisdictions. These might include family counselling and helping lost children. Under a democratic system, the police are really only representatives of the people, trained to enforce the laws.

The police in Canada are not different from other citizens. They do not have special rights or privileges. Like other citizens, they are supposed to act within the law. If they break a law, even while on duty, they will be charged.

In Canada, there are three kinds of police forces—federal, provincial and municipal. The federal police force is the Royal Canadian Mounted Police. The RCMP is known worldwide and they have a reputation for efficiency. In Canada, the RCMP is responsible for enforcing federal laws, such as those dealing with narcotics, smuggling and shipping. As well, except for Ontario and Quebec, which have their own forces, the Mounties act as provincial police forces in the rest of Canada.

The provincial police enforce provincial laws. In rural areas, they also enforce the criminal laws of Canada.

The municipal, or city, police forces are responsible for enforcing the Criminal Code, provincial laws and city by-laws.

There are, in addition, other types of police, such as game wardens and customs officers. Some companies hire their own security guards to protect company property.

The police have a great many hard tasks and responsibilities. As a citizen, you also have a duty to help police officers. In fact, some of your duties are covered by law. The law provides penalties for anyone who obstructs police officers trying to do their duty.

The law also requires you to help police officers do their duty if asked to do so. This applies to cases where an officer is trying to arrest someone. On the other hand, you cannot be forced by a police officer to do an illegal act.

without a warrant anyone they suspect on reasonable grounds of having committed an indictable offence. They may also arrest without warrant anyone they find committing a summary offence. Remember, however, that you must be charged with a specific offence. There is no such thing in Canada as, "We want you to come down to the station and answer a few questions" or arrest "on suspicion" of something.

THE SEARCH WARRANT

Since you have been charged with theft, the police officer will want to search your home for evidence. He or she must have a search warrent issued by the courts. A search warrant is only valid if the details are filled in. Also, it is only good for the day it is issued. A search warrant only permits a police officer to search a place, not a person. However, once inside the place, if the officer has reason to believe a person is hiding anything, he or she may search that person.

Two RCMP officers entered the home of a known drug pusher looking for narcotics. It appeared to the officers that the man was putting something in his mouth. One officer quickly grabbed him by the throat to prevent him from swallowing the evidence. The other put his fingers in the man's mouth to search for the drug capsules. The suspect bit the officer's hand. No drugs were found in the man's mouth. One of the charges against the man was assaulting the officer and resisting arrest. The man's lawyer claimed that lawful search did not include the man's mouth. The judge disagreed. He held that since the officers believed the drugs were in the man's mouth, they had a right to search there.

AT THE STATION

Now that you have been lawfully arrested, you may be taken to the police station. Once at the station, you

Form 5
(Section 443)

WARRANT TO SEARCH

CANADA PROVINCE OF ONTARIO JUDICIAL DISTRICT OF YORK	To the peace officers in the Judicial District of York and in the Province of Ontario

WHEREAS it appears upon the information of ....

that there are reasonable grounds to believe that there are in ....

.... at ....

...., herein called

the premises, certain things, namely:

that are being sought as evidence in respect to the commission, suspected commission or intended commission of an offence against the Criminal Code, namely:

THEREFORE, this is to authorize and require you, between the hours of .... to enter into the premises and to search for the above things, and to bring them before me or some other justice to be dealt with according to law.

DATED this .... day of ...., 19 ...., at the Municipality of Metropolitan Toronto.

____

Provincial Judge or Justice of the Peace
in and for Ontario or ....

These photographs show some of the many aspects of police work.

MTP 17
METRO POLICE
50E98939

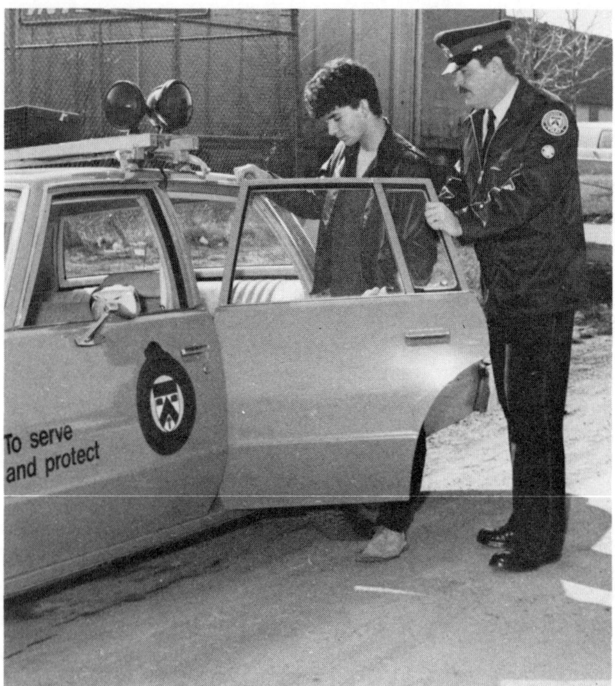

Police officer arrests a suspect.

will be allowed to make a phone call. If you did not have a chance to get a lawyer, you may ask to contact the legal aid duty counsel by phone immediately.

After your arrest, it may be weeks or months before your case actually comes up in court. Rather than spend this period in jail, you may be allowed free on bail. Bail is a guarantee to the court that you will return for your trial.

For simple charges, bail may take the form of a promise to appear "on your own recognizance." For more serious criminal charges, a deposit of money or property will be needed. For a very serious offence, such as murder, where the public safety is involved, bail may be denied.

At the police station, the police may call the bail justice of the peace, who will determine your bail. In the United States, bail bondspersons are people who will put up the money for bail if you cannot afford it. Usually they charge 15 to 20 percent interest for their services. In Canada, bail bondspersons are illegal. You may, however, borrow bail money from friends or relatives.

If you have been set free on bail but do not appear for your trial, you will lose your bail money. As well, you will be arrested on another charge—absconding bail. This is a serious offence.

If you are charged with an offence but cannot afford a lawyer, the Legal Aid program will help pay your legal expenses. The program does not provide the lawyers itself. You are allowed to choose from a list of lawyers in the province. Note that you do not have to be defended by a lawyer. If you wish, you may defend yourself in court, provided that you are competent to carry out your own defence. This is not advisable. As the saying goes, "The lawyer who conducts his own defence has a fool for a client." This is even more true for an ordinary citizen.

Once arrested, you have the right to a trial without unnecessary delay. With the backlog of cases jamming our courts today, it may take as long as a year before your trial comes up in court. If you cannot meet bail conditions, you will be in jail during that period of time. If your lawyer suspects that the Crown is moving slowly and delaying your trial, he may get your release on a writ of habeas corpus. Habeas corpus forces the authorities to justify your arrest. They must show that they are moving as fast as possible to hold a trial. Otherwise you will be released. This is an important safeguard in our legal system. Without it, a person might be kept in jail a lifetime waiting for his or her trial to come up.

Fingerprinting a suspect. Fingerprints may be used as evidence in a court of law.

OUR CIVIL RIGHTS

Citizens of the United States and many other countries for a long time have had their civil rights guaranteed by their constitutions. In Canada, until 1982, these rights had not been set down as specific laws. Of course, as Canadians, we exercised a great number of civil liberties. However, these rights had always been guaranteed by custom rather than by law. In 1982, the government of Pierre Trudeau finally succeeded in passing a Canadian Charter of Rights and Freedoms. The provisions are as follows:

CANADIAN CHARTER OF RIGHTS AND FREEDOMS

—Whereas Canada is founded upon principles that recognize the supremacy of God and the rule of law:

Guarantee of Rights and Freedoms

—**1. The** *Canadian Charter of Rights and Freedoms* guarantees the rights and freedoms set out in it subject only to such reasonable limits prescribed by laws as can be demonstrably justified in a free and democratic society.

Fundamental Freedoms

—**2. Everyone has the following fundamental freedoms:** (*a*) freedom of conscience and religion; (*b*) freedom of thought, belief, opinion and expression, including freedom of the press and other media of communication; (*c*) freedom of peaceful assembly; and (*d*) freedom of association.

Legal Rights

—7. Everyone has the right to life, liberty and security of the person and the right not to be deprived thereof except in accordance with the principles of fundamental justice. 8. Everyone has the right to be secure against unreasonable search or seizure. 9. Everyone has the right not to be arbitrarily detained or imprisoned. 10. Everyone has the right on arrest or detention (*a*) to be informed promptly of the reasons therefor; (*b*) to retain and instruct counsel without delay and to be informed of that right; and (*c*) to have the validity of the detention determined by way of *habeas corpus* and to be released if the detention is not lawful. 11. Any person charged with an offence has the right (*a*) to be informed without unreasonable delay of the specific offence; (*b*) to be tried within a reasonable time; (*c*) not to be compelled to be a witness in proceedings against that person in respect of the offence; (*d*) to be presumed innocent until proven guilty according to law in a fair and public hearing by an independent and impartial tribunal; (*e*) not to be denied reasonable bail without just cause; (*f*) except in the case of an offence under military law tried before a military tribunal, to the benefit of trial by jury where the maximum punishment for the offence is imprisonment for five years or a more severe punishment; (*g*) not to be found guilty on account of any act or omission unless, at the time of the act or omission, it constituted an offence under Canadian or international law or was criminal according to the general principles of law recognized by the community of nations; (*h*) if finally acquitted of the offence, not to be tried for it again and, if finally found guilty and punished for the offence, not to be tried or punished for it again; and (*i*) if found guilty of the offence and if the punishment for the offence has been varied between the time of commission and the time of sentencing, to the benefit of the lesser punishment. 12. Everyone has the right not to be subjected to any cruel and unusual treatment or punishment. 13. A witness who testifies in any proceedings has the right not to have any incriminating evidence so given used to incriminate that witness in any other proceedings, except in a prosecution for perjury or for the giving of contradictory evidence. 14. A party or witness in any proceedings who does not understand or speak the language in which the proceedings are conducted or who is deaf has the right to the assistance of an interpreter.

IN A COURT OF LAW

Months have passed since your arrest, and although you are free on bail, you are impatient to have your name cleared. However, the courts have had a busy time and could not schedule your trial early. In any case, your lawyer needed the time to prepare your case. You have been charged with theft. This is an indictable offence and means you have a choice as to what kind of trial you will have. After consulting your lawyer, you decide to have a trial by judge and jury.

Trial by judge and jury is always interesting. The results of a trial often hinge on the character of the jury. Good lawyers will spend much time studying the psychology of a jury. Your lawyer has informed you of the advantages and disadvantages of the jury system. The advantages include:

- ▶ The verdict must be unanimous. If even one person in the jury thinks you are innocent, you cannot be convicted.
- ▶ Juries tend to be from the same social background as you and might sympathize with your case.
- ▶ Your lawyer has a right to refuse certain people places on the jury. This lessens the chance of bias against you.
- ▶ A good lawyer knows what will appeal to juries and how to impress them.

On the other hand there are disadvantages to the jury system:

- ▶ The jury may be prejudiced against you. They may not like your looks, your background or your social status.
- ▶ If the Crown attorney is better than your lawyer, the jury may be swayed by his or her manner and not the facts.
- ▶ Juries are not experts on the law. They may reach a wrong decision because of their ignorance of the law.

HOW JURIES ARE CHOSEN

Have your parents ever served on a jury? Do you know anyone who has? The chances of serving on a jury are not very high. There are many different kinds of juries. For criminal cases, the jury normally consists of twelve people. The reason for this number is not totally clear. It has come down from England in the Middle Ages. It is thought to be based on the number of Jesus' apostles.

In order to serve on a jury, you must be eighteen years of age or over, a Canadian citizen and sane. You must own property or be a tenant. Everyone who meets these requirements is eligible to serve on a jury with the following exceptions:

- ▶ those over the age of seventy;
- ▶ elected members of government;
- ▶ judges, magistrates, sheriffs, coroners, jail

A judge addresses the members of a jury.

wardens, court officers or police officers;
- firemen;
- ministers, priests, rabbis and members of religious orders;
- doctors, dentists, veterinarians, nurses and people connected with the medical profession;
- members of the armed forces;
- airplane pilots and hostesses;
- sailors;
- people working for newspapers;
- people working in public transportation;
- people working in communications, for example, telephone operators
- lawyers and law students;
- tax collectors;
- people convicted of an indictable offence.

It may seem after this list that the number of people eligible for jury duty is not very large. In fact, millions of Canadians are annually eligible for jury duty. How are members of a particular jury chosen from this list?

Your municipal assessor places a "J" beside the name of all eligible jurors. The municipal clerk then chooses a list from these names, in alphabetical order. He chooses twice as many names, as are needed for the year and sends the list to the county sheriff. The sheriff draws by lot the names of people who will sit on the various types of juries. The court clerk then draws names from a box for each individual jury. Even if your name has survived all these tests, you can still be refused by the Crown prosecutor or the defence attorney for various reasons. Amazingly, some people have been selected for jury duty many times.

Once selected, you cannot refuse to serve on a jury without permission of the court. If you refuse, you are liable to be fined. Some people try to avoid their obligation. They are afraid that a lengthy trial will keep them away from their families and jobs for a long time. Jurors are paid less than $20 per day so this may also mean financial loss.

THE TRIAL

At last a jury has been selected, and your trial is ready to begin. Your lawyer has prepared his or her case and has lined up a number of witnesses on your behalf. These people have been ordered to testify by a subpoena sent out by the court.

The trial begins with the Crown attorney addressing the jury. The jury is told that it will be shown beyond all reasonable doubt that you are guilty of theft and that the evidence presented will prove it. Your lawyer speaks next and presents her opening arguments as to your innocence and the lack of evidence in the Crown's case.

The Crown then calls its witnesses. Each witness is sworn to tell "the truth, the whole truth and nothing but the truth." If a witness lies on the stand, he or she is charged with perjury, a serious offence. After each prosecution witness has testified, your lawyer has the opportunity to cross-examine them. On cross-examination, only questions relating to the original testimony may be asked. Only evidence obtained directly is admitted. If a witness presents facts that were heard second-hand, from someone else, they are not acceptable. This is called hearsay evidence.

During your arrest you repeatedly claimed your innocence. However, if you had confessed your guilt before the trial or made any statement about the case, it would have been introduced as evidence.

Lawyers often use diagrams to help explain their client's case to the judge or jury.

When the Crown attorney rests his case, your lawyer begins to present your case. She attempts to show that the evidence presented by the Crown is flimsy and not sufficient to find you guilty. Several witnesses are called to testify to your good character and honesty. On the advice of your lawyer, you do not take the witness stand yourself. On cross-examination lawyers are allowed to ask leading questions, or questions that suggest an answer. In the hands of a skilled lawyer, such questions can be used to confuse the testimony of a nervous witness.

After the Crown attorney finishes the cross-examination of your witnesses, both lawyers sum up their cases to the jury. You are perhaps somewhat disappointed that your defence lawyer did not prove someone else guilty of the crime. On television shows this happens every week. Unfortunately, in real life this is seldom the case. Cases are lost and won on arguments and weight of evidence and the impressions made on the jury. Perhaps, however, members of the jury, like you, are influenced by the exploits of television lawyers and expect the guilty person to confess. Your lawyer has taken great care to caution them about this attitude in her summary.

During the court proceedings, the judge is under complete control of the trial. He or she may decide what questions, answers and evidence are suitable. As much as possible, a judge must remain fair and impartial in the interpretation of the points of law. At the end of the closing summations, the judge instructs the jury and carefully explains to the jury the laws that apply to this case. They will be instructed about the points on which they must base their decision. The instruction to the jury is very important. If the judge instructs the jury in the wrong way or appears to be unfair, a retrial may be demanded.

The decision of innocence or guilt is left up to the jury. The verdict must be unanimous — that is, all twelve jurors must agree on the innocence or guilt of the accused. The jury has selected a leader called a foreperson who conducts the jury discussion in a closed room. If no unanimous verdict can be reached after a reasonable number of votes, this is called a hung jury. In such cases, the judge may order a retrial with a new jury. If a verdict is reached, it is read by the foreperson.

Judge Rosalie Abella was a Family Court judge and now chairs the Ontario Labour Relations Board.

You await the decision of the jury as they file back into the courtroom. The foreperson reads the verdict — not guilty! The ordeal is over, and you are again a free person.

If you had been found guilty, another of the law's important safeguards would have been available to you: the right of appeal. An appeal is a request for a review of the trial and must be made within 30 days of conviction. Some of the reasons appeals may be granted include:

- The judge instructed the jury in the wrong way.
- Evidence was admitted into court that should not have been.
- The jury was prejudiced.
- New evidence surfaced after the trial.

If the Crown feels the verdict was unfair, it may also appeal on certain grounds. Cases may be appealed all the way to the Supreme Court. There, a decision is final.

THE COURT SYSTEM

The BNA Act of 1867 divided the responsibility for Canada's court system between the federal and provincial governments. The federal government is responsible for the Supreme Court of Canada and the Federal Court. The provinces are responsible for all other courts.

If a jury had reached a "guilty" verdict, it would have been the judge's duty to sentence you. The Criminal Code may set minimum or maximum penalties. It is up to the judge to decide exactly what the punishment will be. Studies show that, in the past, judges have been influenced by the following factors:

- the age of the convicted person;
- the person's character and previous record;
- the circumstances surrounding the crime;
- public pressure against certain crimes in the community;
- the judge's own prejudices.

Even a simple trial may be a long and costly affair. Occasionally, justice is not done. However, the system has a number of safeguards that make decisions as fair and impartial as possible in the vast majority of cases. The system is careful to protect the rights of the individual and society. This sometimes makes it complicated and slow.

Justice Bertha Wilson listens as the court registrar reads the proclamation appointing her to the Supreme Court of Canada during a ceremony in Ottawa.

FEDERAL COURTS

Supreme Court of Canada
The court of final appeal in Canada. It also hears cases between the Dominion and the provinces and cases requiring the interpretation of the BNA Act and the Charter of Rights and Freedoms.

Federal Court
This court hears cases brought against the Crown and cases involving Crown revenues.

COURTS OF THE PROVINCE OF ONTARIO

SUPREME COURT OF ONTARIO	
Appeal Division This court hears appeals from the High Court of Justice and other courts.	Trial Division This court tries important cases, both criminal and civil.

PROVINCIAL COURTS		
Criminal Division This court deals with non-jury criminal trials.	Family Division This court deals with, for example, child custody, child support and young offenders.	Civil Division This court tries small civil claims (less than $1000).

OTHER PROVINCIAL COURTS
Juvenile Courts
Family Courts

This diagram shows the Canadian system of law courts for the Province of Ontario. There are slight variations from this pattern in the provincial court systems of other provinces.

BUILDING YOUR LEARNING SKILLS

FOCUSSING ON THE ISSUE

1 Summarize at least five of the main ideas in this chapter.

2 Answer the following four questions, which pertain to this chapter.
- *a* What is the highest court in Canada?
- *b* A writ of assistance is similar to:
  i summons *ii* a writ of habeas corpus *iii* a search warrant *iv* a subpoena
- *c* What is the Criminal Code of Canada?
- *d* A person who lies in a court of law is guilty of:
  i perjury *ii* hearsay *iii* contempt

3 The following terms appeared in this chapter. Try to recall their meaning and how they are used.

bail	panhandling
Charter of Rights and Freedoms	perjury
	precedent
common law	preliminary hearing
Criminal Code	search warrant
cross-examination	soft drugs
grand jury	subpoena
habeas corpus	summary conviction
hard drugs	summons
hearsay evidence	vagrancy
indictable offence	writ of assistance
Narcotic Control Act	

RESEARCHING

1 Using current newspapers and journals, find out who are the members of Canada's Supreme Court.

2 Research a recent trial. Keep a file of all the information on the case, and follow it to its conclusion.

3 Contact your local police department and ask for up-to-date statistics on crime in your area. Are major crimes on the increase or decrease?

4 Research the origin of habeas corpus.

1·2·3

ORGANIZING

1 Examine the criminal case starting on page 69 of the text. Beginning with the arrest, make a list of the rights you have under the law up to your trial.

2 Make a list of the rights possessed by an accused person during a trial.

COMMUNICATING

1 With your newly found knowledge of court procedure, you are now ready to join Perry Mason as a courtroom lawyer. Set up a fictitious case (it may be murder or theft or a traffic violation) and organize a court case around it, involving members of your class. Roles in the trial must include the following: judge, Crown attorney, defence attorney, court clerk, accused person, witnesses and jury members.

2 Debate this proposition: If a person is old enough to vote and sign a contract at the age of eighteen, the law should allow him or her to drink at the same age.

3 Write an argument in favour of or against this proposition: Accused persons have too many rights in Canada.

ANALYZING

1 A young person convicted of smoking marijuana is guilty of a criminal offence. This person will have a criminal record for life. Do you think marijuana possession should be taken off the Criminal Code as an offence? Why or why not?

2 At times, the RCMP have come under heavy fire from politicians, the media and some segments of the public for a number of illegal activities. Do you think Canada's police officers should be allowed to go beyond the law in order to catch criminals? If so, under what circumstances should this be permitted?

3 Alcoholism has been referred to as an illness, not a crime. Should alcoholics be treated as sick people or as criminals? Should people who commit crimes while under the influence of alcohol or drugs be given more severe penalties?

APPLYING YOUR KNOWLEDGE

1 Explain the difference between an indictable offence and one punishable by summary conviction. Give two examples of each.

2 It has been suggested that a person guilty of a criminal offence stands a better chance of being released in a trial by jury rather than a trial by judge alone. What arguments might support this suggestion? What arguments can you offer against it?

3 Fred, a clerk in a large department store, testified in court that he saw Hardnose Harry picking pockets in his store. Harry was sent to prison for his crime. Several weeks before his scheduled release, Harry was heard to say that the first thing he would do after his release was "get Fred." Is Harry guilty of another crime? Give your reasons for your answer.

chapter 5
YOUNG OFFENDERS

TOPIC ORGANIZER	PAGE
▶ Common Youth Offences	84
▶ The Court System	84
▶ Punishment	86

THEME ORGANIZER

- ▶ It is probable that many young people have at some time in their lives committed an act that the law defines as "delinquent."
- ▶ Under the Young Offenders Act, young people will have the same legal rights as adults.
- ▶ Sociologists try to pinpoint the causes of criminal behaviour, but agreement is difficult.
- ▶ The new law attempts to remove young offenders from the influence of adult criminals by providing separate courts and jail facilities.

INTRODUCTION

Have you ever:

- ▶ driven a car without a licence?
- ▶ skipped school without an excuse?
- ▶ gambled for money?
- ▶ damaged public property?
- ▶ stolen "little things"?
- ▶ drunk alcoholic beverages at a party?

If your answer to any of these questions is "yes," you would have until recently been considered a juvenile delinquent. The old Juvenile Delinquents Act defined a juvenile delinquent as "any boy or girl . . . under the age of sixteen" who breaks federal, provincial or municipal laws.

However, since July 1982, a new statute called the Young Offenders Act has replaced the Juvenile Delinquents Act. This new act will change the way young people in trouble will be dealt with from now on by the police and the courts of law. The new law defines as "young offenders" all offenders between the ages of twelve and seventeen. Young people between the ages of seven and twelve are not considered responsible for their own criminal actions.

Before reading on, study the chart of key words and ideas that follows.

KEY WORDS AND IDEAS IN THIS CHAPTER

Term	Meaning	Sample Use
youth courts	courts that deal only with young offenders	In youth courts, the media and the public are not admitted to hear the cases.
young offender	a young person between the ages of twelve and seventeen who breaks the law	Young offenders make up the fastest growing group of lawbreakers in Canada.
Juvenile Delinquents Act	an act passed in 1908, which specified the offences of juveniles and court procedures dealing with young people	The act specified that a juvenile delinquent was a person under sixteen who broke a federal, provincial or municipal law.
probation officer	an officer appointed by the courts to look after young offenders	Young offenders may have to report to a probation officer.
truancy	the act of a youth who fails to attend school or runs away from home	Truancy is a common feature of today's society. A person under the age of sixteen cannot legally leave home.
vandalism	damaging or destroying public or private property	Vandalism is one of the most common types of youth offences.
Young Offenders Act	an act passed in 1982, which details the offences of juveniles and court proceedings dealing with young people	The act states that a young offender is someone between the ages of twelve and seventeen who breaks a federal, municipal or provincial law.

Young offenders are a major problem in today's society. Crimes committed by juveniles are on the increase. In fact, juveniles make up the fastest growing group of lawbreakers in the country. Many of these crimes are serious: murder, robbery, rape and assault. In the United States, almost a million cases involving juveniles go through the courts every year. Fifty percent of all arrests involve teenagers or young adults. Of those arrested for murder, 44 percent are under twenty-five and 10 percent are under eighteen. Forty-five percent of all arrests for street crimes are of young people under eighteen. In fact, the age of fifteen is the peak age for violent crimes.

Of course, not all young offenders commit crimes of such a serious nature. Many are simply seeking social acceptance from other members of their group. Some commit these offences "just for kicks." A recent survey in Toronto shows the following results (see table on pages 83–84):

SELF-REPORTED DELINQUENT BEHAVIOUR

Type of offence	Age 13–14	Age 15–19
	Percent admitting offence	
Driven a car without a driver's licence	28.6	62.3
Taken little things that did not belong to you	61.0	67.2
Skipped school without a legitimate excuse	13.6	40.8
Driven beyond the speed limit	5.8	51.2
Participated in drag-races along the highway with your friends	6.5	31.1
Engaged in a fist fight with another peer	45.8	56.0
Been feeling "high" from drinking beer, wine or liquor	11.7	39.0

Gambled for money at cards, dice or some other game	42.2	66.0
Remained out all night without parents' permission	19.5	25.8
Taken a car without owner's knowledge	5.2	12.5
Placed on school probation or expelled from school	0.7	5.6
Destroyed or damaged public or private property of any kind	44.8	52.0
Take little things of value (between $2 and $50) that did not belong to you	9.7	16.0

The above are minor offences. Yet several of these, committed often, would be considered serious.

COMMON YOUTH OFFENCES

There are certain kinds of offences that are most commonly committed by adolescents. These are:

Stealing Usually the objects are of small value (under $50). Shoplifting or stealing from lockers in school come under this category.

Vandalism This involves the destruction or damage of property for no apparent reason.

Assault Verbal threats or abusive language can constitute assault. Often this behaviour leads to fights.

Sexual Deviance Intercourse with a female under sixteen years of age is included in this category.

Truancy Runaways from home or school are becoming a common feature of modern society. A person under the age of sixteen cannot legally run away from home. Any adult sheltering a runaway is also breaking the law.

Susan and Debbie were waiting in the office of the manager of a large downtown department store. They had been caught by the store detective putting jewellery and cosmetics in their purses. As they were about to leave the store without paying for the goods, he stopped them. Rather than turn them over to the police, he called their parents. When asked why they had tried to shoplift, the girls said they were bored. There was nothing to do, so for kicks they thought it might be fun to try to steal some things. Besides, many of their friends had done it and had never been caught. The manager allowed the girls to go home with their parents. Susan and Debbie were lucky not to be charged in juvenile court.

Ted and Sean got into trouble of a serious kind. Both had been suspended from school for causing a disturbance and getting into fights. They decided to take revenge. One afternoon, during a class change, they walked back into the school unobserved. They went directly to the boys' washroom and began scratching obscenities on the metal partitions. At the same time, with a pocket knife, they began to remove all the ceramic tiles from the walls. As they were about to leave, they were caught by a surprised vice-principal who was making his rounds of the halls. The damage was estimated at over $500. Ted and Sean were turned over to the police and had to face charges in youth court.

The above cases are examples of two of the most common juvenile offences. In a way, they are crimes that affect everyone. Stores pass shoplifting losses on to consumers through higher prices. This means you wind up paying for someone else's "kicks." At the same time, damage to school property is reflected in higher taxes, which your parents must pay. Is there anything department stores and schools can do to cut down their losses?

THE COURT SYSTEM

Before 1982, young people had few rights in the court system. Under the new law, they have most of the rights of adults when dealing with the courts.

Young offenders will have the right to a lawyer. They must be told their rights the moment they are arrested; and they have the same right to bail as adult offenders.

There is a provision in the new act that allows for the transfer of the young offender to adult court. This may happen if the crime is a serious one, for example, murder or armed robbery, and if the offender has passed his or her fourteenth birthday.

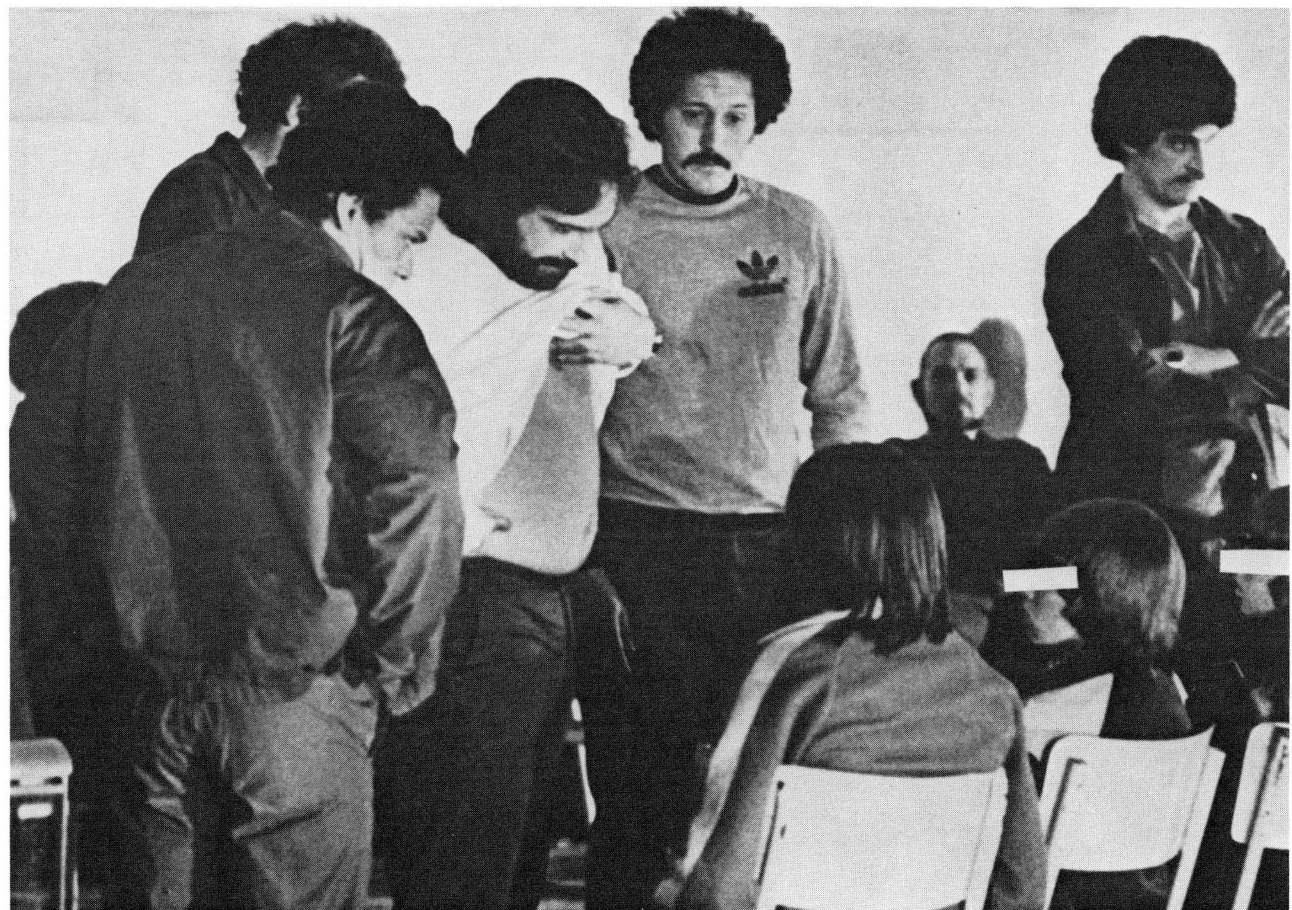

Inmates at Millhaven Penitentiary attempt to discourage young offenders by showing knife wounds sustained in a prison fight.

In the old juvenile courts, the proceedings were intended to protect the identity and future of the young offender. Members of the public and the press were not allowed in the courtrooms and the name of the accused was never published. By contrast, under the new act, trials will no longer take place behind closed doors. The press will be allowed to view proceedings but must not print the name of the accused or identify the accused in any way.

Police will be allowed to fingerprint and photograph young suspects, but they must destroy these records if the defendant is found not guilty. As well, the police must destroy all the records once the offender has served his or her sentence and has not committed another offence for two to five years after being released.

The court may look into the background of the accused, for example, home life or school records. The court uses probation officers and social agencies such as the Children's Aid Society to help in these matters. If the charge is not serious and the accused has had a reasonably clean record, the judge may place him or her on probation. We will see in a later chapter what this sentence involves.

Most young people do not have problems living within the rules of society, despite the pressures and frustration of the teenage years. Yet a minority of Canada's youth insists on breaking the law. They give all young people a bad name in the eyes of some adults. This is reflected in some of our laws, such as curfews and other restrictions on young people.

Sociologists and psychologists have tried to identify causes of criminal behaviour. Many point to a person's social background as a factor. Conditions of poverty, broken homes and an unhappy family life often lead to delinquent behaviour. There are many other unknown factors that form a person's personality. There are many qualities we are born with, others we learn as we are growing. Each of us becomes a unique person with different needs. This is why it is difficult to predict behaviour. In a recent survey, the public was asked what it thought were the factors leading to criminal behaviour.

Would you consider this survey accurate or scientific? Why or why not? Which of the factors below do you think are most responsible for crime?

WHY DO PEOPLE BECOME CRIMINALS?

Cause	Percent of People Surveyed Who Identified Cause
Upbringing	38
Bad environment	30
Mental illness	16
Wrong companions	14
No education	14
Broken homes	13
Greed, easy money	13
Too much money	11
Poverty	10
Liquor, dope	10
Laziness	9
Desire for kicks	8
No religion	8
No job	8
No chance given by society	7
Born bad	5
Feeling of hopelessness	4
Moral breakdown of society	3
Degeneracy, sex	2
Failure of police	2

PUNISHMENT

The creators of the new law felt that young offenders should be held responsible for their actions. At the same time, they felt young people should not be sent into the adult prison system, as they had often been in the past. In the old system, many young people become hardened criminals through their exposure to the tougher adult criminals. In the future, young offenders are to be housed separately from adults when in prison.

Under the new law, alternatives to jail, such as group homes, must also be provided. At the same time, judges may assign a whole range of punishments in order to keep young people out of prison. These include penalties such as repayment in money for damages done to the victim. Another possibility is to have the offender actually work for the victim to restore damages done to his or her property. Other penalties may include fines of up to $1000, community service work or probation for up to two years.

BUILDING YOUR LEARNING SKILLS

FOCUSSING ON THE ISSUE

1 In your own words, summarize three key ideas discussed in this chapter.

2 Answer these questions relating to this chapter:

a A young offender is a lawbreaker who is under the age of:
i fourteen *ii* sixteen
iii eighteen *iv* twenty-one

b A person can legally leave home at the age of seventeen. True or false?

c The most common offence committed by young people is:
i murder *ii* drug abuse
iii stealing *iv* skipping school

d In youth court, only the young offender and his or her lawyer are permitted to attend. True or false?

3 The following terms appeared in this chapter. Try to recall their meanings and how they were used.

assault	runaways
curfew	sexual deviance
delinquency	shoplifting
youth courts	truancy

Young Offenders Act
vandalism
probation officer

RESEARCHING

1 Vandalism is one of the greatest problems in the schools. It is an act in which nothing is gained. Suggest some reasons for the tremendous increase in incidents of vandalism. Try to find out the extent of the damages caused by vandalism in your own school.
2 Carry out a survey to find out how many members of your class belong to a "gang." Try to find out why they joined such a group and the range of activities carried out by this group.
3 The Young Offenders Act has created much controversy among police departments. Contact your local police department and discover their reaction to this act. Inquire as to how the act has helped or hindered police work.

ORGANIZING

1 Make a list of the rights young offenders will have under the new act.
2 Make a list of the differences in the treatment of young offenders and adult offenders in our court system.
3 Examine the chart on page 83. Make a list of the top five offences committed by young people in the thirteen-to-fourteen age range and compare these with the top five offences in the fifteen-to-nineteen age bracket.

COMMUNICATING

1 Check with your local police department to see if they have a youth division. Arrange for an officer to speak about the problems of juvenile offenders in your community.
2 Debate this proposition: There should be no minimum age at which a criminal charge can be laid.
3 Prepare a written argument on this question: In view of the number of alcohol-related driving offences, should the age at which a person receives a driver's licence be raised?

ANALYZING

1 Newspapers are not permitted to print the names of juvenile offenders or to identify them in any way. Do you agree with this practice? Give your reasons.
2 The Young Offenders Act limits the prison sentence a person can receive to three years, regardless of the crime committed. Do you agree with this limit?
3 One suggestion for dealing with juvenile delinquency is to have stricter curfews. Some municipalities are suggesting a 22:00 curfew for those under the age of sixteen. Do you think this is an effective method of fighting juvenile delinquency?

APPLYING YOUR KNOWLEDGE

1 A chart on page 83 of this chapter shows statistics on delinquent behaviour. Without signing your name to the paper, answer the questions along with other members of your class. Compare the results with those in the survey.
2 Law enforcement officials are encouraging sweeping changes to the Young Offenders Act. If you were in a position to change the law, what changes would you make?
3 Police authorities have reported cases where adults, realizing that young people under the age of twelve cannot be charged, are using these children to commit crimes such as breaking and entering and theft. What do you think can be done to solve this problem?

chapter 6

PUNISHMENT FOR CRIME

THEME ORGANIZER

- ▶ Throughout history, almost every society has had a form of punishment for crime.
- ▶ In past centuries, capital punishment was the common method of punishment for dozens of crimes.
- ▶ The question of capital punishment continues to be debated in Canadian society.
- ▶ The prison system is divided into three security levels.
- ▶ One of the aims of the prison system is to punish criminals; the other is to rehabilitate them. Many people argue that the system does neither very well.

HISTORICAL BACKGROUND

INTRODUCTION

Societies have tried to find suitable punishments for breaking the law for a long time. There have been many experiments by various societies in dealing with criminals. In some early societies, the punishment for crimes was left up to the family of the injured party. This often led to a system of revenge and feuds. These feuds might last for generations. In some cases, the criminal paid the injured party or the victim's family instead.

Certain societies, cut off from European influence, continued until recently to have forms of punishment that are very different from ours. Certain aborigine groups in Australia punished a murderer in the following way: The accused was placed, without weapons, facing a row of tribesmen about 15–30 m away. First they would hurl insults at the accused. Finally, they threw their spears. If the accused was wounded, the procedure would stop immediately. If he or she dodged all the spears, one of the victim's relatives would give the accused a ceremonial nick in the thigh with a spear, enough to draw blood. The quarrel was then at an end and everyone went home.

The Comanche Indians of the American Southwest had very few laws. Punishment was carried out by members of the victim's family. In the case of murder, a relative of the dead person might kill the murderer or one of the murderer's sons. In the case of horse theft, one warrior might punish the offender by killing his horses. Comanches generally admitted their guilt, so fair punishment would not lead to more trouble within the tribe. In disputes where there was doubt, the person with the greatest reputation for bravery was considered in the right.

In traditional Inuit groups, disputes were settled by combat. The kinds of combat included wrestling, head butting and song duels. Butting took the form of the two opponents hitting their foreheads together until one of them gave in.

In song duels, the two people took turns singing verses about each other. The verses were intended to insult and ridicule the opponent. This event might go on for several hours a day for more than a month. The winner was decided by the applause of the audience who looked on.

As society became more organized, the government took over punishment for crimes. Little thought was given to the motive for criminal behaviour. The main purpose was to punish wrongdoers harshly. In this way, governments hoped to discourage other criminals. In the Middle Ages, the death penalty was put into effect for almost all crimes. Thus, people were put to death for crimes varying from murder to witchcraft to stealing a loaf of bread. As recently as 1819 in England, the death penalty was in effect for over 200 different crimes.

There were other forms of punishment involving torture. Branding on the forehead or cutting off the hands were common forms of punishment. As recently as the 1960s in Canada, the lash was commonly used on convicted rapists.

The age of the criminal was not a factor in deciding the punishment. In England, there are cases of young children being put to death for petty theft as recently as the eighteenth century. This leads to an obvious problem: if someone were going to be caught for theft, they might as well commit murder in trying to escape, since the punishment was the same for both crimes. In many cases, the punishment did not fit the crime.

It seems that the seriousness of a crime was considered only in the form of the execution a person suffered. Persons convicted of a serious offence, such as treason, might be executed in a very nasty and sadistic way. Forms of execution included: pressing to death; burning at the stake; drawing and quartering; crucifixion; drowning; and being thrown to the lions.

Today only six forms of execution are still officially practised. These are the guillotine, the garotte (an iron collar placed around the neck and tightened by a screw until the victim strangles to death), hanging (this method of execution was used for the last time in Canada in 1962; Parliament abolished capital punishment in 1976), the electric chair, gassing (the condemned person is placed in a sealed gas chamber and deadly cyanide gas is released into the chamber), and shooting (a firing squad executes the condemned criminal).

Before reading on, study the chart of key words and ideas that follows.

KEY WORDS AND IDEAS IN THIS CHAPTER

Term	Meaning	Sample Use
capital punishment	a sentence of death imposed by a court for certain criminal offences	In Canada, capital punishment was abolished in 1976.
maximum security prison	a prison that is heavily guarded to insure that prisoners won't escape	Those convicted of very serious criminal offences and who are considered dangerous to the public are placed in maximum security prisons.
parole	the freeing of a prisoner before his or her full sentence has been served; granted, when the prisoner's conduct and attitude suggest that he or she will not commit another crime	Parole is difficult to get in Canada. Only about 33 percent of those who apply receive this privilege.

rehabilitation	the re-education of a convicted lawbreaker so that he or she will become a useful, law-abiding member of society	One of the chief aims of Canada's prison system is the rehabilitation of criminals.
probation	a type of sentence in which a convicted person can remain out of prison as long as he or she accepts certain restrictions	The rules of parole may require a convicted person to demonstrate good conduct and report to a parole officer.

CAPITAL PUNISHMENT

Capital punishment seems to be on the decline in many countries. However, it is a subject that still produces hot debates and arguments. In Canada, the death penalty was abolished by Parliament. However, a survey has shown that the majority of Canadians are in favour of keeping it.

ARGUMENTS IN FAVOUR

Those in favour of the death penalty, the retentionists, argue in the following way:

- Murderers give up their right to live in society.
- The punishment should fit the crime. This principle of "an eye for an eye" goes all the way back to ancient times. For the ultimate crime, murder, we should reserve the ultimate penalty, execution.
- If there is no capital punishment, murderers would have nothing to lose by murdering again. They would have nothing to lose in trying to escape by murdering their guards.
- Society needs protection from murderers. We can never be sure that they will change their ways. Capital punishment will prevent a murderer from ever killing again.
- Putting a person in jail for life is not much more humane than execution. Besides, the cost of keeping one person in jail for 50 years is estimated at over half a million dollars.
- Capital punishment has a deterrent effect. It would only be used for murder in the first degree, that is, murder that was deliberate and planned. This will cause potential killers to think twice, for fear of losing their own lives. This deterrent effect also builds up in a society over a long period of time. It creates the attitude that murder, because of the method of punishment for committing it, is the most serious of crimes.

ARGUMENTS AGAINST

Those who argue against capital punishment use a combination of the following arguments:

- The death penalty is not a deterrent. Most murders are not planned beforehand. They come about as a result of arguments and fights. In such circumstances, people do not stop to think about the death penalty.
- According to statistics, those countries that still use the death penalty do not necessarily have a lower murder rate.
- Capital punishment is brutal. No civilized society should resort to such a method of punishment. It lowers respect for human life.
- There is the chance that a murderer can be rehabilitated and turned into a useful citizen.
- Juries may be less likely to convict a person if the death penalty is in force because they may be afraid of making a mistake.
- There is always the possibility of executing an innocent person.

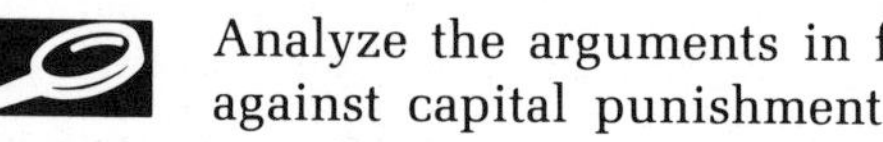

Analyze the arguments in favour of and against capital punishment. Which side do you support?

OTHER FORMS OF PUNISHMENT

Canada has abolished the death penalty, but our courts can hand out a great variety of sentences to lawbreakers. A judge may hand out one of the following penalties for a criminal offence:

Suspended Sentence The court will delay punishment in the hope that the convicted person will not break the law in the future. Generally, this is done in cases of minor crimes and with first-time offenders. If the individual does behave well, no punishment is given. If the individual does not behave well, he or she may be returned to court for sentencing.

Probation This is sometimes attached to a suspended sentence. The individual is placed under the supervision of a probation officer. The convicted person must report regularly to the probation officer. The officer makes sure that the person is fulfilling the conditions set down by the court for parole.

Fine The judge may order the payment of a money penalty for certain crimes. This is the case in matters such as traffic offences. If the offender cannot pay the fine, he or she must serve a term in prison instead.

Training Schools A young person convicted under the old Juvenile Delinquents Act was sent to a training school. The usual age level for these schools ranged from twelve to eighteen. In these schools, young people took the usual school courses. They also learned a trade. Sewing, typing, hairdressing, machine shop, electrical work and cooking were some of the courses offered. Juvenile offenders had to stay in such a school until they could show that they were ready to co-operate with society. As the new Young Offenders Act takes effect, training schools will be phased out.

Prison Going to prison is the normal punishment in Canada for serious crimes. Under the Criminal Code, an offender is sent to a federal penitentiary for

A group home for young people in trouble with the law. In several provinces many young offenders are sent to these small home-like settings rather than to training schools.

serious crimes (crimes that involve a sentence of over two years). Those guilty of less serious crimes go to provincial institutions. For murder in the first degree, the sentence is life imprisonment, which usually means 25 years without parole.

THE PRISON SYSTEM

The prison system is divided into three levels:

Maximum Security	If it is believed that the convicted person will make serious attempts to escape and is dangerous to public safety, he or she is confined to this kind of prison.
Medium Security	If, given the chance, the prisoner would probably try to escape but is not dangerous to the public, he or she serves a sentence in this kind of prison.
Minimum Security	A convicted person who would not try to escape and is not dangerous is often sentenced to this kind of prison. In these prisons, there are usually no locks, bars or walls.

PRISON ROUTINE

A convicted person entering prison is first taken to a reception centre. Here he or she is given all the items needed in prison, including:

- a set of clothing;
- eating utensils;
- toilet articles like paper, soap, towels and toothpaste.

The prisoner is then examined by a committee made up of the warden, a prison psychiatrist, a sociologist, a criminologist, a training officer and a minister or priest. Tests and interviews are given. The prison rules are explained.

The daily routine varies from prison to prison. A typical day may look like this:

07:00	Wake up and wash in the cells. Eat breakfast in the mess hall.
08:00–11:00	Work or study period. If the prisoner

A typical cell in a detention centre in Ontario. People await trial or serve short sentences in these centres.

	does not report for class, the instructor will inform the guards. The guards will make a search. Guards also handle inmates who refuse to work or who cause a disturbance.
11:00–12:30	Lunch
12:30–17:00	Work or study classes
17:00–18:00	Evening meal
18:00–22:00	Free time. Inmates may go to the gym, watch television, play cards, read or write.
22:30	Inmates return to their cells, and the cells are locked.

PRIVILEGES

All inmates have the privilege of writing letters to friends outside the prison. All mail coming in and going out may be censored. Inmates have to buy their own paper and stamps. Inmates can also have visitors. Except for maximum security prisons, inmates are allowed to sit with their visitors in a large reception room. The inmate is thoroughly searched before and after such visits. Visitors are not allowed to hand anything to the inmate.

An inmate who regularly causes trouble and breaks prison rules may be given additional punishment by the warden. The prisoner may be placed in isolation, where association with others is forbidden. Rations may be changed. In the past, physical punishments like whipping were sometimes given. Today such physical punishments are no longer permitted in Canada.

An uncooperative prisoner may also have to serve a longer period in jail. Under a new federal act, all prisoners have the chance to work off one-third of their sentence through good behaviour. This is called earned remission. Therefore, if the prisoner behaves well, he or she will not serve the full sentence. If the prisoner misbehaves, he or she may wind up serving out the entire term.

There are over 9000 prisoners in Canada's federal penitentiaries. Many are not considered dangerous. In some cases they are allowed to go home without guards for a weekend. If they do not return, this is considered an escape. This program has caused concern in the past because of the risks involved. Many in the public and the media have argued that this program should be more tightly controlled. Some say it should be cancelled because of the danger.

Parole is another privilege of the prison system. After serving one-third of the sentence, an inmate of a federal penitentiary, unless convicted of a violent crime, may apply to the National Parole Board in Ottawa to grant a parole. The new federal Parole Act allows each province to set up its own parole board for inmates of provincial prisons. A person released on parole gives his or her word that he or she will behave within the law in society. During the remaining time of the sentence, the person must report to a parole officer, much like someone on probation.

Only about 33 percent of the requests for parole are granted. Interviews are conducted, and reports from the inmate's superiors are considered. A number of factors are taken into account. Past behaviour, personality, the seriousness of the crime, family contacts and job prospects are some of them. The final decision rests on whether the inmate has changed his or her attitude while in prison.

ARE PRISONS USEFUL?

Much of the public would agree that prisons serve a number of useful purposes:

1 They may act as a deterrent. The thought of a lengthy and unpleasant prison sentence may prevent a person from committing a crime.

2 They protect society. Those who commit serious crimes present a danger to society. They should be removed until they can learn to co-operate with others.

3 They provide a setting for rehabilitation. Most people believe that prisons should help the criminal readjust to acceptable behaviour.

4 They are a punishment. The criminal, after all, has broken the law and harmed society. He or she should be punished for this. A person who intentionally commits a crime must suffer the consequences. This purpose is very close to "an eye for an eye."

Do prisons rehabilitate? The evidence suggests that they do not. Some prisoners do not need rehabilita-

CORRECTIONAL SERVICES — CANADA TOTALS, 1985/86[1]

	Federal	Provincial	Total
Correctional Facilities — Government			
Number of facilities	62	170	232
Designated capacity	9 681	17 480	27 161
Total custodial population[2]			
Admissions[3]	6 120	200 940	207 060
Average inmate count	11 214	16 358	27 572
Daily operating cost per inmate[4]	$108.43	$80.03	
Sentenced population			
Admissions	6120	119 629	125 749
Average inmate count	11 214	12 828	24 042
Community supervision — average counts			
Parole/mandatory supervision[5]	14 054	2 677	16 731
Probation supervision	. . .	72 249	72 249
Correctional service expenditures[6]			
Total (millions)	$744.47	$622.23	$1366.70
Per capita	$29.35	$24.54	$53.89

Source: Corpus Information Services

Note: 1 Because of changes in definition, figures should not be compared with data from previous years.

2 Special purpose beds are excluded in both federal and provincial capacities; this amounts to about 2,000 additional bed spaces.

3 All admissions are included regardless of reasons for admission and, within each province, transfers between facilities are generally excluded.

4 Actual counts are used in calculation of per diems in current dollars.

5 Includes provincial offenders in provinces which do not operate their own Parole Boards.

6 Costs of capital construction and grants are generally included; costs expressed in current dollars and refer to gross expenditures.

tion. Their crimes are such that they would probably never commit them again anyway. In these cases, prisons are only for punishment. For the others, rehabilitation does not seem to work. Between 40 and 50 percent of those released from prison will commit another crime and return. Only 20 percent of prisoners are first-time offenders. The other 80 percent have been in prison before. Certainly, this is a high failure rate. One reason for this is that, in prison, inmates often learn the skills to be better criminals rather than better citizens. Many experts are of the opinion that a new system of rehabilitation is needed. A system that will help the inmate deal with a society he or she may not have seen in years is required. Such a system may still be a long way from reality.

Recently, some judges have been imposing a different kind of sentence. They force the convicted person to pay back the injured party or to work in the community rather than going to jail. These sentences are given to offenders who are not considered dangerous or who are not likely to repeat their crime (for example, vandals). Do you approve of this trend?

BUILDING YOUR LEARNING SKILLS

FOCUSSING ON THE ISSUE

1 Summarize three key ideas presented in this chapter.

2 Answer the following questions relating to this chapter:

   a There are approximately how many inmates in Canada's federal prisons?
   i 25 000 *ii* 7000 *iii* 50 000 *iv* 100 000

   b The last execution in Canada took place in:
   i 1958 *ii* 1976 *iii* 1962 *iv* 1967

   c The percentage of applicants who receive parole in Canada is:
   i 33 percent *ii* 10 percent
   iii 50 percent *iv* 80 percent

3 The following terms appeared in this chapter. Try to recall their meanings and how they were used.

deterrent	rehabilitation
parole	suspended sentence
probation	

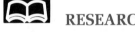

RESEARCHING

1 With the help of information provided by the Justice Department of the federal government, find out the locations of Canada's federal prisons.

2 Are there any offences you feel should be punishable by death? Conduct a survey among your friends, family and classmates to find out their position on this subject. Also, find out how your MP feels about this issue.

3 Do some research on the medieval custom of trial by combat. When was this practice abolished?

4 Gather information on which countries around the world still apply the death penalty.

ORGANIZING

1 Make a list of the kinds of capital punishment still used around the world. In which countries were the guillotine and the garotte used?

2 In chart form, organize the daily routine of a typical day in prison. How much free time does a prisoner normally have?

COMMUNICATING

1 The Parliament of Canada abolished capital punishment in 1976. Present a position paper in favour of or against the return of the death penalty for murder.

2 Debate this resolution: The function of prisons should be to rehabilitate criminals, not punish them.

3 Read the book, *In Cold Blood*, by Truman Capote. In your opinion, was the punishment dealt out by the law justified?

ANALYZING

1 A number of those convicted of criminal offences are placed in minimum security prisons. These people are not considered dangerous to the public. Do you think these people should be given such freedom and trusted so much?

2 Analyze the routine of a typical day in prison. In your opinion, is the routine too harsh or too soft on inmates?

3 Examine the photograph on page 92. Why do you think the prison cell is so barren?

APPLYING YOUR KNOWLEDGE

1 It has been suggested that prisons serve to punish lawbreakers and also to rehabilitate them. Are prisons successful in these two purposes?

2 Recently, a number of judges have sentenced criminal offenders to pay back their victims or work for the community rather than sending them to jail. For which offences do you think such sentences would be useful?

3 What changes would you make to improve Canada's prison system?

chapter 7

CIVIL LAW

TOPIC ORGANIZER — PAGE

THEME ORGANIZER

- The difference between criminal and civil law is often only the question of intent.
- Simple contracts can take several forms, but they can all be binding.
- Some individuals in our society are not allowed to sign contracts.
- The Consumer Protection Act gives individuals some form of protection when buying merchandise.
- Ignorance of the law is not a defence.

INTRODUCTION

Thus far, we have been dealing with criminal law in Canada. At the start of this unit, we mentioned another type of law called civil law. Criminal law, as we have seen, deals with people whose actions in breaking the law bring harm to other individuals or the community. Civil law, on the other hand, deals with disputes and disagreements between people or groups. These have no direct effect on the community. Such cases include disputes over contracts, property or personal relationships. When one party takes another party to court over such matters, it is called a civil suit. Unlike criminal cases, civil cases do not involve society, and there is no Crown prosecutor trying the case. In civil cases, each side hires its own lawyers to contest the points.

Before reading on, study the chart of key words and ideas that follows.

KEY WORDS AND IDEAS IN THIS CHAPTER

Term	Meaning	Sample Use
caveat emptor	a Latin expression that means "let the buyer beware"	Consumers should heed the warning *caveat emptor*. In most cases, the buyer and not the seller is responsible for making sure the merchandise is good.
civil law	the segment of the law that deals with the private rights and agreements between individuals	A dispute over a contract comes under Canada's civil law.
civil suit	court action brought by one person or group against another in matters dealing with civil law	A person may bring a civil suit against another if a contract has not been fulfilled.
contract	an agreement between two parties to purchase something or perform some action; such an agreement is enforceable by law	A contract is legal whether it is verbal, written or implied.
minor	a person under the age of eighteen	A minor may not legally sign a contract in Canada.

WHAT'S THE DIFFERENCE?

Let us examine the difference between these two kinds of laws. Ted the pharmacist fell madly in love with Ellen. Unfortunately for Ted, Ellen was already engaged to be married to her boyfriend of many years, Jack. Jack was a regular customer of Ted's drugstore. He picked up all his prescriptions there. In a final attempt to win his true love, Ted decided on a desperate course of action. He added a small dose of a deadly poison to Jack's next prescription. But Ted's knowledge of poisons was not extensive. The dose he gave Jack was not enough to kill him, although it made him quite ill.

Several days later, the police showed up at Ted's door and arrested him for attempted murder. Why can this be considered a criminal case?

Mary Alice suffered from a persistent allergy for which a prescription medicine was necessary. She had been taking this medicine, obtained from the local druggist, for several years without suffering any harmful side effects. One afternoon, after taking her medicine, Mary Alice became violently ill, and her face broke out in a rash. A doctor was called in, and after a period in the hospital, Mary Alice recovered. The prescription was analyzed. The results showed that the druggist had mistakenly replaced one element in the prescription with another. This small error had caused the whole problem.

Several days later the unfortunate druggist was notified that Mary Alice was starting a civil suit against him for damages of $25 000. Why is this not considered a criminal case?

These two situations illustrate the difference between criminal and civil law. Criminal cases may seem more exciting to the public than civil cases, such as those involving contracts. But it is a fact that more Canadians get into legal trouble over contracts than over anything else. There are thousands of laws dealing with civil cases. Obviously, we cannot deal with them in detail. However, a brief discussion of several examples of the most common problems in civil law will be useful.

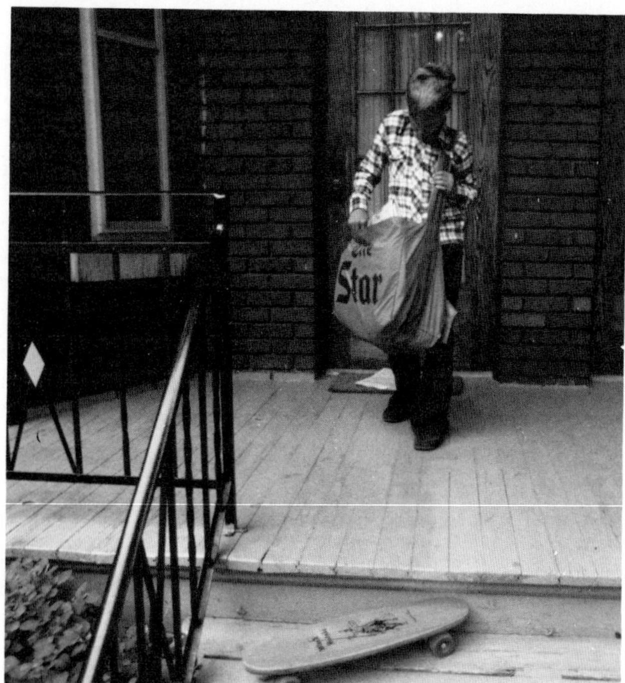

A dangerous situation. If the paper carrier should step on the skateboard and injure himself, who would be responsible? Why would this be considered a civil and not a criminal case?

CONTRACTS

Perhaps the most common legal problem most Canadians have involves contracts. By law, some people cannot be held responsible for signing contracts.

As a minor, you may not legally sign a contract. Within a very few years, however, you may be out on your own. You will face the responsibilities of voting, signing contracts and being liable to be sued in court. Young people at this stage are sometimes taken advantage of by fast-talking salespeople and merchants. Imagine that you have just begun your first job and are in the market for an apartment, a car or new furniture. You will probably sign many contracts over the next few months.

A simple contract can take three forms:

Verbal A spoken agreement between two parties.

Implied Where payment for services is taken for granted; for example, having your car's gas tank filled at a gas station implies that you will pay for the gas.

Written An agreement in the form of a signed document.

Assuming you have the right to sign a contract and that the contract itself does not break any laws, you are legally responsible for upholding your end of the bargain. The following are several common legal problems you may someday encounter.

BUYING A CAR

You have just signed a contract to buy a new car. You are anxiously awaiting delivery. Several months pass by, and still no car. You desperately need a car to get you to your job. Finally, you decide you cannot wait any longer; you would like to buy a car right out of the showroom from another dealer. Can you get out of your contract?

Not really. You should read the fine print in automobile contracts. The agreement you signed would include the following points:

1. There is no time limit set for the delivery of your car. (If you want a time limit, you must agree to one in the contract.)
2. If you fail to take possession of your car from the dealer within 48 hours of notice, you may lose your cash deposit.
3. The dealer may hold the car for 20 days, then resell it. You will be informed of the time and place of the sale. If he or she sells it for less than you agreed to pay, the dealer will require you to make up the difference.

BUYING FROM DOOR-TO-DOOR SALESPEOPLE

You are a homemaker who has just bought a vacuum cleaner from a door-to-door salesperson. The machine seemed to do a good job in the demonstration. You agreed to make 12 payments of $20 each, including interest. This would make the total price of the vacuum cleaner $240. This seems a high price. However, the salesperson promised that if you gave her a list of your friends' names, you might get a better price. You were promised $10 back for each friend who also bought a vacuum cleaner.

The next week, you see a similar machine at a store for about $100 less. At the same time, your spouse, who did not sign the contract, is unhappy with the performance of the vacuum cleaner. Can you return it?

Not unless the vacuum cleaner company agrees. A person does not have to co-sign a contract with his or her spouse. Each partner has full legal rights and responsibilities. The Consumer Protection Act gives a person the right to change his or her mind on a contract signed in the person's home. However, this must take place within two days of the signing. After this, the contract becomes binding.

BOOKS IN THE MAIL

You have just answered an ad that offered free the first book in a series on North American animal life. The ad indicated that you were not obligated to purchase any other books. The free book is not at all interesting. However it is free, so you decide to keep it, but you do not ask for any more books. The next month, a box with the remaining 12 volumes arrives, along with a bill for the books. Do you have to pay?

The answer is no. In Ontario, a person who receives through the mail something he or she did not ask for may actually keep it. To avoid further problems with the company, however, you may wish to send the books back. This can be done in two ways. You may return the box to the post office marked "Refused— Return to Sender." It will then be returned at the company's expense. Or you may send a letter to the company and request them to come and pick up the books.

LEASING AN APARTMENT

You have been living in an apartment for five months and have seven months left on your lease. Suddenly the building is sold to a new owner. The new owner wants to raise your rent by $20 per month. You refuse to pay. The new owner then wants to evict you and claims the right to do so, since you have not signed

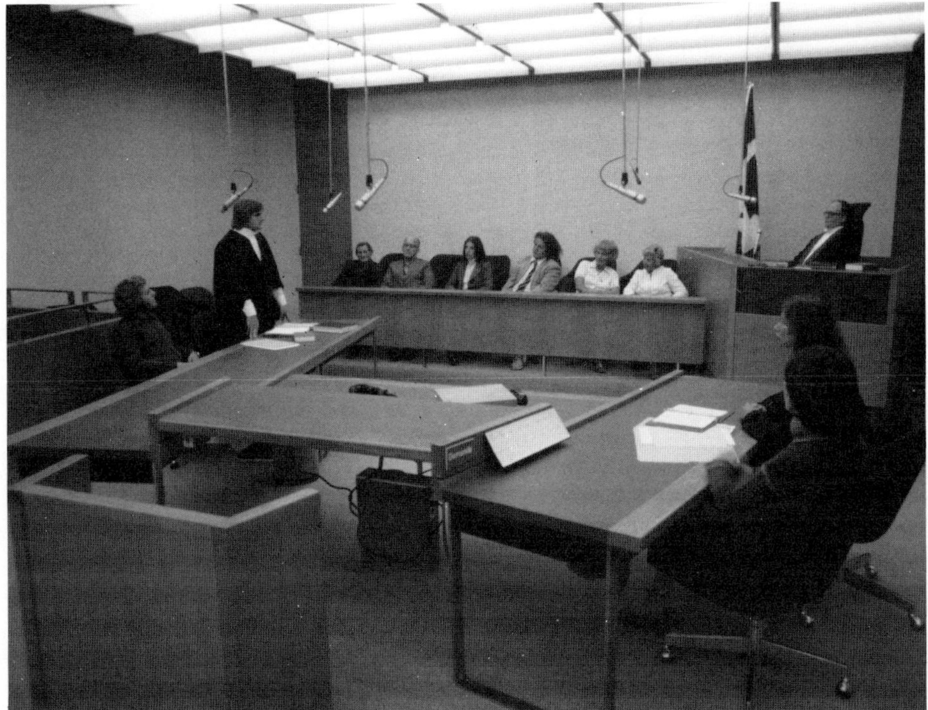

A civil case being pleaded in a courtroom.

a lease. The owner refuses to accept your rent money. Can you be evicted?

The answer is no. The new owner was under obligation to find out about the existing leases on buying the property. This owner must honour any leases signed with the previous owner. You cannot be evicted until your lease expires, and cannot be forced to pay a higher rent. If the new owner refuses to accept your rent, you can pay the court, and the owner can collect the money there.

DEALING WITH REPAIR PEOPLE

Your trusty car has finally let you down, and you have had it towed to the nearest repair station. The mechanic who inspects the car gives a quick estimate of about $100 for repairs. You then sign a work order. Later that day you pick up your car and become furious when you see the bill—$235! Can you refuse to pay?

You cannot refuse payment. The mechanic's estimate was only a guess. At that point, he could not be certain of the damage. When you signed a work bill, you gave him the right to make all the necessary repairs. Now you must pay. If you refuse, he may sell your car to recover his money.

In future cases, you should ask for a full written estimate before authorizing any repairs. You can then refuse to agree to the repair if the costs seem high. You can also state a limit as to the amount you will pay. All these things must be done in advance. Once you sign a work order, you are responsible for its terms.

These are but a few examples of the kinds of difficulties many Canadians become involved in. As much as possible, the law allows individuals to be responsible for their own actions. The moral in every case is to read over contracts and agreements carefully. The law will not always bail you out. Once again, ignorance is no defence. The old Roman warning, caveat emptor ("Let the buyer beware") is still very much to be heeded.

BUILDING YOUR LEARNING SKILLS

FOCUSSING ON THE ISSUE

1 Summarize three key ideas presented in this chapter.

2 Answer the following questions, which pertain to this chapter.

- *a* If you sign a contract to purchase goods in your own home, you may cancel the contract if you change your mind within:
  - *i* five days *ii* one week
  - *iii* one month *iv* two days
- *b* Which of the following may not legally sign a contract?
  - *i* prisoners in jail *ii* minors
  - *iii* a wife without her husband's consent
- *c* If you tell a plumber to fix your sink but do not put your directions in writing, there is no legal contract. True or false?

3 The following terms appeared in this chapter. Try to recall their meanings and how they were used.

caveat emptor	implied contract
civil law	minor
civil suit	verbal contract
Consumer Protection Act	written contract

RESEARCHING

1 Find out a little more about Canada's consumer laws. You may gain reliable information from the following sources: Department of Consumer and Corporate Affairs, Canadian Building, 219 Laurier Avenue, Ottawa 4, Ontario.

2 Gather information on the law regarding the division of property in cases of divorce. How is property to be divided between husband and wife?

3 Try to find out the highest rate of interest that a loan company can charge under the law.

4 What is the minimum wage allowed by law in your province?

ORGANIZING

1 Using an organizer, make a chart listing the three types of simple contracts discussed on page 98. For each, list as many examples as you can of the contracts you or your family have made during the past year.

2 Make a list of your possessions. In case of loss or damage, how many are insured or under warranty?

COMMUNICATING

1 Role play the following scene: You are a temporary clothing-store salesperson. A customer attempts to return a dress she bought the previous day. You notice that there is a stain on the dress. The store's policy is that clothes may be returned for a refund within three days of purchase, but only if they have not been worn. What would you say to the customer?

2 You want to buy a new stereo system and notice a large ad announcing a sale at a nearby store. When you get to the store, the salesperson tells you that the advertised system is not very good, but that they can sell you a much better system, though, of course, at a much higher price. You buy the expensive system, but on the way home you see the same stereo system at a lower price in another store. You want to return the system you bought and have your contract rendered void. Argue your case in front of a court.

ANALYZING

1 The old maxim, "Let the buyer beware," is still very true today. Do you think the government should pass more laws to protect consumers from making foolish mistakes?

2 Most of the products purchased today come with warranties. It is probable that you have a number of such products in your home. Read the warranties closely. How much responsibility does the manufacturer actually have?

APPLYING YOUR KNOWLEDGE

1 What is the difference between criminal law and civil law? Which of the following would be considered a criminal matter and which a civil matter?

a forging your name on a cheque
b mistreating a pet
c refusing to pay your telephone bill
d driving while under the influence of alcohol

2 If you were the judge, what would be your verdict in the following case? Alice entered a contest in which the object was to guess the number of jellybeans in a jar. The prize was a new TV set. A week later she was informed that she and another contestant had tied with the closest answer. There would be a quiz to determine the winner. The contest organizer announced that the last person eliminated would be the winner. They drew lots to determine the order of answering. Alice would answer first. Each contestant answered the first four questions correctly. On the fifth question, Alice missed. So did her opponent. However, since Alice missed first, the organizer announced that her opponent was the winner. Alice protested that this was unfair to her since both contestants had missed the last question. The organizer claimed his decision was according to the rules. The case went to court. How would you decide?

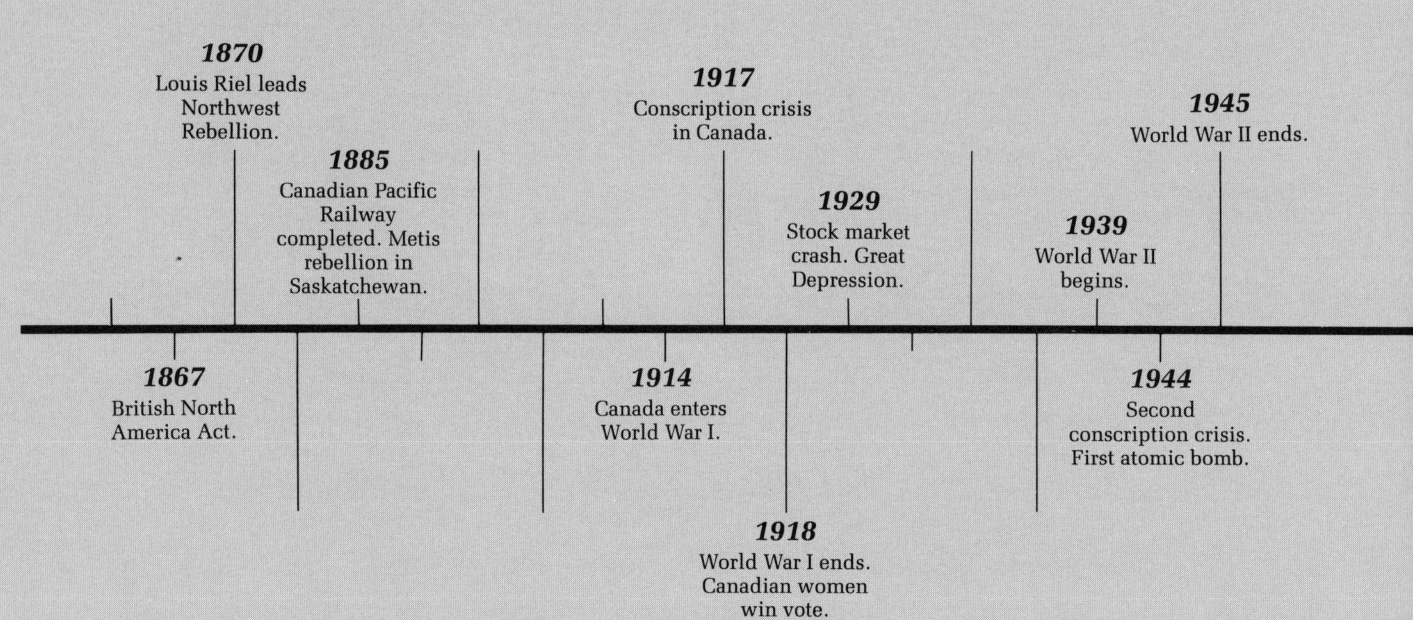
1870
Louis Riel leads Northwest Rebellion.
1867
British North America Act.
1885
Canadian Pacific Railway completed. Metis rebellion in Saskatchewan.
1914
Canada enters World War I.
1917
Conscription crisis in Canada.
1918
World War I ends. Canadian women win vote.
1929
Stock market crash. Great Depression.
1939
World War II begins.
1944
Second conscription crisis. First atomic bomb.
1945
World War II ends.

unit three

CANADA, 1867–PRESENT: AN OVERVIEW

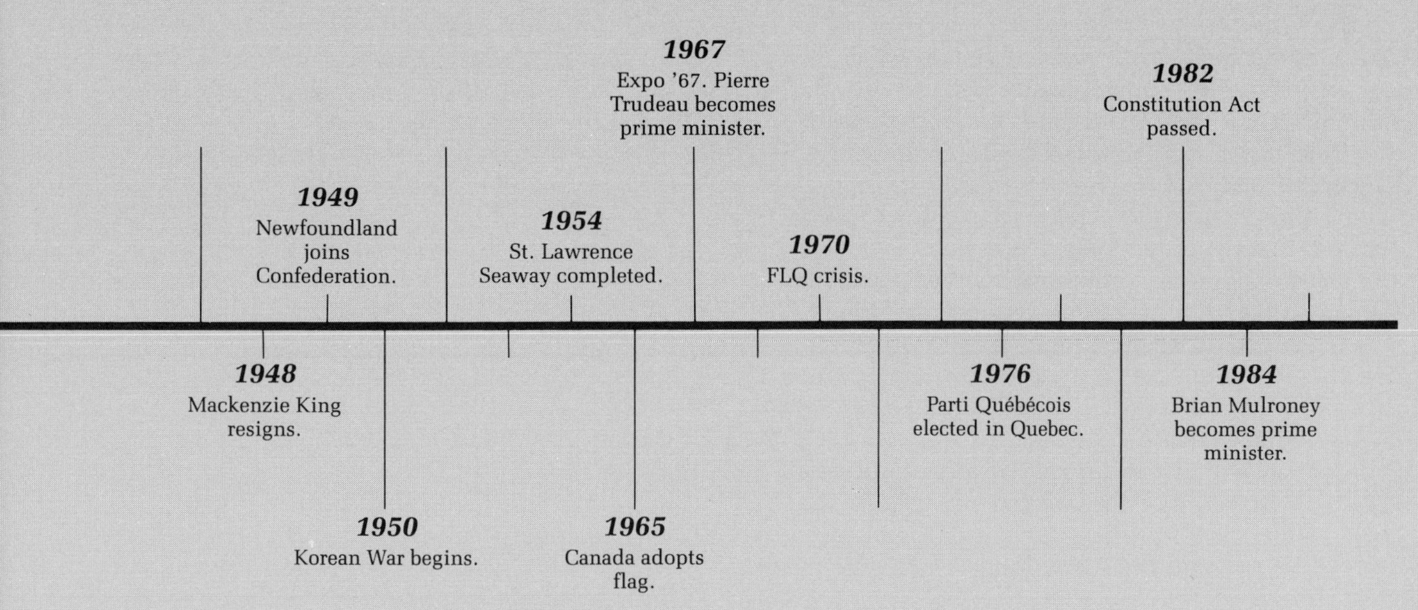
1948
Mackenzie King resigns.
1949
Newfoundland joins Confederation.
1950
Korean War begins.
1954
St. Lawrence Seaway completed.
1965
Canada adopts flag.
1967
Expo '67. Pierre Trudeau becomes prime minister.
1970
FLQ crisis.
1976
Parti Québécois elected in Quebec.
1982
Constitution Act passed.
1984
Brian Mulroney becomes prime minister.

TOPIC ORGANIZER — **PAGE**

THEME ORGANIZER

- Rounding out Confederation: Action and reaction
- Immigration and settlement of the West: Unity in diversity
- Canada in World War I: A war to end all wars
- The conscription crisis: Canada divided
- The Roaring Twenties: The good times roll
- The Great Depression: Economic disaster
- Canada in World War II: In the defence of freedom
- Canada in the Atomic Age: Mankind on the brink
- The discovery of the teenager: Youth makes itself heard
- Women on the march: Gaining economic and social equality
- The political scene: A roller-coaster ride

INTRODUCTION

One hundred and twenty years have passed since that day in July, 1867, when fireworks and parades announced the birth of the new nation of Canada. Since that day, Canadians have lived through remarkable events and experiences.

Canadians fought heroically in two world wars, endured one of the greatest depressions in history and faced challenges to their national existence. At the same time, they contributed to the advancement of science and technology and led the world in the development of natural resources and food production. Canadians today enjoy one of the highest standards of living in the world.

These achievements were not won without great effort and sacrifice. In this unit you will examine the trials, failures and successes of Canadians from their beginnings through their rise to one of the world's great nations.

UNIT PREVIEW QUESTIONS

As you study this unit, keep these questions in mind. They will serve as a focus for your reading. You may want to return to them when you have finished the unit.

1 What were the forces acting as agents for the expansion of Canada from sea to sea? What economic, social and military problems did this expansion create?

2 Can you support the argument that Canada changed from a bicultural to a multicultural country around the turn of the nineteenth century?

3 Canadians fought in two world wars between 1914 and 1945. What was the reaction of Canadians to being conscripted to fight in these wars?

4 What caused the Great Depression of the 1930s? Could another such depression occur in our time?

5 Are there similarities between the attitudes and life-styles of young people today and those of the 1920s?

6 The world entered the Atomic Age in 1945. Should Canada possess nuclear weapons?

7 The struggle for women's rights has been a feature of the twentieth century. What rights have women won in this century? What rights do you think are yet to be won?

chapter 8

CANADA: 1867–1914

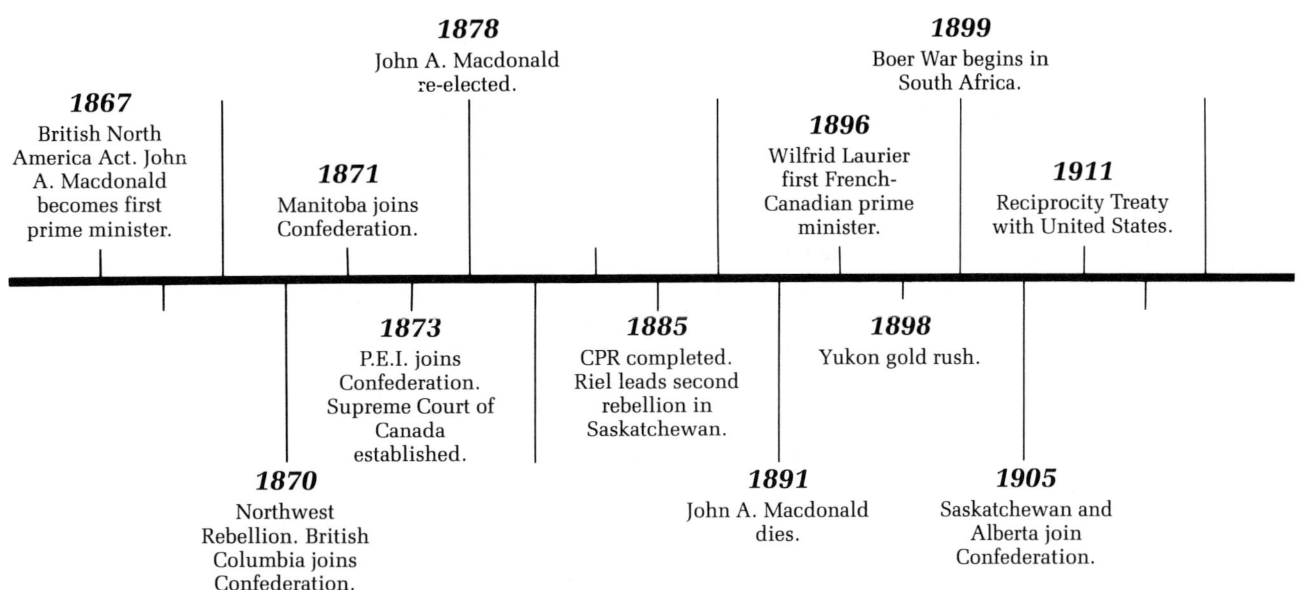

1867
British North America Act. John A. Macdonald becomes first prime minister.
1870
Northwest Rebellion. British Columbia joins Confederation.
1871
Manitoba joins Confederation.
1873
P.E.I. joins Confederation. Supreme Court of Canada established.
1878
John A. Macdonald re-elected.
1885
CPR completed. Riel leads second rebellion in Saskatchewan.
1891
John A. Macdonald dies.
1896
Wilfrid Laurier first French-Canadian prime minister.
1898
Yukon gold rush.
1899
Boer War begins in South Africa.
1905
Saskatchewan and Alberta join Confederation.
1911
Reciprocity Treaty with United States.

TOPIC ORGANIZER

THEME ORGANIZER

- Life in 1867: Life in the slow lane
- Canada from sea to sea: Canada becomes a giant
- Rebellion in the Northwest: A question of minority rights
- Building the CPR: Linking East and West to forge a nation
- The National Policy: John A. Macdonald's dream becomes reality
- The Riel rebellion: Riel—hero or traitor?
- Immigration to the West: Building a multicultural society
- The Laurier era: Entering the twentieth century

INTRODUCTION

The period 1867–1914 was a crucial time in Canadian history. In 1867 Canada was a small, politically unimportant country. The nation was still tied to Britain's apron-strings. By 1914 Canada had become a vigorous young nation. It was about to participate in one of the major wars in human history. The period in between was one of great growth and development, both politically and socially.

In 1867 Canada was made up of four provinces—Ontario, Quebec, New Brunswick and Nova Scotia. By 1914 it contained nine provinces and stretched from the Atlantic to the Pacific Ocean. Only Newfoundland stayed outside the union. It joined Canada in 1949.

These successes were not easily achieved. Canada's giant neighbour to the south, the United States, was growing quickly. It often threatened to absorb Canada. The term used to describe this threat was "U.S. expansionism." Canada was also faced by problems within its borders. These included unifying East and West to form one nation, a rebellion in the West and arguments between English and French. In this chapter we will examine the major developments in the period between 1867 and 1914. We will try to find answers to the following large questions: What forces were at work to change the political and social scene during these years? What sort of country did these forces produce?

Compared to most other countries, Canada is still very young. Yet the difficult decisions made during Canada's "childhood" helped the nation "grow up" quickly. They also shaped Canada's future as a nation.

Before reading on, study the chart of key words and ideas that follows.

KEY WORDS AND IDEAS IN THIS CHAPTER

Term	Meaning	Sample Use
confederation	a union of provinces or states in which power is shared between the federal and provincial governments	In 1867 four provinces united in a federation, an event which we call Confederation, to form the Dominion of Canada.
economic depression	a period during which wages and prices fall; accompanied by high unemployment	From 1875 to 1878, Canada's economy was in the grip of an economic depression.
imperialism	the policy of extending a nation's authority over other countries, often by making them colonies	In 1899 Britain fought a war against the Boers of South Africa. It was an example of the British policy of imperialism.

Industrial Revolution	a period during which most goods began to be produced by machines in factories rather than by hand in the home	After 1867 the Industrial Revolution affected Canadian industry. More and more machinery was used in Canadian factories.
reciprocity	an action between two (or more) parties that is the same on both sides	In 1911 Canada signed a reciprocity agreement with the United States. It involved lowering or removing tariffs. This agreement created political controversy in Canada.
tariff	a list of taxes on certain goods imported from other countries	High tariffs were part of Macdonald's National Policy. The reciprocity agreement of 1911 removed many tariffs.

THE DOMINION OF CANADA IN 1867

CANADA IN 1867 CONFEDERATION DAY

> THE DOMINION OF CANADA
> With the first dawn of this gladsome mid-summer morn we hail the birthday of a new nationality. A united British America with its four millions of people takes its place this day among the nations of the world . . . the Dominion of Canada, on this First day of July, in the year of grace, eighteen hundred and sixty seven, enters on a new career of national existence.

The *Toronto Globe* greeted the birth of the Dominion of Canada with this article. Happy Canadians celebrated their new beginning from Halifax to Ottawa. Picnics, parades, fireworks, 21-gun salutes and, of course, speeches were part of the birthday party. However, not everyone was pleased by the new Dominion. Resistance came from outside Canada and from within. The Halifax *Morning Chronicle* spoke for many Nova Scotians when it printed this July 1 announcement:

> Died! Last night at 12 o'clock the free and enlightened Province of Nova Scotia. . . . Funeral will take place from the Grand Parade this day, Monday, at 9 o'clock. Friends are requested NOT to attend. . . .

The *New York Tribune* spoke for those Americans who still hoped to make Canada theirs when it stated:

> When the experiment of the "dominion" shall have failed, as fail it must, a process of peaceful absorption will give Canada her proper place in the great North American Republic.

In general, though, the mood of most Canadians on this day was one of optimism. The promise of Canada was best worded by the poet Thomas D'Arcy McGee:

> I look to the future of my adopted country with hope, though not without anxiety [worry]. I see in the not remote distance one great nationality, bound, like the shield of Achilles, by the blue rim of Ocean. I see it quartered into many communities, each disposing of its internal affairs, but all bound together by free institutions, free intercourse and free commerce. I see within the round of that shield the peaks of the Western Mountains and the crests of the Eastern waves, the winding Assiniboine, the five-fold lakes, the St. Lawrence, the Ottawa, the Saguenay, the St. John, and the basin of *Minas*. By all these flowing waters in all the valleys they fertilise, in all the cities they visit in their courses, I see a generation of industrious, contented, moral men, free in name and in fact—men capable of maintaining, in peace and in war, a constitution worthy of such a country!

But what was Canada and who were Canadians in 1867? The size of the infant Dominion was not great. Today Canada is the second largest country in the world. In 1867 the young nation was perhaps 10 percent of the size of today's giant. It was composed of

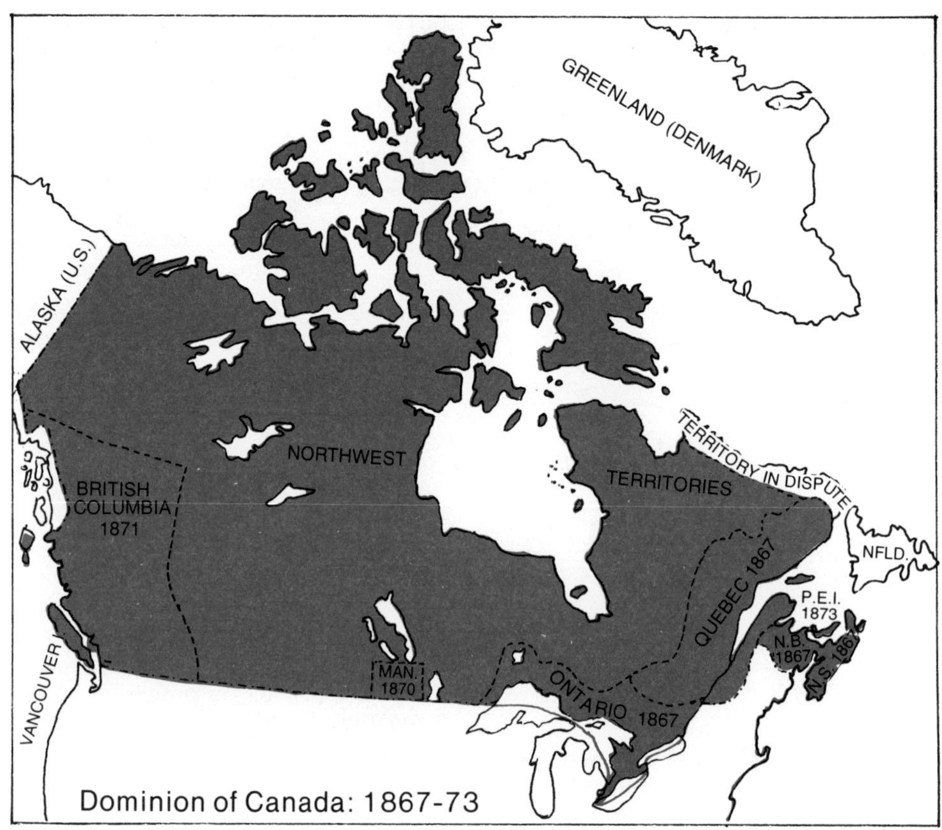

Dominion of Canada: 1867-73

only four provinces: New Brunswick, Nova Scotia, Ontario and Quebec.

The population, too, was small. Of the 3.3 million Canadians, 80 percent lived in Ontario and Quebec. This population was also mainly British and French.

	1867	Today
French	31%	27%
British: English, Irish, Scottish	60.5%	40%
Other	08.5%	33%

What did the future hold for young Canadians in 1867? Many had escaped from poverty overseas, hoping to become wealthy, own land and "move up" in the world. They believed in the progress and growth of their country. These are probably many of the same values shared by young Canadians today. Yet, for the majority in 1867, these goals were only dreams. If you had been a young person living in Canada at that time, you would probably have settled for a life-style much the same as that of your parents and grandparents. Only one Canadian in five lived in a town or city. For the rest, their way of life seemed destined to remain rural. In the Maritimes, shipping and fishing were even then the main features of the economy. In Quebec, the lives of most French-Canadians were still tied to their farms or lumbering. In Ontario, there was a belt of settled communities along the north shore of Lake Ontario from Kingston to Niagara Falls. Outside this belt lay the world of farm, forest and log cabin.

Rural life in the 1800s seems slow by today's space-age standards. There were no paved roads, no automobiles and few machines of any type. The steam locomotive connected only the larger towns and cities. Farmers still had to break open and maintain their own roads.

Wood was the main source of fuel for homes. Light was provided by coal-oil lamps. The women were

FEBRUARY 22, 1873. CANADIAN ILLUSTRATED NEWS 125

FIG. 2 *a*.—Blouse for Girls of 12 to 15. Front.

FIG. 1 *a*.—Rubens Hat for a Little Girl.

FIG. 1 *b*.—High Crowned Hat for a Little Girl.

FIG. 2 *b*.—Blouse for Girls of 12 to 15. Back.

FIG. 3.—Sash of watered Ribbon and Rep Ribbon.

FIG. 5.—Pelargonium Coiffure.

FIG. 6.—Rose-bud Coiffure.

FIG. 4.—Sash of watered Ribbon and Velvet Ribbon.

FIG. 7.—Bretelles of Swiss Muslin, Insertion and Lace.

FIG. 10.—Fancy Case for Skates.

FIG. 8.—Visiting Toilette.

FIG. 9.—Evening Dress.

FASHIONS AND LADY'S WORK.

Women's fashions in 1873. Make up a page like this one on women's fashions today. Use pictures from magazines and catalogues. What do clothes tell you about how people live during a period in history?

"The Great Trophy of Confederation" was designed to honour Canada's tenth birthday, on July 1, 1877. Each of the seven provinces is symbolized in this drawing. Try to identify each one.

expected to cook, spin their own clothes, milk the cows, churn the butter and make the soap for laundry.

Town life seemed a little more lively. You could buy most of life's needs at the general store, even imported cookies and candy. In town you could also expect to find a blacksmith shop, a drugstore, a doctor's office, a local newspaper, a bank and several churches. For entertainment there were taverns.

Taverns were as plentiful as today's corner milk stores. Every town of modest size had at least three taverns. They were the centres of social and political activity. Each tavern had its own special clients. Liberals tended to gather at one tavern, Conservatives at a second and neutrals at a third. Here they discussed the political events of the time. In those days there were no popularity polls and no secret ballot. Studying the taverns' populations was a simple way of judging the popularity of each party.

The larger cities—Montreal, Toronto, Quebec City, Halifax — boasted a few paved streets and gas-lit street lamps. A few of the wealthier houses had running water. Toronto had horse-drawn streetcars. There was almost no Canadian literature or music. However, plays from London or New York could be seen in large cities. These were attended by the wealthier citizens. The average person in this age before movies, television and professional sporting events had to come up with his or her own leisure activities.

Public education was free. However, only a few students went to high school, and fewer still attended university. The core subjects of higher education were Greek, Latin, English, history and mathematics. These prepared the graduate for a career in politics and business. For most of the less fortunate, the future promised dull, tedious labour.

A wind of change, however, was sweeping into Canada. It carried new ideas and new hopes. These hopes were based on the promise of the machine age. The Industrial Revolution had already started in Britain and the United States. It was just beginning in Canada. Young people could now dream of instant wealth. Stories of adventurous people, who started out penniless and almost overnight became millionaires, came north from the United States. The main sources of this new-found wealth were railroads, steel and oil. Within a few years, the names of Andrew Carnegie and John D. Rockefeller stood out as examples of these rags-to-riches stories. This same dream took hold in Canada. If Canadians were to achieve such rewards, Canada would have to continue to progress and to grow. The obvious direction of growth was westward.

ROUNDING OUT THE DOMINION

The motto on the Canadian coat of arms is a Latin phrase, "a mari usque ad mare." It means "from sea to sea." From the very beginning, Canadians realized that if their country was to survive, it must be unified

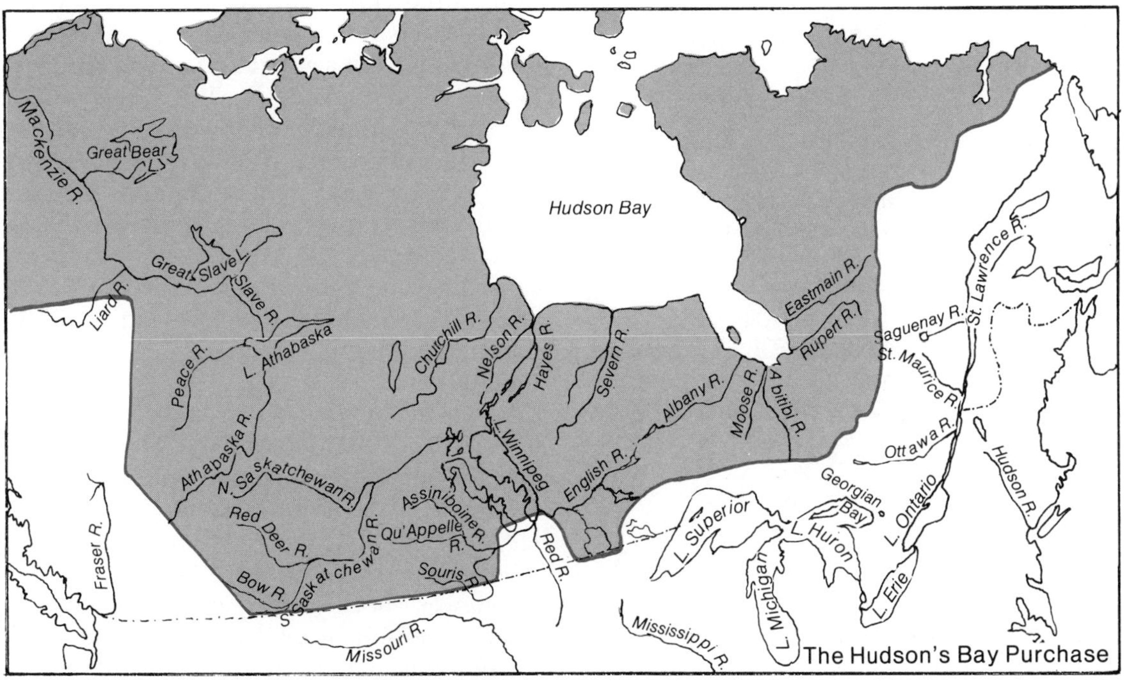

The Hudson's Bay Purchase

from the Atlantic Ocean to the Pacific Ocean. Most Canadians placed their hopes for the future on Prime Minister John A. Macdonald. Macdonald was suited to the mood of the times. He too favoured industrial growth and expansion to the west. Almost immediately, the new prime minister took steps to promote this growth.

Several thousand kilometres to the west was the colony of British Columbia. It seemed eager to join the new Dominion. The main stumbling block was communication. There were no roads linking British Columbia with the rest of Canada. The obvious answer was the building of a railroad that would link British Columbia with the rest of Canada. However, the giant Northwest Territories lay in between. It was owned by the Hudson's Bay Company. Canada had to control this huge expanse of land if it was to become a strong nation. During this period, settlers in the United States were moving west. They came very close to the Canadian border. The threat of an American takeover of the Northwest Territories forced Macdonald's Conservative government into action. The first step was to negotiate the purchase of the Northwest from the Hudson's Bay Company. In 1869 the deal was completed.

THE DEAL

Canada Received	Hudson's Bay Company Received
3.9 million km² = 390 million ha	£300 000 ($1.5 million) 18 000 ha of land around its trading posts 5 percent of all the fertile land in the Northwest

Canada's purchase of the Northwest, at the rate of about one penny for every 3 ha of land, certainly stands out as one of the greatest real-estate bargains of all time.

THE NORTHWEST REBELLION

The purchase of the Northwest also brought the Canadian government its first crisis. The Hudson's Bay Company had given Canada control over not only a vast land, but the people in it as well. This included numerous Indian nations, such as the Cree and Blackfoot. It also included about 12 000 people who lived in the Red River colony.

Louis Riel

The majority of the people at Red River were Metis. The Metis were a proud people. They were part Indian and part French or English. The Metis considered themselves a separate nation. For many years they had led a wandering life. Their economy was based on the annual buffalo hunt. By 1869 the buffalo herds had almost vanished. Great slaughters in the United States had wiped them out. Many Metis wanted to set down roots as farmers in the Red River area. The sale of the Hudson's Bay lands to Canada caused several concerns. Would the Canadian government guarantee the Metis' land titles? Would it respect the French language and Roman Catholic religion?

When the surveyors sent out by Canada reached the Red River, the Metis naturally became suspicious. On October 11, 1869, a group of Metis put a stop to the work of the surveyors and arrested them. The leader of the Metis was a young man of twenty-five whose name was Louis Riel.

Riel was a born leader. He was well educated, having studied law and religion in Montreal. Riel had proved to be a good student, but he was proud and hot tempered. A man who knew Riel described him as follows:

> Riel may have his faults and weaknesses, but he is decidedly an extraordinary man. To begin, his appearance is striking: he has a swarthy complexion with a large head and piercing eyes. He seems quite well educated, and in all gives me the impression of a remarkable man, if unstable.

The Metis decided to keep out the representatives of Canada and set up their own provisional government. This action angered a number of Canadians living in the settlement, including several Ontario Englishmen. One man, Thomas Scott, led a revolt against the Riel government. It failed, and Scott and several English-speaking settlers were jailed. Even in jail, Scott continued to make trouble. He constantly quarrelled with Riel. At last Riel's patience came to an end, and he had Scott executed.

Whether Riel's motives can be defended or not, the execution of Scott proved to be a great mistake. It created a great anti-French, anti-Catholic uproar in Ontario. On the other hand, French-Catholic Quebec sympathized with Riel. The seeds of a new and bitter English-French antagonism had been sowed.

Macdonald now had no choice but to send troops to end the Metis rebellion. Riel feared for his life and escaped to the United States.

One side effect of the Red River rebellion was to focus the attention of Canada on the West. The government now took quick action to guarantee the settlers their land and language rights. In 1870 the Red River settlement was admitted into Confederation as part of the Province of Manitoba. Riel became known as the Father of Manitoba. In time, he was actually elected as member of Parliament from that province, but because of a price on his head, he never served.

BUILDING OF THE CANADIAN PACIFIC RAILWAY

Macdonald's fondest dream was to round out the Dominion from east to west. The cornerstone of this "national dream" was the construction of a great railway to link British Columbia with the rest of Canada. British Columbia agreed to join Confederation in

John A. Macdonald, Canada's first prime minister. He remained in that office from 1867–1891, except for the period 1873–1878.

1871 only if the railway were started within two years of its joining.

This seemed an impossible task for the young nation. The costs would be immense. Macdonald himself estimated the cost at $100 million. Later this was proven to be far too low. The railroad itself, if completed, would be the longest ever built. It would have to cross some of the most difficult territory in the world: forests, swamps, prairies and great mountain ranges. It certainly seemed an ambitious project for a country of less than four million people.

Yet great profits might be made in the building of such a railway. Business people both in Canada and the United States saw potential. Macdonald's government was soon getting offers from companies on both sides of the border to build his railroad.

Meanwhile, Macdonald was busy leading his Conservative party in the election of 1872. He emerged from the election as Canada's prime minister once again. Shortly afterward, the government awarded the contract to build the transcontinental railroad to the Canadian Pacific Railway Company. The Company was headed by Sir Hugh Allan, Canada's wealthiest businessman.

The charter to build the "iron road" cost the Canadian government $30 million in cash and over 20 million ha of some of the best farmland in Canada.

But even as work was beginning on the railroad, a political storm was brewing in Ontario. The Liberal Opposition soon produced evidence that Allan and his backers had given large sums of money to the Conservative party during the 1872 election. In fact, over $325 000 had been donated by the company to ensure Macdonald's re-election. The most damaging evidence was a letter from Macdonald to Allan, which read in part, "I must have another ten thousand; will be the last time of calling; do not fail me; answer today."

The Pacific scandal came crashing down about Macdonald's shoulders. His government was forced

Lord Strathcona drives in the last spike at Craigellachie, British Columbia.

Building the CPR through prairies and mountains.

to resign. In 1873 the Liberal party, under Alexander Mackenzie, governed Canada.

While Alexander Mackenzie was an honest, hard-working and thrifty prime minister, he did lack imagination. Mackenzie was also very unlucky. When he became prime minister, a long period of economic depression was beginning. The CPR was the first to be affected by economic conditions. The Liberal government scrapped most of the plans for its construction. Over the next five years, only a few short sections of track were laid. British Columbia naturally felt betrayed and threatened to pull out of Confederation.

After the Pacific scandal of 1873, it seemed John A. Macdonald's political career had come to an end. But now, in 1878, he appeared as the only man who could save the railway and with it, a Canada that stretched "from sea to sea." Macdonald's Conservatives swept back into power on the promise of a National Policy.

Macdonald's National Policy consisted of three main projects:

1 completion of the Canadian Pacific Railway
2 the raising of protective tariffs to encourage Canadian industry
3 encouragement of immigration to the West

The first order of business was to finish the railroad. A new Canadian Pacific Railway Company, headed by George Stephen and Donald Smith, was founded. The company agreed to finish the railroad by 1891. In return, they received the following generous terms:

- ownership of the railroad;
- $25 million cash;
- 10 million ha in the rich valley of the Saskatchewan;
- exemption from taxation;
- imports carried duty free;
- 1100 km of railroad already completed (valued at $30 million) to be handed over to the company.

A young, energetic American, Cornelius Van Horne, took over construction of the railroad in 1882. In three short years, he engineered the railroad from the head of Lake Superior to British Columbia. The last spike was driven at Craigellachie, British Columbia, on November 7, 1885, six years before the deadline.

THE REBELLION OF 1885

The same year that saw the triumph of the CPR also witnessed the return of Louis Riel. After the troubles at Red River, in 1869, most of the Metis sold their land cheaply to land agents. They travelled far westward, to the valley of the South Saskatchewan River.

Here they continued their farming and hunting life. But with the advance of the railroad, their way of life was again in danger. Once again they voiced their complaints to the government. Once more the Macdonald government ignored the plight of the Metis and their Native Canadian brothers and sisters. Louis Riel agreed to return from the United States and help his people.

At first the Metis drew up a list of simple petitions. They asked for clear title to their lands and justice for Native Canadians. Macdonald, busy with railroad matters, brushed aside their requests. The angry Metis quickly took up arms in revolt. At Duck Lake the Metis took a detachment of mounted police by surprise. After a brief fight, 12 Mounties lay dead; the Saskatchewan rebellion had begun. The Metis were soon joined by the Cree, under Chiefs Big Bear and Poundmaker.

The newly built railroad quickly proved its worth. It brought troops from the East under the command of General Middleton. After more battles at Frog Lake, Cut Knife Hill, Battleford and Batoche, the Metis and their Native Canadian allies surrendered. Riel was captured.

Later that year, at Regina, Riel was put on trial for treason. His lawyers attempted to prove that Riel was insane. The jury, however, believed he was sane and so responsible for his actions:

> He seemed to us no more insane than any of the lawyers and they were the ablest men in Canada. He was even more interesting than some of them.

They found Riel guilty, and on November 16, 1885, he was hanged.

Riel's death caused rioting in Quebec and a new round of bitter English-French feelings. It would take a long time to heal the wounds.

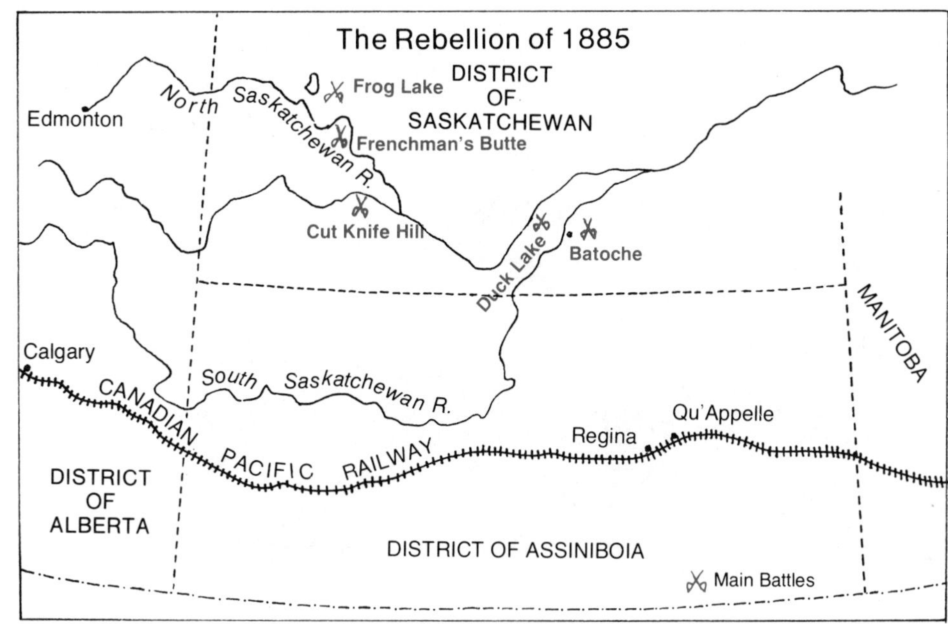

IMMIGRATION TO THE WEST

The second plank of Macdonald's National Policy was the settlement of the West. Free homesteads were offered to draw settlers westward. The fertile lands of the prairies were divided into townships made up of thirty-six 2.6 km squares. A homestead consisted of 25 percent of a square, or 64 ha. Any male over the age of eighteen could file for such a homestead. In return, he had to promise to live on the land for at least three years, build a home and break at least 4 ha of soil each year.

In the decade after 1871, the results of this policy were disappointing. In 1871 the population of the

IMMIGRATION TO CANADA BY CALENDAR YEAR, 1867–1915

Year	Immigrants	Year	Immigrants	Year	Immigrants
1867	10 666	1884	103 824	1900	41 681
1868	12 765	1885	79 169	1901	55 747
1869	18 630	1886	69 152	1902	89 102
1870	24 706	1887	84 526	1903	138 660
1871	27 773	1888	88 766	1904	131 252
1872	36 578	1889	91 600	1905	141 465
1873	50 050	1890	75 067	1906	211 653
1874	39 373	1891	82 165	1907	272 409
1875	27 382	1892	30 996	1908	143 326
1876	25 633	1893	29 633	1909	173 694
1877	27 082	1894	20 829	1910	286 839
1878	29 807	1895	18 790	1911	331 288
1879	40 492	1896	16 835	1912	375 756
1880	38 505	1897	21 716	1913	400 870
1881	47 991	1898	31 900	1914	150 484
1882	112 458	1899	44 543	1915	36 665
1883	133 624				

A "soddy" on the prairies. Settlers often had to make do with these homes for years until more permanent homes could be built. It is estimated that there were thousands of soddies on the prairies. Examine the picture closely. Can you explain how these homes were built?

West was 73 228. Ten years later, the figure was only slightly over 100 000. Instead of a flood, immigration to the West proved to be only a trickle.

The completion of the CPR in 1885 solved the problem of transportation. Before this time, settlers could expect to travel thousands of kilometres on foot and horseback, by cart or by boat, before reaching their destination. Many prospective settlers were naturally frightened of making such a journey. Another spur to immigration was provided by the election of Wilfrid Laurier and the Liberals in 1896. John A. Macdonald died in 1891, still Canada's prime minister. After five more years of Conservative rule, the Liberals swept to power in 1896. Wilfrid Laurier was determined to complete Macdonald's National Policy. His energetic minister of the interior, Clifford Sifton, took charge of immigration.

In the next few years, Europe and the United States were flooded with pamphlets announcing free land in the Canadian West. These pamphlets were so successful that between 1897 and 1914, over one million Americans emigrated to Canada. Another million came from over 30 different countries in Europe and Asia.

The flood of immigrants finally slowed with the outbreak of World War I, in 1914. In the meantime, it had filled the West and had produced two new provinces, Saskatchewan and Alberta, in 1905. Macdonald's dream of a Canada stretching from Atlantic to Pacific had been realized.

THE LAURIER ERA

The new prime minister, Wilfrid Laurier, became the first French-Canadian to hold that office. Stately, elegant and charming, Laurier seemed the perfect person to lead Canada into the twentieth century. His election promised to at last draw together English and French to produce a united Canada. Racial and religious tensions decreased. At the same time, the rest of the world seemed to discover Canada. Laurier came to office at a time when a world-wide depression was coming to an end. Suddenly there were markets all over the world for Canada's minerals, lumber, wheat and manufactured products.

A gold strike in the Yukon drew over 40 000 prospectors to the north. It served to further increase the mood of optimism felt all over Canada. There seemed no limit to what the young country would achieve. One English visitor called Canada "the Cinderella of the Western World." Laurier himself declared that the twentieth century would belong to Canada.

The first crack in the dream came in 1899 in a faraway corner of the world. In South Africa, the Boers, descendants of the original Dutch farmers in that country, were fighting to remain independent from Britain. The Boer's land was rich in diamonds and gold. Britain was determined to gain control of it. Britain asked Canada, as a member of the Empire, to help.

Laurier was placed in a difficult situation. French-Canadians refused to help in what they considered an unjust, imperialistic war. English-Canadians insisted that Canada should do its duty and aid the mother country. A heated debate followed. Again, Canada was divided into two camps, English versus French.

After much thought, Laurier handed down his decision: Canada would not send an official army to South Africa, but it would equip volunteers. Neither side was satisfied with this compromise solution. French-Canadians felt Laurier had done too much; English-Canadians felt that he had betrayed Britain.

Laurier's popularity received a further blow when his government signed the Reciprocity Treaty with the United States in 1911. The treaty demolished one of the cornerstones of Macdonald's National Policy. It removed protective tariffs for Canadian industry. The agreement allowed free trade between the two countries in such products as grain, fish, livestock, fruit and vegetables. Most of the tariff duties were also removed from meat, canned goods and machinery.

The reciprocity agreement had the effect of reducing the price of these goods in Canada. However, many Canadians feared that the competition with United States products would also result in loss of jobs. They believed that economic depression would follow. Then they said, Canada would become ripe for takeover by the United States.

In the election of 1911, Laurier was swept out of office by Robert Borden and the Conservative party. He would never again sit as prime minister of Canada.

It was Borden who would lead Canada into the greatest test of her first half-century — World War I. Over a half million Canadians marched to war in 1914. Of these, 63 000 never returned. Those who survived came home to find that the old way of life had gone forever.

The Yukon Gold Rush: miners crossing the Chilkoot Pass in 1898. The lineup was actually several days long.

At the turn of the century, women participated in almost all sporting activities.

BUILDING YOUR LEARNING SKILLS

FOCUSSING ON THE ISSUE

1 Summarize at least five main ideas presented in this chapter.

2 Answer the following questions relating to this chapter:

a At the time of Confederation, the largest portion of Canada's population was made up of:
i French *ii* British *iii* others

b The CPR was completed in the year:
i 1873 *ii* 1885 *iii* 1891

c Metis are a people who are
i part French, part Indian *ii* part English, part Indian *iii* both a and b

d At the time of its completion, the CPR was the longest railway in the world. True or false?

3 The following terms appeared in this chapter. Try to recall their meanings and how they were used.

a mari usque ad mare
Boers
Confederation
homestead
imperialism
Metis
National Policy
reciprocity
tariffs

RESEARCHING

1 Find out who were the premiers of the four provinces that joined Confederation in 1867.

2 The following individuals played large roles in the building of the CPR. Find out who they were and what roles they played in this great undertaking: Donald Smith, Sir Hugh Allan, Sir Sandford Fleming, Cornelius Van Horne.

3 Do some research on the origins of the immigrants who settled in western Canada at the end of the nineteenth century. Which countries sent the most immigrants to Canada?

4 Gather information on sports in Canada before 1914. Which sporting events were most popular with Canadians?

ORGANIZING

1 Make a list of the payments in land and money granted by the government for the building of the CPR.

2 Place the following events in the sequence in which they occurred:
- ▶ The Boer War breaks out.
- ▶ The Northwest Rebellion erupts.
- ▶ The CPR is built.
- ▶ Canada purchases the Northwest from the Hudson's Bay Company.
- ▶ Gold is discovered in the Yukon.

3 Rank the above five events in order of their importance, according to your point of view.

COMMUNICATING

1 Debate the following statement: The building of the CPR was the most important Canadian achievement before 1914.

2 You are Louis Riel's defence attorney. Present a courtroom defence to justify Riel's actions to a jury.

3 Write a letter to the editor of the *Toronto Globe* in 1885, stating your point of view on the Riel rebellions.

ANALYZING

1 Technological change is proceeding at a much faster rate than in the nineteenth century. Is it likely that many young people will continue to follow in the footsteps of their parents in choosing a career? If you have given any thought to your future career, how closely is it modelled upon that of your parents?

2 The Riel rebellions of 1869 and 1885 represent the clash of an expanding civilization and a more nomadic form of life. Could the rebellions have been avoided? What steps would you have taken if you had been prime minister of Canada during these times?

3 Compare the education of a young person in the nineteenth century with that young people receive today. Which system do you feel better prepares an individual for his or her future?

4 Analyze the immigration statistics on page 117. How do you account for the dramatic decrease in immigration in 1915? How do you account for the difference between immigration in 1881 and in 1882 and 1883?

APPLYING YOUR KNOWLEDGE

1 A tariff system imposes taxes on products coming into the country. This tends to raise the prices consumers have to pay for these products. Apply your knowledge of tariffs, and make a list of the benefits and disadvantages of a tariff system to a country such as Canada.

2 In 1873 Canada suffered a political scandal involving the prime minister. Recently the United States has also been the victim of a political scandal. Compare and contrast the results of the scandals on the two countries and the two leaders involved.

chapter 9

CANADA, 1914–1945: A GENERATION UNDER FIRE

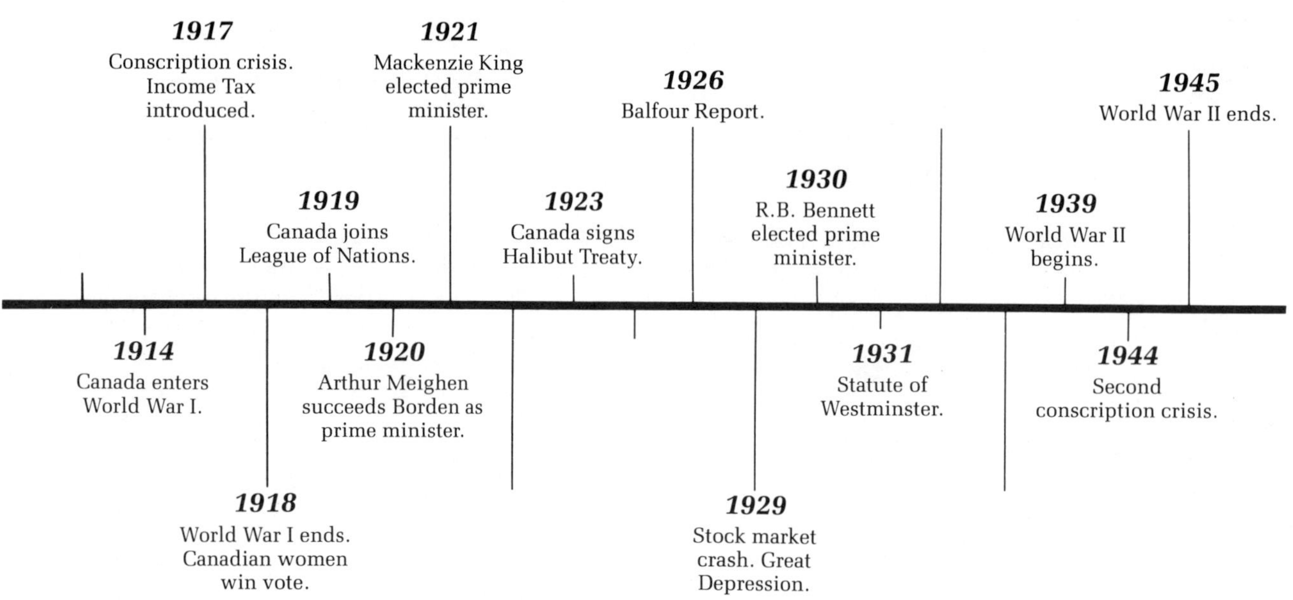
1914
Canada enters World War I.
1917
Conscription crisis. Income Tax introduced.
1918
World War I ends. Canadian women win vote.
1919
Canada joins League of Nations.
1920
Arthur Meighen succeeds Borden as prime minister.
1921
Mackenzie King elected prime minister.
1923
Canada signs Halibut Treaty.
1926
Balfour Report.
1929
Stock market crash. Great Depression.
1930
R.B. Bennett elected prime minister.
1931
Statute of Westminster.
1939
World War II begins.
1944
Second conscription crisis.
1945
World War II ends.

TOPIC ORGANIZER **PAGE**

THEME ORGANIZER

- Causes of World War I: European rivalries create a powderkeg.
- War in the trenches: Poor strategy by the war's generals results in ghastly losses.
- Canada at war: In Europe and on the home front Canadians distinguish themselves in the war effort.
- The Roaring Twenties: In an age of economic prosperity, Canadians reach for the good life.
- The age of Mackenzie King: A short, stocky bachelor sets the tone in Canadian politics for three decades.
- The stock market crash: The crash of the stock market in 1929 ruins many and triggers the Great Depression.
- The Dirty Thirties: The Great Depression of the 1930s brings economic chaos to Canada.
- The new parties: The Great Depression brings to the scene new political parties, most notably the Social Credit party and the CCF (now the NDP).
- World War II: The aggression of Adolf Hitler forces Canada into a second world war within a generation.

INTRODUCTION

The twentieth century, according to Wilfrid Laurier, was to be Canada's century. As the year 1914 unfolded, it certainly seemed that Laurier's statement might come true. Canada was enjoying a period of great prosperity. Her natural resources were at last being developed. Foreign nations were opening their doors to Canadian products.

Canadians had many reasons to feel hopeful about their nation. The tensions between French and English had been extreme during the Riel rebellion (see previous chapter). These tensions now seemed to be coming to an end. Waves of immigrants were opening up the West. The newcomers helped increase Canada's new prosperity. It was an age of exciting new inventions. Both the automobile and the airplane appeared during this period. The future seemed to promise a new, better life-style for Canadians.

Then came the tragedy of World War I. It was followed by a period of upheaval that affected the social, political and economic life of Canadians. Relations between French and English were again strained. The attitude toward women and their role in society changed. Within ten years, the greatest economic depression in history brought Canada to her knees. In 1939 the second major war within a generation began. Once again war tested Canadians as they faced the threat of Nazism.

In this chapter we will survey the great political, social and economic changes experienced by Canadians in the period from 1914 to 1945. Canada began the period as a youthful country, still subject to Britain. She emerged as a mature nation.

Before reading on, study the chart of key words and ideas that follows.

KEY WORDS AND IDEAS IN THIS CHAPTER

Term	Meaning	Sample Use
alliance	an agreement between several countries that they will support each other in case of war	Alliances existed in both world wars. In World War I, France, England, Russia and Italy were allied against Germany and Austria.
arms race	a situation in which countries compete against one another by building ever larger armies and navies and supplying them with the most up-to-date equipment	Prior to World War I, England and Germany were engaged in an arms race. Each side sought to gain the upper hand in naval power. It was one of the factors that led to war.

blockade	shutting off a place to prevent troops or ships from passing through	In 1914 the English navy put into effect a blockade off the coast of Germany.
conscription	compulsory enlistment for military service, usually during times of war	The Canadian government introduced conscription during both world wars. The volunteer system had not brought in enough soldiers. Conscription caused political and social problems.
government bonds	notes issued by a government promising to repay borrowed money, usually with interest	Government bonds were issued during both world wars by the Canadian government to help pay for the cost of the wars.
income tax	a tax placed on a person's earnings	Income tax was introduced as a "temporary measure" during World War I. It is still with us today.
inflation	a period in a country's economy during which prices and wages are constantly rising	A mild inflation occurred from 1922 to 1929 in Canada. It was followed by the Great Depression.
mysticism	the belief that a person can communicate with the spirits of the dead	Prime Minister W.L. Mackenzie King practised mysticism. Many of his decisions were made after consulting the spirits.
Nazi	a member of the German National Socialist Party, whose leader was Adolf Hitler	Nazis believed in the superiority of the German people. The party came to power in Germany in 1933.
plebiscite	the direct vote of all citizens on an issue of major importance	Mackenzie King issued a plebiscite before making a decision on whether to introduce conscription during World War II.
recession	a period of slow economic activity; generally a time of high unemployment also	In the years immediately following World War I, Canada's economy suffered a recession. After 1929, the recession grew into a full-blown depression.
socialism	the theory that a community, through its government, should own or control the key industries in the economy, such as the communication and transportation industries	In its Regina Manifesto, the CCF party of 1932 proposed a program based on socialism. Many of its policies are now in effect in Canada.

WORLD WAR I

1914

As the year 1914 dawned, Canadians had every reason to feel optimistic. The Canadian economy was at last taking its leap forward. The machine age promised more jobs, easier labour, rapid transportation and adventure. Everywhere business seemed to be growing. The markets of the world were at last opening their doors to Canada's mineral, lumber and wheat exports. Prosperity seemed close at hand.

	1901	1911
Population	5 400 000	7 200 000
Wheat exports	$6 900 000	$45 500 000
Mineral exports	$65 800 000	$103 200 000
Manufacturing	$481 000 000	$1 165 900 000
Automobiles	0	$22 000

Of course, life was still hard for many groups in society. It was still common for those working in factories or in construction to labour 12 hours a day or more. Thousands of these workers were killed or injured each year due to unsafe working conditions. Diseases, too, took thousands of lives. Childhood deaths were quite common. Tuberculosis was the most dreaded disease of adults. Hospitals were not today's modern, well-equipped structures. Rather, they tended to be small, dingy, poorly lit buildings.

Thomas Edison's great invention, the electric lightbulb, was making headway in the cities. Even the large cities, however, would seem primitive by today's standards. In Montreal, horses still had the right-of-way over cars on the streets. In Toronto, the fire department's wagons were still drawn by horses. In most places, red flag laws still prevented cars from going faster than 25 or even 15 km/h.

By and large, Canadians were hopeful about their future. Since Confederation, Canada had never been involved in a war. Indeed, at the Canadian National Exhibition in Toronto that year, the theme was "Peace." Few Canadians suspected that the summer of 1914 would bring their country its greatest crisis since Confederation. For, in Europe, on August 4, 1914, the greatest armies in the history of the world

A leisurely Sunday afternoon stroll in High Park, Toronto, before World War I.

were marching against each other. World War I had begun.

BACKGROUND TO WAR

It was to be a war unlike any other in history. In this war, all the resources of the hostile nations were channelled into the war effort. The raw materials, the factories, the civilian populations and the fighting men themselves were all cogs in a great machine. This was total war.

The causes of the struggle had been building for decades. In 1871 German armies defeated the French in the Franco-Prussian War. Since that day, each side prepared for the time when the conflict would be renewed. As each side tried to gain the upper hand, they drew other European powers into the web. They did so through a series of alliances. By 1914 Europe was divided into two main camps. On the German side stood the empire of Austria-Hungary and Italy. This was known as the Triple Alliance. With France were lined up England and Russia — the Triple Entente. (When the war started, Italy joined Britain, France and Russia.)

Each alliance system involved a network of secret treaties. Simply, they promised that if one member of the alliance was attacked, the other two would come to its defence.

The atmosphere of suspicion grew. Germany and England became involved in an arms race. Armies and navies were increased, modernized and equipped with the newest weapons. England's proud navy, faced with the threat of a new, powerful rival in Germany, began an expensive program of rebuilding. Britain's naval budget doubled between 1900 and 1914. She also asked Canada to contribute to this budget. In 1911 this produced a bitter debate in Canada. Should Canada build her own navy or simply contribute to a larger British navy? Laurier and the Liberals were in favour of a separate Canadian navy. Borden and the Conservatives felt Canada should contribute to the British navy. It was one of the issues that helped to defeat Laurier in 1911. As it turned out, Canada did not get her own navy, nor did she aid Britain financially.

It was hoped that, since the two alliances were fairly equal in power, this would discourage the outbreak of war. However, in a far-off corner of Europe called the Balkans, local wars could not be stopped. Serbia was a small country that had recently been given independence from her former protector, Austria-Hungary. Other groups within the Austro-Hungarian Empire began to demand their freedom as well. They were encouraged in this by Austria-Hungary's enemy, Russia. Because of all these rivalries, the area became known as the "powderkeg of Europe."

On the fateful day of June 28, 1914, the heir to the Austrian throne, the Archduke Franz Ferdinand, was shot and killed by a young Serbian terrorist at a town called Sarajevo. Austria believed that the Serbian government was behind the assassination. They made a number of harsh demands. Meeting the demands would have meant the surrender of Serbia. Russia came to Serbia's aid. But Austria refused to back down from her demands. The powderkeg exploded. War was now inevitable.

When war was declared, there were celebrations in all the European capitals. Experts believed the war would be a short one. "Home by Christmas" was the cry of the first volunteers. For most, it would be Christmas, 1918, before they saw their homes again.

THE FIRST BATTLE

Germany came to Austria's aid in this crisis. She had the most powerful army in Europe. However, Germany saw herself surrounded. Russia was on one side and France on the other. Across the channel lay England. Germany felt that her best hope was in landing the first blow.

Russia's army was large but scattered throughout this huge country. It would take weeks or months before this army could be ready to fight on Germany's borders. Germany's main concern was the French army. To meet this problem, the German generals adopted a plan of attack devised years earlier, the Schlieffen plan.

The Schlieffen plan was simple but quite effective. It solved the main problem facing Germany in the war: how to defeat the French armies quickly, then return and face the Russian threat.

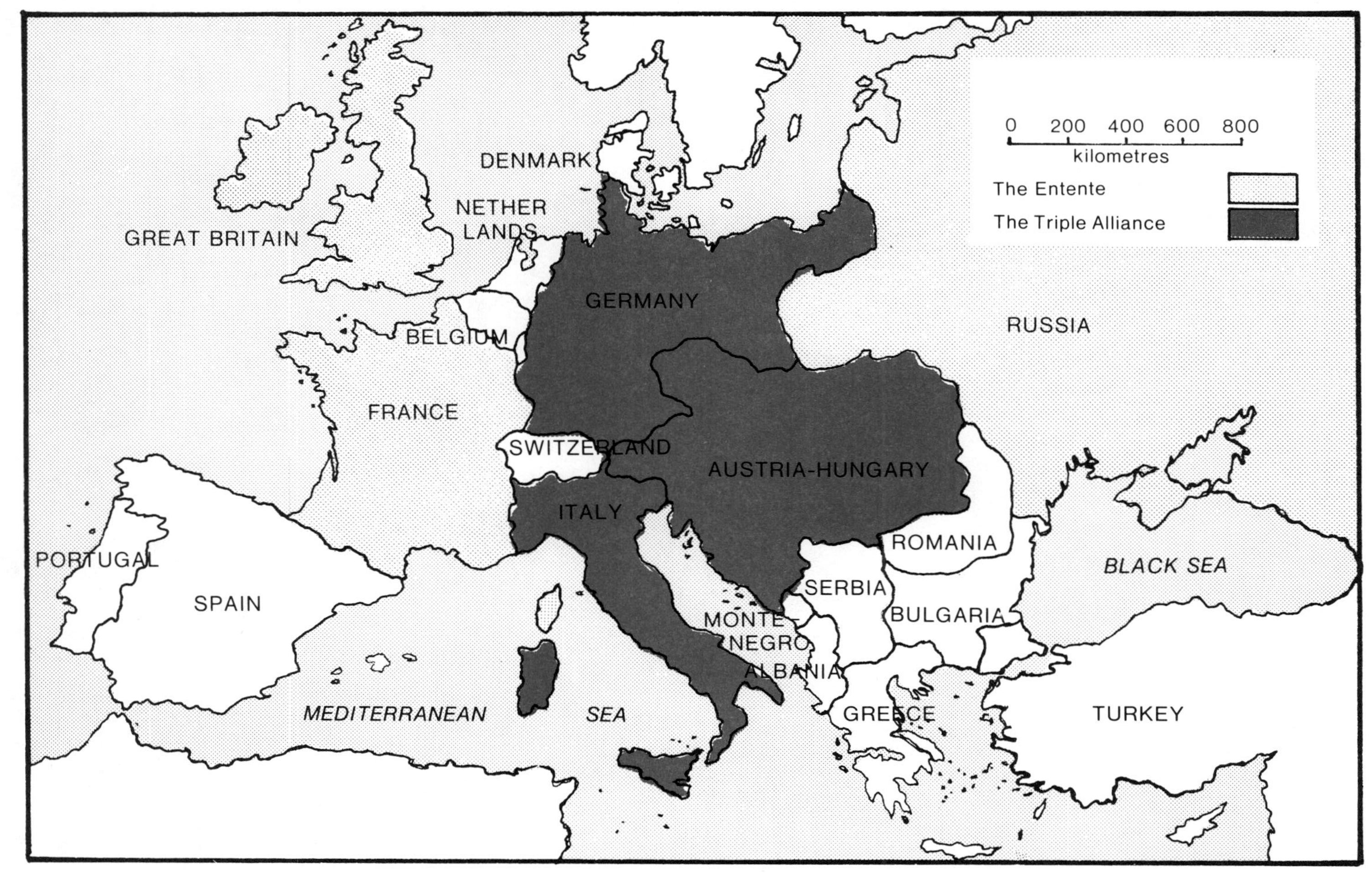
0 200 400 600 800
kilometres
The Entente
The Triple Alliance
DENMARK
GREAT BRITAIN
NETHER LANDS
GERMANY
RUSSIA
BELGIUM
FRANCE
SWITZERLAND
AUSTRIA-HUNGARY
ITALY
ROMANIA
BLACK SEA
PORTUGAL
SPAIN
SERBIA
BULGARIA
MONTE-NEGRO
ALBANIA
MEDITERRANEAN SEA
GREECE
TURKEY

The shortest path to France was directly across the German-French border. However, this area is very hilly and wooded, making transportation very slow. At the same time, the bulk of the French army naturally waited in this area.

To the northwest, through Belgium, the land was ideal for warfare. It was flat, well suited for quick transportation and lightly defended by the French. The Schlieffen plan was designed to send the bulk of the German army through Belgium. It would then swing west of Paris and surround the French armies on the border. The plan's success depended on speed and timing.

Unfortunately for Germany, the commander-in-chief, Von Moltke, made the right wing of the army weaker than the plan called for it to be. At the same time, the German invasion of Belgium quickly brought the British army into action. With the lights of Paris in sight, the German attack slowed down and stopped. The only chance for a short, quick war had vanished. Each side now dug in for a long conflict. From the mountains in the east to the English Channel on the west, the two sides stood in trenches and faced each other across a narrow gap called "no-man's land."

TRENCH WARFARE

The two warring sides prepared for a long conflict. The base of operations became the trench. As the war progressed, trench construction developed into a fine art. For the next four years, soldiers of both armies ate, slept and fought in such trenches.

Canadian soldiers in a trench.

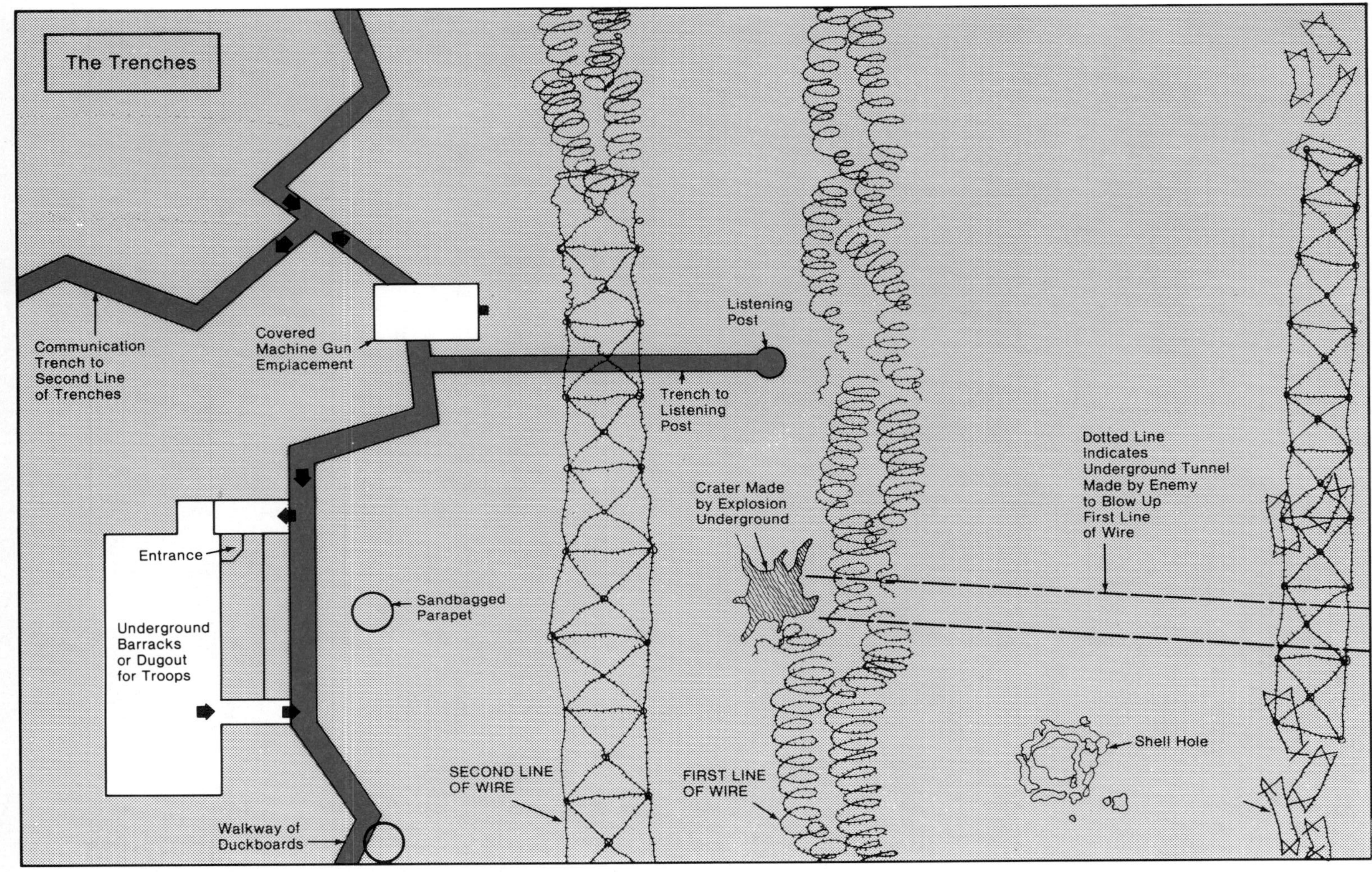
The Trenches
Communication Trench to Second Line of Trenches
Covered Machine Gun Emplacement
Listening Post
Trench to Listening Post
Entrance
Underground Barracks or Dugout for Troops
Sandbagged Parapet
Walkway of Duckboards
SECOND LINE OF WIRE
Crater Made by Explosion Underground
FIRST LINE OF WIRE
Dotted Line Indicates Underground Tunnel Made by Enemy to Blow Up First Line of Wire
Shell Hole

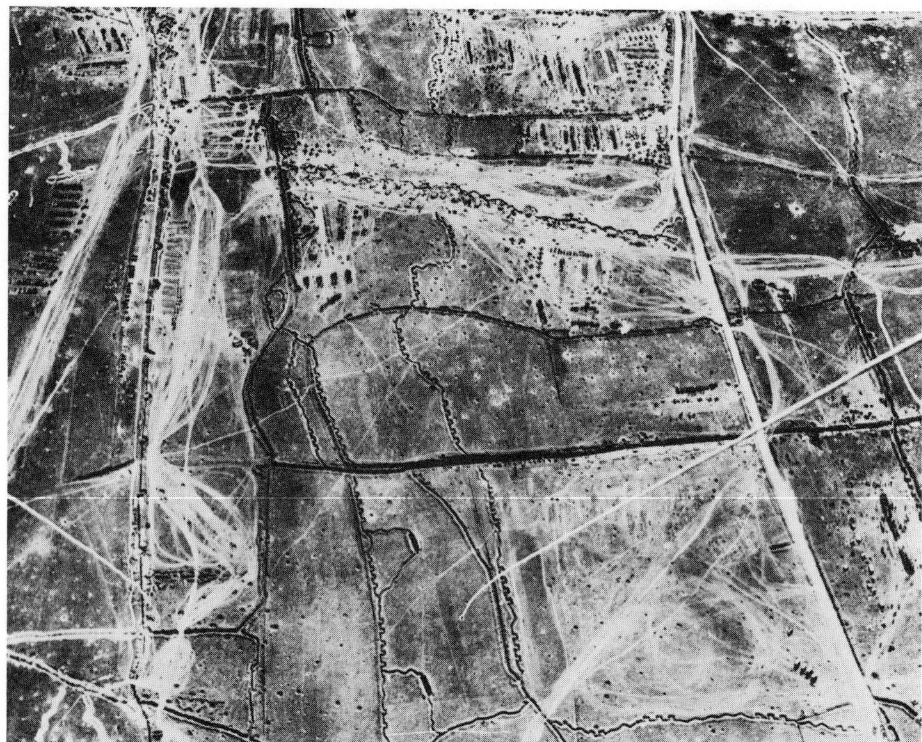

The trench lines at Vimy Ridge in 1917. What details can you observe about trench construction? Can you suggest reasons for this method of construction?

In cold, wet weather, the trenches became slimy, water-logged, muddy pits. The water often rose to waist level. The trenches became infested with flies, rats and other disease-carrying parasites. The stench of decaying corpses and garbage often became unbearable. Often, soldiers had to endure weeks or even months without washing. In such conditions, even small wounds became dangerous and subject to infection and gangrene.

> The familiar trench smell of 1915–1917 still haunts my nostrils; compounded of stagnant mud, latrine buckets, chloride of lime, unburied or half-buried corpses, rotting sandbags, stale human sweat and fumes. . . .

Clothing usually crawled with lice, the food was monotonous — bread and corned beef. Frosty weather, though uncomfortable, helped by freezing the mud. Even so, the frozen clods thrown up by shells could be as dangerous as shrapnel.

Often the opposing trenches were only 25 to 100 m apart. The voices and movements of the enemy were clearly heard. Night attacks were common, but at such close range, the weapons might consist of clubs or knives. Dawn was the usual time for major attacks and "going over the top." Some soldiers prepared themselves for this ordeal by convincing themselves they would soon be killed. One soldier repeated to himself, "In 20 minutes, I'll be dead; in 15 minutes I'll be dead. . . ."

Attackers were cut down by a deadly hail of machine-gun fire, explosive shells and shrapnel. Some became entangled in barbed wire. Only a few reached the enemy trenches. If the attack failed, those who were badly wounded might be left lying for days in "no-man's land," dying slowly.

Many soldiers who were subject to these conditions became "shell-shock" victims. Physically, they were unharmed, but they suffered nervous breakdowns and were no longer fit for fighting.

THE WAR AT SEA

As the war began, Britain was still considered the greatest naval power in the world. The German navy, however, had made great strides in the decade before the war. Their ships were large and efficient. Unlike most British ships, they were made entirely of steel. Control of the seas was vital for Britain. Food and armaments arrived by ship. At the same time, a strong British navy could blockade Germany.

Both sides knew the importance of sea power. They could not risk the destruction of their entire navies in open sea battles. Each side used caution in sending its ships out for action. In fact, there was only one major sea battle in the entire war. The rival fleets met near Jutland on the Danish coast on May 31, 1916. In the battle itself, both sides fought fiercely and skilfully. The German navy did more damage than it suffered. However, it retreated to port after the battle. Although both sides could claim victory, the German navy never again came out of port.

The Germans answered the British blockade with submarine warfare. This was the single greatest threat to British shipping. By July, 1915, some 200 British merchant ships had been sunk by submarines. By 1916 they were sinking 160 ships a month. Germany declared all waters around Britain a war zone. Even neutral ships were in danger. In 1915 the passenger ship *Lusitania* was torpedoed off the coast of Ireland. Over 1200 people died, including 124 Americans. Public opinion in the United States was outraged. It was a factor in bringing the Americans into the war in 1917.

The British blockade of Germany worked well. By 1918 there was a desperate shortage of food in Germany and Austria. Many civilians died of malnutrition as a direct result of lack of vegetables, meat, milk, butter and other essentials.

WAR IN THE AIR

At the start of the war, airplanes were used mostly for reconnaissance. The pilots looked for and reported signs of enemy troop movement. Opposing pilots were, in fact, quite friendly and even waved at each other. This attitude soon stopped. Pilots began to bring up pistols and rifles and shoot at each other. When they mounted machine guns, the first fighter planes were born.

The German air force had several advantages at first. They had more airplanes than Britain and France combined. They also developed more complex weapons. One danger of firing a machine gun was that you might knock out your own propeller.

Billy Bishop in 1917.

The German Fokker airplane had a machine gun timed so that the bullets would not hit the propeller blades.

The common strategy in air battles was the "dog-fight," in which squadrons of planes attacked each other. The objective in these "dogfights" was to attack the enemy from behind or come at him directly out of the sun, so that he would be blinded. There were no parachutes to save the unfortunate pilots who were hit or had run out of ammunition.

Great aces such as Manfred Von Richthofen of Germany and Billy Bishop of Canada were a special breed. On the ground, they could be courteous and chivalrous, while in the air they were ruthlessly efficient. They were also prepared to face death. A French pilot, Charles Nungesser, suffered 17 wounds that left him with one bad leg, an artificial jaw and gold teeth. He had to be lifted into his plane and flew it with only one leg.

Pilots did not suffer the mud of the trenches. They had good food and clean beds, but they also had the highest death rate of any of the services. The average life span of a flier in 1916 was only three weeks.

THE TOP ACES

British	French	German
Edward Mannock (73)*	Rene Fonck (75)	Manfred von Richthofen (80)
Billy Bishop (Canadian) (72)	Georges Guynemer (54)	Ernst Udet (62)

**refers to number of hits*

Of this list, Bishop, Fonck and Udet survived the war.

Air aces were the "knights of the air" and the first heroes of war. They were instantly recognized everywhere and always received special treatment.

Many Canadians excelled as pilots. By the end of the war, almost 33 percent of the British air force were Canadians. Besides Bishop, other Canadians who gained fame as fliers included Raymond Collishaw, William Barker, and Roy Brown, who, it is generally agreed, shot down Germany's "Red Baron," Manfred von Richthofen.

CANADIANS AT WAR

When Great Britain declared war on Germany on August 4, 1914, Canada, as a member of the empire, was automatically at war. Above and beyond this duty, Canadians , both French and English, rushed to Britain's support.

> Canada is in it to the end. She will not stop until "Rule Britannia" and "The Maple Leaf" sound on the streets of Berlin. One contingent has gone, another is in the course of preparation; and they will all go gladly with the same spirit of patriotic determination. It is Britain's war and it is Canada's war.
>
> Premier Hearst of Ontario, 1914

> There are no longer French Canadians and English Canadians. Only one race now exists, united by the closest bonds in a common cause.
>
> *La Patrie*, 1914

Major Jack's painting of Canadian forces in action.

At the beginning of the war, Canada's army consisted of only 3000 men. By October over 33 000 volunteers were training near Quebec City. Over the next four years, out of a small population of eight million, Canadians enlisted in the following numbers:

1914—59 144
1915—158 859
1916—176 919
1917—63 611

By the war's end, over 600 000 Canadians had served in the armed forces, of whom 425 000 went overseas.

In the spring of 1915, the first Canadian troops, the Princess Patricia's Light Infantry Regiment entered the war. Within weeks they suffered the first gas attack of the war at Ypres.

Gas was one of the deadliest weapons introduced in the war. There were two basic types, chlorine and mustard. Chlorine gas killed by suffocation. Mustard gas, which was invisible was more terrible. This gas caused severe burns on the skin and respiratory tract. It also caused blindness.

Of all the troops at Ypres, only the Canadians stood their ground. Ypres was the first of the battles in which Canadians won great fame as soldiers.

> Suddenly we saw the gas rolling up in a brownish-yellow bank. It was between four and twelve feet high and it wouldn't rise higher unless it was pulled up by the wind.
>
> We saw the French-Africans running away, choked with gas, not as a body, but as individuals. We paid no attention to them. We were sorry for them.
>
> I went over to where the line had been broken and where there was confusion. No Canadian troops were running.
>
> The gas was dreadful and suffering was immediate. The only thing we could do was soak our handkerchiefs in urine and hold them over our noses.
>
> Thousands were lying around gasping and crying. They were being drowned by the gas. They didn't know how to protect themselves.
>
> But we held our position.

THE BATTLE OF THE SOMME

In 1916 the three Canadian divisions in Europe were organized as the Canadian Corps. They still fought under the British command, with General Sir Julian Byng at their head.

Soon after, they participated in one of the most tragic battles of the war, the Battle of the Somme. Under General Douglas Haig, British and French troops launched an attack near the River Somme. For days British guns pounded the German positions. Haig was certain that nothing could survive the shelling and that advance would be simple. However, the Germans had known of the attack for a long time and had dug in. As the British attacked, they were met with devastating fire. They fell by the thousands. Some were killed in their own trenches, some in no-man's land, some at the enemy wire. Only a few reached the enemy lines, where they were driven back or killed.

The Newfoundland regiment fighting with the British was destroyed in less than half an hour. Each year on Commemoration Day, July 1, Newfoundland families still mourn their losses from this battle.

By the end of the first day alone, 60 000 British troops had fallen. It was the worst disaster in the history of British warfare. But it was only the beginning. Haig refused to give up his plan and continued to pour troops head-on against the German lines. The slaughter continued without any real gain by either side. When the attack was finally called off five months later, the toll proved frightful. The list of casualties stood at over one million: 420 000 British, 200 000 French and 450 000 Germans. Of the British total, 55 000 were Canadians.

VIMY RIDGE

Canadians continued to fight well in other major encounters in the war. Their crowning glory came on Easter Monday, 1917, at Vimy Ridge. Vimy Ridge was a point of high ground held by the Germans. It commanded the whole countryside around it. It was impossible to break through the German line in this area without first capturing the ridge. Countless Allied attacks on it had failed. The Germans had fortified the ridge with trenches, pillboxes, dugouts and heavy guns.

The task of taking the ridge was given to the Canadians. With sleet driving at their backs, four Canadian divisions charged Vimy Ridge on April 9.

A tank in No Man's Land. What problems might men and machinery encounter when trying to cross this area? What would be the long-term effects of this war on the soil?

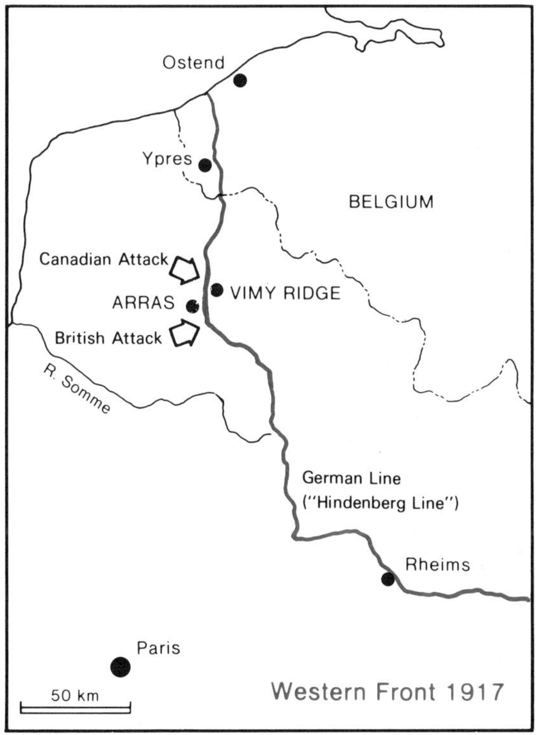

It was a cold grey morning but the visibility was good and I could see far over the waste of desolation which was our battlefield. Shells were still falling up front, but the rear areas seemed deserted, save for some batches of prisoners hastening to the cages, and some walking wounded.

But at zero hour all this was changed. The barren earth erupted humanity. From dugouts, shell holes and trenches men sprang into action, fell into artillery formations, and advanced to the ridge — every division of the Corps moved forward together. It was Canada from the Atlantic to the Pacific on parade. I thought then, and I think today, that in those few minutes I witnessed the birth of a nation.

Brigadier General Alex Ross

By noon Canadian soldiers under the command of a Canadian, Major-General Arthur Currie, had taken Vimy Ridge.

1917 proved to be a fateful year and the turning point in the war. A communist revolution in Russia was successful, and Russia pulled out of the war. This might have been disastrous for the Allies; however, in the same year, the United States entered the war. The injection of fresh American troops into the conflict proved to be decisive.

Canadian forces attacking Vimy Ridge.

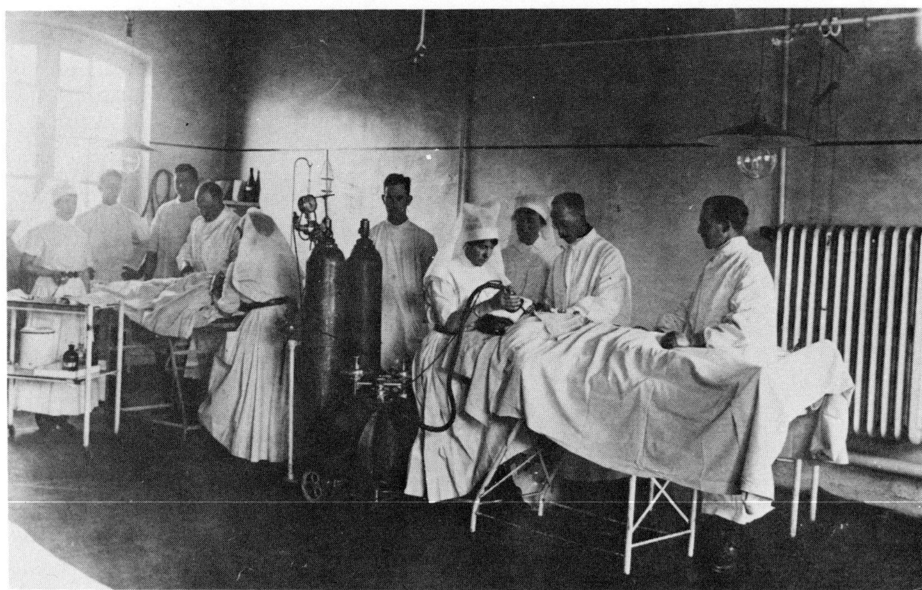

A field hospital behind the lines. Doctors and nurses often worked around the clock on the casualties of war.

In the last stages of the war, Canada continued to play a major role in the fighting. Canadian troops were often found spearheading assaults on German positions. When the Germans saw the Canadians coming, they prepared for the worst.

THE WAR ENDS

At last, on November 11, 1918, at 11:00, the armistice ending the war was signed and the slaughter came to an end.

> I've always thought that the Canadian nation was, in fact, born on the battlefields of Europe. I'm sure that that's true, that the fierce pride developed in the Canadians in their own identity, in their own nationhood, was a very real thing, and it survived over into the peace. Whenever they give the Canadians a chance to show their identity or to be proud of their identity, they are, and they always rise to the occasion.

The cost was high. Sixty-three thousand Canadians had lost their lives. Another 175 000 were wounded. Each country involved in the war suffered great losses. In money terms alone, the war cost the staggering sum of $10 million *per hour*. The loss of human resources was, of course, more serious.

THE DEAD

Allies		Central Powers	
France	1 600 000	Germany	2 600 000
British Empire	1 100 000	Austria	1 700 000
Russia	3 600 000	Turkey	600 000
Italy	700 000		
United States	120 000		
Serbia	1 100 000		
		Total Dead	**13 220 000**

An additional 20 million were seriously wounded. The dead and wounded were young men and women in the prime of life. They became known as the "lost generation." Their energies would be badly missed in the future.

CANADA ON THE HOME FRONT

On the home front, Canada's contribution to the war was as important as that made on the battlefield. Canadian industries immediately switched over to war production. Starting from almost nothing, Canada's factories were producing 33 percent of the shells fired by the British army in 1917. Factories producing airplane parts and high explosives were built in almost 100 different Canadian centres. Maritime dockyards built merchant ships. These replaced the ships lost to submarine attacks. Throughout the war, Canada supplied most of the food consumed by Great Britain and the British armies.

The huge cost of this effort was estimated at $400 for every person in Canada. It was paid in two ways. Much of it was raised through the purchase of government bonds. This still left Canada facing a huge debt. The government turned to taxation to meet the problem. The first tax was the business profits war tax. This was a tax placed on profits made by manufacturers on war contracts. A second tax was in the form of a sales tax on consumer goods. The third and most important step was the Income War Tax Act of 1917. This placed, for the first time in Canada, a tax on income. Canadians have been paying income tax ever since.

The issue of compulsory military service (conscription) in 1917 (see Unit 4, Chapter 11) created a serious political and social crisis. The issue sharply divided English and French in Canada. It left bitter memories long after the war had ended.

THE ROLE OF WOMEN

As the men went off to fight overseas, the jobs they had left in the factories were often taken over by women. By 1918 over 30 000 women were employed in key jobs producing supplies for the war effort. The important role played by women in this war effort forced society to change its attitude toward them.

For years women had been demanding political rights. Now, as a result of the war, men for the first time were willing to listen. In 1918 Parliament passed a bill that gave women in Canada the right to vote in federal elections.

THE EFFECTS OF THE WAR ON CANADA

World War I has been called Canada's greatest crisis. In four short years, on the home front and on the fields of France, Canada matured as a nation. The way of life for most Canadians changed drastically. Those who fought overseas caught glimpses of a different kind of life. They developed a new understanding of what it meant to be Canadian. There would be no return to those leisurely days at the turn of the century.

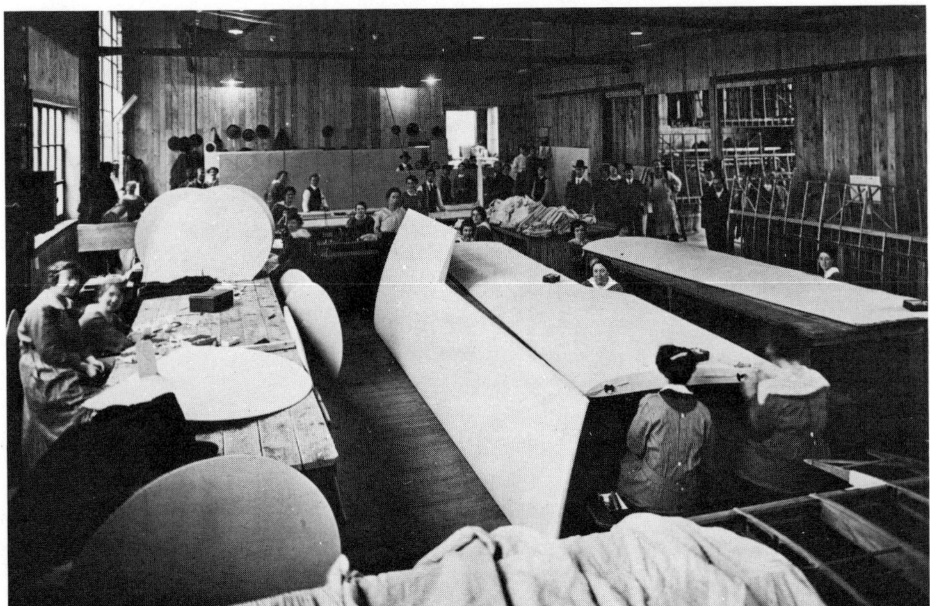

Women building airplanes.

As the Treaty of Versailles was bringing to an end the disastrous war, Canadian soldiers began to return home. Sixty thousand would never again see their country. Many thousands more returned as invalids. Those who did return believed they had fought to make the world "safe for democracy." They hoped that World War I was "the war that would end all wars."

In truth, when the fighting stopped, there was less chance of permanent peace and democracy in the world than before the slaughter began.

The returning soldiers thought they would receive a heroes' welcome. Many were disappointed. After the first celebrations, it was back to normal. Many soldiers found it difficult, after their wartime experiences, to adjust to civilian life. Others who had expected to find their old jobs waiting for them were also disappointed. The Canada they had left in 1914 was greatly changed. The war had unleashed new forces in politics, in economics and in social life. A new generation would have to cope with these changes in the 1920s.

THE ROARING TWENTIES

The usual image of the 1920s is one of high spirits, fun and good times. Terms usually associated with this period are "the Roaring Twenties," "the Aspirin Age" and "the Era of Wonderful Nonsense." Much of this image comes from movies, novels and music. Is this a true impression of the age? Let us look at the main features of this period.

POLITICAL LIFE

In 1919 Sir Wilfrid Laurier died, and his Conservative rival, Sir Robert Borden, who had been prime minister since 1911, retired. Arthur Meighen, a brilliant but cold man, was chosen to succeed Borden as Conservative leader and prime minister. The Liberals chose William Lyon Mackenzie King, a grandson of the man who led the Rebellion of 1837.

At the same time, many people were becoming dissatisfied with the two major parties. Small local parties representing labourers and farmers appeared in

A family swimming and picnic outing in Prince Edward Island.

different parts of the country. One of these, the National Progressive party, enjoyed great success in the federal elections in 1921. With 65 seats, they held the balance of power between the Liberals and Conservatives. For the next few years, they had great influence, especially in the West. With the return of prosperity, however, voters returned to the old parties, and the Progressive movement broke up.

RESULTS OF ELECTIONS IN 1920s

	1921	1925	1926
Liberals	117	101	116
Conservatives	50	116	91
Progressives	64	24	13
Others	4	4	25

WILLIAM LYON MACKENZIE KING

William Lyon Mackenzie King was a short, stocky, plain-looking man. Before his career ended, he proved to be one of the most important prime ministers in Canada's history.

From 1921 to 1930 and from 1935 to 1948 Mackenzie King was Canada's prime minister. His political style was one of extreme caution. He tended to avoid controversy and put off difficult decisions as long as possible. In this way, he hoped to win support from all sides.

King was first elected prime minister in 1921. At forty-seven, he was one of Canada's youngest prime ministers. By the time of his death in 1950, he was famous around the world as the man who had been prime minister longer (21 years) than any other person in the history of English-speaking peoples.

Despite his world fame, Mackenzie King led a very private life. He never married, and although he had many women friends, he seems to have had few romantic interests. King was also a mystic. He felt he was being "guided from above" and often attended seances. He believed he received advice from his mother's ghost. It may be unsettling to many Canadians to realize that some of King's important decisions, especially during World War II, were made after consulting the "spirits."

Mackenzie King

THE ECONOMIC BOOM

Just before the end of the 1920s, experts were announcing that the economy had reached "a permanent plateau of prosperity." The president of the United States, Herbert Hoover, predicted that "we shall soon, with the help of God, be in sight of the day when poverty will be banished from this nation." This tide of optimism swept into Canada as well. Was the optimism realistic, or were Canadians living in a dream world?

Consider these developments. World War I created thousands of new jobs and caused industry to expand. Once the war ended, businesses began to convert to peacetime production. Factories that had been building guns, bombs, tanks and airplanes returned to making stoves, sewing machines and automobiles. During the war, while the men were fighting in

Europe, many factory jobs were taken by women. Employers soon found that women could handle many factory jobs as well as men. They also found they could appeal to the women's patriotic spirit and so pay them lower wages.

When the war ended, these conditions continued, and many soldiers returned home to find no jobs awaiting them. A minor depression resulted in 1920. As unemployment increased, wages and prices fell sharply. Strikes broke out in many parts of the country.

One such strike took place in Winnipeg and affected workers in almost every trade. It was brought to an end only after a riot occurred and the Mounties were called into action.

By 1922 the slump was over, and consumers were scrambling to buy new products. The result was an upward spiral in the economy. Actually, upward and downward spirals are quite common in our system of free enterprise. Economists tell us that if we were to chart our economy over a long period of time, it would not look at all like a straight line. It would look instead like a wave with peaks (economic growth) and valleys (recessions).

This is quite normal. The problem is to prevent a recession from becoming a full-scale depression. We will learn later in this chapter just how such a depression developed.

How does such a spiral begin? If we look at the early 1920s, we can see that there was a great demand for consumer goods. To meet this demand, there was

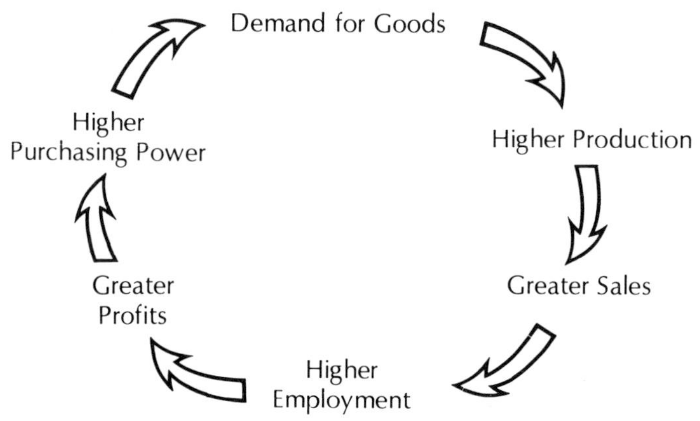

The Model "T" assembly line.

increased production, and therefore, greater sales and more jobs. A by-product of this was greater profit for the owner and more money in the hands of the workers. With this money, the workers continued to buy consumer goods. Thus, a spiral was created, as shown above.

A measure of the economic boom of the 1920s can be seen in the growth of Canadian industry.

	Prewar (1911)	1928
Population	7.2 million	9.7 million
Wheat exports	$45.5 million	$352.1 million
Mineral exports	$103.2 million	$285 million
Manufacturing	$1 165.9 million	$3 769.8 million
Automobiles registered	22 000	1 100 000

Canadian wheat, minerals and pulp and paper reached record sales all over the world. By 1930 Canada stood fifth in the world in the value of her exports.

THE RADIO AND AIRPLANE

The automobile, the radio and the airplane became the great symbols of the 1920s.

Radio The radio brought to Canada the age of instant news and instant entertainment. The first radio station in North America was KDKA in Pittsburgh. Within a short time, however, radio stations spread all over Canada. One of Canada's great traditions, "Hockey Night in Canada," was first broadcast in 1923. Soon Foster Hewitt's familiar "he shoots, he scores" became part of Canadian culture.

By the end of the decade, there were 79 radio stations piping information and entertainment to 300 000 Canadian homes. The most popular entertainers of the period were singers such as Bing Crosby and Rudy Vallee and comedians such as Amos 'n' Andy. Jazz, the music of the twenties, was broadcast. Nonsense songs such as "Yes, We Have No Bananas" also became favourites.

The Airplane The 1920s can also be called the golden age of flight for Canada. It was in the air that young Canadians proved that they were the equals of anyone in the world. Canada produced great flying heroes both before and during World War I. J.A.D. McCurdy, Billy Bishop and Roy Brown were known around the world for their exploits.

In the 1920s, it was Canada's daring bush pilots who carried on the country's great flying tradition. Led by Wilfred "Wop" May, "Punch" Dickins and "Doc" Oaks, the bush pilots were truly responsible for opening up the Canadian North. By 1929 over 250 bush planes were bringing people, food, medical supplies and mail to distant arctic outposts under extremely difficult conditions. Without such daring people, the treasures of the North would have remained beyond our reach.

MORE ACHIEVEMENTS OF THE TWENTIES

The decade was also a period of achievements in other fields. In 1918 women were at last granted the right to vote. This overdue action was largely a result of their role in the war effort and their new role in the work force. Between 1921 and 1930, the number of women employed outside the home rose by 40 percent.

Canadian artists also began to paint the Canadian scene in a new style. Painters Frederick Varley and A.Y. Jackson, along with Arthur Lismer, Lawren Harris, Frank Carmichael, J.E.H. Macdonald and Franz Johnston, made the "Group of Seven" famous throughout the world.

At the same time, Canadians were making their mark in the world of science. In 1922 Dr. Frederick Banting conquered the deadly disease of diabetes with his discovery of insulin. This achievement brought Banting a Nobel Prize.

THE STOCK MARKET

Another indicator of economic boom is the stock market. Most people are confused by the stock market. Have you ever looked at a stock market page? Do you understand the figures, or are you confused by them, like most Canadians?

Actually, the principle of the stock market is quite simple. It is a place where shares in private companies are bought and sold. The buying and selling is done by stockbrokers, who act as agents for private individuals.

HOUSEHOLD DUTIES
REFRIGERATORS
SAVE FOOD!
CONSERVE ICE!
Made to Fill the Need For a Large-Capacity Refrigerator
63-677
45.00
63-677 Ice is nature's refrigerant, but if it is to keep food pure and fresh it must have the help of an efficient refrigerator. One that conserves ice as well as protects food from contamination enables you to effect a double saving and gives you the best return for your money. Made to our own specifications and built on the best scientific principles with carefully insulated walls, this large-size Refrigerator is most suitable where large quantities of provisions must be kept fresh. The refrigeration system is of the direct air-cooling type, and the large galvanized iron-lined ice chamber holds about 200 lbs. of ice. Flues are removable. There is ample room for storage in the large provision chamber, which measures 22½ ins. high, 15 ins. deep and 30¾ ins. wide; fitted with two full-depth removable shelves and one half-depth shelf. The cabinet is well made from clear Northern Ash, paneled construction, and is the single-door, front-icing design that does not necessitate high lifting. Finished in Golden color. Hardware is nickel-plated. Selected easy-rolling casters. Refrigerator only, price 45.00

A refrigerator ad from Eaton's catalogue, 1928. From where would the idea for this refrigerator be obtained? How would this refrigerator work? (Photo courtesy of Eaton's Archives.)

Basically, the stock market works in this way: Let us suppose that you, Joan E. Canuck, invented a better mousetrap. You set yourself up in business as Canuck Consolidated Mousetrap Ltd. Soon the world is beating a path to your door. Business is booming, and you want to expand, but you lack cash. One way to get it is to sell a portion of your company to others. If your company is worth $200 000, you might wish to keep half the company for yourself and sell shares in the other half. The total value of the shares will be half the value of your company, or $100 000.

Price per Share	Total Number of Shares	Total Value
$10	10 000	$100 000

So now you have placed these 10 000 shares of Canuck Consolidated Mousetrap for sale in the stock market. A stockbroker will sell them on your behalf (for a fee, of course). Once the shares are on the market, their price may rise or fall. This depends on the demand for the shares. If your company is doing well and selling a great number of mousetraps, it is likely that many people will want to buy the shares in your company. This demand will push up the price of each share and result in a profit for you. Of course, if sales are poor and the demand is not great, the price may drop. You will then lose money.

In the 1920s, stock prices seemed to be constantly rising. Many people saw the prospects of quick wealth and invested their life savings in the market. Indeed, many fortunes were made in just this way.

THE DIRTY THIRTIES

In the summer of 1929, Canadians in all walks of life were looking forward to more happy times, higher wages, good crops and job security. They were prospering. The nation was prospering. Yet within one year, this scene drastically changed. Canada found itself in the grip of a deadly economic depression.

The stock market crash of October, 1929, signalled the end of the boom years. It marked the beginning of what would be known in Canada and around the world as "the hungry thirties."

What happened to cause such a turnabout? Even the experts are not entirely certain to this day. The causes of the Great Depression are very complex. However, we can identify several of them.

THE EXPORT MARKET

Both Canada and the United States are industrialized nations. We rely a great deal on exports to other countries for our wealth. During the 1920s, the countries of Europe were buying our products at record levels. As a result, businesses continued to grow and produce more goods.

Unfortunately, the export markets soon closed. Europe was still recovering from the effects of the war during the 1920s. It relied on American loans. By 1929 the United States had cut off many of these loans. Europe found itself without any buying power.

The effects soon became obvious throughout North America. The economic spiral of the 1920s was now reversed:

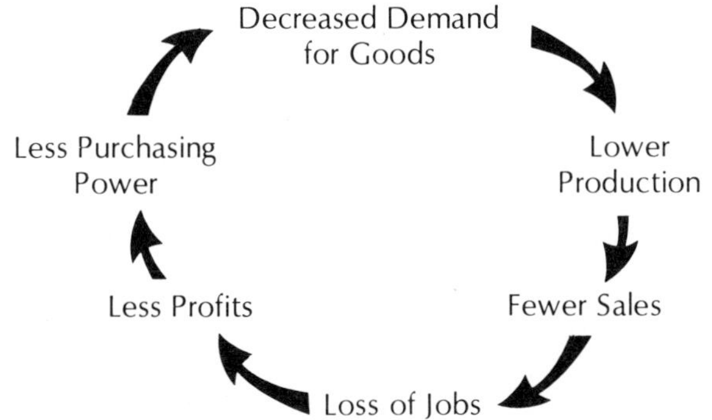

Trade dropped to a fraction of what it had been. Factories found themselves with warehouses full of goods they could not sell. Most cut back production or closed for good, and workers found themselves out of a job. The same effects were felt in the lumber and fishing industries.

THE WHEAT MARKET

The worst suffering was felt in the West, with the collapse of the wheat market. Even during the boom years of the 1920s, the western farmers had not shared in Canada's general prosperity. Despite record wheat sales, competition from foreign producers had kept the price of wheat down. Profits for farmers were low.

WHEAT PRICES (ANNUAL AVERAGES)

1925	1929	1930	1931	1932	1933	1936
$1.43	1.03	0.67	0.40	0.38	0.75	1.02

The Depression brought tragedy to wheat producers. Competition from the United States, the Soviet Union, Australia and Argentina continued to be stiff. At the same time, Europe no longer had the money to buy our wheat. As a result, wheat prices fell from $1.03 per bushel in 1929 to 38 cents in 1932. The West faced ruin. The results were felt across the country.

THE STOCK MARKET

During the 1920s, the symbol of prosperity was the stock market. With prices always rising, investing in the stock market seemed a guaranteed path to instant wealth.

Few people were taking into account the risks involved in gambling on stocks. Investors were so sure that stocks would always rise that they even invested money they did not have. They would buy stocks with a down payment as low as 20 percent. They then paid for the rest with a loan from their broker or from the bank. This was called buying on margin. These investors hoped to make a quick profit on the market, pay back their loan and still have a tidy profit left over.

When the stock market began to fall in October, 1929, panic set in. The stampede soon started. Everyone wanted to sell their stocks before prices dropped further. This panic selling ruined stockholders. It also ruined stockbrokers and banks who had loaned out money for the purchase of stocks.

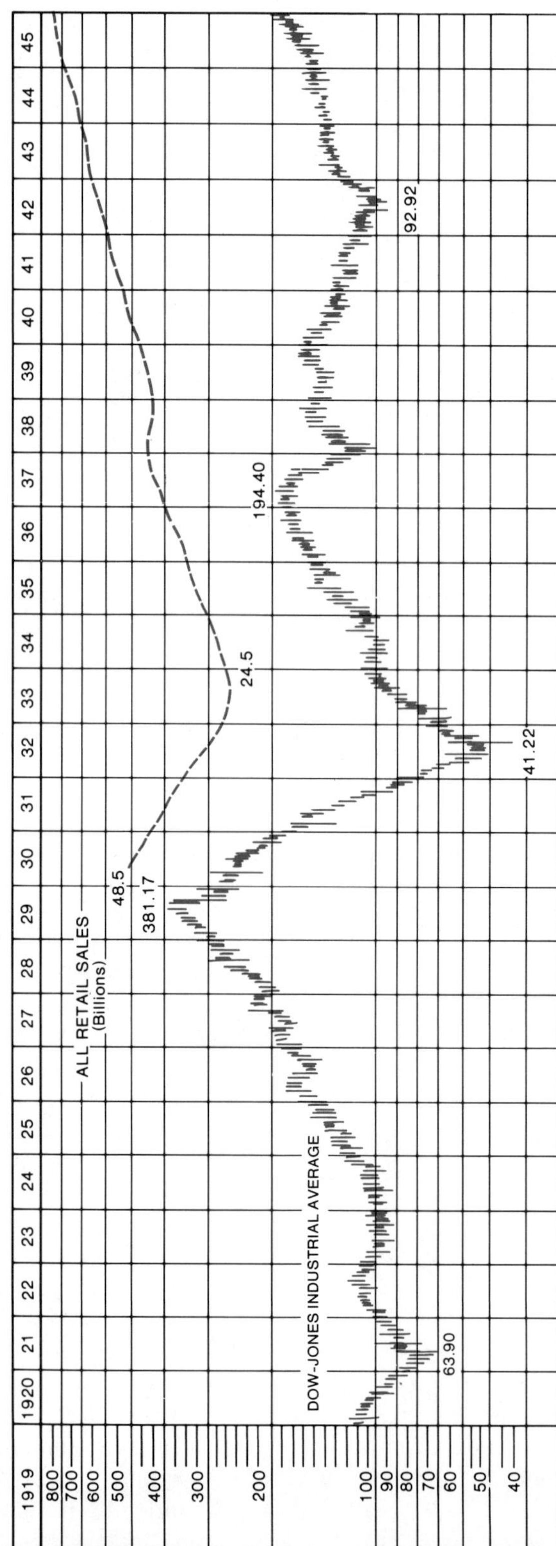

Chart of Stock Market, 1920-1945

STOCK PRICES

	1929		1932	
	High	Low	High	Low
American Telephone & Telegraph	310¼	193¼	137⅜	69¾
General Electric	403	168⅛	130⅝	42½
General Motors	91¾	33½	24⅝	7⅝
National Cash Register	148¾	59	18¾	6¼
Remington Rand	57¾	20⅜	7½	1
Sears, Roebuck	181	80	37⅜	9⅞
United States Steel	261¾	150	52⅝	21¼

EFFECTS OF THE DEPRESSION

If the causes of the Great Depression are hard to discover, the effects are very evident. They can best be seen in the following charts (below and page 146):

PER CAPITA INCOMES, 1928–29 TO 1933, BY PROVINCE

	1928–29 average $ per capita	1933 average $ per capita	Percentage decrease
Nova Scotia	322	207	36
New Brunswick	292	180	39
Prince Edward Island	278	154	45
Quebec	391	220	44
Ontario	549	310	44
Manitoba	466	240	49
Saskatchewan	478	135	72
Alberta	548	212	61
British Columbia	594	314	47
Canada	471	247	48

The statistics do not really show the human suffering during this period. The Depression affected everyone — rich, middle class and poor. Of course, not everyone went broke. There were a lucky few who timed things just right and sold their stocks or businesses before the crash. As prices shot downward, they were even better off than before the Depression.

Most were not so fortunate. There were cases of former millionaires, ruined by the crash, who were forced to live by selling apples or pencils in the street. Others resorted to shining shoes, singing, dancing or begging for enough money to live on.

Many others were worse off still. They could get no jobs at all. At this time in Canada, there was no such thing as unemployment insurance or welfare. Those without jobs had to look out for themselves. Thousands of jobless men took up the practice of "riding the rails." These men jumped on freight trains and travelled back and forth across Canada looking for work, usually without success.

Many relied on relatives who were better off. Others depended on charitable agencies for handouts of food, clothing and shelter. This was called "living on the pogey." Some became so desperate that they asked to be arrested and sent to jail where they received food and shelter.

In the West, the price of wheat fell so low that farmers burned their grain as fuel. It was cheaper than buying regular fuel. Farmers who could not afford gasoline hitched their cars to horses. These became known as "Bennett buggies." R.B. Bennett was prime minister during this period.

To make matters worse, the West suffered through one of the worst periods of drought in its history. In

One of the many farms abandoned on the prairies during the 1930s.

Unemployment Statistics (1929-1943)

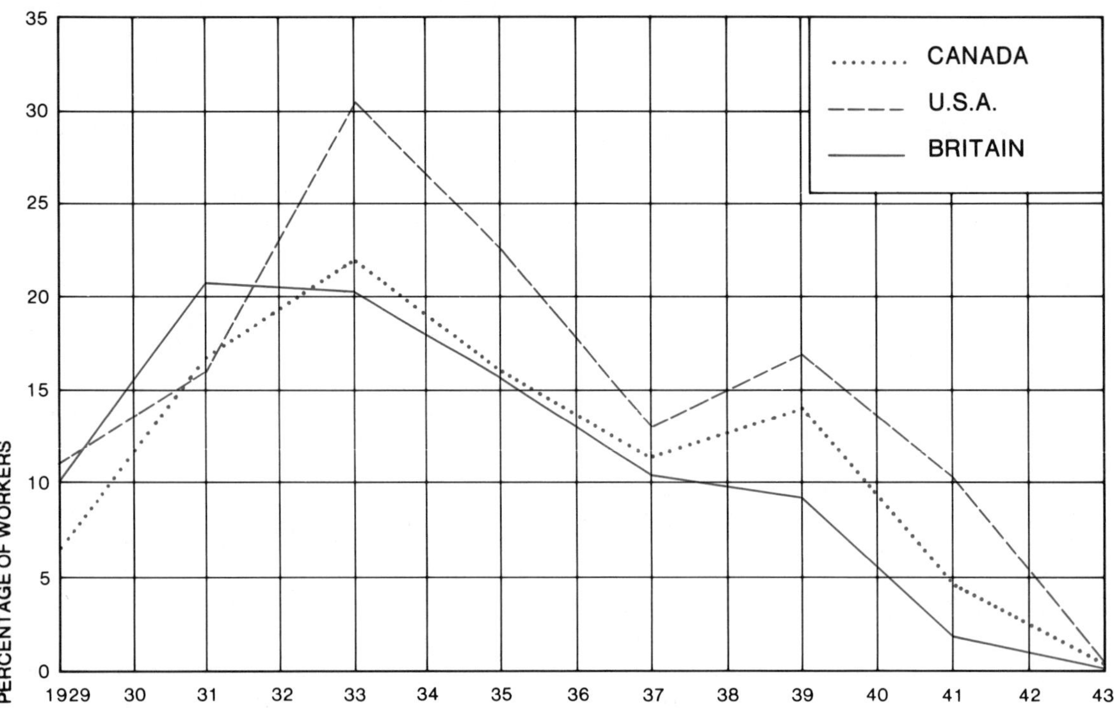

1931 and in the years from 1933 to 1937, droughts crippled the West. Strong prairie winds then stripped the parched topsoil, carried it high in the air and banked it against fences and houses. Many farmhouses were completely covered. Farms were left as sandy deserts. Thousands of farmers simply left the land.

Author James Gray lived through the Depression and wrote of his experiences in *The Winter Years*:

> We received no cash in relief, and for the first year no clothing whatever was supplied. Relief vouchers covered food, fuel, and rent, and nothing else. But we needed other things—many other things like tobacco and cigarette papers, tooth paste, razor blades, lipstick, face powder, the odd bottle of aspirin, streetcar fare, a movie once a week, a pair of women's stockings once a month, a haircut once a month, and a permanent twice a year. Most people tried to find twenty-five cents a week, every week for a newspaper.
>
> Unexpected needs continually cropped up, like needles and thread, darning wool, a bit of cloth for fancy work, a pattern for remaking a dress, a half-dollar every other month for a cooperative half-keg of beer for a neighbourhood party. . . .
>
> Morale was built by taking the children to the zoo to feed the bears, by taking a streetcar ride downtown to wander through Eaton's and The Bay, as women did by the hundreds just to get away from their rooms for an hour or two.

FIGHTING THE DEPRESSION

When the Depression began, the Liberals, under Mackenzie King, were still in power. In the election of 1930, they were toppled from power by R.B. Bennett and his Conservatives. Bennett's plan to fight the Depression was to raise protective tariffs. He hoped to protect Canadian industry by discouraging foreign imports. He also hoped to use this weapon to force countries to lower their high tariffs. This way he would "blast his way into the markets of the world."

Unfortunately, this program failed. Canadian industry continued its tailspin. Finally, as the election of 1935 drew near, Bennett unveiled his "New Deal." This plan was modelled on that of President Franklin Roosevelt of the United States. Bennett's

"New Deal" proposed to create new laws establishing:

- an eight-hour work day
- minimum wages
- an unemployment insurance plan
- elimination of child labour
- control of prices

The voters were suspicious of Bennett and his program. They felt it was just a trick to win the election: after all, he had not solved Canada's economic problems during his first four years in office. In the election of 1935, the voters swept Bennett out of office and brought back Mackenzie King.

NEW POLITICAL PARTIES

The worsening economy naturally encouraged the growth of new political parties. These parties claimed to have bold new ideas to end the Depression. Two main parties began during the Depression. These were the Social Credit and the CCF.

The Social Credit movement started in Alberta. Its leader was William Aberhart, a school principal and radio preacher. Aberhart claimed that the cause of the Depression was the lack of money circulating in the economy. He proposed to credit every citizen with $25 per month. Of course, this idea was very popular in the cash-starved West. The Social Credit took power in Alberta in 1935. They have remained a powerful party in British Columbia and, to a lesser degree, in Alberta ever since.

THE WAY WE WERE

If you are part of the 75 percent of Canadians too young to remember 1932:

- You could buy large eggs for 29¢ a dozen, a loaf of bread for 5¢, a package of cigarettes for 15¢ and a dozen oranges for 25¢.
- If you needed a car, a new Dodge sedan cost $600, and tires for it were $6.
- A gallon of gas to run your car went for 16¢.
- A new dress cost $4, while women's shoes were a further $2 and a pair of silk stockings sold for 68¢.
- A brand-new six-room house with garage might go for $3000. A dining-room suite cost $50, and a new washing machine went for $50.
- Of course, there was the other side of the coin. A job as a secretary paid $20 a week. A school teacher could expect to earn $1200 a year, a bus driver $1400, a waitress $450 and a farm labourer $215.

A family and their covered wagon on the move in 1933. More than 25% of the population of Canada's wheat belt left their homes during the hard times of the 1930s.

The CCF (Co-operative Commonwealth Federation) was formed in 1932. Its program was stated in the Regina Manifesto of 1932. It called for:

- government ownership of banks, insurance companies and other financial institutions
- government ownership of transportation, communication and power companies
- fair business practices
- fair wages
- unemployment insurance
- social insurance against sickness or accidents
- socialized medicine

This program was supported by farmers, workers and those who favoured socialism. Under J.S. Woodsworth, the CCF became very popular in the West, particularly in Saskatchewan. It has also become a force in national politics. In 1958 the party changed its name to the New Democratic Party.

After 1935 the economy improved very slowly. The onset of World War II in 1939 brought an end to the Depression. With the need for war materials, factories returned to full production. Unemployment dropped. The wheat market recovered. The prosperity cycle began once again. It has continued to this day.

WORLD WAR II

Since the end of World War I, Canada had gradually won her independence from Britain. By 1939 Canada had full power over her own foreign policy. Prime Minister King was determined to use this power on Canada's behalf. He was determined not to rush Canada blindly into another war.

By the late 1930s, it seemed as though a second major war within a generation was likely. Adolf Hitler and his National Socialist (Nazi) Party were busy rebuilding and re-arming Germany. They were also retaking territories Germany lost at the end of World War I.

By 1938 Hitler had taken possession of the Rhineland in western Germany. He had also annexed Austria. Now he was threatening Czechoslovakia. British Prime Minister Neville Chamberlain flew to Munich

KEY EVENTS LEADING TO AN INDEPENDENT CANADIAN FOREIGN POLICY

1918 The Paris Peace Conference. Prime Minister Borden succeeded in having Canada and the other dominions take part in the conference on their own and as members of the British Empire delegation. Each dominion signed the peace treaty. Canada's Parliament approved the treaty separately.

1919 The League of Nations. Canada and the other dominions joined the League of Nations as independent members.

1923 The Halibut Treaty. For the first time, Canada signed an international treaty on its own. Until then a British delegate had attended negotiations and signed agreements on behalf of Britain. This treaty with the United States dealt with fishing in Canada's coastal waters.

1923 The Imperial Conference. Commonwealth members agreed that each member should have the right to negotiate its own international treaties. Prime Minister Mackenzie King insisted that the dominions make their own decisions on both domestic and foreign issues.

1925 Locarno Agreements. Germany and France agreed not to use force to settle disagreements between them. Britain agreed to help either country against aggression by the other. The dominions did not have to accept these terms unless they decided to do so on their own. None of the dominions accepted these terms.

1926 The Balfour Declaration. In it the Commonwealth was described as "autonomous (free) communities within the British Empire, equal in status, in no way subordinate to (inferior to) one another in any aspect of their domestic or external affairs, though united by a common allegiance to the Crown and freely associated as members of the British Commonwealth of nations."

1931 The Statute of Westminster. The dominions were given the power to enact extra-territorial legislation. An act of 1865, which said that in any conflict with colonial law, British law was supreme, was repealed. It also stated that no British law would extend to the dominions.

Note: Britain still retained some authority over Canada after 1931. The Judicial Committee of the Privy Council remained a final court of appeal for some Canadian cases. Amendments to the Canadian Constitution (the BNA Act) required approval of the British parliament until 1982. However, Britain kept these powers only because Canada could not agree on another way of dealing with these issues.

to meet Hitler. He returned to England with a promise from Hitler that the Fuehrer had "no territorial ambitions" in Europe. Chamberlain described the agreement as "peace with honour, peace in our time."

This hope was shattered within months when Hitler annexed Czechoslovakia. The final blow to peace came on September 1, 1939. On that day, German airplanes and tanks launched a crushing attack on Poland. England and France, as Poland's allies, had no choice but to declare war on Germany on September 3.

In 1914, when Britain declared war, Canada had no choice but to join her. In 1939 Canada was free to make her own decision. There seemed little doubt what that decision would be. Yet, as a symbol of her independence, Canada waited a full week before declaring war on Germany.

> I have never doubted that when the fatal moment came, the free spirit of the Canadian people would assert itself in the preservation and defence of freedom, as it did a quarter of a century ago.
>
> William Lyon Mackenzie King, September, 1939

CANADIANS ON THE BATTLEFIELD

At the beginning of the war, Canada's army was ill equipped to fight a major war. The army listed 4000 officers and men. The Royal Canadian Navy counted 1800 men and the largest force, the Royal Canadian Air Force, 4500 men. Yet at the declaration of war, volunteers flocked to enlist. Over 58 000 volunteers were taken in during the first month alone. Many others, including veterans from World War I, were rejected. Indeed, out of a population of 11 million, over one million Canadians saw military service. This total included 21 624 women who served in the WAC (Women's Army Corps).

BLITZKRIEG

In Europe the fall of Poland marked the beginning of a period known as the "phony war." England and France waited for the expected blow, but nothing happened. All winter the French troops waited behind their strong fortifications, the Maginot Line, but no shots were fired.

On April 9, 1940, the "phony war" came to an end. Hitler quickly seized Norway and Denmark. On May 10 Winston Churchill became prime minister of England, promising his people nothing but "blood, toil, tears and sweat." On the same day, Germany invaded Holland, Belgium and France. The German attack was precise and efficient. It was known as a blitzkreig, or lightning attack. 400 000 Allied troops were quickly surrounded and trapped against the sea at Dunkirk. It seemed the end was in sight. Then the "miracle of Dunkirk" occurred. Between May 27 and June 4, almost 350 000 men were rescued from the beaches. Boats of all sizes and shapes manned by English civilians crossed the English Channel. This courageous act saved the British army. Even so, the army had lost much of its equipment. France now lay defenceless.

On June 10 Germany's ally, Italy, declared war on France. On June 22, France surrendered. Britain and her dominions stood alone against Germany.

THE BATTLE OF BRITAIN

Hitler next unleashed the *Luftwaffe*, his air force, against Britain. The Royal Air Force was greatly out-

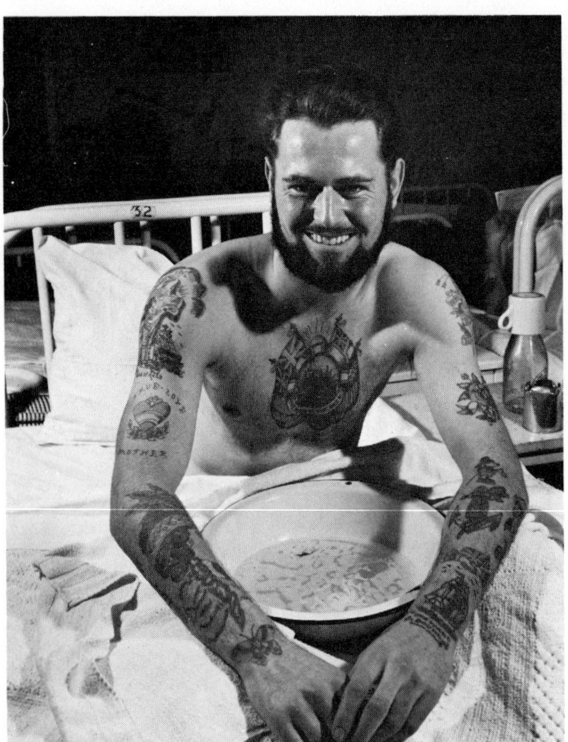

A Canadian sailor recovering after a period of sea duty, proudly displays his tattoo collection. (St. John's, Newfoundland—January, 1943).

numbered. However, with the help of Canadian pilots, it did hold off the German attacks and inflict great damage. The invention of radar was largely responsible for this success. It warned the RAF of coming attacks. The Germans were unaware of this secret. Churchill showered praise on the RAF pilots by declaring, "Never in the field of human endeavour have so many owed so much to so few."

Hitler next ordered his bombers to attack English cities. London, Coventry and Birmingham suffered great losses. However, the German air force continued to suffer many losses. By September 1940 the massive attacks had come to an end. Only the occasional night bombing of cities continued.

THE WAR SPREADS

The war against Germany and Italy spread to North Africa. Here, in early 1941, British troops finally defeated Italian troops in Egypt. Germany sent General Irwin Rommel to the rescue. Rommel defeated the British in a number of daring attacks. The Germans regained much lost territory.

War also came to Greece on October 28, 1940. Mussolini launched his attack expecting easy victory. Once again, however, Hitler had to rescue the Italian army. He sent some of his best troops to Greece. On April 27, 1941, the German army occupied Athens.

One of the major turning points in the war now took place. Hitler, feeling that he had nothing more to fear from Britain, turned to the east. His hatred for the Soviet Union was well known, despite the fact that he had signed a treaty with that country in 1939. On June 22, 1941, Hitler launched a massive attack on the Soviet Union. He expected an easy victory. He told his generals, "We have only to kick in the door and the whole rotten structure of communism will come crashing down."

It was Hitler's greatest mistake. Despite stunning victories at the beginning of the campaign, the German troops soon became bogged down by the Russian winter and heroic resistance from the Russian people. Russia became a huge pit that swallowed some of Germany's finest regiments.

At the same time, on the other side of the world, Germany's ally, Japan, launched a surprise attack on the American fleet at Pearl Harbor. The United States now was committed to war. The invasion of Russia and the attack on Pearl Harbor helped to turn the tide of war against Germany and her allies.

CANADIANS IN ACTION

In December, 1941, the Canadian Army saw its first real action. It took part in the defence of Hong Kong against Japanese attacks. The Canadian position was hopeless. Despite stubborn resistance, Hong Kong fell to the Japanese. Of the 2000 Canadians who took part in the defence, over 500 lost their lives.

Another inactive period for the army followed. In fact, Canadian losses up to this point were light. There were some casualties in the air battles over Europe. Some sailors lost their lives serving in the North Atlantic. As yet, however, there was no repeat of the heavy losses suffered in the trenches in World War I. All this changed in August of 1942.

Canadian soldiers on the beaches at Dieppe.

Since the defeat of France in the summer of 1940, the coastline of Europe had been heavily fortified by the Germans. The Allies were certainly not ready to try an invasion of Europe. However, Britain was being pressured by her new ally, the Soviet Union. The Soviets wanted a new front opened in the west. They felt that this would reduce the huge German build up in the Soviet Union. It would then increase chances for a Soviet victory.

The Dieppe raid was planned mainly as a gesture to the Soviet Union. An attack on the French coastline might also provide useful information for a later invasion. The Dieppe fortifications stood on a cliff overlooking a narrow beach below. The cliff was fortified with pillboxes, barbed wire and heavy guns. In the early dawn light of August 19, 1942, 6000 troops, the great majority of them Canadians, attempted to land on the beach. They immediately came under fire from the waiting Germans. Many never made the beaches. Some penetrated inland but were driven back. In the end, 900 Canadians lay dead, 500 wounded and another 2000 were captured. It was the greatest Canadian disaster of the war.

THE HOME FRONT

Britain's desperate plight in 1940 made an all-out Canadian war effort vital. The War Measures Act of 1914 was still in effect. This gave the government the power to censor the news. It also gave it the power to arrest, imprison and deport people. The government could take over any resources thought necessary for the war effort. Parliament was able to pass several acts that strictly controlled Canadian industry. The production of leather, wool, lumber, steel, aluminum and rubber were regulated. Oil, gasoline and food such as meat, sugar, butter, tea and coffee were rationed. They could be obtained by coupons.

As in World War I, Canadian industry rose to the challenge of supplying the Allies' war needs. Shells, rifles, tanks, airplanes and other army vehicles were turned out in huge volumes. Agricultural production also increased greatly. By 1945 Canada's production had increased to three times its prewar level. Both the Allied cause and Canadian industry benefitted.

This huge war production again created a large debt. Again the answer was to raise income and cor-

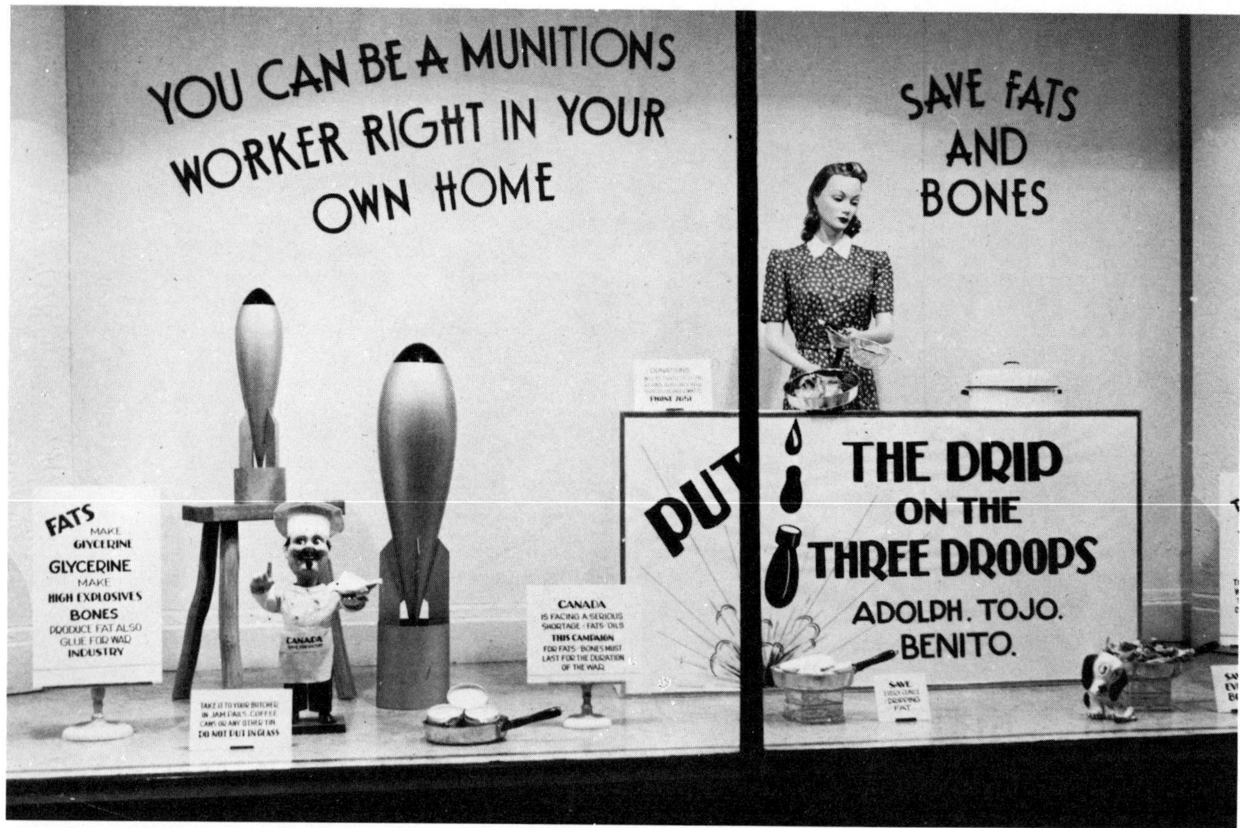

Read these window ads closely. What are they encouraging Canadians to do?

poration taxes. High taxes were also placed on luxury items. The rest of the funds were raised through the sale of Victory Bonds.

THE CONSCRIPTION CRISIS

In the election of 1940, Mackenzie King campaigned on the promise that he would never introduce conscription. In 1917 this issue had bitterly divided Canada. King was determined to avoid such a clash in World War II.

By 1942, however, the prime minister was advised by the military that conscription might be necessary. King turned to public opinion. He called a plebiscite that asked:

> Are you in favour of releasing the government from any obligations arising out of any past commitment restricting the methods of raising men for military service?

Across the whole country, the vote was 64 percent in favour, 36 percent against. However, in the Province of Quebec, the results were 72 percent against and only 28 percent in favour. To soothe French-Canadian feelings, King described his policy as "conscription if necessary but not necessarily conscription." He also said that conscripts would be used for home defence. They would not be sent to fight overseas.

In 1944 a second conscription crisis occurred. By 1944 few men were volunteering for overseas service. Prime Minister King's hand was forced. He decided to send conscripts overseas. In all, 13 000 conscripts served overseas. Feelings in Quebec were very bitter. However, a respected French-Canadian member of Parliament, Louis St. Laurent, helped to calm the situation. This time, violence was avoided.

A shortage of manpower during the war opened up new fields of employment for women. Women held jobs in the non-combative armed forces and in manufacturing for the war effort.

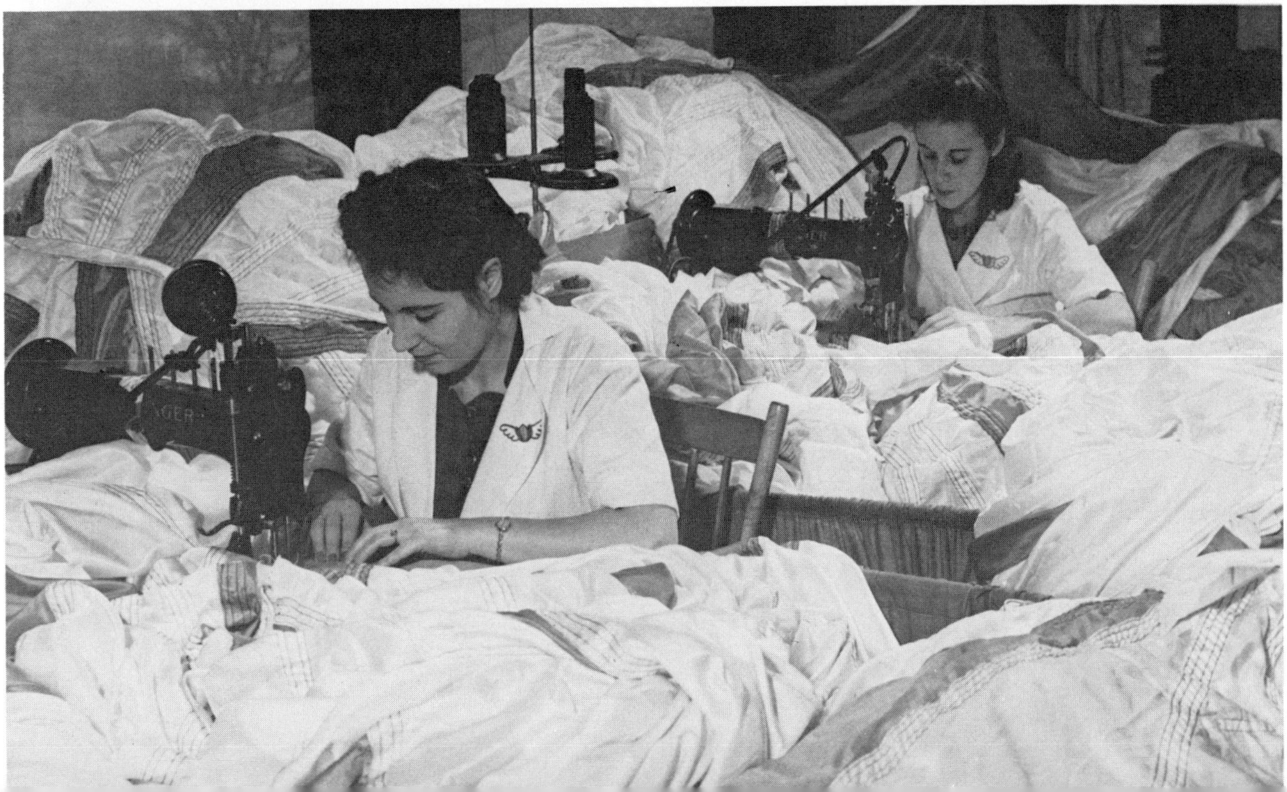

THE TREATMENT OF JAPANESE-CANADIANS

World War II saw many acts of courage and goodwill on the part of Canadians. It also witnessed one of the most shameful acts in Canadian history. On December 7, 1941, Japan attacked American and British forces at Pearl Harbor, in Hawaii, and in the Far East. Canada immediately declared war on Japan, along with Britain and the United States.

In June, 1942, Japanese forces landed on the Aleutian Islands, near Alaska. At the same time, a Japanese submarine was spotted near Vancouver Island. A wave of anti-Japanese hysteria swept British Columbia. About 24 000 Japanese immigrants had settled in that province. Canadian citizens of Japanese origin, many of them Canadian-born, now were considered threats to national security.

The Japanese were removed from British Columbia. Many were placed in internment camps inland. Others were sent to various part of Canada. Their properties were sold publicly for bargain prices, and they were forced to start a new life. The laws against the Japanese were finally lifted in 1947.

THE TIDE CHANGES

The year 1943 saw the changing tide of war favour the Allies. In North Africa, British troops under Field Marshal Montgomery defeated Rommel's Afrika Korps. By this time, American troops under Dwight Eisenhower had also landed in Africa.

In Russia, too, the Germans met disaster. After months of savage fighting, Russian troops trapped a huge German army of over a quarter of a million men. At the end of the battle, only 91 000 Germans survived to be taken prisoner. The retreat from the east had begun.

On July 10, 1943, Allied forces began their attack on Europe by landing in Sicily. The drive up the boot of Italy involved tough fighting. After long periods of inactivity, the Canadian army got its fill of battle.

At Ortona, on the east coast of Italy, Canadians fought a bitter month-long battle. In the mud of winter, the Germans put up a hard resistance. They had to be dislodged street by street and house by house. In this battle, the French-Canadian unit, the Royal 22nd Regiment (the "Vandoos"), greatly distinguished themselves. One correspondent wrote:

> After Ortona Canadians became the acknowledged experts on street fighting. For the rest of the war, officers who had fought there toured Allied military schools lecturing on street fighting. Ortona is a small piece of Canadian history.

For the rest of the war, Canadians continued to play prominent roles wherever major battles were fought. They penetrated the last German defences in Italy.

Japanese camp, Slocan, British Columbia.

Canadian soldiers going through Ortona.

They were also present at the huge Allied assault on Normandy on June 6, 1944, known as D-Day.

For the Normandy operation, the largest invasion force in the history of the world gathered. It consisted of 300 000 men, 4000 ships and 11 000 aircraft. At dawn on June 6, this huge army landed on the beaches of Normandy, and the invasion of Europe was on.

The Canadian army, now under the command of General H.D. Crerar, distinguished itself in many battles during the Normandy invasion—at Caen, Falaise and St. Lambert.

THE WAR ENDS

By early 1945, the German retreat had begun. British and American troops had crossed into Germany from the west and were racing for Berlin. From the east, millions of Soviet troops had cleared Eastern Europe of German occupation. They also drove on Berlin. The Soviet troops reached Berlin first, but by this time Hitler had already committed suicide. Russian and American troops met at the River Elbe, 100 km west of Berlin. On May 7, 1945, General Dwight Eisenhower accepted the surrender of Germany.

It was only now that the full scope of the Nazi atrocities was made known to the rest of the world. As the Allied armies swept through Germany and liberated Poland, they came upon the ghastly remains of Hitler's effort to create a "master race." In his attempt to get rid of those he considered inferior people, Hitler rounded up millions of Jews, Poles, Russians and other East Europeans and placed them in concentration camps. In infamous places such as Buchenwald, Bergen-Belsen and Auschwitz, millions of men, women and children were starved to death, shot and killed in gas chambers. Many were subjected to inhuman medical experiments. In what has been called "the Holocaust," as many as six million Jews lost their lives.

Following the war, many Nazi leaders were placed on trial for these and other war crimes. These were the famous Nuremberg trials. Hitler himself escaped this fate only by taking his own life before he could be captured. Many lesser Nazi officials escaped before they could be caught and tried for their war crimes. In recent years, several of these individuals have been identified and brought to justice. In 1987 the Canadian government passed a bill permitting trials of any war criminal found here to take place in this country. More than 40 years after its end, the bitter legacy of World War II continues to haunt us.

On August 6, 1945, on the other side of the world, another of the war's dreaded legacies was about to be created. On that day, a single American B-29 bomber, nicknamed the *Enola Gay*, flew over the Japanese city of Hiroshima and dropped the first atomic bomb in history. Three days later, a second bomb fell on Nagasaki. On September 2, Japan signed the terms of surrender. World War II had come to an end.

As with World War I, the cost in human terms was horrendous. Great Britain and the United States suffered nearly half a million dead each. German losses were nearly three million. Canada's losses were nearly 45 000. The most staggering figures were those of the Soviet Union, which reported over seven and a half million dead. The spectre of the terrible new weapon, the atomic bomb, remained in the minds of the survivors. The Atomic Age had dawned.

BUILDING YOUR LEARNING SKILLS

FOCUSSING ON THE ISSUE

1. Summarize five key events that occurred in the period from 1914 to 1945.
2. Answer the following questions relating to this chapter:
   - *a* Which countries made up the Triple Alliance in 1914?
   - *b* The passenger ship sunk by Germany in 1915 was:
     i the *Dreadnought* *ii* the *Bismarck*
     iii the *Lusitania* *iv* the *Titanic*
   - *c* Women were granted the right to vote in Canada in the year:
     i 1912 *ii* 1918
     iii 1929 *iv* 1967
   - *d* Outline some of the main features of Bennett's "New Deal."
   - *e* What do the initials CCF stand for?
3. The following terms appeared in this chapter. Try to recall their meanings and how they were used.

alliances	Maginot Line
arms race	mysticism
buying on margin	Nazi
chlorine gas	phony war
conscription	plebiscite
D-Day	red flag laws
government bonds	recession
income tax	socialism
inflation	stockbroker
Luftwaffe	stock market

RESEARCHING

1. Gather information on William Lyon Mackenzie King and his belief in mysticism. Check your resource centre for information from his diaries.
2. Find out how the following World War I weapons were invented:
   a machine gun *b* submarine *c* tank
3. Research the main points of President Franklin Roosevelt's "New Deal" for the United States. Compare them with the main points of R.B. Bennett's "New Deal" for Canada.
4. Gather information on the invention of radar. Why was it such a valuable weapon in World War II?

ORGANIZING

1. Place these events in the correct sequence in which they occurred:
   - ▶ The stock market crashes.
   - ▶ The Battle of Ypres is fought.
   - ▶ W.L. Mackenzie King is first elected prime minister.
   - ▶ Canadian women win voting rights.
   - ▶ "Hockey Night in Canada" is first broadcast.
2. Rank the above events in their order of importance, in your point of view.
3. List the contributions of Canada's men and women in World War I.

COMMUNICATING

1 You are a soldier in the trenches in World War I. Write a letter home to your family explaining the conditions in the trenches.
2 You are a stockbroker in the year 1932. What arguments would you give your client over the telephone as to why he or she should invest now in the stock market?
3 You are a sportscaster in 1929. Do a radio show reviewing the greatest sporting events in Canada during the past decade.

ANALYZING

1 The construction of trenches and the presence of machine guns on the battlefields of World War I made massive attacks across no-man's land practically suicidal. Yet generals on both sides continued to order such attacks. If you had been in command of an army in World War I, what tactics and strategies would you have used to defeat the enemy?
2 William Lyon Mackenzie King was prime minister longer than any other Commonwealth leader in history. Canadian voters were not aware of his private life and beliefs. Do you think they would have continued to vote for him if they had known about this aspect of his personality?
3 Summarize the key points of Bennett's "New Deal" of 1935. How many of his proposals have now become law in Canada?
4 In the following chapters, you will be reading about Canada in the modern world. You will learn about the problems and decisions Canada faces today in national and international affairs. These chapters deal with all aspects of the nation's life—political, social, economic and military. Many of Canada's current problems have their roots in the period we have just studied. Think back and try to make a list of the historical events in the period 1867 to 1945 that may have had an influence on the following areas:
   - English-French relations
   - Canada's foreign policy
   - Canadian-American relations
   - Canada's status as an independent nation

APPLYING YOUR KNOWLEDGE

1 Compare the results of the conscription crises of World Wars I and II. In terms of the military, political and social results, was conscription necessary in each case?
2 Review your knowledge of the stock market. As a class project, every student might bring to school the stock market pages for one day and buy $1000 worth of stocks. Follow the ups and downs of your stocks for one week. At the end of that time, determine which student has made the most money on the stock market.
3 There is much discussion today about whether a depression could happen again. Make a list comparing today's economic conditions with those of 1929. List differences and similarities.
4 Do you agree with Canada's treatment of its Japanese-Canadian citizens during World War II? If not, what do you think Canada should have done?
5 The decision to continue the trials against surviving Nazi war criminals 40 years after the end of World War II has created controversy in Canada. Present a reasoned argument in favour of or against the continuation of such trials.

chapter 10

CANADA, 1945 TO THE PRESENT: LIVING IN THE ATOMIC AGE

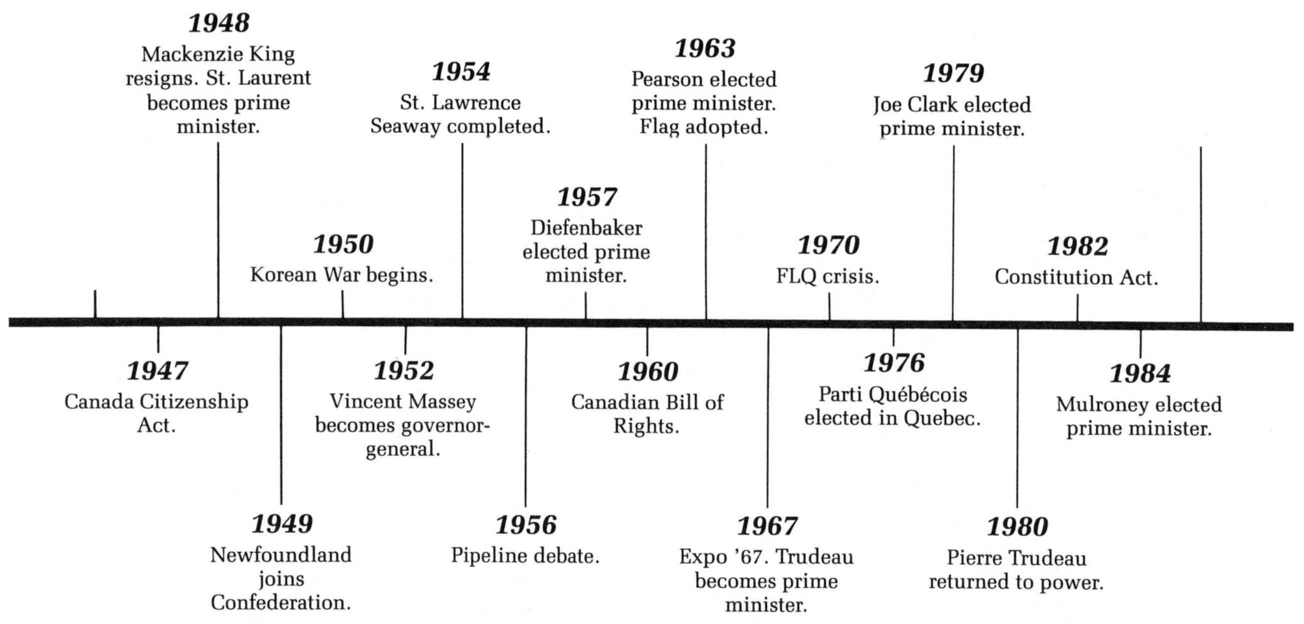

1947
Canada Citizenship Act.
1948
Mackenzie King resigns. St. Laurent becomes prime minister.
1949
Newfoundland joins Confederation.
1950
Korean War begins.
1952
Vincent Massey becomes governor-general.
1954
St. Lawrence Seaway completed.
1956
Pipeline debate.
1957
Diefenbaker elected prime minister.
1960
Canadian Bill of Rights.
1963
Pearson elected prime minister. Flag adopted.
1967
Expo '67. Trudeau becomes prime minister.
1970
FLQ crisis.
1976
Parti Québécois elected in Quebec.
1979
Joe Clark elected prime minister.
1980
Pierre Trudeau returned to power.
1982
Constitution Act.
1984
Mulroney elected prime minister.

TOPIC ORGANIZER — **PAGE**

THEME ORGANIZER

- ▶ The Liberal dynasty: Under Mackenzie King and Louis St. Laurent, the Liberals enjoy a long reign of power.
- ▶ Rounding out Confederation: In 1949 Newfoundland becomes Canada's tenth province.
- ▶ Economic good times: The 1950s see one of the greatest economic booms in Canada's history.
- ▶ The population boom: A great increase in immigration and the birth rate produces a large consumer market.
- ▶ The teenage revolution: A new focus on teenagers results in social change, reflected in clothing, music styles and values.
- ▶ Diefenbaker–Pearson years: One of Canada's great political rivalries emerges in the 1960s.
- ▶ Expo '67: The great Montreal exhibition marks the beginning of Canada's second century with style and patriotism.
- ▶ The Trudeau years: Canada's most dynamic prime minister leads Canada through socially and politically troubled times.
- ▶ The struggle for equality: During the 1970s, attention is focussed on the century-old fight for equal rights for women.
- ▶ The Conservatives return to power: In 1984 Brian Mulroney leads the Conservative party to a record political victory.

INTRODUCTION

> I can recall how much relief we all felt with the news that the war was over. But something funny seemed to happen. The war, no matter how bad it was, was something we had learned to live with for five years. Now we were going back home, but none of us knew what to expect when we got there. Some of us began to worry about what we would find.
>
> When I left Canada in 1940, there was still a depression going on. I thought it would be more of the same when we got back. We heard rumours we might be sent to the Far East to fight Japan, and some of my buddies were actually hoping it was true. Not me though. I was happy to be going home.
>
> returning World War II veteran

Over one million men and women fought for Canada in World War II. The statement of this returning soldier reflects the mixed feelings of relief and concern they felt as the war came to an end. Six years of danger and hardship were over. Now they were returning home to rebuild their lives.

The Canada they returned to in 1945 was very different from the country they left in 1939. The depression was over. It had been erased by the great surge of wartime production, both on the farms and in the factories. Indeed, along with the United States, Canada was one of the most fortunate countries on earth. Its homeland had been spared the destruction of war. Unlike Europe, its cities were standing, and its fac-

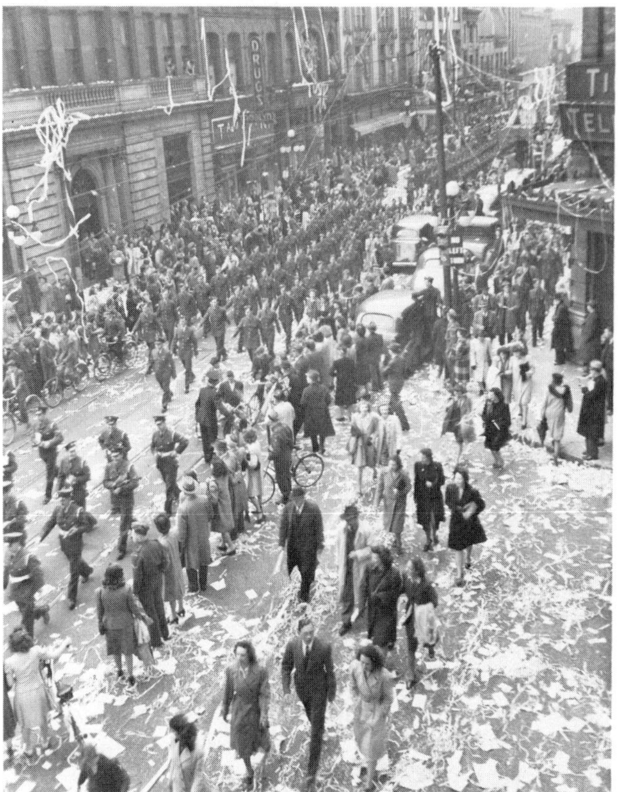

Soldiers and civilians celebrate victory of the war in Europe, May 7, 1945.

tories were intact. Within a short time after the war's end, Canada's industries were again producing consumer goods for buyers at home and overseas.

The years after 1945 would prove to be the most eventful in human history. Canadians were ready to face them with optimism.

Before reading on, study the chart of key words and ideas that follows.

KEY WORDS AND IDEAS IN THIS CHAPTER

Term	Meaning	Sample Use
baby boomers	the generation of Canadians born and raised after World War II	The baby boomers grew up to be the "flower children" of the 1960s.
Beatlemania	a term given to the new values and life-style made popular by the Beatles	Beatlemania produced a revolution in the world of popular music.
generation gap	a term popularly used in the 1960s to explain the difference in values between young people and the older generation	Their opposing attitudes toward the Vietnam War are an example of the generation gap that existed between older people and the young.
hippies	a name given to young people who rejected society's values and wished to have a simpler, more peaceful life-style	Society's image of a hippie was that of a long-haired, shabbily dressed, lazy young person.
just society	the society envisioned by Prime Minister Trudeau and reflected in his policy of equality for all groups in Canada	Federal grants for the cultural activities of Canada's ethnic minorities were one example of the federal sponsorship of the just society.
suffragettes	a name given to those women who fought for the right to vote before 1918	The suffragettes often resorted to defying the law to publicize their aims.
Trudeaumania	a term given to the widespread enthusiasm about Pierre Trudeau and his political style	The large crowds that gathered when Pierre Trudeau made a public appearance were one manifestation of Trudeaumania.
women's suffrage	the right of women in Canada to have full voting power	In 1918 full women's suffrage was made law in Canada.

PUBLIC LIFE SINCE 1945

THE LIBERAL DYNASTY

The end of World War II found the Liberal government of Mackenzie King still in power. In his last election, in June, 1945, the Liberal party under King was returned with a large majority. The prime minister had proved his ability to keep Canadians united during difficult times. It was said that few people loved King or even liked him. They just continued to vote for him.

In 1948, at the age of seventy-seven, Mackenzie King decided to retire. He had served as prime minister of Canada for over 21 years — longer than any leader in the history of the British Commonwealth. To replace King, the Liberals chose Louis St. Laurent, an able, experienced cabinet minister. In November, 1948, St. Laurent became the second French-Canadian prime minister. His selection continued the Liberal policy in this century of alternating between English and French leaders.

St. Laurent, like his French-Canadian predecessor, Laurier, was not only a shrewd politician but also a

Louis St. Laurent, the nation's second French-Canadian prime minister.

man of integrity. He was perfectly bilingual and was at ease dealing with both English- and French-Canadians. In addition, he was a warm, likable person who was immensely patriotic. The press affectionately began to call him "Uncle Louie."

St. Laurent was fortunate to inherit a strong cabinet from Mackenzie King. Outstanding in this group was C.D. Howe. Howe had brilliantly directed Canada's industrial output during World War II and now was engineering Canada's post-war economic boom. In this prosperous atmosphere, the Liberal government was re-elected in 1949 and again in 1953, both times with comfortable majorities.

NEWFOUNDLAND JOINS CANADA

One of the outstanding successes of St. Laurent's government was the completion of Confederation. On March 31, 1949, Newfoundland became Canada's tenth province.

In 1869 Newfoundlanders rejected Confederation and voted to remain a separate British colony. After World War II, Britain was facing severe economic problems. Newfoundlanders were now faced with a choice: Go it alone once more, or join Canada.

AN APPEAL

On Thursday, June 3, the toiling masses in Newfoundland will have the biggest and best chance they ever had in our country's 450 years history.

They will have the best chance they EVER HAD to make Newfoundland a better place for themselves and their families.

Will they use this chance to help themselves?

No, if Water Street can stop them.

No, if the rich and wealthy can stop them.

No, if most of the few fortunate, well-fed, well-clothed, well-housed people amongst us can stop them.

No, if the politicians can stop them.

I do not believe that the toiling masses of our people will listen to the selfish few.

I believe that the great majority of the fishermen, loggers, miners, railroaders, mill-workers, teachers, shop and office workers, civil servants, laborers and others who have to work for their living are closing their eyes and ears to the selfish few.

I believe that the women and mothers of Newfoundland are going to use this wonderful chance on June 3rd.

I believe the children of Newfoundland are going to be remembered by their fathers, mothers, grandfathers, grandmothers, uncles and aunts on June 3rd.

I believe that our people can see clearly now who are their friends, and who are their enemies.

For nearly three years now I have worked hard to bring this wonderful chance to my own brothers and sisters, and to working-men and working-women all over our country. I am the oldest of 13 children, all living. I know how hard it is to bring up a family in this country.

For nearly three years I have fought and worked to get this chance for our people. Water Street and Water Street's politicians have fought me and tried hard to put me down. They have failed.

You have your chance, now. On June the 3rd you can make Newfoundland a better place for yourselves, and a happier place for the children.

Use this chance, fellow-Newfoundlanders. Use this chance, fathers and mothers.

Vote for Confederation.

Make June the 3rd the birth day of a NEW Newfoundland, a new Newfoundland fit for Newfoundlanders to live in.

Your sincere friend,
JOSEPH R. SMALLWOOD

Leading the fight for Confederation was a former journalist and farmer who was now leader of the Newfoundland Liberal party: Joey Smallwood.

Every Newfoundlander under Confederation will know well what it means to be Taxed, Taxed and Taxed, no matter how the Confederates will try to tell you otherwise.

Which side of the Confederation issue is this cartoon supporting?

Because of his energetic leadership, the pro-Confederation forces won the day. The vote, however, was close:

Confederation 78 323
Independence 71 334

And so Joey Smallwood became the last "Father of Confederation." As Louis St. Laurent signed the terms of union, he said, "We the people of Canada look forward to the last great step in Confederation."

THE LIBERAL DOWNFALL

Throughout the 1950s, the Canadian economy boomed. On the whole, Canadians were prosperous. It began to appear as if the Liberal dynasty might never come to an end. But the public began to lose faith as prices rose and inflation became a problem. This began to put financial pressure on the aged and those facing retirement on fixed pensions. Some began to grumble that the Liberals had been in power too long and had become "arrogant."

The biggest blow to the Liberals came with the famous pipeline debate in the summer of 1956. The government had planned to build a gas pipeline from Alberta to the markets in eastern Canada. An American-controlled company was given the contract to build this huge project. When the government granted the company a loan of $80 million, many nationalists were outraged. Why, they asked, should an American company and not a Canadian one be given such money? Weren't we handing control of our resources to outsiders? The bitter debate that followed in Parliament shattered the reputation of the Liberal government.

In the election of 1957, the Conservatives, under John Diefenbaker, won 112 seats, the Liberals only 105. The aging Louis St. Laurent, admitting defeat, turned the government over to the Conservatives, who were led by a lawyer from Saskatchewan named John Diefenbaker. Lester Pearson became the Liberal leader in 1958 and sought to restore the Liberal majority. In the election that followed, in 1958, the Conservative party led by Diefenbaker swept 208 seats while the Liberals won only 49. It was the greatest majority in Canadian history. It also brought to an end an era in politics. The 1950s had been the era of Liberal power. The 1960s brought a struggle for power between Diefenbaker and Pearson.

THE ECONOMY BOOMS

Veterans returning to Canada at the end of World War I faced a sagging economy and few jobs. Those returning home after World War II feared they might find a similar situation. These fears proved groundless, for the period after 1945 saw the greatest economic growth in Canada's history.

NATURAL RESOURCES

Leading the way to prosperity was the great oil boom in the West. The discovery in 1947 of "black gold" at Leduc, Alberta, triggered this spectacular development. In the years that followed, huge drilling operations uncovered large oil and gas deposits in Alberta, Saskatchewan and Manitoba. The search for new oil created a need for drilling rigs, refining plants and pipelines. This sparked growth in other industries as well. The oil industry has become the cornerstone of Canada's economic growth. Before 1945 Canada produced only 5 percent of her own oil needs. Today, with the new offshore discoveries in the Maritimes and in the North, Canada has the capacity to become self-sufficient in meeting her oil needs.

Important mineral finds were also made across Canada. Potash was discovered in Saskatchewan, nickel in Manitoba, iron in Quebec. In mineral-rich Ontario, an explosion of mining ventures saw discoveries of uranium, zinc, nickel, copper and other valuable minerals. By 1960 Ontario was producing almost 60 percent of Canada's metal output, and Canada was becoming one of the world's leading exporters of raw materials.

THE ST. LAWRENCE SEAWAY

One of the greatest of Canada's economic projects came about in co-operation with the United States. This was the so-called "master project of North America," the St. Lawrence Seaway. The dream of opening a passage for large ships from the Great Lakes to the Atlantic Ocean was an old one. Unfortunately, the two-thousand-mile passage from Lake Superior to the Atlantic was blocked at many points by narrow channels, rapids and, of course, Niagara Falls. To build larger canals around these points would be expensive. Since the scheme was meant to open the Great Lakes to ocean freighters, it also meant building huge dams, flooding large areas and moving whole towns. It would require the co-operation of both Canada and the United States to succeed.

The first oil well at Leduc, Alberta signalled the start of Canada's oil industry.

At last, in 1954, the great project was started. Five years later it was finished. The completed seaway provided an efficient route to transport Canada's minerals and wheat to the rest of the world.

One important by-product of this project was the construction of hydro-electric plants along the seaway. These were built into the dams needed to create the seaway. These plants provided cheap electric power to hundreds of communities on both sides of the border. This low-cost power was not only a boon to consumers, it also helped to stimulate industrial growth in eastern Canada and the United States.

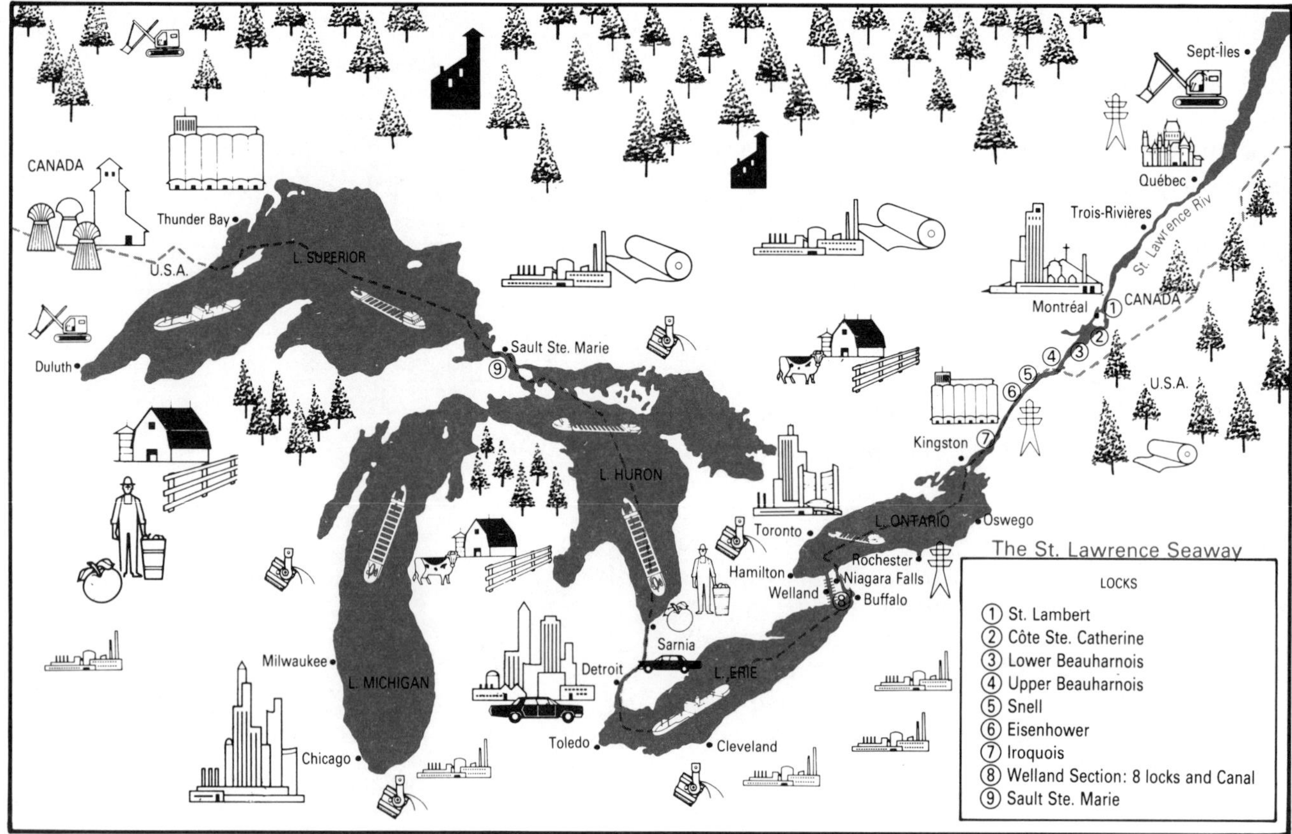

THE GOOD LIFE

The economic prosperity of Canadians in the 1950s was built on oil, minerals, wheat and international trade. Above all, it was built on the huge increase in the population during this decade. At the end of World War II, Canada's population stood at less than 12 million. By 1960 there were almost 18 million Canadians, a 50 percent increase. This rapid increase in population helped change Canada in many ways. It provided a large labour force for Canada's developing industries. At the same time, it created a large new market for consumer products.

The great majority of this new population was concentrated in the cities. As a result, the population boom created a whole new life-style, a life-style that many of today's young people take for granted. It included sprawling suburbs, skyscrapers, shopping malls, subways and fast-food chains.

THE BABY BOOM

Much of the increase in Canada's population was a result of a very high birth rate. For several years after the war, Canada had one of the highest birth rates in the Western world. The children born in this period became known in later years as the "baby boomers." They were a generation of Canadians who grew up in a country full of hope, prosperous and free from war. Probably in no other era had Canadians enjoyed "the good life" so fully.

In addition to the baby boom, Canada's population was swelled by five million immigrants. Many of these poured in from Britain and other European countries ravaged by World War II. Among these were the "war brides," young women who had married Canadian soldiers in Europe. In 1946 these young women, some with small children, began to take up their new lives in Canada.

This population explosion helped to create an eco-

The enormity of the St. Lawrence Seaway project can be seen in the construction of this dam.

nomic boom. In turn, the economic boom helped to change Canada's life-style.

ALL THE COMFORTS OF HOME

Many of the immigrants who sought a new life in Canada had been city people in their native countries. It was only natural that they should head to Canada's large cities. At the same time, the appeal of city life attracted many young Canadians from traditional farming communities.

By 1951 seven out of every ten Canadians were living in a city. Urban sprawl developed. A whole new set of words became part of everyday language: shopping plaza, supermarket, motel, expressway and traffic jam.

Every family could hope to own its own home, perhaps a bungalow or a new split-level design, complete with all the modern conveniences. In 1960 this aspect of the good life could be purchased for under $15 000. Included would be all the latest appliances, such as electric fridges and stoves. However, you might have to wait a while to own these items. Demand often outran production in those booming times.

THE AUTOMOBILE

In the 1920s, the automobile changed our way of life. In the 1950s, it made possible the movement of large numbers of people from the inner city to the suburbs. More Canadians owned cars than at any previous time in our history. The two-car garage became a symbol of suburban living. During the 1950s, Canadians bought three and a half million new cars. And what cars they were!

Perhaps no car-buying generation was ever faced with such a choice. The race was on between carmakers to design bigger, fancier, more powerful cars.

In the 1950s school facilities could not keep pace with the growth in population. Here, children are educated in railway cars.

Suburbia in 1955, complete with cars, bungalows, and the occasional TV antenna.

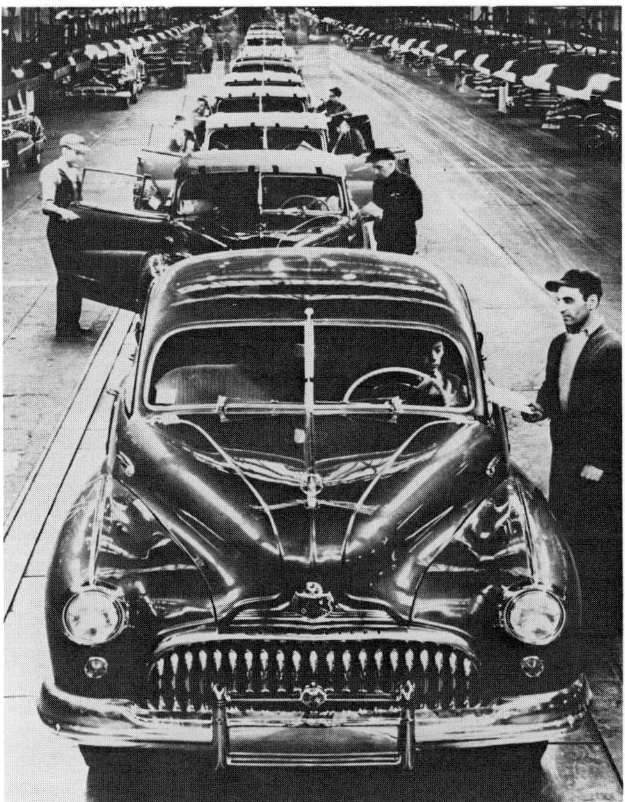

A shiny new car rolls off the production line to meet the growing consumer demand for luxury goods.

The V–8 engine was in great demand in those days of 2000-kg cars and 7¢-a-litre gasoline. For under $3000, you could drive away a new 1959 Chevy sedan with whitewalls and great rear-winged fins. Indeed, fins were the rage in almost all cars made in the late 1950s. Two-tone finishes, chrome strips and power steering were standard features of these cars.

Of course, not all the fads caught on. The "revolutionary" Ford Edsel became the object of countless jokes and proved to be perhaps the costliest mistake in the history of the industry.

THE INVENTION OF THE TEENAGER

The group that benefitted the most from the new prosperity was the pre-adult, high-school age group, which became known as "teenagers." Teenagers had always existed. In previous generations, this group was often expected to work and to help out with the family finances. The movement away from farms and into cities and the sudden prosperity created a whole new phenomenon called "leisure time." The more than one million young people in Canada between the ages of thirteen and nineteen created a whole new life-style to fill this time.

The most obvious change was in clothing fashions. For girls, sweaters, white blouses, pleated skirts, bobby socks and saddle shoes became the standard uniform. Ponytails were the most common hair style, and bleached-blonde hair enjoyed a brief popularity. Those who were more daring might wear shorts in the summer. But the bikini, which had become the rage on the French Riviera in the early 1950s, was still strictly forbidden for the Canadian teenager.

For boys, V-necked sweaters and cardigans were popular, as were bow-ties and white buck shoes. Slicked-back hair with the "wet" look was in style. A minority opted for the "hood" look popularized by movie stars such as Marlon Brando in the film *The Wild One* and James Dean in *Rebel Without a Cause*. They wore white T-shirts, black leather jackets and ducktail hair styles.

Among teenagers themselves, there was much talk about independence and individuality. Despite this, being part of "the group" was as important then as it is now. To be outside the group was to be a loner or an "oddball."

The most popular pastimes for teenagers were "going steady," going to drive-in movies or school dances and "cruising" their town's main street. Afterwards, the group might indulge in hamburgers and root-beers at one of the many new drive-in restaurants, such as A&W.

ROCK-AND-ROLL

For adults the single most alarming aspect of the teenage subculture was the dramatic impact of a new phenomenon in music: rock-and-roll. It all began with a hit song called "Rock Around the Clock" in 1954. The real spokesman of the movement was a young man from Mississippi by the name of Elvis Presley. Sporting long sideburns, a ducktail haircut and a gold suit, Elvis was "king" of rock-and-roll. He frightened some adults, who thought he was a

Teenagers' favourite pastime: dancing to the music of a jukebox after school hours.

Elvis: the magnetic appeal of the ''King'' of rock'n'roll can be seen in the reaction of his audience.

representative of the devil. His famous rolling hips caused young female fans to riot and faint. Elvis's success led the way for other rock-and-roll stars such as Chuck Berry, Little Richard, Jerry Lee Lewis and Buddy Holly. More than any other single item, rock music exemplified the "generation gap" between the old and young in the 1950s. If you were a teenager, you liked rock-and-roll. If you were an adult, you probably didn't.

ROCK-AND-ROLL HITS FROM THE FIFTIES

Song	Performer
"Rock Around the Clock"	Bill Haley and the Comets
"Heartbreak Hotel"	Elvis Presley
"Whole Lotta Shakin' Goin' On"	Jerry Lee Lewis
"At the Hop"	Danny and the Juniors
"Teenager in Love"	Dion and the Belmonts
"Sweet Little Sixteen"	Chuck Berry
"Wake Up Little Susie"	Everly Brothers
"That'll Be the Day"	Buddy Holly
"April Love"	Pat Boone
"Diana"	Paul Anka

A young Paul Anka singing to his Diana, the woman for whom his hit song was written.

Of the many hit songs of the 1950s, only a very few were performed by Canadians. The most famous Canadian rock-and-roll singer was an Ottawa teenager named Paul Anka. His first song, "Diana," not only hit the Canadian charts, it became one of the biggest-selling records of all time and rocketed Paul Anka to stardom. Other popular Canadian singers included Jack Scott, Bobby Curtola, the Four Lads and the Diamonds. It cannot be said, however, that there was a true Canadian music industry. Most of the popular music was American. The Canadian pop-music scene did not become an important factor in the North American music industry until the 1960s.

TELEVISION

On September 8, 1952, the first Canadian to appear on television was broadcast by the CBC to his waiting fellow citizens. There were about 10 000 television sets in Canada on that historic day when Percy Saltzman began to talk about the weather. Those delighted and amazed viewers could not have imagined the impact this little box would have on the future. Some predicted that television was a passing fad. Yet within two years, there were over one million sets in operation in Canada; the Television Age had begun.

Perhaps no other invention (in the twentieth century) has had such an impact on our life-styles and values. The first victims of the television revolution were, predictably, movies and radio. Hundreds of movie theatres closed as more and more people began to watch television on weekends. The movie industry did not fully recover until the 1970s.

Radio was changed forever. It lost its stock programming — comedies, dramas and soap operas.

Canada's most enduring television show, *Front Page Challenge*.

These began to be televised. Radio turned to music, the only type of broadcasting with which it could still draw large audiences. In time, programs such as "Hit Parade," "Top 50" and "Western Jamboree" evolved into today's pop-music programs. In a sense, teenagers' music has helped to keep radio alive.

If television was an entertainment success, it was also, in the eyes of many, a social villian. Experts warned that family ties were being weakened by too much television viewing. Teachers complained that students spent up to 40 hours each week in front of TV sets. They predicted that study habits would break down, homework would be left undone and reading and writing skills would decrease. Time seemed to confirm these suspicions.

Since the fifties, television has been criticized a great deal more, particularly about the sex and violence in its weekly programming. Yet it continues to thrive. In 1986 the cost of advertising during the Super Bowl game reached $1 million per minute. In that same year, it was estimated that the average Canadian home had more than two television sets.

SPORTS

One of the effects of television was to make ordinary events seem more important and ordinary people seem larger than life. Nowhere was this more true than in sports. Hockey and football had always been popular sports in Canada, but it was television that made them national institutions.

Before television, people across Canada could only imagine the games played by legendary players wearing the uniforms of the Montreal Canadiens and the

Hockey Night in Canada **became a Canadian tradition during the 1950s as television brought the games into the nation's living rooms.**

Toronto Maple Leafs. During the fifties, when television began to bring these games to their homes, Canadians in every province started to think of these teams as their own. Millions of viewers thrilled to the exploits of the great Montreal hockey teams of the fifties. Players such as Rocket Richard, Jean Beliveau and Doug Harvey achieved superstar status.

The Canadian Football League also benefitted from television exposure. Football became a national sport, with teams representing every province west of the Maritimes. More than any other single sporting event, the annual Grey Cup game brought together Canadian viewers from coast to coast. Millions watched the Edmonton Eskimos–Montreal Allouette rivalry of the 1950s and saw Edmonton win three straight Grey Cups.

Individual Canadians became heroes as well. Doug Hepburn, of Vancouver, won numerous international weightlifting championships and set world records. Donald Jackson and Barbara Ann Scott won world championships in figure skating. Although many other Canadians made their mark in the world of sports, none captured the hearts of Canadians as

Marilyn Bell and daughter at a plaque commemorating her swim across Lake Ontario. What other great feats have female athletes recently accomplished?

much as a young teenaged swimmer named Marilyn Bell. On September 10, 1954, fighting 12-foot waves, eels and fatigue and cheered on by thousands, Marilyn became the first person to swim Lake Ontario. In so doing, she swam her way to sports immortality. Not until the 1972 Canada–Russia hockey series would a sporting event so move Canadians.

THE DIEFENBAKER–PEARSON YEARS

The 1960s will be remembered as the decade of the youth movement. Terms such as "flower power," "hippie culture," "Beatlemania," "generation gap" and "miniskirts" paint a vivid picture of the times. Socially, this decade was highlighted by unrest and upheaval and a growing involvement of young people in all aspects of public life. Politically, the time was marked by increasing regional tensions and indecision and scandal in government. The political scene was dominated by the battle between two men —John Diefenbaker and Lester Pearson—for control of the government of Canada.

The two men were as different in personality and style as the parties they led. John Diefenbaker, though born in Ontario, spent most of his youth in Saskatchewan. Armed with a law degree, he saw himself as the champion of the underdog and successfully defended many clients in court. As a young boy, he once met Wilfrid Laurier, and politics became his lifelong ambition. But he never forgot the common person. Many years later, as prime minister, he introduced Canada's first Bill of Rights. Diefenbaker always felt this was his most important achievement.

After 15 years of disappointing losses at the polls, Diefenbaker was finally elected to Parliament as a member of the Conservative party. He then set his sights on the party leadership, a goal that he achieved in 1956. In 1957, to the astonishment of most experts, Diefenbaker defeated Louis St. Laurent to become prime minister of Canada. The following year, he led the Progressive Conservative party to the largest political victory in Canadian history.

John Diefenbaker was one of the most magnetic speakers ever to appear on the Canadian political scene. He embellished his speeches with humour, sarcasm, patriotic appeals and thundering phrases. In one speech he appealed to Canadians to share with him a new vision of Canada:

Prime Minister John Diefenbaker displaying his Bill of Rights. The "Chief" always maintained that this was his proudest achievement.

> One Canada, wherein Canadians will have preserved to them the control of their own economic and political destiny. Sir John A. Macdonald . . . saw Canada from East to West. I see a new Canada—a Canada of the North. . . . A new vision! A new hope! A new soul for Canada!

Diefenbaker spoke for the unhappy farmers of western Canada and the unemployed workers of the East. Because of his strong will, however, Diefenbaker made many enemies within his own party, and his nationalistic policies made other countries suspi-

THE END OF AN ERA

John Diefenbaker (''Dief the Chief'') became the favourite subject of political cartoonists. What does each of these drawings say about the Conservative leader?

Lester B. "Mike" Pearson, wearing his familiar bow tie, opens a meeting of the United Nations Assembly.

cious of his aims. His determination to develop an independent policy in foreign affairs caused a hostile reaction in the United States (see Chapter 16).

Diefenbaker's political support melted away. In the election of 1962, he was re-elected, but with a minority government. It would be his last stand as prime minister. Within months the government was rocked by the resignation of the defense minister, Douglas Harkness. The Canadian government had purchased $700 million worth of Bomarc missiles from the United States but refused to arm them with nuclear weapons. As a result, the missiles were useless. Harkness argued that without warheads, the missiles were a needless expense and would serve to weaken Canada's armed forces. Many in the Conservative party agreed with him, but Diefenbaker refused to yield. Harkness resigned in protest.

In April, 1963, another election was held, and this time the Liberals were returned to power. The Liberals were led, as they had been since 1957, by Lester "Mike" Pearson. A veteran of World War I, Pearson had also been a history professor, a hockey and baseball player and a diplomat. He was an excellent scholar and loved adventure, but he soon realized that his future lay in government.

Lacking Diefenbaker's speechmaking powers, Pearson's strength lay in his gift for quiet diplomacy. In 1956, for example, the world was on the brink of war over the Suez Canal crises. Pearson organized a United Nations "peacekeeping" force that probably prevented the crisis from becoming a full-scale world war (see Chapter 19). For this act, he received the Nobel Peace Prize. He was the most famous Canadian outside Canada.

As Liberal leader, Pearson lacked the kind of personal appeal or "charisma" that John Diefenbaker had. Indeed, although he was elected prime minister in both 1963 and 1965, Pearson never had a majority government. During these times, he used his gift for diplomacy to lead Canada through a difficult period that was dominated by the issue of economic nationalism (see Unit 5) and the Quiet Revolution in Quebec (see Chapter 12). He also succeeded, despite much controversy and personal abuse, in giving Canada its own national flag in 1965. His other main achievement, also controversial, was to start the process of making the civil service bilingual.

As Canada entered its centennial year, the bitter political infighting seemed to stop. All Canadians felt a sense of pride and achievement as Montreal was host to a major world fair, Expo '67. This one event did more to unite Canadians than did all the speeches of the politicians.

Expo '67 also marked the end of the Diefenbaker–Pearson era. After resisting several attempts to force him to resign, Diefenbaker was finally removed as Conservative leader in September, 1967. With satisfaction he could look back on that night in 1957 when he was chosen Conservative leader and remarked, "I hope it will be said of me: 'He wasn't always right; sometimes he was on the wrong side, but never on the side of wrong.' "

Three months later, Pearson, too, announced his resignation with a typically low-keyed comment: "Well, c'est la vie!" An era in Canadian politics had ended. A new and more dramatic one was about to begin.

Some of the many choices for a new Canadian flag in 1965. Which would have been your choice?

THE PROTEST GENERATION

In social terms, the 1960s were marked by a rebellion against the materialism of the 1950s. The baby boomers had grown up in an age of prosperity. As a result, they were not as concerned about jobs and security as their parents had been. Increasingly, this generation became involved with social issues. They disapproved of the policies of the older generation on such issues as the Vietnam War, nuclear weapons and race relations. Thousands of young Americans refused to fight in Vietnam and avoided the draft by coming to Canada. The phrase "Don't trust anyone over thirty" typified the attitude of the young.

As outward signs of their protest, young people began to wear long hair. They copied the style of the Beatles, the English rock group that had started a revolution in music. In 1964 "Beatlemania" caused the same sensation in North America that Elvis had a decade earlier. The Beatles became symbols of protest against the adult world. Their life-style, including their experiments with drugs, was imitated throughout North America.

Soon the "hippie" culture was in full bloom. Thousands of young people, worried about war, "dropped out" of society. Some lived in communes or migrated to the hippie districts of San Francisco or Vancouver. Their carefree life-style was sensationalized in the newspapers and on television. It was characterized by "free love" and drug use. Those who advocated this life-style outraged adults and worried parents. However, as economic problems became more serious in the 1970s, the "drop-out generation" began to concern itself more with the everyday task of earning a living. The heady days of "flower power" faded into memory.

The Canadian music industry benefitted from the protest movement of the sixties. A whole generation of musicians chose to write songs about social issues. Performers such as Bruce Cockburn, Gordon Lightfoot, Buffy Ste. Marie and Joni Mitchell created a distinctive Canadian sound that also became popular in the United States. They paved the way for those who made names for themselves in the seventies: Anne Murray, the Guess Who, the Stampeders, Bachman-Turner Overdrive, and Lighthouse.

Right: Long hair and "granny glasses" marked the typical hippie of the 1960s. Below: Young people gather at Mosport for the "Strawberry Fields" Rock Festival (1971), Canada's version of the more famous Woodstock Festival. Bottom right: One of the thousands of young Americans who avoided the Vietnam War by deserting to Canada. This "draft-dodger" later returned to the United States and served a prison term. Some, like boxing champion Muhammad Ali, chose prison rather than fighting in Vietnam.

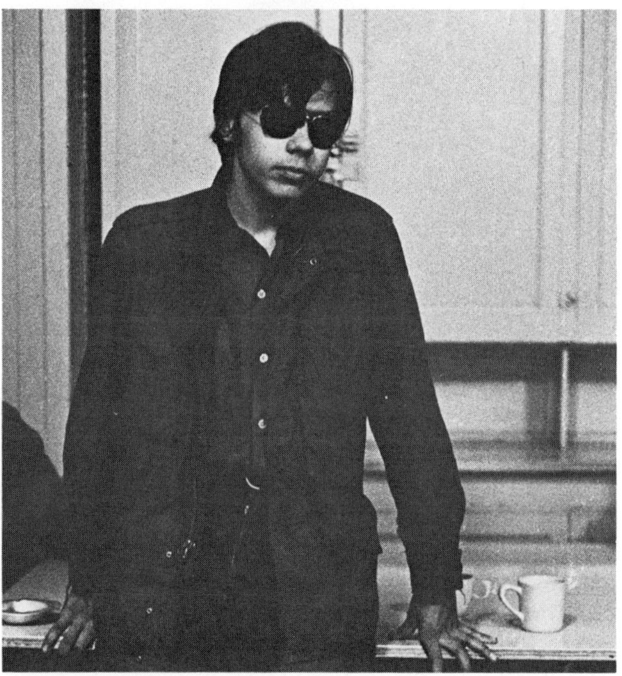

CANADA'S SECOND CENTURY

THE TRUDEAU YEARS

The success of Expo '67 gave Canadians a sense of unity and optimism as no cultural event had done before. The country needed a figure who could represent that feeling in public life. Canadians found this man in Pierre Elliot Trudeau. He seemed to embody the country perfectly: He was of mixed English-French descent and perfectly bilingual. Born of a wealthy family, Trudeau practised and taught law. Before entering politics, he was also a journalist in Quebec. Trudeau was at first a strong supporter of the Quiet Revolution, but when the movement became linked to separatism, he became its bitter opponent.

When Lester Pearson resigned, the Liberal party chose Pierre Trudeau as its new leader and prime minister in 1968. Relatively unknown by the public before now, Trudeau used the general election of that year to create a new style in politics. To those who were suspicious of politicians, he seemed like a breath of fresh air. With a gesture, a smile, a shrug or a witty reply, he turned doubtful audiences into fanatic supporters. His use of television was masterful. From young people and women in particular, he received the kind of adulation usually given only to movie stars and rock-and-roll idols. The press called it "Trudeaumania."

His opponents, Robert Stanfield of the Conservatives and David Lewis of the New Democratic Party, were thoughtful and honourable politicians. They were not, however, "swingers." Stanfield's appearance worked against him in the age of television. So did his manner of giving thoughtful answers to difficult questions. The public preferred snappy, one-line answers. The Canadian public was caught up in the same kind of political enthusiasm that John F. Kennedy had caused in the United States.

The election was a runaway victory for Trudeau and the Liberals. Stanfield might well have recalled the thought expressed by one of Trudeau's opponents

Expo '67 in Montreal was a great Canadian achievement and a source of national pride. Canada's pavilion, the inverted pyramid, is seen in the background.

Pierre Trudeau on the campaign trail in 1968. The hysteria which surrounded his personal appearances was similar to that of rock stars. Compare the crowd reaction in this photo to that for Elvis Presley.

in the Liberal leadership race: "I have been caught in a generation gap."

Probably no politician could have lived up to such expectations as the public had of Pierre Trudeau. In fact, unlike other politicians, Trudeau promised little. Perhaps because of this, the public expected much. Time would tarnish his image, but the summer of 1968 opened a new era of public life in Canada.

THE JUST SOCIETY

Once in power with a large majority, Trudeau worked toward his goal of a "just society." His aim was to increase the role of ethnic groups, women, native people and minority groups in Canada's political life. A new push was made to improve federal–provincial relations; new directions were taken in foreign affairs; and further attempts were made to revise the Constitution by adding to it a charter of rights.

Dramatically, the FLQ crisis of 1970 brought all government activities to a standstill. All the government's energies were channelled into stopping the crisis and halting the spread of separatism (see Chapter 13). Trudeau's use of the War Measures Act, which restricted personal freedom in Canada during the crisis, was severely criticized by the Opposition and the press. The first crack had appeared in the Trudeau image.

Trudeau's concern with social justice encouraged the public debate of social issues. The Trudeau Review, a series of policy documents, was an effort to develop a truly Canadian foreign policy. This angered the United States and led to problems in Canadian–American relations (see Unit 5). At home, the concerns of the women's movement began to be seen as important domestic issues.

A Canadian soldier guarding a public building during the FLQ crisis of 1970. Was the War Measures Act an over-reaction on the part of the Canadian government?

WOMEN IN CANADA

The United Nations declared 1975 International Women's Year. In Canada, as elsewhere, women were asserting themselves in all areas of society. In business, entertainment, sports and politics, women were making headlines across Canada. This movement was the result of a century of struggle for equal rights, a struggle that many women and men feel is still not won.

In the beginning, this struggle was mainly about winning political rights. From the earliest days, injustice towards women was rooted in Canadian law. The Election Act of the Dominion of Canada, 1867, stated that "no woman, idiot, lunatic or child shall vote." For the next 50 years, a number of women's organizations worked to overturn this law and gain the right to vote. Women who belonged to these organizations were called suffragettes.

It was not until World War I that women achieved the right to vote. With many of the able-bodied men in the army, women took over previously all-male jobs in factories and proved they could do the work as capably as men. The part women played in the war effort was a key factor in their winning the right to vote. Still, it took the efforts of several outstanding individuals to achieve this goal. Leading the way was Nellie McClung, Canada's best-known suffragette. Because of her tireless efforts, Manitoba passed the first women's suffrage bill in Canada in 1916. Saskatchewan and Alberta followed in that same year.

Victory at the national level soon followed. In 1917 the government of Robert Borden passed the Wartimes Election Act. This allowed women who were British subjects and had close relatives in the armed forces to vote. In the following year, on May 24, a bill giving women full suffrage was at last passed. Women's first opportunity to use the vote came in the election of 1921. When the results were counted, Agnes Campbell McPhail became the first woman member of Parliament. She served with distinction for 19 years.

Other political victories followed as all the provinces (except Quebec) gave women the right to vote in provincial elections. But there was one brief pause

Nellie McClung and her British counterpart Emmeline Pankhurst, two outspoken and courageous fighters for women's rights.

in this parade of victories. Despite having won full political rights, women were still not considered "persons" according to the BNA Act. In 1927 five women, led by Nellie McClung and Emily Murphy, appealed this law all the way to the Supreme Court of Canada. In an astounding decision, the court upheld the BNA Act. The women then appealed the decision to the highest court in the British Empire, the British Privy Council. In 1929 the Privy Council recognized that women were persons after all, with full social and political rights.

The last barrier to women's suffrage in Canada was overcome on April 25, 1940. Led by Madame Therese Casgrain, the women of Quebec won the right to vote in provincial elections.

In time women began to assert themselves in all areas of political life. They became senators and important cabinet ministers. In 1978 Flora Macdonald made a serious bid for the leadership of the Progressive Conservative party. Many people feel it is only a matter of time before Canada has a woman prime minister.

In recent years, women's struggle has focussed on social and economic issues. Equal pay for equal work,

Three notable women in Canadian public life lead a panel discussion on International Women's Day, March 9, 1982. From left, the PC's Flora MacDonald, the NDP's Pauline Jewett and the Liberal's Celine Hervieux-Payette.

equal pay for work of equal value, daycare centres and abortion rights are issues that have become familiar to all Canadians. They are still surrounded by much legal and social controversy. The next few years will determine how these issues will be resolved.

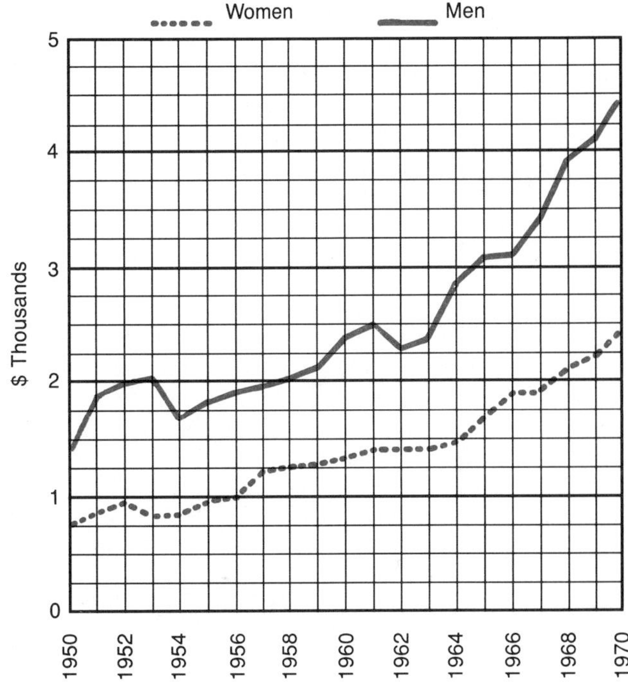

AN ERA ENDS

As the 1970s came to a close, Trudeau's Liberal government was beset by ever-growing problems: rising energy costs, inflation and unemployment, a declining economy, Quebec separatism and Western alienation. In 1979 Canadian voters turned to Joe Clark and the Conservatives to solve these problems. The public soon became convinced that Clark was not the man for the job. In the election of 1980, they returned Pierre Trudeau as prime minister for the fourth time.

During his last term in office, Trudeau concentrated on developing a "made-in-Canada" constitution to update the BNA Act. This had been a dream of Canadian politicians for many decades. On April 17, 1982, after much high-level diplomacy, Queen

A group of provincial premiers discuss strategy during breakfast at the constitutional negotiations.

Elizabeth II at last signed into law the Constitution Act (see Unit 1).

Following this crowning achievement, Trudeau resigned as prime minister in 1984 and passed the mantle of leadership to John Turner. An era had come to an end. Probably no Canadian politician before or since has been so intensely admired or so intensely disliked as Pierre Elliot Trudeau.

THE CONSERVATIVES RETURN TO POWER

With the brief exception of the summer and fall of 1979, the Conservatives had been out of power in Canada for over 20 years. As the election of September, 1984, approached, it initially appeared that John Turner would continue the Liberal dynasty. The Canadian public, however, was in the mood for change. When the results of the election were announced, Brian Mulroney and the Conservatives had won the greatest number of parliamentary seats in Canadian history—211.

It is the Conservatives and not the Liberals who now face the issues of the 1980s: the technological revolution, nuclear weapons, the race for outer space, women's rights, the rights of native people and free trade. These are problems that Canadians and their government must face together in this decade.

Brian Mulroney faces the reality of a difficult job following his record victory in the 1984 federal election.

BUILDING YOUR LEARNING SKILLS

FOCUSSING ON THE ISSUE

1 Summarize five important events that occurred in the period following World War II.

2 Describe two social movements that were important during this period.

3 The following terms appeared in this chapter. Try to recall their meanings and how they were used.

suffragettes	FLQ
Trudeaumania	generation gap
baby boom	hippies
equal pay for equal work	just society

RESEARCHING

1 Find out which teams won the Stanley Cup and the Grey Cup in each of the following years: 1950, 1955, 1960, 1967.

2 Do some research on Canadian singers of the 1950s. Are any of these performers still popular today?

3 Gather information on Canada's prime ministers since 1945. Who was the youngest elected prime minister? Who was the oldest? Which prime minister during this period stayed in power the longest?

1·2·3 ORGANIZING

1 Draw up a chart of Canada's prime ministers since 1945. For each one, indicate what you think his outstanding achievement was.

2 List these events in the order in which they occurred:
- ▶ FLQ crisis develops.
- ▶ The Korean War breaks out.
- ▶ Expo '67 unites Canada.
- ▶ Newfoundland joins Confederation.
- ▶ The Constitution Act is passed.

3 Rank the above events in their order of importance, in your point of view.

COMMUNICATING

1 Debate the proposition: Canada should never arm its missiles with nuclear warheads.

2 It can be argued that clothing and hair styles are a form of communication. Examine the photographs of young people in this chapter. What message are they communicating? Contrast the message of the fifties with that of the sixties.

3 Write a letter to the editor of your local newspaper stating your opinion on the effect of rock-and-roll music on teenagers.

ANALYZING

1 It has been argued that the prosperity of the 1950s resulted in a generation that was too interested in material goods. Is the current trend in society towards materialism?

2 The building of the St. Lawrence Seaway has been called one of the greatest engineering projects in the world. Assess the importance of the seaway to Canada's economy.

3 Obviously, teenagers have been around since the beginning of the human race. Yet it can be said that teenagers as a distinct group were identified in the 1950s. What arguments can be used to support this statement?

4 The advent of television has created a social revolution in modern society. In what ways has television helped to change the attitudes and values of young people?

APPLYING YOUR KNOWLEDGE

1 The oil strike at Leduc in 1947 helped to trigger an oil boom in Canada's West. It has been argued that energy self-sufficiency should be a Canadian priority for the future, even if it means that Canadians must pay more for this energy. What arguments can be used to support or attack this point of view?

2 The concept of equal pay for work of equal value has created controversy in Canada's political and economic circles. What are the arguments in favour of this concept? What potential difficulties might arise in attempting to impose this policy on the work force?

3 In the period after 1945, Canada opened its doors to immigrants from all over the world. Recently, it has become more difficult for immigrants to enter Canada. In view of recent world events, what should Canada's long-term policy be toward immigration?

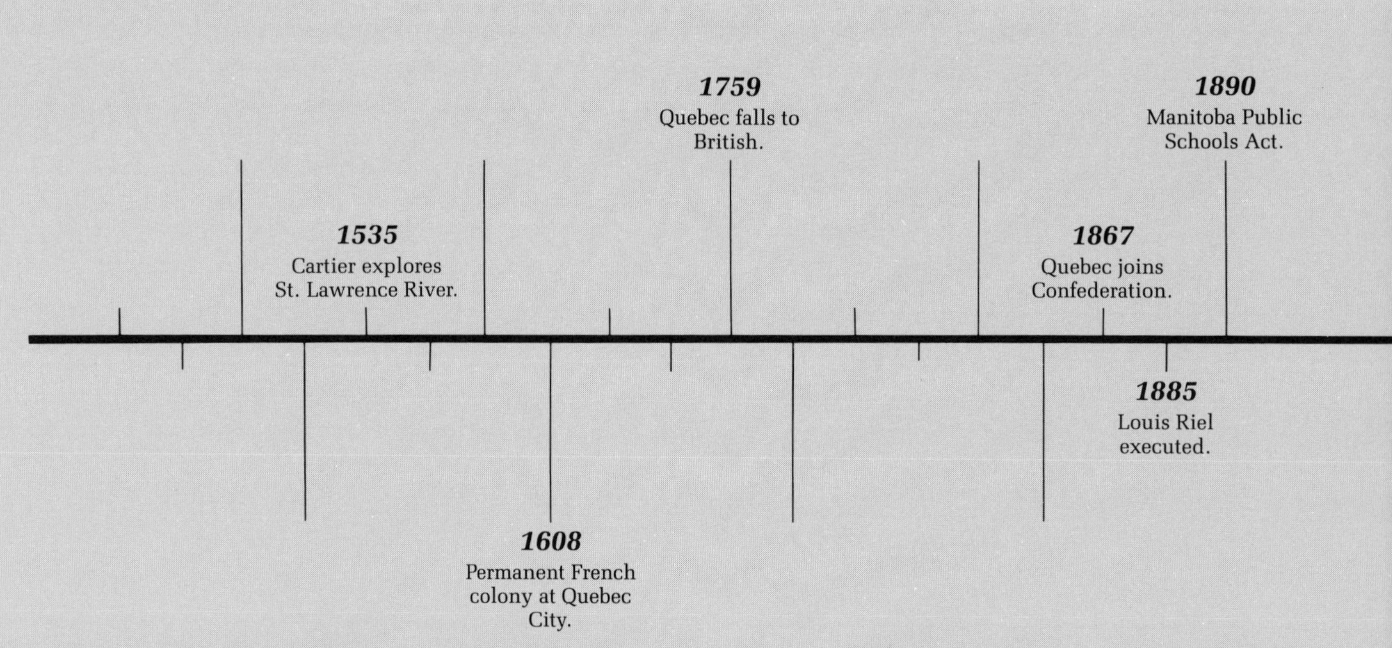

1759
Quebec falls to British.
1890
Manitoba Public Schools Act.
1535
Cartier explores St. Lawrence River.
1867
Quebec joins Confederation.
1885
Louis Riel executed.
1608
Permanent French colony at Quebec City.

unit four

ENGLISH–FRENCH RELATIONS

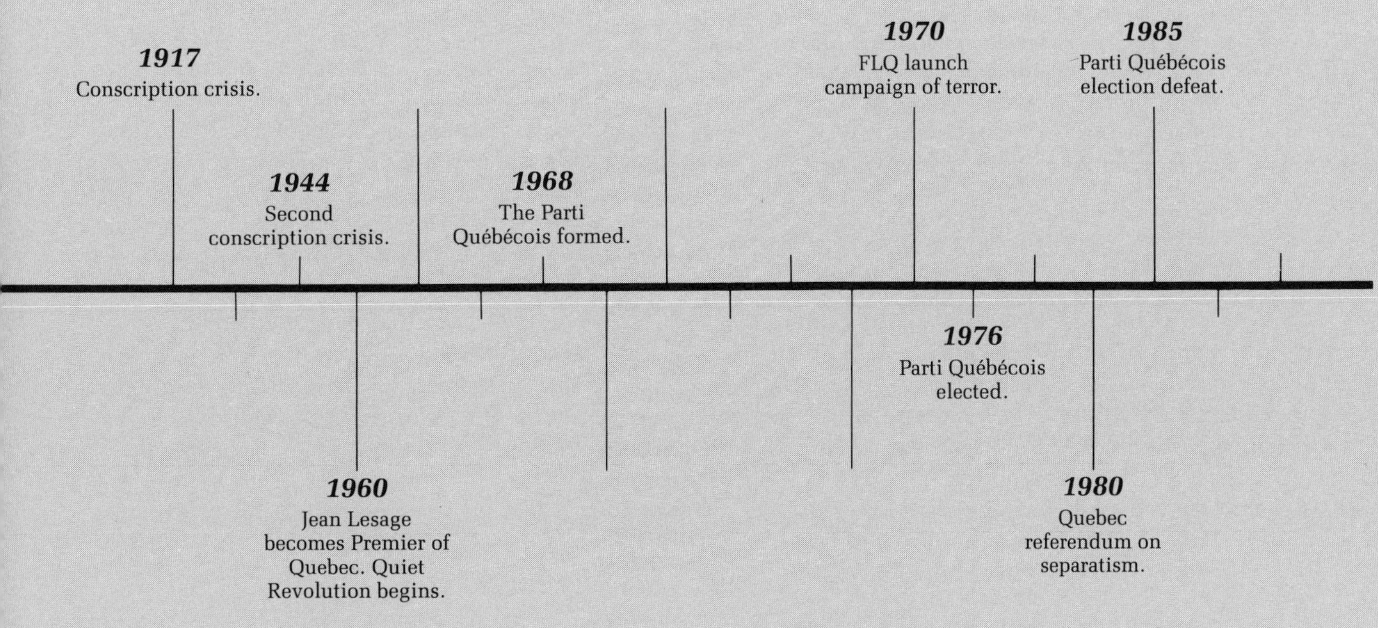

1917
Conscription crisis.
1944
Second conscription crisis.
1960
Jean Lesage becomes Premier of Quebec. Quiet Revolution begins.
1968
The Parti Québécois formed.
1970
FLQ launch campaign of terror.
1976
Parti Québécois elected.
1980
Quebec referendum on separatism.
1985
Parti Québécois election defeat.

TOPIC ORGANIZER **PAGE**

THEME ORGANIZER

- Canada was a French colony long before it became a British possession.
- On several occasions, in different ways, the British attempted to weaken or erase the French culture in Canada.
- French-Canadians have always strongly defended their language, traditions and culture.
- The "French fact" has not always been fully accepted by some English-Canadians.
- Throughout our history, controversial incidents have occurred that have divided our people into "two solitudes," one English and one French.
- From time to time, some French-Canadians have contemplated turning Quebec into an independent homeland, separate from Canada. They envision Quebec as a sovereign nation, with its own flag, anthem, boundaries and armed forces.
- The Quebec separatist movement became a major force in our political life during the 1970s.
- Recently, rapid and sweeping changes have occurred in Quebec and the rest of Canada. These have resulted in French-Canadians feeling more comfortable as members of the Canadian Confederation. Thus, separatism has been weakened, at least for now.

INTRODUCTION

One of the most dramatic events in Canadian history occurred on November 15, 1976. It probably is fair to say that Canada has not been and will never be the same since that date. On that day, a provincial election was held in Quebec. This election was won by the Parti Québécois (party of Quebeckers).

Most Canadians were deeply shocked at this development. The main goal of the Parti Québécois in those days was the ultimate separation of Quebec from the rest of Canada. For this reason, supporters of the party were called separatists. They wished to make Quebec an independent country, with its own flag, national anthem and armed forces. An independent Quebec would conduct its own relations with foreign countries, including Canada. It would have its own place at the United Nations and in other world bodies.

Today the threat of Quebec separatism seems to have faded into the background. But its rapid emergence in the 1970s shook this country to its very roots. Think of it! Quebec officially became part of British North America in 1763. In 1867 it joined Canadian Confederation as one of four charter (original member) provinces. It was and remains today one of our richest, largest and most populous provinces. If Quebec were ever to leave the Canadian union, the results could be disastrous. Imagine a map of the new Canada. What would it look like? What problems would be created by Quebec being an independent country? Now think about our economy and culture. How would the loss of Quebec affect Canada's physical size (and do you know by how much)? If Quebec separated, what would Canada lose besides land area? How would our image in the world be affected?

A number of separatist organizations sprang up in the 1960s. The Parti Québécois was formed in 1968; the election of 1976 was only its third political campaign! Its opponents pointed out that it had won only about 41 percent of the votes cast. Thus, well over 50 percent of Quebec voters had actually voted against the party. Indeed, some voters who did support the Parti Québécois did not actually favour separation. Rather, they were making a protest vote against the party in power. This was the Liberal party, which they felt had done a poor job of running the province. They merely hoped that the Parti Québécois would provide more honest and effective government.

Nonetheless, the 1976 election showed how quickly the separatist party had risen in popularity. Moreover, 41 percent of the vote was enough to give the Parti Québécois 69 of the 110 seats in the Quebec parliament. For the first time in Canadian history, a provincial government was controlled by a political party whose ultimate goal was to take that province out of the Canadian union.

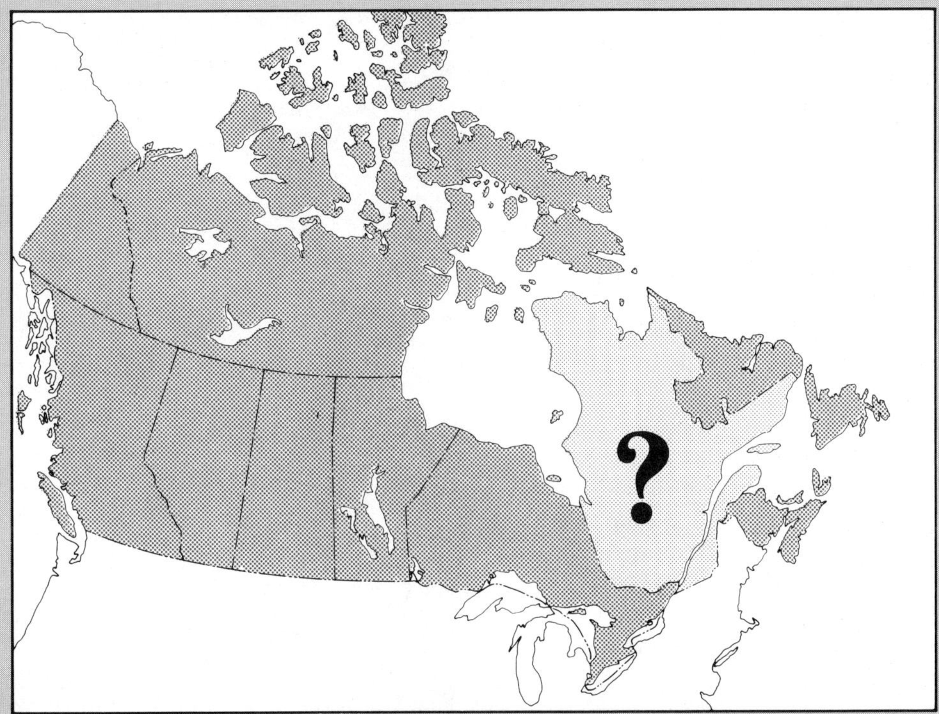

This unit will explore the historical background to Quebec separatism and the reasons for its emergence in the 1960s and 1970s. It will show how this serious challenge was met by Canadians. You will see the separatist tide reach its high-water mark in the early 1980s and then apparently recede, at least for the moment. A vital aim of this unit is to show that the issue of national unity has been and always will be absolutely crucial for Canada. If Canadians stop respecting and caring about each other and about their country, all of us will be in deep trouble. Separatism could re-emerge in Quebec or in other regions of the country where people feel seriously mistreated over a long period of time.

In the next three chapters, we are going to look at the topic of English-French relations in Canada. The first chapter provides a brief review of the historical background of English-French relations. The second studies changes that took place in Quebec from around 1960 to 1975. The last chapter examines the growth of separatist feeling in Quebec and, to some extent, in other provinces.

SEPARATISM IS NOT UNIQUE TO CANADA

Canada is a federal state (review Unit 1). This means that the country is divided into several regions. Each region has its own local government. As well, there is a central government, which handles matters affecting the whole country.

These regions of a federal state usually are called provinces or states. Sometimes, they are distinctive for some reason. They might have special economic interests. Some have unique geographic features. Sometimes they even have dialects, languages or cultures of their own. Such differences can cause a region to feel somewhat apart from the rest of the country. Such feeling can turn into a desire by a region to be completely separate, or independent.

Obviously, this situation exists in Canada. However, it is also found in many other countries. Some Scots want Scotland to be a separate country, not part of the United Kingdom. The Basque people are not completely happy about being part of Spain. Some people in Brittany do not want to be part of France. The accompanying headline appeared recently in a Canadian newspaper. It refers to a separatist problem in Belgium.

Belgian rivals nearer deal on separatism

Belgium is composed of two states. One is Flemish, the other Walloon. This distinction is based on differences of language and culture. To keep the country united, a compromise has been worked out. This includes separate government departments for each group in education, economics and culture. There are separate radio and television networks. Even in the armed forces, there are separate Flemish and Walloon units. Only the top command is unified. Its officers usually speak English as a compromise.

In Canada some people feel that we might have to go as far as Belgium has in order to keep Quebec in Confederation. However, it is not certain that most English-Canadians could accept such an arrangement. Also, such a plan might not meet all the needs of French-speaking Quebeckers.

Identify the two former Canadian politicians portrayed in this cartoon. What point is the cartoon trying to make?

UNIT PREVIEW QUESTIONS

As you study this unit, keep these questions in mind. You may want to return to them when you have finished the unit.

1 How long have the French been in North America?
2 Why have the French in Canada always been so concerned about the survival of their language and culture?
3 For most of our history, what seems to have been the most common feeling among English-speaking Canadians toward French-Canadians? Why has this been so?
4 Why did Quebec agree to join Confederation in 1867? Have French-Canadians received from Canada everything that they could reasonably expect?
5 What advantages or benefits does Quebec get from being part of Canada?
6 What is our federal government (in Ottawa) doing about the challenge of separatism? Can you suggest other policies that could or should be tried?
7 René Lévesque and his followers disliked being called "separatists." Instead, they preferred

"indépendentistes." Why should they stress the idea of independence (freedom) rather than separation? Which term are you inclined to use? Why?

8 There are about 900 000 French-Canadians living outside Quebec (mostly in Ontario and New Brunswick). What would become of them if Quebec separated from Canada? The same could be asked about the 800 000 English-Canadians living in Quebec.

FRIDAY, JULY 1, 1977

A political cartoonist's view of Dominion Day celebrations July 1, 1977. What comment is the cartoon making?

chapter 11

THE HISTORICAL BACKGROUND OF ENGLISH–FRENCH RELATIONS

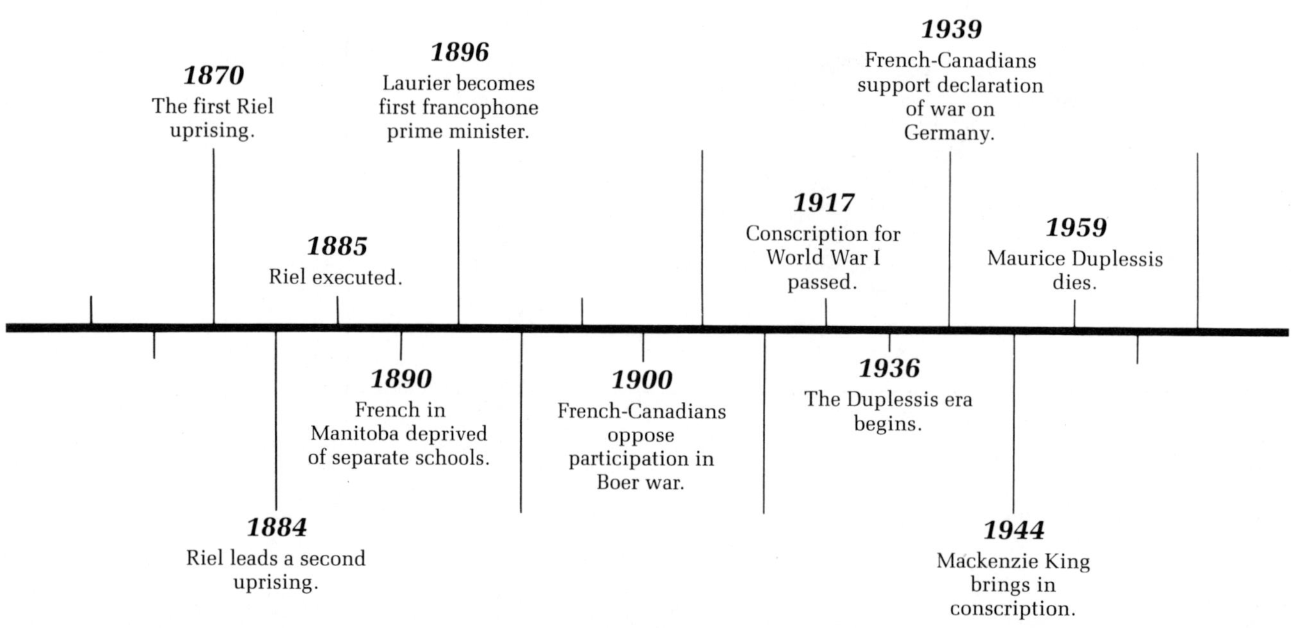

1870
The first Riel uprising.
1884
Riel leads a second uprising.
1885
Riel executed.
1890
French in Manitoba deprived of separate schools.
1896
Laurier becomes first francophone prime minister.
1900
French-Canadians oppose participation in Boer war.
1917
Conscription for World War I passed.
1936
The Duplessis era begins.
1939
French-Canadians support declaration of war on Germany.
1944
Mackenzie King brings in conscription.
1959
Maurice Duplessis dies.

TOPIC ORGANIZER | **PAGE**

THEME ORGANIZER

- The execution of Louis Riel divided Canada along English-French lines.
- While the execution of Riel was legal, the later denial of education rights to the French in Manitoba was a clear violation of the Constitution.
- During World War I, the conscription issue created the deepest English-French division in our history.
- In the 1930s, the rise to power of Maurice Duplessis meant that Quebec would keep most of its traditional ways for another 20 years.
- The second conscription crisis, during World War II, was better handled than the first; thus, it created less English-French conflict and was resolved more quickly.
- After World War II, great pressures for change built up in Quebec. However, Premier Duplessis managed to keep these under control until his death in 1959.
- The death of Duplessis was like the bursting of a dam: A flood of social, economic and political change quickly swept away much of the "old Quebec."

INTRODUCTION

The French tradition in Canada predates that of the English by at least 150 years. The colony of New France was established early in the seventeenth century. Based on farming and the fur trade, it had become a proud, tightly knit community of 60 000 people by 1750. When Britain and France went to war in 1746, the conflict spilled over from Europe into North America. Quebec, the heart of New France, was captured by the British in 1759. In the peace treaty that ended the war in 1763, France surrendered all of its possessions in Canada to Britain.

From this time on, French-Canadians became concerned about their survival as a people. The British conquerors regulated trade, government, law enforcement and all military matters. They also encouraged English-speaking immigrants to come to Quebec as well as to the rest of Canada.

There were great cultural, religious and other differences between the two peoples. To protect their own interests, each group struggled to maintain or increase its power within the political system. French-Canadians remained loyal to Britain during the American Revolution and again during the War of 1812. Having been abandoned by France, they preferred rule by Britain to absorption by the United States.

When Confederation was proposed in 1867, French-speaking Quebeckers had a decision to make. Without Quebec's participation, there could be no meaningful Canadian union. However, if they joined Confederation, French-Canadians would be in a minority position within the country as a whole. A compromise was essential.

After some bitter arguments within their own community, French-speaking Quebeckers decided to support Confederation. A key part of the deal was that there would be separate provinces, each with powers over local matters. Thus, by virtue of their majority within Quebec, the French could retain control of their language, customs, education and other aspects of their identity. It was hoped that mutual respect and trust would help prevent serious crises from occurring in English-French relations.

The years from 1867 to 1960 were very important in the history of Canada. Many of the developments of this period are noted in Unit 3. These years were also important for English-French relations. In 1867, French-Canadians made up approximately 40 percent of Canada's population. By 1960, they accounted for only 30 percent of the population. Generally, this period can be described as one of "ups and downs" in relations between the two peoples. There were quiet times, but these were broken up by events that produced very strong feelings on both sides.

On the whole, the French lost the arguments. This was mainly because they were in the minority. After each setback, they tended to withdraw more and more into a protective shell. Naturally, their outlook became increasingly negative and defensive. This

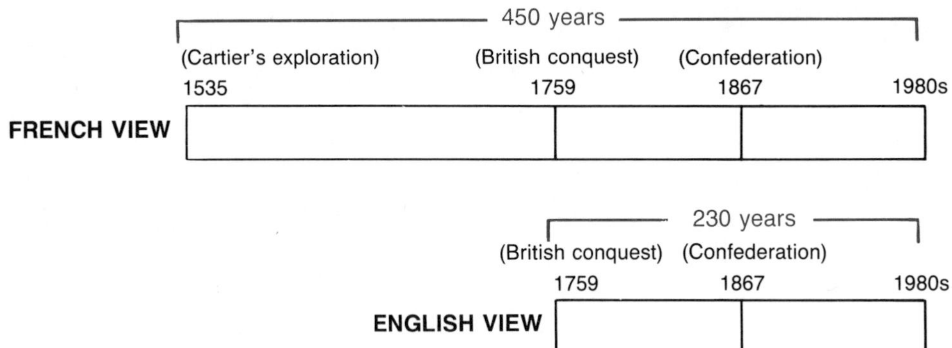

means that their feelings towards Canada became less favourable. They began to take less interest in the affairs of the country. Perhaps they felt that their views were not wanted or would not count for very much. Instead, they concentrated on protecting their language and way of life within Quebec itself. In a sense, they turned that province into a kind of fortress. Here they felt comfortable and at home. They could find shelter from the storms that, from time to time, raged around them.

Before reading on, study the chart of key words and ideas that follows.

KEY WORDS AND IDEAS IN THIS CHAPTER

Term	Meaning	Sample Use
conscription	compulsory enlistment for military service, usually during times of war	Conscription was used to increase Canada's armed forces in World Wars I and II.
constitutional rights	basic rights specifically guaranteed to people in the constitution of their country	French-Canadians believed that their constitutional rights to French language education, guaranteed in the BNA Act, were taken away in Manitoba and Ontario.
corruption	dishonesty; a willingness to ignore principles in return for a reward, such as money	Quebec's troubles in the 1930s were worsened by corruption in its government.
crisis	a very serious or dangerous situation	There have been several crises in English-French relations since 1867. These include the execution of Louis Riel and conscription (twice).
Orangeism	membership in the Orange Order, or sympathy with its beliefs, which tended to be anti-Roman Catholic and, in Canada, anti-French-Canadian	Orangeism was particularly strong in Ontario in the late nineteenth and early twentieth centuries.
postwar boom	a period of prosperity and growth that often follows a major war	A postwar boom occurred after World War I and again after World War II.
treason	any action that betrays or helps to destroy the country of the person who commits it.	Louis Riel was accused of treason for his leadership of rebellions in the Canadian West. He was convicted and hanged.

THE RIEL AFFAIR

Details of this episode already have been provided in Unit 3, Chapter 8. If necessary, review them before reading further.

The Riel affair created very strong feelings in both French and English Canada. Compare opinions quoted below:

This editorial appeared in the *Toronto Evening News* in 1885:

Ontario is proud of being loyal to England.

Quebec is proud of being loyal to sixteenth-century France.

Ontario pays about three-fifths of Canada's taxes, fights all the battles of provincial rights, sends nine-tenths of the soldiers to fight the rebels [Riel's], and gets sat upon by Quebec for her pains. . . .

Hundreds of thousands of dollars are spent in maintaining the French language in an English country. . . .

An anti-French party is springing up in all the Provinces except Quebec. . . .

If we in Canada are to be confronted with a solid French vote, we must have a solid English vote. . . .

If she is to be a traitor in our wars, a thief in our treasury, a conspirator in our Canadian household, she had better go out.

She is no use in Confederation. . . .

As far as we are concerned, and we are concerned, and we are as much concerned for the good of Canada as any one else, Quebec could go out of the Confederation to-morrow and we would not shed a tear except for joy.

If Ontario were a trifle more loyal to herself she would not stand Quebec's monkey business another minute.

Louis Riel

Honoré Mercier, a Quebec politician (later to become premier of that province), gave this speech to a mass rally of 50 000 people in Montreal, also in 1885:

Riel, our brother, is dead, the victim of his devotion to the Metis cause of which he was the leader, the victim of fanaticism and treason: of the fanaticism of Sir John [A. Macdonald] and of some of his friends; of the treason of three of ours [the three French Canadians in the Macdonald cabinet] who, in order to save their portfolios, have sold their brother.

By killing Riel, Sir John has not only struck our race at the heart but also struck the cause of justice and humanity which, represented in all languages and sanctified by all religious beliefs, demanded mercy for the prisoner of Regina, our poor brother of the North-West.

In the face of this crime, in the presence of these failings, what is our duty? We have three things to do: unite ourselves in order to punish the guilty; break the alliance that our deputies have made with Orangeism and seek, in a more natural and less dangerous alliance, the protection of our national interests.

INTERPRETING THE DOCUMENTS

1. Why would English Protestants, particularly in Ontario, be critical of Riel? Why would some of them want him hanged? How would the motive of revenge enter into their thinking?
2. Which of the charges made in the Toronto editorial were accurate and fair at the time they were made? Which were not?
3. Would many English-Canadians today agree with any of the feelings expressed in that editorial? If so, which ones? How would they support their views?
4. What does it mean to "identify" with someone? Why would many French-Canadians identify with Riel as their "brother"?
5. Mercier referred in his speech to "Orangeism." What was this?
6. What threat is made in Mercier's final sentence?

JUSTICE NOT SATISFIED.

SIR JOHN. "Well madam, Riel is gone; I hope you are satisfied."

JUSTICE. "No, I am not. You have hanged the EFFECT of the Rebellion. I must now punish you as the CAUSE."

What is the point made in the above cartoon? Of the Riel affair, Edward Blake (a bitter foe of Macdonald) said: "Had there been no neglect, there would have been no rebellion; if no rebellion, no arrest; if no arrest, no trial; if no trial, no condemnation; no condemnation, no execution. They, therefore, who are responsible for the first are responsible for every link in that fatal chain." Do you agree with Blake?

The final decision about whether or not Louis Riel should hang rested with the prime minister and his cabinet. Macdonald's government allowed Riel's execution to proceed. This decision was greeted with cheers in Ontario but with howls of protest in Quebec. Many French-Canadians felt that this decision had been made for political reasons. They charged that Macdonald valued English votes more than French ones. This made sense, in a way, because the English were the majority. Also, it could be claimed that a decision that pleased the majority was fair and democratic. On legal grounds, it was possible to argue either way. However, most French-Canadians felt that a moral wrong had been done. Somehow, the bargain of Confederation had been broken.

MINORITY RIGHTS IN EDUCATION

When Quebec entered Confederation in 1867, its leaders insisted that education should be under the control of provincial governments. This was provided for in the British North America Act. Furthermore, that act protected the educational rights of minorities. Section 93 clearly stated:

> (1) Nothing in any such (Provincial) Law shall prejudicially [harmfully] affect any Right or Privilege with respect of Denominational [belonging to a church or distinct group] Schools which any Class of Persons have by Law in the Province at the Union.

It went on to say that if any province passed any law harmful to the educational rights of a minority, that minority could appeal to the federal government. This government was given the power to pass whatever measures were necessary to remedy the problem and thus protect the minority. By these terms, the English, Protestant minority in Quebec could enjoy its own separate schools. So could the French, Roman Catholic minorities in Ontario and Manitoba—or so it seemed.

Bad feelings about the Riel episode were still in the air when new trouble broke out in Manitoba. In 1890 that province passed the Manitoba Schools Act. This measure cut off government funds to Roman Catholic schools. Such schools had been guaranteed in 1870, when Manitoba entered Confederation. Most of Manitoba's Catholics were French-speaking. These people felt, quite correctly, that they were being denied their constitutional rights. They appealed to the federal government in Ottawa. However, Prime Minister Macdonald refused to take action. Next, they sought help from the high court in Britain. This body first turned them down, then handed the problem back to the Canadian government. The problem remained unsolved.

In 1896, Wilfrid Laurier was elected prime minister. He was a bilingual French-Canadian. Eventually, he managed to win a few small privileges from the government of Manitoba for its French-speaking citizens. However, the French in Manitoba did not win back all of their educational rights. In fact, in 1916 the Manitoba government passed an Education Act. It did away with the concessions won by Laurier. English became the only language of instruction in the schools of the province. A similar situation developed in Ontario. In 1913 the department of education announced that French could not be used as a language of instruction past the first form (Grade 9). There were about 250 000 French-Canadians in the province at this time. They, too, believed that their proper rights were being denied.

CONSCRIPTION IN WORLD WAR I

Canada's part in this war has already been described in Unit 3. By 1917 World War I was in its third year. It was taking a terrible toll in human life. After a visit to the front lines, Prime Minister Borden was convinced that conscription was necessary. It was the only way to replace the heavy losses that our troops were suffering. For example, in April and May of 1917, Canadian casualties were 23 939. In the same period, only 11 790 volunteers joined the forces.

Conscription would mean that Canadians would be drafted (forced) into the armed forces. Borden's decision produced a crisis in English-French relations. Most English-Canadians agreed with the decision. However, most French-Canadians did not. A long and bitter debate followed. Some of the bad feeling still lingers in the memories of older Canadians who lived through the experience.

SOME OF THE ARGUMENTS PRESENTED BY THE TWO SIDES IN THE CONSCRIPTION DEBATE

Pro conscription (mostly English)

- As a colony of Britain, Canada has a moral and legal duty to do everything in its power to help Britain win this war.
- If Britain loses this war, Canada will suffer. Much of our foreign trade will be lost. The German navy might blockade the St. Lawrence River or even the Pacific coast around Vancouver.
- In April and May of 1917, our casualties were 23 939 but only 11 790 new volunteers enlisted.
- Prime Minister Borden gave Canada's word that we would keep four divisions in the field. Our allies are counting on us.
- If we cannot send replacements, our remaining troops will be in even greater danger. Those who died will have died in vain.
- By seeing this war through to victory, Canada can be proud. We will win the respect of the world.
- You can't back out in the middle of a fight. If we did, in later years we would be looked upon as "quitters" and "chickens" by other countries and by our own children.
- By helping Britain, we help her ally, France. If Canada is ever attacked in the future, we will need the help of these great powers.
- French-Canadians have not been volunteering at the same rate as English-Canadians. Conscription will force them to do their share.

Robert Borden discussing military affairs with army officers.

Anticonscription (mostly French)

- Canada's first obligation is to itself. Britain chose to get into this war; let Britain fight it.
- Germany has no quarrel with us. If it *did* try to harm us, the United States would help us. We cannot do anything big enough to decide who wins or loses the war anyway.
- The losses are unfortunate, but those who volunteered knew the risks they were taking.
- No one realized at the start of this war how long and costly it would become. We have done our share.
- Enough blood has already been shed. Bring the other troops home if necessary.
- Canada does not need fame and should not take pride in fighting wars.
- Let others think what they want. Nothing important for Canada is at stake in this war.

Henri Bourassa, publisher of the newspaper *Le Devoir*, was the leader of the anti-conscription forces.

- We feel no more obligation to France than to Britain. Neither France nor Britain would shed as much blood for us as we have already shed for them.
- French-Canadians are already a minority. They do not wish to throw away their future generations by forcing their sons to fight a British war.

1 As you read the above arguments, which side do you take? Switch the order, so that you read the anticonscription arguments first. Does your opinion change or remain the same? If it changes, why do you think this happens? For a well-founded view, you must do more research.

2 Another reason for French-Canadian opposition was their complaint that they were being asked to join an English army. The recruiting officers usually were English. Very few of the recruiting posters were in French. Training, orders and instruction manuals were mainly in English. The sergeants were mainly English. Most promotions went to English-speaking soldiers. Did the French have good reason to complain? Do you think that a two-language army can function reliably in emergencies?

3 A few French-Canadians went so far as to complain that conscription was an English plot to reduce their numbers. It is a fact that the French could replace their losses only through natural reproduction (births). English Canada would recover much more quickly. This was because the English could replace their losses through immigration *plus* natural reproduction. Should French-Canadians still have been expected to enlist the same proportion of volunteers as the English?

4 As prime minister, what would you have done about conscription in 1917?

Conscription was established by the Military Service Act. This became law on August 28, 1917. Riots and demonstrations broke out in several Quebec centres. Dozens of people were injured or killed before order was restored.

To justify his stand on conscription, Prime Minister Borden called an election in 1917. He won a sweeping victory. However, of the 65 seats in Quebec, 62 were won by the Opposition. Quebec was still solidly against conscription. Once again, French-Canadians had been outvoted and overpowered by the English majority. A few speeches were made in the parliament of Quebec calling for separation of that province from Canada.

THE PERIOD BETWEEN THE WARS

World War I ended with the defeat of Germany in 1918. As the years passed, the bitter feelings about

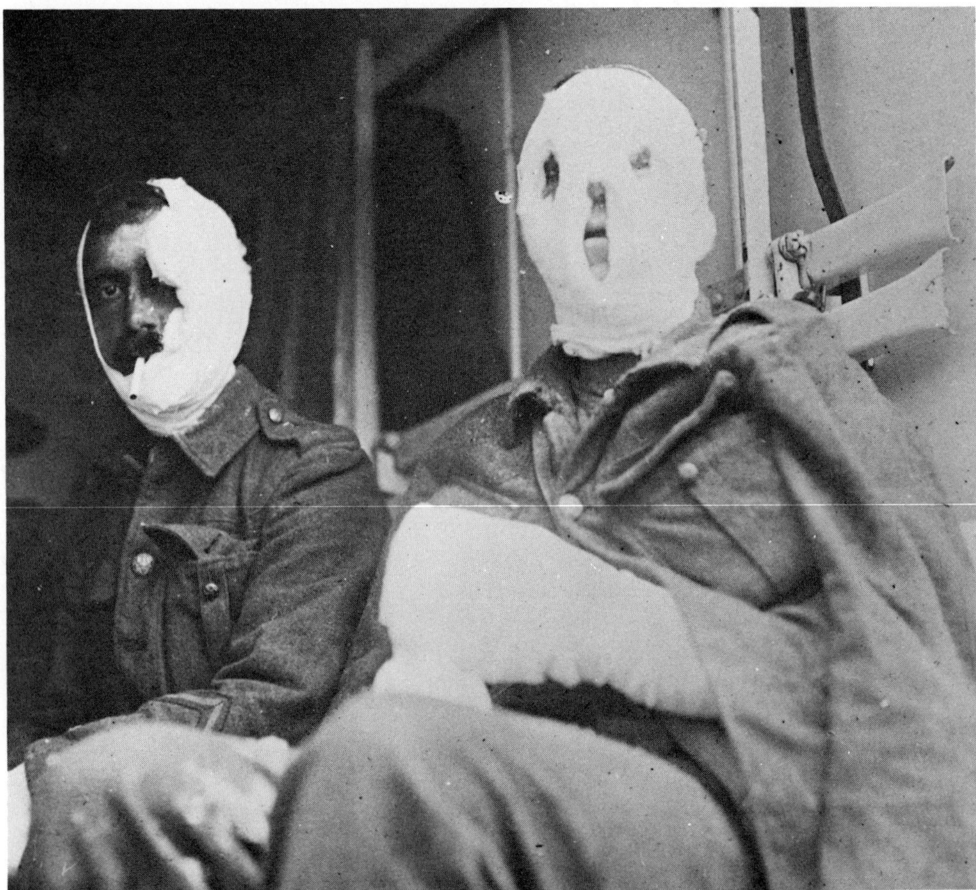

Wounded Canadian soldiers heading back to England, July 1917. If such a photo (or worse ones) appeared in major Canadian newspapers at the height of the conscription debate, what might be the effect on that debate? Would it be more likely to create support for, or opposition to the proposal to draft men into the armed forces? Explain your reasoning as fully as possible.

conscription began to die down. Like other parts of the country, Quebec was somewhat changed by the war. Industries grew larger. More and more people came to live in the towns and cities. Still, for many French-Canadians, the old way of life went on. This was especially true in rural areas. As in all parts of Canada, the younger generation became more interested in education. College graduates tended to follow careers in medicine, law, teaching or the church. This had been a pattern in French Canada for a long time. Some young people moved to the cities. There most of them found jobs in factories or businesses. However, their bosses usually were English. This situation was regarded as normal and did not seem to cause serious problems at the time.

The same could not be said of the Great Depression. This disaster brought great suffering, from one end of Canada to the other. Thousands of people lost their jobs. Many others had to take cuts in pay. Hundreds of businesses went broke. A new politician, Maurice Duplessis, took advantage of these problems to win power in Quebec. He argued that, since the English ran most of Quebec's economy, they were largely to blame for its troubles. Though not completely true, this idea was quite popular with French voters. Duplessis also promised to "get tough" with Ottawa. He wanted more power and tax money from the federal government. His party, the Union Nationale, did a fairly good job of governing Quebec. Progress was made in the fields of education, transportation and hospital care. But no great victories over Ottawa were won. Moreover, Duplessis often accepted support from powerful English interests. Thus, many aspects of life in Quebec did not change very much.

Maurice Duplessis (centre) surrounded by supporters. What institutions, represented here, gave considerable support to the Duplessis government?

WORLD WAR II: CONSCRIPTION AGAIN

As described in Unit 3, World War II broke out in 1939. Canada was in it from the beginning. Once again, we fought on the side of Britain and France. Germany was the main enemy. Our prime minister was Mackenzie King.

At first King promised that there would be no conscription. He wanted to keep the country united. However, battle losses became heavy. The promise could not be kept. Conscription was introduced in 1944. This time the government eased the blow. It said that conscripted men would be used only for home defence. They would not be sent overseas. However, by the end of the war, in 1945, over 13 000 conscripts had been sent overseas.

Despite these facts, conscription was probably not as serious a question as it had been in World War I. This time the enemy was Adolph Hitler, and most people agreed that he had to be stopped. Also, King clearly tried hard to consult French Canada. He was sensitive to French feelings. He chose a French-Canadian, Louis St. Laurent, as his main assistant on this issue. St. Laurent won much support with a speech in Parliament in which he said that:

Prime Minister Mackenzie King reviews a French-Canadian regiment in Britain during World War II.

What is the statement being made by the cartoonist in this drawing?

Believing as I do that, whenever the majority, after full consultation and mature deliberation, reaches a conclusion of that kind [for conscription], it is proper the minority should accept it and loyally assist in carrying it out. . . .

THE POSTWAR ERA

Between 1945 and 1960, English-French relations were quiet. Life gradually returned to normal after the war. The country was quite prosperous. By today's standards, its problems were fairly minor. Maurice Duplessis remained in power in Quebec until his death in 1959. On the surface, everything appeared to be fine.

Beneath this calm exterior, important changes were taking place in Quebec. The war had created an industrial boom. Thousands of new jobs were created in industry and business. More than ever before, Quebeckers poured off the farms and into the cities. Soon the old ways were but a memory for most of them.

In the cities, people were less influenced by the old ties of family and church. Exciting new futures were open to them. Most of these demanded higher education. Many French Quebeckers began to see things about their province that they did not like. For example, they saw that the English minority ran most of the economy. Worse, they ran it in the English language! French-Canadian workers were not as well paid as the English, yet they suffered from higher unemployment. The provincial government was becoming very corrupt. Also, it was not nearly as tough with the federal government as it pretended to be. The power of Ottawa over the lives of Quebeckers seemed to be growing. This federal government was almost completely in the hands of English-Canadians. A feeling began to grow among the French in Quebec that some big changes were needed.

As long as he was alive, Maurice Duplessis was able to keep these new forces for change under control. His power over the province was very great. However, his death had the effect of a bursting dam. New energies, new ideas and new hopes for French Canada were released. They came flooding out in all directions. *La révolution tranquille* (the Quiet Revolution) had begun.

BUILDING YOUR LEARNING SKILLS

FOCUSSING ON THE ISSUE

1 What key ideas about English-French relations are presented in this chapter? (Choose at least three, and then compare your thoughts with those of your classmates.)

2 Formulate five "remembering"-type questions, the answers to which summarize the most important factual information related to your "key ideas" above.

3 The following terms appeared in this chapter. Try to recall their meanings and how they were used.

commute (a sentence)	Orangeism
conscription	postwar boom
constitutional rights	Quiet Revolution
corruption	revenge
crisis	separate schools
Great Depression	treason

RESEARCHING

1 Do research to discover whether it was the intention in 1867 to give the French language equal status with English throughout Canada. Why or why not?

2 Investigate the terms of Confederation as they applied to French-Canadians. Do you think they were offered a fair deal? Explain your answer.

3 The year is 1891. A general election will soon be held in Canada. The intelligence (spy) branch of the British government has asked you to prepare a top-secret report on the two leading candidates for prime minister. They are John A. Macdonald (Conservative) and Wilfrid Laurier (Liberal). Basically, the British want you to describe and analyze the approaches of the two men to the key issue of English-French relations. You are expected to include an assessment of the background, personality and attitudes of each of the two candidates as they relate to this issue. Finally, the British government wants your advice as to which candidate it should secretly support in the forthcoming election with funds and propaganda. Naturally, you are expected to back up your recommendation with strong, clear reasons.

4 As a follow up to question 1 above, who *did* win the 1891 election? Why? Can you discover whether the British government seemed to support either candidate?

5 Gather as much information as possible concerning the violent demonstrations that occurred in Quebec when the federal government passed conscription. What happened? How did the authorities respond? What losses or casualties resulted from these incidents?

6 Try to discover how Prime Minister King's handling of the conscription issue in World War II differed from Borden's handling of the problem in World War I. Can you also uncover reasons for King's different approach?

ORGANIZING

1 Place the following developments in chronological order (time sequence, earliest to latest):
- ▶ The second conscription crisis develops.
- ▶ The Manitoba schools become an issue.
- ▶ Louis Riel is executed.
- ▶ The first conscription crisis develops.

2 Now rank the above from most to least harmful in terms of their apparent effects on English-French relations.

3 Try to think of another way in which the authors might have organized this chapter. Return to your "Focussing" questions and pick a main theme for the chapter. What are the essential supporting facts or materials for this theme? In what order or sequence would you present them to a reader? Why?

4 Try to explain why the authors chose a basically chronological sequence for their order of presentation in this chapter.

COMMUNICATING

1 You are Louis Riel, waiting to speak in your own defence at your trial on a charge of treason. Make some rough speaking notes. Ask classmates for a few other ideas. Organize your thoughts, and then write out a good version of your entire speech. Present the speech to the class or to a group within the class. (Which will be more important, *what* you say or *how* you say it?) Compare your version of the main defence speech with the actual one delivered by Riel.

2 You are John Doe, a Canadian soldier serving in the trenches during World War I. It is 1917, and the conscription debate is raging. You have suffered minor wounds on two occasions. Both times you were patched up and sent back to the battle lines. You have seen many soldiers, both friend and enemy, horribly mutilated or blown to pieces during heavy fighting. You yourself have killed at least three men. Write a letter home to your mother in which you express a strong opinion either for or against conscription.

3 Now you are the mother of John Doe (above). John has written you a letter in which he speaks out on the idea of drafting people into the armed forces. In your letter back to him, break the news gently: His sister, Elizabeth, serving as an army doctor, has been killed during an air raid when enemy planes mistakenly bombed her field hospital. Whatever stand John took on conscription, proceed to support the *opposite* side with as many arguments as you can muster.

4 Imagine that television existed at the time of the Riel trial. You are a TV producer who has been told by the network executives that ratings are down. You are under pressure to plan coverage of the Riel trial in such a way that more viewers will be attracted. Get those ratings (and profits) *up*! With a few classmates, form a small group to plan your trial coverage. People can assume the roles of camera director, studio anchor person, on-the-scene reporters and interviewers. Develop your plan for coverage as fully as possible, and then present it to the class.

ANALYZING

1 If you were guaranteed certain rights and protection under the law and then were denied those rights, how would this affect your feeling toward the law? What development, discussed in this chapter, illustrates this point?

2 If a province or a large group of people can show that its constitutional rights have been violated, is it entitled to walk out of Confederation? Explain your answer.

3 Prepare a graph that you can use to show the trends in English-French relations from 1867 to

1959. Across the bottom, progress in time at five or ten-year intervals. Up the left-hand side, establish a scale of one to ten to indicate the severity of strain in relations at specific times. Plot the key developments appropriately, showing when they occurred and the level of tension they produced (in your opinion). If more than one person attempts this activity, consider having each participant begin with an identical blank graph. This way, once all the graphs are completed, they can easily be compared and discussed. Perhaps the teacher can make an overhead of the basic graph, and then individual student graphs can be superimposed to facilitate comparison and discussion.

4 In your opinion, which prime minister did the best job of handling English-French relations in the time period under discussion? Who was the worst? Explain your decision in each case.

5 Try to discover how Maurice Duplessis stayed in power for so long in Quebec. Did he hasten or slow down the approach of the Quiet Revolution? Defend your choice.

6 Below is the coat of arms of the Province of Quebec.

As you can see, the motto inscribed is "Je me souviens." How does it translate? What does it imply?

APPLYING YOUR KNOWLEDGE

1 Two interesting simulations can be developed from the Riel affair.

a Recreate Riel's trial. Explore the nature of the charges against Riel. Choose witnesses, a jury and key people to act as the prosecuting and defence attorneys. Perhaps your teacher should act as the presiding judge. Afterwards, the whole class can evaluate the trial and discuss the main points that were made by both sides.

b Turn the class into the cabinet of Sir John A. Macdonald. This body had the power to commute (reduce) Riel's sentence. It chose not to do so. Assign appropriate roles, making sure that each province and each major interest group are represented. Take note of the accusation about the cabinet made in Mercier's speech, which is quoted on page 193. The cabinet meeting should be run in a fairly informal way to encourage each person to express an opinion suitable to his or her role. To achieve a high degree of realism, you must keep in mind that the cabinet is made up of politicians. They are most concerned with getting and keeping power and with practical solutions to problems.

2 November 16, 1985, was the one-hundredth anniversary of the execution of Louis Riel. To mark the occasion, a number of publications, including *The Toronto Star*, published articles on the question of whether or not Riel should be granted a posthumous pardon. Such a proposal was made earlier by a member of Parliament from the Regina area.

If necessary, refer to this textbook's section on law to make sure you understand what a pardon is. Next, in light of your previous work on the Riel episode, formulate your own opinion as to whether such a pardon would be appropriate today. Finally, locate the two *Toronto Star* articles. (They appeared on separate pages in the first section of that newspaper.) Answer these questions:

a What is the source of each article?

b Do they basically agree or not?

c Which article is best argued? Why?
d Do you agree with either article? Why or why not?

3 Imagine that Prime Minister Borden has just announced conscription in 1917. Write a short play depicting the conversation within a family having sons of military age. You can make use of some of the ideas developed in the letter-writing exercise in the preceding "Communicating" section; enlarge and extend them. Part of the class should write action and dialogue for a French-Canadian family; part should write for an English-Canadian situation. How are the families' reactions similar? How are they different?

4 You have heard the term "generation gap." Briefly describe what it means. Try to imagine the effect on a rural French-Canadian family of the children moving to the city. Set the scene in the 1950s. How would the life-style of the parents appear to the children? What about the other way around? Which generation would be likely to support the status quo (the way things are and have been for a long time)? Why?

5 There have been occasions when Canadian citizens have honestly been unable to obey the law for reasons of conscience or because of their religious beliefs. Try to discover examples of this dilemma other than the conscription issue. When one of us has truly serious reasons for opposing the law, what courses of action are open to us? Which of these avenues can you support and which do you reject? Why?

6 Earlier you were asked to research the terms of Confederation as they applied to the French in Canada. What possible relevance would these terms have for English-French relations in today's circumstances?

chapter 12

THE QUIET REVOLUTION AND BEYOND

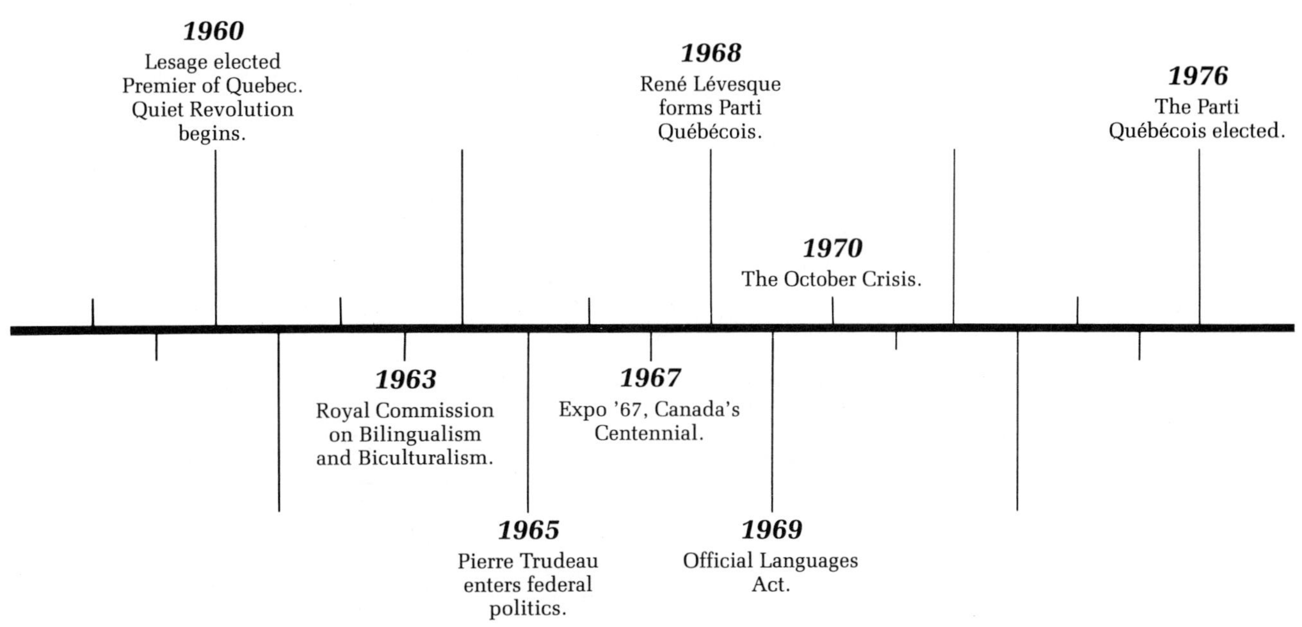

1960
Lesage elected Premier of Quebec. Quiet Revolution begins.
1963
Royal Commission on Bilingualism and Biculturalism.
1965
Pierre Trudeau enters federal politics.
1967
Expo '67, Canada's Centennial.
1968
René Lévesque forms Parti Québécois.
1969
Official Languages Act.
1970
The October Crisis.
1976
The Parti Québécois elected.

TOPIC ORGANIZER

THEME ORGANIZER

- The election of Premier Jean Lesage in 1960 signalled an awakening in Quebec.
- The Quiet Revolution referred to a process of dynamic growth and change that was without parallel in Quebec's history.
- French-Canadians began to question themselves about their identity and their place within Canada.
- The new restlessness in Quebec made some English-Canadians uncomfortable and even angry.
- The Quiet Revolution made Quebec the political focus for French-Canadians across Canada. This helped to produce the greatest challenge ever made to Canadian Confederation.
- French-Canadians sought complete equality and fulfilment as a people. This would have to take place either within Canada or within a separate, independent nation of Quebec.
- Our federal government responded with a series of initiatives for change. Some French-Canadian extremists criticized these initiatives for being much too timid; English-Canadian radicals attacked them for being far too generous.
- The key question became: Could English- and French-Canadians find a common view of Canada and accept the changes necessary to achieve full equality for the French culture here?
- The Quebec separatists won power in the 1976 provincial election. The possibility of Quebec leaving Confederation forced many Canadians to re-examine their positions on the key question.

INTRODUCTION

As we have seen, English-French relations followed a fairly steady pattern from the time of the conquest in 1759 to the death of Maurice Duplessis in 1959. Most of the time, each group went its own way. These periods of calm were sometimes broken by serious and even violent conflict. Then feelings cooled down. Many English-Canadians regarded Canada as a one-language country. English was the official language of government and business. Both of these fields were dominated by English-speaking people. There was no trouble as long as the French accepted that "this is how it is."

However, by 1960 the mood of Quebec was changing. The French majority there was no longer ready to accept things as they were. In the words of one French-Canadian, "We have survived enough. The time has come to give this survival a positive sense, to fix a goal for it and to justify it." In short, changes had to be made. The French of Quebec would no longer accept English control of their economy. They would no longer accept the second-class position of their language, either in Quebec or in the rest of Canada.

Before reading on, study the chart of key words and ideas that follows.

KEY WORDS AND IDEAS IN THIS CHAPTER

Term	Meaning	Sample Use
Anglophone	a person who speaks the English language	Some Anglophones tended to the view that Canada was a country of and for the English; they opposed official bilingualism and the goals of the Quiet Revolution.
backlash	a movement or feeling against a current trend	There was a backlash in English Canada against efforts to please French Canada.

consultation	seeking advice	Quebec has long wanted more consultation between the federal government and the provinces before important decisions are made.
controversy	argument or difference of opinion	There was a controversy over whether air-traffic controllers in Quebec should be able to work in French as well as English.
Francophone	a person who speaks the French language.	Francophones tended to support the Quiet Revolution and want more rights for French-Canadians living outside Quebec.
independence	being on your own without needing to rely or depend on others	Some French-Canadians would like independence for Quebec. It would then no longer be a province of Canada.
Red Ensign	a flag of British origin and design that served as Canada's flag until we adopted our own distinctive flag in 1965	The replacement of the Red Ensign with the maple leaf flag was a sign of Canada's "coming of age"; another symbol of our earlier ties with Britain was removed. This was particularly pleasing to those French-Canadians who did not want to be reminded of the British conquest of New France in ages past.
revenue	money that makes up a government's income	Quebec and the other provinces would like a larger share of Ottawa's revenue.
subsidy	financial aid	Quebec and the other provinces would like increased subsidies from the federal government.
terrorist	a person who uses violence to try to gain a political goal	Terrorists believing in Quebec's independence carried out bombings, kidnappings and other violent acts in Quebec in the 1960s.

WHY THE QUIET REVOLUTION HAPPENED

The following conditions existed in Canada in the early 1960s. They explain many of the reasons for Quebec's unrest.

- Quebec's rate of unemployment was one of the highest in Canada.
- In Quebec many French-Canadian workers were earning less than non-French workers doing the same job.
- The English minority in Quebec had many more rights and privileges than French minorities had in other provinces.
- Many French-Canadians had to speak English to keep their jobs in Quebec.
- Ottawa, Canada's capital, was almost an all-English city.
- Most of the top jobs in the federal civil service were held by English-Canadians.
- There were only a handful (five or six) of

French-Canadian cabinet ministers. None of them had a really important department to run.

- The prime minister of Canada could speak hardly any French. He seemed to be unaware of the new feelings of Quebeckers.
- The birth rate among French-Canadians was falling rapidly. The great majority of new immigrants to Quebec were sending their children to English schools.
- French-speaking Quebeckers did not seem to have their share of top jobs, even in Quebec.

Here are some statistics to illustrate a few of the points made above:

Occupation and Ethnic Origin — Quebec, 1961 (Percentages)

Source: (*Report of the Royal Commission on Bilingualism and Biculturalism,* Volume 3A, 1969)

QUEBEC LABOUR INCOME

Average Labour Income of Male Workers from Selected Ethnic Groups 1961

	Income	Index
All ethnic groups (average)	$3469	100.0
British	4940	142.4
Scandinavian	4939	142.4
Jewish	4851	139.8
German	4254	122.6
Polish	3984	114.8
Asian	3734	107.6
French	3185	91.8
Italian	2938	84.6
Indian	2112	60.8

THE REVOLUTION BEGINS QUIETLY

As we have seen, the Quiet Revolution did not happen overnight. The forces of change had been at work for many years in Quebec. The death of Maurice Duplessis in 1959 released them in full force. This was made clear in the Quebec election of 1960. The Union Nationale party was defeated. It had been in power for 18 of the previous 23 years. The Liberal party, led by Jean Lesage, now took over. His government began to work on these goals:

- Clean up the corruption in Quebec's government;
- Improve public services, such as hospitals and transportation;
- Increase wages and pensions;
- Develop natural resources;
- Reform education;
- Develop new industries that are under French control where possible.

This was a very ambitious and costly program. To make sure he had public support, Lesage called another election in 1962. The Liberal party slogan was *Maîtres Chez Nous* (masters in our own house). The Lesage government was re-elected by the voters. Encouraged, it pressed on with its programs.

These photos depict both the older rural aspects of Quebec and the newer urbanized Quebec.

Educational reform was a vital part of the Quiet Revolution. Studies showed that many school buildings were inadequate. Teacher training and educational equipment were somewhat old-fashioned. Supplies were scarce. Perhaps most important, the curriculum (program of study) was out of date. More attention had to be paid to science, mathematics and business courses. Such a change in emphasis would provide young French-Canadians with the training needed to qualify for important jobs in industry. In a modern economy, it was not enough for French-Canadians to be doctors, lawyers and teachers. If they were to have influence, they would also have to become engineers, architects, technicians, computer experts, managers and so on. Realizing this, the Lesage government poured millions of dollars into Quebec's educational system.

Even this was not enough. If the Quiet Revolution was to succeed, other things had to happen. The rest of Canada would have to recognize the equality of the French language to the English language. The nearly one million French-Canadians outside of Quebec would have to be treated respectfully, as the equals of English-Canadians. The federal government in Ottawa would have to contain more French-Canadians in important positions. It also would have to grant more powers to Quebec, plus funds to make use of those powers.

THE REVOLUTION BECOMES LESS QUIET

When the Lesage government began to press for these goals, the rest of Canada woke up. The revolution was growing loud. Things had been peaceful for 15 years. English-Canadians had been lulled into thinking that change was not necessary. They were not in the habit of reading newspapers from Quebec. They did not see the tension building. Therefore, they were rather unprepared for what began to happen. The new demands of Quebec came as a shock to most of them.

Ottawa felt most of the pressure. Premier Lesage accused the federal government of interfering in provincial affairs, particularly in education. He asked for the right to pull Quebec out of several federal programs, such as pensions and medical plans. Quebec preferred to handle these alone. He also wanted Quebec to have more control over its own economic development. This was important for many reasons. It would make it easier for French-Canadians to play a greater part in the Quebec economy. This, in turn, would help the French preserve their language and culture in the province.

Premier Lesage was not yet through: He wanted more. To pay for Quebec's greater powers, he needed more money. Therefore, he asked Ottawa for a larger share of the revenue (money) brought in by the federal income tax. In addition, he wanted Ottawa to pay bigger subsidies (grants of money) to Quebec.

Finally, Mr. Lesage demanded more consultation between Ottawa and the provinces. By this he meant that the federal government should pay more attention to provincial feelings. It should tell provincial governments about its plans. It should ask their advice and even gain their support more often. It should not simply act on its own in matters that affect provincial interests.

Naturally, such demands raised a lot of eyebrows. Still, many other provincial leaders tended to agree with Quebec on these questions. Some of them felt that Ottawa was becoming too powerful. More co-

Jean Lesage

French President Charles de Gaulle tours Quebec in 1967.

operation was needed. More money, of course, was always welcome. Still, to many English-Canadians, Quebec was going too far, too fast. Demands like this could weaken the central government. They could even threaten the unity of the country. Just what was Quebec after? Where would its demands end?

In 1966 opponents of the Quiet Revolution saw a ray of hope. Quebec held another election, but this time the Lesage government was defeated. Many Quebeckers had become alarmed at the huge spending programs of their government. The changes were too great and too many even for them. The Union Nationale returned to power. It was led by Daniel Johnson. Now, perhaps, things would return to normal. Such thoughts did not last long. Premier Johnson did not intend to give up the main goals of the Quiet Revolution. He kept the pressure on Ottawa for the same things that Lesage had wanted.

Mr. Johnson also revealed a new plan to help achieve these goals. It involved closer ties with France. English Canada had kept fairly close ties with *its* mother country. Why shouldn't Quebec renew old bonds with France? The latter might be helpful as a trading partner. It also could supply investment funds to build Quebec's economy. Perhaps it would give moral support to the Quiet Revolution. Some English-Canadians panicked. They feared that Quebec might be seeking France's help in becoming partly or fully independent.

This fear reached a peak in 1967 when French President Charles de Gaulle visited Quebec. From the balcony of Montreal's city hall he shouted, "Vive le

Montreal, May 17, 1963. Bomb disposal expert Sgt. Walter Leja is seriously injured by the explosion of a terrorist bomb placed in a mailbox.

Québec Libre!" ("Long Live Free Quebec!") English Canada went wild. Letters poured into editors demanding that de Gaulle apologize, be sent home or worse. He was asked to leave Canada by the Canadian prime minister, Lester Pearson. Many French-Canadians were excited by de Gaulle's sympathy for them. But few of them wanted to separate from Canada. They were shocked by the violence of English-Canadian reactions.

Violence of another sort had also begun in Quebec. As early as 1963, a handful of radicals swung into action. They broke into stores and army warehouses to steal guns and ammunition. They painted separatist slogans in prominent places. They planted bombs in public buildings. Such actions were condemned by the vast majority of French-Canadians. Still, they were well publicized in the English press. It was time for Ottawa to act.

OTTAWA RESPONDS

At first the federal government was not sure what to do. By 1963 its plans were somewhat clearer. Quebec and the other provinces were consulted more, just as Premier Lesage had asked. The provinces were granted more powers and more money to carry them out. As a result, Quebec set up its own system of pensions, student loans, youth allowances and other programs. Partly to please Quebec, a new Canadian flag was adopted in 1965. The maple leaf emblem replaced the old Red Ensign. The latter was too closely identified with our colonial ties to Britain. Therefore, it was disliked by many French-Canadians. They felt that Canada, as an independent country, should have a distinctive flag of its own.

In another important move, Ottawa set up a special commission in July, 1963. This was called the Royal Commission on Bilingualism and Biculturalism. It had two jobs: first, to examine the condition of the French language and culture in Canada; second, to suggest ways to improve this condition. The federal government made another vital point: In future, the English and the French would be regarded as equal founding peoples of Canada. Their relations would have to develop in a spirit of partnership. The last traces of the old "conqueror-and-conquered" relationship would have to go.

These were brave words and noble thoughts. However, these hopes could only come true if all Canadians *wanted* to see them realized. A few commentators said that it had to happen or Canada would be finished within 20 years. Few people took them seriously.

THE "BI AND BI" COMMISSION

In 1965 the Royal Commission on Bilingualism and Biculturalism made an early report. It described English-French relations as poor. It threw challenges to both sides.

To the English

- Stop acting as though Canada is a one-language country, run by and for the English.
- End your prejudice and discrimination against the French.
- Accept the French language and culture as part of Canada's culture and way of life.

To the French

- Stop harping on past injustices.
- Don't blame the English for all your troubles.
- Claim your full rights under the law, and use them more effectively.
- Start showing more attachment to Canada, not just Quebec.

In the next few years, the "Bi and Bi" Commission made several important recommendations. Here are some of them:

- Declare Canada officially bilingual (done);
- Make English and French the official languages of the Parliament of Canada and the federal courts (done);
- In communities where the English or French minority is large enough, provide government services in both languages (partly done);
- Give students in all provinces a chance to study both languages (done where provinces agreed);
- Employ more French-Canadians in the federal government (done);
- In Quebec make French the main language of work in government and business (done);
- Ontario and New Brunswick should declare themselves officially bilingual provinces (done in New Brunswick);
- All provinces should provide services in French or English to their minorities (partly done);
- Declare the region of Ottawa-Hull the national capital area and make it officially bilingual (done).

REACTING TO THE "BI AND BI" REPORT

1 Do you agree with most of these recommendations? Which ones do you agree with? Why?

2 Do you strongly disagree with any of these ideas? If so, why?

3 Do you think the "Bi and Bi" Commission wanted all Canadians to become bilingual? Explain your answer.

4 Do you personally believe that all Canadians should become bilingual? Would this be possible?

5 Look up the most recent Canadian census. Make up a chart showing the four or five largest ethnic groups in each province. Which province, other than Quebec, has the most French-Canadians? Germans? Italians? Ukrainians? Chinese? Greeks?

6 Some people suggest that if French is going to have official recognition, so should the languages of other large ethnic groups. These would include German, Italian and Ukrainian. How do you feel about this idea?

TRUDEAU: A NEW VOICE IN OTTAWA

An exciting new personality came into politics in the mid-1960s. He was young, intelligent and fluently bilingual. His name was Pierre Trudeau. For years, as a professor and writer, he had been a critic of government. In 1965 he joined the Liberal party and was elected to Parliament. By 1968 he was prime minister of Canada.

The newly elected prime minister, Pierre Elliott Trudeau, conducts a working lunch with Jean Marchand (left) and Gerard Pelletier (right). These men were brought into the Trudeau Cabinet to help bring a "new deal" to French-Canadians.

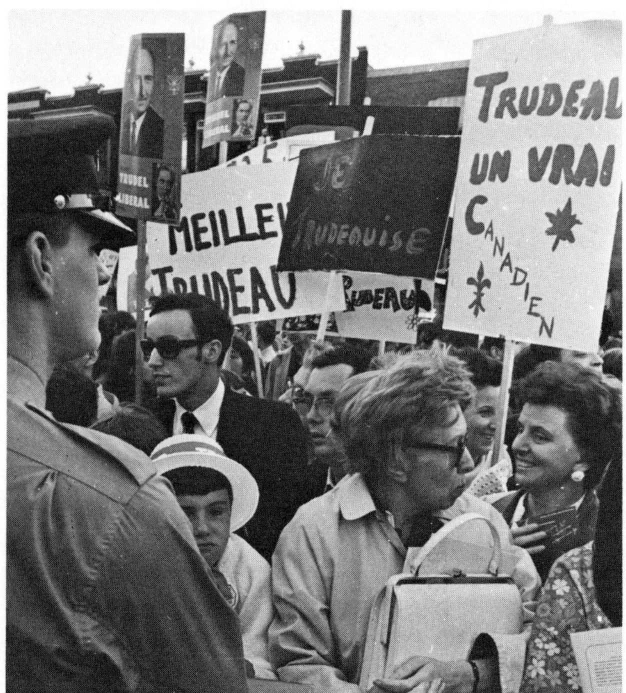

This photo indicates the popularity of Pierre Trudeau with French-Canadian voters in the late 1960s.

To English-Canadians he seemed the perfect person to heal the country's wounds and restore unity. They especially liked his view that Quebec should remain in Canada. Mr. Trudeau was strongly opposed to separatism. He called it a backward step. He said it would be harmful to Canada but even more costly to Quebec. He also denied that large changes were needed in the Canadian Constitution (the BNA Act). In his opinion, Quebec had all the basic powers needed to protect and advance the French language and culture. Quebeckers, he claimed, should use their energy and determination to exercise their existing rights and thus to achieve their full potential. Also, Trudeau called upon English-Canadians to recognize the "French fact" in Canada. This required their genuine acceptance of French-Canadians throughout the nation as full and equal partners in Confederation.

Most French-Canadians were happy about the election of Mr. Trudeau as prime minister. They, too, rejected separatism. However, many of them disagreed with his statements about the Constitution. There was a growing feeling, especially in Quebec, that some basic changes were needed.

NO SPECIAL STATUS FOR QUEBEC

Pierre Trudeau rejected the suggestion that Quebec needed and deserved special status in the Constitution because of its unique situation. Clearly, he thought that equality was the main goal for which all French-Canadians should strive. Basically, he felt that equality already existed—on paper. The task was to make it real in the hearts and minds of all Canadians.

1 Try to discover the main changes proposed by supporters of special status for Quebec.

2 Do you agree with any of these ideas? Why or why not?

3 Pierre Trudeau regarded equality, not special status, as the proper goal of French-Canadians. One reason for this was simple fairness. Another was political reality. Which goal would have been easier to persuade the rest of Canada to accept? Explain your answer.

4 What great gamble was Mr. Trudeau taking by rejecting special status for Quebec? Looking back, did his gamble pay off? If so, for whom? Were there any losers? Elaborate on your conclusions.

Instead, Mr. Trudeau concentrated on fostering bilingualism. He brought many prominent French-Canadians into the government. They were given key positions in the cabinet and the civil service. Large sums of money were spent to provide language instruction to civil servants who could speak only one language. By 1976 this spending had reached almost $150 million per year. This policy was criticized by some Canadians for two reasons. First, it obviously was expensive. Second, they argued that it was not working. This latter criticism is the more important. The amount spent to promote bilingualism in the civil service was only one-third of 1 percent of the total 1976 budget. Surely this would not be too high a price to pay if the program worked? Unfortunately, it appeared to be failing.

DIFFICULTIES WITH BILINGUALISM

The Trudeau government learned that the saying is true: It really is difficult to "teach an old dog new tricks." Most unilingual adults are poor students when it comes to learning a second language. Perhaps there was another way? The federal government began to think that it would be better to concentrate on the younger generation. In other words, provide teachers and funds to expand language programs in elementary and secondary schools across Canada. However, this plan posed problems too. One of these was that education was a provincial responsibility. Provinces had always guarded this right very jealously, Quebec most of all. Time was another factor. Could the country wait until a new generation of bilingual Canadians grew up?

Other problems with bilingualism were emerging as well. A backlash was developing in English Canada. People were complaining of the "favouritism" being shown to Quebec. As evidence, they pointed to the numbers of French-Canadians being appointed to key government jobs. They claimed that Quebec was receiving more money from Ottawa than it was paying in through taxes. Montreal was the site for Expo '67 and the 1976 Summer Olympic Games. (Actually, this was largely because of the efforts of Montreal itself. Both projects were very expensive and left Montreal with serious financial problems.)

Perhaps most importantly, English-Canadians felt that French was being "rammed down their throats." An Ontario father kept his child home from classes after "O Canada" was sung in French over the school's public address system. A Toronto radio station broadcast a short commentary entitled, "Hey, Quebec: Go Suck a Lemon!" Phone calls and letters poured into the station. They did not condemn the prejudice and intolerance shown in the program. Rather, the vast majority of them said, "Right on!" Equally strong letters began appearing in English-language newspapers. A few excerpts appear below:

> "For generations, Quebec has been Canada's baby, spoon-fed, diapered and powdered at the expense of the rest of the Canadian taxpayers."

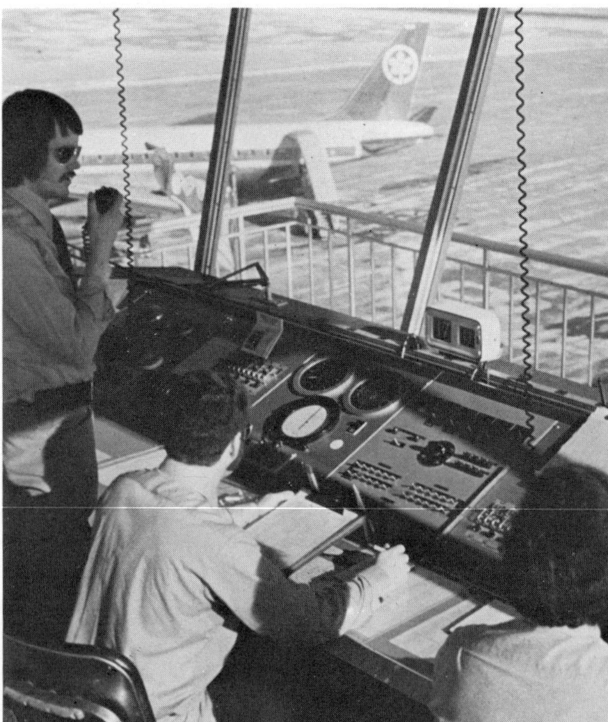

In 1976 pressure grew to let French-speaking pilots and air traffic controllers communicate over the air in French. Many English-Canadians protested. Investigate this issue. How was it resolved?

> "Giving in to continual French demands in . . . English-speaking provinces, while we observe what is happening in Quebec, is folly to the ultimate degree."
> "Given your choice of a bilingual Ontario or Quebec separation, I vote for the break-up of Canada. Mais oui!"

Ironically, bilingualism was also opposed by many French-Canadians. As one observer said, "We are not asking to speak French in Vancouver. We are asking to live in French, in Quebec." Another added, "We don't want to feel at home in Winnipeg or be served in French in your post-office. You write 'luggage' on your airport doors. We'll write 'bagage' and serve you in French in our post-office."

There were English-Canadian supporters of bilingualism. However, they seemed to be in the minority. Also, their position was made more difficult by some rather drastic developments within Quebec.

COULD A FRENCH-CANADIAN FEEL AT HOME IN YOUR COMMUNITY?

Most Canadians want our country to stay together. They do not want Quebec or any other province to leave Confederation. Some people claim that French-Canadians would identify more with Canada if they could feel "at home" outside Quebec.

Examine your own community. How comfortable would you feel in it if you spoke only French? To answer this question, consider these points:

- Could you do your shopping in French?
- Could you deal with the government, police or other services in French?
- Could you speak French at work?
- Could you or your brothers and sisters go to a French school?
- Does your community have a French-language newspaper? radio station? TV channel? theatre? library?
- What else would be required for you to feel "at home" in the community?

Obviously, it would be impossible for all or even most communities in Canada to make both English- and French-speaking people feel "at home." Fortunately, it also is unnecessary. Still, perhaps bilingualism should be further advanced than it is. How large do you feel a community should be before it can be asked to support bilingual facilities? How large should a cultural minority be before it can expect bilingual services? Apply these standards to your own community. How is it doing?

THE QUIET REVOLUTION GETS NOISY IN QUEBEC

In 1970 the Union Nationale government lost power in Quebec. The Liberal party, led by Robert Bourassa, took over. Besides being a fellow Liberal, Mr. Bourassa shared Prime Minister Trudeau's belief that Que-

Robert Bourassa

bec should stay in Confederation. The signs seemed encouraging.

Then, in October of 1970, a series of shocking events occurred (see Chapter 13). A radical separatist group kidnapped James Cross, a British trade official. A few days later they kidnapped Quebec's minister of labour, Pierre Laporte. Eventually, Mr. Cross was freed, but Mr. Laporte was killed. The crisis was finally overcome, but not before some extreme statements were made on both sides. Most French-Canadians were repelled by these criminal acts. However, some of them sympathized with the emotions and frustrations of the terrorists. Some English-Canadians could not understand this combination of feelings.

Bilingualism and English-French relations generally suffered a more serious blow in 1974. Mr. Bourassa's government passed the controversial Bill 22. This act made French the only official language of Quebec. Here are some of its terms:

- Business firms would be pressed to operate in French. Those that did not would not receive any government contracts.
- Immigrant children wishing to attend English schools would have to take tests in that language. If they could not pass, they would then have to attend French schools.
- Present English schools could not expand unless granted government approval.
- Official documents, business contracts, product labels, menus and billboards had to be printed in French. Special permission would be required to print them also in English.
- Employers had to be able to communicate with their employees in French.

Bill 22 did not ban English from the parliament or courts of Quebec. It *did* require that English be taught in French schools.

This act offended many English-Canadians. It created hardships for the 20 percent of Quebec's population that was non-French. Obviously, it did a great deal of damage to the bilingualism program of the federal government.

The newly elected premier of Quebec, separatist René Lévesque, speaks to supporters just after the announcement of his victory of November 15, 1976.

NOVEMBER, 1976: SEPARATIST VICTORY!

For weeks in advance, the polls kept saying it would happen. Few people believed them—until it *did* happen! On November 15, 1976, the Bourassa government was overwhelmingly defeated by the separatist Parti Québécois. Details of this development are provided in the next chapter. It is enough to say here that the entire country was stunned. Even the Parti Québécois itself was somewhat surprised at its great success.

English-French relations, it seemed, had come to a cross-roads. Or had they come to the end of the road?

BUILDING YOUR LEARNING SKILLS

FOCUSSING ON THE ISSUE

1 The term "Quiet Revolution" is quite unusual. Why was it appropriate for what was happening in Quebec during the 1960s?
2 What became the largest single question facing Quebeckers during the Quiet Revolution?
3 What are the most important understandings to have about English-French relations during the Quiet Revolution?
4 Name four French-Canadian politicians who were very important to the Quiet Revolution in some way. Outline the role that each played in that process. Evaluate the significance of each individual's contributions.
5 The following terms appeared in this chapter. Try to recall their meanings and how they were used.

air traffic controller	francophone
anglophone	independence
"Bi and Bi" Commission	Quiet Revolution
Bill 22	Red Ensign
consultation	revenue
controversy	subsidies
curriculum	terrorist

RESEARCHING

1 Try to find media coverage of the 1960 provincial election campaign in Quebec. What were the main issues? How did the two major contending parties stand on those issues? Who won? Why?
2 Who was the prime minister of Canada when the Quiet Revolution really broke out into the open in Quebec? Investigate the attitude he took and the actions he carried out in the face of the changes that were occurring.
3 Examine the rapid rise of Pierre Elliott Trudeau in federal politics. How and why did it happen? Was "Trudeaumania" real?
4 Various students should each poll a number of adults to discover their feelings about Canada becoming officially bilingual. Ask them:
   a how they felt when the Trudeau government first began to really promote this goal;
   b how they feel about this issue today.
   c have their views changed much? Why or why not?
5 Examine newspaper and magazine commentaries on the dramatic election victory of the Parti Québécois in November, 1976. Try to obtain samples from various provinces. What are the most frequent viewpoints expressed? Where does the most extreme commentary on each side of the issue come from?
6 As we have seen, some French-Canadians complained that they did not have enough representation in the federal cabinet. This is a key body because it advises the prime minister. Its members also set government policy for the entire country. As well, they provide leadership for the various departments of government. Do some research to see how the membership and ethnic make up of the cabinet have changed over the years. The *Canada Year Book* would be very helpful. Ask your teacher and librarian for other suggestions regarding sources. Try to discover the names of the members of cabinet under the following prime ministers:
   a Mackenzie King (in the years immediately after World War II)
   b Louis St. Laurent (around 1955)

c John Diefenbaker (around 1960)
d Lester Pearson (around 1965)
e Pierre Trudeau (around 1969 and 1978)
f Joe Clark (1979)
g Brian Mulroney (1986)
h Brian Mulroney (1988)

What has happened to the overall percentage of French-Canadians in the cabinet? How can you account for this? What has happened to the number of *key* cabinet positions held by French-Canadians? Do the same reasons apply? Does the political party or ethnic background of the prime minister seem to be a factor? Can French-Canadians fairly argue today that they are under-represented in the cabinet? Why or why not?

1·2·3

ORGANIZING

1 Place the following events in *reverse* chronological order, from most to least recent in time:
   - ▶ The Official Languages Act is passed.
   - ▶ Maurice Duplessis dies.
   - ▶ The "Bi and Bi" Commission is appointed.
   - ▶ The Parti Québécois comes to power for the first time.
   - ▶ Pierre Trudeau is elected prime minister of Canada.
   - ▶ The Parti Québécois is formed.
   - ▶ The FLQ murders Pierre Laporte.

2 Design an organizer chart that lists the causes of the Quiet Revolution under three headings: political, economic and social. Then fill in the chart as completely as possible.

3 Separate the following points into *causes* and *results* of the Quiet Revolution. Make a special note of any developments that you think fall into both categories.
   - ▶ Canadians became more concerned about the unity of their country.
   - ▶ Quebec was falling behind other provinces in some ways.
   - ▶ French-Canadians became more anxious about their cultural identity.
   - ▶ Unemployment was higher in Quebec than in most other provinces.
   - ▶ Some English-Canadians wished that French Canada did not exist.
   - ▶ French-Canadians faced discrimination in the federal civil service.
   - ▶ French-Canadians questioned whether they could truly feel that Canada was their homeland.
   - ▶ French was treated as a second-class language in Canada.

4 Make a list of at least six steps that you think separatist sympathizers might have taken to organize the Parti Québécois in the 1960s. Next, try to arrange these steps in order of importance.

COMMUNICATING

1 Design a symbol that, in your opinion, clearly expresses the hopes and feelings of a Quebec separatist. This symbol might be used on a flag or a campaign poster. Compare your design with the symbol actually adopted by the Parti Québécois. Can you interpret their symbol?

2 Make a list of at least five ways in which a political party can make its views known to the public *other than* by advertising through the mass media.

3 What do you think are the most important communication skills for a successful politician in Canada today?

4 Develop the dialogue for an emotional scene in a French-Canadian household in the 1960s. A conservative, middle-class mother is shocked when her teenage daughter comes home on a college vacation and announces that she has become a separatist sympathizer. If your efforts are successful, perhaps you could enlarge the script and cast of characters and have members of the class enact the play.

ANALYZING

1 In your opinion, what was the single most important cause of the Quiet Revolution? Explain your choice.

2 The visit of French President Charles de Gaulle to Quebec in 1967 was highly controversial.

How did it affect English-French relations, and how significant were those effects on the progress of the Quiet Revolution?

3 Why did the federal government's efforts to promote bilingualism run into difficulties?

4 What was the main purpose of Quebec's Bill 22?

5 Should it be possible for a unilingual French-Canadian to get an important government job in Ottawa? Why or why not? Find out whether it is in fact possible.

6 Is effective communication the most crucial skill for a politician in Canada? Explain your answer.

7 Give reasons for the election victory of the Parti Québécois in 1976. Rank these in order of importance.

APPLYING YOUR KNOWLEDGE

1 Imagine that you are a federal civil servant in Ottawa. You speak only in English and have just been told that, in your job, bilingualism is now required. The ability to speak French also would improve your chances of future promotion. Failure to learn French will cause you to be moved to another, perhaps less important job. What thoughts run through your mind as you drive home from work that evening? What will you decide to do? What factors will influence your decision? Is it fair for the government to put you in this position? Explain your answer.

2 Consider the possibility of making contact with some French-Canadian students from Quebec. This can be done by individuals or as a class project. Students in the class who study French could be in charge of writing the necessary letters. Others could think of the questions to ask and the kind of information, photographs or other materials to be exchanged. Such activities should be attempted only with the advice of your teacher and the permission of your school principal.

3 What do you think the policies of René Lévesque's new government were after it won the election of 1976? What dangers or mistakes might he have to guard against?

4 What key factors do you think might determine whether the Parti Québécois will succeed or fail in splitting Quebec away from Canada?

5 Looking back, how could English-Canadian teenagers have contributed to the maintenance of Canadian unity in the late 1970s? Would any of your suggestions still be helpful today?

chapter 13

QUEBEC SEPARATISM

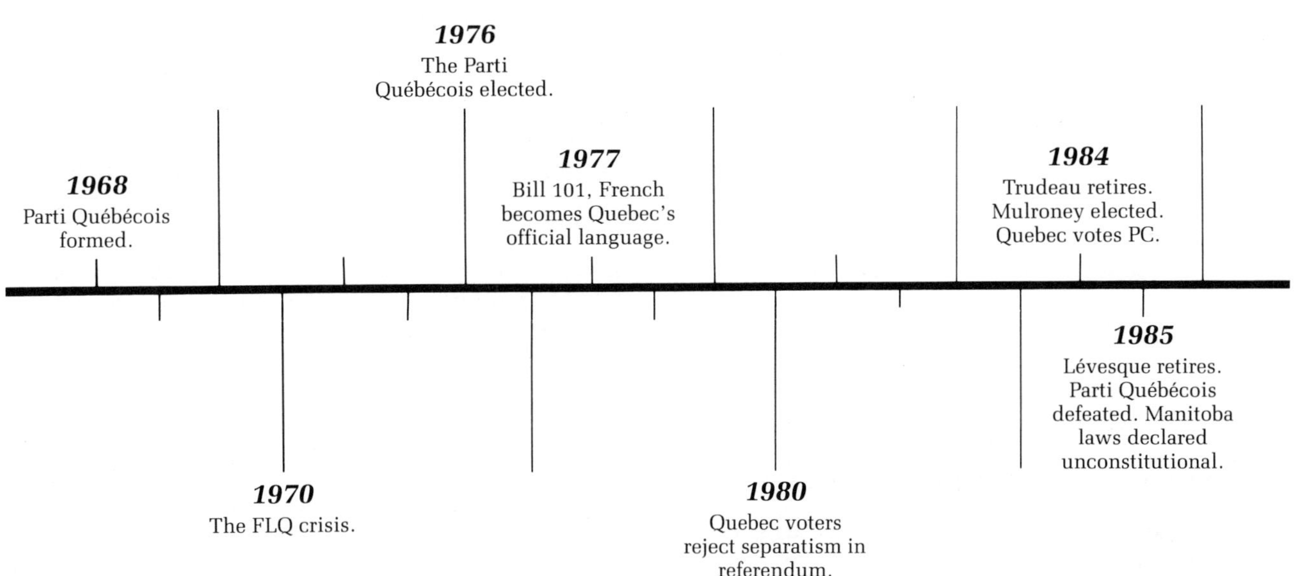

1968
Parti Québécois formed.
1970
The FLQ crisis.
1976
The Parti Québécois elected.
1977
Bill 101, French becomes Quebec's official language.
1980
Quebec voters reject separatism in referendum.
1984
Trudeau retires. Mulroney elected. Quebec votes PC.
1985
Lévesque retires. Parti Québécois defeated. Manitoba laws declared unconstitutional.

TOPIC ORGANIZER

THEME ORGANIZER

- The idea of having their own, separate nation has a strong emotional appeal for some French-Canadians.
- Quebec has much of what it needs to survive as a nation.
- It is legal for a Canadian to be a separatist, provided he or she uses only peaceful, democratic methods to achieve this goal.
- The separation of Quebec would seriously weaken Canada economically, politically and militarily.
- In exchange for their independence, Quebeckers might have to accept a significantly lower standard of living.
- The radical terrorist movement, the FLQ, was rejected by an overwhelming majority of French-Canadians.
- The turning point for French-Canadian separatists came with the strong rejection of their proposal in the 1980 provincial referendum.
- Although its strength has ebbed, Quebec separatism remains a challenge to Canada.

INTRODUCTION

> I feel alive again! We're free at last! We showed those English! Now we can walk with our heads up!

November 15, 1976. In Montreal and Quebec City, the night air was full of shouts and cheers in French. There was dancing in the streets. Large groups of people, most of them young, laughed, cried, cheered and sang. One of their favourite chants, which they repeated over and over, was, "*Québec aux Québécois!*" ("Quebec to the Quebeckers!"). These enthusiastic crowds were supporters of separatism. They were celebrating the spectacular election victory of the separatist Parti Québécois.

The Paul Sauvé Arena in downtown Montreal was literally packed to the rafters with Parti Québécois workers and supporters. They were waiting for the arrival of their leader, René Lévesque. Suddenly he appeared, moving through the happy crowd, surrounded by aides and bodyguards. He climbed up onto the platform and raised his arms. The crowd cheered wildly and nonstop for almost five minutes. Finally, they quieted enough for him to speak. A rather small, frail man, he appeared very tired. But the strength of a great victory energized him. Overcome with emotion, his eyes filling with tears, the new premier of Quebec began to speak. The words were calm and gentle.

He urged his supporters to keep a friendly, reasonable attitude to Canada. As he spoke, the CBC television cameras in the studio moved close up to the commentators. Most of them tried to play down what was happening. But their facial expressions did not match their words. One of them, Premier Richard Hatfield of New Brunswick, looked stricken. His province has the highest percentage of French-Canadians outside Quebec. New Brunswick guarantees equal rights to French and English, including equality of educational opportunity. Premier Hatfield was very frank. He admitted to being surprised, disappointed and worried by the election results. It was clear that a new chapter in English-French relations was about to be written.

Before reading on, study the chart of key words and ideas that follows.

KEY WORDS AND IDEAS IN THIS CHAPTER

Term	Meaning	Sample Use
customs union	a trade agreement between two or more countries; they agree to eliminate tariffs or duties in their trade with each other	If Quebec separated, it would want to continue trade with Canada through a customs union.

exile	a situation in which a person is sent away from his or her home, either for a certain period of time or indefinitely	Certain members of a terrorist group, the FLQ, were exiled from Canada because of their actions during the October Crisis of 1970.
federalist	in Canada, a person who wants all provinces to remain united within one country	Most Canadians are federalists. They are opposed to Quebec separatism.
indépendentist(e)	a French term, meaning a person who wants independence or freedom for his or her country	Quebeckers who favour separatism refer to themselves as indépendentists rather than separatists.
regionalism	a tendency of people to identify with and be loyal to their region rather than to their country as a whole	Separatism is an extreme form of regionalism.
secession	the act by which a province or state withdraws from a federal union	The separatist government of René Lévesque wanted Quebec's secession from Canada.
separatism	the desire of a province or region of a country to split away from the rest of the country and operate independently	Since the 1960s, there has been some support for separatism in Quebec and, to a much lesser degree, in certain parts of western Canada.
separatist	a person who wants his or her province to secede from Canada	The separatist movement grew steadily in Quebec through the late 1960s and early 1970s. In 1976 the separatists won power in the Quebec provincial election.
sovereignty association	proposed by the Parti Québécois as the ideal relationship between Quebec and Canada; though sovereign (separate and independent) Quebec would be "associated" with Canada in various ways; the two countries would share a common currency (the dollar) and a free trade agreement; they could co-operate in mutual defence	During the referendum of 1980 on separation, the Parti Québécois asked Quebec voters to support sovereignty association with Canada.

SEPARATISM: IS IT LEGAL?

Separatist feelings are not new to Canada. They have been expressed, from time to time, since Confederation. Also, they are not found only in Quebec. They have been voiced in the Maritimes and in the West, particularly in British Columbia and Alberta.

The main reason for this is that Canada is divided into regions. Each of these areas tends to have its own identity. This means that it feels somewhat different from the rest of the country.

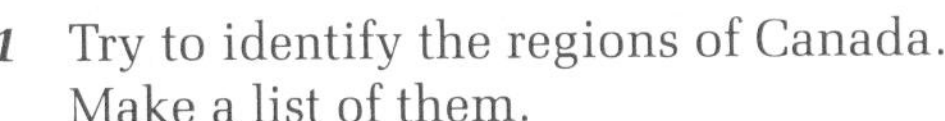

1 Try to identify the regions of Canada. Make a list of them.

2 What factors have produced this regionalism? Explain why they have had this effect. (A full answer should include ideas about geography, history, ethnic groups, culture and economics.)

3 From what region of Canada do you come? How strong is your own per-

"JE SUIS FÉDÉRALIST."

"French Canadians could no more constitute [make up] a perfect society than could the five million Sikhs of the Punjab [a region of India]. We are not well enough educated, not rich enough, nor, above all, numerous enough, to man and finance a government possessing all the necessary means for both war and peace."

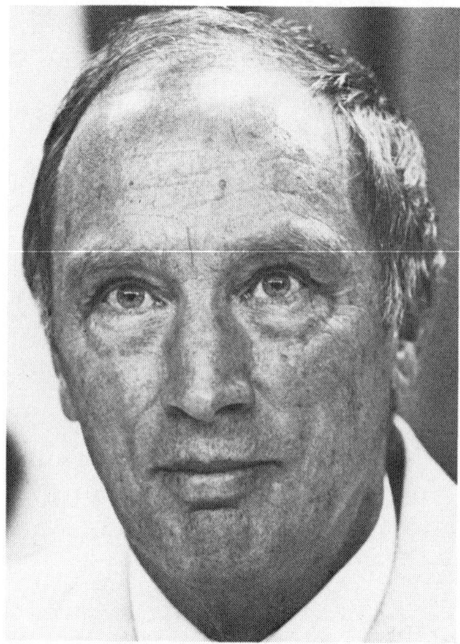

Pierre Trudeau

The two sides of the issue of Quebec separatism were symbolized by these two politicians for several years. Both were fluently bilingual and highly intelligent. Both were dynamic leaders. Each had a great deal of political power. Here the similarities end.

Pierre Trudeau's background was French and Scottish. His father was a very wealthy businessman. The young Pierre went to private schools. He spent much of his youth studying and travelling the world. For several years he was a professor and teacher of law. He also edited and wrote for *Cité Libre*. This publication often criticized the government of Quebec's premier, Maurice Duplessis. He also wrote books on Canadian government and politics. In 1968 Mr. Trudeau became prime minister of Canada. He remained strongly opposed to Quebec separation.

"JE SUIS SÉPARATIST."

"French Canada is a true nation. It has all the elements essential to national life: it possesses unity as well as human and material resources, including equipment and personnel, which are as good or better than those of a large number of the people of the world."

René Lévesque

René Lévesque was not born into a wealthy family. Perhaps this is why his ties with average people seemed closer and more emotional than Trudeau's. He was a war correspondent in World War II. Later he became a well-known CBC television commentator. He entered Quebec politics in 1960. Lévesque was soon made a member of the Lesage cabinet. Gradually he came to the belief that Quebec could not fulfill itself within Canada. When he could not persuade the Liberal party to share his views, he left it. In 1968 he helped to form a new separatist group, the Parti Québécois. He was made its first leader that year. In the same year, Mr. Trudeau became prime minister of Canada.

What is the point being made in this cartoon?

sonal sense of regional identity? Why is this? Do you think that you are typical of your region? Why or why not?

4 Why might it be a good thing for Canadians to have these regional loyalties and identities? On the other hand, what problems might these create?

COULD A PROVINCE SECEDE FROM CONFEDERATION?

From time to time this question has come up. Could a province pull out of the Canadian union? There are different opinions on that question. However, most legal experts agree that such an action would be illegal. This claim rests mainly on one simple fact: There is no mention of such action in the British North America Act. The BNA Act is the basis of our Constitution. It lays down the rules by which our system of government must operate. If the Constitution does not mention withdrawal of provinces from the union, then such action cannot be taken. Arguments that support this view are based on what happened in 1867. When the provincial leaders discussed Confederation, they had in mind a union that would last forever. They were not planning a temporary arrangement.

Still, there are points to be made for the other side. It is true that the BNA Act does not mention secession (withdrawal by one or more provinces). Therefore, it does not forbid such an action. Also, Canada claims to be a democratic country. It tries to serve the best interests of the Canadian people. What if some of those people, living in one or more provinces, are unhappy? What if they feel that they could do better by forming their own country? Why should they not be allowed to do so? Why should Canada force a province to stay in the union against its will?

Today there are some people in certain provinces who are in favour of getting out of Confederation. This feeling is strongest in Quebec. It also has a little support in the West and in Newfoundland. Some Quebeckers have pointed out that Quebec joined Confederation without taking a vote among the people. They are quite correct. Such a vote would be called a plebiscite or referendum. No such vote, strictly on the question of joining Canada, was held in Quebec or in any other province, for that matter. The decision was made by politicians elected earlier by the people. Therefore, some Quebec separatists argue that Quebec could leave Confederation the same way it came in. That is, it could leave by a decision of the Quebec government, not by a direct vote of the people.

Another question that comes up is this: If a province wants to leave Confederation, should the decision be made by its voters alone or by all Canadian voters? What is your opinion on this issue? How could you defend your view?

Finally, we come to what is perhaps the most difficult point of the problem: *What if the people of a province want to secede, but the rest of Canada is opposed to the idea? Could the courts solve the problem? How important would legality* (the legal right to do something) *be, especially to the province that wants to leave? Should Canada use force to keep a province in Confederation?*

A few years ago, these questions would have been considered wild and foolish. Today, unfortunately, this is no longer true. The danger of one or more provinces seceding from Canada is very real. These questions matter to all of us. Think about them carefully.

THE RISE OF THE PARTI QUÉBÉCOIS

The rise to power of the Parti Québécois in Quebec was truly amazing. No political party in Canada's history has ever risen so far, so quickly. Separatist ideas go back a long way in the history of Quebec. Still, until recently, very few people held these ideas. As we have seen, some Quebec leaders were opposed to Quebec joining Confederation in 1867. At the time of the Riel affair and the first conscription crisis, a few voices muttered about Quebec leaving Canada. In the 1930s and 1940s, Lionel Groulx spoke and wrote about separation.

However, the thought of separation never really took root in Quebec until the 1960s. Its development was prompted by the Quiet Revolution. As we have seen, the main goal of this movement was not to take Quebec out of Confederation. Yet there was a threat beneath the surface. If Quebec's goals were not achieved, separation might occur. Some English-Canadians were openly hostile to the Quiet Revolution. In the previous chapter, we read some of their statements on bilingualism and other issues. Such remarks encouraged separatist feeling. As one French Quebecker said, "We want the French language and culture to flourish freely in Quebec. If this is too much to ask, then we might as well forget about Canada."

This chart shows the gradual rise in public support for separatism in Quebec.

RESULTS OF SELECTED POLLS ON SEPARATISM SINCE 1962

	In Favour	Opposed	Undecided
1962	08%	73%	19%
1965	07%	79%	14%
1968	10%	72%	18%
1970	14%	76%	10%
1973	17%	64%	19%

A number of small separatist parties were born in Quebec in the early 1960s. They were led by such people as Marcel Chaput, Pierre Bourgault and Gilles Grégoire. None were very successful. Altogether they received only 9 percent of the votes in the 1966 election. However, the movement was strengthened in 1968. In that year, most of the separatist organizations agreed to combine and form one party. Its name: the Parti Québécois. Its leader: the dynamic and popular René Lévesque. Even at this stage, few Quebeckers took the separatists very seriously. Lévesque's predictions about rapid success made many of them laugh. Look at those predictions. How accurate was Lévesque?

The separatists *did* become the government of Quebec in 1976. Still, it is important to remember that they won only 41 percent of the votes. In other words, 59 percent of Quebeckers voted against the Parti Québécois. Lévesque had a big advantage in the election: Quebec voters were disgusted with the Liberal gov-

LÉVESQUE'S PREDICTIONS

Prediction	Year of Quebec Election	Results of Quebec Election (other parties not shown)		
		Party	% of Vote	Number of Seats
In 1968 René Lévesque said: 1. "In our first election, we will win at least 20 percent of the votes."	1970	Liberals Parti Québécois	45 23	72 7
2. "In our second election, we will win about 25 percent of the votes, and we will form the official opposition [i.e., win the second-largest number of seats]."	1973	Liberals Parti Québécois	55 31	102 6 (enough to become the official opposition)
3. "In our third election, we will form the government of Quebec."	1976	Liberals Parti Québécois	33 41	28 69

A separatist demonstration in Montreal, 1967.

LET'S NOT SPEAK OF SEPARATION, OUR AIM IS TO REPLACE A STUPID, CORRUPT, INCOMPETENT, DISHONEST GOVERNMENT
CAMPAGNE 76

INDEPENDENCE INDEPENDENCE INDEPENDENCE
CAMPAGNE 77
TUES., MAR. 1, 1977.

This cartoon refers to the election strategy of René Lévesque in the 1976 Quebec election. What is the point it makes?

ernment of Robert Bourassa. The Liberals had promised to cure unemployment in Quebec. However, unemployment grew quickly between 1973 and 1976. Taxes and the provincial debt also increased. Scandals rocked the government. They even damaged the personal reputation of Mr. Bourassa. In the 1976 election, the Parti Québécois did not stress separatism. Instead, it asked for support because it could provide good government. A Parti Québécois government would be honest and work better than that of Mr. Bourassa. These reasons were probably as important to Lévesque's victory as his support of separatism. They may even have been more important.

CAUSES OF QUEBEC SEPARATISM

The main reasons for the growth of separatist feeling in Quebec can be found in the statements quoted below:

A "The fact is, we are considered as second-class citizens, constantly held in contempt by our English counterparts. . . . After having all of this thrown at me day after day, you tell me how I can be anything else but a separatist. How can I refuse this last chance to be myself? How can I refuse to be a part, as a full citizen, of a culture, of a country? . . . We are only human, and we can take just so much."

B "We believe that a country like Quebec, which is three times as large as France, five times as large as Italy, thirteen times as large as Cuba, that such a country which stands among the first producers in the world of hydro-electric power, wood, pulp and paper, iron ore, minerals of all kinds, that this country which is linked to the ocean by one of the main seaways of the world, can live by itself and prosper."

C "I think of Quebec first because this province is the only one in which I feel completely at home, the only one which allows me to live freely in French twenty-four hours a day."

1 What reasons for separation are stated or implied in A? In B? In C? How do you react to each of these arguments?

2 Do you agree with the suggestion in B that an independent Quebec could survive on its own?

3 Most French-Canadians have a deep emotional attachment to Quebec. Why is this?

4 The last two prime ministers, Pierre Trudeau and Brian Mulroney, have both been bilingual Quebeckers. Would this tend to help or hurt the separatist cause in Quebec? Explain your answer.

5 What additional reasons can you find for the growth of separatist feeling in Quebec?

This young girl sits in front of a doorway in a Montreal slum. Some Quebeckers believe that a radical change in government would improve conditions such as this.

WHO WERE THE SEPARATISTS?

A survey published by *The Toronto Star* in 1977 identified some characteristics common to most separatists.

	% of Respondents			
	Total	**Extreme Separatists**	**Extreme Federalists**	**Middle-grounders**
Sex				
Male	50	54	48	49
Female	50	46	52	51
Age				
18–30	34	56	16	39
Average	39	33	45	37
Marital Status				
Single	21	29	09	30
Married	66	56	78	58
Education				
High school or less	61	49	69	59
Technical/or community college	22	40	12	18
University/graduate school	17	11	19	23
Union Household	41	58	30	39
Employer				
Self-employed	10	09	14	07
A company	57	47	67	55
Government (municipal, provincial, federal)	31	41	19	37
Own Property	49	38	60	45
Ethnic Background				
French	73	88	60	77
English	27	12	40	23

continued from page 229	Total	Extreme Separatists	Extreme Federalists	Middle-grounders
Speak English With Little or No Difficulty (% of French)	60	72	46	61
Place of Residence				
Urban	86	93	84	85
Voting Behaviour				
Provincial Election—November, 1976				
Parti Québécois	60	98	27	64
Liberal	26	02	48	22
Union Nationale	11	—	20	10
Créditiste	02	—	02	04
Parti Nationale Populaire	01	—	03	—

The underscored numbers show where there are significant differences between those in one of the three groups and the population as a whole.

PORTRAITS OF TWO SEPARATISTS

In 1977, Richard Cyr was a 26-year-old heavy machinery operator in Montreal. He was a high-school graduate. He also had studied at a vocational college. He was married and had one child. He earned about $14 000 per year. He owned no property but hoped to have his own home one day. He was a union member.

He said that he spoke no English. He did not want French-Canadian children exposed to bilingualism or even to English media. He was confident that an independent Quebec could survive. Separation might lead to a civil war. Most of the fighting would be with the English in Quebec who "are our number one problem." He said he was not religious. He did not care if the rest of Canada adopted bilingualism. He stated that he would not change his mind unless something shocking happened—"like I dropped dead!"

Madeleine Longpré is from east-end Montreal. In 1977 she was in her mid-fifties and married to a construction worker. Her husband earned about $8000 per year. She said that Quebeckers have waited too long. They would not change their minds about separating. She claimed that there was growing anti-English feeling in Quebec. She blamed the English hold on the best jobs for this. She had no hope of Canada becoming bilingual because the English were too "hard-headed." Anyway, it would take too long. The French were "fed up with waiting." She felt that Quebec was rich but lost out by staying in Confederation. She was prepared to suffer a 10 percent cut in her family's income for the sake of Quebec's independence.

A DISSENTING VOICE

Alain Marcoux was a 25-year-old worker in Trois Rivières. He was strongly against separatism. He was worried about job opportunities. He had seen many friends lose their jobs in the slow Quebec economy. He did not speak English but wished that he could. He felt that speaking English would increase his chance for a better job. He did not feel that French culture (or identity) was threatened. It was too deeply rooted in Quebec. He felt that many young French-Canadians were too romantic about independence. They did not realize its dangerous results. He believed that the English and French could live together if both sides would try harder.

QUEBEC SEPARATISM: THE RADICAL FRINGE

Most of those Quebeckers who support separatism are opposed to violence. They believe that Quebec should leave Canada peacefully and democratically. The Parti Québécois is a legal party in Canada.

However, since the early 1960s, separatism also has drawn a few radicals (extremists) to its cause. One such radical group was known as the *Front de Libération Québécois* (Quebec Liberation Front), or FLQ for short. Its members believed that Quebec could become independent only by using violence. This group was responsible for most of the terrorist acts in Quebec in the 1960s. These acts included robberies and bombings. In a few cases, people were killed or badly injured.

FLQ activity reached a peak in October, 1970. Some of its members kidnapped James Cross, a British trade official, from his Montreal home. A few days later, the FLQ also seized Quebec's labour minister, Pierre Laporte, while he was playing with some children on his street. Through these actions, the FLQ hoped to bring attention to their cause. They wanted publicity from the media. Perhaps they also hoped that the government and English-Canadians would react harshly. This might create sympathy for the FLQ among French-Canadians. The FLQ might then be seen as heroes.

Their aims were only partly fulfilled. They did receive publicity. But almost all of it was bad. The Trudeau government brought in a drastic measure known as the War Measures Act. In effect, this act suspended everyone's civil rights. It let police arrest and jail people without charging them. Tension was very high for many days. Most Canadians were shocked when the police found the body of Pierre Laporte. It was stuffed in the trunk of a car in a Montreal parking lot. He had been strangled, apparently with the chain of his crucifix.

Mr. Cross was later released, shaken, but unharmed. In exchange, the government had to agree to let his abductors escape to Cuba. They were exiled from Canada for life. A total of 23 people were convicted and jailed for terrorist acts. These included Jacques Rose and Bernard Lortie. They were sentenced to eight years and life in prison respectively for their part in the Laporte kidnapping.

Most experts felt that these actions destroyed the FLQ and damaged the separatist cause in Quebec.

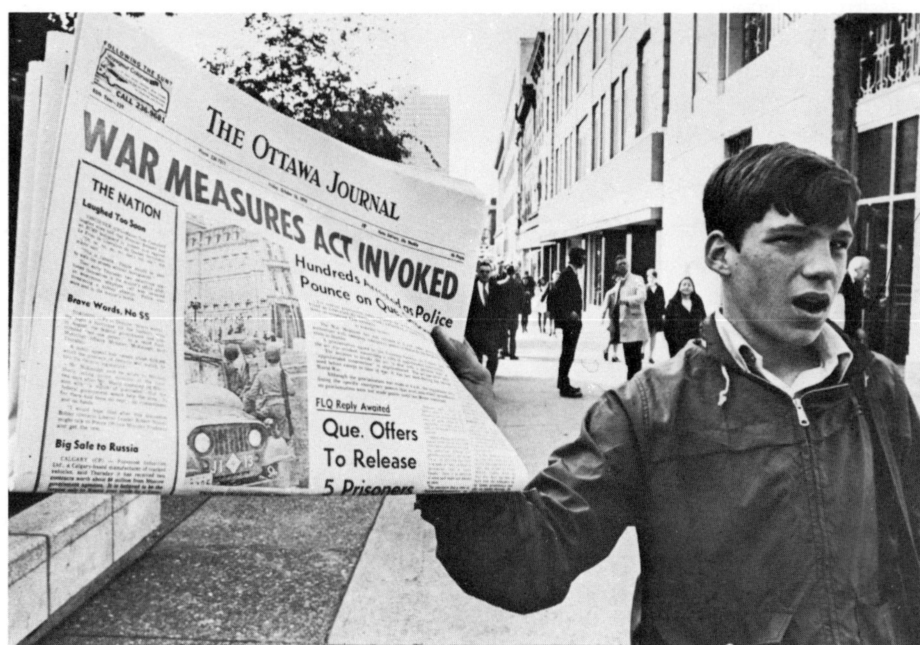

A newspaper carrier holds up a newspaper with a banner headline announcing the use of the War Measures Act, October 16, 1970.

FLQ kidnapper, Marc Carbonneau, who was exiled from Canada in 1970.

Pierre Laporte

They might have been right on the first count. It appears they were quite wrong on the second. Perhaps this is partly because of the public reaction to the invoking of the War Measures Act. Most of the media attacked the government's use of this act. They described it as unnecessary. It was, they said, harmful to human rights in Canada. Civil liberties groups agreed. No doubt, the heavy-handed actions of the government had some public support. However, in Quebec, the use of the War Measures Act probably created some sympathy for the separatist cause.

In the late 1970s and early 1980s, several of the former FLQ members who had been exiled came back to Canada. They gave the authorities advance notice of their plans. All understood that they faced immediate arrest and probable prison sentences. The typical sentence received was two years less one day. This meant that they could avoid serving time in federal penitentiaries. Usually these former terrorists served eight months or less and then were released on parole.

None of the FLQ terrorists, including those convicted of the murder of Pierre Laporte, served long prison terms. Even Paul Rose, who received two life sentences, was out on parole in less than ten years. Francois Simard, also sentenced to life but released on parole, wrote a book about the murder, or "execution," of Laporte. He described the killing as tragic but said it was necessary to show that the FLQ were committed and sincere.

1 Why, in your opinion, have the authorities handled the cases of the returning FLQ exiles with a minimum of publicity and severity?

2 Do you agree with the treatment given the FLQ exiles? Why or why not?

3 Do further research into the circumstances of the death of Pierre Laporte. Would it best be described as a murder or an execution? Why? What penalty, if any, should have been paid by those directly responsible for the death of Mr. Laporte? Explain your answer.

WHAT IF QUEBEC SEPARATED?

The separation of Quebec from Canada is not a certainty. Still, it *could* happen. Therefore, it is important to think about its possible effects on the rest of the country. Here are some:

- Canada would lose its largest province (about 14 percent of its total area).
- Canada would lose about 25 percent of its population. (Up to 800 000 English Quebeckers might leave the province, but almost as many French-Canadians from outside Quebec would probably return.)
- Canada would lose about 25 percent of its gross national product (total value of goods and services produced).
- Canada would lose about 15 percent of its fresh water, 14 percent of its mineral production and large quantities of hydro-electric power.
- The value of the Canadian dollar would probably fall.
- Atlantic Canada would be physically cut off from the rest of Canada.
- The defence of Canada might be in danger.
- Some experts believe that the rest of Canada might begin to fall apart. Other provinces might want to separate.

Opponents of Bill 22 demonstrate in favour of English schools in Montreal. Many such opponents were immigrants to Canada. Why would many of these same people be even more upset by Bill 101?

These comments from letters to a Toronto newspaper suggest other concerns:

- "In my opinion, the existence of Quebec and French-Canadians in Canada is one of the few differences between our country and the United States."
  (What does this imply about Quebec's contribution to Canada's identity? Do you agree?)
- "It (Quebec's separation) would be the end of Canada, and we would be part of the United States of America in a short time."*(Do you agree with this opinion? How is it linked to the one above?)*

Consider the results of the following opinion poll:

> "If Quebec should leave confederation, how serious do you think this would be for the future of the rest of Canada — very serious, fairly serious or not very serious?"

(The table also gives results for a similar poll conducted in 1966, but in that study, "very" and "fairly" serious categories were combined.)

	Very serious	**Fairly serious**	**Not very serious**	**No opinion**
National — 1977	46%	27%	22%	05%
— 1966	48		28	24
Quebec — 1977	40	31	22	07
— 1966	51		20	29
Rest of Canada				
— 1977	48	26	22	04
— 1966	47		31	22
By region in 1977				
Atlantic	63	14	18	05
Quebec	40	31	22	07
Ontario	51	28	20	02
Prairies	35	29	27	09
British Columbia	48	23	28	02

1 This Gallup poll was taken in February, 1977. What had happened to the public mood on the question since 1966? In what region of the country was there the most concern? The least concern? How do you account for these facts?

In late 1977, some of Quebec's Inuit population protested against Bill 101. They demanded the right to English-language education for their children. They indicated that if Quebec separated from Canada, they (the Inuit) would secede from Quebec. At the same time, René Lévesque's government rejected their demand. Here, an Inuit leader confronts a member of the Quebec Provincial Police.

2 Try to find a recent poll with responses to the same or a similar question. If this is unavailable, conduct your own poll to obtain a sampling of current opinion on this matter.

BILL 101: QUEBEC'S LANGUAGE CHARTER

In the previous chapter, there was mention of Bill 22. This was a measure taken by the Bourassa government. Its aim was to strengthen the position of the French language in Quebec. The Parti Québécois criticized it when it was introduced. When that party came to power in 1976, it was determined to scrap Bill 22. This was done in the summer of 1977 with the passage of Bill 101.

Bill 101 was designed to make French the only official language in Quebec. It was much clearer than Bill 22. It also was easier to enforce in the courts. Here are some important things that the bill does:

- gives every Quebecker the right to work in French;
- gives every Quebecker the right to receive an education in French;
- gives every Quebecker the right to be informed and served by the provincial government in French;
- gives every Quebecker the right to speak in French in any public assembly;
- gives every Quebecker the right to require that the government, public services, professional corporations, employees' associations and various other enterprises communicate with him or her in French;
- states that most government documents will be issued only in French (although people can communicate with the state and receive a reply in another language);
- requires all businesses with 50 or more employees to earn "francization certificates" by 1983 (to certify that their operations are conducted basically in French);
- says that any employee may require his employer to put written communication in French;

- states that no employer can dismiss or demote a salaried worker solely on the grounds that he or she does not speak English well;
- requires that public notices, from both government and industry, must be only in French;
- strictly limits the right of Quebec schoolchildren to be educated in English.

The Quebec government was bitterly attacked by English-Canadians for this bill. Premier Lévesque defended Bill 101 on the grounds that the British North America Act gave each province the right to pass laws regarding language. He said that continuing immigration into Quebec was starting to threaten the position of the French majority. Very few of these immigrants were French-speaking. Many of them came from such countries as Italy, Portugal and Greece. Most were sending their children to English schools. Also, the birth rate among French-Canadians had declined. These two facts posed a serious problem. Bill 22 had said that immigrant children who wished to attend English schools had to pass a language test. This test was proving unworkable. Bill 101 tried to limit English education to the children of parents who truly belonged to the English community. It made the following provisions:

- All children who were legally in the English school system when Bill 101 became law could remain there. Also, their younger brothers and sisters could attend English schools.
- Children whose mother or father was educated in English primary schools could attend such schools in Quebec.
- Children who were originally from other Canadian provinces could attend English schools in Quebec, *but only if the governments of those provinces would guarantee French education to their French-speaking minorities.*

When Bill 101 was passed, only one province guaranteed the right of education in French. This was New Brunswick. Ontario and certain other provinces rejected Quebec's offer of reciprocal (mutual) guarantees in education rights. In 1976, New Brunswick had about 106 000 students in English schools and 54 000 in French schools. Ontario had about 750 000 people of French descent. Of these, about half used French in the home. Ontario had promised "adequate" provision of French education where the number of students made it practical. In 1977 there were 24 publicly supported secondary schools and 304 elementary schools in Ontario offering education in French. Western provinces had lower percentages of French-Canadians. Therefore, they had fewer French schools. Manitoba had, in effect, removed French educational rights in the 1880s. Some of these rights were restored in the early 1970s. There were few French schools in Saskatchewan, Alberta and British Columbia. However, these provinces were working to improve this situation.

1. After the passage of Bill 101, some people suggested that the other nine provinces should do away with French educational rights and stop all support of bilingualism. What do you think of this idea? Why?
2. The government of Quebec argued that the English minority in Quebec still had more rights and protection than the French minorities in the other nine provinces. Would you agree?
3. Does a provincial government have the right to tell any of its people the language in which their children will be educated? Explain your answer.

HOW WOULD QUEBEC SEPARATION TAKE PLACE?

As we have seen, the separatist threat grew in Quebec, especially after the election of 1976. Both supporters and opponents of the idea had to face this difficult question: If Quebec *did* separate from the rest of Canada, how would this actually take place? Those who thought seriously about it realized that there were several smaller questions within the larger question. For example:

- Would the decision be made only by the voters of Quebec? Or should all Canadian voters have a say?
- Should the issue be decided in an election? Or would a referendum (plebiscite) be the best format for allowing the public to voice its opinion?
- If Quebec favoured separation but the rest of Canada did not, how could the matter be resolved? By peaceful negotiation? By the use of military force? By third-party mediation (such as the World Court)?

Understandably, René Lévesque had given much thought to these questions. In his opinion, his election victory in 1976 was, technically at least, sufficient to indicate that Quebeckers wanted Quebec out of Confederation. After all, this was the ultimate goal of his party, which had won a large majority of seats in that election. But he realized that he needed further justification, because in the election campaign, he had de-emphasized separation as an issue. Only about 41 percent of the votes cast had been for his party. Many of these would not have supported an immediate move to separate from Canada. So instead, Lévesque decided to use his first term in power to strengthen his position. He would provide good government, resist federal efforts to "make peace" and work on building public sympathy.

His strategy with both English- and French-Canadians was to encourage them to regard their relationship as a failing marriage. The two sides could and should remain good friends. However, the marriage (Confederation) simply was not working. Both sides were becoming angry and frustrated. Each was trying to make the other into something that it was not. The solution was a friendly divorce. Each side would have its freedom, but the two of them could continue a worthwhile relationship. The name he gave to this proposed new relationship was sovereignty association.

In this scheme, Quebec and Canada would each be sovereign, or independent. However, they would still be "associated" by maintaining several important ties. For example, they would use a common currency and money system. Also, they would agree to limit or remove all barriers to trade between themselves. (This would create a customs union between the two countries.) Border regulations would be kept to a minimum to make it easier for goods and people to cross their common boundaries. Their armed forces would co-operate in a plan of mutual defence. Lévesque was confident that such a solution could be achieved without violence. However, he insisted that the decision on whether or not Quebec would separate could be made only by the voters of Quebec. He therefore proposed a plebiscite, or referendum, on this one question, to be held near the end of his first term in office (no later than 1981).

Federal politicians, led by Pierre Trudeau, rejected much of this thinking. Most believed that all Canadians had a right to participate in any decision about a province separating to become an independent nation. Naturally, they preferred that no such question should ever come to a vote. Mr. Trudeau went

1 What is the point being made in this cartoon? 2 What is the most likely year for the publication of this cartoon? (Explain your choice.) *a* 1984 *b* 1978 *c* 1970

The media have an important role to play in public issues, including Quebec separatism. Press coverage could greatly influence opinion on both sides. What comment is this cartoon making about the press? Note also the newspaper headlines on the following page. They give the flavour of press common in the late 1970s.

so far as to suggest the following: The Parti Québécois should give the minorities within Quebec the option to secede: Let the English and the various native peoples vote on the question of whether to separate from Quebec!

A few Canadians called for the use of force to keep Quebec in Confederation. There were several arguments against this. The bloodshed might be terrible. The other costs would be enormous. Would the effort really be worthwhile if a province wanted out so badly? Also, Canada might not be strong enough to do the job. The armed forces were fairly small and weak. There were probably fewer than 10 000 combat-ready troops in the entire country. And many of these were French-Canadians! (The armed forces have one almost entirely French-Canadian regiment. This is the "Vandoos," the Royal 22nd Regiment. It is a tough, well-respected fighting force based at the Citadel in Quebec City.)

Most Canadians agreed that, if Quebec actually came to the point of separation, force should *not* be used to settle the matter. Prime Minister Trudeau stated this publicly and was supported by Joe Clark, the leader of the Opposition in Parliament. But this left us with the problem of what the terms of separation would be. Many English-Canadians opposed the idea of sovereignty association. They argued that such a scheme would benefit Quebec far more than Canada. If Quebec wanted to leave, it could go ahead. But it must accept the risks of such an action. It could expect no special help from Canada. Rather, Canada should insist upon some terms of its own, such as:

Quebeckers willing to suffer setbacks to achieve aims

Separation—if it comes—can and should be peaceful

'Levesque's got us over a barrel'

Majority believe separation would entail higher taxes

Ottawa claiming bilingual victory in public service

Quebec states its case

More Quebeckers oppose separation

Language bill: Quebec road signs in French only

Toronto trial in French refused for Quebecker

Tell Quebec we care,

Canadian civil war result if Quebec splits, teacher says

Quebec language bill is a step backwards

Jobs, not language, issue in Quebec,

91 head offices quit Quebec

Unity desire outside Quebec not making large impact

- a guaranteed land corridor between Ontario and the Maritimes, to include railroad and highway links;
- a guaranteed right to use the St. Lawrence River and Seaway;
- fair compensation for federal assets (buildings, equipment and other items paid for by all Canadians) in Quebec;
- the transfer from Quebec of nationally owned companies (such as Air Canada and the CNR).

Would you add anything to this list?

Examine the collection of newspaper headlines from the 1970s that deal with Quebec separatism:

1. How many of these headlines refer to the possible undesirable effects of Quebec's separation from Canada? Which problems do they highlight?
2. Find a headline in this collage that predicts violence if Quebec attempts to separate. Find another that contradicts this view.
3. How many of the headlines refer to the language issue? State three points that they make about this issue.
4. Make up three headlines that could have been written in the 1970s. Add them to this collage.
5. Now add four more about English-French relations and separatism that would be appropriate to today's situation within Quebec. Is their tone very different from those of the 1970s? If so, how and why?

COULD AN INDEPENDENT QUEBEC SURVIVE?

Canadians differ widely in their views on this question. Their opinions seem to reflect their wishes. Those who favour independence tend to believe Quebec could survive on its own. Many of those opposed say that it could not.

What do you think? Make a list of the things that a country needs to survive. Then find out whether Quebec has them.

Obviously, the Parti Québécois feels confident that Quebec *could* survive as an independent country. They point out that almost 100 new nations have been created since 1945. Quebec would have more people, more resources and better technology than most of those countries. Separatists claim that Quebec has a clearly defined territory, a common language and culture, plus its own history. Montreal is one of the world's great cities. Also, it is the second-largest French-speaking city in the world. Above all, separatists argue that Quebeckers *want* to live together in an independent country with its own special identity. So far, the opinion polls do not support this claim.

An independent Quebec would need strong trading ties. At present, Quebec sells more than 50 percent of its manufactured goods to the rest of Canada. Quebec could not afford to lose this market. On the other hand, Canada counts on selling about 25 percent of its goods in Quebec. Perhaps the two countries would be forced to be reasonable with each other.

An independent Quebec would also need investment funds to develop its industry. The United States is an important source of such funds. It is difficult to tell whether Americans would be willing to invest in the economy of a separate Quebec.

REFERENDUM 1980: A TIME OF DECISION

Since taking office in 1976, Premier René Lévesque faced a dilemma. What should he do about the issue of separation? The ultimate goal of his Parti Québécois was a free and independent Quebec. Its more extreme members began to pressure him to work for this. Emotionally, Lévesque probably agreed with them. But he was a practical politician. He sensed that the voters of Quebec were not ready for such a step. Moreover, in the 1976 election campaign, he had promised not to actively work for independence. Perhaps he also questioned whether Quebec could actually survive on its own without too much economic hardship.

To help formulate a strategy (plan), Lévesque quietly ordered several private tests of public opinion. The results were very informative: Only about 20 percent of Quebeckers favoured outright separation.

About 38 percent supported the idea of sovereignty association. But 54 percent were willing to have the Quebec government try to negotiate sovereignty association with the federal government of Canada. These polls also showed that a majority of Quebec voters:

- had no clear idea of what sovereignty association actually involved;
- believed it meant that Quebec would somehow remain a part of Canada;
- thought that Canada probably would agree to such a scheme.

Imagine that you were René Lévesque in this political situation in the late 1970s. Devise a plan of action on the issue of separatism that will:

- appease (satisfy) your more radical supporters;
- deal with your own personal longing for independence;
- not cause you to lose the next Quebec election;
- avoid offending the rest of Canada too much (after all, a separate Quebec might need some friendly support in order to survive).

To add realism to this simulation, you could:

- Have small groups of students develop two different "Lévesque strategies." These could be compared and evaluated to determine which approach is best. Perhaps parts of each plan could be adopted.
- Once the strategy is determined, try to anticipate how the Canadian federal government would react to it.
- Predict various scenarios by which the "battle for public opinion" would be fought.

In the next few pages, we will discover what Lévesque's strategy actually was and what happened when he attempted to carry it out.

Lévesque's strategy was strongly influenced by the polling information he had received. Eventually he announced that a referendum would be held on the question of sovereignty association before the end of his first term (1981 at the latest). Prime Minister Trudeau immediately expressed his disapproval of this idea. He believed that a referendum was not the proper way to settle a political issue. It tended to divide voters too deeply. Also, it weakened parliamentary democracy by reducing the importance of elected representatives of the people. Nonetheless, Lévesque announced that the referendum would take place in the spring of 1980.

Speculation began to grow about a vital issue: How would the referendum question be worded? This was revealed in a dramatic announcement on December 20, 1979. The question would read as follows:

> The government of Quebec has made public its proposal to negotiate a new agreement with the rest of Canada, based on the equality of nations; this agreement would enable Quebec to acquire the exclusive power to make its laws, administer its taxes and establish relations abroad — in other words, sovereignty — and at the same time, to maintain with Canada an economic association including a common currency; any change in political status resulting from these negotiations will be submitted to the people through a referendum; on these terms, do you agree to give the government of Quebec the mandate to negotiate the proposed agreement between Quebec and Canada?
>
> OUI ____ NON____

1 Be sure you know the meaning of the key words used in this passage, for example: negotiate, exclusive power, sovereignty, common currency, political status, referendum, mandate.

2 What would it have meant to vote "OUI" on this question? What would it have meant to vote "NON"?

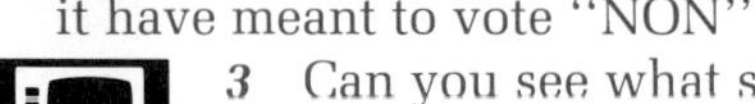

3 Can you see what strategy the separatists were using by wording the question in this way?

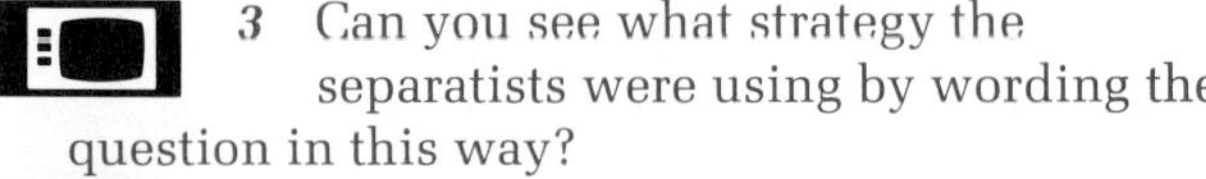

4 Many prominent Canadians, including Prime Minister Trudeau, were opposed to Quebec separating. How could they have tried to influence the vote?

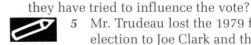

5 Mr. Trudeau lost the 1979 federal election to Joe Clark and the Conservatives; however, he returned to power in 1980. Could his return have had a significant effect on the outcome of the Quebec referendum? Explain.

Using the information from the text, determine the time (year) and circumstance of this photograph. Also, suggest a caption for it and explain your choice.

This photo was taken in Quebec in 1980. What clues support this fact? The caption suggested by the owners of the photo was: "A House Divided." What famous American politician once made a crucial speech with the same title? In what circumstances? How, then, was the photo caption appropriate for the Quebec situation?

While Lévesque began to prepare for the referendum, the federal government was not totally ready for the challenge. As indicated above, the Trudeau Liberals lost the 1979 election. They were defeated by Joe Clark and the Progressive Conservatives. Previously, Clark had criticized Trudeau for straining relations with the provinces to the breaking point. During the election campaign, he had promised a "fresh face to federalism." The details of this proposal remained unclear. Still, Clark hinted that his government would seek more co-operation and share more powers with the provinces. Once in office, Mr. Clark faced many problems in addition to the Quebec issue. While his new, inexperienced government struggled to establish itself, René Lévesque's referendum strategy swung into high gear.

When the wording of the referendum question was announced, it came under immediate attack. Opponents accused the Lévesque government of deliberately confusing Quebec voters. Why was the question so long? Why was sovereignty association not defined more clearly? Prime Minister Clark and most of the provincial premiers stated their opposition to a referendum. Some critics branded the notion of sovereignty association a "pipe dream" and a "political fantasy."

1 What is a "pipe dream"?
2 Why might the Lévesque government try to be unclear about the meaning of sovereignty association?
3 Why might sovereignty association have been a "political fantasy"?

Some people said that sovereignty association was impossible. Here are some of their arguments:

- A separate Quebec would have approximately 6.5 million people; the rest of Canada would have over 17 million. Ontario alone had almost 8.5 million people. Why would 17 million Canadian voters give 6.5 million Quebeckers an equal say in such matters as trade, money, banking and transportation? Why would 8.5 million Ontarians agree to 6.5 million Quebeckers having a greater voice than themselves in such matters?
- While part of Canada, Quebec benefitted from high tariff protection. Quebec industries, such as the clothing, shoe and textile industries, were shielded from foreign competition. As a result, Canadians paid higher prices for such goods. Why would they allow this to continue if Quebec separated?
- Quebec was receiving more revenues from the federal treasury than it was contributing. Even so, it had the highest rates of taxation in Canada. If it separated, Quebec would be forced to raise taxes further. Surely the voters would not accept this.
- If Quebec separated, Canadians would be angry and hurt. While they might not resist by force, neither would they be helpful. Quebec would have to make it alone.

To help their cause, the Lévesque government published a so-called "white paper." This was presented as a history of the French-Canadian people. The story was told in terms of "good guys and bad guys." It made scapegoats of the English in Canada. French-Canadians were portrayed as long-suffering heroes who had courageously resisted the English bullies and exploiters.

As we have seen in earlier chapters, a partial case could be made for this interpretation of Quebec's history. However, the white paper grossly distorted the history of English-French relations for political purposes. Its errors and exaggerations were quickly attacked. Some of the strongest attackers were French-Canadian. One of these was Claude Ryan, the leader of the Quebec Liberal party. Another was Pierre Trudeau. He had been returned as prime min-

During the Quebec referendum campaign in 1980, both sides competed for the votes of women. One separatist sarcastically described French-Canadian women who supported union with Canada as "Yvettes." This was a reference to a clichéd female character who obeyed her husband, stayed home to keep house and was not a bright, independent thinker.

How is this cartoon related to the "Yvette" incident? What is the main point of the cartoon? In what way was it a prediction of the referendum result? Was it an accurate prediction? If you had made the sarcastic reference to "Yvettes," would you feel that the referendum result proved you to be wise? Why or why not?

ister in a surprise federal election held in February, 1980. The sworn enemy of René Lévesque was back. On election night, a triumphant Pierre Trudeau greeted his cheering supporters with the quip, "Welcome to the 1980s!"

Now the battle lines for Quebec's referendum were clearly drawn. Each side made heavy use of the media to promote its views. Prominent French-Canadian entertainers, athletes and other personalities were enlisted to support separatist or federalist arguments. The debate raged on radio and television talk shows, in assembly halls and even in private homes. As Pierre Trudeau had predicted, the referendum was dividing friends and families.

The referendum question itself (see page 240) provided the main focus for the debate. Voters could say "yes" (*oui*) or "no" (*non*) to allowing the Quebec government to try to negotiate sovereignty association with Canada. A shrewd promise was contained within the wording of the question. It said that the Lévesque government would not take Quebec out of Confederation without a second referendum. Thus, Quebec voters would get another chance to voice their opinions before the final step would be taken. Obviously, the strategy here was to reduce voter anxiety. In a sense, a "yes" vote on the first referendum was not going to cost the voters anything. What did Quebec have to lose by *trying* for a new deal?

Both Claude Ryan and Pierre Trudeau urged a "no" vote, but for vastly different reasons. Ryan wanted to try his *deux nations* concept. Briefly, this involved winning special status for Quebec within Confederation. Quebec would be recognized as a "nation," equal to the rest of Canada. He proposed a long list of extra powers that Quebec would need to function in this role. For this to be achieved, it would be necessary to completely rewrite the Constitution of Canada.

This left Pierre Trudeau with a problem: What could *he* offer the voters for saying "no" in the referendum? After much thought, he made his promise. If the voters rejected sovereignty association, he

The Winner: Liberal leader Pierre Trudeau waves to the crowd in the ballroom of Chateau Laurier Hotel in Ottawa after winning the federal election of 1980. At right is Liberal Party president Alasdair Graham.

Quebec Liberal leader Claude Ryan is the centre of attention as he campaigns in Radisson near James Bay during the referendum campaign in 1980. Several school children followed Ryan as he went from house to house knocking on doors in this community of 1200.

would undertake a major reform of the Canadian Constitution. Most of the details could be worked out later. However, there would be heavy emphasis on equal rights for all Canadians. Moreover, the Constitution would be "brought home." By this he meant that the final legal ties with Britain would be broken. Our former mother country would no longer have any power over our courts or over the Constitution itself.

The Trudeau position was a far cry from that of Claude Ryan or René Lévesque. Could he sell it to the voters of Quebec? From Ottawa Trudeau led the charge into his home province. He brought along several of his cabinet ministers, especially the more prominent French-Canadian members. These included Jean Chrétien and Marc Lalonde. They made many pro-Canada speeches across Quebec. Their crowds were large and enthusiastic. They swept aside separatist criticism that they were interfering. They spoke as French-Canadians who had made it to the top of the federal power structure. Surely their own careers were proof that their people could flourish freely within Confederation. Because of his less dynamic personality, Claude Ryan seemed to fade into the background.

The "no" side was further strengthened by the activities of Joe Clark and of several provincial premiers. These people criss-crossed Quebec, campaigning against sovereignty association.

Obviously, their combined efforts paid off. On May 20 the referendum results were decisive. There was a record turnout at the polls — 82 percent of all eligible voters. The results were as follows:

	Oui	**Non**
French-Canadian Quebeckers	60%	40%
English-Canadian Quebeckers	9%	91%
Others	16%	84%
Overall	40.6%	59.4%

René Lévesque and the separatist movement had suffered a major setback. For the moment, at least, the crisis for Canada had passed. All sides needed time to fully assess the results of this referendum. Both Lévesque and Trudeau faced further challenges. Lévesque still had to govern Quebec. He would need to call an election within a year. And Trudeau had to make good on his promise of constitutional reform.

QUEBEC AND THE NEW CONSTITUTION

The referendum results held valuable lessons for all Canadians. Perhaps most important was that a large majority of Quebeckers did not want or were not ready to separate. No doubt, many still felt a strong loyalty to Canada. Perhaps others were reluctant to "take a chance." Independence might be too costly, especially in terms of higher taxes, fewer jobs and lower living standards. Still, more than half of French-speaking Quebec voters had opted for a *try* at negotiating sovereignty association.

Indeed, the Parti Québécois made a rapid and impressive recovery from its referendum defeat. In 1981 it won its biggest-ever election victory. Below are the results (shown in comparison with the 1976 election):

	1976		**1981**	
	Seats Won	% of Votes Won	Seats Won	% of Votes Won
Parti Québécois	71	41.4	81	49.5
Liberals	26	33.8	41	45.5
Others	13	24.8	—	05.0

A dejected René Lévesque hears the results of the referendum. What do you think would have happened to Quebec and Canada if the "Oui" supporters had won the referendum?

These results in 1981 made Trudeau's task of constitutional reform more difficult. Perhaps Quebec voters saw René Lévesque as a kind of insurance policy. They would not let him take Quebec out of Canada. However, they wanted him as premier to "keep Ottawa honest." This way, they might enjoy the best of both worlds.

Constitutional reform became the great challenge of Pierre Trudeau's career. He was bombarded by demands from all sides. Hundreds of interest groups wanted a say in the proposed changes. In this chapter, we are concerned with the effects of the new Constitution on English–French relations.

One important change involved the amending formula. This is the method by which the Constitution can be changed. Quebec had always been concerned about this issue. It was most anxious about any change in the division of powers between the federal and provincial governments. A new amending formula had been proposed at the Victoria Conference in 1971. Quebec had rejected it. Premier Robert Bourassa insisted that Quebec should have the right to veto (cancel) any proposed change to the Constitution that it did not like. However, this idea was unacceptable to the rest of Canada. If Quebec could have such power, why could not Ontario or large regions such as the West or the Maritimes?

In the 1980s, Trudeau tried again. Eventually, Ottawa plus nine of the provinces agreed on the terms of a new Constitution. The package included a new amending formula. However, no province or region was given the power of veto over proposed amendments. Still, an important concession was made. It involved amendments in which the powers of one or

Quebec Leader Robert Bourassa (second from left) waves to supporters at the National Assembly, after the swearing in of three new Liberals elected on June 18, 1984. From left, Marcel Parent, Robert Bourassa, Guy Pratt and Giles Fortin.

more provinces might be altered. In such cases, where a province objected to the change, it could "opt out" and not be affected by that change.

Neither Claude Ryan nor René Lévesque could accept the proposed new Constitution. Both believed that it fell far short of giving Quebec a "fair shake." Therefore, Lévesque made good on an earlier threat: He refused to place Quebec's signature on the new Constitution. Nevertheless, it became the law of the land in April, 1982. Within a few years, Ryan, Trudeau and Lévesque all had retired from politics. The new Constitution seemed to pose no great problems for Quebec. But quiet efforts continued into the late 1980s to bring Quebec completely "into the fold." Obviously, some compromise would be necessary. Could Ottawa make concessions that would please Quebec yet not offend the rest of the country?

IS SEPARATISM STILL A THREAT TO CANADA?

As Canada approaches the 1990s, separatism remains an important issue. At the moment, it seems to be in retreat, not only in Quebec but elsewhere in the country. Early in 1985, the Mulroney government signed new agreements on oil-pricing and revenue-sharing with Newfoundland and certain western oil producers. This helped to reduce discontent with Ottawa in these regions. The election defeat of the Parti Québécois in December of the same year also was significant. Short of funds and deeply divided, the once-feared separatist party faced possible collapse. Only a few years earlier, it had seemed to be on the brink of achieving its goal; now its main concern was its own survival.

But the movement has the potential for survival, especially in Quebec. A way must be found to overcome Quebec's last objections to the new Constitution. Severe economic problems could rekindle doubt about the value of remaining in Canada. Carelessness or indifference could once again fan the flames of separatist emotion. Because of strong opposition, the government of Manitoba in 1984 was forced to drop its attempt to extend French-language rights in that province. Ontario, with almost 500 000 French-speaking citizens, continues to reject official bilingualism. French-speaking Quebeckers follow such developments with great interest. Much progress has been made by and for this generation of French-Canadians. Still, they must wonder when they will be accepted across the country as full and equal partners in the Canadian nation.

QUEBEC IN THE 1980s

Soon after the 1981 election, René Lévesque ran into serious political problems. Quebec was hit hard by the economic recession of 1982–83. Unemployment rose above 400 000. To improve social programs and win voter favour, the Lévesque government went on a spending spree. The provincial debt rose rapidly, and taxes had to be increased. Each year about 25 000 English Quebeckers were leaving for other provinces. They were taking their skills, capital and businesses with them.

The growing discontent of workers was another serious problem. These people had been among the strongest supporters of the Parti Québécois. Robert Bourassa returned to the leadership of the Quebec Liberal party. By late 1984, polls showed that he had the support of almost 70 percent of Quebec voters.

Events elsewhere in Canada played a part in these developments. Brian Mulroney, a bilingual Quebecker, was chosen as the new leader of the Progressive Conservative party in June, 1983. A major rival, John Crosbie, was rejected chiefly because of his inability to speak French fluently. One year later, Pierre Trudeau retired from politics. This showed his confidence that separatism was no longer a threat. His successor, John Turner, was chosen partly because of his bilingual ability but also because of his reputation for skill in business matters. All Canadians, including Quebeckers, clearly were concerned more with economic issues than with separatism.

Meanwhile, the Parti Québécois began to show signs of serious division. Early in 1985, after bitter debate, the party decided to put the goal of separatism into the background. René Lévesque supported this move. He argued that the main concern of the party must be to stay in power. Therefore, it must address issues of greatest interest to the voters. His opinion polls told him that these issues were Quebec's high rates of unemployment and taxation. Several key members of the party disagreed with their leader on this point. Some announced their retirement from politics. Others actually decided to vote with the Opposition in an attempt to defeat Lévesque's (and their own) government.

Beset by troubles, Mr. Lévesque began to show signs of ill health. Rumours of his retirement began to spread. He confirmed these rumours by stepping down from the party leadership in the summer of 1985. On September 29, Pierre Marc Johnson, a son of the late Quebec premier Daniel Johnson, became the new leader of the Parti Québécois. Almost immediately, the new leader called for a provincial election. During the campaign, he stressed economic issues and downplayed separatism. Nonetheless, the Parti Québécois was soundly defeated by the Liberals, led by Robert Bourassa, on December 2, 1985.

This was an amazing comeback for Mr. Bourassa. His political career was apparently ruined in 1976 when he suffered a crushing defeat by René Lévesque and the separatists. Now it seemed that Quebec politics had come full circle. A leader stressing continued membership in Canada had overwhelmingly defeated the separatist party! His return was well timed. In the mid-1980s, Quebec enjoyed a strong economic recovery. French-Canadians started many small and medium-sized businesses. They also rose to powerful positions in large corporations within the province. Talk of separatism almost disappeared.

Quebec took another large step toward full membership in Confederation through the Meech Lake Accord of 1987 (see page 12). By the terms of this agreement, all of Quebec's major objections to the Constitution were resolved. Perhaps most significant was the recognition of Quebec as a "distinct society" within Confederation. Some critics of the Accord, including Pierre Trudeau, described it as a "disaster." The federal government of Brian Mulroney had surrendered far too much power to Quebec and the other provinces. However, by late 1987 it appeared that the Accord would receive the final approval of Ottawa and of all ten provincial governments.

The Meech Lake Accord was a great victory for Premier Bourassa. However, the mellowing mood of Quebec was abruptly shaken one evening in early November, 1987. The late news was suddenly interrupted by the announcement that René Lévesque had died of a massive heart attack. Immediately, old emotions were rekindled in a blaze of media publicity. Tens of thousands of mourners filed past Lévesque's casket, which was draped in the flag of Quebec. Many eyes were clouded with tears; quiet voices murmered a heart-felt "Merci" or "Au Revoir." There was a dramatic moment when former prime minister Pierre Trudeau paid his last respects to his greatest political foe.

Apparently, Lévesque's death, and elaborate state funeral, renewed old rivalries within the Parti Québécois. Insiders revealed that the party was again torn between the ideal of total separation and a more moderate approach. Within days an emotional Marc Johnson announced that he was resigning the party leadership. Speculators predicted that his eventual successor would be Jacques Parizeau. This brilliant, hardline separatist had quit the party in disgust over Lévesque's backtracking on the issue of independence for Quebec.

BUILDING YOUR LEARNING SKILLS

FOCUSSING ON THE ISSUE

1 Why was the Quebec provincial election of 1976 so important?
2 After that election, what became the central question in English-French relations?
3 Two key facts about the Quebec separatist movement are:
   a In 1976 the Parti Québécois won a stunning and decisive election victory over the pro-federalist Liberals of Robert Bourassa.
   b in 1985 the Parti Québécois was divided, unpopular and suffered an overwhelming defeat by the same Robert Bourassa.

Formulate two questions, the answers to which would highlight the key developments within that nine-year span.

4 The following terms appeared in this chapter. Try to recall their meanings and how they were used.

assets	indépendentist
Bill 101	radical
customs union	referendum
exile	secession
federalist	separatist
FLQ	sovereignty association

5 Look again at the photograph that appears on page 229. What does this photograph portray? How does it illustrate a major cause of the separatist movement? Does it also suggest a reason for the apparent failure of separatism?

RESEARCHING

1 Form two study groups to investigate the lives and backgrounds of René Lévesque and Pierre Trudeau. Each group should uncover information concerning family, upbringing, education, jobs and other experiences. Try to form impressions about the character and personality of the man your group is studying. (Possible sources are biographies, autobiographies, magazine and newspaper articles.) This research will later be used in a simulation activity.

2 Examine the press coverage of the terrorist acts committed by the FLQ in the early 1960s. Try to find a pattern in the incidents. Compare media coverage and commentary from within and outside Quebec.

3 Try to trace the development and expression of separatist feeling in Quebec throughout the province's history.

4 Read through the British North America Act to see if there is any reference to the right of a province to secede or to the possibility that the Canadian union was not considered permanent.

5 During the FLQ crisis of October, 1970, Prime Minister Trudeau referred to "bleeding hearts" in the country. Try to discover:

a the situation in which he made the remark;
b what he meant by his words;
c the criticism against which he was defending himself at the time.

6 Choose one prominent member of the FLQ and prepare a report for the class on that person.

7 Regions of Canada other than Quebec might have reasons to be unhappy with their situations. Try to find out which regions these would be and why they might be discontented.

1·2·3 ORGANIZING

1 Develop a summary chart on the question of whether or not a separate Quebec could survive as an independent nation. First, design the chart. It should show the positive and negative points. It also should categorize the deciding factors under five headings: political, economic, social, military and "other." Now fill in the chart as fully as you can, using point form.

2 Which of these names does not belong with the others: Marc Carbonneau, Paul Rose, Pierre Vallières, René Lévesque, Bernard Lortie?

3 Imagine that you have been asked to present a report to the class on a prominent member of the FLQ. On what aspects of that person's life would you expect to gather information?

4 Let us assume that you gather information on question three, above, under these headings: job experience; reasons for joining the FLQ; early childhood; current status; activities with the FLQ; education; results of activities with the FLQ.

a In what order would you present these aspects of the person's life?
b How would you know which aspects to emphasize?

5 Conduct an opinion poll in your school or neighbourhood on this question: How serious would Quebec's separation be for the rest of Canada — very, fairly, or not very serious? Compare your results with the poll on page 233.

COMMUNICATING

1 What comment is this cartoon making about a serious political problem facing the separatist movement? Do you think the cartoon requires a caption? If so, suggest one. If not, why not?

2 Write up a declaration of principles and beliefs that would express your feelings if you were a member of the FLQ. You can compare your version with the real FLQ Manifesto, which was published in 1970.

3 Why do you think the colour red is often chosen as a symbol by most revolutionary groups?

4 Pierre Trudeau referred to the death of Pierre Laporte as a "murder." The FLQ called it an "execution." What different messages do these words convey? Which word do you think was more appropriate?

5 Canadians who oppose Quebec leaving Confederation tend to call those who do want to leave *separatists*. However, Quebeckers who favour separatism prefer to call themselves *indépendentists*. What differences are suggested by the two terms?

ANALYZING

1 What factors explain the decline of the Quebec separatist movement in the 1980s? Rank these in order of importance. Compare your answer with those of other classmates. Try to reach a consensus on this question.

2 Whose problem would be more serious — Quebec's without Canada or Canada's without Quebec? Explain your viewpoint.

3 It has been suggested that all Canadians be asked to take an oath of loyalty to Canada. Those who refuse would be deported (forced to leave Canada). Would this be wise? Would it be legal? Would it be possible?

4 Should the Parti Québécois be legal in Canada? Why or why not?

5 One political change that might please some French-Canadians would be the abolition of the monarchy in Canada. Why might it please them? What other groups in Canada might also approve? Should it be done?

6 Assess the impact of the FLQ crisis of October, 1970, on the separatist movement. Did it help or hurt? Why?

7 In the early 1960s, a French-Canadian said, "What actually threatens Canada is not change and questioning but a stubborn refusal to accept change and difference." What do you think this person meant? What was being referred to? Is this opinion correct? Did Canadians listen seriously to this statement and others like it? Support your answer with evidence.

8 For several years, unemployment has been higher in Quebec than in most other provinces. Some experts say that this should show Quebec that, if it separated, things would get even worse. Others argue the opposite. They say that high unemployment will cause more Quebeckers to support separatism because they will feel that they have nothing to lose. Which argument makes more sense to you? Why?

9 In June of 1985, the Supreme Court of Canada announced a major decision. It declared most of

Manitoba's laws unconstitutional on the grounds that they were printed only in English. Both the prime minister of Canada and the premier of Manitoba seemed pleased by this decision. Try to discover the basis of this court ruling. What effects will it have in Manitoba? In other provinces? Will this decision tend to harm or improve English-French relations? Explain your answer.

APPLYING YOUR KNOWLEDGE

1 Draw a political map of Canada or North America as you think it will appear in the year 2000. Boundaries are the most important point of this exercise. Will there still be a Canada? If so, of what provinces or regions will it consist?

2 While in power, René Lévesque admitted that many people in the Parti Québécois wanted Quebec, after independence, to take a neutral position in foreign policy. However, he said that he expected that Quebec probably would end up joining the North American Air Defence System with Canada and the United States. He even admitted that there was a possibility of Quebec joining the North Atlantic Treaty Organization. Why might an independent Quebec want to join these two alliance systems?

3 Why would Brian Mulroney's election as prime minister in 1984 be significant for English-French relations?

4 Would it be fair to conclude that all future prime ministers will have to be bilingual? Why or why not?

5 How would an independent Quebec affect Canada's military security? How is this consideration related to question two, above?

6 It has been said that separatism will always be a factor in federal politics as long as Quebec remains in Confederation. Do you agree? Why or why not?

7 Refer back to the data collected on Pierre Trudeau and René Lévesque in "Researching." Two students should now assume the roles of these two politicians. Perhaps each could choose one classmate to act as an aide/adviser. The class should select a format that will best enable these two colourful personalities to convey their beliefs and to confront one another as the bitter opponents they were. Possibilities include: a debate (formal or informal); a radio phone-in session (that could be taped for playback and review); a double interview in "Meet-the-Press" style.

8 This proposed exercise combines several learning skills. (Afterwards, try to identify them.) Clip newspaper stories on English-French relations for a three- or four-week period. Cut the headlines off the articles. Use a numbering or lettering system so that the headlines can later be reunited with the proper articles. Put the articles away. Next, put all the headlines together and use them to try to identify:

a the current issues in English-French relations;

b the present trends in those relations;

c the attitude of the press to those issues;

d the attitude of politicians to the issues.

Allow each student in your class to choose one headline. Using his or her knowledge of the subject, plus the ideas developed so far in the exercise, try to recreate the original article. Finally, match each headline with its original article. How close did the student "author" come to the original?

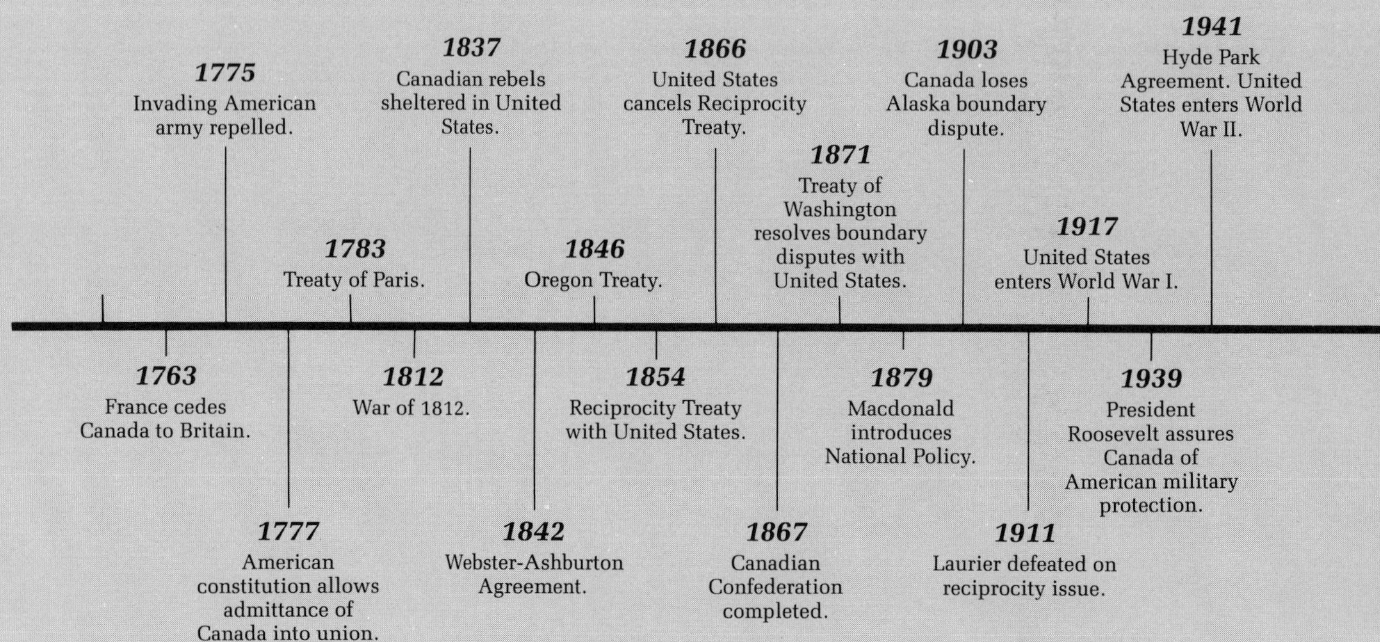
1775
Invading American army repelled.
1837
Canadian rebels sheltered in United States.
1866
United States cancels Reciprocity Treaty.
1903
Canada loses Alaska boundary dispute.
1941
Hyde Park Agreement. United States enters World War II.
1871
Treaty of Washington resolves boundary disputes with United States.
1783
Treaty of Paris.
1846
Oregon Treaty.
1917
United States enters World War I.
1763
France cedes Canada to Britain.
1812
War of 1812.
1854
Reciprocity Treaty with United States.
1879
Macdonald introduces National Policy.
1939
President Roosevelt assures Canada of American military protection.
1777
American constitution allows admittance of Canada into union.
1842
Webster-Ashburton Agreement.
1867
Canadian Confederation completed.
1911
Laurier defeated on reciprocity issue.

unit five

CANADIAN–AMERICAN RELATIONS

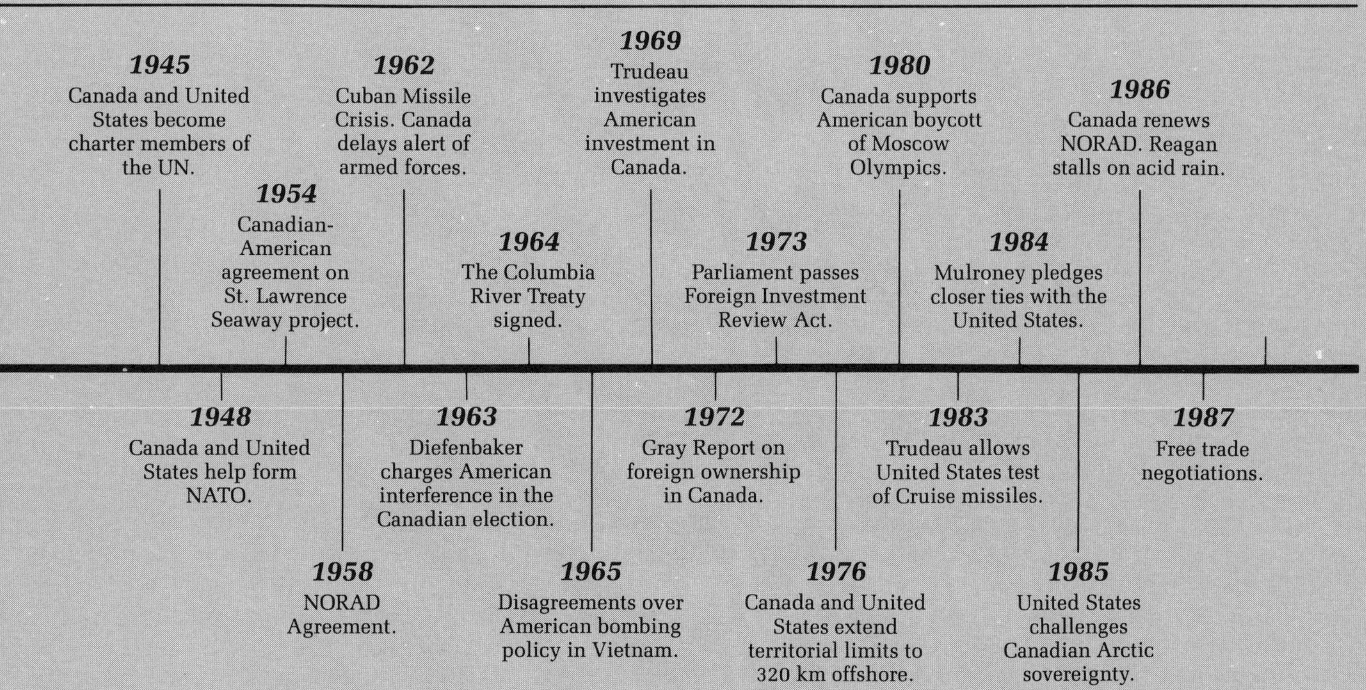

1945
Canada and United States become charter members of the UN.
1948
Canada and United States help form NATO.
1954
Canadian-American agreement on St. Lawrence Seaway project.
1958
NORAD Agreement.
1962
Cuban Missile Crisis. Canada delays alert of armed forces.
1963
Diefenbaker charges American interference in the Canadian election.
1964
The Columbia River Treaty signed.
1965
Disagreements over American bombing policy in Vietnam.
1969
Trudeau investigates American investment in Canada.
1972
Gray Report on foreign ownership in Canada.
1973
Parliament passes Foreign Investment Review Act.
1976
Canada and United States extend territorial limits to 320 km offshore.
1980
Canada supports American boycott of Moscow Olympics.
1983
Trudeau allows United States test of Cruise missiles.
1984
Mulroney pledges closer ties with the United States.
1985
United States challenges Canadian Arctic sovereignty.
1986
Canada renews NORAD. Reagan stalls on acid rain.
1987
Free trade negotiations.

TOPIC ORGANIZER

THEME ORGANIZER

- In their early history, Canada and the United States tended to be enemies.
- This rivalry lasted over 200 years and was due to serious political, economic and cultural differences.
- Canada has been invaded twice by the armed forces of the United States.
- Relations gradually began to improve in the mid-nineteenth century.
- By the early twentieth century, the idea of war between the two countries was almost unthinkable.
- Throughout the twentieth century, ties between Canada and the United States have grown steadily stronger.
- Our two countries have fought on the same side in two major wars and other smaller wars. Today we are military allies in two key organizations: NATO and NORAD.
- We are each other's largest trading partner.
- Through capital investment and other economic measures, the United States exerts tremendous influence in the Canadian economy and government.
- Some people feel that Canada is in danger of being engulfed by the United States through:
  - **a** political pressure
  - **b** military dependence
  - **c** economic dependence
  - **d** strong cultural influences that threaten to erase our distinctive identity
- While we remain "best friends," some serious issues have been raised between our two countries, including:
  - **a** pollution control
  - **b** sovereignty in the Arctic
  - **c** off-shore territorial limits and fishing rights
  - **d** trade policy
  - **e** the degree of our support for American policy on nuclear weapons

INTRODUCTION

NEWS RELEASE:

OTTAWA, JULY 1, 2000. At noon today, the Maple Leaf flag was lowered for the last time from the flagpole on Parliament Hill. Officially, from 13:01, the former English-speaking provinces became part of the United States. It had been just 35 years since the Maple Leaf was first unfurled as Canada's own emblem.

Many famous Canadians and Americans gathered for today's brief ceremony. They were joined by thousands of ordinary citizens. The former prime minister of Canada made a short but emotional speech. He talked about what Canada had achieved since its birth in 1867. He described the great strength and other qualities of the Canadian people. Finally, he spoke of his own mixed feelings about the new union with the United States. He said that he was sorry to see the end of Canada. But he thought that all Canadians were excited about joining the greatest nation on earth. He ended his speech with a hope. This was that the new union would add to the strength, happiness and wealth of all Americans—old and *new*.

Then the band began to play. It was made up of United States Marines and former members of the Canadian Armed Forces. "O Canada" echoed across the Ottawa River for the last time. It could probably be heard on the other side by citizens of the Republic of Quebec. The band played slowly and with great feeling. It was a dramatic moment. Some people were crying. A member of the Royal Canadian Mounted Police lowered the maple leaf flag while the band played. The flag was carefully folded. It was handed to an American soldier. The flag will be placed in a Washington museum.

Next, the American flag was slowly hauled up the pole. The band played a stirring version of "The Stars and Stripes'." At first, some of the crowd did not sing. But by the end, most people were singing loudly. Then the president of the United States spoke to the crowd. He praised the former country of Canada. He welcomed the people of Canada into membership in the United States. He said this was a natural union. It was to be expected. He ended by asking everyone to sing "America the Beautiful."

How do you feel about this imaginary scene? Does it bother you? Would you like to see it happen? Could it really happen? Some people will consider it far-fetched, pure fantasy. But there are some Canadians who believe that Canada's survival is in danger. There is still the possibility that Quebec might break away from the Canadian union. This could lead other provinces to do the same thing. One or more of these might then ask to join the United States. After all, Canada already is very dependent on the Americans. Why bother to keep trying to pretend we are different from them?

Perhaps these are wild ideas. But we must look at all the possibilities. The next few years will probably decide the future of Canada. Most important to that future are our relations with the United States. This unit will examine those relations, both past and present. It will also look at what might lie ahead.

WHAT GALLUP POLLS SHOW ABOUT CANADIAN–AMERICAN RELATIONS

Over the years, several Gallup polls have been taken on the question: WOULD YOU SAY THAT RELATIONS BETWEEN CANADA AND THE UNITED STATES ON THE WHOLE, ARE EXCELLENT, GOOD, JUST FAIR OR POOR? The following percentages show a trend in Canadian opinion on this question.

Rating	1955	1960	1964	1974	1981	Today?
Excellent	19	15	11	07	06	
Good	56	54	57	44	39	
Just fair	17	24	26	37	41	
Poor	02	03	01	06	09	
Don't know	05	04	05	06	05	

Note: *Figures might not add up to 100 percent due to rounding.*

1 What seems to be the trend in Canadian thinking about our relations with the United States? What reasons can you suggest for this trend?

2 Take your own opinion poll. For best results, you should try to question about 100 people. Ask the same question of everyone. Record their answers carefully. Try to get a broad sample. That is, ask people of different ages, sexes, occupations, ethnic groups and so on. Have at least ten friends or classmates conduct a similar poll. Then average your findings.

3 See how your figures compare with those of earlier years such as 1974 and 1964. Is the trend that you noted in question one continuing?

4 Try to find a recent Gallup poll done on the same question. How do its figures compare with yours?

UNIT PREVIEW QUESTIONS

As you study this unit, keep these questions in mind. You may want to return to them when you have finished the unit.

1 What ties do we now have with the United States? How strong are they?
2 How and why have these ties developed?
3 How important is the United States to us? How important is Canada to the United States? Why?
4 Are relations between our two countries becoming better or worse? Why?
5 Is Canada too dependent on the United States? If so, in what ways? What can be done about the situation?

chapter 14

THE HISTORICAL BACKGROUND OF CANADIAN–AMERICAN RELATIONS

TOPIC ORGANIZER **PAGE**

THEME ORGANIZER

- Canada and the United States began as colonies of powerful European rivals, France and Britain.
- Even after Canada became a British possession, its relations with the Americans remained poor.
- The United States has always been much richer and more powerful than Canada.
- Canada was invaded by the Americans in 1775 and again in 1812.
- After the War of 1812, Britain and the United States tried to avoid conflict. The British ceded large areas of land to the Americans at our expense.
- Canadian Confederation was prompted partly by concerns about the growing economic and military power of the United States.
- The period between 1905 and 1918 marked a major change in Canadian-American relations. The United States replaced Britain as our main trading partner and source of foreign investment. Also, we became allies during World War I.
- World War II further strengthened the growing ties between the two countries, especially economic and military.
- Since World War II, these ties have grown stronger than those between any two other countries in the world. This development has been welcomed by many Canadians, but it has also been criticized by some who fear domination or even a complete takeover by the United States.

INTRODUCTION

Former prime minister Pierre Trudeau compared living next door to the United States to sleeping with an elephant. He said, "No matter how friendly or even-tempered is the beast, one is affected by every twitch and grunt."

The comparison was, in many ways, a good one. The United States is truly a giant—the world's richest and most powerful country. Physically, Canada is about the same size. However, the United States has 10 times our population, about 12 times our economic production and *many* more times our military strength.

The United States is far more important to Canada than any other country. It is our closest neighbour. Moreover, it is our major trading partner. The United States is our main source of foreign money for investment and our chief military ally. Therefore, Canadian-American relations are very important to both countries, but especially to Canada.

Canadians often have mixed feelings about the United States. Indeed, it has been said that we have a "love-hate" relationship with Americans.

1 What do you think is meant by a "love-hate" relationship? Do you have such mixed feelings about anyone or anything? If so, what and why?

2 Do you have any positive feelings about the United States or its people? Such feelings might involve friendship, love, respect, admiration, gratitude or pride. If you do have such feelings, describe them as fully as possible. Then try to say why you feel this way.

3 Do you have any negative feelings about Americans or their country? These could include anger, dislike, hatred, fear or jealousy. If so, describe and then analyze your feelings.

4 If it is helpful, discuss your thoughts on questions two and three, above, with your family and friends. Then compare your findings with those of classmates. Make lists of both the positive and negative feelings and the reasons for both.

5 Try to interpret (analyze) your findings. Then evaluate (judge) them. For example, are most of the feelings based on the present or on past developments? (In other words, how important does history seem to be as a factor in Canadian feelings about their neighbour?) Also, are most of your findings based on the first-hand experience of people? If not, what are they based on — media reports? rumour? prejudice? (In other words, how well founded are the feelings you have listed?)

There are many reasons why Canadians might have positive feelings about the United States. In part, we owe our security and our high standard of living to the United States. Some of us have friends or relatives in that country. Many of us have travelled there. We share a common language. Many of our political and religious beliefs are similar. Most Americans are friendly, generous hosts and polite visitors. It seems that we even have a common sense of humour—we laugh at the same jokes. This seems a minor point, but perhaps it is quite significant. Think about it!

Unfortunately, Canadians also have reasons for some negative feelings about the United States. In the past, the United States has been a threat. Americans have invaded us twice. They have seemed ready to do so on several other occasions. A good portion of Canadian history has involved our reacting to the

The American attack on Quebec, December 31, 1775 (as portrayed by C.W. Jeffreys). Although carried out under cover of darkness and in a raging snowstorm, the attack failed. Over 100 Americans were killed and 430 were captured.

American presence. Perhaps this is still true today. Presently, Americans own huge chunks of our country and its economy. Their culture threatens to overpower us. American television, films, music and magazines play a large part in our lives. Many Canadians feel that Americans do not know enough about us. We would like more respect from them. Indeed, it seems that often they take us for granted. The United States is not an enemy country. Yet it still threatens our independence in many ways.

To deal with the following items, it would be helpful to talk with several Americans. If this is impossible, try to have friends or classmates join you in pretending to be Americans for a while. This should be done seriously.

1 What do you think Americans should know about Canada? Why? How much of this do they appear to know? Why is this? Could the situation be improved?

2 An American president, Richard Nixon, once made a public statement that showed he did not know of Canada's economic importance to the United States. At that time, we were the Americans' main source of imported oil. Then, as now, we were a leading trade partner. How could the president have made such an error? How does this affect your ideas on question two in the previous set of questions?

3 Would Americans likely be more informed and concerned about Quebec separatism or a communist uprising in a small African nation? Which development would be more vital to their interests?

4 What criticisms might Americans make of Canada? How valid would these be? (Explain your answers, and be aware that you are biased!)

For many reasons, there has been a recent growth of anti-Americanism in Canada. There also is evidence that some Americans are becoming more critical of us. Today relations still are basically quite good. However, if certain trends continue, trouble might lie ahead. It is very important for Canadians (and Americans) to know about the present state of relations between their two countries. They also should know the reasons for this situation. These matters will be dealt with in this unit. In the first chapter, we will look at the history of Canadian-American relations from earliest times to around 1970.

Before reading on, study the chart of key words and ideas that follows.

KEY WORDS AND IDEAS IN THIS CHAPTER

Term	Meaning	Sample Use
annexation	the act whereby one country takes over another	Some Canadians fear annexation by the United States.
anti-Americanism	being against the United States or things American	There has been anti-Americanism in Canada both in early and recent times.
competition	the act of trying to defeat or be better than someone else	Since 1945 the United States and the Soviet Union have been in competition with each other.
investment	money, effort or something of value that a person puts into a project	Large sums of money (capital) are needed to get a business started or to help it grow. In Canada much of this money is foreign. How might this foreign investment threaten our independence?
loyalty	the act or feeling of being faithful to someone or something	United Empire Loyalists were Americans who showed loyalty to Britain during the American Revolution. Many of them came to Canada.
Manifest Destiny	an American belief that the United States would one day take over all of North America	The belief in Manifest Destiny helped to start the War of 1812. It also contributed to anti-Americanism and fears of annexation in Canada.
negotiations	bargaining	Canada and Britain held serious negotiations with the United States in 1871 before the Treaty of Washington was signed.
reciprocity	an action between two (or more) parties that is the same on both sides	Canada tried to gain reciprocity in trade with the United States. This involved the lowering or removal of tariffs by both countries.
technology	the methods and materials used to do or make something	The United States has developed the most advanced technology in the world. Much of this is available to Canada. It tends to make our life easier and richer.

THE BEGINNINGS

Both Canada and the United States were "discovered" by European explorers. These explorers sailed from Spain, Holland, England and France. The first three nations set up colonies in what would later become the United States. France started settlements farther to the north. These were mainly in the St. Lawrence valley and in the present provinces of Nova Scotia and New Brunswick. They called their colony New France.

By 1750 there were 13 American colonies along the Atlantic Coast. They were controlled by Britain. Their relations with New France were poor. The two peoples had different languages and cultures and often competed in trade. Britain and France were enemies in Europe. These bad feelings spilled over into their North American colonies.

CANADA AND THE UNITED STATES GO SEPARATE WAYS

The British conquered New France in 1759. When the Americans rebelled against Britain in 1776, they expected that the Canadians would join their fight for freedom. However, Canada remained loyal to Britain on that occasion and again during the War of 1812. In both cases, an American victory could have led to a takeover of Canada. English- and French-speaking Canadians joined the British in defending our soil. Such efforts created a sense of unity and pride among Canadians. Our people began to feel that they all belonged to one country.

The War of 1812 was to be the last official warfare between Canada and the United States. Neither country lost land as a result of the war. For the rest of the nineteenth century, Canadian-American relations gradually improved. Trade ties increased, particularly in the period from 1854 to 1865, when a reciprocity treaty was in existence. There were some moments of tension. In the 1860s, Canadian Confederation was prompted partly because of our concerns about the growing economic and military power of the United States. By uniting, the Canadian colonies hoped to strengthen themselves against possible hostile American actions.

However, when relations were strained, both sides showed that they were anxious to avoid a serious confrontation. Disputes, mostly relating to boundaries or fishing rights, were settled peacefully. Sometimes, to avoid conflict, the British ceded large territories to the United States, often at our expense.

THE TWENTIETH CENTURY

Canadian–American relations improved steadily between 1900 and 1945. Canada and Britain were allies against Germany in World War I (1914–1918). The United States came into the war on their side in 1917. This was the first time that Canada and the United States had been military allies. Thus, World War I helped to create a strong new bond between us.

There was another important result of this war. Before it began, Britain was our major trading partner. It also was our main source of foreign investment. The war gave Canada's economy a chance to grow tremendously. To do so, it needed a lot of new investment. Britain was pouring its money into its own war effort. Therefore, we relied more than ever on American investment. By the end of the war, the United States had replaced Britain as our leading trade partner and supplier of foreign investment.

During the 1920s and 1930s, Canadians and Americans shared many common experiences. (Many of these are described in Unit 3, Chapter 9.) First came the prosperous, exciting Roaring Twenties. These

Aging war veterans of the War of 1812, photographed at a reunion.

This is a Canadian political cartoon published during a federal election campaign of the late 19th century. Try to discover which election this was. To which issue in that election does the cartoon refer? What is the point of the cartoon? Who are the people portrayed? Which Canadian political party does it seem to support?

were followed by the "hard times" of the Depression in the Dirty Thirties. At the end of this came World War II (1939–1945). In this war, Canada was an ally of Britain from the beginning. The United States joined the allies late in 1941.

During this war, Canadian–American relations became closer than ever before. There was great trust and goodwill between the two countries. We co-operated closely in military matters. Together we planned war production for our industries. The United States promised to defend us against any enemy invasion. Actually, the Americans did this mainly in their own interest. Still, Canadians were grateful for the promise of help from such a powerful friend. Together the two countries made plans for the defence of North America. This close relationship lasted long after the war ended. It is still in effect today.

We also have kept our close economic ties with the United States. We have enjoyed great benefits from this relationship. Americans buy large quantities of raw materials from us. They provide investment funds to help us develop our economy. American technology is available to us. In most fields, it is the best and most advanced in the world. The American economy produces many goods and services that Canadians enjoy. These also are available to us.

In the late 1940s, world tension began to increase again. This was mainly due to competition between the United States and the Soviet Union. This conflict became known as the "cold war" (see Unit 6, Chapter 19). In this situation, Canada clearly sided with the United States. The cold war grew even more serious during the 1950s. Understandably, our military and economic ties with the United States grew stronger than ever.

By the early 1970s, this trend had begun to change. World tension seemed to ease somewhat. American relations with communist countries, especially China and the Soviet Union, slowly improved. The

How does this modern cartoon compare to that of the 1890s on page 260 in terms of: *a* theme? and *b* interpretation of the issue?

danger of world war declined. As Canadians came to feel more secure, we placed less value on American protection.

Furthermore, we began to see some of the bad aspects of our close ties with the United States. Perhaps we had become too dependent on the Americans. Maybe they had too much influence over our government, culture and economy. These ideas received considerable publicity in our media. They revived a certain amount of anti-Americanism among some Canadians. Our government responded with policies aimed at reducing American influence here.

In the 1980s, the pendulum seemed to swing back toward closer ties between the two countries. Another round in the arms race renewed fears of war. Economic hard times hit Canada, driving up unemployment. These conditions left most Canadians in no mood to "talk tough" to our American neighbours. Also, Pierre Trudeau retired from politics in 1984. Brian Mulroney, our new prime minister, stressed the importance of friendlier relations with the Americans. He pledged closer economic and military co-operation with the United States.

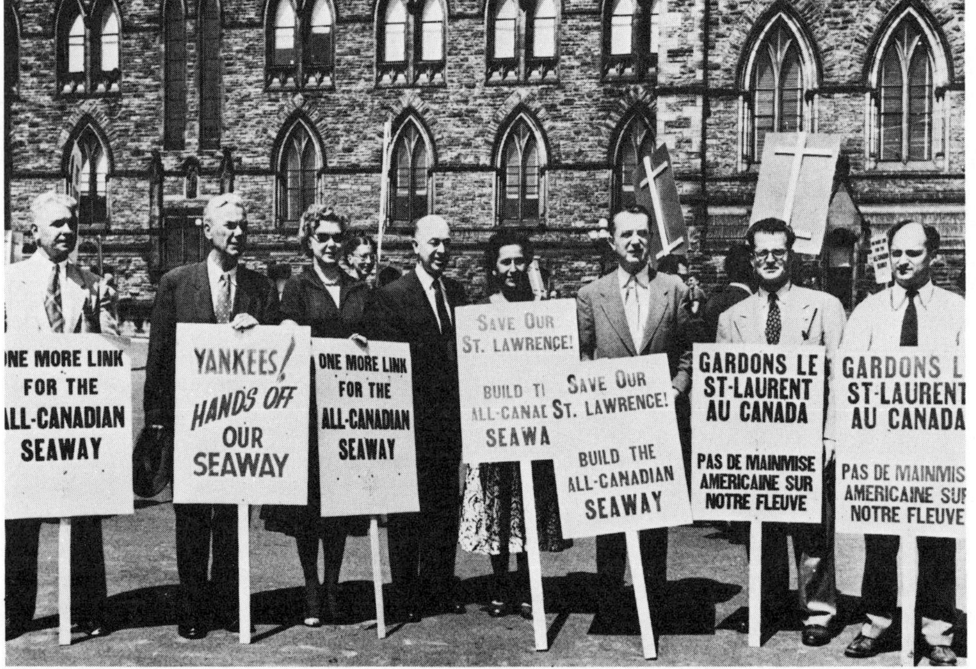

Canadians demonstrate for an all-Canadian St. Lawrence Seaway, 1954. Why would they have such a goal? For what reasons did our government reject this idea?

Quebec City: St. Patrick's Day, 1985. The "first families" of Canada and the United States singing "When Irish Eyes Are Smiling."

ANNEXATIONISM

Would you like to join or be taken over by the United States? If Canada were to be annexed to the United States, this would mean that we would become part of that country. Annexationists are people who would like to see this happen. Such feelings have been expressed in Canada from time to time.

1849

The editor of *The Saint John Morning News:*

> Geographically speaking, we belong to the United States. We are connected by an imaginary line. We have sprung from the same stock, we speak the same language, profess the same literature, are not lacking the enterprise of our neighbours.

1. This article is saying that Canada is an artificial political unit. What is the "imaginary line" to which it refers? Look at a political and a physical map of North America. Does the political boundary fit or clash with natural geographic regions? Does this mean that we will one day become part of the United States?
2. According to this article, what things do Canadians have in common with Americans? What else can you add to this list?
3. Which American state is closest to you? What Canadian province is farthest from you? Do you have more in common with the people of that American state or that Canadian province?
4. Do you feel that you have more in common with Americans or with French-Canadians? Why?

1959

Farley Mowat, Canadian novelist:

> In short, I now conclude that the only solution to our trouble with the Americans is to jine 'em; from which it follows that I no longer believe we can lick 'em . . . in almost every important social, intellectual and economic aspect we have already become pseudo-Americans.

1. What are "pseudo-Americans"? Do you agree with Mowat that this is what we have become?
2. In what important ways are Canadians different from Americans? Are these differences enough to keep us apart from Americans? Explain your answer.

BUILDING YOUR LEARNING SKILLS

FOCUSSING ON THE ISSUE

1 What trend does this chapter trace for you?
2 What periods seemed to be turning points within the time span covered?
3 Formulate three questions, the answers to which incorporate the important information and ideas in this chapter.
4 The following terms appeared in this chapter. Try to recall their meanings and how they were used.

annexation	loyalty
anti-Americanism	Manifest Destiny
border dispute	negotiations
competition	reciprocity
investment	technology

RESEARCHING

1 Canadian public opinion about the United States was somewhat divided at the time of the War of 1812. Try to discover the nature of this division and the reasons for it.
2 In preparation for a debate or panel discussion, research this question: Who won the War of 1812? Look at the causes of the war, bearing in mind what each side hoped to gain or prevent (in short, its goals). Also concentrate on summaries of the war's results, reading between the lines to see the significance of the outcome and comparing the results to the goals of each side.
3 Read the speeches made in favour of Confederation by prominent Canadian politicians of the time. Look for remarks that show their concern about military, economic or other dangers being posed by the United States.
4 Make a list of occasions on which Britain "sold out" Canadian interests to the United States in order to avoid war with that country. Now try to develop a problem-solving model based on this data. (You can refer to the Introduction to this text for ideas about a general approach.)

1·2·3 ORGANIZING

1 Organize the following events in a three-column chart. Choose appropriate headings, and then list the events accordingly.
   - ▶ the reciprocity treaty
   - ▶ the War of 1812
   - ▶ World War II
   - ▶ the Alaska boundary dispute
   - ▶ the St. Lawrence Seaway project
   - ▶ annexationism
   - ▶ the American Revolution

2 Now, using the same events listed above, devise a second organizer chart, again using three columns but having a totally different basis for separating the various items.
3 It is 1871, and you are Prime Minister John A. Macdonald. You have just arrived in Washington on the eve of a major conference between the United States and Great Britain. Within the next 12 hours, you want to do the following things:
   - ▶ pay your respects to the American ambassador;
   - ▶ huddle with your delegation to go over last-minute plans and details;
   - ▶ pay your respects to the British ambassador;
   - ▶ write home to an aide asking that he send you your favourite sweater, which you forgot to pack.

   In what order should you do these things? Explain your decisions. Compare your opinions with those of classmates. Can you agree on the most effective sequence?

COMMUNICATING

1 As we know, the Americans were successful in their attempt to break free of British control. History textbooks in Britain and Canada tend to refer to this development as "the American Revolution." American textbooks call it "the War of Independence." What different views of the same historical development are communicated by these terms?
2 Work on the preparation of two propaganda leaflets for distribution in Upper Canada (Ontario) during the War of 1812. One should be

American and urge the local inhabitants to support the invading United States troops. The other should be pro-British and urge loyalty to and assistance for the mother country in defence of the colony. Try to make effective use of slogans, titles or headlines and sketches, as well as clear, concise arguments.

3 If you did question two in "Researching" (above), you can now set up a debate or panel discussion on this question: Who won the War of 1812?

4 It is 1864. Debates are in full swing on the merits of Confederation. Write a newspaper editorial with a view to convincing readers that Confederation would strengthen the Canadian colonies against American pressures. (You can make use of work done for question three in "Researching," above.)

5 Dig a little more deeply into the Alaska boundary dispute. Then, with a classmate, complete the following exercise: Both of you are American newspaper reporters assigned to cover the settling of the dispute. One of you writes for a moderate, responsible and fair-minded newspaper. The other works for a sensation-seeking "rag." Each of you write a story describing the outcome of the dispute. Use language appropriate to your paper's readership and standards. Reflect suitable degrees of truth and/or exaggeration.

6 Have some classmates imagine that they are Canadians who have moved to the United States. Have others play the part of Americans who have moved to Canada. Interview the members of both groups. Ask them:

a why they moved;

b how they find life in their adopted country.

Use a tape recorder if possible. Replay the taped interviews several times. List the similarities and differences between Canadians and Americans and their ways of life.

ANALYZING

1 Why do Canadians have a love-hate relationship with the United States?

2 Categorize the following statements as to whether they are fact or opinion:

a The United States became our major trading partner in World War I.

b Britain won the War of 1812.

c If the United States had attacked Canada in the 1860s, Britain would have decided not to defend us.

d Being allies in two world wars greatly strengthened the ties between Canada and the United States.

e The United States will never again invade Canada.

3 In the twentieth century, Canada gradually drew closer to the Americans and away from the British. Why did this happen? Has this change been good or bad for Canada? Explain your answer.

4 In 1961 President John F. Kennedy spoke in Ottawa. He said, "Geography has made us neighbours. History has made us friends." In what ways was he correct?

5 "Given the American commitment to Manifest Destiny and the reluctance of Britain to defend us, it is amazing that Canada did not simply become annexed to the United States." To what extent do you agree with this statement? Why did we survive? Can you identify a single predominant reason?

APPLYING YOUR KNOWLEDGE

1 The Americans decided to fight for their independence from Britain; Canada decided to remain a loyal British colony. Does this suggest basic differences between the two peoples? How did these different decisions affect future Canadian-American relations?

2 Create a series of fictional headlines dealing with the military aspect of Canadian-American relations over the years. Include an appropriate date and by-line with each, as in the following example:

1775
INVADING AMERICAN FORCES DEFEATED AT QUEBEC
100 Enemy Killed, Almost 200 Wounded

Put these headlines in chronological order. See

if classmates can make additions and/or corrections to them. Then make a general statement about the trend in these relations. What are the future possibilities of our military relations with the United States? Which do you think is a. most likely? b. least likely? In each case, explain your reasoning.

3 Do you think that having the United States as a neighbour helps keep Canada united? Why or why not?

AN APPLICATION OF THE PROBLEM-SOLVING APPROACH

At the beginning of this textbook, you were provided with an outline of the main steps involved in posing and then attempting to solve a significant question. This is known as the problem-solving approach to learning. Here is an exercise using this approach to the material that you have been studying in this chapter. It was suggested to you earlier in "Researching," question four. If you made an attempt at that exercise, you might compare your work with this example.

Step 1 **Identifying the Problem**
Over the years, to what extent was Canada's future sacrificed by Great Britain in the interests of maintaining peace with the United States?

Step 2 **Posing the Key Questions**

a In what situations or at what times were sacrifices made by Britain to the United States?
b What did these sacrifices, or concessions, involve?
c Why were they made?
d Did Canada lose or gain from these sacrifices having been made?
e How significant were the losses and/or gains for Canada?
f Is it possible that Canada might not exist today if those sacrifices had not been made? Or would the Canada of today have been a far greater nation than it is? If so, in what respects?

Step 3 **Collecting the Data**
Your main sources will be reference books and possibly books of documents that contain copies of key treaties and agreements.

Step 4 **Evaluating the Data**

a How does your information relate to your key questions? Does some go beyond your expectations?
b How reliable are your sources?
c How should the data be organized?
d What are the strongest and weakest points?

Step 5 **Analyzing the Data**

a What evidence supports the theory that Britain damaged Canada's future by making concessions to the United States?
b What evidence suggests the opposite?
c Is any of the evidence inconclusive?
d Does any data suggest extenuating circumstances? (That is, were there perhaps good or even compelling reasons for British actions at the time? Did Britain act for the benefit of Canada or Britain or both?)
e Which case appears to be the strongest? Why?
f Is the case built mostly on facts or on speculation and opinion?

Step 6 **Solving the Problem**
Considering your answers to the above questions, what is your conclusion on the central issue?

Step 7 **Applying the Knowledge Gained**

a If you find Britain basically NOT GUILTY of "selling out" Canadian interests to the United States, then you can regard Canada's past ties with that country in a more favourable light. You might be prepared to suggest that modern Canadians have greater affection and/or respect for Britain for that reason.

b In the case of a GUILTY verdict, presumably the reverse would be true. It might also lead to a consideration of whether Canada could build a good case with the United States today for the return of "lost" lands and fishing rights. Did Britain have the right to cede these to the United States? Did Britain have any legitimate right to these in the first place? Should Canadians be influenced by such a past in their present or future dealings with the United States?

chapter 15

CANADIAN–AMERICAN RELATIONS: ECONOMIC LINKS

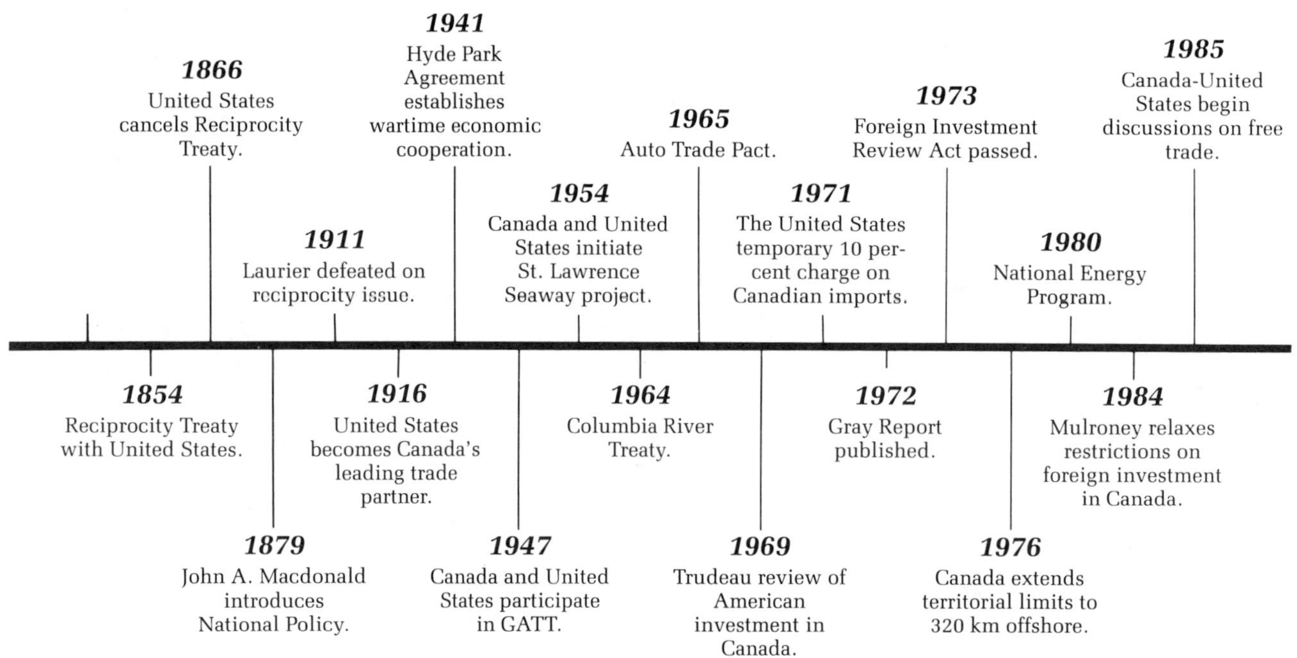

1854
Reciprocity Treaty with United States.
1866
United States cancels Reciprocity Treaty.
1879
John A. Macdonald introduces National Policy.
1911
Laurier defeated on reciprocity issue.
1916
United States becomes Canada's leading trade partner.
1941
Hyde Park Agreement establishes wartime economic cooperation.
1947
Canada and United States participate in GATT.
1954
Canada and United States initiate St. Lawrence Seaway project.
1964
Columbia River Treaty.
1965
Auto Trade Pact.
1969
Trudeau review of American investment in Canada.
1971
The United States temporary 10 percent charge on Canadian imports.
1972
Gray Report published.
1973
Foreign Investment Review Act passed.
1976
Canada extends territorial limits to 320 km offshore.
1980
National Energy Program.
1984
Mulroney relaxes restrictions on foreign investment in Canada.
1985
Canada-United States begin discussions on free trade.

TOPIC ORGANIZER **PAGE**

THEME ORGANIZER

- Canada's economic prosperity depends heavily on foreign trade.
- Over 75 percent of all our foreign trade is done with one country: the United States.
- By the late 1980s, the main issue in our trade relations had become the question of whether or not to enter into a near total free-trade relationship with the United States.
- Capital investment is crucial to the growth of any modern economy.
- Canada relies far more heavily on foreign investment than any other major industrialized nation.
- This foreign investment has advantages, but it also raises serious questions, such as whether Canada's economy is controlled by Canadians or by foreigners.
- About 80 percent of all foreign investment in Canada comes from one country: the United States.
- Various Canadian governments have made modest attempts to curb foreign investment here; these efforts have usually been abandoned in the face of strong American pressure.
- Today there is more foreign investment in Canada than ever before.
- Canadians are divided about what, if anything, should be done about this trend.

INTRODUCTION

"No nation, no people, have helped more than the U.S. to make Canada what it is today—one of the most desirable places to live in the world. . . ."

"You are a serf, no more than that . . . and Massa lives away down south."

These statements conflict. They express different views on Canada's economic ties with the United States.

1 What is the opinion expressed in the first statement above? Give some examples to support that view.
2 What is the opinion expressed in the second statement above?

Both statements have some truth. It is true that Canada has very close economic ties with the United States. These are much closer than with any other country. As a result, Canada enjoys many benefits. We have one of the highest standards of living in the world.

Our close economic links with the United States, the world's richest nation, help explain this. Without these links, the quality of our life would go down. Naturally, we do not want this to happen. Therefore, we depend on the United States a great deal. This dependence creates some problems for us.

We will explore our economic ties with the United States in this chapter. We will look at the good and the bad features of this "American connection."

Before reading on, study the chart of key words and ideas that follows.

What point is this drawing trying to make?

KEY WORDS AND IDEAS IN THIS CHAPTER

Term	Meaning	Sample Use
balance of payments	the relationship between the value of imports and exports	The total value of Canada's imports is usually greater than that of its exports. This represents a yearly drain of money out of the country.
capital investment	money put into a business	Many foreigners invest money in Canada. This has both good and bad effects on our economy.
continentalism	the belief that Canada and the United States are part of one North American unit	Some Americans would like Canadians to support continentalism. Then the United States could claim a share of our natural resources.
entrepreneur	someone who organizes, manages and takes the risks of a business venture	Americans are among the world's best entrepreneurs. Canada also has some entrepreneurs but needs more.
export	a product or service that we sell to another country	Canada exports huge quantities of raw materials and smaller amounts of semi-finished and finished goods.
foreign investment	money invested in Canada by non-Canadians	There is over $100 billion worth of foreign investment in Canada today.
foreign trade	trade between Canada and other countries	Foreign trade is vital to our economy. Our main trading partner is the United States.
free trade	a trading relationship in which there are no tariffs (customs duties)	Canada and the United States have tried to work out a free-trade deal that would eliminate all remaining tariffs over a period of years.
import	a product or service that we buy from another country	Our major imports include finished products, capital and technology.
non-merchandise trade	trade that does not involve goods, for example, tourism, interest payments or services	Canada tends to have a large deficit in such trade. This more than cancels out our surplus in merchandise trade.
standard of living	the amount of comfort and convenience a person can have; this is determined by his or her income and the cost of goods and services that are available	Canada has one of the highest standards of living in the world. This is partly due to our ties with the United States, which is the richest country in the world.
trade deficit	an unfavourable balance of trade (imports cost more than our exports are worth)	Canada tends to have an overall deficit because of our heavy reliance on foreign capital and technology. Also, Canadian tourists spend more money abroad than foreign tourists spend here.
trade surplus	a favourable balance of trade (exports are worth more than the cost of our imports)	We tend to have a surplus in merchandise trade.

OUR TRADE WITH THE UNITED STATES

WHAT IS TRADE?

Most of us know what the word "trade" means. Children often make several "deals" in one day: "I'll trade you my cap pistol for your toy car"; "you give me three sticks of gum plus two pennies, and I'll give you half of my popsicle." Sports fans know what it means if two teams make a trade: "The Edmonton Oilers trade Wayne Gretzky to Toronto Maple Leafs for Wendel Clark, plus cash and a player to be named later." Trade involves an exchange between two or more parties. Each wants something from the other. Each is willing to pay for what is wanted.

FOREIGN TRADE

Trade goes on within each country. It also takes place between countries. This second type of exchange is called foreign trade. Goods or services that we sell to other countries are called exports. They are desirable because they create employment and bring more money into Canada. Goods or services that we buy from other countries are called imports. They may be enjoyable or even necessary, but they cause money to leave Canada in payment for them.

The relationship between the value of imports and exports is called the balance of trade. If the value of exports is greater, then more money is coming in than going out. This is called a surplus, or a favourable balance of trade. When the reverse is true, we have a deficit, or an unfavourable balance of trade.

Canada relies very heavily on foreign trade. Indeed, we are one of the world's leading trading nations. Here are some statistics on that trade:

VALUE OF TOTAL IMPORTS TO CANADA BY GEOGRAPHIC REGION
(expressed in thousands of dollars)

Region	1979	1983	Today
Western Europe	6 808 790	7 526 609	
Eastern Europe	326 979	250 095	
Middle East	1 925 961	864 863	
Other Africa	418 136	677 684	
Other Asia	4 287 485	7 827 892	
Oceania	612 715	521 188	
South America	2 225 581	2 047 003	
Central America	693 331	1 765 030	
United States	45 571 224	54 103 299	

VALUE OF TOTAL EXPORTS FROM CANADA BY GEOGRAPHIC REGION

Region	1979	1983	Today
Western Europe	8 442 561	7 834 806	
Eastern Europe	1 235 045	2 122 471	
Middle East	833 309	1 445 653	
Other Africa	801 336	949 821	
Other Asia	6 183 495	8 706 172	
Oceania	679 499	609 971	
South America	1 711 507	1 488 751	
Central America	1 190 539	1 445 497	
United States	44 534 675	66 332 528	

Source: *The Canada Year Book (1985)*
Note: *These totals reflect merchandise trade only.*

1 Compose four or five questions, the answers to which summarize the main points illustrated by these charts.

2 What is the single most striking piece of information to be gathered from these charts?

3 What two areas, other than the United States, are our most important sources of foreign trade?

4 In terms of percentage increase, with which region did we enjoy the largest rate of export growth between 1979 and 1983?

5 With which regions, if any, did we have a trade deficit in those years?

6 Between 1979 and 1983, did we become more or less dependent on trade with the United States?

7 Through research, try to update this chart. What significant changes can be observed?

8 Suggest reasons why we have not diversified our trade by doing more business with countries other than the United States.

CANADIAN IMPORTS AND EXPORTS (1983)

Category	$ value of imports (millions)	% of 1983 total	$ value of exports (millions)	% of 1983 total
Coffee	401	0.5	—	–
Live animals	132	0.2	340	0.4
Food, feed, beverages and tobacco	4 870	6.4	10 074	11.4
Inedible crude materials (metal ores, concentrates and scrap; coal, crude petroleum, natural gas)	7 201	09.5	14 393	16.3
Inedible fabricated materials (wood and paper, textiles, iron and steel, petroleum products, chemicals)	14 006	18.5	30 011	33.9
Inedible end products (industrial and agricultural machinery, motor vehicles and parts, communications and office equipment)	48 397	64.0	33 472	37.8
Special transactions	981	01.3	216	0.2

Source: *The Canada Year Book (1985)*
Note: *Some commodities have not been included.*

1 In which category did Canada have the strongest exports?

2 In which category did we import most heavily?

3 Does this chart suggest that Canada was still, to a large extent, a "hewer of wood and drawer of water" in international trade?

4 Is this trade pattern a healthy one for Canada? Why or why not? How could it be improved?

5 Try to update this chart. Has our trade pattern become stronger or not?

CANADA'S FOREIGN TRADE PICTURE (1963–1986, MERCHANDISE TRADE ONLY)

	Imports		Exports		
Year	(millions of $)	% change from previous year	(millions of $)	% change from previous year	Trade balance (millions of $)
1963	6 578	04.5	6 990	10.0	412
1964	7 488	13.8	8 303	18.8	815
1965	8 633	15.3	8 767	05.6	134
1966	10 072	16.7	10 325	17.8	253
1967	10 873	08.0	11 420	10.6	547
1968	12 360	13.7	13 679	19.8	1 319
1969	14 130	14.3	14 871	08.7	741
1970	13 952	−01.3	16 820	13.1	2 868
1971	15 617	11.9	17 820	05.9	2 203
1972	18 668	19.5	20 150	13.1	1 482
1973	23 325	24.9	25 421	26.2	2 096

CANADA'S FOREIGN TRADE PICTURE (CONTINUED)

	Imports		Exports		
Year	(millions of $)	% change from previous year	(millions of $)	% change from previous year	Trade balance (millions of $)
1974	31 722	36.0	32 442	27.6	720
1975	34 716	09.4	33 328	02.7	– 1 388
1976	37 494	08.0	38 475	15.4	981
1977	42 363	13.0	44 554	15.8	2 191
1978	50 108	18.3	53 182	19.4	3 074
1979	62 871	25.5	65 641	23.4	2 770
1980	69 274	10.2	76 159	16.0	6 885
1981	79 482	14.7	83 811	10.0	4 329
1982	67 856	– 14.6	84 530	00.9	16 674
1983	75 587	11.4	90 964	07.6	15 377
1984	95 842	26.8	112 384	23.5	16 542
1985	105 032	09.6	119 241	06.1	14 209
*1986	111 500	06.2	122 000	02.3	10 500

Source: *Statistics Canada*
**estimated*

Using the data from this chart, answer the following questions:

1 What year saw the greatest percentage increase in Canadian imports? In exports?
2 In which years did the total value of Canadian imports actually decline?
3 In which year or years did Canada experience an unfavourable balance of trade (a deficit)?
4 In which year or years did we achieve our greatest favourable balance of trade (surplus)?

5 Through research, try to update this chart.
6 Also through research, try to discover what circumstances might have helped to explain each of the major developments highlighted in the first four questions. For example:
   a What situation contributed to our rather disappointing performance in 1982?
   b Did the "energy crisis" of the 1970s have a significant impact on our foreign trade?
   c Overall, what has been the trend in the values of the Canadian and American dollars since the late 1970s?
7 Using the data from the chart on pages 272 to 273, draw a bar or line graph to illustrate "Canada's Foreign Trade Picture (1963–1986)."

8 Is there an apparent connection between currency values and trade patterns? (See also the chart on page 272.) If so, why?
9 When our exports increase, what tends to happen to our imports? What conclusion can we draw about the relationship of trade to world prosperity? Why is that logical?
10 Could a country reasonably expect to greatly increase exports and, at the same time, greatly reduce imports? Why or why not?

Refer to the chart entitled "Canada's Foreign Trade Picture" on page 272. As you can see, it deals only with merchandise trade. Therefore, it does not give you the complete picture of our foreign trade.

This is because trade involves more than just goods or merchandise. For example, when foreign tourists visit Canada, they spend money here. This has the same effect on our economy as if we exported cars to the United States or wheat to China. Similarly, when Canadians visit other lands, money leaves our country. So this has the same effect on our economy as an import. Any transaction that causes money to come

A huge variety of consumer goods and commodities can be containerized for efficient ocean transport aboard vessels like this Danish container ship unloading at Vanterm, the Port of Vancouver's largest container terminal.

into or leave Canada is part of our overall balance of payments situation. Those transactions that do not involve goods are referred to as non-merchandise trade.

Unfortunately, in non-merchandise trade, Canada has run a huge deficit for many years. Our tourism account is partly responsible for this. Canadians spend more money travelling abroad than visiting foreigners spend here. Also, as you will soon learn, there is very heavy foreign investment in our country. When foreigners earn interest or profits on their money here, they often take it back to their own country. This counts as an import to us because money is leaving Canada. In both 1985 and 1986, our deficit in non-merchandise trade was over $18 billion!

So when all aspects of our foreign trade are calculated, our overall balance of payments in recent years has looked like this:

CANADIAN BALANCE OF PAYMENTS

Year	Balance (in billions of dollars)
1981	$ − 6.13
1982	+ 2.91
1983	+ 2.94
1984	+ 3.36
1985	− 0.58
1986	− 8.81

Source: *Statistics Canada*

1 In which years did we have deficits? Which year gave us our greatest surplus?

2 What is alarming about the trend shown in 1985 and 1986?

3 Does this chart suggest that we should encourage or discourage foreign tourists to visit Canada? Why?

4 Does this chart present an argument for or against foreign investment in Canada? Explain your answer.

FREE TRADE WITH THE UNITED STATES: GOOD OR BAD FOR CANADA?

In 1985 Prime Minister Brian Mulroney made an announcement that surprised many Canadians. He stated that his government would try to negotiate a free-trade agreement with the United States. Free trade would mean the end of tariffs between our two countries. Goods could cross the border each way without having any customs duties imposed on them. If completed, such a deal would have a tremendous impact on our country. But while he was campaigning to become prime minister in 1984, Brian Mulroney did not indicate that he was planning such a bold step.

From time to time in our history, we have considered entering a special trade arrangement with the United States. In 1854 we signed a reciprocity treaty with the Americans. This removed or lowered tariffs on a long list of goods. The agreement provided great economic benefits to some parts of Canada but was cancelled by the Americans in 1865.

During the Canadian election of 1911, Wilfrid Laurier proposed a new reciprocity treaty with the United States. His opponent, John A. Macdonald, had once supported a similar idea. Now he reversed himself. He attacked Laurier's proposal as disloyal to Britain, our mother country and chief trading partner at the time. He predicted that reciprocity would eventually lead to our outright annexation by the United States. This and other issues led to the defeat of Laurier's government in that election.

Mr. Mulroney's dramatic announcement in 1985 touched off a lengthy debate in Canada. To some extent, that debate is still going on today. Unfortunately, it has been largely a "media debate." Experts for one side or the other have tried to make their case on television, on radio talk shows, in the newspapers. The public has remained somewhat aloof, although their vital interests are at stake. Perhaps the issue is

What is the message of this cartoon? Write an appropriate caption.

too complex. Many of the questions involved can only be answered by the passage of time. Thus, any judgements or conclusions are educated guesses at best.

Here are some of the main arguments put forth on each side of the free trade issue:

IN FAVOUR

- We would have easier access to the huge American market.
- There would be more job opportunities for Canadians.
- Sales and profits for Canadian companies would increase greatly.
- We would no longer have to fear American economic retaliation, such as protective tariffs against our goods.
- Weak Canadian industries would have to become "lean and mean" (more efficient and competitive) or else go under.
- Consumers would benefit greatly. Free trade would increase competition in our market.

Trade ambassador Simon Reisman talks with reporters during a break with provincial officials regarding free trade with the United States. The meeting was held in Ottawa.

This, in turn, would mean lower prices plus a greater variety and better quality of products.

- Canadian businesses would be stimulated to spend more on research and technology. Thus, Canadian industry would become more modern and "high tech."

AGAINST

- Many "Canadian" companies are actually branch plants of American corporations. They were established partly to sell in the Canadian market without having to pay customs duties. If such duties no longer existed, these branch plants might gradually be closed down. Their operations would be transferred to the United States. Canadian job losses would be catastrophic: At least 280 000 jobs could disappear this way.
- Canada cannot compete effectively against huge American companies. They will flood our market with cheaper products and put many truly Canadian companies out of business.
- Because of heavy foreign investment, we are weak in many areas of technology and scientific research. This would limit our ability to develop modern industries that could compete with those of more advanced countries.
- Economically we would become even more dependent on the United States. Even more than before, we would be reduced to selling off our natural resources in return for finished products.
- Exposed to unlimited American foreign competition, our financial and cultural industries will weaken. Again, our independence will suffer.
- These trends eventually will lead us into complete political union with the United States.

Even from these few arguments, the importance of the free trade issue becomes clear. The long-term results of any such deal will be of vital concern to Canadians. These could affect not only our jobs and our standard of living but also our cultural identity and our political sovereignty (independence).

Supporters of free trade accused their opponents of being pessimists and even cowards. Canadians, they said, should be confident about their own abilities and potential. They should boldly grasp this great opportunity. Critics of free trade were depicted as "losers" who could only think in negative terms.

To counter such arguments, the opponents of free trade tried to suggest positive alternatives. These included such ideas as:

a Try to diversify Canadian trade. Seek greater markets in countries other than the United States.

b Try to become more independent and self-sufficient; reduce our need for trade with foreign countries. Turn our raw materials into high-quality, high-tech finished products for our own consumption.

c Develop a long-range economic plan. This should seek to reduce foreign investment. It also should promote research and technology. This will help the growth of modern Canadian industries that can compete in world markets.

SOME OF THE PROBLEMS OF NEGOTIATING A FREE-TRADE DEAL

The Canadian and American negotiating teams began to work in earnest in 1985. Naturally, each team was trying to get the best possible terms for its own country. For almost two years they appeared to be making little progress. Several important difficulties emerged. The chart on the following page shows a few of the more troublesome issues and the viewpoints of each side.

At one point, in the autumn of 1987, it appeared that the negotiations were doomed to failure. The chief Canadian negotiator, Simon Reisman, walked out of the discussions in Washington. He returned to Ottawa, explaining that an impasse had apparently been reached. The Americans were refusing to budge on our key demand. Canada was insisting on a *guarantee* that our imports to the United States market would not be blocked or limited by special American laws. Congress has the power to pass such laws and has done so frequently. Within a few days, the negotiations were resumed. After each side made some

What Canadian fear regarding free trade is being expressed?

Issue	American View	Canadian View
What aspects of trade should be "on the table" (open to negotiation)?	All aspects of trade between the two countries are negotiable.	Most items are negotiable, with the exception of certain policies and programs that we regard as special, for example, the Auto Pact (see pages 279 to 282) and our "cultural industries" (see below).
Could there be restrictions on investing in each other's country?	There should be no such restrictions.	Canada must have the right to limit foreign investment in certain key industries such as banking and communication.
What should happen to the Auto Trade Pact, which guarantees production and jobs in Canada?	This pact is outdated and unnecessary. Also, it contradicts the very idea of "free" trade. It should be phased out over a period of a few years.	The protective guarantees of the Auto Pact are essential to Canadian prosperity. The pact should not be included in a free-trade deal.
Should either government continue to give financial help to industries such as publishing and broadcasting, which are considered vital to the country's identity and independence?	All such assistance must end. Businesses and industries must "stand on their own two feet" and compete in the open market. We are "prepared to have America's culture on the table and take the risk of having it damaged by Canadian influence. . . ."	Canada must be able to continue its support of such industries. "Will the prime minister tell the Americans that *Anne of Green Gables* is not a threat to American culture?" "(American) comments portray a stunning ignorance of Canada. . . . completely insensitive and totally unacceptable. . . ."
Should a free-trade agreement influence or determine the value of each country's dollar?	The Canadian dollar is too low in value. This gives Canadian exports an unfair advantage in the American market. Canada should let its dollar "float" higher. This would result in fairer trade.	Canada must keep the right to regulate the value of its own money. The American dollar *should* be higher in value than the Canadian; it is based on a much larger and richer economy.
Could either government continue to give financial help to underprivileged regions in its country (for example, subsidies or tax concessions to help an industry develop in a poor region)?	Such assistance must stop. It interferes with free competition by giving an unfair advantage to the companies receiving government subsidies.	Canada has both rich and poor regions. This threatens our unity. We have a tradition of helping poorer areas through government assistance. This encourages businesses to set up in areas where they might not otherwise do so. We must be able to continue such policies.

concessions, the negotiating teams agreed on a set of proposals.

It took months to work out all the details of the free-trade deal. In the meantime, its broad outlines were gradually revealed. Unfortunately, Canadian and American politicians were playing to different audiences. Some statements made by American politicians to their voters made the deal look bad for Canada. Moreover, both of our opposition parties made savage attacks on the free-trade proposals. Most damaging of all was the supposition that the Mulroney government had caved-in to American pressures. Many thought that Canada had agreed to remove almost all restrictions on American investment here and had given the United States much easier access to our non-renewable energy supplies. Worst of all was the belief that the Americans had tricked us in the matter of guaranteed protection for our imports to the United States. Several experts stated that the Americans really had *not* given up their right to pass laws restricting such imports. Their "guarantee" was worthless.

By late 1987, the details of the free-trade agreement had been completed. The proposal was ready for presentation to the American Senate, whose approval was necessary before the deal could be put into effect. Although not required by law, Prime Minister Mulroney indicated that he would submit the plan to the Canadian House of Commons. Here, his party had a solid majority. Any meaningful resistance to his free-trade plan would come in the next Canadian federal election.

The negotiations were tough, and occasionally bitter. Sometimes the conflict from the private meetings leaked out to the press. Canadians gradually developed the suspicion that Canada would be making more concessions than the United States if a deal was concluded. The Americans were negotiating largely from a position of strength. Their industries were larger and more competitive, their technology more advanced. Their foreign trade was more diversified. Therefore, they did not need us as much as we needed them. Moreover, the Mulroney government was trailing badly in the opinion polls. To regain respect and popularity, it felt obliged to "deliver" a free-trade agreement.

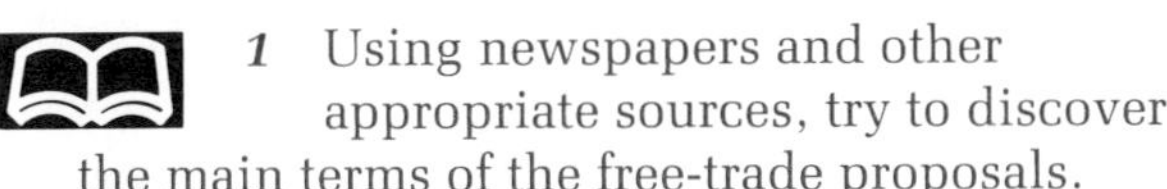

1 Using newspapers and other appropriate sources, try to discover the main terms of the free-trade proposals.

2 Which, if any, of these proposals were agreed to and put into effect?

3 Can you figure out what compromises were made by the two sides in order to reach an agreement?

4 Based on the above, which country made the greater concessions? Explain your answer.

5 In its merchandise trade with the United States, Canada in 1985 had a surplus of $20.7 billion. In 1986 there was another huge surplus of $16.2 billion. How could a free-trade deal improve upon this situation? (Clue: Without a free-trade deal, what might the United States have introduced to protect itself against Canadian imports?)

6 To better assess the outcome of the free-trade discussions, refer to the problem-solving exercise at the end of this chapter.

THE AUTO PACT: THE FREE-TRADE ISSUE IN MICROCOSM

Much can be learned about the complex issue of free trade by studying the Auto Trade Pact between Canada and the United States. This agreement was signed in 1965. It was designed to improve the efficiency of the North American auto industry. It also was supposed to guarantee a fair share of production and jobs for Canadians. Under its terms, we experienced both good and bad years. However, by the 1980s the benefits of this pact for Canada were clear and increasing.

Therefore, some Americans were anxious to end the pact or at least change its terms. When free-trade discussions began in 1985, these people saw their opportunity. Certain guarantees (see below) had been built into the Auto Pact. These contradicted the idea of free trade. Thus, American negotiators insisted that any free-trade deal would have to include a re-examination of the pact. The jobs of more than 100 000 Canadian auto workers could be threatened by a change in the pact. The Canadian government shared their concern. However, it also had to consider the broader view: *Overall, did the potential benefits of free trade outweigh its risks, both obvious and hidden?*

At the end of this chapter, there is a problem-solving exercise. It follows the model introduced at the beginning of this textbook. It is based on the question of whether or not free trade with the United States is desirable for Canada. What follows here is some material to help you understand the connection between the Auto Pact and the free-trade issue. This also could help you if you later decide to tackle the larger problem-solving exercise.

- In 1964 the auto industry in Canada was weak, inefficient and foreign dominated.
- In 1964 Canadians were producing 4 percent of North American motor vehicles. Yet they were buying 7.5 percent of that production. Thus, we had a deficit in auto trade of $711 million with the United States.
- In 1965 about 83 000 Canadian jobs depended directly on the production of cars and car parts.
- Some terms of the 1965 Auto Pact were:
  1 Companies producing cars in Canada could

import new vehicles and parts for new vehicles into this country duty-free.

2 In return, any such company must assemble, in Canada, vehicles equal in value to their total sales here in a given year.

3 Further, any such company must put a minimum of $60 worth of Canadian parts or labour into its cars for every $100 worth of vehicle sales in Canada.

4 The pact can be cancelled by either country on one year's notice.

- By 1986 the value of two-way trade in motor vehicles and parts between Canada and the United States had reached almost $70 billion. This represented about 33 percent of the total trade between the two countries.
- By 1986 there were 130 000 jobs for Canadians in the auto and related industries. Of these jobs, about 112 000 were located in Ontario.

1 Which of the above items are statistics? Which could be classified as facts? Which are opinions?

2 What benefits did Canada seem to derive directly from the Auto Pact?

3 Why would the Americans have agreed to this pact?

4 One goal of the pact was to reduce the price of cars for North American consumers, especially Canadians. Based on the terms of the pact, how might this occur?

5 Why would over 85 percent of the jobs in the Canadian auto industry be located in Ontario?

6 Try to discover which province obtained the second-highest share of jobs from the auto industry.

7 Over 90 percent of auto industry jobs were in central Canada. What would be the political significance of this? If you were prime minister, how might this fact influence your decisions about trade and the Auto Pact?

The following chart shows the trade balance in cars and parts between Canada and the United States in the first years of the Auto Pact.

1 In which of the years shown did we have our largest deficit? Approximately how much was that deficit?

2 In what year did we have our first surplus? When did we have our largest surplus? About how much was it?

3 Using the *Canada Year Book* or other sources, update the above chart as fully as possible. Among other things, you should discover that:

- In 1980 we had our first deficit in auto trade with the United States — a whopping $2 billion!
- By 1982 this had been reversed into a $2 billion surplus.
- By 1985 our surplus had reached $5 billion!

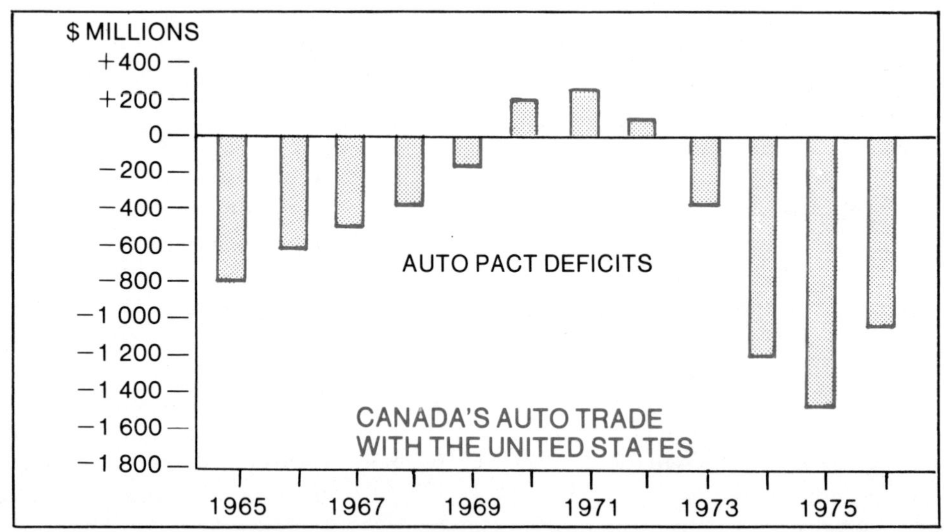

4 Why would Americans strongly resist changes in the Auto Pact in the 1970s? By the 1980s, why would one observer be saying, "Canada's position on the automotive agreement stinks. If I were on the United States' side now, I would be screaming bloody murder."

5 Try to discover the reasons for the dramatic shift in the auto trade balance between 1980 and 1982. (Clue: Note the world energy situation and sales of certain model sizes.)

6 Why was the Auto Pact incompatible (did not fit) with the idea of free trade?

7 If the Auto Pact was abolished, what changes might occur in the car industry in Canada?

WHY IS THERE NO TRULY CANADIAN CAR?

The manufacturing of automobiles is a major industry for several countries. Such an industry is capable of creating jobs, stimulating technology and, if successful, generating huge profits. To an outside observer, it would appear that Canada has what it takes to have an auto industry that is truly its own. So why don't we?

In the early twentieth century, several small Canadian automobile companies were established. These included Derby at Saskatoon, Gray Dort at Chatham, Ontario, and Forster at Montreal. Some went bankrupt, but others were simply brought out by large American companies. For example, Sam McLaughlin sold his very substantial company at Oshawa, Ontario, to General Motors.

Today and for many years previously, Canadians love cars. We have more cars per capita than almost any other country in the world. Thus, Canada is an excellent market for this product. Many other countries make their own distinctive automobiles. Yet we do not. The capital, technology, profits and control of this key industry in our country lie in foreign, principally American, hands. Without their goodwill, and perhaps without the protection of the Auto Pact, tens of thousands of Canadians could be thrown out of work within a short period of time.

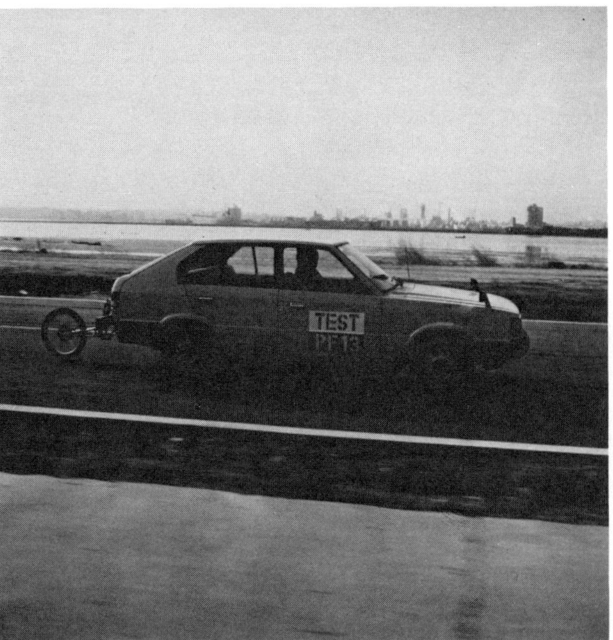

Hyundai automobiles were introduced to Canada in 1984. Slight modifications made the cars suitable for the Canadian climate. Under Canadian government regulations, developing countries such as Korea enjoy reduced import duties allowing them to sell their products at a lower price.

Here is a list of a few of the foreign-made cars sold in Canada. Beside it is a list of the countries that design and make them. In your mind, link the items in the two columns. Then follow up with the remainder of the exercise.

Column A	**Column B**
Toyota	Korea
Volvo	Germany
Mercedes	France
Jaguar	Italy
Hyundai	Sweden
Lada	Japan
Peugeot	Britain
Ferrari	Soviet Union

1 Try to think of two examples from countries other than the ones listed above.

2 What factors must be present for a country to be able to develop and support its own automobile

The new Toronto Stock Exchange, one of the most modern facilities of its kind in the world.

industry? Which of these factors does Canada possess?

3 Honda is one example of a foreign car company operating a branch plant in Canada. It is well known for the very high quality of its products. In 1987 Honda announced that the Canadian workers at its plant in southern Ontario were turning out the best Hondas in the world. They had even surpassed the quality standards of the Honda workers in the home plants in Japan. What is the irony in this situation?

4 Suggest reasons why there is no truly Canadian car today. Would free trade with the United States help or hinder the development of such a company? Explain your answer.

The following questions deal with the importance of Canada's trade with the United States:

1 Imagine that the United States stopped buying from Canada. Suggest reasons why this might happen. Use the charts in this chapter to help answer these questions. Where else might Canada look for customers? Which countries might want our products and be able to afford them? Why is it unlikely that they could replace the United States as our main customer?

2 What if Canada could not replace the United States as a customer? How would you be affected? Why? (Make your answers as full as possible.)

3 Imagine that the United States stopped selling

its goods and services to Canada. Could we get the same things from other countries? If so, from whom? If not, why not?

4 What if we could not buy similar things from other countries? How would you be affected? Why? (Again, give a full answer.)

5 Discuss or debate this point: *There are more advantages than disadvantages in Canada's close trade ties with the United States.*

AMERICAN INVESTMENT IN CANADA

THE NATURE OF INVESTMENT

It is a hot summer day. The temperature is climbing above 30°C. Three young children get a smart idea. They will set up a cold-drink stand in their neighbourhood. They will charge 10¢ a glass. First they need $2 to buy tins of frozen lemonade. They only have $1. They ask their mother for the other dollar. She says no. They offer to give her half of any profits (gains) from their business. She changes her mind and gives them $1. She has just made an investment. She is now part-owner of a new lemonade business.

When money is used this way, it is called capital. Most businesses and industries need large amounts of capital to get started and to keep going. People invest (put their money) in businesses to make profits. If the business in which they invest succeeds, they will share in the rewards.

Canada is a highly industrialized country. Hundreds of large businesses employ thousands of workers. There are thousands of smaller operations, too. Billions of dollars have been invested in these companies, large and small. Much of this capital has been invested by Canadians. Some, though, comes from other countries. This money is called foreign investment.

KINDS OF FOREIGN INVESTMENT

Foreigners invest in Canada in several ways. They may loan money to Canadian businesses. They may also loan money to a government in Canada, national, provincial or local. This is done by buying the bonds put out by those governments.

Foreigners sometimes buy stocks (shares of ownership) in Canadian companies. Sometimes foreigners buy an entire Canadian company. Or they buy a big enough share to take over control of the company. Such an action is called a takeover. Foreigners also can buy buildings, land or other kinds of property in Canada. Sometimes foreign companies set up branch plants in Canada. Such plants are called branches because they are part of the main "tree" (the foreign parent company).

Relative to its size, Canada's economy has much more foreign investment than any other major industrialized country. By 1987 the total of foreign long-term investment was over $230 billion. Of this, just over 75 percent was American. On average, the total foreign investment in Canada grows by $10 to $15 billion annually.

Some Canadians are very upset by these figures. They argue that Canada is in danger of losing control of some of its key industries. Others claim that this foreign investment offers tremendous advantages to us. Before considering the arguments, examine the following charts and graphs. Keep in mind the meaning of these two terms:

direct investment This is made to gain control of an operating company. It includes takeovers and the setting up of branch plants.

portfolio investment This involves the purchase of bonds and shares for the interest they yield or for possible capital gain as shares rise in value. It includes buying government or corporate bonds and buying shares on a Canadian stock exchange.

The following questions deal with the graph on page 284, "Foreign Long Term Investment in Canada."

1 Which of the three categories of investment was largest before 1975? Which grew to be largest in later years?

2 Calculate the approximate percentages (of the total) of each type of investment in 1984.

3 Was the trend to greater portfolio and less direct investment desirable? (It might help to review the meanings of these terms.) Explain your answer.

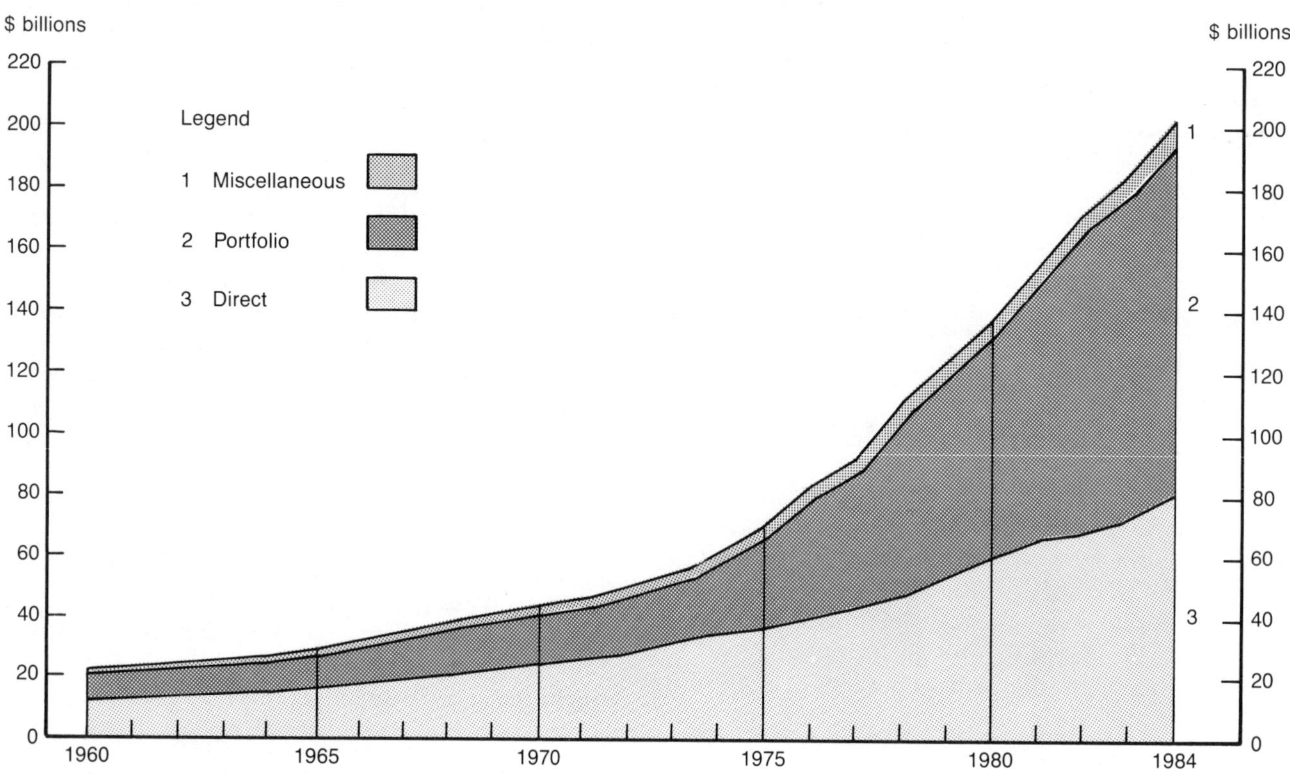

Source: Statistics Canada

FOREIGN LONG-TERM INVESTMENT IN CANADA (in millions of dollars)

Invested in Canadian:	American 1977	American 1982	British 1977	British 1982	All Other 1977	All Other 1982	Total 1977	Total 1982
Government bonds (all levels)	8 010	15 189	598	1 592	4 204	14 967	12 812	31 748
Manufacturing	18 215	27 315	1 630	2 337	2 269	5 113	22 114	34 765
Petroleum and natural gas	11 111	21 027	1 096	2 396	1 641	6 845	13 848	30 268
Mining and smelting	4 733	5 021	487	671	876	2 085	6 096	7 777
Utilities (mainly railroads and electric power)	11 093	19 456	553	776	3 955	9 663	15 601	29 895
Financial industries	5 611	11 413	1 569	2 641	3 724	8 713	10 904	22 767
All other	6 979	10 016	826	1 211	2 419	4 129	10 224	15 356
Total Long-Term Foreign Investment	65 752	109 437	6 759	11 624	19 088	51 515	91 599	172 576

Source: *Statistics Canada*

FOREIGN DIRECT INVESTMENT IN CANADA BY AREA OF OWNERSHIP (in millions of dollars)

Country	1976 Amount	1976 % of total	1980 Amount	1980 % of total	1984 Amount	1984 % of total
United States	31 917	79.1	48 686	79.0	62 359	76.3
United Kingdom	3 968	09.9	5 333	08.7	7 342	09.0
West Germany	691	01.7	1 698	02.8	2 112	02.6
Netherlands	769	01.9	1 189	01.9	2 040	02.5
France	600	01.5	824	01.3	1 292	01.6
Switzerland	555	01.4	816	01.3	1 284	01.6
Japan	336	00.8	605	01.0	1 752	02.1
All others	1 475	03.7	2 493	04.0	3 595	04.3
Totals	40 311	100.0	61 644	100.0	81 776	100.0

Source: *Statistics Canada*

1 What is the main idea expressed in this chart? What does it tell you about the role of the United States in our foreign investment picture?

2 What do five of the countries listed in this chart have in common?

3 What do you notice about the trend in Japanese direct investment?

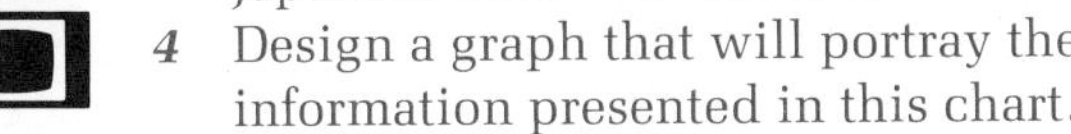

4 Design a graph that will portray the information presented in this chart.

5 Using the same data, re-design this chart in a way that conveys the information as well or better than the original.

The pie graphs on pages 286 and 287 show how the assets and profits of Canada's leading companies were distributed in 1983. Remember that a company's assets are the things of value that it owns (for example, land, buildings, equipment). The small circles show the distribution for the 25 largest companies in Canada. Many of these are foreign controlled. The medium-sized circles show the distribution for the top 500 companies in the country. The large circles show the distribution for *all* companies here.

WHAT HAS BEEN DONE ABOUT FOREIGN INVESTMENT

In recent years, Canadians have become more aware of foreign investment in their country. It is an issue that receives much attention in the media. Many prominent people have expressed opinions on the

FOREIGN OWNERSHIP AND CONTROL IN MAJOR INDUSTRIES IN CANADA (1980)

% of foreign ownership	Industry	% of foreign control
48	Manufacturing	51
48	Petroleum and natural gas	50
49	Mining and smelting	41
38	Railways	2
35	Total Industries (not including financial industries)	27

Source: *Statistics Canada*

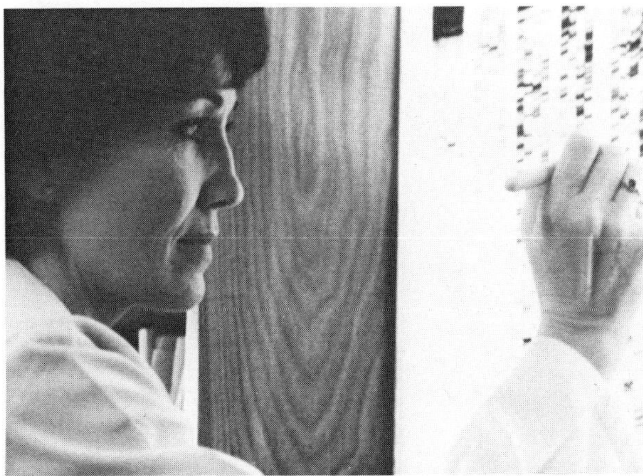

A Canadian research technologist at work. Our dependence on foreign investment and technology limits such job opportunities in Canada.

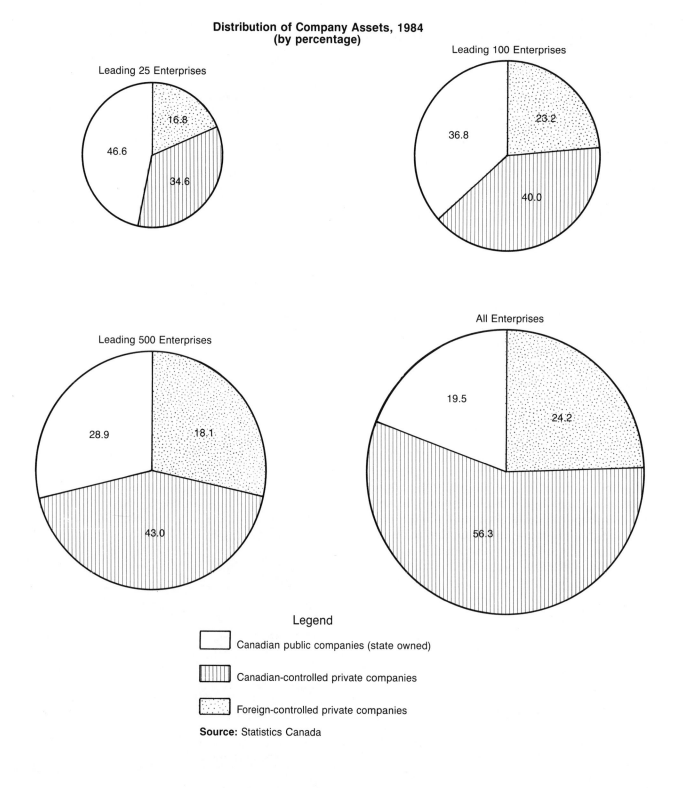

Distribution of Company Assets, 1984
(by percentage)

Leading 25 Enterprises

46.6

16.8

34.6

Leading 100 Enterprises

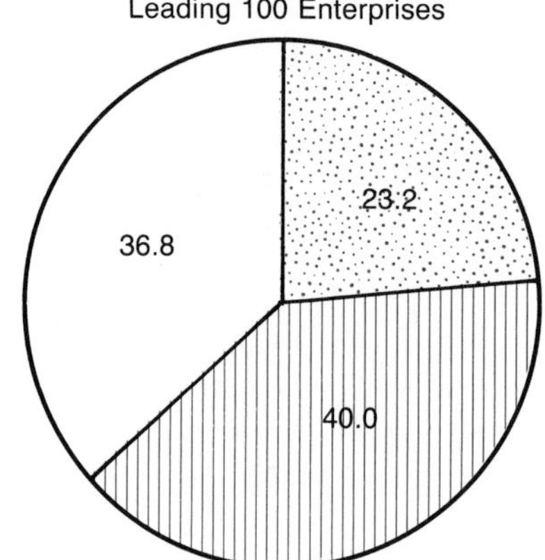

Leading 500 Enterprises

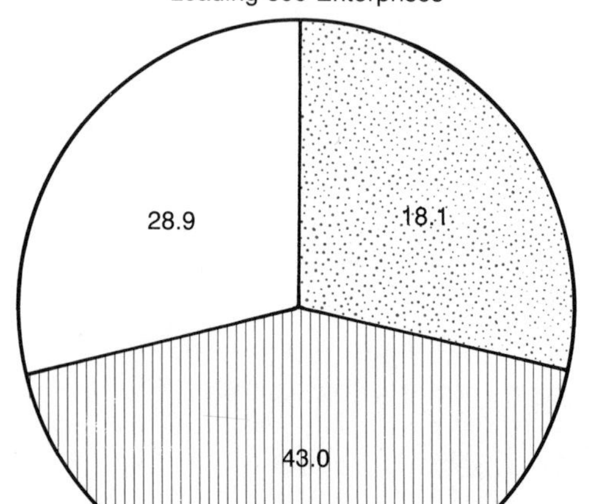

All Enterprises

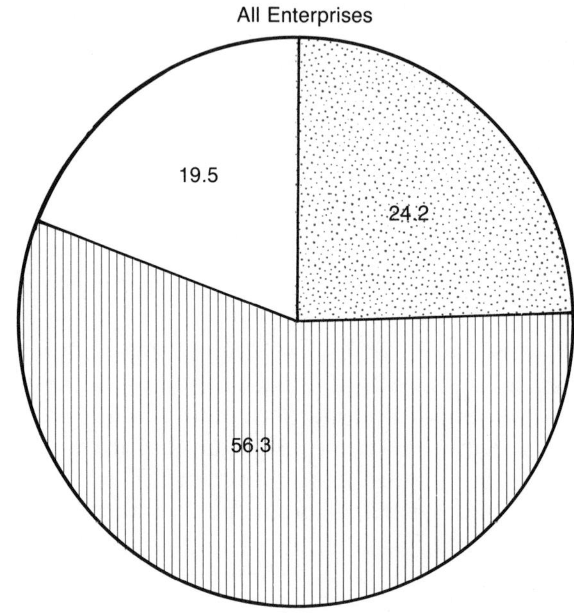

Legend

Canadian public companies (state owned)

Canadian-controlled private companies

Foreign-controlled private companies

Source: Statistics Canada

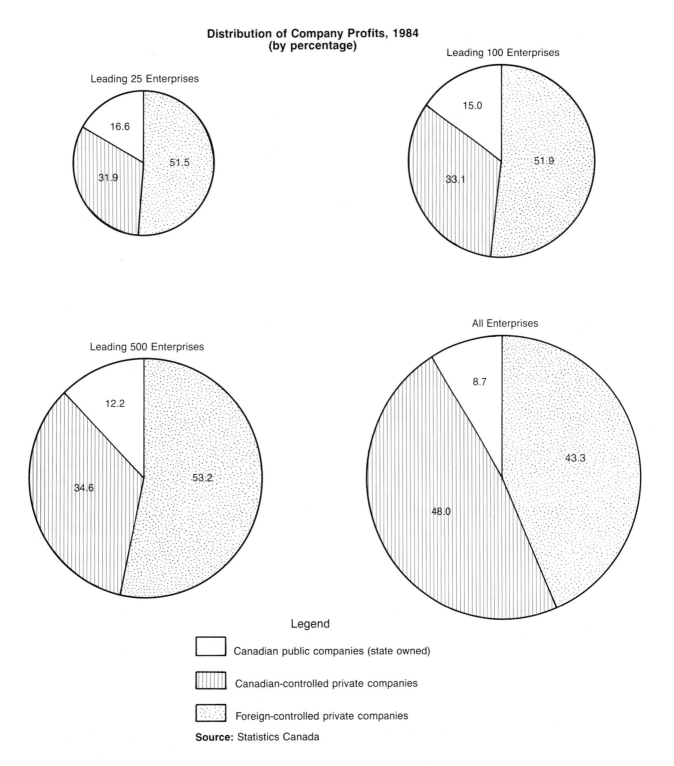

Distribution of Company Profits, 1984
(by percentage)

Leading 25 Enterprises

16.6

31.9

51.5

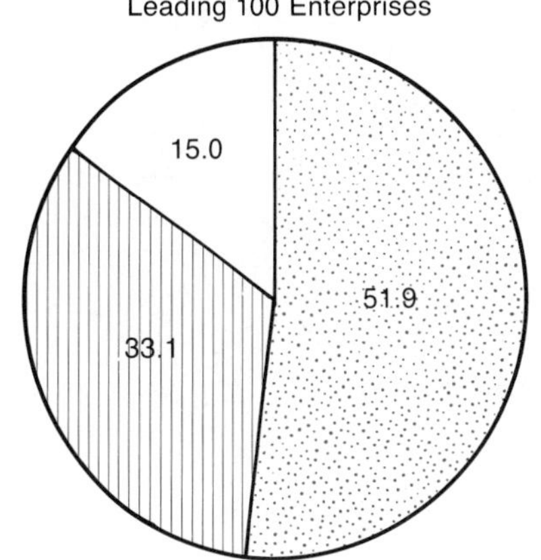

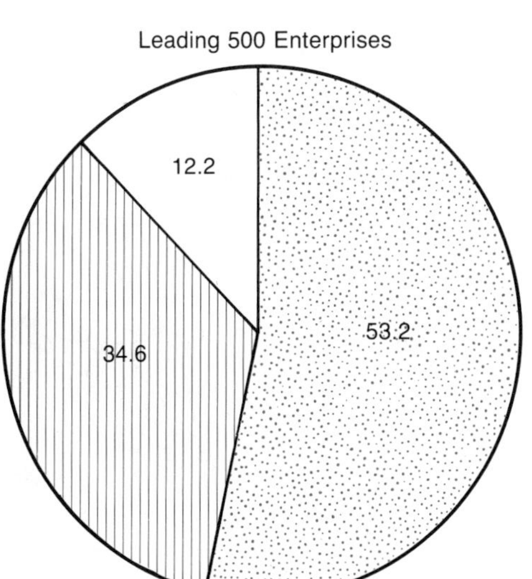

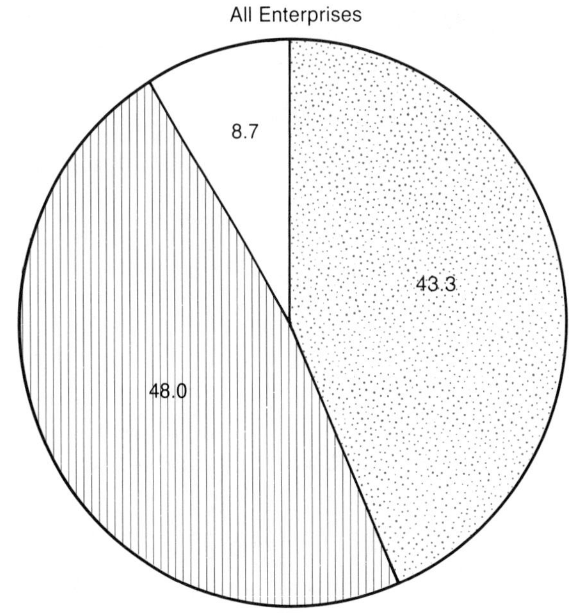

Legend

Canadian public companies (state owned)

Canadian-controlled private companies

Foreign-controlled private companies

Source: Statistics Canada

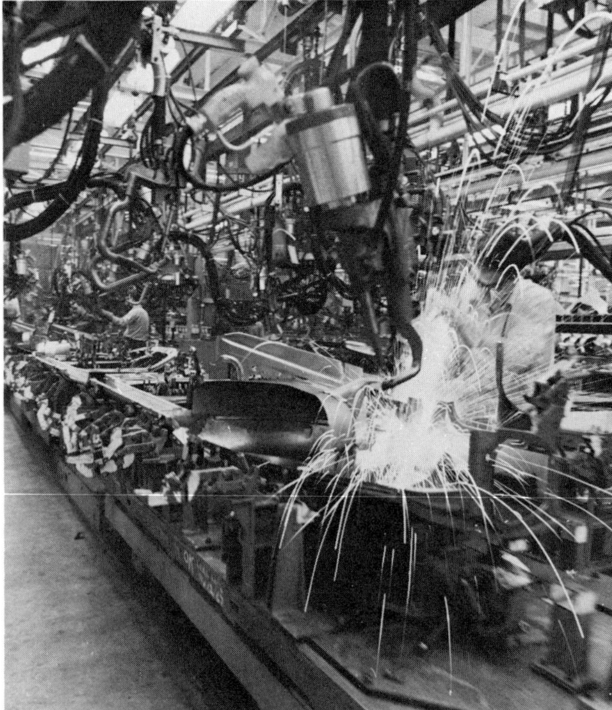

An automatic welder on the Ford Motor Company assembly line at St. Thomas, Ontario. The Ford Company employs thousands of Canadian workers. However, critics of the Auto Trade Pact suggest that Canada should obtain many more jobs from that agreement.

matter. These opinions differ widely. As a result, some Canadians wonder if there really are "right answers" to the questions being raised and what those answers might be.

In the 1970s and early 1980s, the trend seemed to be towards more concern about foreign investment. Therefore, the federal and provincial governments began to pay more attention to the issue. They even took a few modest steps to exercise some control, such as:

- insisting that no more than 25 percent of Canadian banks could be owned by non-Canadians.
- granting broadcasting licences for radio and television only to Canadian citizens or to companies with at least 80 percent Canadian ownership.
- making it more difficult for foreigners to get oil and gas leases in the Yukon and Northwest Territories.
- preventing foreigners from buying land in some provinces; for example, Prince Edward Island placed restrictions on foreign (and non-resident) ownership of ocean-front land.
- passing a *Foreign Investment Review Act* which gave the federal government the power to examine foreign bids to take over Canadian businesses. These bids could be rejected by the government if they did not appear to benefit Canada as a whole. (Over 95 percent of such

This cartoon illustrates the different approaches of two prominent Canadians to economic relations with the United States.
1 Who are the two people portrayed here? What are their official positions?
2 According to the cartoon, what is different about the approach of the two men?
3 How do the responsibilities of the two men differ? How might this be connected to the approaches they take to the issue?
4 Does the cartoon fairly portray the style and/or policies of each man? Why or why not? (In the case of Mr. White, newspaper research into his labour negotiations of 1984 and 1985 would be helpful in answering this question.)

bids were still approved and allowed to proceed.)

- giving special loans or tax advantages to Canadian-owned companies. For example, a few years ago, the government of Ontario made a large loan to a Canadian publishing company. As a result, the company remained in Canadian hands.

WHAT COULD BE DONE ABOUT FOREIGN INVESTMENT

- Place limits on future foreign investment in Canada.
- Buy back some existing foreign investment here.
- Identify key industries and insist on Canadian control of them.
- Nationalize (authorize direct government takeover of) certain large foreign-owned companies, such as Imperial Oil and General Motors.

CURRENT TRENDS

In the early 1980s, the Trudeau government announced a new program called the National Energy Policy. Its main goals were to promote self-sufficiency and increased Canadian ownership in our energy industries, particularly the petroleum industry. One of the results of this policy was the creation of Petro-Canada.

This program was attacked by some opposition politicians and even more strongly by American-based oil companies. Some of these companies ran expensive advertisements in newspapers and magazines, warning of the dangers for Canada in the National Energy Program. American government officials complained about this new energy policy and also about Canadian efforts to strengthen the Foreign Investment Review Agency. They described such actions as "unfriendly" and threatened retaliation against Canadian companies in the American market.

During the federal election campaign of 1984, Brian Mulroney's Progressive Conservatives called for a new approach to the issue of foreign investment.

Mr. Walter Gordon was one of the first prominent Canadians to call for major limits on foreign investment. He was finance minister in the Pearson government of the early 1960s. His ideas proved to be too controversial, so he was unable to put them into effect. Eventually, to save embarrassment he was moved to a less "sensitive" position. In frustration, he later left politics to return to private business. For many years he continued to warn Canadians not to sell out their future to the highest foreign bidders.

They took the position that Canada needed *more*, not less, investment from all sources. They promised to abolish the Foreign Investment Review Agency and to dismantle the National Energy Policy. Within one year of winning the 1984 election, they had "delivered" on both of these promises. Some Canadians hailed the new approach as indicating that "we are open for business again"; others expressed the fear that we were "giving away the store."

SHOULD WE BOTHER?

- A university in western Canada recently tested the benefits of foreign investment. Its conclusion: The benefits were not as great as Canadians thought. If Canadians had invested the same funds in their economy as foreigners had, their standard of living would not have suffered much. The Canadian economy would only be about six months behind its current level of development.

- Each year billions of dollars flow out of Canada in profits and dividends to foreign investors. This causes a large deficit in our balance of payments; we must make this up in sales of exports or in cash.
- Much of the "new" money invested yearly in Canada by non-Canadians actually comes from within Canada. Perhaps as much as 90 percent comes from profits on Canadian businesses plus loans or grants from Canadian banks and governments.
- In 1981 overall foreign control of Canadian industry stood at 26 percent. This compared with 3 percent in Britain, France and the United States and less than 1 percent in Japan.
- Foreign investment supposedly creates employment. Then why is Canada's unemployment rate so high compared to that of countries with far less foreign investment than we allow?
- Canada's political independence declines as our economic dependence on foreigners increases.

1 Many other countries have tougher laws against foreign investment than we do. These include Britain, France, Italy, West Germany, Mexico and Japan. Why do you think Canada does not follow their example?

2 What could the United States do to try to discourage us from reducing foreign investment? (Make your answer as complete as possible.) Could we resist such measures? Why or why not?

3 To greatly reduce foreign investment in Canada would cost billions of dollars. Where would the money come from? Do a series of interviews to discover the opinions of your friends and neighbours on this issue.

4 Try to discover what our political parties have to say about American investment in Canada. Which answers do you prefer?

PRESENT TREND

Over the years, Canadians have been asked about their attitudes towards foreign investment. Here are the results of one survey. The question asked was: *Do you think there is enough American capital invested in Canada now or would you like to see more?*

Year	Enough now	Like to see more	Don't know
1964	46%	33%	21%
1967	60	24	16
1970	62	25	13
1972	67	22	11
1975	71	16	13
1977	69	20	12
1980	64	20	17
1982	56	36	08

1 In what year did feelings against American investment seem to peak?

2 What factors might explain why Canadian opposition to American investment declined greatly in the early 1980s?

3 Based on the figures above, what do you expect happened to the willingness of Canadians to pay for buying back control of their economy? Why? How would this affect the policies of our political parties?

4 Try to find the music and *Canadian* lyrics (words) to the song "This Land Is Your Land, This Land Is My Land." Sing the song together with your class. Now consider this title: "This Land Is *Their* Land" (a reference to foreign ownership in Canada). As a class, try to make up new lyrics for the song. Make them reflect the extent of foreign control of our economy and how you feel about it.

When continental resource sharing is discussed, the focus usually is on energy resources. Chief among these are coal, oil and natural gas. Also important but rarely publicized is the valuable resource of fresh water. The United States consumes 30 to 40 times as much fresh water as Canada. Its daily consumption is well over 500 billion litres. Evidence suggests that American water supplies are being seriously reduced. For example, both Florida and California are facing growing shortages and falling water tables.

THE SHARING OF CONTINENTAL RESOURCES: "WHAT'S OURS IS OURS, AND WHAT'S YOURS IS OURS."

Each year the United States uses vast amounts of natural resources. It has a large population. It demands many goods and services. Many countries, including Canada, want the products of American industry. As a result, the United States is by far the world's biggest industrial producer. Many of the energy resources that Americans consume come from Canada. The American factories have huge appetites. Every year they grow hungrier.

American businessmen know how important Canada's natural resources are to their industries. This is one reason why they have bought up so many of those resources. They would like a guaranteed supply of our raw materials. The American government has tried to "sell" Canada a continental resources sharing plan. Here is the main idea: Our natural resources should not be regarded as "Canadian" or "American." They should be held in common. There should be no border between our two countries when it comes to resources. We have seen examples of how co-operative Canada has been with the United States about our resources. But we still say no to the idea of a continental resources sharing plan.

1 List the advantages to Canada of such a plan.
2 How do you feel about such a plan? Why?
3 The Americans can be tough bargainers in economic matters. In 1970 President Nixon cut in half the daily amount of Canadian oil allowed into the United States. This cost us millions of dollars per day. One reason for this action was to make us agree to a North American energy-sharing plan. We refused.
   a Why did this action cost us money?
   b Would the United States likely take similar action today? Canada did agree to sell an additional 189 billion cubic metres of natural gas to the Americans over the next several years. Why would we do this? (Afterwards, President Nixon removed the limits on imported Canadian oil.)

Thus, some Americans have proposed vast water diversion projects. The main idea would be to divert (redirect) water from the Great Lakes by systems of special channels and dams. Obviously, the dollar costs of such systems would be astronomical. However, there could be other costs as well, particularly to Canada. These could include environmental damage. Also, some experts claim that significant diversion of water from Canada could reduce our capacity to generate hydro-electricity.

1 In the late 1980s, water levels in the Great Lakes were unusually high. How could this circumstance be used by supporters of water diversion projects?
2 What kinds of environmental damage might be caused by such projects? Would this damage be serious or fairly minor and therefore "acceptable"?
3 If any water diversion projects are adopted, who should pay for them?
4 Would it be fair for Canada to charge money for "Canadian" water flowing to the United States? Why or why not?

5 If a truly serious water shortage developed in the United States, could Canada refuse to help? If not, why not? If so, should we refuse? Explain.

SHOULD WE SELL CANADA TO THE UNITED STATES?

From time to time, Canadian politicians have been accused of "selling out" Canada. Usually such charges refer to some concession made on negotiations relating to trade, investment, defence or similar issues. Such charges most often come from the media or opposing politicians. Frequently they are greatly exaggerated.

Recently, however, a Canadian businessman made headlines with a rather startling suggestion. He proposed that Canada offer itself for sale to the United States for a cool $15.6 trillion. This was his estimate of the value of Canada's assets, such as land, resources and equipment.

Such a price would make it possible to pay $1 million in cash to every Canadian citizen eighteen years of age or older. If Canada became part of the United States, we would no longer need to worry about our trade ties or foreign investment or the value of our dollar against the American currency.

The person who suggested this scheme quickly indicated that he was only joking. He was tired of hearing certain groups talk about separating from Canada. He wanted Canadians to appreciate their country more and not to do things that would only weaken or divide us.

1 Do you think the United States would be interested in buying Canada? Give reasons for your opinion.
2 Is there any way to set a realistic price for such a purchase?

3 If a generous American offer to purchase was made, would you support or oppose it? Why? What should be done with the money if the offer were accepted?
4 Suggest at least three reasons why no such offer has ever officially been made. Rank these reasons in order of importance.
5 How would you interpret the statement that the United States really has no reason to offer to buy Canada?

CONCLUSION

We have seen that the economic ties between Canada and the United States are very close. In many ways, this is a happy and pleasant relationship. But Canadians are becoming more aware that we pay a big price for this. We must count on American trade, investment and goodwill. We seem to be growing more dependent on these things. A few people are telling us that this threatens our *political* independence. This topic will be discussed more fully in a later chapter. We should note that these warning voices seem to be in the minority. They have not really captured the public's attention. Both federal and provincial governments let us slip closer into the American embrace. Do you agree with this viewpoint? Why or why not?

BUILDING YOUR LEARNING SKILLS

FOCUSSING ON THE ISSUE

1 What are the two key aspects of Canada's economic relations with the United States?
2 Why do we have such close economic ties with the United States?
3 What are the main advantages and disadvantages of such close ties?
4 Identify the person in this photograph. How did he help to focus the debate on our proper economic ties with the United States?

5 In 1985 Canada sold 78.8 percent of all its exports to the United States. Also, 72 percent of all our imports came from the United States. What potential problem in our trade pattern is emphasized by these facts?

6 The following terms appeared in this chapter. Try to recall their meanings and how they were used.

balance of trade	market
branch plant	nationalize
capital investment	quota
continental resource sharing	royalty
deficit	standard of living
entrepreneur	stocks
export	subsidiary
foreign investment	surcharge
foreign trade	surplus
free trade	takeover
import	trade

RESEARCHING

1 Try to discover why the United States government cancelled the reciprocity treaty with Canada in the 1860s.

2 Trade reciprocity with the United States became a major issue in the Canadian general election of 1911. What arguments were offered on both sides of this highly controversial issue? (Your findings will be used in a later exercise.)

3 Try to find trade statistics that will show the major trends in Canadian foreign trade over the past 20 to 25 years. (Statistics Canada, *Canada Year Book* and this textbook all offer some help.) Choose intervals of three, four or five years, beginning around 1960. Then, to help your communicating and analyzing skills, construct line graphs that will depict this data in a clear and meaningful way. Try to make general statements about the trends shown on each graph.

4 A similar exercise can be done on the theme of foreign investment in Canada. The same sources will be of help. Try to collect data and design bar graphs to show (in selected years):
a the percentage of American investment out of the total foreign capital invested in Canada;
b if possible, an analysis of other significant sources of investment funds (for example, Japan, West Germany or Saudi Arabia);
c the percentage of foreign ownership and/or control in major Canadian industries, such as manufacturing, oil and gas, mining and smelting.

5 In the 1970s and early 1980s, energy was an important issue in Canadian-American relations. Using magazine and newspaper accounts, try to determine:
a why energy was an issue;
b specific energy-related problems between the two countries;
c how these problems were connected to the themes of trade and investment;
d how the problems were dealt with.

6 In 1971 the Canadian government published the *Gray Report*. This had been produced by a special committee led by Herb Gray. Mr. Gray was a cabinet minister in the Trudeau government. This report made a number of recommendations about foreign investment in Canada. Shortly after, Mr. Gray lost his cabinet position. Students who are interested in economics could discover the details of the Gray Report. They should report these to the class. Consider these questions:
a What, if anything, was done about the recommendations of the *Gray Report*? Why?
b Why might Mr. Gray have been removed from the cabinet?
c How does this incident compare with the experience of Walter Gordon?

1·2·3 ORGANIZING

1 In point form, develop an organizer chart on foreign investment in Canada that summarizes:
a reasons for foreign investment in Canada;
b five major advantages of this investment;
c five major disadvantages of this investment.

2 To organize this chapter, the writers have used one of these approaches: chronological, thematic, order of priority. Which was used? How can you tell? Was this the best choice? Why or why not?

3 Within the section on foreign investment, what was the sequence (order) of the ideas of information presented to you? Was it logical?

Suggest a sequence that, in your opinion, would have been better. Why do you think so?

4 Imagine that you are prime minister of Canada. You have been convinced by your advisers that Canada must reduce its trade dependence on the United States. This will mean seeking expanded markets for Canadian goods in other foreign countries. Consider these possible actions:

- ▶ call in the American ambassador for a "friendly chat";
- ▶ inform the United States that you are suspending all trade with them until further notice;
- ▶ do a full study of Canada/United States trade patterns;
- ▶ send a flock of Canadian trade representatives to foreign countries to promote Canadian goods;
- ▶ telephone the American president and tell him or her of your intentions;
- ▶ launch a study to determine what potential we have to increase trade with other countries.

a Which action would be totally inappropriate? Why?

b Organize the remaining actions into an order of priority (first things first). Give reasons for the sequence you have chosen. Compare your ideas with those of classmates.

c Is there a "right" order? Is there a definite first step? last step?

COMMUNICATING

1 With the class in an appropriate seating arrangement, try the following exercise:

Step 1 The teacher or a student makes up a brief newsflash relating to Canadian-American relations. It should be between four and six sentences in length. The message should be written down for later reference.

Step 2 The creator of the newsflash *whispers* the message to the person next to him or her. This person passes on the story, again by whispering, to the next person, and so on until the last person has received the message.

Step 3 The last person writes down his or her version of the message and then repeats it aloud to the class. Compare this with the original. What happened? Try to trace the stages at which things began to get mixed up. Why does this happen?

Step 4 (optional) This exercise can be repeated with variations. For example, involve fewer people. Shorten or lengthen the message. Set up a competition between two groups, each trying to communicate the same message with the greatest accuracy. And so on.

Step 5 Try to identify five factors that can influence the effectiveness of communication.

2 You are a professional speech writer. You are offered a substantial amount of money to write a speech for a very prominent politician. This person wishes to convince his or her audience that seeking more foreign investment would be Canada's best policy. Do the best job you can on the speech — you are being very well paid.

3 OK! You have submitted the speech and collected your money. The politician was very pleased with your work; the audience received the speech enthusiastically. But you are troubled. You did not believe a word of that speech; in fact, you think the very opposite! Write an anonymous letter for the editorial page of the local newspaper. Imagine sending a copy of the letter to the politician who hired you. (By the way, you have a perfect right to your opinion on foreign investment, whatever that opinion is. Instead of letting all your hard work go to waste, why not really send a letter expressing your views to your member of Parliament? And a copy to your local newspaper —it might get published!)

4 Re-examine all the cartoons in this chapter. Which one communicates its message best? Worst? Tell why in each case.

5 Design a cartoon that communicates your opinion on some aspect of Canadian–American relations. Decide whether or not to use a caption. Compare you cartoon with that of one other classmate. Try to interpret and then improve upon each other's work. Have a third person judge which cartoon is best. Then put your cartoon up against those of other students in the class. Choose the best three cartoons and discuss the reasons for the decisions.

ANALYZING

1 Which of the following statements can be proven to be facts, and which are opinion?
  - *a* About 75 percent of all foreign investment in Canada is American.
  - *b* Canada and the United States have developed many ties that are so close that Canadian independence is in danger.
  - *c* American investment in Canada is part of a conspiracy to take over this country.
  - *d* Canada allows more foreign investment than any other major industrialized nation.
  - *e* The benefits of foreign investment, in jobs alone, far outweigh any disadvantages.
  - *f* When foreign firms operating in Canada put the profit motive first and the laws of their home country second, Canada's political independence suffers.
  - *g* By relying on foreign investment, we discourage the growth of Canadian technology.

2 Suggest several reasons why there is such a huge volume of trade between Canada and the United States.

3 How could Canada gain more control over its own economy? Why are these steps difficult to take?

4 Which issue is more important to the Canadian economy, trade or investment? Develop at least a one-page argument to support your opinion.

5 Obviously, Canada has extremely close economic ties with the United States. Are the effects of these close ties mainly positive or negative? Explain your answer in detail.

6 Do you think it is right that any private individuals, Canadian or foreign, should own natural resources in Canada? Why do you feel this way? (This could be a good topic for a class discussion or debate. A relevant case study would be the Denison Mines affair of 1970.)

7 American investment is spread all over the world. More than 25 percent of it is in Canada. This amounts to many billions of dollars. Would it be fair for us to change the rules of investment in Canada after the American money has been invested here? Would it be *wise*? Is it reasonable to have controls that are at least as tough as those imposed by other countries, such as Britain, Japan and Mexico, where Americans invest? Why might it be more difficult for us to apply similar rules?

8 This exercise is designed primarily to help you develop your powers of analysis. However, it also involves the skills of researching, communicating and, at the end, applying your knowledge. Examine the cartoon on page 296.
  - *a* What do you think is the point of this cartoon?
  - *b* How does it relate to the theme of continental resource sharing?
  - *c* In your opinion, is the cartoon effective? Why or why not?
  - *d* Why do you think the cartoonist chose to use a cat and a goldfish for the illustration? List the artistic touches that enhance the cartoon's message.
  - *e* In answering the last question, did you consider the shape of the cat's tail? the magnifying effect of the bowl on the cat's left eye? the facial expressions of both the cat and the fish? the cat's ribbon?

APPLYING YOUR KNOWLEDGE

1 Canada spends relatively little on research and the development of technology. Instead, we import about $20 billion worth of technology each year.
  - *a* What effect does this have on our balance of payments?
  - *b* How might it affect future employment in Canada? Why?
  - *c* We also rely heavily on foreign investment. Does this encourage or discourage the

growth of Canadian research and technology? Explain your answer.

d Would free trade tend to encourage or discourage the growth of our own research and technology? Explain.

2 Try to involve other people in a discussion of the United States' influence on the Canadian economy. Parents or other relatives and friends would be ideal participants. See if they are aware of the nature and extent of this influence. What do they think about it? If many of you feel concerned, what can you do about it?

3 Looking ahead, are Canada's economic ties with the United States likely to grow stronger or weaker? Why do you think so?

4 Does our present economic relationship with the United States threaten our independence as a nation? If so, how? If not, why not?

5 Refer back to question two under "Researching." You were asked to discover arguments offered both for and against the idea of trade reciprocity with the United States. These arguments applied to the situation in 1911. To what extent are they still applicable today? (Now consider following up with the exercise below.)

6 An excellent application of the reciprocity arguments can be made to the free-trade debate that raged in Canada in the late 1980s. Canada began exploring this idea with the United States in 1984, after Brian Mulroney became prime minister. You can easily turn this issue into a problem-solving exercise. The key question is: Should Canada adopt free trade with the United States? By now, you should be familiar with the problem-solving method. If so, develop the outline of an approach on your own. If necessary, refer to the model provided in the Introduction to this text.

CANADA AND FREE TRADE

A PROBLEM-SOLVING APPROACH

Step 1 **Identifying the Problem**
Perhaps the main question is whether or not a free-trade policy should be adopted.

Step 2 **Posing the Key Questions**
There are many things to be considered. We should look at our overall trade picture. How important is foreign trade to us? How healthy is our present trade with the United States? What dangers does it face? What would be the potential advantages and disadvantages for us in a free-trade deal with the United States? What risks are involved? Would the potential gains justify taking such risks?

Step 3 **Collecting the Data**
Much relevant material will be found in newspapers, specialized reference books, government publications and magazines. With the latter, make your effors more productive by using the periodicals index in your library. It might be possible to interview people who are knowledgeable in this field.

Step 4 **Evaluating the Data**
Remember to keep an open mind, especially at the beginning of your investigation. Reflect on the nature and quality of your sources. NOW YOU'RE ON YOUR OWN. GOOD LUCK!

PS An excellent method for concluding this study would be either to:

a conduct a full-fledged debate on the main question; OR

b simulate a meeting of the federal cabinet. The purpose of the meeting will be to decide Canada's policy on free trade with the United States.

If you attempt the cabinet simulation, give each class member a role. Some will be key ministers (for example, finance, trade and commerce). All provinces and regions should be represented. So should special interest groups such as organized labour and business.

If a class consensus emerges, you might consider communicating with the appropriate authorities, especially in government. This communication could take the form of a petition, an invitation to a politician to attend your class or a letter-writing campaign. Try to find other people or organizations who share your views, and join forces with them. You have a perfect right to participate in peaceful demonstrations. If there is no class consensus, you still are free to take action as an individual.

chapter 16

CANADIAN–AMERICAN RELATIONS: MILITARY AND POLITICAL ASPECTS

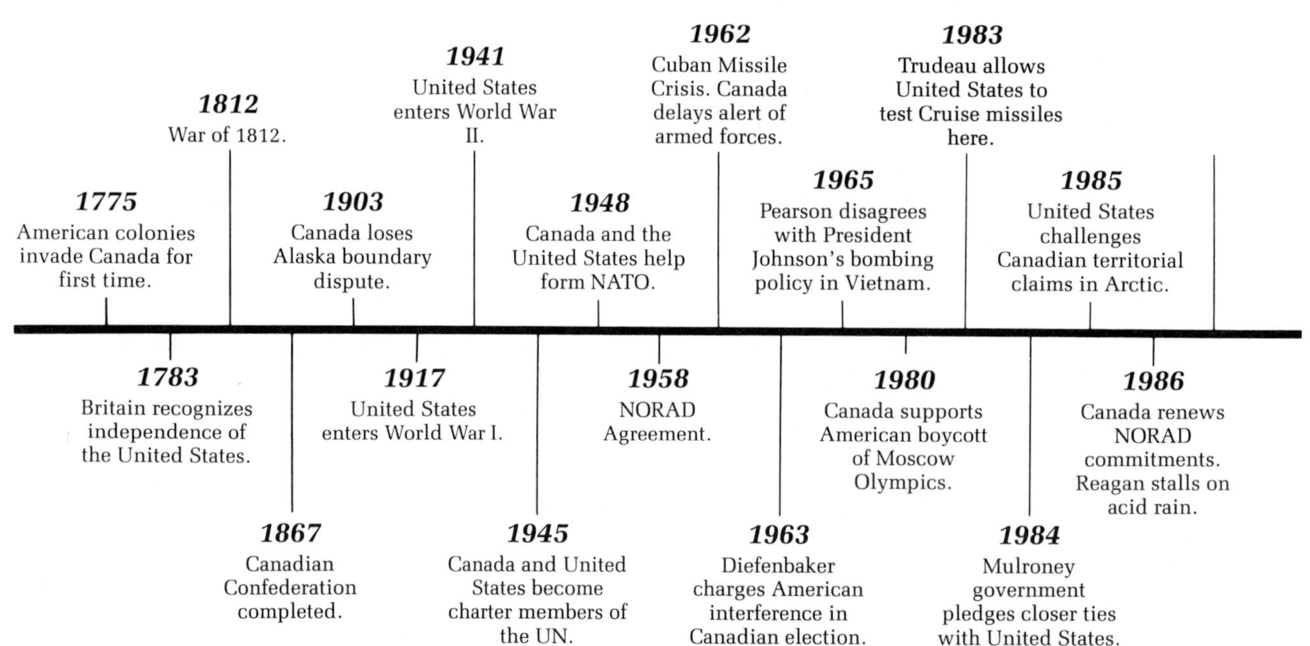

1775
American colonies invade Canada for first time.
1783
Britain recognizes independence of the United States.
1812
War of 1812.
1867
Canadian Confederation completed.
1903
Canada loses Alaska boundary dispute.
1917
United States enters World War I.
1941
United States enters World War II.
1945
Canada and United States become charter members of the UN.
1948
Canada and the United States help form NATO.
1958
NORAD Agreement.
1962
Cuban Missile Crisis. Canada delays alert of armed forces.
1963
Diefenbaker charges American interference in Canadian election.
1965
Pearson disagrees with President Johnson's bombing policy in Vietnam.
1980
Canada supports American boycott of Moscow Olympics.
1983
Trudeau allows United States to test Cruise missiles here.
1984
Mulroney government pledges closer ties with United States.
1985
United States challenges Canadian territorial claims in Arctic.
1986
Canada renews NORAD commitments. Reagan stalls on acid rain.

TOPIC ORGANIZER

THEME ORGANIZER

- After World War II, Canada and the United States hoped for a new era of world peace.
- The development of the cold war led us to maintain our close military ties.
- Canada and the United States are still allies because of their membership in NATO and NORAD.
- The United States maintains huge military forces, including an expanding array of nuclear weapons.
- The United States wants us to increase our defence spending, but Canadians fear involvement in a major nuclear conflict with the Soviet Union.
- Canada has occasionally created friction with the Americans by criticizing or refusing to support American military actions around the world.
- Canadians are divided over whether or not we should participate in the testing of American nuclear weapons such as Cruise missiles and the Star Wars defence system.
- The United States exercises tremendous influence on the activities and decisions of the Canadian government — much more than most Canadians realize or Canadian politicians will admit.

INTRODUCTION

Most of us have heard about "the longest undefended border in the world." Of course, this refers to the Canada–United States border. The fact that it *is* undefended shows the trust and good feelings that exist between us. For almost 100 years, there has been no serious danger of war between Canada and the United States. Indeed, since World War I, the two countries have been strong military allies.

1 What does it mean to be a "military ally" of another country?
2 What advantages could there be in having an ally like the United States? Why might this also be a disadvantage or a danger?
3 Why are Canada and the United States military allies? Think about economic, geographic and historic reasons. You should also consider values and beliefs shared by the two countries.

Canada's military ties with the United States became very strong during and after World War II. These ties were slightly strained in the early 1960s. This happened again in the early 1970s. However, today Canada and the United States seem to be entering a new period of co-operation. In this chapter, we will study some of the reasons for these developments.

Before reading on, study the chart of key words and ideas that follows.

KEY WORDS AND IDEAS IN THIS CHAPTER

Term	Meaning	Sample Use
acid rain	rain or snow that has been polluted by acids	The destruction of freshwater lakes by acid rain is a major issue between Canada and the United States.
cold war	a war of words and ideas; not "hot" because the two sides do not actually shoot at each other	After World War II, a cold war developed between the United States and the Soviet Union. Each country had several allies on its side.
deter	to persuade another person or group *not* to do something (usually done by threatening to take counter action)	The United States and the USSR have huge weapons systems. Each has enough power to destroy the other. Each nation's weapons deter the other from attacking.

espionage	various spying activities	Espionage is a key part of the cold war. Most countries spy on suspected enemies (and even friends). They do this to discover new weapons and secret plans. This reduces the chance of being surprised by future developments.
military ally	a friendly country with whom we have a defence agreement that requires us to defend each other and sometimes to co-operate in an attack on an enemy	Canada and the United States have been military allies for many years.
obsolete	out of date or old-fashioned	Countries develop new weapons very quickly. Because of this, their existing weapons become obsolete. Out-of-date weapons are of limited use, even though they might be very expensive.
Star Wars	a proposed high-tech system of defence against nuclear missiles; better known as the Strategic Defence Initiative (SDI)	Canadians were divided as to whether such a plan would increase or decrease the chances of war.

THE COLD WAR

As we saw in Unit 3, Canadians and Americans fought side by side in two world wars. In World War II (1939–1945), the very survival of North America was at stake. This experience made strong bonds between our two peoples. When the war ended, many dangers to world peace remained. Therefore, Canada and the United States chose to remain allies.

THE SOVIET THREAT

The new danger in North America seemed to come from the Soviet Union. This country had been our ally in the war. This did not prevent problems from developing. The reasons for this are explained in more detail in Unit 6, Chapter 19. Still, it is necessary here to give at least a brief summary of them. Since 1918 the Soviet Union had been under a Communist government. Its leaders did not share our beliefs in democracy and human rights. This was a difference in basic values. It created tension and mistrust on both sides.

At the end of World War II, the Soviet Union was the strongest power in Europe. It used this power to take over several countries in central and Eastern Europe. The Communists believed in spreading their system as far as possible. Some democratic countries feared that the Soviet Union might attack them next. This was not really very likely. Still, it was possible. Their concern was real. Canada and the United States had to be prepared, just in case.

THE NATURE OF THE COLD WAR

This tense situation came to be called the "cold war." It was "cold" because there was no actual shooting between the two sides. Instead, the conflict was more like a war of words and nerves. Nonetheless, both sides built up their armed forces. They spent huge sums of money on planes, tanks, guns and other weapons. They also engaged in espionage. This way, they hoped to learn about each other's latest military equipment and plans for using it.

THE FORMATION OF NATO

These actions caused the cold war to become more tense and dangerous. Canada and the United States

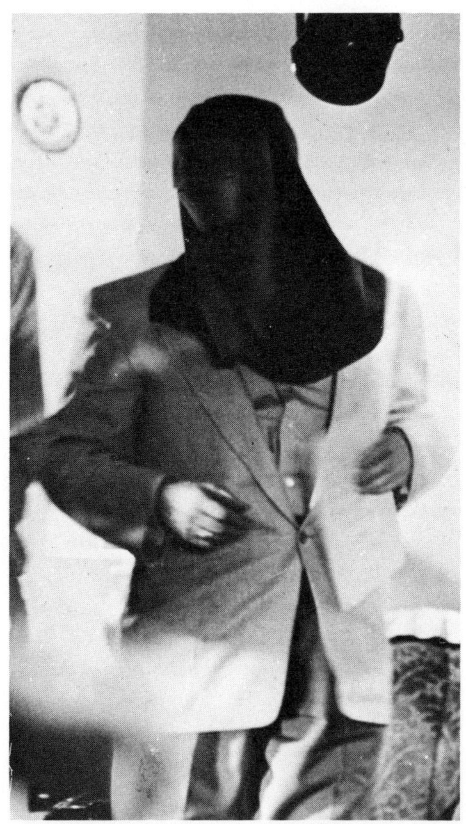

In 1945 Igor Gouzenko was a clerk in the Soviet embassy in Ottawa. After defecting he gave the Canadian government evidence of a large Soviet spy ring operating in Canada and the United States. This news increased suspicion of the Soviet Union. In this rare photograph taken in 1954, Gouzenko's identity is protected by a hood. Why was this necessary? Until his death in 1982, he lived in an unknown location in Canada under RCMP protection. He used an assumed name and had undergone extensive plastic surgery to alter his facial features.

became even more concerned about their own safety. Several countries in western Europe had similar feelings. Therefore, in 1949 they joined together in a new and larger alliance. This was called NATO (North Atlantic Treaty Organization). Details about NATO are included in Unit 6, Chapter 19.

The main goal of NATO was and is to provide security for its members. NATO officials worked out plans for their common defence. Basically, the idea was to present a united front against any enemy. Such unity would deter (discourage) an enemy attack.

In fact, the main enemy was expected to be the Soviet Union. NATO was geared to protect western Europe against a Soviet attack. Canada and the United States did not want that area to be taken over by the Russians. Thus, by protecting western Europe, we protected ourselves.

CANADA AND THE UNITED STATES FORM NORAD

NATO did not do enough to protect North America from a *direct* Russian attack. This fact became clear in the 1950s. During this period, many new weapons were developed. The first two atomic bombs had been dropped on Japan in 1945. They destroyed the cities of Hiroshima and Nagasaki. They killed or wounded over 100 000 people. By the early 1950s, both the Soviet Union and the United States had developed hydrogen bombs. These were much more powerful than the bombs dropped on Japan. Moreover, aircraft were becoming larger and more powerful. They could fly farther and faster. New jet bombers could carry hydrogen weapons from the Soviet Union to the United States and vice versa.

To meet these dangers, it was essential to improve the air defence of North America. Radar had been developed during World War II. It could warn of approaching aircraft. In the early 1950s, Canada agreed to help build and operate new radar stations on our soil. If radar spotted attacking planes, jet fighters could be sent up to intercept (stop) them. Several lines of radar stations were built across Canada. The line farthest north was called the DEW (Distant Early Warning) Line. It was completed in the early 1950s.

Still, this was not enough to deal with a modern nuclear attack. Even the radar lines were obsolete (out of date) almost as soon as they were built. This was because of the development of long-range missiles. This took place in the late 1950s and early 1960s. The largest of these missiles were called ICBMs — Intercontinental Ballistic Missiles. They were huge rockets with hydrogen warheads attached to them. An ICBM launched from certain places in the Soviet Union could hit Toronto or New York City

Above: This type of atomic bomb was dropped on Hiroshima, Japan, in 1945. Right: An atomic explosion. Below: The ruins of Nagasaki after the dropping of an atomic bomb on that city.

A radar installation on the Pinetree Line.

within 30 minutes. Radar stations were of little use against such weapons.

These developments created major problems for NATO and for North America. Now Canada and the United States were just as vulnerable to sudden attack as Europe was. If you had been responsible for North American air defence at this time, what would you have done?

UNITED STATES OFFENSIVE MISSILES (1960 TO 1980)

Here are some of the offensive missiles of the United States. The Polaris and Poseidon missiles are fired from submarines. Over the years, they have improved both in accuracy and range (distance they are able to travel). They have largely been replaced in recent years by more advanced missiles with multiple warheads. Missile-firing submarines are considered to be almost invulnerable to enemy attack. They can fire their weapons while submerged, and these warheads can strike targets over 5000 km away.

The Minuteman and Titan missiles are land-based and are fired from underground silos. While more vulnerable to enemy attack, their range is great (up to 16 000 km). They can carry much larger warheads. In recent years, they, too, have been fitted with multiple warheads.

THE CREATION OF NORAD

By the late 1950s, it was clear that North America needed a better system of air defence. This system was created in 1958. It is called NORAD (the North American Air Defence system). It provided for the complete co-ordination (linking) of Canadian and American air defence plans. It organized radar warn-

United States Offensive Missiles

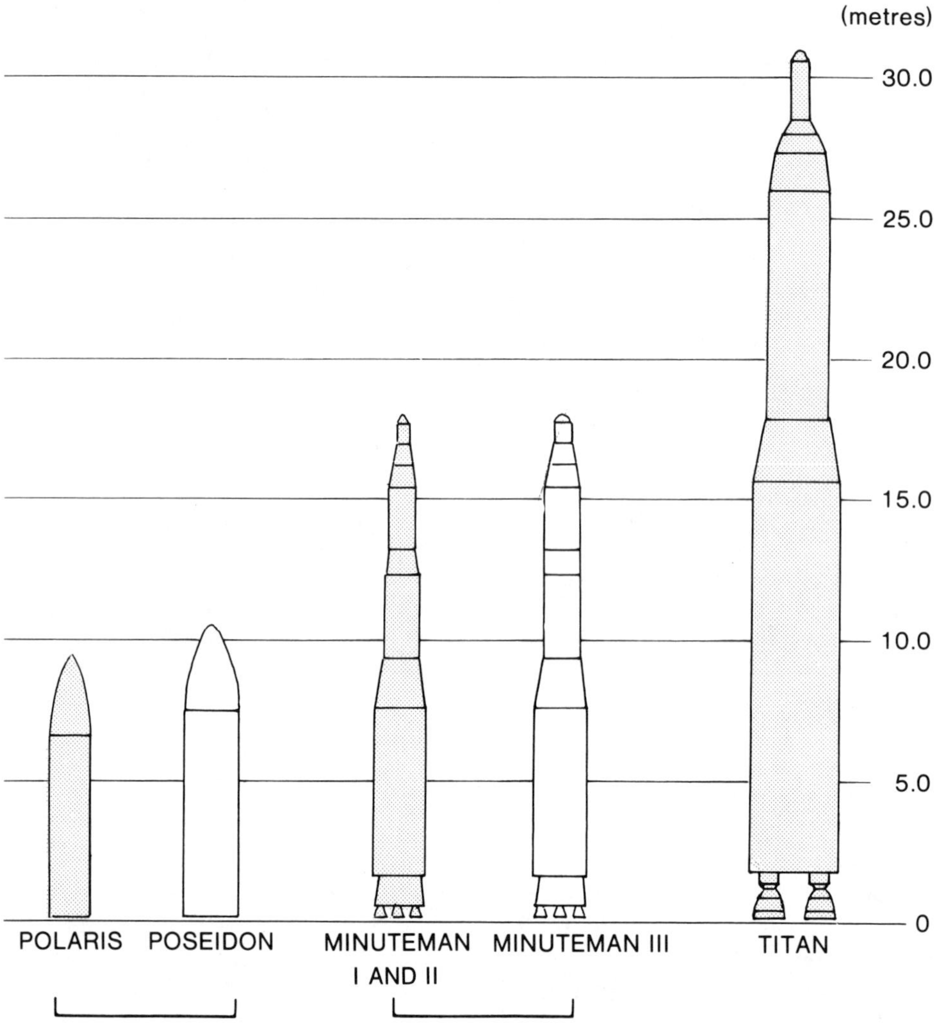

ing systems. These were connected with air bases from which jet interceptors could rush up to meet enemy bombers. Huge new research projects were begun. These developed new communications systems, such as satellites, to provide quick warning against missile attacks.

The headquarters of NORAD are situated near Colorado Springs in the United States. A large mountain has been hollowed out at the centre. Inside are located vital computers and communications equipment. The headquarters are in constant contact with all NORAD bases and forces—on land, at sea and in the air. If they received warning of an attack on North America, they would control the response of all NORAD defensive and offensive weapons.

By the terms of the NORAD agreement, an American is in overall command. The assistant commander is a Canadian. In a war situation, the president of the United States has the final decision as to the use of NORAD forces. He or she could commit Canadian forces to battle or order American forces to enter Canadian territory. Most likely, enemy missiles or bombers would be intercepted in our airspace. Naturally, this could have disastrous results on life in this country.

Canada has contributed to NORAD in other ways.

This photo shows the launching of a new Trident-class submarine, the USS Alabama, in May of 1984. These vessels cost over $2 billion each. They have a top speed of 30 knots and, if necessary, could go for twelve years without refuelling. A Trident submarine carries 24 missiles, compared with 16 for the older Polaris-type subs. By 1989, the United States expects to have sixteen of these newer-type submarines in service. At that time, they will be equipped with special "Trident" missiles. These will have a range of almost 8000 kilometres and will be able to strike within 150 metres of their target! Each missile will be capable of carrying up to ten warheads of 475-kiloton power. (The bomb used on Hiroshima was about 12.5 kilotons in power.) In theory, if a Trident submarine were carrying its maximum load of warheads, and each struck its target, that one submarine alone could destroy all of the significant cities of the Soviet Union.

The controversial B-1 bomber. In 1977, President Carter decided not to proceed with the production of this new long-range aircraft. This decision was reversed by President Reagan. One hundred such planes could cost billions of dollars. The B-1 will probably be obsolete by the time it is fully in service.

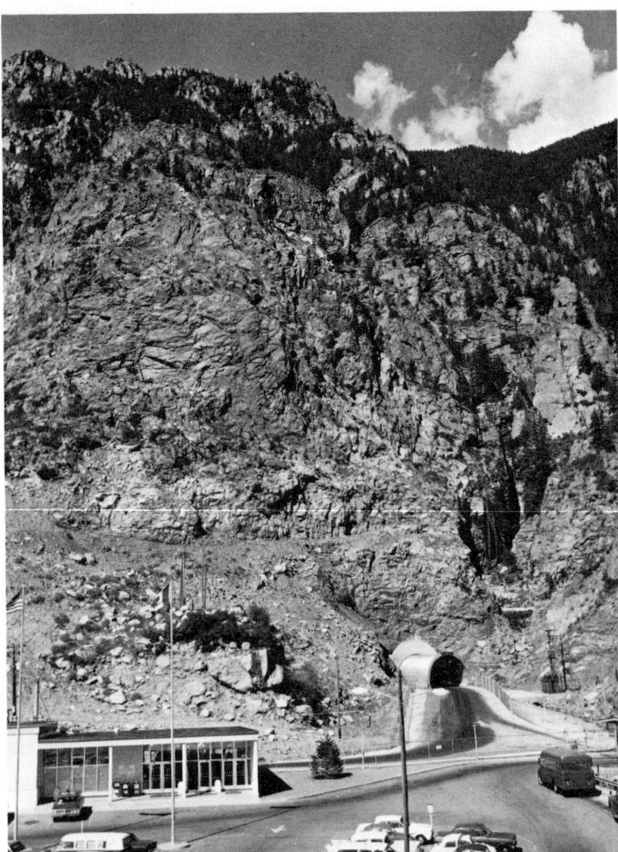

The main entrance to NORADs underground headquarters near Colorado Springs. Inside there are eleven steel buildings, some of them three stories deep. They are under more than 400 m of granite. In recent years the accuracy, power and sheer number of Soviet missiles have increased greatly. Therefore, experts think that these underground NORAD headquarters could be totally destroyed in a nuclear attack. Other arrangements have been made to keep open the communications lines to the Commander-in-Chief, the President of the United States.

We keep several squadrons of jet interceptors. Most of these planes are based in Quebec and New Brunswick. They could meet an enemy bomber attack. Until 1972 we kept BOMARC missile bases at North Bay, Ontario, and Macaza, Quebec. These had nuclear warheads. They, too, were designed to destroy bombers. However, the BOMARCs have become obsolete. The bases have been removed.

SHOPPING LIST FOR A MODERN-DAY WARRIOR

(or What Every Well-Equipped Nation Is Wearing These Days)

In this chapter, we have been describing some of the weapons of modern warfare. On every day of every year, millions of dollars are spent developing, testing or buying various kinds of weaponry. It has been estimated that up to 50 percent of the scientific work done by the United States and the Soviet Union is connected in some way to war. Here is a list of only a few of their latest projects:

- Each of the two superpowers could launch several thousand nuclear warheads against the other. One American expert estimates that 400 such warheads would destroy 75 percent of the industry of the Soviet Union and 33 percent of its population.
- Sensor devices are being tested. They would make the ocean "transparent" and reveal the hiding places of submarines. Then special torpedoes moored to the ocean floor could be released. These would "listen" to the sound of the enemy vessels and use that sound to aim themselves and destroy those vessels.
- "Smart bombs" and missiles are being developed. These have very accurate, built-in aiming devices to score direct hits on almost any target. Their guidance systems include radar, laser beams and television cameras.
- The United States has developed a small Lance missile with a warhead that can release millions of neutrons. These would bring slow, agonizing death to many people.
- The United States has developed a nuclear-tipped Cruise missile. It is launched from a bomber. It is 4.3 m long and flies at 885 km/h. However, it can fly at treetop level and automatically adjust its path for terrain. This means it is almost impossible

to detect or effectively destroy. A Cruise missile can fly 2400 km and strike within 30 m of its target. This missile is discussed further on pages 311 to 313.

- Many countries have chemical and bacteriological weapons. These can release gases that paralyze or kill, poison drinking water, ruin food supplies and spread various kinds of incurable diseases. The United States suspects the Soviet Union of developing a "new generation" of such weapons. Thus, it is increasing its own research in this field.
- Both superpowers are developing Stealth technology. This involves methods of treating the outer shell of planes and missiles so they cannot be "seen" by enemy detection systems.
- Both superpowers regard space as the next theatre of conflict. They are racing to develop a variety of Star Wars weapons to help them do battle in outer space. Already, each side has hunter-killer satellites. These can use laser guns to destroy unarmed satellites now in space.

The arms race is increasing in speed and cost. Meanwhile, millions of human beings go without adequate food, clothing, shelter, education or medical attention. As one concerned person said at the United Nations, "Time is not on our side."

CANADIAN SUPPORT FOR AMERICAN ACTIONS

Since World War II, Canada has supported most American military actions. We joined American forces fighting in Korea (see Unit 6, Chapter 19). We agreed with the build-up of US soldiers in Vietnam in the early 1960s. We later became somewhat critical of American actions in Vietnam.

The United States has not been completely happy with Canada as an ally. For example, it feels that we should spend more money on defence. The Americans spend a much bigger percentage of their budget on defence than we do. Thus, it feels that we are not paying enough toward the costs of NATO and NORAD. For example, today there are almost 200 000 service men and women in NORAD, stationed at about 400 separate bases. Almost 95 percent of them are Americans. The United States also gives 20 times more money than Canada does to NORAD. The approximate figures are $4 billion to $200 million.

The Cuban Missile Crisis strained Canadian–American relations. In 1962 the United States learned that the Soviet Union was placing missiles in Cuba. These weapons could hit American targets in seconds. They also could reach parts of Canada. The Americans ordered the Soviets to remove the missiles. If they did not obey, they would face nuclear war. In time the Russians did remove their weapons. Meanwhile, NORAD forces were put on full alert.

The deadly "Cruise" missile developed in the late 1970s by the United States.

A Soviet ship en route to Cuba, 1962. Crates of missiles can be seen lashed to the forward deck.

This map shows the potential range of the Soviet missiles being set up in Cuba in 1962. These missiles were removed because of American pressure.

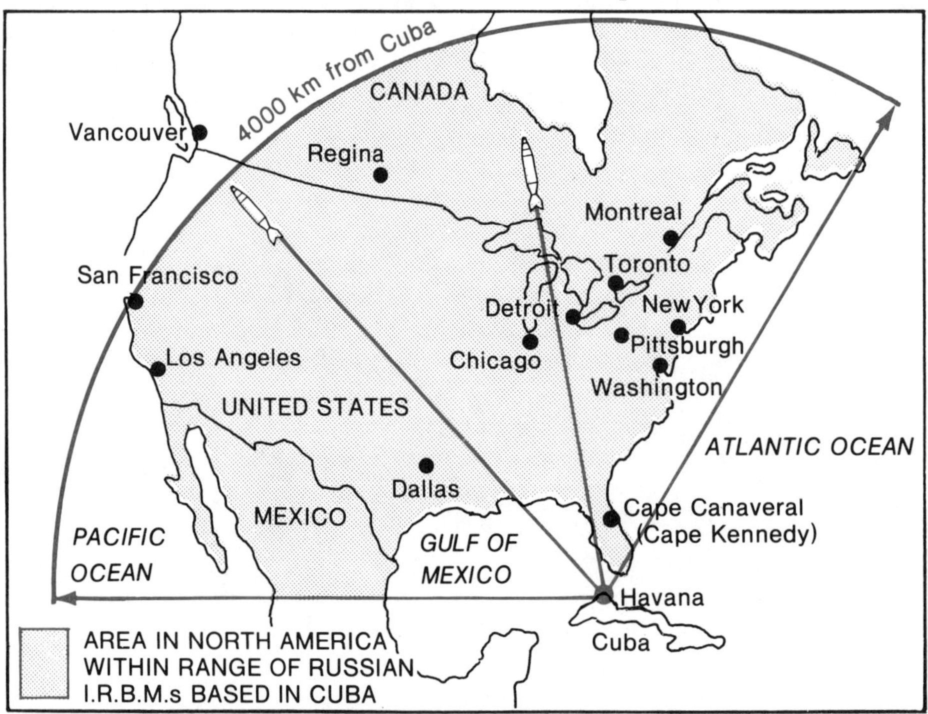

President Kennedy asked that all Canadian forces be put on alert. For various reasons, Prime Minister Diefenbaker hesitated to do this. He and President Kennedy did not get along well together. Their personalities clashed. Also, the Americans were pressing Canada to adopt nuclear weapons. Mr. Diefenbaker did not want to do this. Perhaps by refusing to "jump" when the Americans said to, he hoped to show that Canada had some independence.

The Americans resented this for a long time. They showed this by their actions towards Canadian forces. Canadians with NORAD were given less important duties. They also received less information about military developments. In 1973 American forces were again put on full alert. This time the trouble was in the Middle East. Canada's defence minister was informed eight hours later of President Nixon's decision!

Other military matters have strained Canadian–American relations at times. In the mid-1960s, Canada became critical of American actions in Vietnam. Prime Minister Pearson once spoke out in public against American bombing there. Lyndon Johnson, the president of the United States, was furious. In a private meeting with the prime minister, he attacked Mr. Pearson's "interference" in American affairs. Witnesses said that the two men almost came to blows.

Prime Minister Pearson (left) and President Johnson appeared to be happy in this meeting in 1966.

Canada has traded with some countries that the United States did not officially approve of. These included Cuba and China. Both have Communist governments. This fact largely explains American dislike of them. Moreover, Canada decided to officially recognize Communist China at a time when the United States did not.

Canada made these decisions for several reasons. We are an independent country. We cannot be expected to always do what the United States wants. This is especially true when we do not agree with American policy. Also, Canadian politicians must please Canadian voters. Sometimes they can do this by "tweaking the noses" of the Americans — or appearing to do so. Still, our government must be very careful in this regard. It is constantly walking a tightrope, and this can be tricky! We cannot afford to push the United States too far. As one analyst has said:

> It is not in the Canadian interest that the U.S. should be weakened and humiliated — even when it follows policies Canadians think foolish. . . . The price Canadians pay for the national independence they have is that they do not push it too far. . . . Canadians know that they would not survive if the United States ceased behaving towards them like a civilized country.
>
> John W. Holmes, *The Better Part of Valour: Essays on Canadian Diplomacy*

CONCERN OVER THE NORTHWEST PASSAGE

In 1969, the American supertanker *Manhattan* made an historic trip through the Northwest Passage (see map). Its purpose was to see if Alaskan oil could be shipped by this route to ports on the American east coast. Canada is concerned about these plans. There is great danger of oil spills from the tankers. This would seriously harm the Arctic environment. Also, Canada claims to control the waters involved. The United States argues that these are international waterways. If this is true, they can be used by anyone.

This dispute was rekindled in August, 1985. The United States announced that an American Coast

THE NORTHWEST PASSAGE

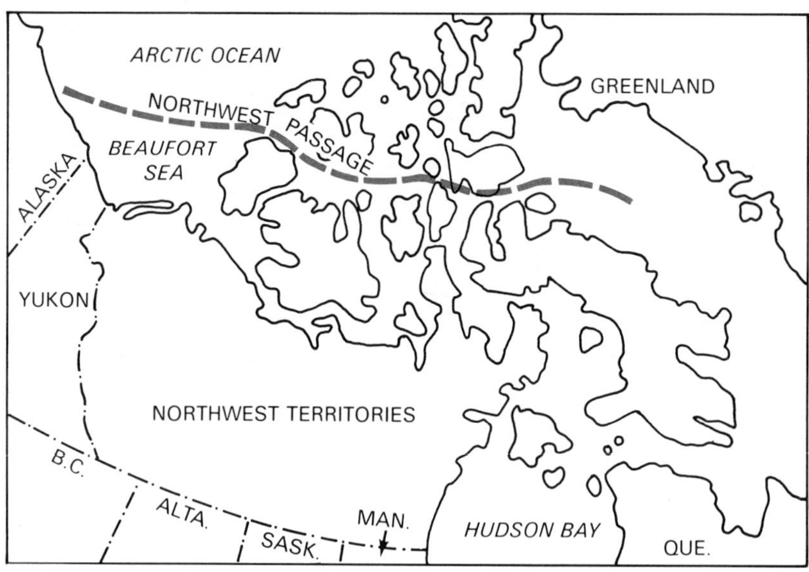

Guard icebreaker, the *Polar Sea*, would sail through the Prince of Wales Strait, which is part of the Northwest Passage (see the map on page 311). The American government made a point of not asking Canada's permission for this voyage.

The Canadian government of Brian Mulroney was deeply embarrassed. It had been considering a free-trade agreement with the United States. Improved Canadian–American relations was one of the main foreign policy goals of the Mulroney government. To help save face, at the last minute our government "authorized" the voyage of the American icebreaker.

A small group of Canadian nationalists criticized this voyage as "insulting and demeaning" to Canada and a challenge to Canadian sovereignty. They planted large Canadian flags on islands and ice floes along the route of the *Polar Sea*. They also hired a small plane from which they dropped packages onto the deck of the American ship. These contained more Canadian flags and a message of protest.

While the controversy slowly faded, this incident focussed attention on several Canadian weaknesses. It showed that, "when push came to shove," we had no effective choice but to accept American actions. Moreover, we had and still have glaring military weaknesses. We claim vast areas of northern territory but are unable to defend or even patrol them adequately.

In 1985 Canada had no naval vessels or submarines capable of operating in ice-filled waters. The Soviet Union, on the other hand, possessed a rapidly growing northern fleet that included powerful modern surface vessels plus at least 46 nuclear-powered submarines. To deflect some criticism, our government said it would consider building and arming the world's largest icebreaker (100 000 horsepower) to help maintain our claims in the Arctic. In the meantime, Canada could only continue its periodic overflights with spotter aircraft. But even if such a flight did detect a "hostile presence," we had few soldiers to spare and no ships capable of getting them to the potential danger zone.

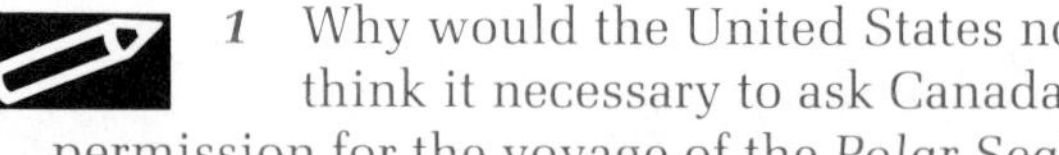

1 Why would the United States not think it necessary to ask Canada's permission for the voyage of the *Polar Sea*?

2 The American government knew in advance that this voyage would embarrass the Mulroney government. Why, then, would Washington proceed?

The Voyage of the Polar Sea

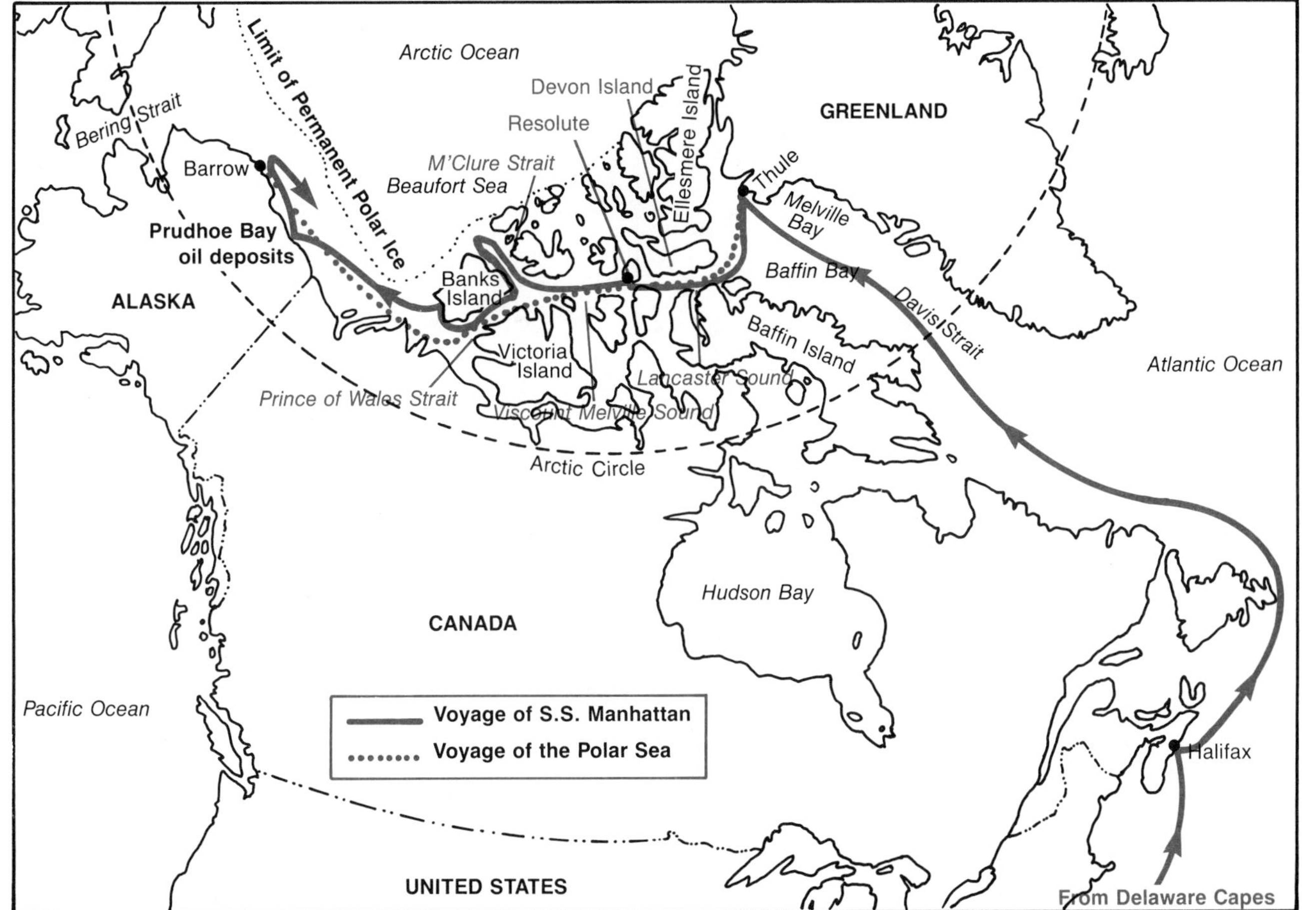

3 What are the weaknesses in Canada's relationship with the United States that permit such incidents to occur? What do these weaknesses imply about Canada's status as a nation?

"REFUSE THE CRUISE"

The development of the Cruise missile by the United States is described on page 306. This weapon created a major controversy in Canada in the early 1980s. The Americans asked our government for permission to test the missile's guidance system in Canadian air-space. In their view, the terrain and temperatures in our North were similar to those over parts of the Soviet Union. They needed to know if the guidance system could work reliably in these conditions.

Supports of the Cruise argued that it was needed to deter a Soviet attack. It was cheap to produce and almost unstoppable. Furthermore, it would be deadly accurate if its guidance system could be perfected. On the other hand, opponents in both Canada and the United States condemned this new weapon. First, it would provide no lasting military advantage. The Russians would quickly develop similar weapons of their own (as they have done). Worse, the Cruise would make it almost impossible to achieve a complete ban—or even a freeze—on the development of nuclear weapons. This is because the Cruise is so small. Hundreds could easily be hidden in such locations as warehouses, trucks or even private homes.

This would make it impossible to check up on how many nuclear weapons each side had. If countries could not be sure of this, would they ever agree to limit nuclear weapons? Why cut back on your weapons if you can't be sure what the other side is doing?

Canadians became deeply divided over whether or not we should allow Cruise missile testing in our country. Demonstrations and petitions were organized by supporters of each point of view. The Trudeau government finally agreed to permit the tests. Canada had a duty as a member of NATO and NORAD, it argued, to help our American allies perfect this important new weapon. Subsequently, the brief tests were conducted by American air force personnel. The missiles used were unarmed, so there was no danger of a nuclear accident.

In 1985 and 1986, the Americans asked permission to resume their Cruise testing program. This time it was the Progressive Conservative government of Brian Mulroney that gave its consent. Again there was a public outcry. Some of the protests turned to laughter when two of the tests ended in embarrassing

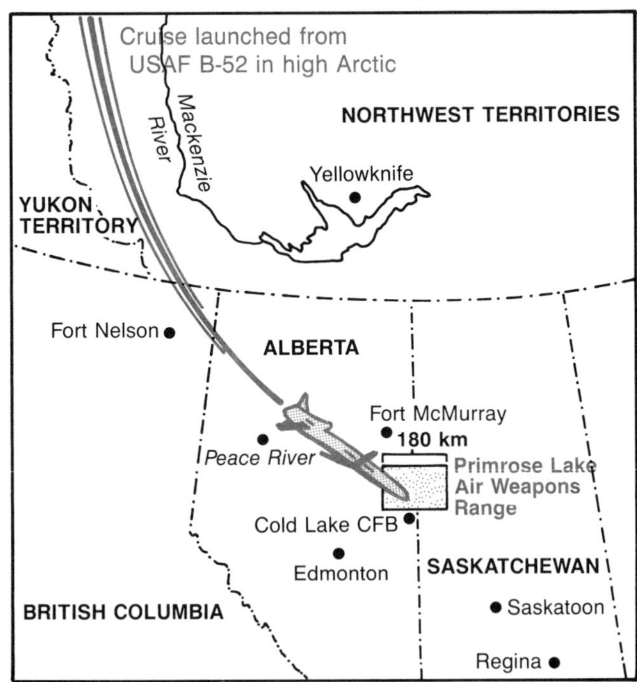

Source: *Maclean's*, March 4, 1985

Alberta high school students protest Cruise missile testing by "crashing" their own papier mâché model into the roof of their school.

failures: One missile crashed to earth well short of its target, having apparently run out of fuel; another missile fell straight down from the bomber from which it had been launched. No official reason was given, but it has been said that the missile's engine refused to start. Meanwhile, some technical experts began to suggest that the Soviet Union was developing a new radar that would be capable of detecting low-flying Cruise-type missiles. Despite such discouragements, the United States pressed on with its Cruise program. In this, it had the full support of the Canadian government. Opposition, though vocal, was not widespread or effective. In fact, it died down rather quickly.

STAR WARS

As we have seen, in the 1980s the United States became very concerned about the huge build-up in Soviet military power. Under President Ronald Reagan, the United States dramatically increased its spending on national defence. In addition to more modern missiles, aircraft and submarines, President Reagan called for an ambitious new project that was

Star Wars

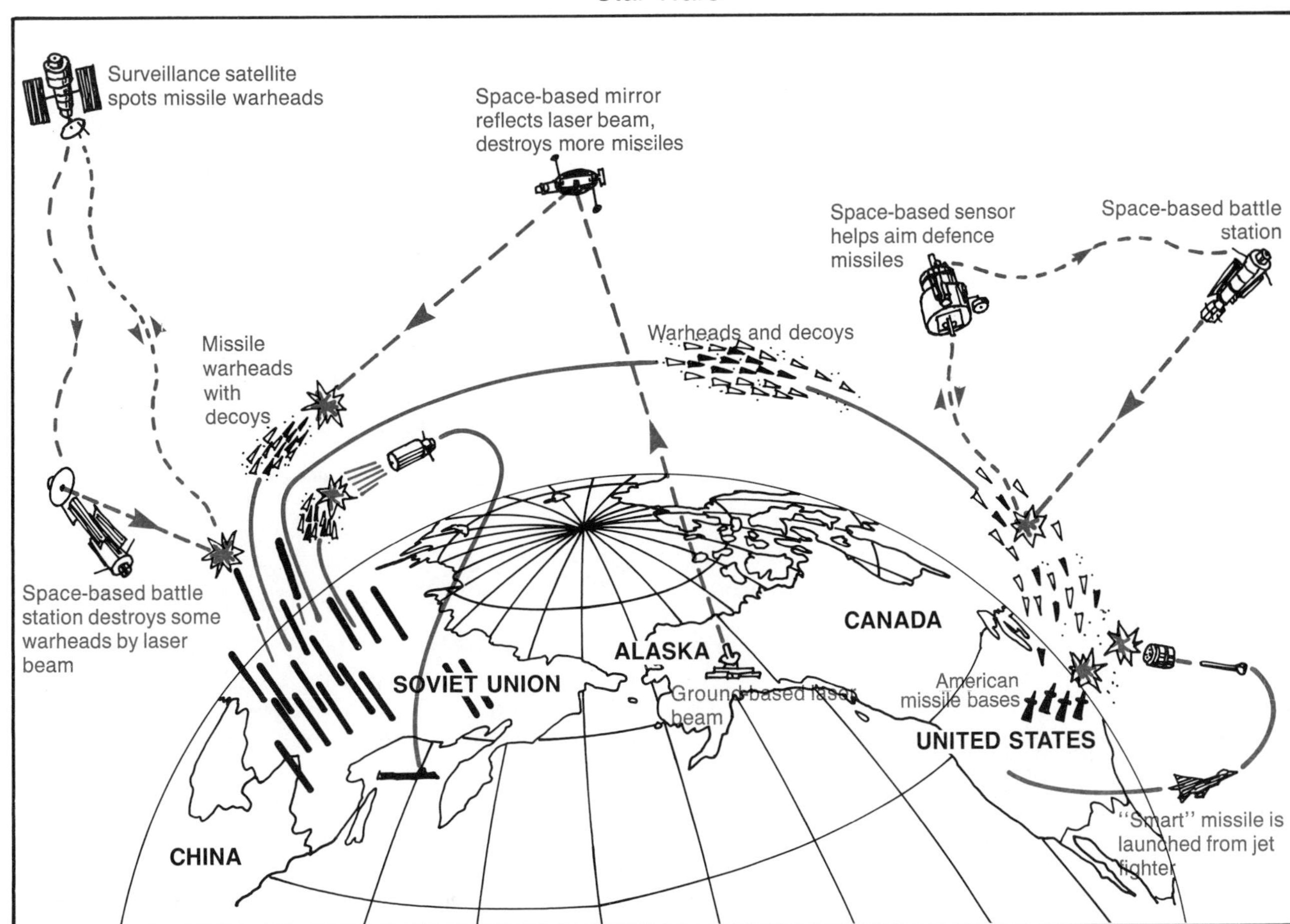

Source: *The Toronto Star* (March 9, 1985)

The diagram above gives some idea of the complex defence system known as "Star Wars." It is intended to shoot down missiles from space. In 1987 "Star Wars" was still in the design stage.

nicknamed Star Wars. Its formal name was Strategic Defence Initiative (SDI).

Reagan's proposal was based on his faith in the superiority of American scientific know-how. He challenged American scientists to create a near-perfect defence against intercontinental ballistic missiles. The president justified SDI partly on the grounds that it was designed purely for defence rather than for attacking anyone. Also, it could become a useful "bargaining chip" in arms-control talks with the Soviet Union. If the Soviets really wanted the United States to cancel Star Wars, they might make some important concessions in return.

However, critics of the SDI plan called it a gigantic error. Some believed that the plan was scientifically impossible to complete. If this was so, huge sums of money would be wasted trying to make the project work. And even if Star Wars *could* be completed, it would only force the Soviet Union to take dangerous steps of its own, such as:

a launch a pre-emptive attack before the United States could put a complete missile defence system into position;
b build an enormous supply of additional ICBMs so that it could confuse and overwhelm the new American defence system;
c develop its own version of Star Wars and thereby make all American offensive missiles useless.

In 1985 the United States invited its major allies, including Canada, to participate in the development of Star Wars. Opinion in Canada was divided. The Mulroney government compromised. While private companies could participate in Star Wars if they wished, the government itself would not do so.

1 Suggest at least three reasons why the United States would want its allies, including Canada, to participate in Star Wars.

2 What potential advantages might Canada enjoy by participating in Star Wars research and development?

3 Why might such involvement also be dangerous?

4 In your opinion, should the government of Canada have become involved in Star Wars or not? What is the key reason for your view?

5 What decision or decisions has our government made regarding Canadian involvement in Star Wars since 1984?

6 Some defence experts claim that if Star Wars is developed, Canada will not be able to avoid involvement. In what sense could this be true? (Clue: Think of how the defence system would work. Would it be more effective if Star Wars equipment were actually positioned on Canadian soil?)

7 Examine the cartoon below. What statement is it making about possible American military strategy? How does this cartoon relate to the Star Wars issue?

News Item: NUKES FOR CANADA IN U.S. PLANS

AMERICAN POLITICAL INFLUENCE IN CANADA

The United States can put great pressure on Canadian politicians. Usually, our neighbours are very friendly. But they know what they want. They can be very persuasive. As the saying goes, "They can make us offers we *cannot* refuse."

To get their way they could harm our economy. They could put hundreds of thousands of Canadians out of work. Our standard of living could be sharply lowered. They could literally ruin certain businesses, industries or whole communities. Just the threat of using such powers would probably be enough to make a Canadian politician co-operate. We can see that Canada pays a steep price for having a branch-plant economy.

INTERFERENCE IN ELECTIONS

American political leaders have, in the past, interfered in Canadian elections. They have helped candidates who favour American interests. Sometimes they have wanted to see an "undesirable" Canadian politician beaten. This happened in 1963. American interests gave large funds to the campaign of the Liberal party. They hoped to help defeat the Progressive Conservative government of John Diefenbaker. (Some reasons for their attitude have been suggested earlier in this chapter.) The Diefenbaker government was defeated.

1 American business corporations and labour unions have given money to Canadian politicians and political parties. Why would they do this? Should it be allowed?

What is the point of this cartoon? Could you conceive of another cartoon to illustrate the point? Try to create at least the idea for the cartoon, if not the actual final drawing. Compare your idea with those of classmates. Which is the most effective cartoon? Why? Over what specific issues could the Mulroney government be accused of "falling prey" to the American Eagle?

2 It has been suggested that the United States government sometimes pressures American companies to make political contributions in Canada. Why would it do this?

3 In the past, American presidents have offered their own expert political advisers to certain Canadian leaders. Why? Should this be allowed?

4 Examine media accounts of the 1984 Canadian federal election. Why was the Reagan administration pleased with:

a Pierre Trudeau's retirement from politics,
b John Turner's selection as the new leader of the Liberal party;
c the defeat of the Liberals by Brian Mulroney and his Progressive Conservative party?

One Canadian professor has suggested that no Canadian government can survive without American approval and support. This claim may be exaggerated. Still, it makes us stop and think.

All things considered, can we really call ourselves a sovereign, independent country?

ACID RAIN: THE "ACID TEST" OF OUR INFLUENCE IN WASHINGTON

We know that the United States can exert great influence over governments in Canada. But is the reverse also true? If it was, we could use our influence to obtain better trade deals and other concessions. In recent times, the issue of acid rain has demonstrated how little power we really have over the Americans. It also shows how badly we *need* some sort of influence over them.

Acid rain is a product of industrialization. When coal is burned in power plants, smelters or steel factories, it gives off certain gases. Chief among these is sulphur dioxide. These emissions become part of the atmosphere. They combine with water droplets in the atmosphere to form sulphuric and other acids. Then they fall to earth as rain, snow or fog.

Wind currents can carry this pollution hundreds or even thousands of miles from its sources. Industrial plants in the Ohio River valley, Pennsylvania and West Virginia are among the worst sources of acid rain. Other serious offenders include the Inco plant at Sudbury, Ontario, and the Noranda smelter in northwestern Quebec. Together they were respon-

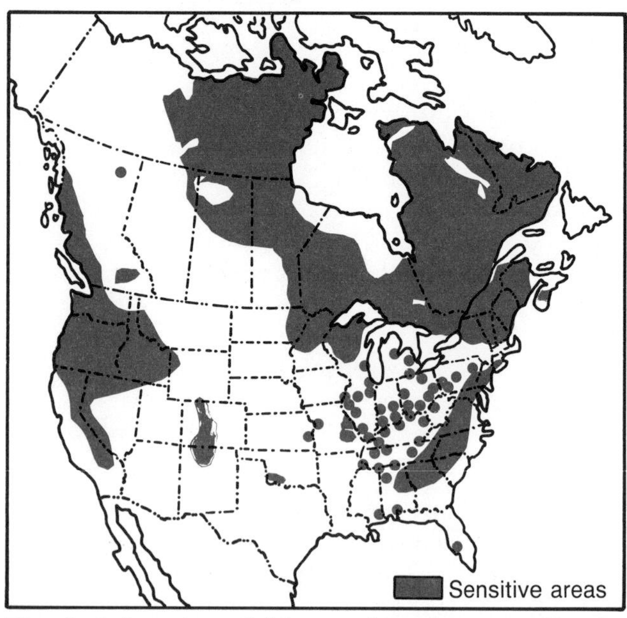

The shaded sections of this map show the areas of North America which are most sensitive to the effects of acid rain. The dots indicate the main sources of sulphur dioxide.

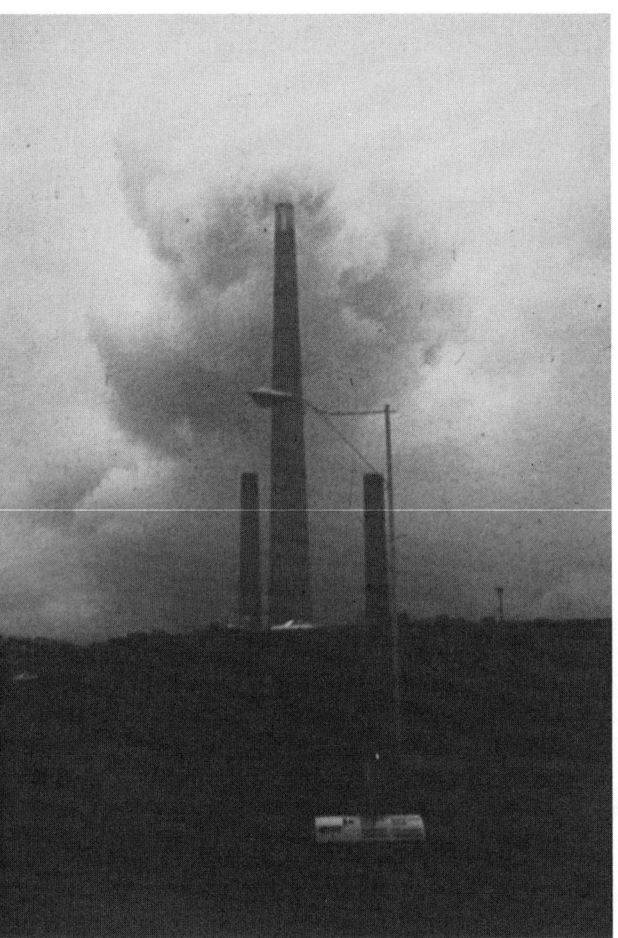
The damage from acid rain develops slowly, and is unseen at first. But eventually trees are harmed, aquatic life is killed and damage appears on buildings, automobiles and other exposed surfaces. Already, thousands of Canadian lakes are either "dead" or in serious trouble. Our environment officials predict the loss of almost 50 000 lakes by the year 2000 if nothing is done. Another concern relates to our food supply. As the earth soaks up these pollutants, they will begin to appear in our fruit, vegetables, meat and dairy products, not to mention our drinking water.

sible for about 60 percent of the acid rain originating in Canada in 1987. Ontario's coal-burning power plants were another important source of this pollution. Recently, huge spending programs were undertaken to greatly reduce emissions from these plants. Costs are being shared by the federal government, and the companies and provincial governments directly concerned. By 1994 it is hoped that acid rain from these sources will be reduced by about 75 percent.

Unfortunately, there has been less progress on the American side of the border. Environmentalists and groups of concerned citizens have tried to apply pressure for action. States that are suffering from the effects of acid rain support such measures. But some states depend for their prosperity on the mining or burning of coal. Tens of thousands of jobs are at stake. It would cost billions of dollars each year to clean up the effects of acid rain and reduce future emissions. Recent American presidents have tended to drag their feet on this issue. Most notable among these was Ronald Reagan. He was well known for his refusal to believe that acid rain is a serious problem. He protested that further research was necessary. He did his best to reduce funding for such research and for proposed clean-up projects.

In the mid-1980s, President Reagan and Prime Minister Mulroney discussed acid rain at a series of top-level meetings. Mr. Mulroney was pressured by concerned people in both countries. They urged him to "get tough" with the president over the acid-rain issue. But this was easier said than done. Also, Mr. Mulroney seemed more anxious to secure other objectives with the Americans. Chief among these was a free-trade deal.

Thus, while some progress has been made, the problem still remains. Apparently, it will be solved only when and if our two countries are led by politicians who can agree that a solution is essential.

1 If acid rain is to be reduced, who should pay the costs? No matter how the bill is divided, who will *actually* be paying? Why is this?

2 Do you believe that the Canadian people would be willing to pay noticeably higher taxes to help solve the acid-rain problem? Conduct your own opinion survey to see if your belief is correct. (This exercise will be meaningful only if you do enough advance research to provide valid questions and statistics about the volume and sources of acid rain and the estimated costs of clean-up.)

3 Some of the companies that are major contributors to acid-rain pollution in Canada are American-controlled. What is ironic about this situation?

4 Canada is steadily reducing its acid-rain emissions. Does this give us more or less right to criticize the Americans for "dragging their feet" on this issue? Why?

5 Another pollution issue between Canada and the United States is the rapid growth of toxic wastes in the Great Lakes. If you happen to live in the Great Lakes basin, you might research this topic. As a political problem, how does it compare with acid rain? Together, what serious impact might these problems have on your life?

BUILDING YOUR LEARNING SKILLS

FOCUSSING ON THE ISSUE

1 Try to make a short series of statements that sum up the main points of this chapter. Each statement should contain only one major idea. The statements should have a logical sequence.

2 The authors suggest the photos appearing on pages 301, 302, 307, and 309 as illustrations of the main points of this chapter. Suggest reasons for their choices. Turn through the pages of this chapter and look for additional or better choices they might have made.

3 The following terms appeared in this chapter. Try to recall their meanings and how they were used.

ABM system
acid rain
atomic bomb
BOMARC
branch-plant economy
cold war
deterrence
DEW Line
espionage
hydrogen bomb
ICBM
military ally
Minuteman
NATO
NORAD
obsolescence
radar
"smart" bomb
Star Wars

RESEARCHING

1 Investigate the story of Igor Gouzenko. How did the Canadian government almost bungle this glorious opportunity to expose Soviet spying in North America? Why did Prime Minister King at first not want to know what Gouzenko had to reveal? What can you discover about Gouzenko's subsequent secret life in Canada?

2 NORAD headquarters in Colorado have experienced several frightening false alarms. Some of these involved Canadian officers who came very close to having to make difficult and dangerous decisions. Try to uncover at least one such story, and share the details with the class.

3 In connection with question two above, a very effective film was made in the 1960s. It was based on a book entitled *Failsafe* and took the same title. The theme was the danger of accidental nuclear war. Obtain a copy of this film on videotape, either by renting it from a commercial outlet or by taping it when it is next shown on television.

4 Try to discover three issues *not* discussed in this textbook on which the Canadian and American governments are in significant disagreement. Newspapers and magazines will help. Check the vertical files and periodicals index in your library. What is Canada's position on each issue? Do you agree with these positions?

5 In the early 1960s, John Diefenbaker's government fell apart. Some of its problems related to our military and political relationship with the United States and our policy regarding nuclear weapons. Gather as much information about this situation as possible. You will be using it in later exercises.

1·2·3 ORGANIZING

1 To follow up on question five above, under what headings will you organize your findings? In what sequence will you place them? Why?

2 Place the following events in proper chronological order.
- Prime Minister Diefenbaker delays support for the United States during the Cuban Missile Crisis.
- Canada joins NORAD.
- The Trudeau government agrees to permit Cruise missile testing in Canadian airspace.
- Prime Minister Pearson gets "shaken up" by President Johnson for publicly criticizing American bombing policy in Vietnam.
- Igor Gouzenko defects to Canada from the Soviet embassy in Ottawa.
- The American supertanker *Manhattan* makes its historic trip through the Northwest Passage.

3 Examine the following list. Which item does not belong? Why?
- Cruise
- hydrogen bomb
- ICBM
- Minuteman
- Polaris

4 Which item does not belong in this list? Why?
- Cruise
- ICBM
- Polaris
- NATO
- hydrogen bomb

5 Design and develop an organizer chart that summarizes the key ideas of this chapter. How many columns will you need? What will be their headings? Which important points belong in each column?

COMMUNICATING

1 For ages nations have engaged in what is called propaganda. This is a special way of advertising or communicating messages. The purpose is to influence the thinking and thus the actions of large groups of people. The information presented might be true, distorted or even false. But the object is always to create strongly positive or negative thoughts and feelings in those who receive the messages. Study some forms of propaganda (for example, commercial ads, taped recordings of political speeches or government news agencies such as Voice of America). What media of communication are being used in the examples you have uncovered? In each example, what is the message? What techniques have been employed to try to deliver the message effectively? Could you improve on them in any ways?

2 As a follow-up to the above exercise, you, alone or with some classmates, can develop some propaganda of your own. It should be in favour of the Canadian–American military alliance. Your work could include radio or television news items, leaflets or government bulletins. Another student or team of students could take the *opposite* stand on the same issue and also develop appropriate propaganda items. Once the work is finished, each side should examine and evaluate the work of the other. Comment on strong points and offer suggestions for improvement where possible. Can you find any examples of real propaganda for comparison purposes?

3 Igor Gouzenko was a cipher clerk in the Soviet embassy in Ottawa. Therefore, he was involved in a special kind of secret communication that most governments use. This is called a code system. Morse code is a very simple example of such a system. The trouble is, Morse code is

internationally known and thus is not suitable for secret communications. Governments often require top secrecy when communicating with armed forces commanders, diplomats, spies or other employees. To ensure secrecy, governments develop their own complicated codes using numbers or letters or combinations of these. They must work out a system to represent letters, numbers and punctuation marks in code. A cipher clerk must be an expert in such a code and be able to put messages into code (encode) or translate them out of code (decode) as required.

If time permits, work out a simple code with friends or classmates. Practise sending messages by whatever means available. You might then wish to do further research into this business of secret codes. There is an interesting story about how the Allies broke a top-secret German code in World War II and the uses to which they put this discovery. You might also try to find out how codes are designed today, how messages are sent and received and what machines are used to encode and decode messages.

4 Practise note-taking from audio and/or visual sources of information. A few students could prepare and bring to class audio or video cassette tapes of certain news stories. (Ideally, these should relate to the topic of Canadian–American relations.) Play a tape for those students participating in this exercise. The first time through, students should concentrate on identifying the key issue(s) and supporting points. Then they should think of an organizational plan for their notes (headings, subheadings, sequence). Next, play the tape again. Concentrate on filling in the notes as completely as possible (point form is strongly suggested). A third playing of the tape is optional. Then students should compare notes and add to their own where desired.

Next each student should formulate a series of questions testing factual knowledge of the tape's contents. Finally, formulate a key question that asks the student to analyze, sum up or otherwise comment upon the tape's overall theme. All questions should be clearly phrased. Now attempt someone else's test. Results can be scored. *Most importantly*, a discussion should follow regarding "do's" and "don'ts" of note-taking, organization, question-framing and effective two-way communication.

ANALYZING

1 Compare the reasons for Canada's joining NATO with those behind our later formation of NORAD with the United States. Make separate lists of the similarities and differences. Do you see any cause-effect relationship?

2 Identify three major issues from this chapter on which Canada and the United States were in disagreement. Summarize the effects of each dispute on the overall relationship. Which of the three was most serious? least serious?

3 Look more deeply at the matter of Canada's continuing membership in NATO and NORAD. Could or should Canada withdraw from these alliances? Try to find detailed arguments by "experts" on each side of this question. Which arguments impress you the most? Why? How feasible would a withdrawal by Canada be? Would it be easier to get out of one than the other? If so, why?

4 Think back on the main points made in this unit. Can our government consider itself fairly independent of the United States? Could it be more so? Explain your answers.

APPLYING YOUR KNOWLEDGE

1 Since we are allies, is it likely that the United States would spy on Canada? Why or why not?

2 If we declared ourselves neutral in the cold war, could we actually remain neutral if trouble occurred? If a major war broke out and we were attacked, would the United States defend us whether we wanted to be defended or not?

3 If the United States invaded Canada (which is highly unlikely), the Soviet Union almost certainly would not help us. Think of at least three reasons why not.

4 In a previous exercise, it was suggested that you research the circumstances of the downfall of

the Diefenbaker government in the early 1960s. If you did so, you discovered that some of the key reasons for the government's fall related to our military ties with the United States (support in the Cuban Missile Crisis, the adoption of nuclear weapons). You can now apply your knowledge in a simulation.

Set up the class to act as the Diefenbaker cabinet. Key roles will be played by such people as George Hees, Douglas Harkness, Alvin Hamilton and John Diefenbaker himself. (Their portfolios and attitudes on the issue should be researched if they are not fully known at this point.) Each member of the class will be a cabinet member with the right to speak on the debate OR an "expert" who can testify to the cabinet on some point on which they need guidance. These experts can be neutral on the key question, or they can themselves be trying to influence the cabinet's ultimate decision. The question: *Should Canada accept nuclear weapons from the United States?* At the time, these weapons would have included atomic warheads for our BOMARC missiles, nuclear bombs for our Starfighter aircraft in Europe and atomic shells for our field artillery.

The discussion should be within a 1960s context. Once your cabinet decision is made, compare it with the real ones made by the Diefenbaker and Pearson governments.

Finally, apply your understanding to the situation today. Which of the arguments for or against Canada having nuclear weapons are still relevant today? Which are weak or even irrelevant? Which are even stronger now than they were in the 1960s?

Do you know the policy of our present government on this issue? Once you do, if you don't agree, consider actions that you could take on this vitally important question.

5 You are prime minister of Canada, and the American president secretly says to you, "You don't have to officially adopt nuclear weapons for your armed forces; just let us store some of ours, secretly, within Canada in case we have to use them sometime." What will your decision be? Why? (There have been rumours in the press from time to time that Canada *has* quietly done this for the United States.)

chapter 17

AMERICAN CULTURAL INFLUENCE: CAN WE TELL "US" FROM "THEM"?

TOPIC ORGANIZER **PAGE**

THEME ORGANIZER

- An important part of being an independent country is having a clear, strong national identity.
- This identity includes many things: people, geography, history, institutions and culture (which includes language, the arts, customs and traditions).
- Canada does possess a distinctive national identity.
- However, this identity is in constant and growing danger from the powerful influence of American culture.
- This American influence is exerted mainly through the mass media: television, films and magazines.
- Canada needs the policies, leadership and determination that will protect and nourish our arts, education system and our own mass media, all of which contribute strongly to our distinctive identity as Canadians.

INTRODUCTION

"Canadian independence from the United States? BIG DEAL! There isn't any important difference between the two countries anyway."

1 Have you ever heard that kind of statement before? Who would be more likely to say this — a Canadian, an American or someone from a third country? Why? Who would be least likely to say it? Why?

2 Can you state important differences between

Canada and the United States? Between Canadians and Americans?

3 Set up a simulation in your classroom. Create a team of four or five investigators. The rest of the students should represent people from several different countries. Obviously, these should include Canada and the United States. The job of the investigators is to pick out the Canadian and American members of the group. Set up your own rules. However, you cannot ask direct questions such as, "What is your nationality?" Afterwards, the investigators will report to the class. Why did they choose the questions they used? What clues did they use?

4 Imagine that you could no longer live in Canada. In what other country would you choose to live? Why? Compare your answers with those of classmates, friends or family.

5 Use the ideas gained in questions three and four above to help you with your next task: Make a list of important similarities and differences between Canadians and Americans. Include points about values, life-styles, customs, culture, government and economics. Which seem to be greater, the similarities or the differences? Which are more important? Why?

6 How important do you think it is for Canada to be and feel different from the United States? Why? How is this question connected to the idea of Canadian independence?

Before reading on, study the chart of key words and ideas that follows.

KEY WORDS AND IDEAS IN THIS CHAPTER

Term	Meaning	Sample Use
Americanize	to make something American in nature or style	Canada is becoming Americanized in some ways. For example, we drive American cars, wear American-style clothes and use American chain hotels, motels and restaurants.
cultural identity	a people's awareness of who and what they are	Canadians are developing a cultural identity. Sharing experiences, customs and arts helps this feeling to grow. The strong impact of the United States on Canadian life can make it hard to develop our own identity.
independence	the ability to get along without relying on anyone or anything else	Canada and the United States both gained independence from Britain. We are now trying to be independent of the United States. The Americans have considerable influence in our affairs.
mass media	means of communication that reach huge numbers of people; include radio, television, newspapers and magazines	The mass media are important in shaping the ideas of the people. The media can help develop our culture, identity and unity. We are often exposed to American media and their influence.

nationalism	a feeling of pride in and loyalty to a particular country or nation	Nationalism is strong in the United States. It is also strong in Canada, although Canadians do not express their nationalism as openly as Americans do. Nationalism must remain strong in Canada if our country is to survive.
pop culture	"popular" culture that appeals to the great majority of people; includes television, most movies and popular music; does not include opera, ballet or classical music	Our pop culture is strongly influenced by the United States. Canadian identity is stronger in our "formal" arts, such as painting and literature.

THE IMPORTANCE OF BEING DIFFERENT

We have been looking at the ties that exist between Canada and the United States. These ties are mainly economic, military and political. We have seen some of the benefits of these ties. Some of the problems have also been discussed. Perhaps the biggest danger in the American connection is that we could lose our independence. Canada could lose its independence as a country in one of two ways.

First, we might be taken over by force. This seems unlikely. Still, we are very important to the United States. They need our natural resources. We also are a valuable market for their goods and services. In a way, we are their "northern shield." We stand between them and their major rival, the Soviet Union. The United States must have our military help. This is mainly needed to patrol our airspace and coastal waters. It is unlikely that we would try to end our economic and military ties with the United States. (The reasons for this have been explained in previous chapters.) However, if we did try, we might force the Americans to act against us.

Canada could disappear as a nation in a second way. It is a quiet, slow and fairly pleasant process. It is also the more likely and dangerous way we could lose our independence. At the end of Chapter 15, we referred to the "American embrace." It is cozy and very strong. As we settle into it, we feel more and more comfortable and safe. But if we do not take care we might wake up too late. We might discover that we have sold our riches, that we have also lost control of our government and forgotten how to defend ourselves. Then that little scene in Ottawa, where the maple leaf flag is lowered and replaced by the stars and stripes, might actually take place.

1 Think back to that imaginary scene that introduced this unit. How did it make you feel?

2 Read that imaginary scene to your family and friends. How do they feel? Ask them to explain their reactions.

3 Look for opinion polls on the question of Canada becoming part of the United States. How do Canadians in general seem to feel about the idea?

4 Think about those Canadians who would not mind or who would actually prefer joining the United States. What do you think are their reasons?

5 Now consider those Canadians who are against the idea. Why do they feel this way?

6 What seems to be the main difference between those in favour of joining the United States and those against?

You have probably discovered a key idea. Some Canadians have a much stronger sense than others of a true Canadian identity. They believe that Canada *is* different from other countries, including the United States. There are things about Canada that are special.

Irving Layton

Margaret Atwood

Gabrielle Roy

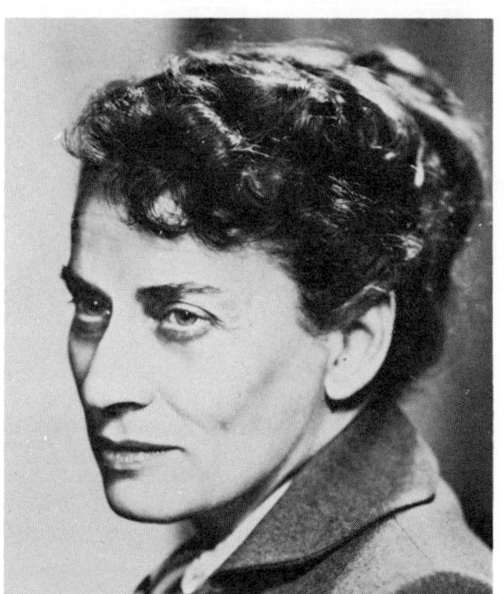

Farley Mowat

Mordecai Richler

Margaret Laurence

You may have studied the works of some of these Canadian writers.

The Stratford Festival Theatre in Stratford, Ontario, is famous for its Shakespearean plays.

The audience waits for the beginning of a performance in the Grand Théâtre de Québec.

These are worth preserving. If our country is to survive, a majority of Canadians must feel this way.

At times, it is difficult to find this Canadian identity. American ideas, ways of doing things and goods seem to be everywhere in Canada. You can easily see this for yourself. Do a survey. Ask people to name their favourite motel chains, fast-food restaurants, types of cars, TV programs and entertainment stars. Look carefully at the products in your home and school. How many of them are American? Do you see the problem?

It is true that the arts are flourishing in Canada. There are many fine Canadian writers, dancers, painters, poets and musicians. However, in many cases very few Canadians know about their works.

On the other hand, there is another type of culture. We will call it "popular culture." Popular culture is known to and enjoyed by large numbers of our people. We will now look at American influence on this level of our culture. We will also consider what we are doing about that influence.

ENTERTAINMENT

TELEVISION

Television is by far the most popular form of entertainment in North America. Studies show that by the time you entered high school, you had already spent more hours watching television than you will ever devote in your lifetime to attending school.

1 To fully appreciate how much time people spend in front of "the tube," conduct a survey of your own classmates. Ask each person to estimate his or her viewing hours per week. Make a grand total for the class and then take a simple average. (An average of 30 hours is quite normal.)

This point is, television influences us all. It is a major source of the ideas, values and impressions that we develop from a very early age. It has a powerful impact on our life-style and, indeed, on our identity.

2 Now, consider what you watch on television. Conduct another poll, this time to determine the favourite shows of your classmates. Each person should list his or her "top 20," placing them in rank order from 1 to 20. Collate the results to determine the overall "top 20" for the class. You might broaden the survey to include family members, neighbours or anyone who is willing to spend time filling out the list.

1·2·3

3 Once you have finalized the "top 20," try to find a recent overall rating for Canadian viewers or for your locality.

a What is the rank of your top *Canadian* program?

b How many of your "top 20" are Canadian shows?

c Of these, which deal with specifically Canadian themes or content? (Or how many could just as easily be mistaken for American productions?)

d If you take away sports programs, how many Canadian shows are left in the "top 10"? in the "top 20"?

Typically, an average of only two or three Canadian shows make the top 20 favourites. American producers have tremendous advantages over their Canadian competitors. They know their shows will have much larger audiences. As a result, advertisers will pay comparatively high prices to sponsor popular American shows. Therefore, production budgets can be very generous. More money can be spent paying top

TORONTO
DETROIT
"STAY WITH THE LEAFS, WE GOTTA GET OUR 60% CANADIAN"

stars, using costly special effects and exotic locales for background. As a result, $350 000 to $500 000 might be spent on a typical half-hour American show. A similar top Canadian show would be fortunate to receive $100 000 for production expenses. Naturally, many viewers will continue to find the American shows more attractive. And so the cycle goes on.

SOAP OPERAS: A SLICE OF POPULAR CULTURE

In recent years, the soap opera has become the most popular type of show on television.

1 What is a soap opera? How did the term develop?
2 Do you watch "the soaps"? If so, which ones? Which do you like best? Why?
3 How do you account for the popularity of soap operas? (Give several reasons.)
4 Do you think soap operas are realistic? In what ways are they "larger than life"?
5 Is it possible that soap operas influence people in their daily lives? If so, which influences would be positive? Could there be negative influences? If you think so, explain what they are as fully as possible.
6 Are there any successful Canadian soap operas? If so, name them. If not, why not? How important is it for there to be Canadian productions in this field?

Carl Marotte stars as gifted hockey player Pierre Lambert in the thirteen-part CBC drama series "He Shoots, He Scores." What other Canadian series have been successful in the United States?

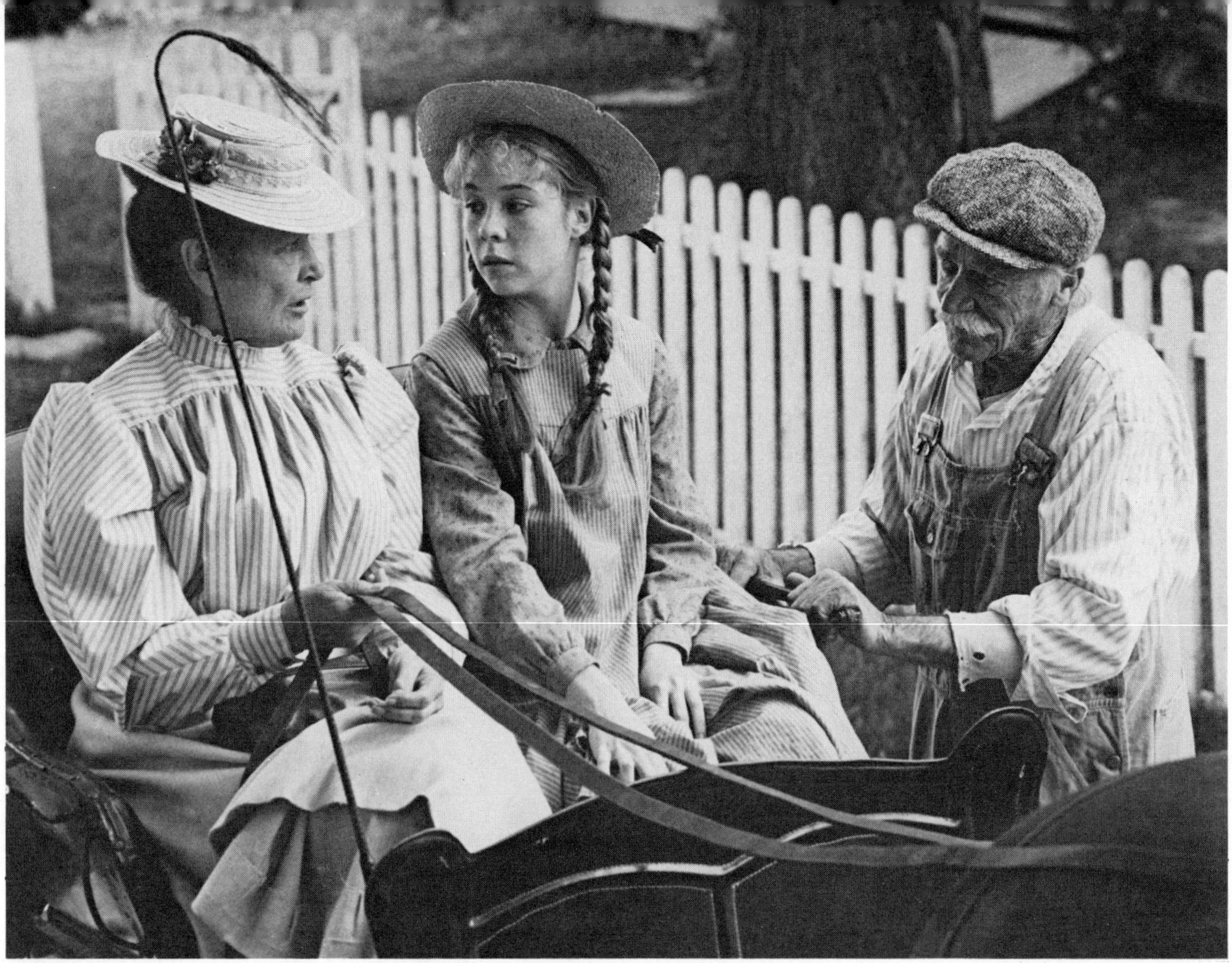

The release of *Anne of Green Gables* illustrated that Canadian films can achieve success in the United States. What other Canadian films have been successful there? *Courtesy of Sullivan Films Inc.*

FILMS

Movies are another popular form of entertainment. Look up movie advertisements in your local newspapers. How many Canadian-made films can you find? Are there other non-American films playing? If so, do they outnumber the Canadian movies? How many of the non-American films have you seen? How many would you like to see?

It seems that Canadians prefer American movie stars, too.

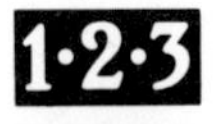

1 Choose your top ten favourite movie stars. How many are Canadian?

2 Compare your choices with those of friends, relatives or classmates. What is the trend?

3 Can you name five Canadian movie stars?

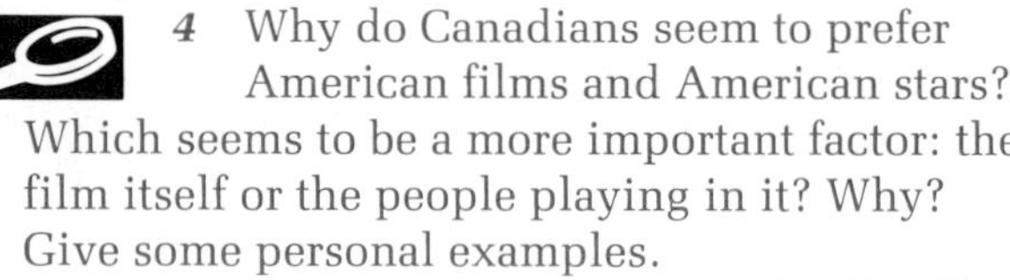

4 Why do Canadians seem to prefer American films and American stars? Which seems to be a more important factor: the film itself or the people playing in it? Why? Give some personal examples.

5 How might our heavy exposure to American shows and stars in television and movies affect us?

6 A recent study done in the United States showed that violence was increasing rapidly in American movies and television. This was true even on children's shows and during family viewing time. Did you consider this in answering question five above?

CANADA'S FEATURE FILM INDUSTRY

How can we develop a Canadian identity in films? In the 1970s, our government poured millions of dollars into the building of a feature film industry. This helped Canadians to create such fine films as *Goin' Down the Road*, *Wedding in White*, *Kamouraska*, *Mon Oncle Antoine*, *The Rowdyman* and *Why Shoot the Teacher?*

Most of these films were Canadian in every sense. They were written, produced, directed and performed by Canadians. They also dealt with Canadian places, events and themes. *Kamouraska* won some international recognition. This was probably because it dealt with universal themes such as loneliness, jealousy, infidelity and greed. However, it had a distinctive French-Canadian setting. Even more well received was *The Apprenticeship of Duddy Kravitz*. This film was based on the novel by a Montreal writer, Mordecai Richler. An American actor was brought in to play the title role. Perhaps this had something to do with the film's box-office success. More likely, this success was due to the quality of the story. The fact that the story took place in Canada was downplayed in American promotion. Thus, its themes and humour could be more easily shared by the large American audience.

Feature films are commercial (business) ventures. Therefore, they must make profits for their investors. To succeed, they need large audiences. Not many Canadian films have markets outside Canada. This is especially true if they deal with Canadian themes and star Canadian performers. Even *within* Canada, they must compete with American and other foreign films. Thus, Canadian film-makers face several difficult choices. They can make low-class movies that feature sex, violence, the supernatural and other cheap thrills. They can use American stars to "hype" (stimulate) the box-office. Or they can seek help from the Canadian government. The government now offers tax advantages for films made in Canada. Unfortunately, this has attracted more foreign than Canadian producers to make films here.

In 1984 a survey was done among Canada's leading

A scene from *Mon Oncle Antoine*. This film won international recognition in several film festivals.

film critics. They were asked to name the all-time best Canadian-made films. Here are the results:

1 *Mon Oncle Antoine* (1971)
2 *Goin' Down the Road* (1970)
3 *Les Bons Debarras* (1979)
4 *The Apprenticeship of Duddy Kravitz* (1974)
5 *Les Ordres* (1974)

By comparison, the all-time top-five Canadian-made films for money-making, up to 1984, were:

1 *Meatballs* ($4.2 million)
2 *The Apprenticeship of Duddy Kravitz* ($2.3 million)
3 *Black Christmas* ($2 million)
4 *Murder by Decree* ($1.9 million)
5 *Why Shoot the Teacher?* ($1.8 million)

1 How many of the above-mentioned Canadian films have you seen? Have you heard of any of them before? Ask your parents the same questions.

2 Name some other Canadian feature films. How many have you seen? Do you know whether they made profits?

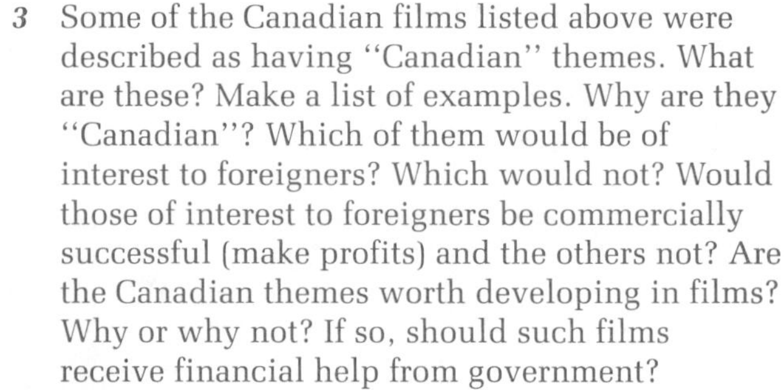

3 Some of the Canadian films listed above were described as having "Canadian" themes. What are these? Make a list of examples. Why are they "Canadian"? Which of them would be of interest to foreigners? Which would not? Would those of interest to foreigners be commercially successful (make profits) and the others not? Are the Canadian themes worth developing in films? Why or why not? If so, should such films receive financial help from government?

4 Is it important to have a Canadian feature film industry? Explain your answer. If you say yes, how could we encourage its growth? Should Canadians produce "garbage" movies with mass appeal? (Would you feel differently if you were an investor in Canadian films?) Should we import foreign directors and stars? Should we penalize foreign films and performers in Canada?

THE MASS MEDIA

The mass media are means of communication that reach large numbers of people. Thus, they include

Press coverage of a political party rally in a Canadian city.

radio, television, newspapers and magazines. The mass media affect our thoughts and values, and so they have an influence on our culture. In Canada the media are strongly influenced by the United States. We have seen how many Canadians prefer American television and films to our own.

This is a serious situation for two reasons. First, the media *are* mass. They reach huge numbers of people. The most gifted Canadian high-school teacher might reach 5000 to 6000 students in his or her career. A popular half-hour show on television will draw several million viewers. Second, we are exposed to the media for long periods of time.

Review the survey of television viewing habits you did for the exercise on page 326.

1 What was the average number of hours your classmates spent watching television in one week?

2 Extend your survey. Find out the amount of time spent doing these things in one day:
   a listening to radio;
   b reading newspapers;
   c reading magazines.

   What are individual totals for a week? What is your total? Take an average. Add it to the results of your first survey. How big a role do the mass media play in your life? In that of your classmates?

3 On which medium do you and your friends spend the most time? the least time?

4 Rank the five most popular magazines among your classmates. How many are American? Canadian?

5 Which of the five media under consideration (film, television, radio, newspapers, magazines) do you think has the most Canadian content or shows the most Canadian influence? Which as the least? How do these estimates relate to the popularity of these media among your peers?

Canadians rely heavily on American mass media. This must affect our culture. It seems to make us more "American" in outlook and style. It becomes harder and harder to develop a distinctive culture of our own.

This problem will not be easy to solve. Here is an example to show you why. Imagine that you own a radio or television station in Canada. Of course, you want to attract the biggest possible audience. Then you can ask higher rates from advertisers. What would you do to gain a large audience? Would you tend to use Canadian or American material and performers? Now pretend you are a Canadian advertiser. Naturally, you want to reach the most people. You want to advertise in magazines and on radio or television programs with large numbers of readers, listeners or viewers. Will these be mainly Canadian or American?

POPULAR MUSIC

Who are your favourite popular music performers and groups? Many of the top song-writers, record companies, studios, back-up musicians and tour organizers are Americans, too. Make a class list. Are most of your favourites American or Canadians? Do you know which they are? The biggest market for pop music is the United States. Therefore, it must appeal to American tastes. The American style in popular music is copied by foreign performers and writers.

However, Canadians have made a very strong impact on popular music. Here are some famous examples.

Bryan Adams
Paul Anka
The Band
Robert Charlebois
Bruce Cockburn
Burton Cummings
Glass Tiger
Corey Hart
Dan Hill
Gordon Lightfoot
Loverboy
Murray McLauchlan
Joni Mitchell
Anne Murray
Platinum Blonde
Carol Pope
Rush
René Simard
Triumph
Neil Young
Gilles Vigneault

1 What names can you add to the list?

2 Do you think that popular music plays an important part in a country's culture? If so, can you explain why?

3 Pick a Canadian pop musician, group or song that you consider to have a Canadian identity.

Canadian pop musicians turn on the power! In a now-famous 1985 recording session, some of the biggest names in our pop music industry gathered to record "Tears Are Not Enough." The number quickly climbed to the top of the charts and helped raise a large sum of money for famine relief in Ethiopia. How many of these prominent Canadian performers can you identify?

From left to right: Front row, Anne Murray, Geddy Lee, Joni Mitchell and Neil Young; Middle Row, Burton Cummings, Carroll Baker, Veronique Beliveau and Bryan Adams; Back Row, Murray McLauchlin, Liberty Silver, Mike Reno, Robert Charlebois and Ronnie Hawkins.

What makes the musician, group or song Canadian? Is it style? lyrics?

4 Which do you consider most important for developing a distinctively Canadian culture: television, films or pop music? Explain your answer.

SPORTS

North Americans are enthusiastic about sports. This is especially true of professional sports. Vast numbers of people are involved in or affected by sports. Sports have become big business. Sports are an important part of our culture and way of life.

Can you find the differences between what is Canadian and what is American in "pro" sports?

1 Name your five favourite sports. Can any of these be considered native to Canada? What sports, if any, orginated in Canada? How popular are they in this country?

2 Which are your three favourite teams in your top five sports? Is the first choice in each your own

THE "TALENT DRAIN" OR "GO SOUTH YOUNG WOMAN/MAN"

Many talented Canadians have had to go south to win success. This has been true of people in many fields: business people, actors, musicians, comedians, film directors, athletes and writers are some examples.

1 Rich Little, Paul Anka, Michael J. Fox, Norman Jewison, Anne Murray, Donald Sutherland and others have found fame in the United States. How many names can you add to this list?

2 Why do you think this happens? Does it make Canadian culture stronger or weaker? Does it affect the Americans' influence over us? Explain your answer.

3 What (if anything) can be done about this situation?

Sometimes, talented Canadians have simply been ignored in their own country. More often, though, the chances for success are simply greater south of the border. The American market is ten times larger than ours. Salaries, too, are bigger. More money can be spent on production. Often, Americans are more willing to risk money on new ventures than we are.

Michael J. Fox moved to Los Angeles and became a teenage idol for American youth. What other Canadian stars moved to the United States to further their entertainment careers?

Something else limits chances for talented Canadian performers. Canadians often import American talent for big jobs in Canada. The Canadian National Exhibition is held each summer in Toronto. Its managers bring in many Americans to star in the big grandstand shows.

Some Canadian cities have cultural centres. These are used to stage plays, shows or other forms of entertainment. Often, Canadian performances lose money. How do these centres survive? Some receive government grants. But most bring in American headliners to attract bigger crowds and earn more money. A performer is paid mainly on the basis of audience appeal. Thus, foreign stars are usually paid more than Canadians, even while performing in Canada. Canadian-made films often star American or other foreign actors. Even in business, large companies sometimes bring in American executives to fill key positions. Why do you think this is done?

You can see why talented Canadians often seek their fame and fortune elsewhere, mainly in the United States. Perhaps nothing can change these facts. We could look at it from another angle. Are you proud when you hear about Canadians who have "made it" in the United States? Perhaps their success can boost Canada's image and make our culture stronger. It still seems sad, though, to see them leave Canada for "greener pastures."

1 On the other hand, some Canadians do *not* "make it" in the United States. Try to think of some examples. Are these "failures" victories for Canadian culture? Or are they just failures? Why?

2 Occasionally, talented Americans choose to live and work in Canada. Can you give some examples? Does their work retain an American character, or does it become Canadian in nature? Or does it have a more universal appeal? Why might some American artists prefer to live here?

hometown team? How many of your favourites are based in the United States?

3 Look at the sports pages of a major newspaper. If it is the baseball season, find out how many baseball teams are Canadian. Explain your findings. Hockey is a Canadian game. If it is the hockey season, find out how many professional hockey teams are Canadian. How many are American? Why is this?

1·2·3 4 Name your five favourite stars in each of your five top sports. How many are Canadian? American? Did you choose them as favourites because of their nationality? If not, why did you pick them? When you are watching a contest between Canadian and American teams, do you think about national pride? Do you think it is part of the competition? Why or why not?

Paul Henderson scores the winning goal against the Soviet Union in the final game of the first ever Canada—USSR hockey tournament, 1972. Find some people who remember watching this goal being scored. Ask them how they reacted. What were their feelings? Why? What does this say about the importance of sports in helping to shape a country's identity?

In 1977 Prime Minister Trudeau made a speech in Washington, DC. He used professional sport as an example of Canadian-American harmony. He noted that Washington hockey fans support their NHL team without thinking that most of the players are Canadians. Similarly, Montreal and Toronto baseball fans cheer their almost entirely American teams.

However, not long before, the Trudeau goverment had interfered in professional football in Canada. It stopped the new World Football League from setting up teams in Canada. This league was mainly American. But the backers of a proposed Toronto team were Canadians. Mr. Trudeau claimed that the Canadian Football League (CFL) had to be protected. Its championship game for the Grey Cup was a major Canadian custom. It was a part of our culture. It had to be preserved. Politics can be funny! Football is essentially an American game. Even in Canada, many of the top players, coaches and managers are Americans. Yet a football game is thought of as a part of our culture.

1 Are you a fan of Canadian football? If not, pose these questions to someone who is. How do you choose favourite players? By their ability? nationality? for some other reason?

2 Do you believe that a certain number of players on each Canadian team must be Canadians, regardless of ability? Or would you rather see your team go after the best possible players and ignore their nationality? Explain your answer. If you prefer the second choice, how would you give Canadians the chance to play professional football? Look at this issue from another angle. What would happen to American hockey teams if fans in the United States insisted that their teams be mainly American?

3 Do you think that Canadian athletes playing in the United States represent a threat to American culture? Do American teams or athletes threaten

our culture? Is it fair to compare the two situations? Explain your answers.

4 Should the Canadian Football League try to expand into the United States? Do you think that it would succeed? Why or why not?

5 Was the Canadian government right to stop the World Football League from establishing teams in Canada? How important are sports to the growth of a Canadian identity?

EDUCATION

Education helps shape our thoughts, ideas and values. There has been concern about American influence in this field. Many of the textbooks used in Canadian schools are written by Americans. More of them are published by American companies or Canadian branches of such companies. American ways have affected Canadian education. The "credit system" used in many Canadian high schools is an American idea. Many of the lecture methods we use also began in the United States.

Between 1977 and 1981, 40 percent of professors and 25 percent of all faculty hired by Canadian universities were foreign citizens. Of these, the great majority were Americans. The large number of American professors in Canadian colleges worries some people. Most of our colleges and universities have Americans on their staffs. Sometimes they hold key positions. Often Americans make up high percentages of the staff. There are two sides to this issue. Some people say that Canadian students must have the best professors. Why limit our choices to Canadians? Better professors will make our educational system stronger. This will enrich our culture. There is another side to the issue. Perhaps these foreign teachers present biased views. Shouldn't we offer jobs to Canadians first?

Many people want tighter controls on education. Politicians know this. Some provinces have limited the use of foreign textbooks. For example, Ontario publishes a booklet entitled *Circular 14*. It lists the textbooks approved by the government for use in Ontario schools. With a few rare exceptions, these texts must be Canadian. This means that the books must be written by Canadian citizens. They must also be manufactured in Canada. Teachers are encouraged to use Canadian learning materials wherever possible. Special permission is needed to use a textbook not listed on *Circular 14*. It is usually more difficult to gain such permission for foreign texts.

Other measures have been taken to increase the Canadian content of our educational system. Some universities have placed limits on the hiring of foreign (mainly American) professors. Several years ago, the Canadian Studies Foundation (CSF) was created. Its members came from across Canada. They were experts in the field of education. The CSF tried to encourage more study of Canada in our schools, particularly in the areas of history and geography. The CSF also helped to develop new units and courses of study featuring things Canadian. Many provinces have responded. Now there is a much greater emphasis on the study of Canada. Another CSF goal was a core curriculum for all Canadian students. This would mean that all students would study the same basic things in certain required courses. So far, this goal has not been achieved.

1 Look through your own textbooks. Examine the pages at the beginning. They contain the name of the publisher. Often they show where the book was published and printed. The names of the authors are found here, too. Sometimes their job titles are included. How many of your textbooks are published and printed in the United States? How many are written by Americans?

2 This textbook has been written by Canadians but published by an American subsidiary. Does this affect the content?

3 The authors wish to state that there has been no pressure whatsoever to present a pro-American viewpoint in this book. On the contrary, Canadian values and ideas have been stressed. Which do you think is more important, that your books be written by Canadians or published by Canadian-owned companies? Explain your answer.

4 Do you feel that you study too much about Canada in school? How much of the history,

geography and literature of other countries do you study? Do you feel it is enough? Why or why not?

5 How much American history have you studied in school? Do you think that this is appropriate, considering the importance of the United States? Have you ever criticized Americans for their lack of knowledge about Canada? Can you honestly say that you are better informed about their country than they are about yours?

WHAT CAN BE DONE?

Obviously, American culture has a powerful influence on Canada. What can we do about this? There are several choices. One would be to change the tastes of Canadians. This would be very difficult. On the other hand, we could do nothing about American cultural influence in Canada. This would be dangerous. Instead, governments in Canada have taken steps to compromise between these extremes.

Governments have given money to promote Canadian culture. Theatres and art schools have been built with these grants. The money has been used to hire teachers and to support struggling artists. Considerable money is being given to people in the feature film industry. "Canadian content" rules have been passed for television and radio broadcasting. These require stations to include specific amounts of Canadian material in their programming. There also are strict limits on the amount of foreign ownership in Canadian broadcasting.

In the early 1960s, the Canadian government began to help Canadian magazines. It ended certain tax privileges for American publications. Advertisers in these magazines had been allowed to deduct their advertising costs from their income taxes. This was

stopped. The American publications protested. They were supported by the United States government. Therefore, two powerful magazines, *Time* and *Reader's Digest*, were exempted from (not included in) these new rules. However, in 1975 the Canadian government put new demands on these two magazines. Sixty percent of their content would have to be Canadian. Seventy-five percent of the business would have to be Canadian owned. *Reader's Digest* met these terms. *Time* did not. It closed down its Canadian offices. The American version of *Time* is still available in Canada and selling well.

The effort to develop a distinctive Canadian identity goes on. There are two parts to the struggle: One involves building our own positive Canadian culture; the other means resisting powerful foreign influences, especially that of the United States. Recently, a well-known Canadian writer and editor spoke to an American audience in Washington. His remarks summed up the theme of this chapter. He said that, on the subject of Canadian culture, there are two groups in Canada. These are the nationalists and the "I don't cares." He expressed the fear that the latter group was winning. But, as he pointed out, we *must* be nationalistic. Otherwise, someone else's nationalism will roll right over us.

BUILDING YOUR LEARNING SKILLS

FOCUSSING ON THE ISSUE

1 What is the main point or theme of this chapter?
2 For each of the photographs on pages 328, 332, 333, and 334, state one important idea from this chapter that the photo symbolizes.
3 From your work on this unit you have learned that, if Canada were ever to be absorbed by the United States, it would come about in one of two ways. What do you think these would be? Elaborate briefly on each of the possible scenarios.
4 State five ways in which American culture affects Canada.
5 The following terms appeared in this chapter. Try to recall their meanings and how they were used.

Circular 14	mass media
compromise	national identity
CSF	popular culture
culture	prime time
cultural identity	soap opera
feature film	

RESEARCHING

1 Prepare a survey of the feature films currently showing in the theatres of your town or city. (What is your easiest source of information about what's playing?) Prepare two lists of the ten most popular films, one reflecting adult tastes and one reflecting the preferences of you and your peers. For each film, try to discover some significant Canadian input, such as:
   a theme or story
   b setting
   c leading actors/actresses
   d producer
   e director
   How much Canadian content is there in today's leading films?
2 Have members of the class list their favourite five or ten pop-music performers (singles or groups). Rank these in overall popularity with the class, from first to tenth. How many Canadian performers are represented? Are they in your "top ten" because they are Canadian or because of their music, appearance or publicity?
3 Each of the following items was written, spoken and/or sung by a Canadian. They express various viewpoints about the United States. Track them down, copy the words to each on separate pages and save them for a later exercise.
   a "American Woman," a song by Burton Cummings and others, copyright 1970 by Shillelagh Music Company;
   b "Homo Canadensis," a poem by Al Purdy, from *Cariboo Horses*, published by McClelland & Stewart;
   c "The Americans," a radio comment by the late Gordon Sinclair, copyright 1973 by Conestoga Music, Toronto.

4 It has been suggested that for many years, Canada has been victimized by a process known as "the brain drain" to the United States. Investigate this phenomenon. What was it? Does it still go on? What were/are its causes? Has it had any major effect on Canada? (Also, see "Applying Your Knowledge" exercises on page 339 for a suggested follow-up.)

1·2·3

ORGANIZING

1 List these famous Canadian personalities in four separate columns and choose a suitable heading for each column.

Margaret Atwood	Brian Orser
Wayne Gretzky	Anne Murray
Bryan Adams	Donald Sutherland
Carling Bassett	Oscar Peterson
Gaetan Boucher	Ben Johnson
Mordecai Richler	Liona Boyd
Margot Kidder	Bruno Gerussi
Gordon Lightfoot	Lise Payette
Pierre Berton	John Candy

2 Link the events listed below on the left with the appropriate locales, listed on the right:

Shakespearean Festival	Montreal
Canadian National Exhibition	Calgary
Shaw Festival	Charlottetown
Winter Olympics	Quebec City
Anne-of-Green-Gables Festival	Toronto
Expo '86	Niagara
Winter Carnival	Stratford
Expo '67	Vancouver

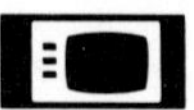

COMMUNICATING

1 Refer to question three in "Researching," above. For each of the three examples of communication considered there, decide:

a what the message is;

b which message or messages you most and least agree with;

c regardless of your personal preference, which vehicle communicates most effectively; least effectively. Explain your choice in each case.

2 Create a poem, song, cartoon, short story or slogan to communicate your own view of the United States and its people. Various classmates can share their creations with each other. Compare and evaluate the various items.

ANALYZING

1 What would it take to make the arts in Canada achieve their maximum potential? Why are these conditions unlikely to be met?

2 A recent comment in an American newspaper said that Canadians "worry too much" about the strength of their culture. It pointed out that Canada has produced many fine artists and writers. Per capita (per person in our population) we might have more talented people than the United States. What do you think of this argument?

3 Do you think there is too much anti-Americanism in Canada? Why does some of this feeling exist? Is it good for Canada? Why or why not?

4 "Even the most intelligent Americans . . . neither know nor care that they share this continent with a Canadian culture distinct from their own." What is the point of this remark? Do you agree with it? How does it relate to anti-Americanism in Canada? Would it make any difference if Americans were aware of Canadian culture and our desire to be different from Americans?

5 It has been suggested that one way to keep Canadian culture distinctive is to keep Quebec in Confederation. What is meant by this? Do you agree with the idea?

6 "What the United States wants it will get. And if we don't give them what they want, they'll take it anyway. And what they want — is most of what we've got." What is the main feeling in this comment? Do you agree with it? Why might Canadians be more hopeful than this?

APPLYING YOUR KNOWLEDGE

1 Discuss the following ideas in class: Consider the everyday lives of "average" Canadians and

Americans. What similarities and differences are there? Which are greater, the similarities or the differences? Are the differences important? What are the implications of your answers for Canadian culture and identity?

2 Which do you think is more important to Canadian independence: economic freedom or cultural freedom? Explain your answer.

3 Why will it probably always be more exciting and attractive for many of our artists to migrate to the United States than to continue their work in Canada?

4 "We like the Americans we know; we just don't like the United States." What does this mean? What material from this unit on Canadian–American relations can you use to illustrate this statement?

5 Debate one of these statements:

RESOLVED that international competition in sports helps to build Canadian unity. (Think of examples such as the Olympic Games and World Cup hockey.)

RESOLVED that a country's pop music is more important than its literature in developing a sense of cultural identity.

6 In the "Researching" section, question four asked you to find out about "the brain drain." If you did so, now consider these questions:

a Should Canada be concerned about this phenomenon?

b If so, what actions or policies could we pursue to reduce or reverse its negative effects?

c Can you foresee problems with these approaches?

7 It has been suggested that Canadians have three main options (choices) regarding future relations with the United States: Keep the same ties as we now have; move toward closer union; try to become more independent. What would be the advantages and disadvantages of each choice? Which do you prefer? Conduct a poll to see how many people agree with you. Which path do you think our government is following at present? What makes you think so? Does Canada really have a choice about the strength of its ties with the United States? Explain your answer.

8 Given all of the above, what should Canadians be doing about our relationship with the United States?

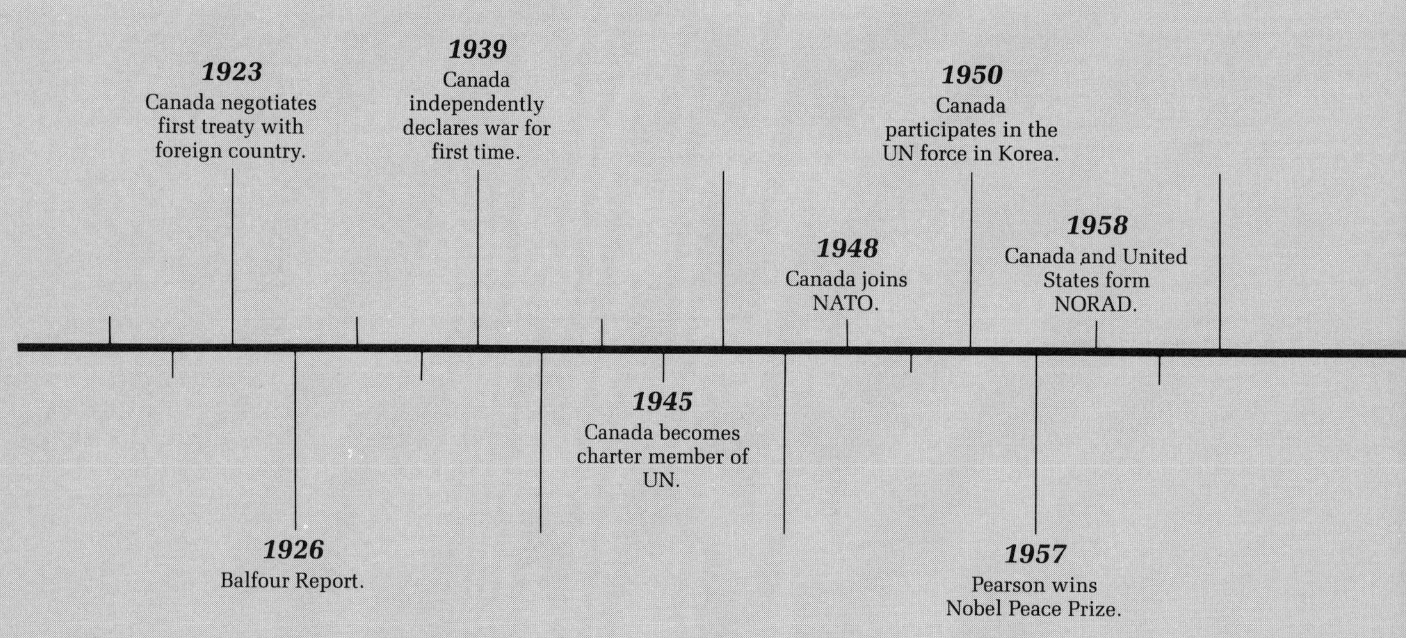
1923
Canada negotiates first treaty with foreign country.
1926
Balfour Report.
1939
Canada independently declares war for first time.
1945
Canada becomes charter member of UN.
1948
Canada joins NATO.
1950
Canada participates in the UN force in Korea.
1957
Pearson wins Nobel Peace Prize.
1958
Canada and United States form NORAD.

unit six

CANADIAN FOREIGN POLICY

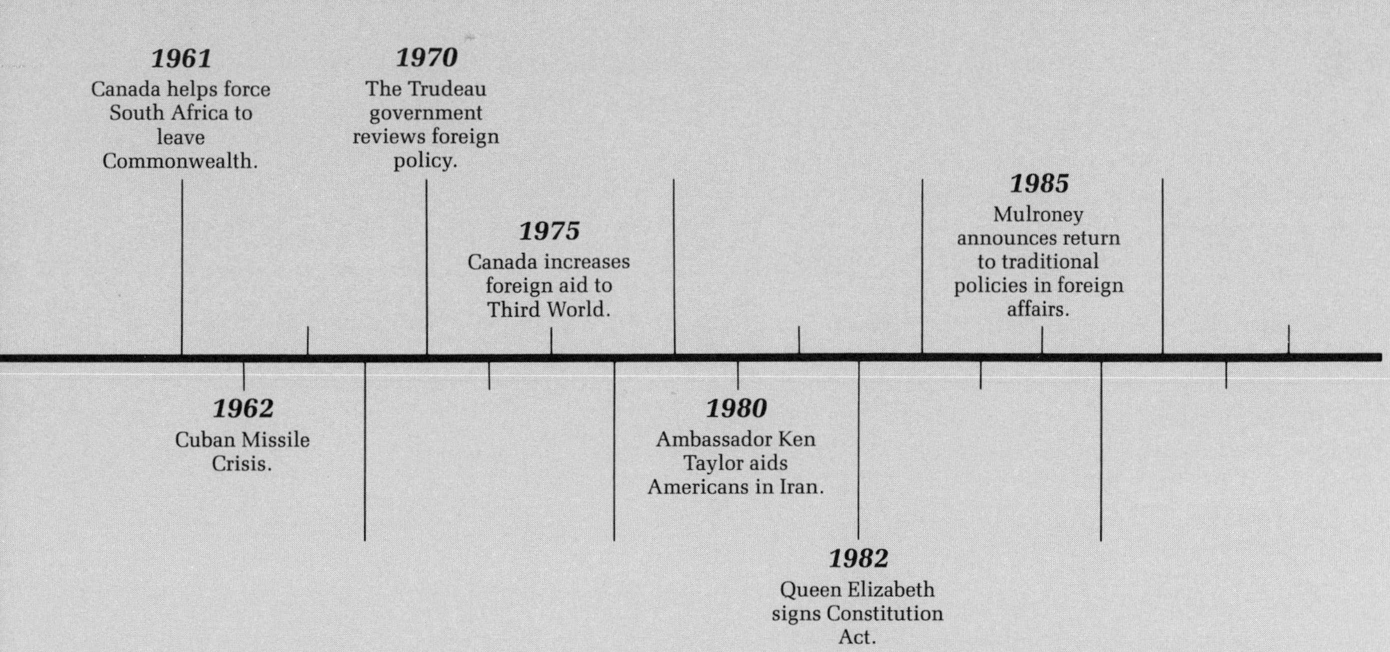

1961
Canada helps force South Africa to leave Commonwealth.
1970
The Trudeau government reviews foreign policy.
1975
Canada increases foreign aid to Third World.
1985
Mulroney announces return to traditional policies in foreign affairs.
1962
Cuban Missile Crisis.
1980
Ambassador Ken Taylor aids Americans in Iran.
1982
Queen Elizabeth signs Constitution Act.

TOPIC ORGANIZER

THEME ORGANIZER

- Foreign policy is the systematic way in which a country pursues its relations with other countries.
- Every nation in the world has a foreign policy.
- The basic goal of every country is to survive.
- At the heart of international relations is the crucial issue: Will we have war or peace?
- Canada gradually claimed the right to make its own foreign policy as it won independence from Britain in the 1920s and 1930s.
- Since World War II, Canada has played a fairly important role in world affairs.
- As the world has changed, Canada has tried to adjust its foreign policy to meet new conditions.
- Today Canada faces difficult decisions on several issues.

INTRODUCTION

Today Canadians are well aware that they are citizens, not just of Canada, but of the whole world community. This awareness is shared by almost all of the other peoples on earth. Only the most isolated tribes in very remote areas might fail to appreciate this reality.

There was a time, not too long ago, when this was not the case. It was possible for many people throughout the world to go about their lives with little knowledge or understanding of the world at large. Methods of transportation and communication were much less advanced. Therefore, time and distance were much greater obstacles than they are today. Also, many people received little or no education.

All this has changed. This is due partly to the rapid growth of modern technology. Transportation and communication have been revolutionized. Mass public education, at least to the high-school level, is almost universal. The mass media, aided by computers and communication satellites, have produced an information explosion. There have been great increases in international trade, travel and cultural exchanges. Consequently the world has become, in a real sense, a "global village."

All of these trends and more have contributed to the growing sense of a world community. This, in turn, has highlighted the importance of how nations conduct their relations with one another. The way a country deals with other countries is called its foreign policy. In an age when possible destruction awaits our planet through nuclear war or ecological disaster, it is essential that we understand our country's role in the world. That is the theme of this unit.

UNIT PREVIEW QUESTIONS

As you study this unit, keep these questions in mind. You may want to return to them when you have finished the unit.

1. What does Canada stand for in the world?
2. What do we want from our ties with other countries?
3. How do we try to achieve these aims?
4. What do other countries think of Canada?
5. How important is Canada in world affairs?
6. What changes, if any, should we be making in our dealings with other countries?

chapter 18

UNDERSTANDING FOREIGN POLICY

TOPIC ORGANIZER	PAGE
▶ Goals and Methods in Foreign Policy	344
▶ Factors That Influence Foreign Policy	346
▶ Making Judgements About Foreign Policy	348
▶ The Importance of Foreign Policy	350

THEME ORGANIZER

- ▶ Foreign policy is a country's planned approach to its relations with other countries.
- ▶ Goals and methods for reaching them form the central core of foreign policy.
- ▶ Many factors influence a country's choice of goals and methods.
- ▶ While the details of foreign policy often change, two constants remain: Countries pursue their own interests first, and, above all, they try to survive in the world.
- ▶ A foreign policy usually is evaluated in terms of its effectiveness in achieving desired goals.
- ▶ A country's foreign policy also can be judged by its positive effects on the world as a whole.
- ▶ As the world becomes a "global village," foreign policy becomes increasingly important.

INTRODUCTION

The term "foreign policy" means the interactions and ties that one nation has with other nations. Every country in the world has a foreign policy. Canada is no exception to this rule. Our main task in this unit is to try to discover what Canada's foreign policy is all about.

Here is a way to help you understand foreign policy. Think of a country as a person. Have you ever heard the saying, "No man is an island"? This suggests that no person can live a full or normal life if he or she is completely alone. Now, some quick wits among you are probably saying, "There are several countries that are islands, and I can name some." This is true, but only in a geographic sense. Countries, like people, cannot act as though no one else exists in the world. Such isolation cannot be, especially in our modern world.

1 What word do we use for a person who tries to live completely alone? Why might someone try to live in this way?

2 Try to imagine yourself in such a position. Why would it be practically impossible to live strictly alone? (Among other things, your answer should include references to modern methods of communication and transportation.)

3 Why would it be impossible for a country to be completely isolated from other countries?

4 Despite what we have said above, some people can live in more isolation than others. Suggest some reasons for this.

5 Now apply this thinking to countries. Why do certain countries need a lot of contact with other countries? Why do others need fewer outside ties? Which kind of country is Canada? Why?

Before reading on, study the chart of key words and ideas that follows.

KEY WORDS AND IDEAS IN THIS CHAPTER

Term	Meaning	Sample Use
blockade	to cut off all travel to and from a country, usually by surrounding it with land, sea and air forces	A blockade can be used to weaken or punish a country or to defeat it in war. It cuts off a country's foreign trade.
diplomacy	the art of conducting relations with foreign countries; involves the negotiation of treaties, alliances and other agreements; requires wisdom, skill and patience	Diplomacy is used to carry out a country's foreign policy. A diplomat is a nation's representative to other nations.
disarmament	the act of getting rid of armed forces and weapons of war	Disarmament can be a step toward reducing tension between countries. It tends to increase the chances for peace.
foreign policy	the relations a country has with other countries; includes the setting of goals and the determination of methods for achieving them	Foreign policy is the theme of this unit. We want to know what Canada's foreign policy is and how effective it is.
ideology	a body of ideas used as the basis for a political system	Democracy, communism and Christianity are examples of ideologies. A country's ideology influences its foreign policy.
national self-interest	whatever is best for one particular country	Just like people, countries usually put their own (national) interests first. This is a form of selfishness.
security	safety	The main goal of a country's foreign policy is security. The country wants to survive and to be safe from conquest or destruction.

GOALS AND METHODS IN FOREIGN POLICY

Let us now return to our main idea. There are over 200 separate countries in our world. Each of them has to have at least some dealings with other countries. Naturally, every country wants its foreign policy to work well and succeed. This takes careful planning (not to mention some good luck). For example, a country must decide what its goals are. Then it must consider what methods to use in order to achieve these goals. In making these decisions, several other things must be kept in mind. How weak or strong is this country compared to others? How rich or poor is it? How might other countries react to its plans? Which goals are most important? And so on. From this, you can see how complicated foreign policy can be.

To help our understanding, let us think of a country as a person. Its foreign policy can be compared to your relations with other people. Let us imagine that you have some plans for this coming weekend. You really could use a car. So you hope to persuade your parents to lend you the family auto. This is your goal. Now you must decide on the method or methods by which you will achieve this goal after your parents respond to your request by saying, "Well, maybe." Think of some possibilities.

How many possible methods have we predicted here?

- You smile more.
- You start keeping your room clean.
- You suddenly become useful around the house, doing dishes and cutting the lawn.
- You don't play your music as loudly as usual.
- You stop fighting with your brothers and/or sisters.
- You are nice when relatives visit.
- If your parents resist, you try to make them feel guilty.
- You threaten to leave home.

1 What other suggestions can you make?
2 Rate all of the possible methods. Put them in order from most effective down to least effective. Have a reason for each decision.
3 Would some of these methods be good under certain conditions but poor under others? Which ones? Why?
4 Try to find methods whose effectiveness depends on the personalities of the people involved.

As does your social life, a country's foreign policy has goals and methods. The following is a list of terms that relate to foreign policy. Be sure you know their meanings before proceeding with the chapter. (Get help from your classmates, your teacher or a dictionary if necessary.)

alliance
blockade
build-up of arms
diplomacy
disarmament
financial aid
foreign trade
immigration
peace
prosperity
security
spying
threat of force
tourism
war

Most of us probably would choose peace as the most important goal of foreign policy. Certainly, it seems to be the most desirable. War is costly and terribly destructive. In a major war using today's weapons, every living thing on the face of the earth could be wiped out. In spite of this, most countries do not have peace as their main goal. Instead, they choose what they call security. This might seem strange, but it is quite natural. A country, just like a living person, has an instinct for survival. It wants to live and not be destroyed. Therefore, it will do almost anything to live, including fight. Like people, most countries prefer not to fight. However, they will do so to protect themselves. True, they might lose and be destroyed. However, victory permits survival. Sometimes it even brings great rewards. By winning a war, a country might gain land, riches, people and glory. For these reasons, there are times when certain countries do attack others. Thus, it is sometimes possible to judge other countries. Like people, their actions are "good" or "bad," depending on the intentions and results of their actions.

Perhaps this is the most important point to remember about foreign policy: *The main goal of every country is to survive.* This causes it to seek security. In the end, all other factors give way — peace, war, good, bad, right, wrong. Obviously, this creates a kind of "jungle" in world affairs. The rule of "survival of the fittest" applies. Until this changes, all of us must live with the possibility of world destruction through war. This is why the conduct of foreign policy is so important today.

FACTORS THAT INFLUENCE FOREIGN POLICY

No two countries have exactly the same foreign policy. This is because the situation of each country is unique (special). There are several factors that can influence the foreign policy of a country.

One of the factors is ideology. This means the ideas or values for which a country stands. Some nations, like Canada and the United States, believe in democratic government. This means that they want people to have rights and freedoms. Thus, they tend to have friendly relations with other democratic countries. However, they are sometimes in conflict with countries that do not share these beliefs, for example, countries that believe in government by dictatorship.

Another factor in foreign policy is history. Your nation might have a long record of peace and friendship with another country. This is bound to affect your relations with each other. So would a long record of war or bad feelings.

Foreign policy is not a one-way street. Therefore, how other nations feel and act toward your country affects its foreign policy. For example, you might want to have friendly relations with a neighbouring country. You set this as a goal of your foreign policy. You try to encourage trade, tourism and military co-operation. These are methods of reaching your goal. However, the neighbouring country has been persuaded by a third country to help conquer you! Clearly, your policy is going to have to change when you discover this fact!

1 How could you discover that your nation is in danger of attack?
2 What if you fail to discover this?
3 Can you see now why countries spy on each other? Why might even friendly countries, which seem to have good relations, spy on each other?

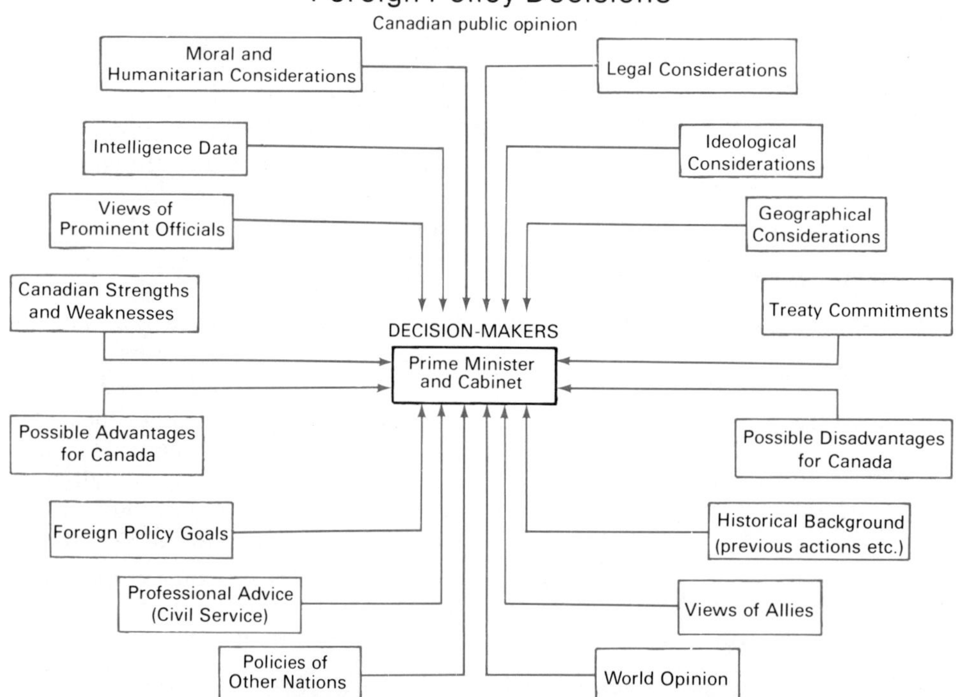

In a democracy, public opinion can influence foreign policy, sometimes strongly. Here, demonstrators gather outside the Parliament Buildings in Ottawa.

4 Is there any way the nations of the world could do away with spying on each other? Why or why not?

There are many other factors that influence a country's foreign policy. Some of these are:

- ▶ geography,
- ▶ public opinion (the views of the people),
- ▶ military power,
- ▶ personal views of leaders,
- ▶ the type of economy in the country.

Set up a chart similar to this in your notebook.

HOW CERTAIN FACTORS INFLUENCE FOREIGN POLICY

Factor	How it influences foreign policy	Example of an application to Canada

1·2·3 *1* Take each of the five factors mentioned above and list them down the left-hand column of your chart. (Leave plenty of space between each one.)

2 Try to explain how each factor could influence a country's foreign policy.

3 Next, try to create an example of how each factor has or could have an influence on Canadian foreign policy.

4 Compare your answers with those of classmates. Add their best ideas to your chart.

5 Below are listed several facts about Canada. Read each one carefully, and then:

a try to decide which of the five factors is being illustrated by the statement;

b state how this fact could influence Canadian foreign policy;

c if you have not thought of the idea, add it to the third column of your chart beside the appropriate factor.

- ▶ A majority of Canadians trace their ancestry to Western Europe, particularly to Britain and France.
- ▶ Canada relies heavily on foreign trade; we need markets for raw materials and other products.
- ▶ Canada is next door to the richest and most powerful country in the world.

- ▶ From the 1960s to the 1980s, the Canadian armed forces were neglected and underfunded. They now need many new weapons and more recruits.
- ▶ The prime minister, assisted by the cabinet, is responsible for planning and carrying out Canadian foreign policy.
- ▶ Canada is a democracy, so the government must answer to the people every few years in an election.

MAKING JUDGEMENTS ABOUT FOREIGN POLICY

We make judgements about the actions of people every day. We judge our parents, friends, teachers, bosses and business associates. Usually we judge them in terms of ability, intelligence, attractiveness, personality, moral qualities (honesty, loyalty) and the degree of success we think they achieve.

We can judge a country's foreign policy in a similar way. Basically, there are two standards of judgement. One of these is effectiveness (whether or not it works). This can be assessed by comparing a country's goals with the degree to which these goals are met. If most or all of the goals are achieved, then the foreign policy has been very effective. In short, it has been successful. The less progress made toward the goals, the less effective the policy.

Earlier, we gave the example of you seeking ways of getting the use of the family car. You were asked to judge the value of several methods available to you. How would we decide whether or not your policy was effective? (CORRECT! Did you get the car or not?) Still, you might have finished somewhere between complete victory and defeat. Maybe you were allowed to use the car once a week. These same ideas of victory, defeat or something in between apply to foreign policy. Remember: The main goal of every country is to survive. Beyond this, it wants to prosper and to give its people the best possible life. In the end, its success or failure must be measured by the extent to which it does these things.

In a sense, these are selfish goals. You want the car for yourself. A country wants security or prosperity for itself — ahead of other countries, if necessary.

Today's world is full of tension and conflict. Therefore, it is more important than ever before that our leaders carry out foreign policy with great care and wisdom.

Thus, many of a country's actions are said to be based on its self-interest. To be exact, this is national self-interest.

There is a second standard for judging a country's foreign policy. This is called idealism (the opposite of self-interest). It refers to the beliefs of those who work for the good of the world as a whole. Countries, like people, have different motives (reasons) for doing things. Sometimes they act selfishly. However, at times they do things that are of great help to others. Often, there is a mixture of motives behind their actions.

For example, let us imagine that a young girl notices an elderly man struggling along the street with an armful of groceries. She helps him carry his parcels home. Why did she do this? To help the old man? To have a chance at a reward of some kind? To make herself feel good? To relieve her guilt feelings for having ignored his problem once before? Will she ever really know why she did this? Does it really matter, so long as she and the old man both benefit?

Above: Canadian officers discuss their part in the United Nations peacekeeping force on Cyprus. Left: Canada supports disarmament. A Canadian sentry watches a German soldier check piles of weapons surrendered in World War II. Below: For self-protection, Canada still keeps armed forces at the ready.

A Canadian Foreign Aid Worker teaches English in China. What other objectives of foreign aid are visible in the photo?

The same issues come up when judging a country's foreign policy. Let us say that country "A" is rather poor and backward. Country "B" volunteers to send assistance. Part of this assistance consists of teachers and other experts who will train and educate the people of country "A." Why has country "B" done this? Is it an honest attempt to help? Will the teachers be agents and spies for their government? Will they fill the children's heads with foreign ideas? Does country "B" want to make a friend or a dependent out of country "A"? How should we judge this policy? In terms of its results? In terms of the "good" or "bad" intentions behind it? Probably each of us will judge on the basis of our own personal attitudes and values. This is why there can be much difference of opinion over the quality of a country's foreign policy.

To sum up this section, foreign policy can be judged in two main ways: how well it achieves its goals and the amount of good it does for the world as a whole. Throughout history, nations have asked, "Did it [an action] work?" more often than "Did it help people?" Or, to put it another way, winning is more important than playing the game. Try to remember these ideas as you study the following chapters on Canadian foreign policy.

THE IMPORTANCE OF FOREIGN POLICY

As we all know, the world today is full of problems and dangers. Among these are ignorance, disease, starvation, illiteracy, pollution, overpopulation and the threat of nuclear war. We in Canada are fortunate. Most of these problems are far less serious here than in other lands. Still, we are not just Canadians. We are members of a single human race. We are, whether we realize it or not, citizens of the entire world. Thus, the problems of the world are partly our problems. They will not disappear. We cannot pretend that they do not exist.

In some ways, the planet Earth is getting smaller. New means of transportation and communication are causing this to happen. Today we can fly across Canada more quickly than most people could travel 200 km just 80 years ago. In 1988 Calgary hosted the Winter Olympics. The events were telecast live, by satellite, to viewers as far away as Tokyo and Moscow.

However, these same wonders can bring up the bad side of life as well as the good. While we sit in front of our TV sets eating cake and ice cream, the news camera zooms in on the face of a starving child in Africa. At other times, we can see "in living colour" the effects of floods, earthquakes, wars or other human disasters, all in the comfort of our air-conditioned family rooms. The missile, another marvel of science, can drop destruction upon us from the other side of the world. This can happen in less time than it takes some of us to get to work or school.

We hope that these problems can be solved or at least made less dangerous. This can happen only if the nations of the world agree to co-operate in finding solutions. To do so, *they must improve their relations with each other*. In this simple fact we find the real importance of foreign policy.

BUILDING YOUR LEARNING SKILLS

FOCUSSING ON THE ISSUE

1. What is foreign policy?
2. What is the difference between a goal and a method in foreign policy? Give at least two examples of each.
3. What are the main factors that influence a country's foreign policy?
4. What are the two main standards by which a foreign policy can be judged?
5. The following terms appeared in this chapter. Try to recall their meanings and how they were used.

alliance	motive
blockade	national self-interest
diplomacy	peace
disarmament	prosperity
effectiveness	security
idealism	spying
ideology	war
isolation	

RESEARCHING

1. Start collecting media articles on Canadian foreign policy. Clip stories, photos, cartoons and editorials from newspapers and magazines.

ORGANIZING

1. Set up your file of clippings in a logical way. You might organize the items according to the country or region with which they deal.
2. Think of one or two alternative methods of organizing your file.
3. As your file grows, try to design a cross-reference system to help you find items more quickly.

COMMUNICATING

1. Using headlines and captions for assistance, decide what your clippings are telling you about Canadian foreign policy.
2. Practise writing summaries of major articles. Your summaries should express the main ideas and supporting points in half a page or less.
3. Once your file is large enough, prepare a three- or four-page "Official Summary of Canadian Foreign Policy." This should clearly communicate the basics of our foreign policy at the present time.

ANALYZING

1 Based on your summary (question three, above), what seem to be the two or three most important goals of Canadian foreign policy today? What are the main methods that we appear to be using to try to achieve these goals?
2 Can you identify areas of success and/or failure? Explain your judgements.
3 Why is foreign policy so important in human life today?
4 How can a nation both defend itself and work for world peace at the same time?
5 Some people believe that in relations among countries, "might is right." What do they mean by this? How would such people judge a foreign policy — by its effectiveness or its idealism? Explain your answer.
6 Why is the view that "might is right" dangerous?
7 Some people who talk about the shrinking earth say we are now living in a "global village."
   a What does this term mean?
   b What does it suggest about human life today?
   c How is this term connected to the idea of the importance of foreign policy?
8 Some issues in a country's life are foreign, while others are domestic (internal). Below is a list of issues. Decide the nature of each, foreign or domestic, and say why this is so. Could any be both? If so, explain how.

alliance	peace
crime	revolution
fishing	riot
immigration	trade
industry	treaty
labour strike	war

APPLYING YOUR KNOWLEDGE

1 Organize a class debate on this idea: RESOLVED: that in foreign policy, might *is* right.
2 Imagine that you are the leader of a country called OZ. You are responsible for creating and carrying out the foreign policy of the Land of OZ. Invent names for three or four other countries to make up a "world." Give each country, including OZ, certain characteristics. Specify size, population, wealth, type of economy, military power, history and geography. (If necessary, review the section on "Factors That Influence Foreign Policy.") Now create a set of goals for the foreign policy of OZ. Then suggest the most effective methods of securing these goals. Explain your suggestions. Finally, compare your ideas with those of classmates, friends or members of your family at home.
3 There are several simulation games that deal with some of the ideas presented in this chapter. Among these are "Diplomacy," "Dangerous Parallel," and "Crisis." Perhaps your teacher or librarian could help you locate and organize one of these simulations.
4 Refer back to the list of terms that you reviewed in "Focussing on the Issue," question five. You can test and then use your knowledge by working on the following chart. Set it up in your notebook, using the model supplied on page 353.
   a List the terms, in any order, down the left-hand column.
   b Write in (briefly) the meaning of each term.
   c Pretend that you are the foreign minister of a country. This could be Canada or some other nation, real or imaginary. With each term, try to think of how it could be used as part of your foreign policy (refer to the example provided). Would this term be a *goal* or a *method* of policy? Put a check mark in the appropriate column. If you think it could be both, check the "Both" column instead.
   d How many items have you classified as "Both"? Would this tend to suggest that foreign policy is simple or complicated? Explain your answer.
   e Now defend your decisions. In the right-hand column, give an example of the item being used in the foreign policy of your country.
   f Of all the items you have checked as "Methods," which is the most dangerous? Why? Could it also be the method of carrying out foreign policy that works best? How?

UNDERSTANDING FOREIGN POLICY

Term	Meaning	Goal of foreign policy?	Method of foreign policy?	Both method and goal?	Example of use
Example: foreign trade	an exchange of goods between two or more countries			✓	*As a goal:* Country "A" wishes to increase its foreign trade. It uses diplomacy to try to negotiate trade arrangements with other countries. *As a method:* Country "A" wishes to improve its relations with another nation. It tries to do this by offering attractive trade proposals.

g Review the items you have checked as "Goals." Which do you think is the most important? Why? What methods would help achieve this goal?

h With regard to the goal you selected in "g" does it seem to you that most countries today have chosen this as their main goal? If not, why not?

5 How good are you at judging motives behind foreign policy? Reproduce the chart on the following page in your notebook. Make it large, and leave plenty of space between lines.

a Various foreign policy actions are listed down the left-hand column. First you must judge the reasons behind such actions on the assumption that they are Canadian actions. Put check marks in any of the four appropriate columns under "Canadian Motives."

b Next, judge the motives of such actions, assuming they were performed by the Soviet Union. Check off the appropriate columns.

c Do you find different reasons for the actions, depending on whether they are done by Canadians or Russians? If so, why?

d Look at your assessment of Canadian motives. Do you think a Russian would agree? Why or why not?

e What does this exercise tell you about trust in foreign policy? What does it tell you about judging foreign policy?

f If possible, choose two other actions, add them to the above list and complete the chart.

g Canada actually does perform several of the above actions in its foreign policy. This will be described more fully in later chapters.

	CANADIAN MOTIVES				SOVIET MOTIVES			
Action	**Self-interest**	**Idealism**	**Attacking**	**Defending**	**Self-interest**	**Idealism**	**Attacking**	**Defending**
1. Build-up of armed forces at home								
2. Setting up of military bases in other countries								
3. Sending financial aid to poorer countries								
4. Sending spies into other countries								
5. Trying to increase trade with other countries								
6. Investing money in the economies of other countries								
7. Making a military alliance with one or more other countries								
8. ?								
9. ?								

chapter 19

CANADA'S SEARCH FOR PEACE AND SECURITY

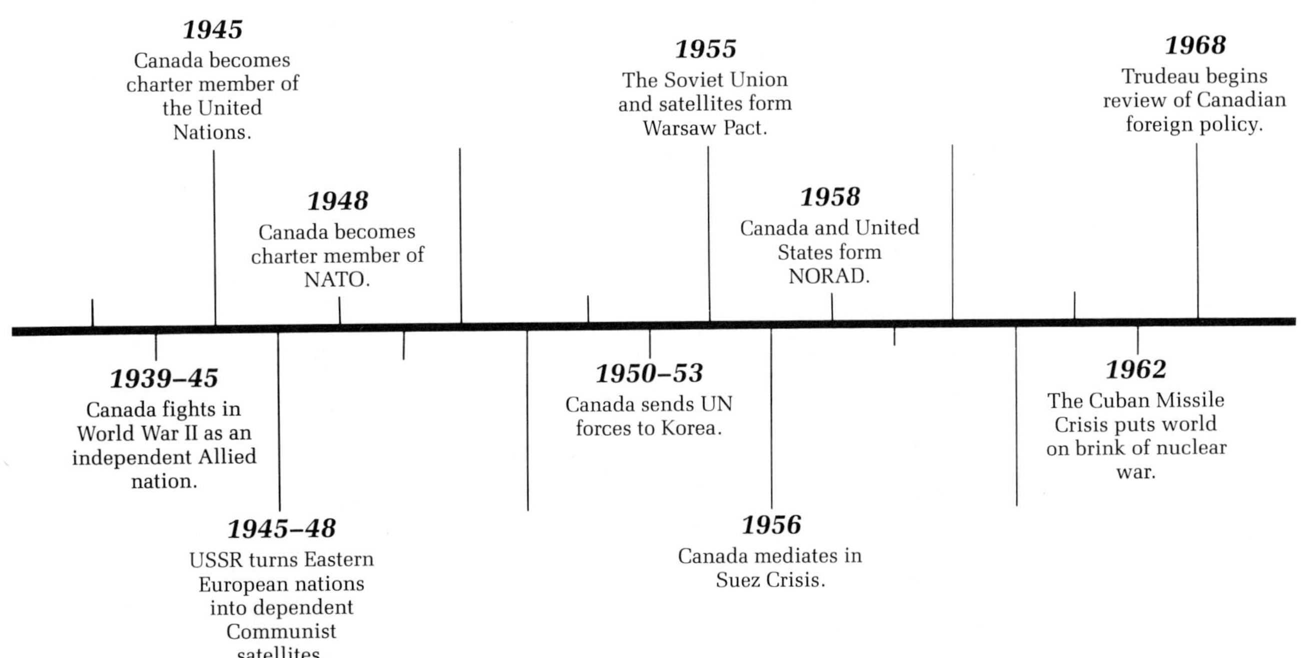
1945
Canada becomes charter member of the United Nations.
1948
Canada becomes charter member of NATO.
1955
The Soviet Union and satellites form Warsaw Pact.
1958
Canada and United States form NORAD.
1968
Trudeau begins review of Canadian foreign policy.
1939–45
Canada fights in World War II as an independent Allied nation.
1945–48
USSR turns Eastern European nations into dependent Communist satellites.
1950–53
Canada sends UN forces to Korea.
1956
Canada mediates in Suez Crisis.
1962
The Cuban Missile Crisis puts world on brink of nuclear war.

TOPIC ORGANIZER

THEME ORGANIZER

- By the end of World War II, Canada was a significant "middle power" in the world.
- For postwar security, we put our trust first in the United Nations.
- Canada has been a leading supporter of UN efforts to preserve peace and help underdeveloped countries.
- A cold war gradually developed between the United States and the Soviet Union.
- As world tension increased, weaknesses in the structure of the United Nations became apparent.
- Canada joined two military alliances (NATO and NORAD) to increase its security against possible attack.
- By the 1960s, the world was changing rapidly; it became necessary for Canada to review its foreign policy.

INTRODUCTION

As we have seen, all nations want to be secure, or safe. This is the only way to be sure of survival. Each nation must decide for itself the best way to achieve this security. This is one of the main jobs of the government of a country.

So far, the government of Canada has done a good job of keeping our country secure. Since Canada was formed in 1867, no foreign enemy has set foot on our soil. The task of protecting Canada has not always been easy. Since 1900 we have been involved in two terrible world wars (see Unit 3, Chapter 9). Fortunately, we were on the winning side in both of those conflicts.

When World War II ended in 1945, many Canadians believed that our security was now guaranteed. There would be no more troubles or major wars in the world. That hope has proven to be false. The world is still a very dangerous place. Canada, though reasonably secure, would be foolish to think itself completely safe. Therefore, while we continue to work for peace, we must protect ourselves in case of war.

Before reading on, study the chart of key words and ideas that follows.

KEY WORDS AND IDEAS IN THIS CHAPTER

Term	Meaning	Sample Use
aggression	the act of attacking, hurting someone, taking property or invading a country	The United Nations tries to stop aggression because it can lead to war.
arms race	a competition among countries to develop new weapons and build large quantities of them	Many countries are involved in the arms race today. Chief among these are the United States and the Soviet Union.
buffer state	a country located between two other countries that might come into conflict	Today Poland acts as a buffer state between the Soviet Union and Western Europe.
collective security	the safety provided by numbers, as when several countries band together and promise to defend each other against attack	Canada tried to gain collective security through the United Nations. When this failed, we turned to military alliances such as NATO and NORAD.

demobilization	reduction of the size of armed forces	Demobilization took place quickly in Canada after World War II ended.
economic sanction	stopping trade or other business with a particular country	The United Nations sometimes asks its members to apply economic sanctions against an aggressor. These sanctions are meant to discourage its bad behaviour.
international law	law that applies throughout the world, not just in one country	The United Nations would be more effective if countries would agree to obey international law.
middle power	a country that is neither a superpower nor a weak nation but something in between	For a few years after 1945, Canada played the role of a middle power.
peacekeeping	getting between two fighting groups and acting firmly but fairly toward both to prevent more violence	Canada is a world leader in peacekeeping. It does this mainly by supporting the United Nations' work in world trouble spots.
refugee	a person who is fleeing from his or her homeland	Canada has admitted thousands of refugees since 1945. It provides a new and safe home for these people.
superpower	a nation with great power and wealth	The United States and the Soviet Union are superpowers today. Some other countries, such as China, could become superpowers in the future.
veto	the power to block action by simply saying "no"	Several countries have veto power in the United Nations. This makes it very difficult for the UN to work effectively.
world government	a government for the whole world; would have ruling power over all countries	Some people think world government is needed to prevent war. It could save the world from destruction.

CANADA'S WORLD POSITION BY 1945

It has been said that Canada "came of age" in World War II (1939–1945) and became a truly independent country. Also, the war gave a boost to our economy. By the end of the war, Canada was one of the leading industrial nations of the world. It was a major producer of arms and ammunition.

We came of age in yet another sense. Several great military powers had been crushed, at least temporarily. Among these were Germany and Japan. On the other hand, the Canadian armed forces had been built up to record size. Over 1 million Canadian men and women were in uniform by the end of the war. This combination of factors lifted Canada to high rank among the nations of the world. For a while, at least, we were the fourth or fifth strongest military power in the world!

This was a source of great pride to Canadians. So was the fine record of service built up by our forces during the war. Over 40 000 Canadian soldiers lost their lives in the defence of their country. The Canadian people and their government felt that this sacrifice gave us the right to have a strong voice in world

The Honorable C.D. Howe, Minister of Munitions and Supply, inspects a shell offered by a munitions worker. During World War II, Canada became a leading manufacturer of munitions. Thousands of women such as the one shown here made a major contribution to Canada's war effort.

affairs. The prime minister, Mackenzie King, was determined that Canada should play an important part in the postwar world.

Obviously, we could not have as much influence as the "great powers." Among these, the United States and the Soviet Union were in a class by themselves. Next came Britain, France and China. However, on the next level down were medium-sized nations such as Canada. They were not superpowers, but neither were they weak or unimportant. Thus, a key part of Canada's foreign policy after 1945 was to play the role of a middle power. In the following sections, we will see how this was done.

CANADA'S ARMED FORCES

Canada has never maintained large armed forces in peacetime. When World War I began in 1914, there were fewer than 5000 battle-ready troops in the entire country. Also, there was very little modern equipment or weapons. Almost the same situation existed in 1939, at the start of World War II. When that war ended, a decision had to be made about our forces. Should they be kept at their current high level? Should they be reduced a bit? Should they be severely cut back to our normal peacetime level? (The name for this last action is demobilization.)

The government of Mackenzie King decided to demobilize the Canadian armed forces. This does not mean that they were completely disbanded. However, by 1947 their numbers had been reduced to around 100 000 (from a wartime high of 1 million plus). This was done partly because the greatest danger seemed to end with the war. Also, it was very expensive to keep large armed forces. The people were sick of war and tired of paying for it. Therefore, there was very little criticism of demobilization.

Since the late 1940s, Canada's security needs have changed from time to time. They seemed to be greatest through the 1950s and early 1960s (for reasons we will soon discover). In this period, our armed forces were kept around the 90 000 level. The defence budgets were high enough to pay for new weapons and equipment. However, world tension began to decrease in the late 1960s and early 1970s. So too did our armed forces. The numbers fell below 80 000 for the first time since before World War II. Budgets were cut back. Weapons and equipment slowly became

Comparison of Soviet Bloc and Western Forces After World War II

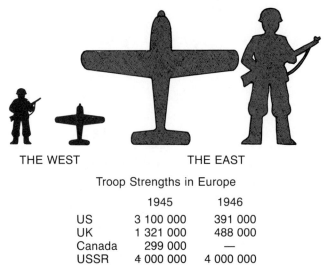

Troop Strengths in Europe

	1945	1946
US	3 100 000	391 000
UK	1 321 000	488 000
Canada	299 000	—
USSR	4 000 000	4 000 000

scarce and outdated. Beginning in 1976, the Canadian government moved to improve the situation. Defence budgets were once again increased, if only slightly. Plans were made to buy new aircraft, tanks and naval vessels. There were further modest spending increases in the 1980s.

If you have read the chapter carefully so far, you should have noticed a problem. How could Canada expect to play a key role, as a middle power and yet reduce its military strength to a low level? How, indeed, could it even expect to remain secure?

The fact is that Canada was *not* able to play a middle-power role for very long. We grew weaker. At the same time, other nations recovered or developed for the first time. It seems that we Canadians were a little too idealistic about the world. First, we forgot that the idea of "might is right" still counts for something. In the crunch, the countries with the most "muscle" get the biggest say. These countries also have more influence on less powerful nations. For example, a developing nation might choose as its ally a country that can provide it with military arms for self defence. Second, we pinned too many hopes on a new world organization, the United Nations.

THE FORMATION OF THE UNITED NATIONS

Most of us have heard the expression, "You can't take the law into your own hands."

1 What does this mean?
2 Give an example of someone trying to do this.
3 Why would someone want to do this?
4 Why is it not legal to do this? Should it be?

The idea we are getting at is that, in Canada, we have a set of laws (described in Unit 2). These laws are designed to protect all of us. For them to work, we must all basically agree to obey them. Those who break the law must be punished. Otherwise, the laws will become meaningless. The law controls our actions and punishes wrongdoers. But this does not occur in world affairs. There are a few rules that many nations have agreed to obey. These are called international law. They deal with such things as navigation on the oceans and conduct in war. However, any country can ignore these rules if it wishes. There is no effective way of enforcing them as yet.

Each nation is "a law unto itself." Its actions are based on what it wants to do. There is no law to limit its actions. They are limited only by their own power and the wishes of other nations. This is why "might is right" is often true in foreign policy. This is also why so many wars occur.

As World War II was ending, several countries decided to try to do something to prevent future wars. Their idea was to create a world organization. All nations would some day belong to it. This was the start of the United Nations. The hope was to create a body that would try to enforce certain rules upon all members (just like a government does within a country). In this way, war could be prevented. Problems among nations could be solved peacefully.

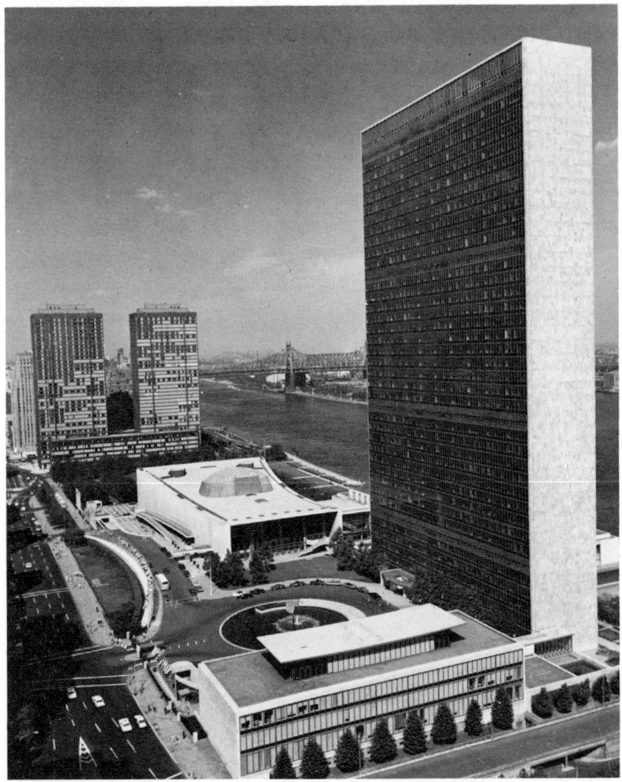

The United Nations Building, New York City

Organization of the United Nations

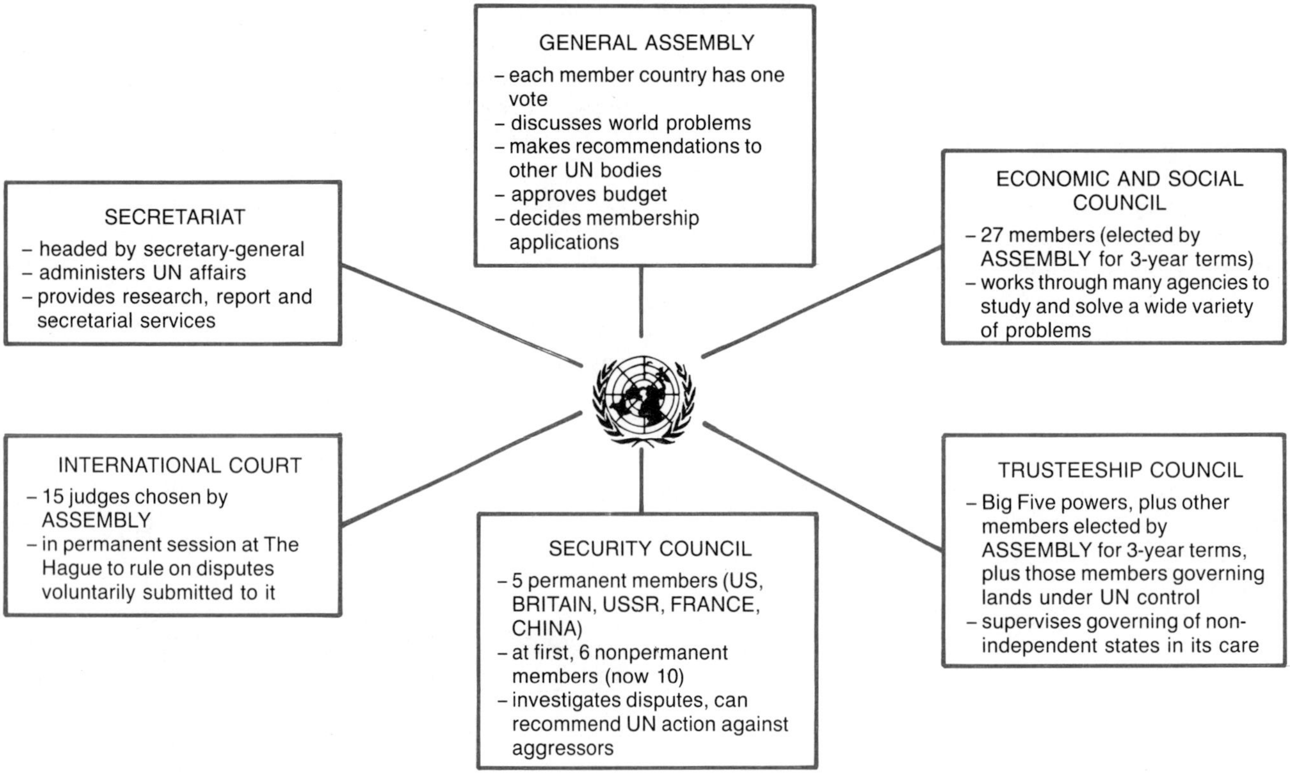

GENERAL ASSEMBLY
- each member country has one vote
- discusses world problems
- makes recommendations to other UN bodies
- approves budget
- decides membership applications

SECRETARIAT
- headed by secretary-general
- administers UN affairs
- provides research, report and secretarial services

ECONOMIC AND SOCIAL COUNCIL
- 27 members (elected by ASSEMBLY for 3-year terms)
- works through many agencies to study and solve a wide variety of problems

INTERNATIONAL COURT
- 15 judges chosen by ASSEMBLY
- in permanent session at The Hague to rule on disputes voluntarily submitted to it

TRUSTEESHIP COUNCIL
- Big Five powers, plus other members elected by ASSEMBLY for 3-year terms, plus those members governing lands under UN control
- supervises governing of non-independent states in its care

SECURITY COUNCIL
- 5 permanent members (US, BRITAIN, USSR, FRANCE, CHINA)
- at first, 6 nonpermanent members (now 10)
- investigates disputes, can recommend UN action against aggressors

In 1945 the San Francisco Conference created a charter (or constitution) for the United Nations. This charter was approved by 51 nations. It came into effect on October 24, 1945. The Charter begins as follows:

> *We the peoples of the United Nations determined* to save succeeding generations from the scourge of war, which twice in our lifetime has brought untold sorrow to mankind, and to reaffirm faith in fundamental [basic] human rights, in the dignity and worth of the human person, in the equal rights of men and women of nations large and small, and to establish conditions under which justice and respect for the obligations arising from treaties and other sources of international law can be maintained, and to promote social progress and better standards of life in larger freedom . . . *have resolved to combine our efforts to accomplish these aims.*

1 Make a list of the ideals for which the United Nations stands.

2 What goals, other than preventing war, does the UN have, according to its charter?

3 Why is the prevention of war its main goal?

4 What does the word "scourge" mean? Why can war be called a scourge?

5 To what events does the "twice in our lifetime" phrase refer?

As we have learned, the main goal of the United Nations is to prevent war. It can work toward this goal in a number of ways. The United Nations is a complex organization. The more important facts about the UN are summarized in the accompanying chart.

HOW THE UN WORKS FOR PEACE

Here are the main methods that the United Nations can use to keep peace and prevent war.

1 The United Nations tries to persuade countries to reduce their armed forces.
2 The United Nations sets up many agencies to fight world problems such as poverty, disease and illiteracy.
3 Serious disputes between countries can be discussed by the General Assembly and by the Security Council. Perhaps one of these bodies can arrange a peaceful solution.
4 The disputing countries can take their problem to the International Court.
5 If, for example, a country threatens to do something that is harmful to the world community, the United Nations can call for economic sanctions against it. This means that other countries would not trade with that country. This could hurt its economy. Therefore, it might correct its actions.
6 If one or more countries attacks another, the United Nations can threaten to use force against the attackers.
7 If necessary, the United Nations can ask member countries to contribute soldiers and weapons to a United Nations armed force. This force can be used against aggressor (attacking) nations.

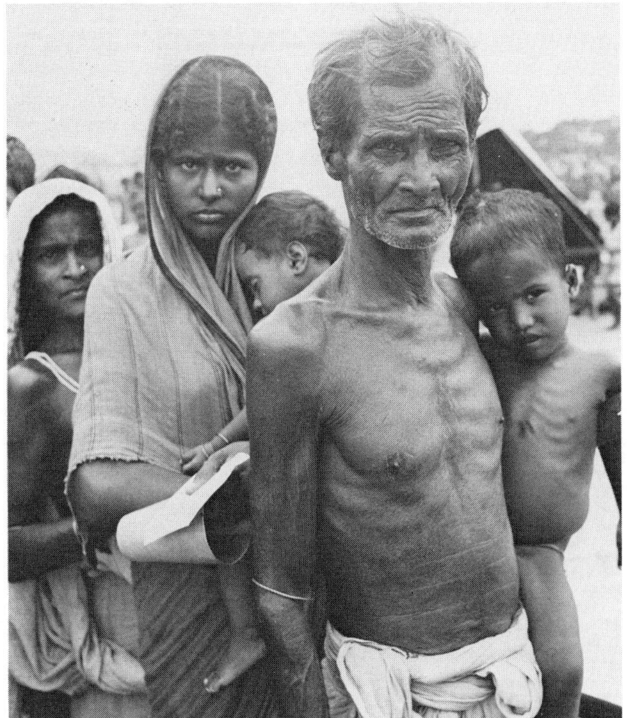

Refugees from East Pakistan. Canada has helped to meet the needs of such people for shelter, food, water, and health care.

CANADA'S SUPPORT OF THE UNITED NATIONS

Canada has always been one of the strongest supporters of the United Nations. We are one of its 51 charter (original) members. Each year we make a large contribution of money to the UN budget. We have supported UN efforts to achieve disarmament.

Canada also has worked through the United Nations to help poor countries. Most of you probably remember "trick or treating" on Halloween. Perhaps a few of you would confess to still doing this. Do you remember the UNICEF boxes that some of you carried around? You asked people to put money in them. This, whether you knew it or not, was to support a United Nations project, the United Nations International Children's Emergency Fund. It has helped children in countries ravaged by war. It also helps children in countries that have been struck by epidemics, floods, earthquakes and other disasters.

In total, there are over a dozen United Nations agencies providing economic and social assistance throughout the world. To date, Canada has contributed well over $100 million to those agencies. Canadian money has gone for the relief of drought, sickness, starvation and other human problems. We have helped to build dams, bridges, roads, schools, hospitals and other facilities in poor countries. In addition, we have welcomed thousands of refugees to Canada.

Canada also has made important military contributions to the United Nations. In 1945 we argued for the creation of a special United Nations force. We suggested that every member should contribute. They could provide money, soldiers, ships, aircraft, guns or whatever they could afford. This force would be kept at the ready. It could be sent into action anywhere at any time to keep world peace. Unfortunately, this idea was not accepted.

However, in 1950 the United Nations decided to create a similar kind of force. This was needed to

The Korean War

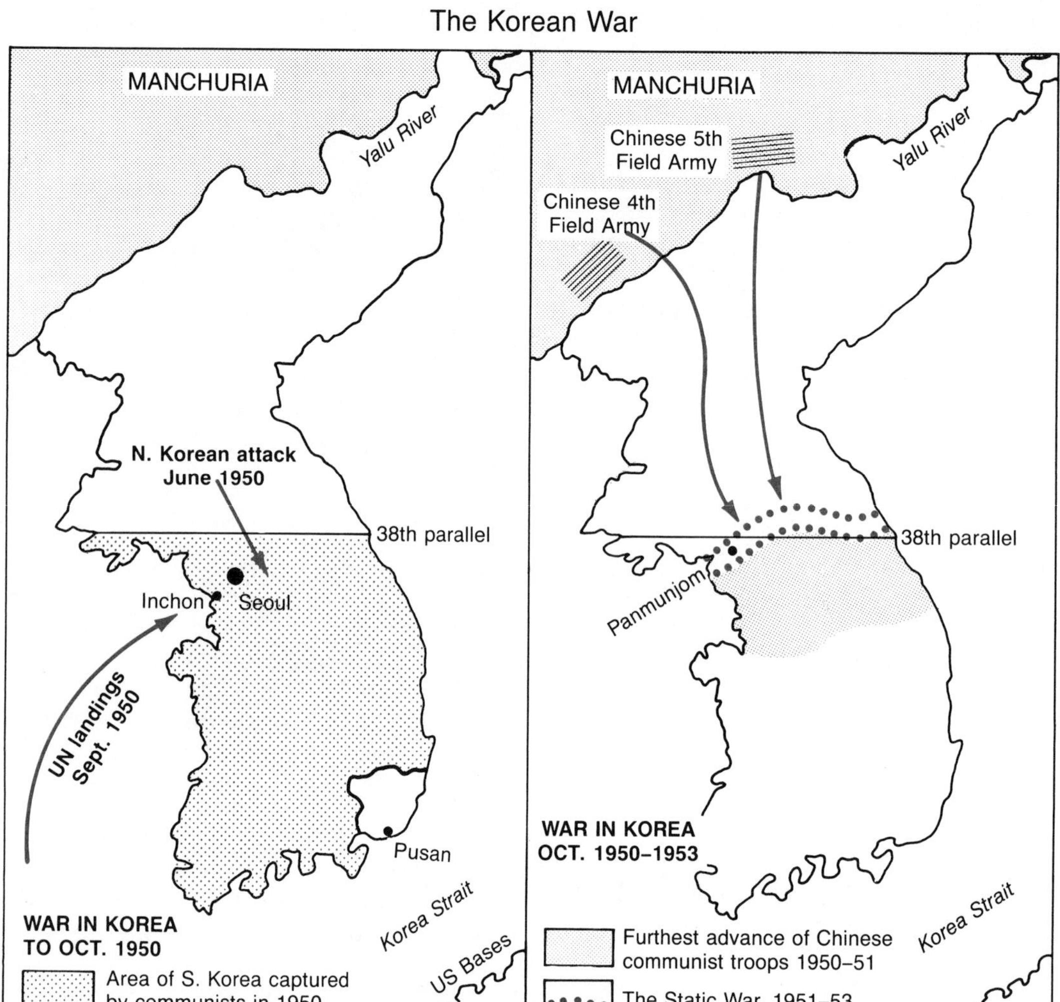

meet a special problem in Korea. This country is a peninsula in Asia (see map). After World War II, it was divided into North and South Korea. The dividing line was the thirty-eighth parallel of latitude. The North was Communist and was supported by the Soviet Union. South Korea was protected by the United States.

In June of 1950, North Korea attacked South Korea. It seems that the North was encouraged to do this by the Soviet Union. The United States asked the United Nations to take action against this aggression. The Security Council met in special session. Eventually, it reached a decision. A United Nations armed force was sent to Korea to turn back the invaders.

Over 300 000 troops served in the United Nations forces in Korea. About 85 percent of these were American. Over 30 other members of the United Nations contributed in the same way to this force. Canada sent an army brigade of about 8000 soldiers. It also provided three naval destroyers and an air transport squadron. Only the United States and Britain made larger contributions to the UN force. Over 1500 Canadian soldiers were casualties in the Korean War. Of these, 406 were killed.

The Korean fighting was finally ended by a truce (agreement to stop shooting) in July, 1953. The United Nations action saved South Korea. Perhaps even more important was the fact that the United Nations had shown that it could be effective. In time, most of the UN forces went home. Canada's idea of a permanent UN force was still not accepted. However, our support of the United Nations in its hour of need was very valuable.

Canada has helped the United Nations in yet another important way. This is in the difficult job of peacekeeping. Since World War II, several trouble spots have developed in the world. On many occasions, this has led to fighting. Sometimes the United Nations can persuade the two sides to stop fighting. This involves arranging a truce. However, this agreement to stop shooting does not always last. Therefore, the United Nations offers to provide a force to stand between the two sides. This UN force supervises the truce. It reports any violations by either side. It also helps to solve misunderstandings. In this way, the UN force can usually prevent the conflict from breaking out again. This work is also called "truce supervision."

Canada is an ideal country for this type of role. We have a reputation for being quite impartial (fair-minded). We are not a large power; therefore, we are not feared. Our government is keenly interested in peace. Our people want Canada to play a helpful role. They also seem willing to pay the cost. As a result, Canada has been very active in truce supervision and peacekeeping for the United Nations. We now are known throughout the world for this role. You could say it has become part of Canada's identity. In this role, our forces have appeared in such countries as Egypt, India, Vietnam, Cyprus, Lebanon and the Congo. A good example of the way we carry out this role is our involvement in the Suez Crisis of 1956.

THE SUEZ CRISIS

In 1956 a major conflict developed in the Middle East. The immediate cause was an invasion of Egypt by British, French and Israeli armed forces. In that year, Egypt decided to nationalize (take state control of) the Suez Canal Zone. The Suez Canal was and is a vital waterway linking the Red Sea with the Mediterranean. Britain once controlled this area and much of Egypt as part of its vast worldwide empire. It was still part of an international commission that directed

Canadian soldiers on UN patrol in Egypt. Their jeeps contrast sharply with the more traditional form of desert transportation.

the management of the Suez Canal. After the Egyptians gained their independence, they grew resentful of foreign control of the canal zone, which was within their territory.

France, like Britain, had been a leading colonial power in the Middle East. As two of the most powerful nations in Western Europe, they decided to reverse Egypt's takeover of the canal zone. This would guarantee continued free passage of oil and other vital materials in the trade between Western Europe and the Middle East.

Most Arab nations sympathized with Egypt. Britain and France received military support from Israel, a young nation that the Arab states had sworn to destroy. French and British paratroopers were dropped into the canal zone in October, 1956. To support them, Israel attacked Egypt through the Sinai peninsula.

These actions provoked an emergency debate at the United Nations. Most members sympathized with Egypt. The Soviet Union, anxious to win favour with Arab nations, threatened to intervene (come in) on the side of Egypt. The United States was deeply embarrassed. It was a supporter of Israel and an ally of Britain and France. Still, it agreed with the Russians that the attack on the canal zone was wrong. Canada was similarly embarrassed, especially since Britain was our former mother country.

Finally, a way out was found. It was presented by Canada at a dramatic, all-night meeting of the General Assembly. The spokesman was Lester Pearson, our secretary of state for external affairs.

Pearson suggested the calling of an immediate end to the shooting. Next, he asked for a United Nations Emergency Force (UNEF) to preserve the truce. It would also supervise the withdrawal of all invading forces from Egypt. Next, the UNEF would patrol tense border areas. This plan was adopted, and its terms were carried out. The UNEF grew to about 6000 troops. They were supplied by several countries, including Canada. Ours was the largest single contribution (about 800 men). The first commander of the UNEF was a Canadian, General E.L.M. Burns.

Lester Pearson won the Nobel Prize for Peace in 1957. This was a great honour — for him and for Canada. The Nobel Prize is an award that is widely recognized around the world. The UNEF remained in place until June, 1967, when President Nasser of Egypt forced it to leave. There have been further major conflicts in the Middle East. Canada has always been ready to contribute to peacekeeping efforts there.

CANADA'S DISAPPOINTMENT WITH THE UNITED NATIONS

Thus far, the record of the United Nations might appear to you to be very good. In some respects, the record has been good. However, we must remember two key facts. First, the main goal of the United Nations is to prevent war. It has not achieved this aim. Second, Canada was counting on the UN for a measure of security. This could work only if the United Nations was able to prevent wars. In time, the weaknesses of the UN began to show. When that happened, Canada had to make other arrangements for its security.

WHAT WENT WRONG?

The United Nations has proved to be a disappointment for several reasons. To begin with, it does not have enough power. It cannot force any nation to do something it does not want to do. It can only ask, advise or suggest. The UN has no permanent armed force of its own. In the General Assembly, each country has one vote, regardless of size, wealth or power. It has become, in some ways, a debating society, where smaller, weaker or poorer nations can have their say. Therefore, it is often ignored by the big powers.

The big powers pay somewhat more attention to the Security Council. However, this body also has a serious weakness. Each of the five permanent members has the power of veto. This means that each of these countries can block any action with which it disagrees. In other words, all five permanent members must agree to any action before it can be taken. Look back at the chart on the organization of the United Nations. Name the five members of the Security Council. As you might imagine, they often disagree. Unanimous (united) agreement is almost always impossible. It is true that there has been no world war since 1945. This might be partly due to the existence of the United Nations. More likely it is due to the wish of the big powers to survive. With modern weapons, a world war might destroy the whole world.

The basic problem of the United Nations is that it is not a world government. None of its members gives up any of its independence when joining. Each member is free to leave the UN. It can support or reject UN policies as it sees fit. Earlier in this chapter, we saw that things cannot run this way in an individual country. All members of a society must agree to obey its laws. These laws must be enforced upon everyone. It seems that the countries and people of the world will not see the world as one society. They will not obey one set of laws. For these reasons, the United Nations has not become what its founders, including Canada, hoped it would be.

THE COLD WAR TOUCHES CANADA

The weaknesses of the United Nations became all the more apparent with the development of the "cold war." That phrase probably strikes you as unusual. Perhaps that is because wars are normally described as "hot" because of the fighting and violence involved. The term "cold war" refers to a situation that developed in the world after 1945. It centred around the two great superpowers, the United States and the Soviet Union. These two countries did not actually go to war with each other. However, they became bitter enemies. Their conflict took the form of arguing, spying and competing with one another. Thus, their war was one of words and threats. Relations between them became very hostile — or frigid, you might say. Hence, the term "cold war" was used to describe the situation.

Ironically, the cold war began to develop as World War II was drawing to a close. In that war, Canada, the United States and the Soviet Union were allies. That is, they fought on the same side. Their common enemy was Germany. Once Germany was defeated, it was hoped that we could remain on friendly terms with the Soviets.

Unfortunately, this did not happen. One reason was that there were great ideological differences between the two sides. The Soviet Union is a Communist country. The West (Canada, the United States, Britain, and their allies) believes in democracy. Because of this difference, there was bound to be some mistrust and suspicion.

There was another important problem. Both the United States and the Soviet Union had become superpowers. They were the two most powerful nations in the world. Each wanted to be "number one." Each wanted to expand its power and to influence as many countries as possible. Naturally, this meant there would be rivalry (competition) between them.

The two sides also disagreed about the peace terms in Europe. The Soviet Union had borne the brunt of the land war against Hitler's forces. Millions of Soviet citizens had been killed. Cities were torn apart. Toward the end of the war, the Russian forces swept toward victory. They rolled over much of Eastern Europe. They wanted to keep their influence in this region. This would protect their western borders against a new German attack. It also would give security against a possible attack by Western Europe or the United States. The Russians wanted to offer very harsh terms to Germany. They insisted that Germany

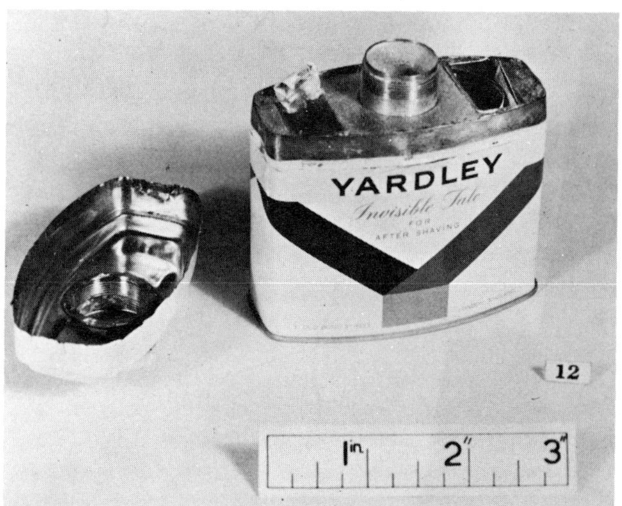

Evidence at a spy trial in Britain during the cold war. A tiny radio transmitter was hidden in this can of aftershave powder.

The Communist Countries of Europe in 1988

RUSSIA

OTHER COMMUNIST COUNTRIES

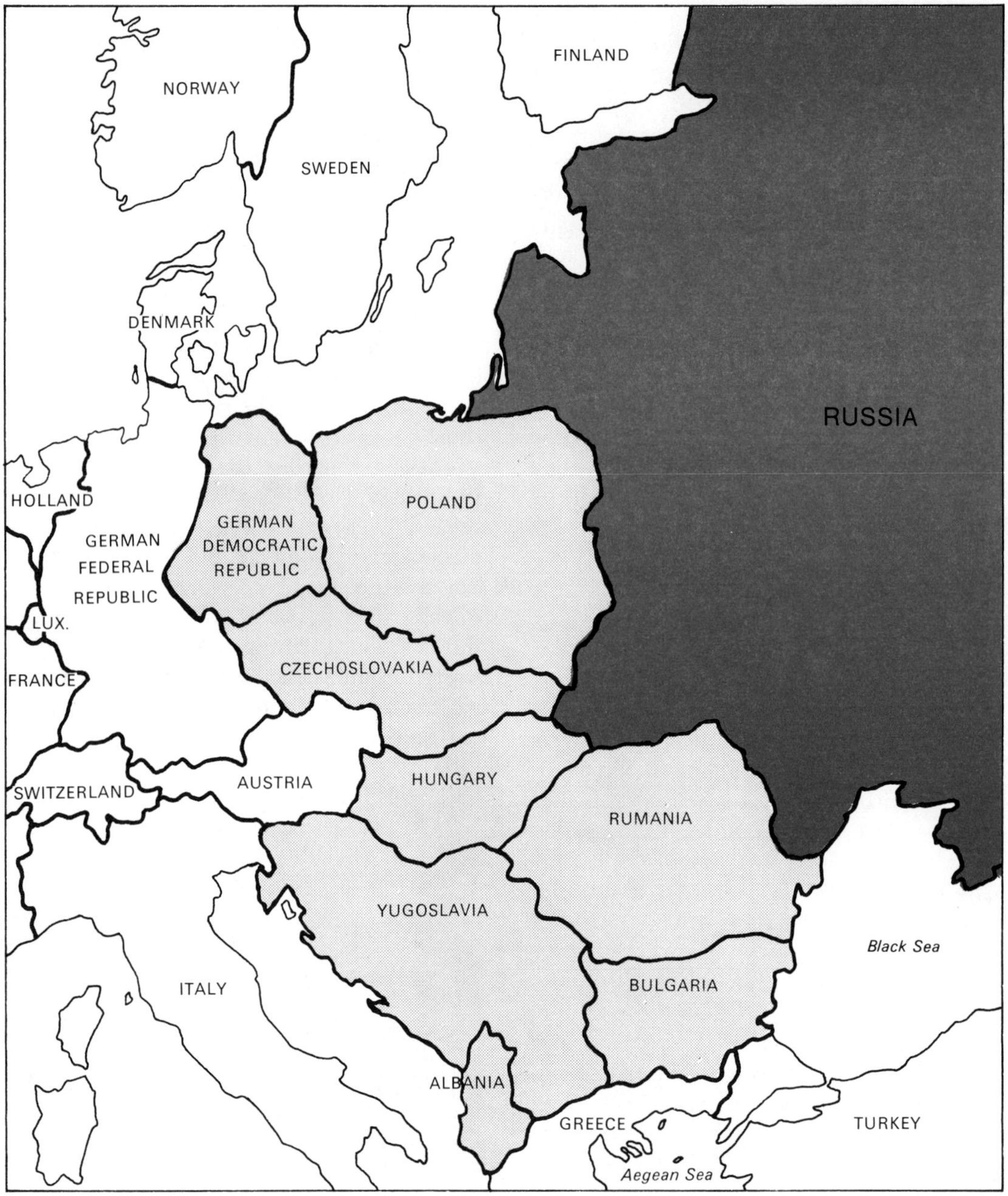

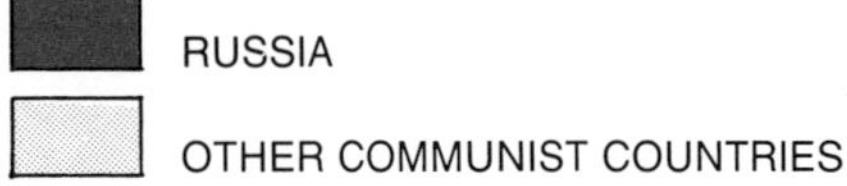

should remain weak and divided. This way, Germany could never again be a threat to peace or to the Soviet Union.

The Western allies did not completely agree with this approach. The United States was supported in this by Canada, Britain and France. They felt that the Soviet forces should withdraw from Eastern Europe now that the war was over. Furthermore, they began to realize how Germany could be useful to them. They did not want Germany to threaten world peace again. However, if allowed to keep some military strength, Germany could act as a buffer state (shield) to protect the West from Russian influence or expansion.

For these reasons, the cold war began. Problems arose in different areas. The wartime allies were unable to agree on a settlement in Europe. The West kept large forces in France, Holland, Belgium and western Germany. Russian forces remained in such countries as Poland, Hungary, Czechoslovakia and eastern Germany. In addition, the Soviet Union gave support to local Communist parties in these countries. With Soviet help, these parties gradually took over the governments of most East European nations. Russian agents also tried to arrange Communist takeovers of Greece and Turkey. (The latter country controls the Bosporus and the Dardanelles, the vital straits between the Black and Mediterranean Seas.)

In the late 1940s, Communist parties did well in elections in France and Italy. They also tried to stir up strikes and other troubles in several Western countries. From the Russian viewpoint, such actions were necessary and proper. They helped to spread communism, a system in which the Soviet government believed strongly. Also, they helped to strengthen Soviet security. However, the West did not share this view. Canada, the United States and their allies saw great danger in these developments. Some people came to believe that there was a Communist conspiracy (plot) to take over the whole world. Also, Communist rule brought dictatorship. This destroyed freedom and democracy wherever it went. These were ideals that the West was determined to defend.

THE FORMATION OF NATO

The proper name for NATO is the North Atlantic Treaty Organization. It was formed in 1948. Its aim was to meet the threat of Russian expansion. Canada was one of the first countries to join NATO. We did

To strengthen its ground forces, Canada purchased new "Leopard" tanks in the late 1970s. These were made in West Germany. They are faster and more powerful than the old Centurion tank. Some of the Leopards are on duty with NATO forces in Europe.

this with some regret. This is because we seemed to be admitting that the United Nations could not give us proper security. Forming this military alliance seemed to be a step backward. However, the danger from the Soviet Union appeared to be increasing. Our first responsibility was the protection of our country. The following countries belong to NATO:

Belgium
Canada
Denmark
Federal Republic of Germany (West Germany)
*France
*Greece
Iceland
Italy
Luxembourg
Netherlands
Norway
Portugal
Spain
Turkey
United Kingdom
United States

*Both France and Greece later withdrew from the NATO military command. Each country took back complete control over its own armed forces. However, both countries are committed to the common defence of all NATO members.

1 Locate each of these countries on a world map. In terms of position, what do most of them have in common? How does this help explain the title of their organization?
2 Who are the four most powerful members of NATO? Of these, which is strongest? Why?
3 How powerful is Canada in relation to its NATO allies?

4 Why would Canada and the United States be concerned about what happens in Europe? Why would it not be better for North America to simply defend itself and let Western Europe do the same?

HOW NATO WORKS

The main idea behind NATO is collective security. This means "One for all, and all for one." Each member of NATO promises to help all the other members. This includes financial and economic aid. It also means military help if necessary. Thus, if Canada is attacked by a hostile country, every other NATO member is bound to help us. In return, we must go to the aid of any other NATO member that is attacked. In this way, NATO provides group protection, or collective security. No enemy country can attack one NATO member without having to take on *all* members.

NATO's European members had the most to fear from an attack by the Soviet Union. Therefore, large NATO forces were stationed in Western Europe. For the most part, they have been under a unified command, usually headed by a top American officer. NATO headquarters are situated at Castean Mons in Belgium. NATO forces are equipped with a variety of weapons ranging from conventional arms to nuclear weapons. NATO hopes that its strength will act as a deterrent (discouragement) to potential enemies. Knowing that an attack could mean total destruction, such an enemy would not dare begin a war.

From the beginning of NATO, Canada has contributed to its forces in several ways. At first, we agreed to keep a full army brigade (8000 to 10 000 soldiers) in Western Europe. Later, we added several squadrons of jet fighter aircraft. Units of the Canadian navy also were assigned to NATO duty. These ships helped to patrol the seas, keeping track of Soviet fleets and submarines. All of this cost Canada millions of dollars per year. It seemed to be a good investment for our security.

A Canadian CF-18 jet fighter on a routine training mission over Southern Germany as part of Canada's NATO commitment.

THE SOVIET RESPONSE TO NATO

The Soviet Union was very upset by the creation of NATO. It argued that no such alliance was needed because the Soviet Union was *not* an aggressor. It posed no threat to Western Europe. On the contrary, the Russians argued that the creation of NATO was itself an aggressive act. They saw NATO as a threat to the security of Eastern Europe. Therefore, the Soviet Union persuaded many countries of that region to form their own alliance. This finally was done in 1955. The organization was called the Warsaw Pact. Its members are: Albania, Bulgaria, Czechoslovakia, East Germany, Hungary, Poland, Rumania and the Soviet Union.

All of this happened within ten years of the end of World War II. In that terrible conflict, over 100 million human beings died. Nonetheless, the world by 1955 was once again divided into two hostile armed camps. The cold war was on.

Soviet troops taking physical training. Soviet forces in Europe are more numerous and better prepared than the conventional NATO forces which they face.

CANADA AND THE UNITED STATES FORM NORAD

The cold war went on throughout the 1950s. The Korean War (discussed in the previous chapter) was one aspect of the cold war. So, too, was the Communist takeover in China in 1949. For a while, China and the Soviet Union appeared to become allies. This created a powerful combination against the West. Communist influence seemed to be spreading in Europe and Asia.

New developments in weaponry made the tension and danger even worse. Both the Soviet Union and the United States enlarged their armed forces. They became locked in an arms race. They were competing to see who could build the most and biggest weapons. These included very powerful hydrogen bombs. One such bomb was capable of wiping out a large city.

Normally, such bombs, or "warheads," were carried to their targets by jet bombers. However, during the 1950s, guided missiles became more important. Missiles fired from 10 000 km away could hit North America in about half an hour! Canada and the United States had plans for the defence of North America. However, these plans were several years old. These new weapons made the plans out of date. To meet this danger, Canada and the United States formed the North American Air Defence System (NORAD) in 1958. The details of this system are described in Chapter 16. Since 1958 Canada has reviewed its position every few years. On each occasion, we have decided to remain in NORAD. It is still one of the key links in our system of security and defence.

A NEW WORLD TAKES SHAPE

Fortunately, the tension of the cold war began to ease somewhat in the 1960s. There were several reasons for this. Both the United States and the Soviet Union had come to accept each other as superpowers. Each could destroy the other but would be destroyed in return. It was clear that they simply had to get along somehow. Also, each got to know the other a little better. Perhaps this reduced their fear and suspicion somewhat. New leaders came forward in many countries. They did not have the same prejudices. They seemed more willing to work with one another, and to accept change.

There were many signs that the cold war was beginning to thaw, at least a little. There was increased trade and travel between East and West. Cultural exchanges became more common. Government leaders held more conferences and made more agreements. For example, several countries signed a treaty that banned the use of nuclear weapons in outer space or on the ocean floor. They also agreed to try to stop the spread of nuclear weapons to other countries. The United States and the Soviet Union even began meetings to discuss limiting the numbers and types of their nuclear weapons.

The world was changing in other ways as well. Many new nations emerged. This was especially true in Asia and Africa. Nations of Western Europe, such as Germany, had recovered from World War II. They wanted to regain an important voice in world affairs. So did Asian nations, such as China and Japan.

Our government could not ignore these changes. The Canadian public was beginning to take a greater interest in world affairs. They could see that our foreign policy was becoming outdated. We still talked and acted like a middle power, yet we had not been one for many years. If world tension was declining, then possibly NATO and NORAD were outdated, or at least less important than they used to be. Perhaps we should be giving more attention and money to the poor, underdeveloped countries of the world.

For these and other reasons, by the late 1960s, Canadian foreign policy was ready for a complete review. When Pierre Trudeau took over as prime minister in 1968, that review became inevitable.

BUILDING YOUR LEARNING SKILLS

FOCUSSING ON THE ISSUE

1 Why was World War II an important experience for Canada?

2 What two different strategies did Canada employ to try to ensure its security and its survival in the years following the war?

3 Why was Canada so anxious for the United Nations to succeed?

4 Why did the cold war begin? How did this development affect Canada's foreign policy?

5 Why did the Canadian government begin a review of its foreign policy in the late 1960s?

6 U Thant, a former secretary general of the United Nations, once said, "In modern war, there is only one victor, and his name is Death." How does this statement express the main theme of this chapter?

7 The following terms appeared in this chapter. Try to recall their meanings and how they were used.

aggression	middle power
arms race	NATO
buffer state	NORAD
collective security	peacekeeping
conventional weapons	refugee
demobilization	superpower
deterrent	veto
economic sanction	Warsaw Pact
international law	world government

RESEARCHING

1 For up-to-date information on the United Nations and its activities, write to: Information Division, United Nations New York, New York 10017 USA.

2 Try to discover whether or not Canada has any non-conventional weapons, such as nuclear warheads, chemical weapons or germ-warfare equipment. Use your findings as the basis for a panel discussion or debate. (See "Communicating.")

3 Do research on the latest missiles and other weapons being developed by the United States and the Soviet Union. Your information can be used to support a class simulation. (See "Communicating.")

ORGANIZING

1 Put the following events in proper chronological order:
- Formation of NORAD
- Suez Crisis
- Korean War
- End of World War II
- Trudeau's review of foreign policy
- Formation of NATO
- Beginning of the cold war
- Formation of Warsaw Pact

2 The following is a list of several countries in the world today:

Argentina	Japan
Britain	Nigeria
Canada	Poland
China	West Germany
India	United States
Italy	Soviet Union

To the best of your ability, rank order these countries according to their power, from most to least powerful. Then try to put them in columns under these headings: superpower, major power, middle power, small power. Compare your opinions with those of classmates. Have your teacher develop a class consensus.

3 Which of these countries does not belong to NATO today: France, Portugal, Norway, Austria, Canada, Britain?

4 Imagine that two students are assigned essays on the United Nations. One has to trace its birth and development; the other has to evaluate its effectiveness. For each essay, suggest five or six headings under which notes could be made. Then suggest an appropriate sequence (order) in which those headings could be presented. Compare your ideas with those of classmates.

COMMUNICATING

1 On page 360 the chart showing the organization of the United Nations also displays the United Nations symbol. What does it represent?

2 Why is a bird, the dove, widely regarded as a symbol of peace?

3 Write a one-page article, in the form of a newspaper editorial, in which you argue either that:

a Canada should take all necessary steps to reclaim its status as a middle power; OR

b As an example to the world, Canada should give up all of its weapons and armed forces.

Then find a classmate who has chosen to write

on the theme you did not choose. Compare your arguments. Evaluate each other's editorial for clarity and strength of the argument.

4 Refer back to "Researching," question two. Divide your class into two groups: Half will be Americans and half Soviets. Each group will discuss its strategy privately. Imagine that you are preparing for a meeting with the other country to try to agree on limiting or abolishing certain weapons. Argue if you must, but agree on a plan for your team. What will you agree to give up? What do you want the other country to give up in exchange? Now hold your conference.
   a What happened? Why did it happen? What does this tell you about the arms race and the problems of disarmament?
   b Compare your results with what has actually happened in arms talks between the Soviets and the Americans. Such talks go on almost constantly and usually are reported in the press. See what you can find.
   c Based on your experience of the above exercise, what problems of communication seem to exist between the two sides? Do they necessarily *want* to communicate effectively with one another? Explain your answer.

5 Debate one of the following resolutions:
   a The United Nations is now little more than a glorified and costly debating society and should be dissolved; OR
   b Without the existence of nuclear weapons, World War III would already have happened.

ANALYZING

1 In the Suez Crisis of 1956, the United States was on one side and Britain on the other. Why would this be embarrassing and difficult for Canada?

2 Why would NORAD put its command headquarters inside a mountain?

3 It has been suggested that Canada should leave NORAD because we are becoming too dependent on the United States. What do you think of this idea?

4 If Canada cancelled its security agreements with the United States, would the Americans defend us anyway, whether we wanted this or not? Explain your answer.

5 Why is Germany considered a buffer state? Could Canada play this role? Why or why not?

6 Part of NATO's strategy always has been to have a wide variety of weapons available. This permits it to make a flexible response to any aggression. The following is a partial list of the actions that NATO could take in the event of a Soviet attack on Europe. Put these in order of seriousness, from least to most serious:
   - send troops, guns, tanks and other conventional weapons to meet the invaders;
   - warn the Soviets to withdraw their troops;
   - release nerve gas that would paralyze the enemy troops;
   - drop conventional bombs on Soviet cities and industrial centres;
   - use chemical weapons on the Soviet troops;
   - give the Soviets a time limit for the withdrawal of their forces;
   - launch missiles armed with nuclear warheads against the Soviet Union;
   - fire small tactical nuclear warheads at the Soviet troops;
   - drop bombs on the Soviet Union that would release deadly gases and germs.

APPLYING YOUR KNOWLEDGE

1 What is meant by a world government? Why is the United Nations not a world government? With the help of classmates, try to plan the structure of a world government. You will have to think about rules, various governing bodies, budget, law enforcement and voting arrangements. If you succeed in creating a model, try it out. Set up an imaginary world crisis, and take it to your world government for solution.

2 Based on your experience of question one above, what is the most difficult part of making a world government work? Could this problem ever be solved? Why or why not?

3 Why do you suppose each permanent member of the United Nations Security Council insisted on having veto power? Canada opposed the idea. Suggest a reason for our attitude.

4 Many people criticize the United Nations. An American once said that such people reminded him of "the poor Roman who felt sorry for himself because he didn't have a shoe, until he saw a man who didn't have a foot." What was he saying about critics of the United Nations? Do you agree?

5 In the 1950s, before NORAD, the United States operated a Strategic Air Command. It kept armed bombers in the air at all times. Why would it do this? One of its pilots once said, "The moment we get the order to fly into Russia and drop our bombs, we will have failed in our main mission." What did he mean by this?

chapter 20

FOREIGN POLICY FOR A CHANGING WORLD: CANADA'S SEARCH FOR NEW ROLES

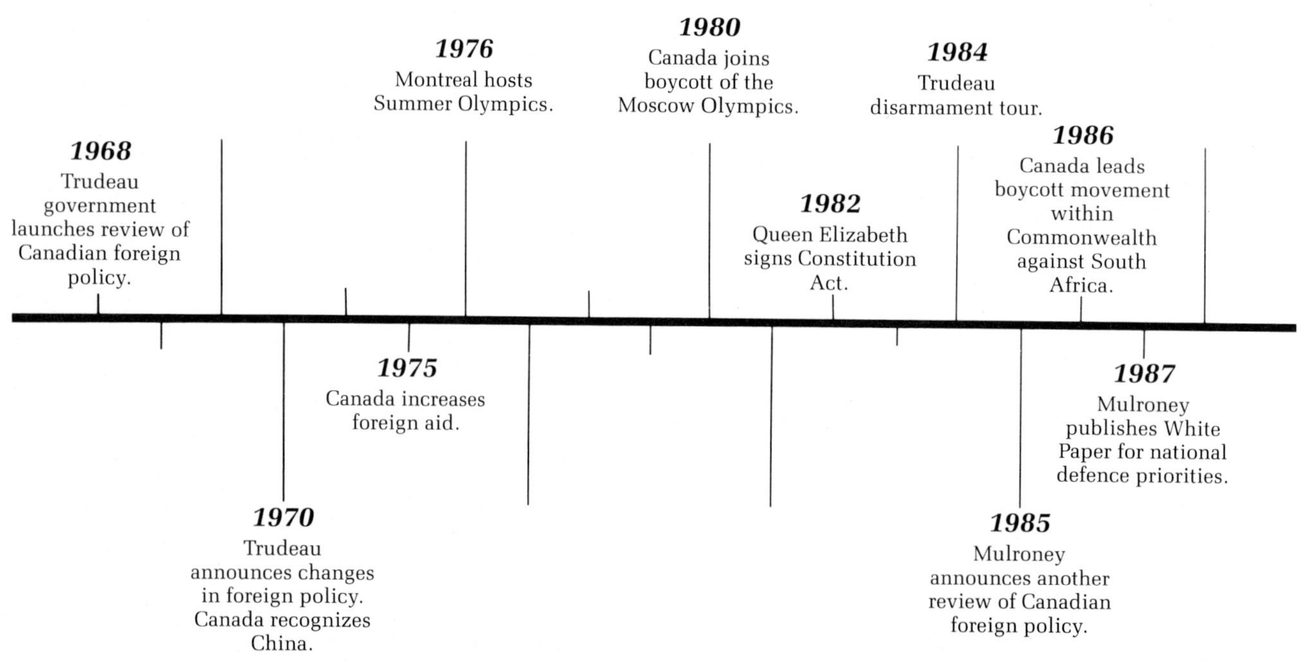

1968
Trudeau government launches review of Canadian foreign policy.
1970
Trudeau announces changes in foreign policy. Canada recognizes China.
1975
Canada increases foreign aid.
1976
Montreal hosts Summer Olympics.
1980
Canada joins boycott of the Moscow Olympics.
1982
Queen Elizabeth signs Constitution Act.
1984
Trudeau disarmament tour.
1985
Mulroney announces another review of Canadian foreign policy.
1986
Canada leads boycott movement within Commonwealth against South Africa.
1987
Mulroney publishes White Paper for national defence priorities.

TOPIC ORGANIZER

THEME ORGANIZER

- The Trudeau review of foreign policy was badly needed and long overdue.
- This review resulted in our foreign policy becoming more realistic.
- We abandoned the pretense of being a middle power and concentrated more on economic assistance to less fortunate countries.
- We remained in the British Commonwealth but placed less importance on this tie than we did previously.
- The major threat to the world today is nuclear war. We have tried to encourage the superpowers to reduce the tension, mistrust and weapons competition between themselves.
- Our government continues to believe that it is in Canada's interest to belong to NATO and NORAD rather than withdrawing from these alliances, possibly to become neutral in the cold war.
- Canada is a leading critic of dictatorial regimes that repeatedly violate human rights.
- We have opened our doors to many immigrants, including refugees.
- Although our influence is limited, we could be doing more to help solve the world's major problems. The more we contribute, the more influence we are likely to have.

INTRODUCTION

As we learned in the previous chapter, the world was changing rapidly in the 1960s. Despite this fact, there had been no major review of Canadian foreign policy. Our goals and methods had remained basically the same for over 15 years. In 1968 the way was cleared for such a review to begin. In that year, Prime Minister Lester Pearson retired from politics. He had been the main architect (designer) of Canada's foreign policy since 1950. Pierre Trudeau was Canada's next prime minister.

Mr. Trudeau was an exciting new personality in politics. He was well educated, fairly young and very intelligent. He had played no part in the formation of earlier Canadian foreign policy. Therefore, he could look at it in an open, unbiased way. He was quite prepared to make changes in it if necessary. This attitude seemed to have the support of the Canadian public. And so, in 1968, Mr. Trudeau made an important announcement. There would be a complete review of Canadian foreign policy.

In this chapter, we begin by looking at the Trudeau review of foreign policy. Then we will see the results of this review. Next we will consider some issues that still face Canada in world affairs. Finally, we will briefly summarize what we have learned in this unit about Canadian foreign policy.

Before reading on, study the chart of key words and ideas that follows.

KEY WORDS AND IDEAS IN THIS CHAPTER

Term	Meaning	Sample Use
ambassador	a person sent by one country to represent it in a foreign nation	Canada sends ambassadors to most other countries in the world.
apartheid	a policy of systematic oppression of the black majority by the ruling white regime in South Africa	Canada has been a leader among nations trying to pressure the South African government to abandon apartheid.
British Commonwealth	an organization of former British colonies that co-operate in trade and other matters	Canada plays an important role in the British Commonwealth.

Canadian International Development Agency (CIDA)	an organization set up by our government to help poorer countries in the world	Through CIDA Canada sends much valuable aid to other countries each year.
Canadian University Service Overseas (CUSO)	an organization that sends university students to countries needing various kinds of assistance	CUSO is one of many ways in which Canada helps less fortunate countries.
Colombo Plan	an organization created in 1950 to provide aid to Southeast Asia	Canada was a leading supporter of the Colombo Plan.
colony	an area that is not independent but rather is controlled by a foreign state	Canada is a former colony of Britain.
developed nation	one that is industrialized and therefore has a reasonably high standard of living	Canada, the United States and most Western European nations are examples of developed nations.
diplomatic recognition	a sign of official acceptance of one country by another	In 1970 Canada gave diplomatic recognition to the government of Communist China.
foreign aid	help that one country gives to another	Foreign aid is an important part of Canadian foreign policy.
la Francophonie	French-speaking parts of the world, mostly former colonies of France	Quebec is interested in la Francophonie. The Trudeau government increased foreign aid to member countries.
gross national product (GNP)	the value of all goods and services produced by a country's economy in one year	Canada's GNP is well over $350 billion per year. We give about half of one percent of this in foreign aid.
MAD (mutual assured destruction)	a situation that exists between the United States and the Soviet Union, in which each can wipe out the other because of their massive nuclear arsenals	Disarmament activists seek the elimination of MAD policies.
nonalignment	the policy of not taking sides in world affairs	Many nations in the world are aligned — with the United States, the USSR or China. Others follow a policy of nonalignment. Many of these belong to the Third World.
refugee	a person who flees to a foreign country to escape danger or persecution in his or her own country	There are over 10 million refugees in the world today.
Third World	refers to nations that are nonaligned and usually underdeveloped	Most Third World countries are found in Africa and Asia.
tied aid	foreign aid that has "strings attached"	Some of Canada's aid is tied aid: We lend money to countries and then insist they buy Canadian products with some or all of the money.

underdeveloped nations	countries that have had little industrial or urban growth, are quite poor and need foreign aid	Underdeveloped nations are found mostly in the Third World. Many are bitter. They think the developed countries take advantage of them. They want a bigger share of the world's riches.

SETTING UP THE TRUDEAU REVIEW

Prime Minister Trudeau invited the whole country to take part in this review. He encouraged the press and the public to say what they thought. He personally took part in debates on the subject in many parts of Canada. People were invited to talk to government committees. Many people took advantage of this chance. They included professors, businesspeople, teachers, soldiers and diplomats.

To help guide the review, Mr. Trudeau set down a few guidelines. Any decisions made should meet certain conditions. His guidelines are listed below.

1 Canada needed to broaden its ties with other countries. We should not be too dependent on any one other nation.
2 Canadian foreign policy should not be controlled by our armed forces.
3 Our foreign policy should reflect life in Canada. It should be based on our ideals and values, on public opinion and on our needs.
4 The goals of our foreign policy should be realistic (sensible).
5 Any foreign policy decision must:
- **a** help our economy grow;
- **b** keep us independent;
- **c** maintain peace;
- **d** protect our security;
- **e** be morally right (be fair and honest);
- **f** help all peoples gain a better life;
- **g** protect our environment (fight pollution and save resources).

UNDERSTANDING THE GUIDELINES

1 Why would Canadians be concerned about being too dependent on one country? How could the government help to broaden our ties?

2 Why would it be dangerous for any country to let its armed forces control foreign policy?

3 How do we set realistic goals in foreign policy? Why should we consider our economic and military strength in doing this? Can we do whatever we want in foreign policy? Why or why not?

4 In May, 1968, Prime Minister Trudeau said this about Canadian foreign policy: "We shall do more good by doing well what we know to be within our resources to do, than to pretend, either to ourselves or to others, that we can do things clearly beyond our national capacity." In simple terms, what was he saying? To which one of his guidelines (above) does this comment refer? Why do you think so? Do you agree with his view?

5 Look at number five again. List these factors in order of importance, as you see them. Be sure you have reasons for your decisions. Compare your ideas with those of your classmates.

FINDINGS AND SUGGESTIONS OF THE TRUDEAU REVIEW

The results of the review of foreign policy were published in 1970. The publication was called *Foreign Policy for Canadians* (available in most libraries). It took the form of six separate booklets. The first provided a general plan for Canadian foreign policy. The other five booklets were called "sector papers." They dealt with Europe, the Pacific, Latin America, the United Nations and foreign aid to poorer countries. Below are some of the key ideas from *Foreign Policy for Canadians*.

EUROPE

- Canadians have strong ties with Europe. About 96 percent of all Canadians are of European ancestry. About 14 percent of all Canadians were born in Europe.
- Canada has diplomatic and trade ties with every European country.
- Canada's future relations with Europe are very important.
- Europe can help Canada reduce its dependence on the United States.
- We should trade more with Europe.
- We should encourage more Europeans to invest in Canada.
- We should take advantage of the thaw in the cold war. We should be seeking closer ties with Central and Eastern Europe, not just with Western Europe.

THE PACIFIC

- Canada is not just an Atlantic-coast nation. We also are a country on the rim of the Pacific.
- Tremendous changes are taking place in Asia.
- Canada's relations with Pacific nations are important. This is especially true of such countries as China, Japan, Australia, Indonesia, Malaysia and the Philippines.
- Canada should increase its exports to and investments in the Pacific region.
- Canada should encourage an exchange of people, culture and ideas with Pacific nations.
- Canada should increase its aid to poor Pacific nations.
- Canada should avoid large military commitments in this region.

LATIN AMERICA

- We live in the same hemisphere as the Latin American peoples. Nonetheless, we have not felt particularly close to them in the past.
- Canada has few historical or cultural ties with Latin America.
- Canada should seek stronger ties with countries of Latin America. This is especially true of trade. Latin America has a large, rapidly growing population. It could become an important market for Canadian goods. Also, Latin America has many valuable resources, such as oil, that Canada needs.
- Canada and Latin America share a common concern about strong American influence. This could be a base on which to build closer ties and thus reduce our dependence on the United States.

UNITED NATIONS

- Canada has been one of the strongest supporters of the UN.
- The UN has been a disappointment to Canada, particularly in the preservation of peace.
- Canada should not count on the UN as much as it has in the past.
- Canada should continue to support the UN. However, less emphasis should be placed on peacekeeping. More stress should be placed on helping poor nations, working for disarmament and winning more respect for human rights and international law.

FOREIGN AID

- Canada has had a fairly good record in this regard. However, it still does not meet the amount of aid suggested by the United Nations.
- Canada can and should increase its foreign aid to poorer countries.
- Canadians think that their foreign aid is more generous than is really the case.
- Canada's foreign aid should stress development assistance. This means that it should aim to help countries become more self-sufficient. Previously, much of our aid was to help deal with immediate problems such as starvation or disease.

This kind of slum area is all too common in underdeveloped countries. Canada has increased its aid to such countries in recent years.

- Our foreign aid should become broader in scope. It should not all be given out through the United Nations and the British Commonwealth.

CANADA AND THE BRITISH COMMONWEALTH

Another important part of Canada's foreign policy is our membership in the British Commonwealth. At one time, Great Britain controlled a huge world empire. The statement "The sun never sets on the British Empire" was literally true. The empire stretched right around the world. When the sun was setting on one part, it was rising on another.

However, after World War II the sun *did* set on the British Empire. Almost all of the areas that Britain held as colonies (dependent lands) are now independent. Still, many of them have decided to remain associated with Britain and with each other. They do this through membership in the British Commonwealth. This organization contains 25 percent of the world's population. It occupies 20 percent of the world's land area. All major continents and racial groups are represented in it. Usually, relations among its members are friendly and harmonious. The Commonwealth acts as an example to the world of how peoples of different languages, races and cultures can co-operate. In this sense, it is similar to the United Nations.

Canada has been a member of the Commonwealth from the very beginning. We developed some important trade ties within it. Our association with the Commonwealth nations reduces our dependence on the United States, if only slightly. Membership in the Commonwealth also could help Canadian security. Other members might be willing to help Canada in time of trouble. In addition, Canada has given a great deal of foreign aid to certain Commonwealth countries. This was given mainly to poorer nations in Africa and Asia.

For example, the Colombo Plan was created in 1950. Its goal was to ensure economic progress throughout Southeast Asia. Canada has been a major supporter of this plan. We have given tens of millions of dollars for such projects as a cement plant in Pakistan, a nuclear reactor in India and power, irrigation and transportation systems in several countries.

By the late 1960s, Canada had become one of the leading members of the British Commonwealth. Despite this, our role in that organization came under review in 1968–1970. In *Foreign Policy for Canadi-*

The Commonwealth

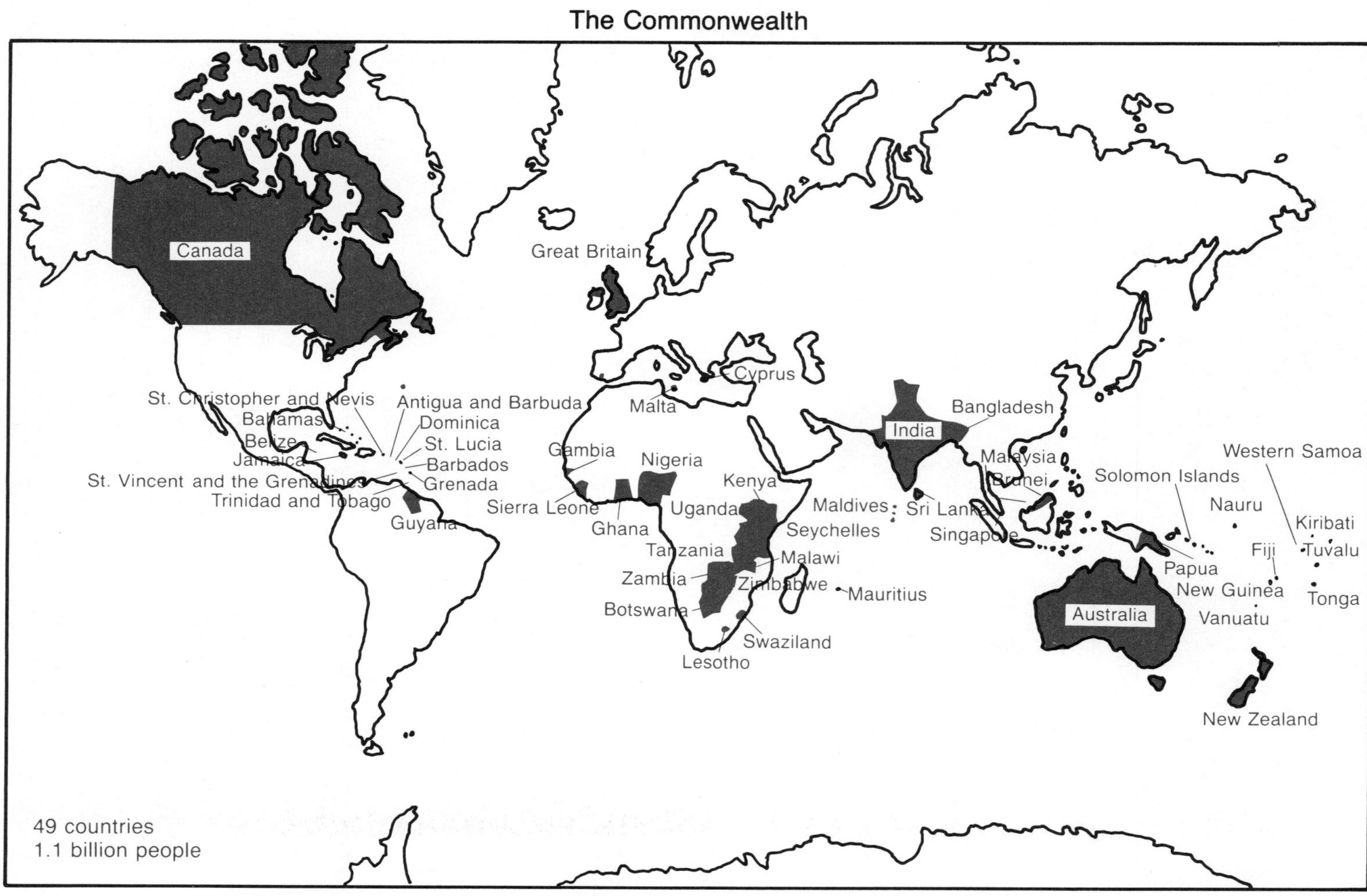

ans, there was no sector paper on the Commonwealth. Instead, individual member countries were considered as part of the region in which they were located. Canada still plays an active part in the British Commonwealth. Many Canadians feel that membership in the Commonwealth is part of Canada's identity in the world community. However, this feeling is not regarded as a vital part of our foreign policy.

RESULTS OF THE TRUDEAU REVIEW OF FOREIGN POLICY

Even before the results of the review were published, the Trudeau government had begun to take action. One of the most important steps concerned defence policy. In April, 1969, Prime Minister Trudeau announced changes in Canada's NATO role. Over the next few years, we would abandon our nuclear role. That is, Canadian forces working with NATO would no longer have nuclear weapons. Also, the number of Canadian ground troops in Europe would be reduced by almost 50 percent. Further, Canada's defence budget was frozen at $1.82 billion per year until 1972. This made Canada one of the lowest spenders on defence of any NATO country.

In 1970 the Trudeau government made another very important move. It gave official diplomatic recognition to China. This means that we accepted the Communist government of China as the legal government. We also exchanged ambassadors with China. This was important for several reasons. First, we showed our independence from American policy. (The United States did not yet recognize Communist China.) Second, we showed that we accepted the fact that some countries preferred to live under communism. (This is an example of the realism that Mr. Trudeau called for.) Third, we showed that we regarded Asia as a vital area of the world. China is a key power in that area and will become even more important in the future.

During his 1973 visit to China, Trudeau meets Mao Zedong (deceased 1976), the revolutionary leader who turned China into a communist state.

As we said earlier, *Foreign Policy for Canadians* was published in 1970. After this, our government responded to it in several ways. Many of these are summarized below.

GOVERNMENT RESPONSES TO THE TRUDEAU REVIEW

CANADA AND EUROPE

- The Trudeau government carried on with the reduction of Canadian forces in Europe. The army brigade was reduced to about 5000 soldiers. Nuclear weapons were abandoned.
- Canada dropped its opposition to Britain's entry into the European Economic Community. Instead, the government appointed a special ambassador to the EEC. Canada has also tried to arrange new trade terms. Canada seeks certain favours as well as investment capital from European nations. (French and Swedish auto manufacturers already have established branch plants in Quebec and Nova Scotia. French, German and Swiss money is being invested in Canadian industries.)
- Canada now attends the meetings of the important Council of Europe.
- Canada has signed agreements to share scientific and technological information with various European countries. It also belongs to the Committee on the Challenges of Modern Society.
- The Trudeau government signed trade, scientific and cultural agreements with the Soviet Union. We want to sell products to the USSR and its Eastern European allies.
- Prime Minister Trudeau visited the Soviet Union. His goal was to strengthen goodwill and to see how the Soviets have developed their far northern areas. Canada hopes to borrow Soviet know-how in this field.
- Canada's relations with France became somewhat strained. France seemed to show sympathy for the separatist movement in

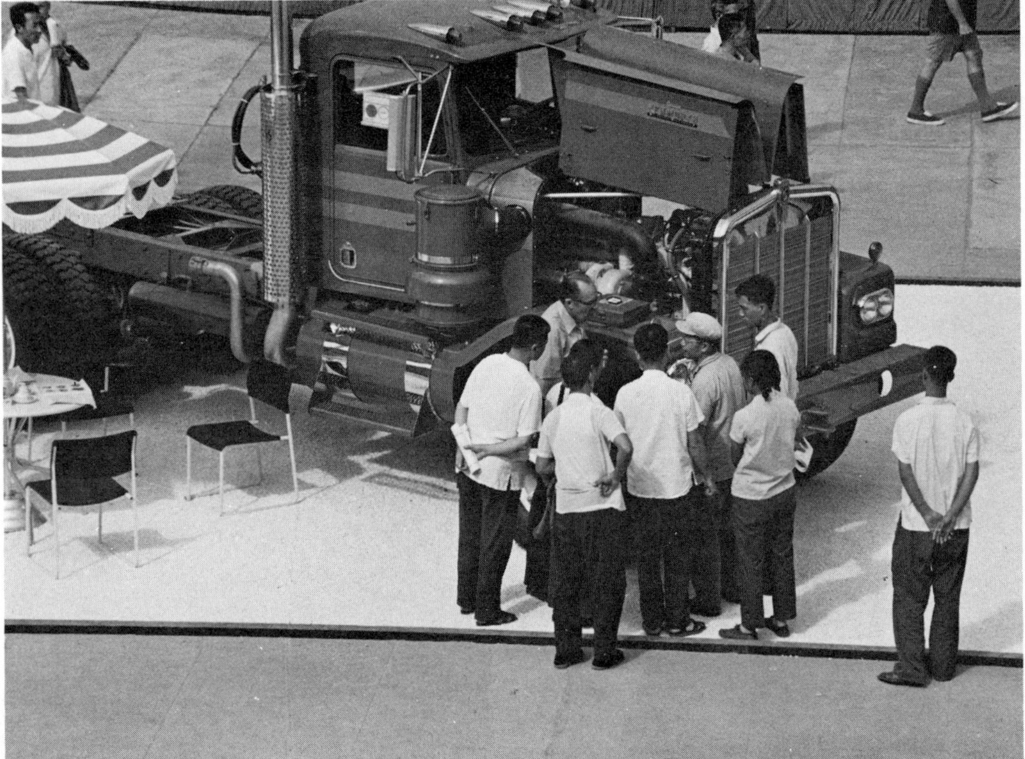

A representative from Canadian business shows a truck to interested Chinese at a trade exhibition in Peking.

Quebec. Canada regarded this as unwanted interference in its internal affairs.

CANADA AND THE PACIFIC

- Prime Minister Trudeau travelled more widely in the Pacific than any previous Canadian prime minister. His travels underlined the importance of this region to Canada.
- Canada kept its close ties with Commonwealth members in the Pacific region.
- Japan was recognized as our second-most-important trading partner and source of foreign investment.
- The federal government greatly enlarged port facilities on the coast of British Columbia.
- Trade with Australia and New Zealand increased significantly.
- Canada established diplomatic relations with Communist China. Trade and cultural exchanges with China increased.
- Canada altered its immigration policy to admit more Asians.
- The federal government sponsored Asian studies programs in Canadian universities. It also set up a Pacific Economic Advisory Committee.
- In 1973 Canada agreed to serve on the International Commission of Control and Supervision (ICCS), created to observe the Vietnam peace settlement. (Canada soon found it necessary to withdraw from that body.)
- Canada increased its foreign aid to Pacific nations.
- In the autumn of 1973, Ottawa announced a three-year wheat deal with China that had a potential value of $1 billion. This coincided with an official visit to China by Prime Minister Trudeau.
- By the late 1970s, Taiwan and Hong Kong had become major sources of imported goods to Canada. These imports were low-priced. Some of them threatened the jobs of Canadian workers in similar industries, such as clothing. The government put limits on the amount of textiles (mostly clothing) that could be imported. Its aim was to protect Canadian businesses and workers. The government also considered limiting textile imports from certain Asian countries. This move, too, was designed to help Canadian companies and workers.

CANADA AND LATIN AMERICA

- Canada was very cautious in dealing with the nations of this region. This is because we had commitments elsewhere. Also, the United States has a special interest in Latin America.
- Canada had investments in and trade ties with many Latin American countries. These ties were growing stronger. However, they were still not very strong.
- Canada continued to reject membership in the Organization of American States (OAS).
- Canada increased its development aid to Latin America.
- Canadian ties with Mexico were growing. Mexico is now our second largest market in Latin America. We consult each other on common problems. These include pollution, drug traffic and laws of the sea.
- Canada admitted hundreds of political refugees from Chile after a revolution took place in that country.
- Canadian trade and tourism with Cuba increased.

CANADA AND THE UNITED NATIONS

- Canada no longer counted heavily on the UN to handle threats to world peace.
- Canada maintained and increased its support for UN aid programs.
- Canada continued to assist, when asked, in peacekeeping operations. One example of such assistance was the force sent to the Middle East in 1973.
- Canada's overall feeling about the UN was expressed by Mitchell Sharp in September 1969: "Canada believes that the United Nations must fail to reach its goals if it cannot come to grips with its own problems . . . The UN . . . is drowning in a sea of words. . . . This has led governments to attach less importance to the United Nations' activities. . . ." Similar thoughts were expressed by External Affairs Minister Joe Clark in October, 1984. In a frank,

hard-hitting speech, he outlined the UN's main weaknesses. He also pledged Canada's continuing support for the United Nations' efforts to maintain world peace.

CANADA AND INTERNATIONAL DEVELOPMENT

- The government body responsible for running Canada's assistance program was the Canadian International Development Agency (CIDA).
- The Trudeau government made foreign aid a major feature of its foreign policy. The goal of the 1975–76 federal budget was to set aside ¾ of 1 percent of Canada's gross national product for such assistance. To date, we have not achieved this goal. Indeed, by the mid-1980s, we were slipping farther away from it (see page 386).
- The countries receiving development aid from Canada were located in Asia, Africa, Latin America and the Caribbean.
- A greater share of Canadian aid was directed to French-speaking countries, especially in Africa.
- In Asia, the state of Malaysia became a special object of Canadian aid.
- Peru, Brazil and Colombia are examples of Latin American nations with which Canada developed new aid programs.
- In the Caribbean, Canada increased assistance to fellow Commonwealth countries.

HELP FOR FOREIGN COUNTRIES

As we all know, Canada is one of the richest countries in the world. Canadians live better, fuller lives than do most of the people of the world. If you don't agree that life in Canada is very good, ask yourself the following questions:

- Have I ever had to worry about where my next meal was coming from?
- If I became injured or sick, would it be impossible to get medicine or decent medical attention?
- Have I ever seen a child suffering from serious malnutrition?
- Have I ever seen a person actually dying of starvation or thirst?
- Is it impossible for me to get a good education, even if I want it badly?
- Is it fairly normal to see dead bodies in the streets of my neighbourhood?

For most of us, the answer to each of those questions is no. However, to millions of human beings, the answers would all be yes. In comparison with us, many countries in the world are poor; they are often referred to as underdeveloped nations. More recently, they have been referred to as countries of the Third World.

These countries want but do not have the standard of living enjoyed by the industrialized nations of the world. They are called the Third World because most of them are nonaligned. This means that they have no firm commitments either to the East or the West. In the cold war, they do not support either side. Most of these countries are in Africa and Asia. There also are many underdeveloped countries in Latin America. However, most of these are aligned with the United States—at least, up to a point.

Here are some statistics that show how badly the underdeveloped nations need help:

- 500 million people in the world live in absolute poverty.
- Each day about 10 000 people die from malnutrition, and another 25 000 die from water-borne diseases such as typhus. Many of these are children.
- About 30 percent of all adults alive today cannot read or write.
- The average income for a person living in Haiti is about 3 percent of the average income in Canada.
- Nigeria has one doctor for every 35 000 people; Canada has one for every 750 people.
- A Canadian consumes about 2.3 kg of food per day; the average person in India consumes about 0.5 kg, most of which is rice.
- In Canada, about 1 child in 40 dies before it is one year old; in South America and Asia the figure is 1 in 10.
- On a per capita (per person) basis, the developed countries consume twenty-five times the resources that underdeveloped countries use.

- About 20 percent of the world's population enjoys about 80 percent of its hardware.
- In 1984 the world spent over $600 billion on military items; this is over 30 times as much as was sent in aid to less developed countries.
- Canada has 0.5 percent of the world's population. However, we claim:
  - 7.3 percent of the world's land surface;
  - 15 percent of the world's known fresh water;
  - 10 percent of the world's productive forest;
  - 10 percent of the world's nickel supply;
  - 21 percent of the world's recoverable uranium;
  - 8 percent of the world's coal;
  - the riches of the world's longest coastline (29 766 km).

1 What seem to be the main problems of the Third World?

2 Experts tell us that the gap (difference) between rich and poor nations is growing larger, not smaller. Why would this be?

3 It appears that we Canadians have far more than our share of the world's key resources. Why is this?

4 As you ate your third hamburger or second milkshake, did you ever think about the possibility that a young person somewhere in the world was starving to death? Do you think Canadians feel guilty about the richness of their lives compared to those of most other peoples? Should they? Explain your answers.

Most of the developed nations of the world try to help underdeveloped countries. They do so for two main reasons: self-interest and idealism. These motives were discussed in Chapter 18. If necessary, review that discussion.

1 Give an example of foreign aid based on the motive of self-interest.

2 Now give an example of aid based on idealism.

3 Which motive do you suspect is most common? Why?

Education is an important aspect of Canadian foreign aid as Canadian technology and knowledge are passed on to developing nations. Why does education play such an important role in development?

4 Which motive do you think is most often behind Canada's aid? Which motive should be? Explain your answers.

Since World War II, Canada has spent tens of millions of dollars on foreign aid. Before the Trudeau review, most of this went to poor Commonwealth countries or was distributed through the United Nations. We still provide help through both of these channels. However, since 1970 some important changes have occurred in our aid program.

First, as recommended in the Trudeau review, we did increase the amount of our aid. Years ago the United Nations suggested a guideline for foreign aid from wealthy nations. It was suggested that these nations give ¾ of 1 percent of their gross national product (GNP) per year. Thus, if a country had a GNP of $100 (unlikely!), it should give 75¢ in foreign aid. Canada accepted this principle and established it as a long-term goal of our foreign aid program.

1 Go to a library and look at the latest figures on Canada's gross national product.

2 Write the figure down. Calculate: what is ¾ of 1 percent of that amount? This is how much the United Nations says Canada should contribute to foreign aid. Check out your sources. Have we actually achieved this target? If not, how far short are we?

3 Do you think that the UN guideline of ¾ of 1 percent of GNP to foreign aid is reasonable? Why or why not?

In 1961 Canada was contributing only ⅕ of 1 percent of its GNP to foreign aid. By 1974 this had grown to ½ of 1 percent. Still, about 50 percent of this aid was tied. In other words, there were "strings attached." For example, we might lend $10 million to country X but insist that half of that money be spent buying Canadian-made farm machinery. In this way, we made a lot of money. We collected interest on the loan. Also, we helped our own industry and trade. We increased our exports, created jobs in Canada and made profits on manufacture of the machinery. However, by the late 1970s, much less of Canada's foreign aid was tied. Also, many of our loans were either made interest-free or were "forgiven," that is, we did not ask to be paid back.

In addition to increasing the amount of our foreign aid, we began to distribute it more evenly. Between 1945 and 1965, the bulk of our assistance went to two Commonwealth countries: India and Pakistan. In Africa we tended to favour Nigeria and Ghana. One goal of the Trudeau government was to increase aid to former French colonies. French-Canadians often felt that we favoured former British colonies and ignored the French-speaking world (la Francophonie).

Much of Canada's aid was now being disbursed (distributed) through the Canadian International Development Agency (CIDA). By 1977 its yearly budget was around $1.1 billion. We also operated the Canadian University Service Overseas (CUSO). This organization has sent thousands of university-trained volunteers to underdeveloped countries. They work in these countries as teachers, doctors, technicians, or as advisers on various problems.

Unfortunately, our foreign aid program was cut back in the 1980s. This was due mainly to a serious economic recession. Unemployment grew rapidly in our own country. The government's expenses began to increase at a much faster rate than its income. Growing budget deficits caused an alarming expansion of our national debt. Cutbacks in many areas of government spending were inevitable. As well, private contributors of foreign aid also faced hard times.

Consequently, by 1982 we ranked as one of the stingiest of all industrialized countries in the giving of foreign aid. Our total contributions had fallen to 0.42 of 1 percent of our GNP. Remember, ¾ of 1 percent was our goal. The federal government was now talking about not achieving that goal until 1990. By 1985 further cuts in aid had occurred. These totalled hundreds of millions of dollars. Moreover, 1995 became the new date for achieving the United Nations' recommended target of ¾ of 1 percent of the GNP. Not only that, but the federal government began increasing the percentage of our aid that was tied. By 1986 almost 80 percent of government aid had "strings attached" to it.

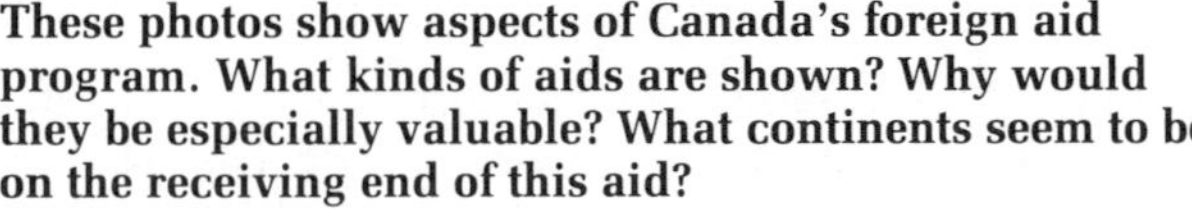
These photos show aspects of Canada's foreign aid program. What kinds of aids are shown? Why would they be especially valuable? What continents seem to be on the receiving end of this aid?

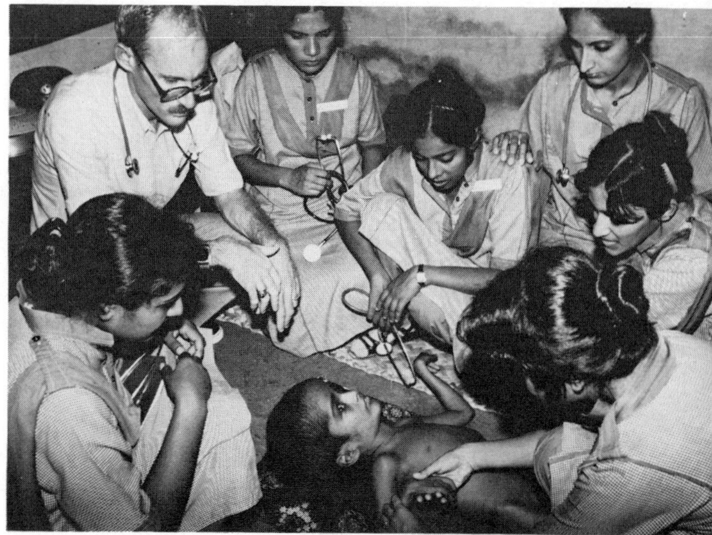

THE INCREASING DANGER OF NUCLEAR HOLOCAUST

Since the development of the first atomic weapons, there have been several occasions when a nuclear war seemed possible. So far as we know, our closest call came in 1962 with the Cuban Missile Crisis (see pages 307–309). At that time, such a war probably would have killed a minimum of 25 percent of the world's population. However, since then the variety, numbers and destructive power of the world's nuclear weapons have grown tremendously. Consequently, an all-out nuclear war today would, beyond any doubt, annihilate the human race as well as most other forms of life on this planet.

This 1947 photo shows two victims of the American atomic bomb blast on Hiroshima. At the time no one knew that the long-term effects of radiation would result in deaths years after the attack.

NUCLEAR WAR: WHAT WOULD IT BE LIKE?

The real nature of a nuclear war probably is beyond description and human understanding. An award-winning film, *If You Love This Planet*, includes graphic scenes of the survivors of Hiroshima. This Japanese city was largely destroyed by an atomic bomb in the last days of World War II. Although these scenes are shocking, the makers of the film could not begin to show the full horror of the bomb's effects. Moreover, the atomic bombs dropped on Hiroshima and Nagasaki were quite small by today's standards.

A 1983 television special entitled *The Day After* tried to show the effects of a modern nuclear weapon on a major American city (see page 390). This program was watched by one of the largest audiences in television history. Viewers were warned in advance that certain scenes were extremely graphic and could be very upsetting. Indeed, many viewers were deeply affected by the program. However, some people actually criticized the film, not because it was too harsh, but because it was not realistic enough! It gave viewers only a hint of the true horrors of a nuclear war.

Each year, the superpowers add hundreds of nuclear warheads to their stockpiles. A 1 megatonne weapon has the explosive force of 1 million tonnes of TNT. This is 70 to 100 times more powerful than the atomic bombs dropped on Japan in 1945. Today a 1 megatonne warhead is no more than a medium-sized weapon. Hundreds of American warheads are in the 3 to 5 megatonne range, and some are larger. The Soviet Union tends to use even larger warheads.

This is why an international team of scientists recently agreed that an all-out nuclear war probably would end all human life on this planet. They predicted that such a war likely would produce a phenomenon that they called "nuclear winter." Their theory suggests that, after the explosion of thousands of large nuclear weapons, fantastic amounts of smoke and dust would be thrown into the atmosphere. This would form a kind of ring around the earth. The sun's rays would not be able to penetrate this ring, possibly for several years. Can you imagine the results?

The earth, it is believed, would literally go into a deep freeze. Temperatures would drop, perhaps lower than −40°C, and remain there. All vegetation would die. So would any humans who had managed to survive the actual bomb explosions. Some scientists speculate that a few forms of life might survive: rats and, more likely, cockroaches.

But we have been talking about a total nuclear war. What if only a limited war were fought? Perhaps each side would use a few nuclear weapons but then step back in horror and stop the fighting before losing all control. Or there could be a mistake or an accident or a terrorist action in which only one or two nuclear explosions were set off. What would it be like if your community experienced a nuclear explosion? With the help of some basic data, you are about to figure this answer out for yourself.

Before proceeding, draw a map of your own town or city. Use a definite scale. If you have a standard size sheet of notepaper, we suggest a scale of 1 cm to 1 km. The middle of your page (mark it with a dot) will be "ground zero," or the point at which the nuclear warhead explodes. (For maximum effect, such weapons are usually set to go off in midair, 1 to 3 km above ground level.) We will assume that the weapon is on-target, so that ground zero, in the centre of your page, represents the middle of your town. Using the centre as your reference point, draw in major streets and intersections as space allows and keeping to your scale. You might note the location of certain landmarks, such as your house, school and the homes of friends or relatives. *We will now examine the effects on your community of a 1 megatonne warhead.*

Using ground zero as a base, take a compass and begin to inscribe concentric circles on your page. Use the radii indicated in the left-hand column of the following chart. Also, lightly shade the area inside each ring as suggested in the chart.

Radius from ground zero	Shade colour (lightly)	Description of immediate effects
2.5 km	red	At the very centre of this zone, people would simply cease to exist. They would be instantly vapourized, converted into tiny particles of radioactive dust. The explosion would create winds of 1000 km/h. Even the strongest buildings would be blown away. Farther from the centre of this zone, people, cars and debris would all become flying missiles or be crushed by an incredible over-pressure equal to 1000 tonnes. Anyone sheltering in a basement with thick concrete walls would die within seconds from a lethal dose of radiation.
5.0 km	orange	Again, there would be no survivors. Winds would reach 500 km/h. There would be an over-pressure of 500 tonnes (10 times that of the atmosphere). Probable causes of death are: —50 percent due to blast effects —30 percent due to flash burns —20 percent due to flying debris
7.0 km	yellow	This zone would be blanketed by fire. Winds would reach 300 km/h and be strong enough to hurl a large adult into a wall with deadly force. A few people in this zone would survive for a short while, but they would most certainly be badly injured or very ill.
8.5 km	green	Within this zone a huge, spreading fireball will develop. It is likely that no one will escape without at least third-degree burns. Many will die of asphyxiation as the firestorm consumes most of their oxygen.
10.0 km	blue	Winds would approach 200 km/h. Most buildings would be heavily damaged. There would be many survivors initially, but most would be badly injured, burned or exposed to massive doses of radiation.
14.0 km	purple	The majority of people here would still be alive but, again, many would be injured. Those who were able would leave quickly. The area would be unsafe, perhaps for years, because of radioactivity.

The possible realities of nuclear attack were vividly depicted in the film *The Day After*. While many felt that the film was sensationalist, most experts agree that the suffering and destruction of a nuclear war are beyond comprehension. ***Photo © 1987 American Broadcasting Corporation, Inc.***

Of course, very few Canadian communities are likely to suffer a direct attack such as this. Their main concern would be the radioactive fallout that would descend upon them in the weeks and months following a major nuclear exchange. However, the experts admit that our largest cities are probably each targeted with at least one Soviet warhead and possibly three or four. It is estimated that a 1 megatonne warhead, exploded over Toronto during a working day, would instantly kill at least 700 000 people. An additional 1 million people would be badly injured. All of the downtown skyscrapers would be reduced to rubble.

There could be no organized community assistance program after a nuclear explosion. Power lines would be down. There would be no water pressure and thus no fire protection. Roads would be unusable because they would be interrupted by collapsed bridges and overpasses and blocked by millions of tonnes of debris. The hospitals, with their staffs and supplies, would be destroyed. At present, there are fewer than 4000 hospital beds available for serious burn cases in all of North America. Naturally, most of them are located in large downtown hospitals.

Most of the people still alive within your map area after the explosion would be doomed. Those who could would probably try to vacate the area. Local food and water would be hopelessly contaminated. But even those who could flee would soon begin to show the symptoms of radiation sickness. Over the next weeks and months, most of them would surely suffer agonizing deaths.

These are, to be sure, appalling facts. Yet you have lived with them all your life. So have more than 50 percent of the world's present population. Humans are highly adaptable creatures. Probably this explains why our species has survived so long. But have we really adapted to the threat of nuclear war? It is not likely. What most people have done, quite understandably, is to put the matter out of their minds. It is simply too horrible to contemplate. Anyway, what can one person do about the situation?

While this is a normal reaction, it does not solve the problem. When people cease to think or care, when they give up, they actually become part of the problem. Therefore, while thoughts about the true nature of nuclear war are fresh in your mind, we ask you *not* to turn them off. Take time to discuss the issue with your classmates, your friends and your family. Probably there will be agreement on at least one point: *No one wants nuclear war*. The question then becomes: *How can we best prevent it?*

Usually two different views of this issue emerge. Some people believe that the best method of prevention is the one now being used by the two nuclear superpowers. They keep developing and building new weapons. This way, they say, each side maintains a "believable deterrent." The other side dare not attack for fear of totally unacceptable punishment in return. This concept is known, ironically, as MAD, for Mutual Assured Destruction. Supporters of this concept defend it on the grounds that it *has* worked: There has not been a nuclear war. President Reagan of the United States appeared to share this view. He was fond of quoting an old Roman saying: "If you want peace, prepare for war."

Opponents of this view fear that we have avoided nuclear war more because of good luck than good planning. They point to such dangerous developments as the increasing amounts of explosive power, the shrinking of warning time and the spread of nuclear weapons to other countries. They fear that the chances of nuclear war by accident are mounting daily.

HOW DID THIS SITUATION DEVELOP?

It is truly bizarre that, in their search for greater security, the most powerful nations on earth have created the means for their mutual total destruction. How could this have happened? Surely the peoples of the world do not have a mass suicide complex? The money spent on the build-up of today's nuclear arsenals probably would be sufficient to end poverty, ignorance and most diseases throughout the world! Moreover, as we have seen, there appeared to be a partial thaw in the cold war in the late 1960s and early 1970s. What went wrong?

Basically, there seems to be too much hostility and fear among the nations, both great and small. Local wars have continued to rage in Asia, Africa, the Middle East and Latin America. Some of these, notably in Vietnam, Afghanistan and Lebanon, have threatened to bring the superpowers into direct confrontation. Moreover, bombings, assassinations and other terrorist acts have occurred more and more often. Poor countries struggle with massive debts and overwhelming social problems. Ours has become an increasingly dangerous world. The major powers renewed the nuclear arms race as a means of maintaining their power and prestige.

During the cold war, each side felt that the other could not be trusted and was building too many new weapons. Therefore, each side felt justified in "defending itself" by adding to its own collection of new and more powerful aircraft, warships and nuclear weapons. Ironically, both sides wanted more security. Yet their arms build-up made nuclear war more probable and more likely to destroy all life on earth if it were ever fought.

In the late 1970s, the Soviet Union decided to install new SS–20 missiles in Eastern Europe. These missiles were much improved over earlier models. They posed a new threat to Western European nations

Medium Range Nuclear Missiles

NETHERLANDS
48 cruise

USSR and WARSAW PACT
243 or 270 SS-20s

BRITAIN
160 cruise

BELGIUM
48 cruise

WEST GERMANY
96 cruise
108 Pershing II

ITALY
112 cruise

WARSAW PACT

SS-20

441 deployed overall

243 (Soviet figure)
or 270 (NATO figure)
in Europe, rest
near China
Length: 16.5 m (54 ft.)
Range: 4989 km (3100 mi.)

NATO COUNTRIES

WARSAW PACT COUNTRIES

NATO

PERSHING II

108 deployed
Length: 10.4 m (34 ft.)
Range: 1803 km (1120 mi.)

CRUISE

Ground-launched
cruise missile
208 deployed
256 more planned
Length: 6.4 m (21 ft.)
Range: 2494.5 km (1550 mi.)

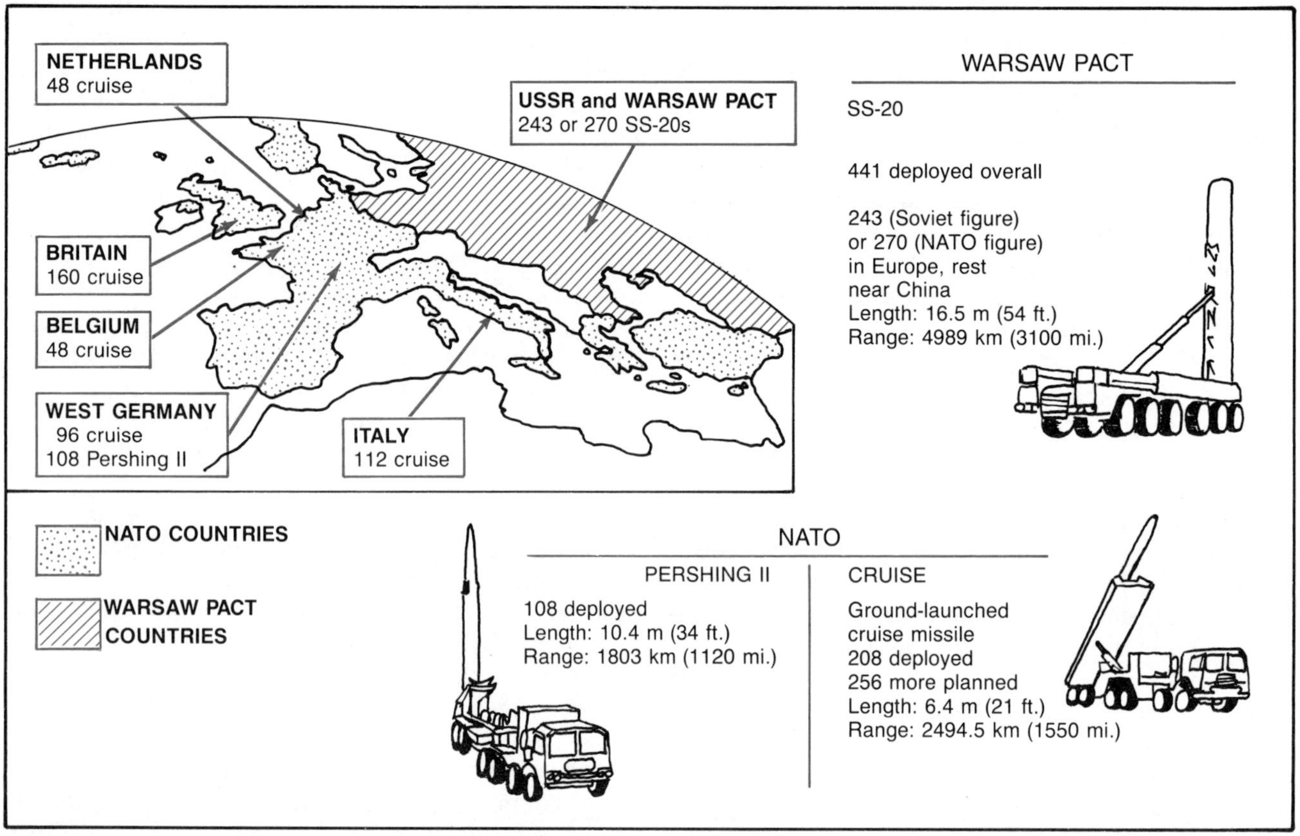

Sources: Department of Defence, *Janes Weapons Systems*

This chart shows the number of medium-range nuclear missiles scheduled for deployment in European countries that would be barred under US and Soviet proposals.

and to their major ally, the United States. The Americans felt they had to respond to this challenge. Accordingly, by 1983 they began to place new Pershing II missiles in Britain, Italy and West Germany. These missiles were deadly accurate. They could strike targets in Eastern Europe and parts of the western Soviet Union in less than 10 minutes. The Soviets declared that such a short warning time was intolerable. They would have to place their own missiles on a "launch-on-warning" basis. Such a situation would increase the chances of a nuclear war beginning because of an accident or a miscalculation.

In addition, both sides began to deploy large numbers of Cruise-type missiles (see pages 311–313). The danger posed by this type of weapon was not its speed or even its explosive power. Rather, the main concern was its small size. Cruise-type missiles are very easy to conceal. Therefore, they make it much more difficult to secure an agreement to limit or abolish them. How could one side trust the other to abide by an agreement? Would it not be very tempting to conceal a few hundred of these missiles? Then, if the other side destroyed its own missiles, the hidden weapons could be brought out and the enemy blackmailed into surrender. If no such limitation agreements are reached, both the Soviet Union and the United States are expected to have several thousand Cruise-type missiles in their possession by 1990. Some experts fear that, by then, no meaningful agreement on limitation will be possible.

These and other arms developments touched off huge protest rallies in Canada, the United States and many European countries in the 1980s. Such activities were much more limited in the Soviet Union because of its dictatorial government. In Canada, the debate about our proper role in arms control broke out again in 1984. Prime Minister Trudeau was retiring, but he made a final effort to bring the Soviets and Americans to the negotiating table. His "peace initiative" was highly publicized but achieved little, at least in the short run. His successor, Brian Mulroney, also supported negotiations to limit or abolish nuclear weapons. But he also clearly indicated that Canada was a loyal NATO ally. We would continue to support the United States' efforts to maintain a strong nuclear deterrent until the Soviet Union became serious about arms control.

By the late 1980s, there were encouraging signs of progress on arms control. President Reagan met with the new Soviet premier, Mikhail Gorbachev, in Iceland in 1986. While no specific agreements were reached, a new tone of conciliation was evident. The following year, Soviet and American representatives discussed proposals to reduce or eliminate short- and medium-range missiles in Europe. Both sides were hopeful that agreements here might eventually lead to significant reductions in their total nuclear arsenals.

THE ISSUE OF PEACE AND SECURITY IN TODAY'S WORLD

During the 1970s and early 1980s, Canadian foreign policy was shaped largely by Pierre Trudeau. As we have seen, he changed the direction of that policy in many ways. When Brian Mulroney became prime minister in 1984, it was time to look again at our

1 What is the theme of this cartoon?
2 What are the two sides portrayed here?
3 State three important ideas about disarmament negotiations which are suggested by this cartoon.
4 Suggest a one-word caption which would clearly express the theme of the cartoon.

international relations. The world was continuing to change rapidly. Moreover, the politics and personal views of Mr. Mulroney differed greatly from those of his predecessor.

Accordingly, in 1985 our Minister of External Affairs, Joe Clark, announced a new review of Canadian foreign policy. Part of this review involved a re-examination of our defence policy. Official statements of the new policies were expected by 1987 or 1988.

The security and survival of the nation are at the root of all such policies. The difficulty lies in deciding on the best methods by which to achieve these goals. For years, Canadians have been somewhat divided about which methods work best. Here are some of the ideas on this issue from two different viewpoints:

SIDE A

- Canada is a prosperous and free country. Others might attack us out of envy or greed.
- Since we have a lot to lose and the world is a dangerous place, we should maintain a high level of defensive forces.
- We must stay in NATO and NORAD to further protect ourselves.
- Our allies would never forgive us if we deserted them. Also, they could punish us, for example, in our trade relations with them.
- The United States is our best friend and ally. We should support stands on major world issues.

SIDE B

- Canada is a huge, thinly populated country. We could never develop or pay for armed forces large enough to defend ourselves.
- Our national debt is already massive. Increasing spending on armed forces would only be a waste. It also might provoke potential enemies.
- The United States would never permit another power to take over Canada. Any country that takes on the United States risks total destruction. This is protection enough for us.
- Our armed forces are negligible. We could set an example for the world by reducing or eliminating them.
- Perhaps by leaving NATO and NORAD altogether we could achieve neutrality and true independence.

1. Try to add arguments to each side of this question.
2. On the whole, which side has the more practical, common-sense arguments in your opinion? Explain your answer.
3. With which side do you agree? Why?
4. Based on your knowledge of current affairs, which side does our present government policy seem to favour? Support your opinion with facts.

The Mulroney government knew that it was inheriting certain problems in the area of security and defence. While the Trudeau government set spending records and amassed a huge national debt, it largely ignored the armed forces. Consequently, their numbers, strength and morale declined considerably. Shortly after taking power, the Mulroney government received a report by a specially appointed commission on the state of our national defence. Here are some of its findings:

GENERALLY

- The Canadian Armed Forces (CAF) were suffering from "benign neglect."
- The quality of the people was top rate, but their numbers were far too low (down from 127 000 in 1962 to 84 000 in 1984).
- The CAF were incapable of carrying out their key roles of national defence, coastal surveillance and assistance to NATO allies.
- For their size, the CAF had more generals than almost any other armed forces in the world.
- The CAF had so few reserves that they would not be able to replace even moderate losses in the early stages of a war.
- In all branches of the service, much essential equipment was either hopelessly outdated or not available.
- There were not even enough arms and ammunition available to allow the forces to train properly, let alone fight a war.

SPECIFICALLY

THE NAVY

- Despite having the world's longest coastline, we had let our once-proud navy become a laughing stock.
- Our 20 aging warships were literally falling apart; also, none of them could defend itself against missile attack. In modern warfare, they would not last 24 hours at sea.
- We had only three submarines; these were aging and diesel-powered. The Soviet Union had 400 submarines, half of which were nuclear-powered.
- Although trade is our lifeblood, we had virtually no minesweeping capability to keep our harbours and sea-lanes open in the event of war.
- Although we have a huge, resource-rich Arctic to protect, we had almost no icebreaker capability.

THE AIR FORCE

- We had far too few jet fighter aircraft.
- We had no modern weapons for defending our fighter bases against air attack.
- We needed more and better anti-submarine patrol aircraft.
- We lacked airlift capacity to move even small numbers of troops to battle areas.

THE ARMY

- We had far fewer combat troops than any other country of comparable size or wealth.
- We were desperately short of heavy equipment, especially tanks, artillery and transport vehicles.

The chief recommendation of the special commission was that the defence budget be increased substantially. The Mulroney government agreed but was faced with the need to curb spending so as to reduce the deficit. So a compromise was made. Whereas the defence budget totalled about $7 billion in 1982–83, by 1987–88 it had grown to just over $10 billion. Still, such an increase barely covered the cost of salary raises and a few purchases of new equipment. Six new frigates were purchased for the navy at a total cost of about $4 billion. Modern tanks cost $3 million apiece. Top-quality jet fighters go for $15 to $25 million each. Experts continue to urge the purchase of several submarines and the expansion of the regular forces to the 200 000 level. Clearly, such steps would call for the spending of vast additional sums.

Our government is under heavy pressure from our allies, especially the United States, to spend more on defence. The following chart compares some aspects of the Canadian and American armed forces as of 1987. Remember that the United States is approximately ten times our size in population and wealth.

1 When the Americans complain that we are not doing our fair share are they justified?

2 Does it make sense to spend over $10 billion per

Item	United States	Canada	Ratio (US/Canada)
Regular armed forces	2 200 000	86 000	25:1
Reserves	1 700 000 + 560 000 (National Guard)	24 000	95:1
Warships	319	23	14:1
Aircraft and Helicopters	7 273	267	27:1
Tanks	15 012	114	132:1
Defence budget (in 1986 US dollars)	$292.5 billion	$7.2 billion	40:1

Career opportunities for women in the Canadian Forces are becoming greater today. Research the official policy on career equality within the Forces and discuss the future prospects.

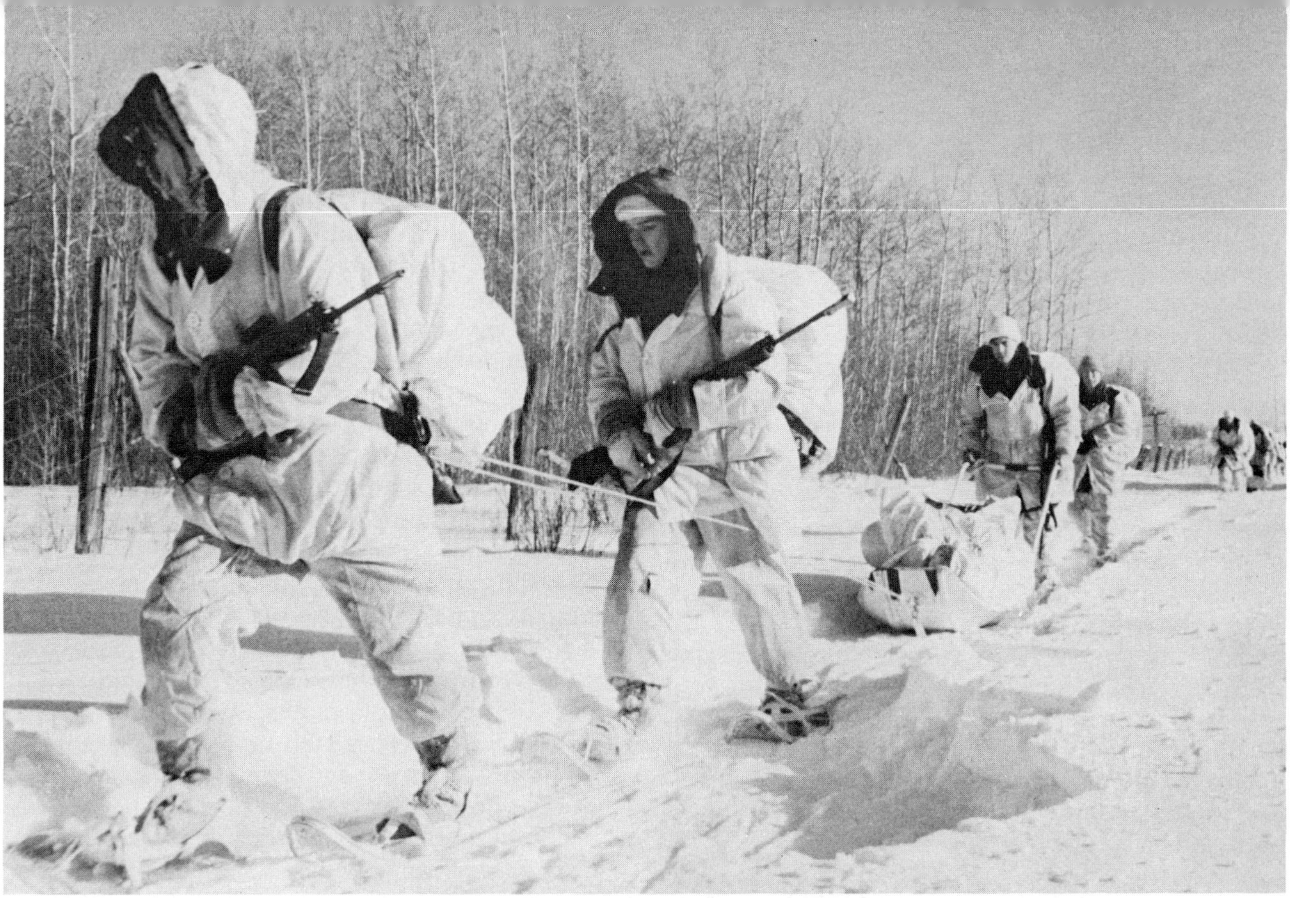

year on armed forces that cannot come close to giving Canada proper protection?

3 If we cannot defend our territory, do we have the right to call ourselves an independent nation?

4 Do you think that the Canadian people are concerned enough about this issue to accept large tax increases for more adequate armed forces? Would these expenditures really make us more secure?

WHAT SHOULD BE DONE WITH CANADA'S NATO FORCES?

Since NATO was formed in 1948, every Canadian government has said that this alliance is a cornerstone of our foreign policy. It is a key part of our security and defence. Still, as we have seen, the Trudeau government substantially reduced our military contribution to NATO. To compensate, we promised to send troops and aircraft to aid Norway in the event of a Soviet attack. Our contribution to NATO shrank to a mere armoured brigade plus three squadrons of fighter aircraft.

These forces are so small that they could have no real effect if war broke out in Europe. Rather, they are a symbol of our support for the alliance. If our troops were attacked, we would automatically be at war on the side of our NATO allies against the attacking forces.

Membership in NATO has cost Canada hundreds of millions of dollars. In the past, most Canadians believed that this money was well spent. Much of it supported the armed forces that we kept in Europe. These included air and land units stationed in West Germany. Units of the Canadian navy helped to patrol North Atlantic waters. Canadian money also helped some of the poorer NATO countries develop their economies and defence forces.

However, in recent years some Canadians have begun to question the value of NATO. The danger of a Soviet attack on Western Europe seems to have declined. Perhaps the large costs of keeping our troops in Europe could be better spent on problems here at home. Such people suggest that our money and troops are being wasted; we should bring the forces home, where they could be of more use.

Others claim that we must keep troops in Europe. This will show our allies that we still support them. They can trust us. Also, if we pull out, some countries might cut off their trade with us. The United States keeps large armed forces in Europe. They want us to help share the load. If we refuse, we will probably lose our voice in large NATO decisions. If trouble comes, we could find ourselves with no allies and few friends.

1 Pose two questions that clearly express the decisions facing Canada with regard to NATO.

2 Look up current statistics that show the value of Canada's trade with NATO countries. The *Canada Year Book* would be one useful source. How valuable is this trade? Could we afford to risk losing it? Does it justify our annual expenses in NATO?

3 NATO and Warsaw have attempted to reach an agreement limiting their short- and medium-range missiles. The chart

below indicates the possible strengths of the two sides after the proposed reduction. Is there any category of weaponry in which NATO would be superior? To what type of weaponry would NATO have to resort to effectively stop a Soviet attack?

	NATO	Warsaw Pact
Nuclear Weapons		
Land-based battlefield ballistic missiles**	207	1 000
French medium-range land-based ballistic missiles	18	0
Nuclear-capable artillery	3 032	3 884
Surface-to-air missiles	443	0
Submarine-launched ballistic missiles (including English)	200	18
Land-based strike aircraft	1 534	2 004
Carrier-based strike aircraft	126	0
Conventional Forces††		
Total military manpower	5.9 million	4.4 million
Tanks	21 600	32 000
Artillery	17 200	23 000
Attack helicopters	1 100	960
Combat aircraft	6 250	6 550

**does not include U.S. and Soviet strategic nuclear weapons*
***range less than 300 miles*
†range between 600 and 3 400 miles
††includes French and Spanish forces
Source: © 1987 The New York Times Company. Reprinted by permission.

4 What implications are there for Canada in these figures?

5 Some Americans and Europeans have accused Canada of trying to get a "free ride." What does this mean? Do we want the benefits of NATO membership, but not the responsibilities? Is the charge a fair one?

6 With the class, fully discuss the arguments for and against Canada removing its troops from Europe. Also consider the possibility of Canada leaving NATO altogether. What do you think our government should do about these questions? Why?

7 Try to find out what the government is presently doing about these matters.

ISSUES INVOLVING HUMAN RIGHTS

VIOLATIONS OF HUMAN RIGHTS

The tradition of respect for human rights and freedoms is so well established in Canada that, to a large extent, we take them for granted. As described in Chapter 4, we have an excellent human rights code. While we still have certain abuses to correct, our problems pale in comparison with those of many other nations. At this very moment, as you read these words, in various parts of the world people are being

- arbitrarily arrested;
- kept in jail for indefinite periods without being charged;
- illegally deprived of their property;
- badly beaten;
- tortured, both physically and psychologically;
- deliberately starved;
- murdered by government forces;
- prevented from leaving their own country;
- discriminated against on the basis of their race, religion or political beliefs.

We could fill several pages with specific examples of such violations of human rights. Here are just a few:

- In South Africa, the black majority has been

1 What country is being portrayed here? Find three pieces of evidence to support your conclusion.
2 Who is the person depicted on the bow of the ship? How does his famous policy of "glasnost" apply here?
3 What is the main point of the cartoon?
4 From the text, find printed material to substantiate the accusation made in the cartoon.
Reprinted with special permission of King Features Syndicate, Inc.

cruelly exploited and oppressed for many years.

- In the Soviet Union, many citizens of the Jewish faith have been forbidden to emigrate to Israel or anywhere else. Critics of the Communist regime languish in jails, toil in labour camps or live as "nonpersons" in exile in secluded areas of their homeland.
- In Chile people of all ages have been arrested, tortured and even killed for resisting the brutal dictatorship of Augusto Pinochet. Chile is a predominantly Roman Catholic country. In 1987 demonstrators were gassed and beaten while Pope John Paul II celebrated Mass in a public square.
- In Argentina thousands of people are still missing years after the military government that ordered their kidnapping and murder was removed from power.

Many of the offending countries belong to the United Nations. Upon joining, each member must agree to the terms of the United Nations Charter and its Declaration of Human Rights. However, as in other areas, the United Nations lacks the power to punish members who violate its rules. Whether members of the UN or not, many countries in the world are *not* democracies. Instead, they have governments that are dictatorial in varying degrees. Consequently, it is quite possible for violations of human rights to occur in such countries.

Gross violations of human rights by other nations pose difficult decisions for Canadian foreign policy. On the one hand, we could dismiss them as none of our business. Strictly speaking, they are the internal affairs of the countries in which they occur. However, such an attitude is unacceptable to the consciences of most Canadians. It contradicts the basic human values in which we believe and that we hope the world will one day share.

Thus, the Canadian government has little difficulty in making critical judgements about those governments that violate human rights. The problems come when we try to decide what we can or should *do* about such governments.

For example, let us imagine that a certain country makes headlines by severely mistreating large numbers of its citizens. Over a prolonged period, grisly stories about these abuses appear in the world press.

1 Make a list of steps that, in theory at least, the government of Canada could take to try to curb these abuses.
2 Rank these possibilities in order of severity, from least to most severe.
3 Separate the steps into two categories, from the Canadian standpoint: practical and impractical. In each case, have a reason for your decision.

4 Overall, what factors would determine whether or not Canadian foreign policy could influence the behaviour of the offending country?
5 Think of obstacles that might limit or block the actions contemplated by our government.

Note: To help you with the above, review appropriate parts of Chapter 18.

Here are some steps you might have considered for question one, above.

- Reduce or cut off our trade with the offending country.
- Demand that the United Nations investigate and debate the issue.
- Threaten to invade the offending country.
- Reduce or eliminate any aid to or investment in the offending country.
- Launch a media blitz to publicize and condemn the human rights violations.
- Go to war with the offending government.
- Send a note of protest to that government.
- Urge our friends and allies to take actions similar to ours.
- Cut off formal diplomatic relations with the offending country.

If any of these suggestions did not occur to you, add them to your rank order (question two) and categories (question three). In terms of possible obstacles for our government (question five), did you consider the following?

- The offending country might actually be a friend or ally.
- We might have major trade or investment ties with such a country and thus stand to lose a lot of money if we reduced our contacts.
- We might have no significant economic ties with the country and thus lack economic leverage against it.
- Our own government might have major political and/or economic problems at home. It might not want to become involved in a controversy where its chances of success were very slim.
- Our own armed forces are very weak.
- The offending country might occupy a strategic position or possess vital minerals that are essential to us or our allies.
- The offending country might have close ties with one or more of our allies and/or trading partners. Foremost among these is the United States. Would we risk a conflict with the Americans in order to try to protect human rights?
- Would we be prepared to risk a war to try to help strangers in a foreign country?

SOUTH AFRICA: A CASE STUDY IN THE VIOLATION OF HUMAN RIGHTS

The case of South Africa illustrates many of the ideas we have been considering. In that country, the white minority has ruled the black majority for decades. The white regime rules with an iron first. The blacks are denied basic human rights, including an equal voice in their own government. They have no voting rights whatsoever. They are subjected to all manner of discrimination and abuse. They are kept in the lowest jobs and have inferior housing, education and medical services. The blacks are forced to live mainly in slum ghettos well away from the comfortable, sometimes luxurious white neighbourhoods. This policy of segregation and suppression is called apartheid.

For years, Canada and most other democracies have condemned apartheid and its ghastly

WHITE PERSONS ONLY

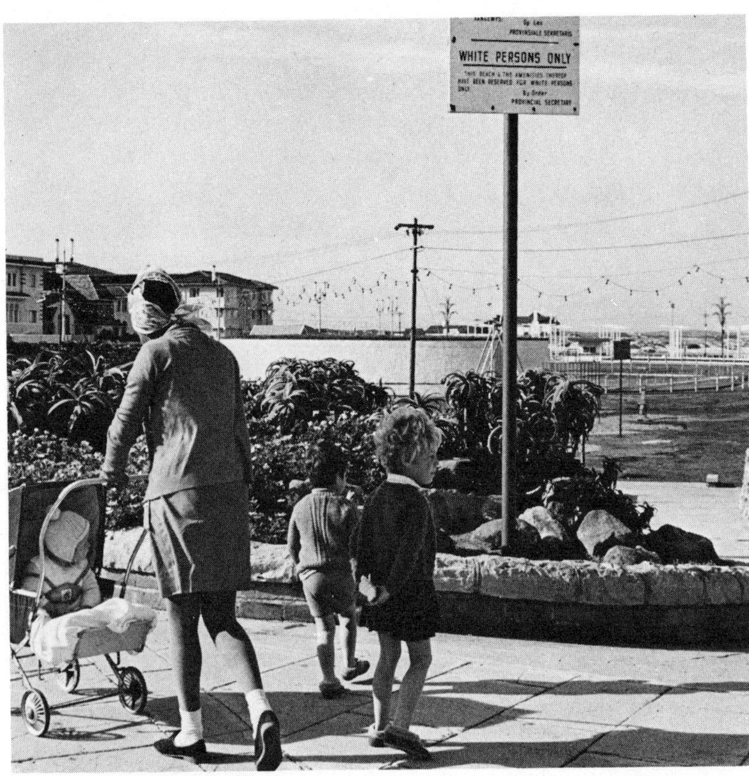

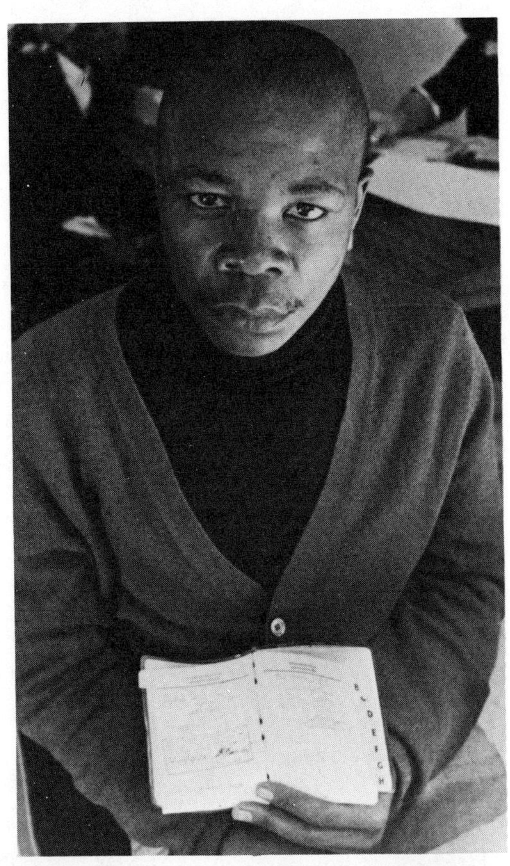

These photos show how non-whites suffer racial discrimination in South Africa. What information can you gather about South Africa's racial policies from the photos?

NON WHITES ONLY
OUT

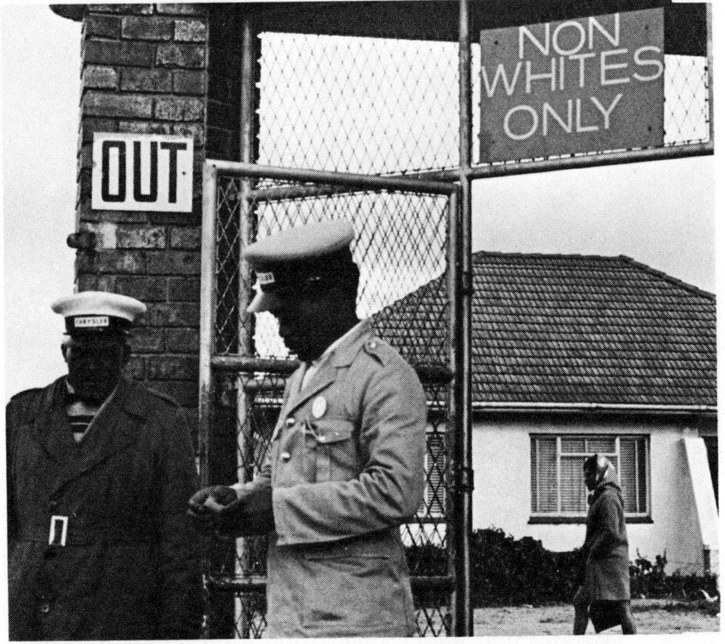

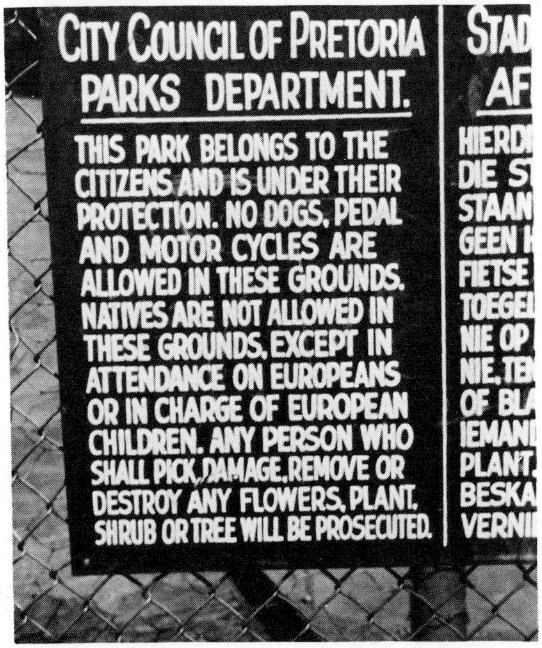

CITY COUNCIL OF PRETORIA
PARKS DEPARTMENT.
THIS PARK BELONGS TO THE CITIZENS AND IS UNDER THEIR PROTECTION. NO DOGS, PEDAL AND MOTOR CYCLES ARE ALLOWED IN THESE GROUNDS. NATIVES ARE NOT ALLOWED IN THESE GROUNDS, EXCEPT IN ATTENDANCE ON EUROPEANS OR IN CHARGE OF EUROPEAN CHILDREN. ANY PERSON WHO SHALL PICK, DAMAGE, REMOVE OR DESTROY ANY FLOWERS, PLANT, SHRUB OR TREE WILL BE PROSECUTED.

consequences. Indeed, Canadian criticism was instrumental in pressuring South Africa to leave the British Commonwealth in 1961. We have supported United Nations measures, including economic sanctions, against the South African government. However, such measures have not been very effective.

The issue is complicated by certain circumstances. South Africa occupies a strategic position. It has the potential to control navigation around the Cape of Good Hope. Moreover, it possesses titanium and other rare raw materials that are absolutely vital to Western technology and industry. American, British and Canadian business interests have invested billions of dollars in South Africa. It is feared that a black takeover might lead to the country becoming nonaligned in the cold war or, worse still, a Communist government.

In recent times, there has been a major escalation of violence in South Africa. Black resistance to systematic oppression is mounting rapidly. In response, the white regime passed strict new laws increasing police powers to deal with the "state of emergency." In 1986 alone, approximately 25 000 South Africans, almost all blacks, were jailed indefinitely. (About 10 000 of these were adolescents or children.) The majority were eventually released without any charges being laid. There are well-documented cases of police abuse of these people. The abuses range from the use of tear gas, rubber bullets and vicious dogs against innocent civilians to whippings, torture and even murder of blacks suspected of resistance to government policy.

In 1986 the Mulroney government helped tighten Commonwealth sanctions against South Africa. However, our goal of drastically reduced trade with that country has not been reached. In 1987 our two-way trade with South Africa still was worth about $500 million. This was actually an increase over previous years. Moreover, Britain and the United States disappointed us by not supporting the idea of a strict economic blockade.

REFUGEES

A refugee can be defined as a person who flees to a foreign country to escape danger or persecution in his or her own country. Today there are an estimated 10 to 15 million such people in the world. This tragic problem has been caused mainly by oppressive regimes and their large-scale violations of human rights.

The United Nations Declaration of Human Rights states that "everyone has the right to leave any country, including his own." Sometimes an oppressive regime is quite happy to have citizens who criticize or oppose it leave the country. But more often, it wants to detain such people for punishment. By the imprisonment, torture or execution of dissidents, the regime can discourage other potential opponents.

CENTRAL AMERICAN REFUGEES, 1985

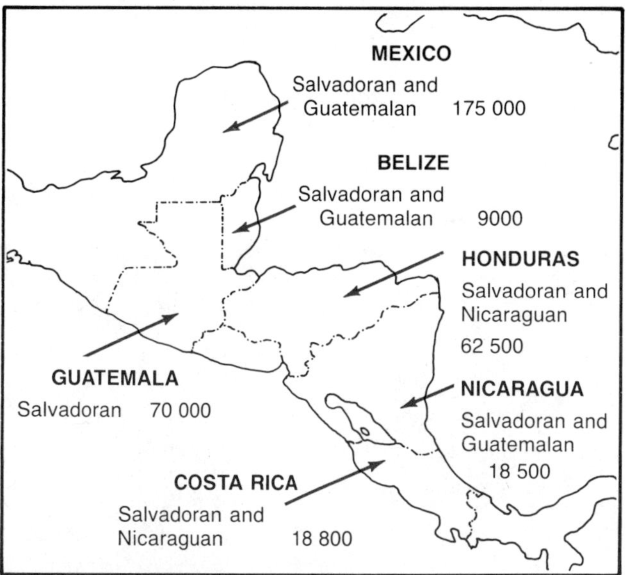

Source: *World Refugee Survey, 1985*

This map illustrates the huge refugee problem which existed in Central America by 1985. A major cause was the continuing civil war in El Salvador. Over 500 000 people have become refugees throughout the course of this war. The violence of this conflict was graphically illustrated in the controversial movie, *Salvador*. Among other atrocities, this film depicted the massacres committed by the infamous "death squads." The fighting caused thousands of people to be chased off family farms, swept from combat zones and pushed across borders.

Also, it is bad publicity for a country to have thousands of its citizens fleeing to seek refuge elsewhere.

Since World War II, Canada has opened its doors to over 400 000 refugees. Indeed, in 1986 the United Nations gave its highest award for refugee aid, the Nansen Medal, to the "entire people" of Canada for our efforts in this cause. In the immediate postwar period, we accepted many refugees from Europe. In more recent years, people from Vietnam, Lebanon, Iran, Chile, El Salvador and many other countries were welcomed here.

By late 1986, both the Canadian and American governments were becoming concerned about the growing flood of people trying to enter their countries by claiming refugee status. For example, Canada admitted only about 1600 refugees in 1980. By 1986 the number had grown to 18 282. The majority were coming from Central and South America. According to our government officials, approximately 75 percent of the refugee claims made for entry into Canada were false. Most of the illegitimate applicants were classed as "economic migrants." Such people were believed to be leaving their own countries not to escape persecution but to improve their standard of living.

Such false claims were spoiling the chances of legitimate refugees. Moreover, the influx of people was straining our relief centres. Some Canadians believed that the numbers were too high for our country to absorb comfortably. When the United States made its entry requirements harder to meet, the pressure on Canada to do likewise increased immediately. Refugee applications began to flow into Canada at the rate of 1000 per week. In this situation, the Mulroney government felt it had no choice but to tighten its entry requirements as well. Some Canadians regarded the changes as reasonable and fair. However, others were critical. One person said, "They

This family fled Guatemala in 1987 after receiving a series of anonymous death threats. They wait in a New York hotel room after being refused entry to Canada. Canada's immigration policy is being reviewed due to the number of refugees seeking admission.

(the government) seem to have no idea of the conditions refugees are facing.'' Another expressed his concern more bluntly: ''Locked doors mean death.''

IMMIGRATION POLICY

The refugee situation is related to but should not be confused with the matter of immigration policy as a whole. Technically, this is a matter of domestic, not foreign, policy. However, it does involve our relations with other countries and peoples. It also reflects Canadian values and affects the image that we project to the world.

It is a cliché, but it is also a fact, that Canada is largely a land of immigrants. Immigrants have helped to build our railways, settle the West and dig our mines, and they have enriched our culture in many ways. Most experts agree that a steady stream of immigration helps to maintain healthy economic growth. Immigrants bring valuable skills and needed capital and are consumers of goods and services.

SOURCES OF IMMIGRANTS TO CANADA (by area of origin)

Area	1982	1985
Europe	47 878	18 844
Africa	5 101	3 547
Asia	48 519	38 488
Australasia	1 246	1 128
North and Central America	11 542	11 412
Caribbean	9 550	5 504
South America	6 257	4 343
Oceania	1 002	—
Not stated	360	—
Total	131 455	84 302

Source: *Statistics Canada*

A REFUGEE CASE STUDY

In August of 1986, Canadian officials discovered 155 Tamils adrift in lifeboats inside Canadian waters off the coast of Newfoundland. They were from Sri Lanka, where political violence had caused the deaths of many of their people.

Originally, the Tamils claimed that they had travelled directly from their homeland. Normally, this condition must be met before Canada will grant refugee status and allow foreigners to live permanently in our country. However, the Tamils soon admitted that, in fact, they had each paid $3500 to a West German sea captain to transport them from Europe to Canadian waters. Only then were they set adrift in the lifeboats.

The case caused considerable controversy. Some Canadians believed that because they had lied, had money to buy their passage and had not fled directly to Canada, the Tamils should not be admitted as refugees. Rules are rules. An example should be set so that we would not be regarded as ''an easy mark'' and thus face a flood of such cases. Others disagreed, arguing that the Tamils had nowhere to go but back home, where a violent end might await them.

After some deliberation, the Mulroney government decided to allow the Tamils to remain in Canada. However, within a few months, a rumour began to circulate that other Tamils were planning a similar strategy. This might have contributed to the government's decision to tighten our refugee policy early in 1987.

Do you agree with our government's decision to admit the Tamils as refugees? Why or why not?

The numbers of immigrants to Canada have fluctuated wildly over the years. The record was set in 1913, when 400 870 newcomers arrived on our shores. Numbers have been much lower during wartime and in periods of economic depression. For much of the 1970s and 1980s, the figures ranged between 90 000 and 190 000, though they were usually closer to the lower figure. Some experts now claim that Canada should aim for an annual total of about 250 000 immigrants, which is roughly 1 percent of our population. They point to our declining birth rate, aging population and yearly loss of at least

DESTINATION OF IMMIGRANTS BY PROVINCE (approximate percentages)

Province	% of immigrants heading there
Ontario	43
British Columbia	17
Quebec	16
Prairie provinces	22
Maritimes	02

Note: *There has been little change in these percentages for the past 20 years.*
Source: *Statistics Canada*

40 000 people who emigrate to other countries. They predict that, without greatly increased immigration, our population will actually decline, and our economy will suffer as a result.

However, immigration remains a somewhat controversial issue in Canada, as it does in many other countries. People sometimes fear large numbers of "foreigners" in their midst. Differences in race, religion, culture or political views might play a part in this. Sometimes there is a feeling that immigrants take jobs from Canadians, when in fact their presence usually creates *more* jobs. Whatever the reason, when a government senses a strong backlash of feeling against large-scale immigration, it sometimes adjusts its immigration policy to suit the public mood.

Today the basis of Canada's policy rests on the Immigration Act of 1976. This act establishes the following principles for deciding who will be permitted to immigrate to Canada:

- non-discrimination
- family reunion
- humanitarian concern for refugees
- promotion of national goals

The act goes on to say that, in addition to all of the above, we must take into account Canada's needs in population and labour skills at any given time.

Clearly, this act allows much leeway for judging the applications of potential immigrants. Still, there have been periodic complaints that immigration officials can be heartless, for example, by refusing to admit certain relatives of people already living in Canada. Some Canadians favour a fairly loose application of the rules to permit more refugees and regular immigrants to settle here. Others want a strict application of standards to ensure that we keep numbers low, admitting only "high quality" immigrants who have valuable labour skills.

CONCLUSION

Today Canada is a respected but not very influential country in the world. We do not seek to conquer any territory or dominate any other people. Our record in support of human rights, the United Nations, disarmament and peace gives us cause to be proud.

Still, we could do much more. Our aid to less fortunate countries is not overly generous, considering our wealth and comparing our contributions to those of other prosperous nations. Probably we could open our doors to many more immigrants, particularly refugees. We could give more help in the fight against world poverty, ignorance, pollution and disease. Above all, we must do our utmost to help the world avoid nuclear war in the face of the terrifying arms race, which is still underway. If *that* problem is not solved, there will be no point in worrying about the others.

BUILDING YOUR LEARNING SKILLS

FOCUSSING ON THE ISSUE

1. Why did it become necessary to review Canadian foreign policy in the late 1960s?
2. State three important changes that the Trudeau review caused in our foreign policy.
3. Why is "O Canada, we stand on guard for thee" not an accurate portrayal of our defence preparedness?
4. Explain how Canada's position on human rights, refugees and immigration are connected to each other.
5. What are the main issues in Canadian foreign policy today?

6 The following terms appeared in this chapter. Try to recall their meanings and how they were used.

apartheid	GNP
CIDA	MAD
CUSO	nonalignment
developed nation	refugee
diplomatic recognition	Third World
foreign aid	tied aid

RESEARCHING

1 Canada's latest White Paper on defence policy was published in 1987. Try to discover its main recommendations. To what extent has the government acted on them?

2 Prepare a brief paper outlining the role of women in the Canadian armed forces in the twentieth century. In the process, try to assess what progress, if any, has been made toward sexual equality.

3 If your work in question two, above, does not cover the issue, investigate the policy of the Canadian Armed Forces on women in combat roles. Your findings will be used in a forthcoming assignment.

4 Try to find two or three case studies on people who applied for immigration to Canada, either for themselves or for family members, and were rejected. Your data can be used later in a debate or panel discussion.

5 Finland is a nation that, like Canada, is the immediate neighbour of a superpower. Still, it has taken a position of neutrality in the cold war. Try to find information on this matter. (A Canadian, Gwynne Dyer, has written on this topic.) Your information will be used in a later exercise.

6 Develop a file of articles on Canadian foreign policy today. It will be used later.

1·2·3 ORGANIZING

1 Set up your file on Canadian foreign policy in a systematic way. For example, separate the articles according to the regions of the world with which they deal. Indicate two other methods of organization that you think might be better. Why are they better?

2 Based on question one, above, set up an organizer chart that could be used to review, summarize and evaluate Canadian foreign policy in point-form style.

3 Which of these terms does not belong with the others: CIDA, Colombo Plan, MAD, CUSO, Third World?

4 Imagine that you are the local director of refugee settlement in the largest city in your province. You have just been informed that a busload of refugees will be arriving at your headquarters within 24 hours. Make a list of at least five steps you would have to take to prepare for their arrival. Rank the steps in order of difficulty. Then rank them in order of importance.

COMMUNICATING

1 Write a newspaper editorial in which you outline a major issue in foreign policy today. Indicate why it is an important issue, what our policy on the issue should be and why you advocate such a policy.

2 Persuade other members of your class to join you in an expanded exercise on the Canadian national anthem.

a First, each person should try to write out our national anthem's words. Did anyone succeed? Do the results communicate any message?

b Next, give every participant a copy of the correct words.

c Acting as a group and posing as foreigners, try to reach a consensus on what this anthem says about Canadians. Do you think that the words of the anthem accurately reflect Canadian attitudes and values today? If not, try, individually at first, to write a new, more appropriate anthem. Now reassemble the group to compare ideas.

3 Form two groups of students interested in working on Canadian immigration policy. Divide yourselves on the basis of those who support tightening the rules and reducing numbers of immigrants and those who believe

the opposite should be done. Each group should develop a clearly written set of rules and standards to be presented as "Canada's New Immigration Policy." (Include, for example, requirements for entry.) You must have factual arguments to support positions taken. The two groups can then discuss their views with each other. Your work can later become the basis for a panel discussion or simulation before the entire class.

4 Organize class debates or panel discussions on one or more of the following topics:
   a Are the Canadian Armed Forces right in allowing women full equality in combat roles?
   b Should Canada try suspected Nazi war criminals in this country instead of returning them to Europe?

ANALYZING

1 Would we become more secure by spending less money on defence?

2 Joseph Stalin was once the dictator of the Soviet Union. While contemplating a certain course in foreign policy, he was advised against it. The reason: This action would be opposed by the Pope. Stalin supposedly replied, "And how many divisions does the Pope have?" What is a division? What point was Stalin making? Give an example from the world today that would support his point. Should this point have any bearing on Canadian foreign policy?

3 In 1987 a Canadian journalist published an article claiming that Canada is a major exporter of arms. The journalist stated that our annual sales of weapons and ammunition are worth hundreds of millions of dollars. A significant percentage of these arms end up in poor countries ruled by tyrants who violate human rights and/or make war on other states. Should we allow such sales of weaponry? Make your answer as full as possible.

4 The first woman to reach the rank of general in the Canadian Armed Forces achieved that promotion in 1987. Is this an encouraging or a discouraging development? Why?

5 The world's population continues to grow very rapidly. Is this a particularly significant development for the field of foreign policy? Why or why not?

6 Develop a list of the world's most important problems. List these in order of seriousness, from most to least serious. To the solution of which of them could Canada make a meaningful contribution? How?

7 It has been said that next to avoiding nuclear war, the greatest concern in Canadian foreign policy should be to protect our independence from the United States. Do you agree? Explain your answer.

APPLYING YOUR KNOWLEDGE

1 If the world's population grows by a billion people every ten to fifteen years, what implications does this have for our foreign aid program?

2 Should we regard ourselves primarily as Canadians or as citizens of the world? Explain your answer.

3 If you did research on the neutrality of Finland ("Researching," question five):
   a How is Finland's situation similar to ours? How is it different?
   b Could we change our foreign policy in any way, based on the Finnish example? If so, how? If not, why not?

4 In 1987, speaking on the subject of peace, Canadian astronaut Mark Garneau commented on how beautiful yet fragile the earth looked from a spacecraft. It seemed to him incredible that a mere speck in the universe could hold so many dreams, fears and forms of prejudice. What was he trying to tell us? How does the concept of the "global village" fit in here? What signs do you see that the world is moving in this direction? Are you encouraged or discouraged about this?

CREDITS

Photo Credits

Public Archives Canada

12 — PA-57522	132 — C-29484	261 — C-6541
17 — C-9952	133 — C-5121	262 (lower) — 93725
19 — C-17825	134 — PA-2195	309 — PA-159610
21 — C-74147	135 — PA-1020	358 — C-7487
109 — C-59029	137 — PA-25166	194 — C-9202
110 — C-65915	138 — PA-44006	196 — C-19139
112 — C-16408	139 — C-20049	197 — C-9092
113 — C-5329	150 — PA-151546	198 — 1679
114 — C-3693	151 — C-14160	199 (lower) — C-5761
115 — C-24996	152 — C-29450	199 — C-53641
115 — C-9695	154 — C-29464	200 — C-24354
118 — PA-38503	155 — 27991	212 — PA-157323
119 — C-5142	159 — PA-114440	214 — C-25003
120 — PA-74583	161 — C-20048	224 (left) — PA-142647
125 — PA-61143	163 — C-75818	227 — C-5306
128 — C-568	166 (upper) — PA-111570	229 — PA-43770
130 — PA-2366	172 — PA-112659	258 — C-70261
131 — PA-1651	193 — C-18082	260 — C-61889

ABC-TV/Dean Williams — 390; Courtesy of Judge Rosalie S. Abella — 78; Courtesy of *The Albertan*/Calgary Sun — 237; Blaine, *The Spectator*, Hamilton — 173; Courtesy of Canada Mortgage and Housing Corporation — 166 (lower); Canadian Forces Photos — 303 (Sgt. Tim Smith), 306, 368, 396, 397 (lower), 397 (upper/Sgt. Dan Bryantowich); Canapress Photo Service — 10, 23, 25, 26, 31, 79, 85, 153, 168 (lower), 169, 171 (lower), 175, 178, 179, 180 (lower), 181, 182, 241, 243, 244, 245, 246, 263, 276, 282, 301, 305 (upper), 307, 312, 332, 333, 381, 388, 404; Courtesy CBC — 170, 171 (upper), 327 (right); CFTR RADIO, Rogers Broadcasting Ltd — 7; CIDA — 350 (Gary Chapman), 385 (Dilip Mehta); 387 (bottom left/Paul Chiasson), 387 (bottom right/Dilip Mehta); A. Donato/*Toronto Sun* — 188, 242; Eaton's Archives — 142; Photo by Environment Canada — 316; Ford of Canada — 140, 288 (right); Glenbow Archives, Calgary, Alberta (ND-3-6343) — 147, 180 (upper); Courtesy of the Estate of Walter Gordon — 289, 292; Hyundai Auto Canada Inc — 281; Photos by Interactive Image Technologies Ltd — 35, 63, 74, 76, 77, 98, 99; P. Kuch, *Winnipeg Free Press*, Public Archives Canada (C-90421) — 177; Photos by Joan Latchford — 176 (top right, bottom right); *London Free Press* — 326, 327 (left); All rights for reprint reserved by the Metropolitan Toronto Police Museum — 72, 73, 74; Metropolitan Toronto Police — 71; Miller Services Limited — 38 (Fotoblohm), 167, 168 (upper), 176 (left/J. Phillips), 232 (left), 288 (left/Blaine), 302 (bottom), 308, 314 (Uluschak), 347, 365, 369; Dept. of National Defense — 349 (middle, lower), 367; National Film Board of Canada — 224 (right), 231, 329, 330, 382; Courtesy of the New Democratic Party (photo by Ronald Stephenson) — 21; Courtesy of Ontario Hydro — 165; Courtesy of Ontario Ministry of Correctional Services — 91, 92; Denny Pritchard/*Star Phoenix*, Saskatoon — 277; Public Archives of Nova Scotia — 136; Gouvernement du Québec — 210, 217 (upper), 232 (right), 325 (lower); Quebec Ministry of Tourism — 209 (upper, lower); Saskatoon Archives Board (R-A 613(3)) — 145; Courtesy of Stratford Festival/Photographer Stephen Evans — 325 (upper); A Kevin Sullivan Production produced by Sullivan Films Inc., in association with CBC Inc., PBS/Wonderworks, ZDF/TV60, City TV, and with the participation of Telefilm Canada — 328; Tom Toles in *The Buffalo News*, 3/16/87 — 393; The City of Toronto Archives (1983-130-129) — 49; Reprinted with permission from The Toronto Star Syndicate — 189, 211, 217 (lower), 225, 228, 233, 234, 236, 250, 262 (upper), 275, 296, 315, 334, 336, 398; Transport Canada Photo — 216; Courtesy of the Office of the Rt. Hon. John Turner — 21; Courtesy United Nations — 174, 348, 349 (top), 359, 361, 363, 379, 387 (upper), 402; Courtesy of the US Dept. of Defense — 305 (lower); Courtesy of the US Information Agency — 302 (upper, middle); Courtesy of Vancouver Port Corporation — 274

Acknowledgements

24 — From *Memoirs of a Bird in a Gilded Cage* by Judy LaMarsh. Used by permission of The Canadian Publishers, McClelland and Stewart, Toronto.

45, 46 — From the *Constitutional Conference Proceedings*, Second Meeting, February 10-12, 1969.

64 — "Average Annual Homicide Rates per 100 000 Population, by Province, 1980–1986." *Canadian Crime Statistics 1986*, Cat. 85-205/1986, p. 35. Reproduced with permission of the Minister of Supply and Services Canada.

65 — "Rate per 100 000 Population of Criminal Code Offences, by Provinces, 1986." *Canadian Crime Statistics 1986*, Cat. 85-205/1986, p. 30. Reproduced with permission of the Minister of Supply and Services Canada.

94 — By permission of Corpus Information Services (a Division of Southam Communications Ltd) to reproduce material from the *1988 Corpus Almanac and Canadian Sourcebook*.

146 — From *The Winter Years* © 1966 by James Gray. Reprinted by permission of Macmillan of Canada, a Division of Canada Publishing Corporation.

161 — Compliments of Hon. J. R. Smallwood.

224 — From *Federalism and the French Canadians* © 1968 by Pierre Elliot Trudeau. Reprinted with permission of Macmillan of Canada, a Division of Canada Publishing Corporation.

228 — Published with permission of Baxter Publishing Company.

271 — "Value of Total Imports to Canada by Geographic Region" and "Value of Total Exports from Canada by Geographic Region." *The Canada Yearbook, 1985*, Cat. 11-402. Reproduced with permission of the Minister of Supply and Services Canada.

272 — "Canadian Imports and Exports (1983)." *The Canada Yearbook, 1985*, Cat. 11-402. Reproduced with permission of the Minister of Supply and Services Canada.

284 — "Foreign Long-Term Investment in Canada (in millions of dollars)." *Canada's International Investment Position, 1981-1984*, Cat. 67-202. Reproduced with permission of the Minister of Supply and Services Canada.

284 — "Foreign Long-Term Investment in Canada by Type of Investment." *Canada's International Investment Position, 1981-1984*, Cat. 67-202. Reproduced with permission of the Minister of Supply and Services Canada.

285, 286, 287 — "Distribution of Company Profits (1983)" and "Foreign Ownership and Control in Major Industries in Canada (1980)." *Corporations and Labour Unions Returns Act — Report for 1984*, Part I — Corporations, Cat. 61-210. Reproduced with the permission of the Minister of Supply and Services Canada.

285 — "Foreign Direct Investment in Canada by Area of Ownership." *Canada's International Investment Position, 1981-1984*, Cat. 67-202. Reproduced with permission of the Minister of Supply and Services Canada.

309 — From *The Better Part of Valour: Essays on Canadian Diplomacy* by John W. Holmes. Used by permission of The Canadian Publishers, McClelland and Stewart, Toronto.

311 — "Route of the Polar Sea." Reprinted by permission, *Maclean's Magazine*.

316 — "Sensitivity to Acid Rain." Canadian Embassy, Washington, D.C.

402 — "Source of Immigrants." *Canadian Statistical Review*, July 1987, Cat. 11-003, Vol. 62, No. 7. Reproduced with permission of the Minister of Supply and Services Canada.

INDEX